PREFACE

Congress Reconsidered, third edition, is a new book. Twelve of the eighteen chapters are totally new since the second edition, and the other six have been substantially revised and updated. Every essay was written specifically for this book. Yet for all the changes, this edition shares a common purpose with the earlier two.

When, as APSA Congressional Fellows, we discussed putting together a collection of original essays on Congress, it was in response to the major institutional upheavals of the mid-1970s. The Congress we observed then was significantly different from the one we had read about. Accordingly, our major goal in the first edition, published in 1977, was to bring a diverse audience of students, faculty, journalists, and political professionals up to date concerning the new reforms and their meaning, as described and analyzed by scholars in close contact with the institution.

Clearly, the congressional revolution of the 1970s has ended. The changes it brought about are no longer unfamiliar. Many have been consolidated into the ongoing institutional framework; others have been modified; a few have been discarded or have fallen into disuse. Therefore, the second edition of *Congress Reconsidered,* published in 1981, focused on Congress's ability to adapt to the changes of the 1970s.

Like the first two editions, this edition attempts to present scholarly research on the workings of the contemporary Congress and to do so in a way that appeals to a broad audience. Like its predecessors, it examines Congress as an institution responding to changing conditions internally and to alterations in its broader political and social environment. There are, however, important differences. First, this edition provides a greater historical perspective on congressional change. Second, coverage of recent trends in congressional elections has been expanded. Congressional constituencies and election research, previously discussed in a single chapter, now are treated in a whole section of the book. Finally, this edition examines more closely the institutional development and leadership of the U.S. Senate. For years congressional scholars focused on the House of Representatives. Fortunately, the rebirth of Senate scholarship allows us to present a book that has a balance of coverage of the two chambers that previously was not feasible.

To place the 18 essays in *Congress Reconsidered* in the context of partisan changes, we begin by taking a close look at the 1984 election results. The prologue analyzes Ronald Reagan's landslide victory, evaluates the Senate and House outcomes, and explores the impact of this election, as well as that of the 1980 and 1982 contests, on parties, leaders, and policymaking in Congress.

The book is then divided into six parts. The first, "Patterns and Dynamics of Congressional Change," contains revised overviews of the Senate and House and a new essay that examines the changing career choices of five postwar congressional classes. Part II, "Elections and Constituencies," analyzes the key factors that decide congressional elections, compares the constituency service of U.S. representatives and British MPs, and examines the competing influence of parties and PACs in financing House campaigns. Part III, "Committee and Subcommittee Politics," includes an updated review of committee activity and policymaking, a discussion of the increasing role of subcommittees in Congress, and an analysis of the changing impact of the House Ways and Means and Senate Finance committees on federal fiscal policy.

Congressional leadership and party politics are addressed in Part IV, which contains companion pieces on Senate and House leadership and an analysis of the historic decline in party voting in the House. "Congress, the Executive, and Public Policy," Part V, includes an update on agenda and alignment change; an assessment of the effectiveness of the new budget process; a study of the development, criticisms, and current status of the legislative veto; and an examination of the conflict between Congress and the executive over the making of foreign policy. The book concludes with two historical studies. The first shows how changing time and workload constraints have affected the operation of Congress in general and the effectiveness of filibusters in the Senate in particular. The second describes the shifting bicameral relationship of the House and Senate since the first Congresses.

In preparing this book we have been fortunate, as we were on the previous two editions, to have the input, assistance, and encouragement of others. Once again, our contributors have been critical to the success of this project. Their first-rate essays have made our task as editors more manageable. We also are grateful for the institutional support we have received from our universities, as well as from the Hoover Institution, the University of Houston Center for Public Policy, and the Dirksen Center. And our departmental colleagues have created a professional environment that directly and indirectly has been a stimulus in the preparation of this volume.

To a number of individuals, including James Anderson, Cheryl Dodd, Richard Fenno, Edward Harpham, Tom Mann, and Leroy Rieselbach, we extend special thanks. They have helped in different ways, and some may not be fully aware of how much we value them personally and professionally.

Much of the credit for the quality of this book rests with the fine staff of CQ Press. It has been delightful to work with Joanne Daniels. Her good judgment, openness to suggestion, no-nonsense professionalism, and wry sense of humor make an unbeatable combination. We were fortunate to have Barbara de Boinville's editorial attention, skill, and creativity in the preparation of the third edition as well as the second. In addition, we owe a continuing debt to Jean Woy, who persuaded us to work with CQ Press about five years ago. Needless to say, it's been a good decision.

Ten years now have passed since we were APSA Congressional Fellows, yet we continue to accrue benefits from participation in the program. It not only gave us the chance to collaborate on *Congress Reconsidered,* but more importantly it has served as a crucial stimulus to our research and professional careers.

Finally, we acknowledge the professional and personal debt of each to the other during the past decade. Dodd at last accepts with some resignation that he will not become a great country and western singer, and Oppenheimer realizes that his name will not appear on the NBA draft list. So we settle, respectively, for dancing the two-step to Willie Nelson and playing noon-hour pickup hoop games. Thankfully, the ability to carry a tune and make a jump shot are not prerequisites for the study of legislative politics.

L.C.D.
B.I.O.

THE ELUSIVE CONGRESSIONAL MANDATE: THE 1984 ELECTION AND ITS AFTERMATH

Lawrence C. Dodd and Bruce I. Oppenheimer

The 1984 election confronts both Congress and the nation with an uncertain political future. President Ronald Reagan, having won re-election by the greatest electoral landslide in history (525 electoral votes), should have emerged with a decisive mandate to govern. Yet the electorate tarnished his personal victory by reducing the Republican majority in the Senate and maintaining a Democratic majority in the House. Control of Congress thus eludes Reagan for a third straight election. The nation now enters its longest period of divided congressional rule, and its longest period without a president and Congress of the same party, in the past one hundred years. For either party to achieve governing control of Congress, it must concentrate on winning the 1986 elections and, in the interim, build voting alliances with disgruntled members of the opposite party. Success will depend on how well each party deciphers the hidden messages of 1984.

Senate Elections

Perhaps the most significant message of the Senate results is the increased value of incumbency. In the 1976, 1978, and 1980 elections, 40 percent of Senate incumbents were defeated. By contrast, only 9 percent of Senate incumbents running in 1982 and 1984 lost their seats.

One consequence of this low turnover is that the Senate's partisan distribution at the beginning of the 99th Congress (1985-1986) is the same as at the beginning of the 97th Congress (1981-1982)—53 Republicans and 47 Democrats. It was, however, slightly narrower than the 55-45 balance in the 98th (1983-1984). As Table 1 shows, small regional shifts did take place: Republicans gained one seat in the West and South, and Democrats gained two seats in the Midwest. Moreover, a comparison of members in the 97th and 99th Congresses reveals that the Senate has become a little less conservative. Of the 13 senators in the 99th who were not members of the 97th, five could be described as modestly more liberal than the senator holding that seat four years earlier—Jeff Bingaman (N.M.), Albert Gore, Jr. (Tenn.), Tom Harkin (Iowa), Jay Rockefeller (W.Va.), and Paul Simon (Ill.). Only three could be seen as more conservative—Chic Hecht (Nev.),

Dan Evans (Wash.), and Mitch McConnell (Ky). Nevertheless, the overall partisan and ideological shifts have not been dramatic.

Why have the 1982 and 1984 Senate elections produced so little change? Have Senate seats become relatively safe once again, or have other factors been at work? Despite the prima facie evidence from these two contests that the plague of electoral vulnerability has passed in the Senate, a reasonable argument can be made to the contrary.

Consider the Senate elections of 1982 and 1984 as the result of two offsetting conditions. First, in both contests one party was far more exposed than the other. In 1982 there were 20 Democratic seats (seats either held by incumbent Democrats seeking re-election or left open through the retirement of incumbent Democrats) and only 13 Republican seats being contested. In 1984 the situation was reversed: 19 Republican and 14 Democratic seats were up for grabs. In each election one party had far more at stake than the other in terms of potential seat losses. Thus, Democrats were expected to be be particularly vulnerable in 1982, and Republicans were expected to be particularly vulnerable in 1984.

Short-term conditions reinforced these expectations. Just as Reagan's success in enactment of his economic program in 1981 encouraged potential Republican challengers in 1982 and discouraged Democrats, high unemployment figures in 1983 served to entice strong Democratic candidates in 1984

Table 1   The Partisan Distribution of Senate Seats, 1977-1985, and Contested Seats, 1986

Congress	East	Midwest	South	West	Total
95th (All Seats)					
Democrats	14	16	19	13	62
Republicans	10	8	7	13	38
97th (All Seats)					
Democrats	13	10	15	9	47
Republicans	11	14	11	17	53
99th (All Seats)					
Democrats	13	12	14	8	47
Republicans	11	12	12	18	53
100th (Seats Open for Contests)					
Democrats	2	3	4	3	12
Republicans	4	7	4	7	22

NOTE: *East:* Conn., Del., Maine, Md., Mass., N.H., N.J., N.Y., Pa., R.I., Vt., W.Va. *Midwest:* Ill., Ind., Iowa, Kan., Mich., Minn., Mo., Neb., N.D., Ohio, S.D., Wis. *South:* Ala., Ark., Fla., Ga., Ky., La., Miss., N.C., Okla., S.C., Tenn., Texas, Va. *West:* Alaska, Ariz., Calif., Colo., Hawaii, Idaho, Mont., Nev., N.M., Ore., Utah, Wash., Wyo.

(such as Paul Simon, William Winter, Albert Gore, Jr., and James Hunt), while leading prominent Republicans (such as Lamar Alexander, Arch Moore, and Pete du Pont) to pass up the opportunity to seek Senate seats.

The 1981 predictions of Republican Senate gains in 1982 and the predictions in 1983 of Democratic control of the Senate in 1984 were derailed by a second offsetting condition—a change in short-term partisan forces. The 1982 recession and the 1984 recovery created situations in which the exposed party received the benefit of the partisan swing in the electorate. In 1982 these partisan forces were sufficiently strong to enable vulnerable Democrats to hold their seats and some seemingly safe Republicans to survive upsets by challengers who were not considered particularly strong. Similarly, the two-seat net gain by the Democrats in 1984 could easily be viewed as a Republican victory. With the exception of the switched-seat races, most of the close 1984 Senate contests involved Democratic incumbents.

If there is a lesson to be drawn from the 1982 and 1984 Senate elections, it is not that Senate incumbents are once again nearly as safe as House incumbents, but that Senate contests, especially when compared with House races, are highly competitive. It is now possible for a candidate of either party to win a U.S. Senate seat in nearly every state. Short-term partisan forces appear to be crucial in determining the results of Senate contests. In 1982 and 1984 they may have been sufficient to offset incumbent vulnerability.

As Table 1 indicates, most of the contested seats in 1986 are Republican, largely as a result of the 1980 Republican landslide that resulted in the loss of 12 seats previously held by Democratic incumbents. Many of these new Republican senators—for example, Alfonse D'Amato (N.Y.), Jeremiah Denton (Ala.), James East (N.C.), Paula Hawkins (Fla.), Robert Kasten (Wis.), Mack Mattingly (Ga.), and Don Nickles (Okla.)—appear vulnerable to the strong challengers that they are likely to face. Of course, Democratic incumbents, particularly those in highly competitive states, such as Alan Cranston (Calif.) and Alan Dixon (Ill.), will be tested as well. In short, incumbent vulnerability and high turnover, particularly among Republicans, is likely in 1986.

House Elections

The 1984 House elections, like the Senate contests, are most notable for the small turnover. Despite the Reagan landslide, Republicans made a net gain of only 14 seats, which placed the Democrats in control of a 253-182 majority. The reasons for the low turnover in the House, however, are different from the reasons for it in the Senate. In the House, the Democrats were the more exposed party, yet the partisan trend that worked against them did not result in a sizable seat loss.

Some would correctly note that the House results resemble those of 1972 when President Richard Nixon was re-elected with an even larger percentage of the popular vote (60.7) than Ronald Reagan in 1984 (58.9), yet the GOP gained only 12 House seats. These elections differ, however, in that the Democratic House candidates in 1972 were more prone to distance themselves from their party's presidential nominee than were the 1984 candidates. The irony is that nearly all the Democratic incumbents in 1984 survived without deserting the sinking ship.

There are three immediate reasons why House Democrats fared so well in 1984 given the party's exposure level and the short-term forces of the election. First, there were few open seats. Voluntary retirements, which peaked at 48 in 1980, dropped to a two-decade low of 22 in 1984. Due to these retirements, three primary defeats, and two vacancies because of deaths, there were only 27 House seats in which an incumbent was not running for re-election. As congressional elections research indicates, it is open seats that attract the fiercest contests and in which partisan shifts are most likely to occur.[1]

Second, few weak Democratic incumbents ran in 1984. A large number of incumbent House members were defeated in the previous two elections. Combined with the numerous voluntary retirements of the last decade, this may have significantly reduced the number of weak incumbents who remained in the House. Despite expectations of a Reagan landslide and the belief by some observers as the election drew closer that Republicans would make sizable House gains, no one had a very long list of Democratic incumbents who appeared vulnerable.

Finally, reapportionment and redistricting in 1982 created uncertainties for incumbents. Many had to cultivate support in large areas previously excluded from their districts. Reapportionment thus forced many seasoned incumbents to act as though they were newcomers and devote extra effort to wooing voters. Such behavior may well have generated a "reapportionment surge" somewhat akin to the more traditional "sophomore surge" that characterizes new members. The advantages of first-time incumbency can produce a measurable increase in the percentage of the vote a member delivers in his or her first race for re-election.[2] A similar surge, experienced by Democratic incumbents reapportioned in 1982, could have helped offset national partisan forces that favored Republican challengers.

All three explanations of why House Democrats fared so well in 1984 are related to the continuing advantage of incumbency in House races. As Figure 1 shows, few House contests were even close. Ignoring the unopposed Democrats, represented by the bar on the far right of the figure, we see a bimodal distribution. One mode is in the 25 to 30 percent Democratic grouping indicating Republican victors with 70 to 75 percent of the two-party vote. The other mode for Democratic victors clusters in the 55 to 70 percent of the vote. What is perhaps most significant is the small number of seats—only 48—in the 45 to 55 percent range. If all Republican candidates had run 5 percentage points better, the party would have won only 25 additional seats— still short of a House majority. (And had all Democrats run 5 percentage points better, they would have won 23 additional seats.) In 1984 President Reagan's

Figure 1   Frequency Distribution of Democratic Percentages of Two-Party
Vote in House Districts, 1984 Election

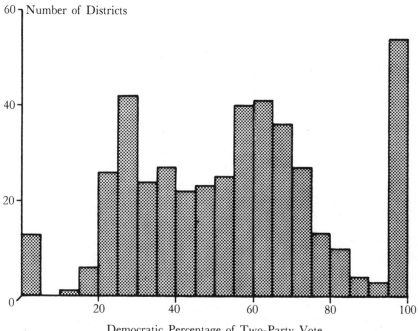

Democratic Percentage of Two-Party Vote

SOURCE: *Congressional Quarterly Weekly Report,* November 10, 1984, pp. 2923-2930.

coattails may have extended to House elections, but the number of competitive
seats, unlike in the Senate, was very small. The major impact of the Reagan
landslide may have been only in moving the modes for the two parties to a position somewhat more favorable to Republicans than previously was the case.

The 1984 election marginally altered the parties' geographic strength in
the House. The biggest change occurred in the South—primarily in Texas
and North Carolina—where Republicans made a seven-seat net gain, largely
offsetting Democratic gains in the South in 1982. The 99th Congress has 47
Southern Republicans, a new high, and 82 Southern Democrats—not
drastically different from the 78-43 party split among southern House
members in 1981.[3] The Democrats hold a majority of House seats in the East,
Midwest, and West as well. (See Table 2.)

How has the Democratic party been able to continue its hold on the
House after losing the presidency twice decisively and relinquishing control of
the Senate in 1980? Numerous factors help explain their staying power,
among them the advantages of incumbency, reapportionment and sophomore

Table 2 The Partisan Distribution of House Seats, 1977-1985

Congress	East	Midwest	South	West	Total
95th					
Democrats	82	68	91	51	292
Republicans	35	53	30	25	143
97th					
Democrats	68	58	78	39	243
Republicans	49	63	43	37	192
99th					
Democrats	65	62	82	44	253
Republicans	43	51	47	41	182

NOTE: The regional categories are the same as in Table 1.

surges, the ability of members to represent effectively the parochial interests of their districts, and the fact that many districts are not competitive in partisan terms. Another reason may lie in the voting rates and demographic makeup of the districts that Democrats and Republicans win.

In the 1984 House election, significantly more votes were cast in House districts won by Republicans than those won by Democrats. This difference is possible because House district lines are drawn on the basis of population and not according to the number of voters. Democrats traditionally do disproportionately well among less affluent groups and thus in less affluent districts with lower registration and turnout rates. Republicans run well among high participation groups and districts. In addition, because of birth and death rates, Democratic districts may contain a higher percentage of the population below voting age than do Republican districts. With fewer eligible voters and lower turnout, Democratic districts tend to produce fewer total votes in Senate and presidential elections than a small group of Republican districts.

Variation in the number of voters in different districts can be quite large. In Texas, for example, a Democrat won a House seat in 1984 for which fewer than 97,000 votes were cast, and a Republican won a seat for which more than 275,000 votes were cast. Both districts contained roughly the same number of residents according to the 1980 census. While this is an extreme example, it illustrates the potential size of the discrepancies in total vote.

The broad implications of such variation can be seen by examining the 1980 presidential vote in New York. Reagan won the statewide vote by a 4 percent margin over President Jimmy Carter, while the Democrats won 22 of New York's 39 congressional districts (56 percent). However, had the same number of votes been cast in each congressional district, and with the same percentage of support for the two candidates, the adjusted statewide total would have given Carter a 4 percent victory margin over Reagan.[4]

The electoral anomalies of 1980, 1982, and 1984 thus may result from the tendency of the House to reflect the broad political interests of the nation's aggregate population, while the Senate and presidency more nearly reflect the sentiments of the national voting public. Although these tendencies are built into our constitutional system, their stark emergence in recent elections, with presidential landslides barely affecting overall House results, may be rooted in specific developments. These include the Supreme Court's decision to strictly enforce the equal population provision for legislative apportionment, recent immigration patterns, and the greater declines in birth and death rates among the nation's affluent classes than among its disadvantaged.

The apportionment of the House by population rather than by voters thus can deprive Republicans of a congressional mandate even when they generate impressive vote totals at a statewide and national level. To break the Democrats' grip on the House, the GOP must make inroads into the less affluent population centers. The Democrats, for their part, may be hard pressed to regain control of the Senate and the presidency until they look beyond the nation's population centers and attract support in middle-class districts whose residents cast the bulk of the nation's votes. The efforts of the Democrats and Republicans to expand their bases of support will focus on Congress as they use their institutional power to shape a record to take to the electorate in 1986 and 1988.

Governing in the 99th Congress

Both parties face serious obstacles in building positive records in Congress. These obstacles are rooted in the divided control of Congress and in the partisan and ideological tensions within and between the two houses. The problems confronting the Senate reflect the changes that have taken place since the Republicans won their Senate majority in 1980. At that time, the Republicans, who had not controlled the Senate for almost 30 years, were anxious to use their power to fulfill the conservative promises that had helped produce the party's victory. Since the overwhelming majority of the party had been elected in 1978 or 1980, Senate Republicans could approach the 97th Congress with few re-election worries and with a willingness to support the party and its president. Their fervor for the Reagan administration's program allowed them to overcome their collective inexperience, suppress the obstructionist tendencies they had learned as a minority party, and work together as a relatively cohesive governing body.

Very different circumstances, however, confronted Senate Republicans at the beginning of the 99th Congress. Twenty-two of them, more than 40 percent, face re-election in 1986. They will run in an off-year election of a second-term president, traditionally a disastrous time for the president's party. They may well run during a recession. And some of these incumbents, first elected on Reagan's coattails in 1980, lack solid bases of personal support in their states and are vulnerable to strong challengers. Many Republican senators thus began their service in the 99th Congress preoccupied with their immediate political futures and inclined to cast votes that meshed more with constituents' attitudes than their party's programs.

A great loss to the Senate GOP was the retirement of Majority Leader Howard Baker (Tenn.) to prepare a race for the presidency. His departure deprived the party of proven leadership that could help it maintain its precarious coherence during Reagan's second term. Robert Dole (Kan.) was elected as Baker's successor on November 28, 1984, in one of the most wide open contests for Majority Leader in recent decades. Dole is an articulate and pragmatic moderate with extensive legislative skills but no proven experience as a floor leader. In addition, new chairmen took the helm of key committees, with Richard Lugar (Ind.) becoming chair of Foreign Relations and Robert Packwood (Ore.) replacing Dole as head of Finance.

As committee and party leaders seek to unite the party, their greatest asset should be Reagan and his 49-state mandate. The Senate GOP's greatest liabilities are the lack of a clear-cut program to enact, electoral contests in 1986 for nearly half of its members, and a Majority Leader who lacks previous floor experience.

Unlike Senate Republicans, Senate Democrats in the 99th Congress face a brighter future than they did in the 97th. They have maintained a sizable number of seats despite the conservative national tide of the last few years. Moreover, as we have noted, most Senate contests in 1986 involve seats currently held by Republicans. This gives the Democrats an opportunity to increase their numbers and possibly regain Senate control. In addition, because most Democratic incumbents do not face re-election in 1986 they may be less influenced by short-term electoral forces and thus more able to withstand pressures to support Republican programs.

The Democratic party thus has the opportunity to build a more cohesive front against the Republicans than it did in the 97th Congress. This front undoubtedly will be strengthened by the liberal newcomers elected in 1984, by the more difficult policy choices that the president may present to Congress (cuts in social services and tax increases are less popular than the tax cuts of Reagan's first term), and by the fact that the president's victory did not seem to mandate particular legislative proposals. The Democrats also benefit from the return of an experienced floor leader, Robert Byrd (W.Va). Senate Democrats, in league with House colleagues, could play a stronger role during the second Reagan administration than they did during the first.

The House remains the major obstacle to Republican control of the national government, and the 1984 election results make it unlikely that the GOP will soon overcome this obstacle. Its failure to take advantage of Reagan's landslide and win a substantial increase in House seats gives moderate-to-liberal Democrats the opportunity to thwart the administration's policy initiatives.

But House Democrats, whose 253 seats put them 35 votes over the constitutional majority of 218, face difficulties of their own in the 99th Congress. Although the party has a formal majority, approximately 20 to 30 of its members are strong conservatives, mostly from the South, who are naturally attracted to many of President Reagan's proposals. The loss of their support would reduce the Democratic majority to approximately 10 to 15 votes. This margin of safety includes moderate conservatives from the South, Southwest, and West, who could prove unreliable if the party caucus takes an uncompromisingly liberal stance.

Much depends on the skill of the party's leaders. At the beginning of the 99th Congress, House Democrats had the same leadership team that had led them since 1976—Speaker Tip O'Neill (Mass.) and Majority Leader Jim Wright (Texas). The effectiveness of this team may be limited by O'Neill's plans to retire in 1986. Most analysts expect Wright to succeed him, but the race for Majority Leader could be wide open. A protracted struggle for the position, and the weakened bargaining clout that a lame-duck team often experiences, could complicate the building of a cohesive party.

Thus, the Democrats face a period of extended risk and transition. Their margin of control is sufficiently narrow (35 seats) that the Republicans may be able to exploit intraparty conflict and wrest effective control of policy away from them, much as they did in 1981. In addition, President Reagan began his second term with such popular support that the Republicans, with good economic times at home and peace abroad, conceivably could pull an unprecedented upset in the 1986 elections and challenge Democratic control of the House in the 100th Congress.

House Republicans' prospects for success revolve around their ability to work together, develop a coherent policy agenda, and sell it to conservative Democrats. Their prospects are somewhat dimmed by members' expectations of difficult re-election battles in 1986 and their consequent desire to fashion voting records that reflect the special political complexions of their districts and not necessarily the party line.

Conclusion

The 1984 election is a story of opportunity lost. The Republican party, failing to benefit extensively from Reagan's coattails, lost one of its best chances in modern times to mount a serious challenge to Democratic control of the House. Such a victory, coupled with the Reagan landslide and Republican Senate majority, might have allowed the party to complete the Reagan revolution begun in the 97th Congress. The Democrats, by contrast, passed up an opportunity to regain majority status in the Senate or at least to improve their electoral chances for the future.

The elections of 1978, 1980, and 1982, as well as 1984, demonstrate the continuing inability of both parties to elicit a clear governing mandate from the public. Elections for the presidency and Congress appear out of sync, with landslides in one institution offset by close elections and contradictory results in the other. Moreover, the two houses seem unable to mesh, with neither party able to mount a sufficiently strong nationwide campaign at the congressional level to win outright control and a governing mandate in both chambers. Even when we examine coalitional politics within each house, acknowledging the tendency of conservative Democrats to vote with Republicans, we see no clear pattern emerging within each house, much less across the two chambers. One reason may be the design of House districts.

As we have noted, demographic trends and apportionment decisions create numerous House districts with an unusually low number of voting residents. These primarily working-class districts elect a large group of Democratic representatives but, because they lack a sizable base of voters, cannot contribute proportionately to Democratic control of the Senate and the presidency. The Republicans, who gain their support from a minority of the nation's population centers but from a majority of the nation's voters, can lose the House while winning the Senate and presidency.

Three additional factors may contribute to the anomalies we have observed in Senate, House, and presidential elections. First, the rise of the mass media has enabled presidential nominees to appeal directly to the public without working through local party organizations—thus limiting the impact of a presidential landslide on congressional campaigns. Second, the increased fragmentation of the power and resources in Congress since the 1970s helps modern incumbents, particularly representatives, perform valuable services for their constituencies and thereby gain the personalized support that can shield them from national voting trends. Finally, voters may be hesitant to give a clear mandate to one party or ideology because they are genuinely uncertain about how to address the complex economic and international problems facing the nation.

The current congressional stalemate does not appear to be a chance occurrence. It is rooted in the demographic characteristics and apportionment of House districts, in the character of modern electoral politics, in the structure of Congress, and in the nation's search for a persuasive policy vision. The deep-seated nature of the stalemate suggests that the struggle for a governing mandate could well preoccupy the two parties and shape the conduct of congressional politics through the end of the decade.

NOTES

1. See Gary C. Jacobson, *The Politics of Congressional Elections* (Boston: Little, Brown & Co., 1983).
2. For a discussion of "sophomore surge," see Albert D. Cover and David R. Mayhew, "Congressional Dynamics and the Decline of Competitive Congressional Elections" in *Congress Reconsidered*, 2nd ed., edited by Lawrence C. Dodd and Bruce I. Oppenheimer (Washington, D.C.: CQ Press, 1981), pp. 62-82.
3. The South gained eight House seats due to reapportionment in 1982.
4. We do not take into account here post-1970 population shifts in New York.

Part I

PATTERNS AND DYNAMICS
OF CONGRESSIONAL CHANGE

1. THE SENATE THROUGH THE 1980s: CYCLES OF CHANGE

Norman J. Ornstein, Robert L. Peabody, and David W. Rohde

Few political institutions have captured the attention of the American public as the U.S. Senate has. From televised hearings on crime, communism, and Watergate, from media coverage of Senate-based presidential contenders, and from movies like *Mr. Smith Goes to Washington* and *Advise and Consent,* the public is much more aware of the Senate than it is of "the other body," the House of Representatives. Curiously, though, the public's awareness of the Senate has not been matched by a comprehensive and systematic analysis of how the Senate operates and how senators behave. We know a lot about the Senate of the 1950s, thanks primarily to the efforts of two outstanding political scientists, Ralph K. Huitt and Donald R. Matthews.[1] And we have some good work tracking change in the Senate in the 1960s.[2] But, like the rest of the American political system, the Senate has changed considerably in the past quarter century and continues to change—in the nature of its membership, in its formal and informal leadership, in its internal processes and structures, and in its policy directions. While many of the changes are ongoing trends over two decades, many others are cycles, moving the Senate back toward earlier patterns of behavior. This essay attempts to sort out the changes, showing how the Senate is different, how it has stabilized, and why.

The Membership

It will come as no surprise that the membership of the Senate has changed substantially since the mid-1980s and, indeed, even since the mid-1970s! Only four senators who served in the last Congress before change swept the institution in 1958 (the 85th) remained in the Senate in 1984. Meanwhile, 58 of the 100 members of the 98th Senate (1983-1984) were new to the chamber since Jimmy Carter's election in 1976. Change in membership, however, has meant more than simply substituting one legislator for another. With respect to a variety of criteria and categories, different kinds of senators have replaced those who served earlier, and this has affected the operation of the Senate and the policies it has produced. We will consider

13

three aspects of this change: partisan division, ideology, and sectional party affiliation.

The most obvious of the changes has been in the party affiliation of the membership. From the end of World War II through most of the 1950s, the partisan division of the Senate was unusually close; neither party ever controlled the body by more than a few votes. However, in the election of 1958, the Democratic membership of the Senate jumped from 49 to 64 seats. Through the 1970s, the number of Democrats was usually in the sixties. In the 94th and 95th Congresses, Democrats held 62 seats, and in the 96th they held 59. But 1981 brought a stunning reversal, as Democrats saw their two decades of dominance transformed into a narrow Republican majority that remained in party control of the Senate through 1984. After nearly two decades of being in the majority, Senate Democrats were suddenly thrust into the foreign condition of minority status, while Senate Republicans, long accustomed to being in the minority, suddenly had the power—and responsibilities—of the majority. After four years of this status, the parties were still sorting out their respective roles.

A second aspect of change relates to the regional character of the two parties. Through the 1950s, Democratic membership was concentrated in the South and West, while Republicans came primarily from the East and Midwest. For example, in 1957 the Democrats held every Senate seat from the South and 13 of the 22 seats from the West, but they had only 5 of 20 eastern seats and 3 of the 22 midwestern seats. By the 1970s, however, these regional patterns had changed. In the 96th Congress (the last they controlled), the Democrats held majorities in every region except the West (where Republicans held 14 of 26 seats), including 11 of 20 in the Midwest. These dramatic gains by Democrats were offset somewhat by losses in the South. In 1979 the Democrats changed regional patterns once again. By 1984, Democrats were down to only 50 percent of the 22 southern seats and 50 percent of the 20 seats in the East. Republicans dominated the Plains and the West, holding a full 68 percent of the 38 seats in these regions.

These changes have combined to alter substantially the relative power of various groups within the Senate. Until the 1960s, Southern Democrats dominated the Democratic party in the Senate, and through that dominance and frequent alliance with conservative Republican members, they were able to control the Senate. With the narrow partisan division of the 1950s, southerners accounted for more than 40 percent of the total Democratic membership. With the large influx of Northern Democrats after the 1958 election, the percentage fell to 34. This was followed by a fairly continuous decline as the Republicans began winning seats in the South. In 1984 southerners accounted for only 24 percent of Senate Democrats. But despite their overall lower level of representation, Southern Democrats were on the rebound, thanks to the workings of seniority. Even though the southerners had continued to decline as a share of the Democratic party in the Senate (the 24 percent level was their lowest total in modern times), the Southern

Democrats who were in the Senate had steadily accumulated service. Nine of the twenty most senior Democrats in the 98th Congress were from the Deep South, and all nine were ranking members on important committees (and thus would become committee chairmen if the Democrats remained a majority). The majority Republicans had seen a much more diverse regional base, but they too had noticeable regional emphases, especially in the South and the Rocky Mountain region.

The partisan and regional changes in the Senate contributed to changes in the ideological character of the membership. Table 1-1 shows the proportions of liberals, moderates, and conservatives among various groups of

Table 1-1   Ideological Divisions in the Senate, 85th Congress (1957-1958) and the 1st Sessions of the 94th Congress (1975), 96th Congress (1979), and 98th Congress (1983)

	Northern Demo- crats	*Southern Demo- crats*	*All Demo- crats*	*Repub- licans*	*All Members*
85th Congress (1957-1958)	*(N=27)*	*(N=22)*	*(N=49)*	*(N=47)*	*(N=96)*
Liberals	67%	9%	41%	2%	22%
Moderates	19	27	22	26	24
Conservatives	15	64	37	72	54
94th Congress (1975)	*(N=46)*	*(N=16)*	*(N=62)*	*N=38)*	*(N=100)*
Liberals	85%	—	63%	16%	45%
Moderates	15	19%	16	26	20
Conservatives	—	81	21	58	35
96th Congress (1979)	*(N=43)*	*(N=16)*	*(N=59)*	*(N=41)*	*(N=100)*
Liberals	58%	—	42%	7%	28%
Moderates	37	31%	36	32	34
Conservatives	5	69	22	61	38
98th Congress (1983)	*(N=35)*	*(N=11)*	*(N=46)*	*(N=54)*	*(N=100)*
Liberals	47%	—	39%	—	20%
Moderates	47	55%	39	30%	34
Conservatives	6	45	22	70	46

NOTE: The classification is based on a variation of the conservative coalition support score published annually by Congressional Quarterly. The support score of a member was divided by the sum of his or her support and opposition scores, which removes the effect of absences. Members whose scores were 0-30 were classified as liberals, 31-70 as moderates, and 71-100 as conservatives. The number of persons used to compute each percentage is shown in parentheses. The scores for 1957-1958 were calculated from the appropriate roll calls listed in the *Congressional Quarterly Almanac* for those years. The scores for 1975 were taken from the *Congressional Quarterly Weekly Report,* January 24, 1976, p. 174; and the 1979 scores from *Congressional Quarterly Weekly Report,* January 26, 1980, p. 198. The 1983 scores are from *Vital Statistics on Congress, 1984-1985,* ed. Norman J. Ornstein et al. (Washington, D.C.: American Enterprise Institute for Public Policy Research, 1984).

senators in the 85th Congress (1957-1958) and in the first sessions of the 94th Congress (1975), 96th Congress (1979), and 98th Congress (1983).

Democrats in the 85th Congress were divided almost evenly between liberals and conservatives, whereas the Republicans were overwhelmingly conservative. This produced a conservative majority in the Senate in 1957-1958. The subsequent sharp increase in the number of Democrats and almost matching decline in the number of Republicans produced a liberal plurality by 1975.

Not all of the ideological change was due to these numerical shifts, however. The makeup of various subgroups in the Senate had also shifted, as Table 1-1 indicates. For example, in the 85th Congress, Northern and Southern Democrats had their distinct ideological character, but there was also substantial heterogeneity within each group. By the 94th Congress this was no longer true; there were no northern conservatives and no southern liberals, and the proportion of moderates in each group had also declined. Moreover, over the same period the Republicans in the Senate became considerably more heterogeneous.

In the 96th Congress these trends began to reverse, particularly among Northern Democrats. Due to the election of conservative Northern Democrats—such as J. James Exon and Edward Zorinsky of Nebraska, Dennis DeConcini of Arizona, and David Boren of Oklahoma—and the shift to a more conservative voting pattern by a number of senior senators, this party group became much more heterogeneous ideologically. Thus, overall, the Senate in the 96th Congress stood about midway between the 85th and 94th ideologically, but with a strong moderate group.

In the 1980s, election patterns changed both parties, and the Senate, even more. The early 1980s continued to diminish the liberalism of the dwindling group of Northern Democrats; they went from a nearly 6 to 1 liberal/moderate ratio in 1975 to a 1 to 1 split nine years later. However, the conservative cadre of Southern Democrats was moving at the same time—and toward the same centrist location. Even with the convergence, the two regional wings of the Democratic party remained distinctive, while the party overall had a moderate-liberal cast.

For the Republicans, the dramatic 1980 election gave the GOP a majority. Most of the newcomers were staunch conservatives. By 1983 the Republican party had become as conservative overall as it had been in the 1950s—but with more members. However, the more senior GOP holdovers from the earlier period remained more moderate, and they took a disproportionate share of chairmanships and key power positions by virtue of their seniority. Thus, traditional patterns of power distribution moderated the sharpness of the conservative trend in the Senate. Overall, the Senate of 1984 was more conservative than at any time since 1957-1958, but still less conservative, in total membership and in the exercise of power, than its 85th Congress predecessor.

Norms and Rules

The Senate is a decisionmaking institution, and as such it has a set of formal rules that regulate its operations. It is also a group of individuals, and "just as any other group of human beings, it has its unwritten rules of the game, its norms of conduct, its approved manner of behavior." [3] The Senate has both formal and informal rules, and while there has been a great deal of continuity in both categories during the past two decades, there have also been some significant changes.

The unwritten rules or norms of the Senate are patterns of behavior senators think other senators should follow. Many members share similar expectations about how a senator ought or ought not to behave. In his study of the Senate in the mid-1950s, Matthews cited six norms or "folkways": legislative work, specialization, courtesy, reciprocity, institutional patriotism, and apprenticeship.

The first norm required that members devote a major portion of their time to their legislative duties in committee and on the floor and not seek personal publicity at the expense of these legislative obligations. Second, a senator was expected to concentrate on matters pertaining to committee business or directly affecting constituents. The third norm, courtesy, required that the political conflicts within the Senate should not become personal conflicts. References to colleagues in legislative situations should be formal and indirect, and personal attacks were deemed unacceptable. Reciprocity, the fourth folkway, meant that members were expected to help colleagues whenever possible and to avoid pressing their formal powers too far (for example, by systematically objecting to unanimous consent agreements). A senator was to understand and appreciate the problems of colleagues and to keep bargains once they were struck. The fifth norm of institutional patriotism required that a member protect the Senate as an institution, avoiding behavior that would bring it or its members into disrepute. Finally, new senators were expected to serve a period of apprenticeship. A freshman senator, it was felt, should wait a substantial amount of time before participating fully in the work of the Senate. During this time freshmen were expected to learn about the Senate and seek the advice of senior members.

Many of these folkways provide substantial benefits to the collective membership, and it is not surprising that most of them are still recognized in the Senate today. But, as patterns of power and ambition inside and outside the Senate have changed, the sanctions available for violation of the norms have diminished; thus, violations are much more frequent. The norms of legislative work and specialization are two that clearly persist as expectations. The Senate, like the House, is characterized by division of labor through the committee system. This system allocates legislative responsibilities to members, and these responsibilities have grown substantially since the 1950s. The Senate's ability to make policy and to function effectively depends in large measure upon each member living up to his or her individual responsibilities.

The norms of legislative work and specialization express the expectations of members that each of them ought to do so.

The way to have influence in the Senate, according to one senator, was "just year after year of patience—willingness to carry at least your fair share of the work." Another said on the same point, "I believe the principle could be stated very simply—that is, keep up with your work." When asked about specialization, a third senator commented:

> I believe that senators do specialize in their activities as far as their committee ... that doesn't mean that they can't learn a lot about other things ... but you are expected to know in greater detail and greater accuracy about the things that your committee has jurisdiction over. That is an obligation.[4]

If legislative work and specialization still exist as norms—as expectations—why are they observed much less frequently today than they were in the 1950s? For one thing, the Senate has become a veritable breeding ground for presidential candidates. Many members are absent from the Senate for extended periods of time to explore or promote presidential campaigns. To enhance their presidential possibilities, senators will often turn to the mass media, rather than to their committees or the Senate floor, as a forum for their policy ideas. Even if senators are not actively seeking the White House, the chance to become a national celebrity, through appearances on the "CBS Evening News," "Nightline," or "20/20," or through profiles in *Newsweek* or *People,* is increasingly tempting. Legislative drudgery or committee detail in the back halls of Congress are not the routes to extensive public and media attention.[5] Thus, more and more senators are involved in a wide spectrum of policy areas extending beyond their committee assignments and often well beyond their Senate work.

Like legislative work and specialization, the folkways of courtesy, reciprocity, and institutional patriotism continue in the Senate but are violated more than in the past. Courtesy permits political conflict to remain depersonalized, allowing yesterday's opponent to be tomorrow's ally. (As one Republican senator said, "It's the catalyst that maintains a semblance of order.") However, the ideological divisions in the contemporary Senate have frequently pitted one or more of the staunch liberals (such as Howard Metzenbaum of Ohio) or, more often, the extreme conservatives (such as John East of North Carolina or Don Nickles of Oklahoma) against colleagues in public and often bitter exchanges. Late in 1982, for example, a mainstream conservative Republican, Allan Simpson of Wyoming, said on the Senate floor of the uncollegial behavior of his colleague Jesse Helms (R-N.C.), "Seldom have I seen a more obnoxious and obdurate performance." Despite the lapses, the norm of reciprocity, particularly its aspect of individual integrity, continues to be important in an institution that operates informally and in which virtually all agreements are oral. Institutional patriotism tends to be reinforced by the increase in competition between

Congress and the executive branch for control over foreign policy and the budget, but the partisan divisions between House and Senate, and the public disapproval of Congress as an institution, have made it easier for senators to criticize the Senate with impunity.

As we have seen, five of the folkways that were operative in the Senate two decades ago still describe "expected" behavior within the body today. Even this is not true, however, of the sixth norm, apprenticeship. Unlike the other folkways, it is difficult to discern what benefits apprenticeship provided to the Senate as an institution or to its members individually. As Matthews noted, apprenticeship had its roots very early in the Senate's history.[6] Nevertheless, the only group that could be seen to benefit from the observance of this norm by the 1950s were the senior conservatives in both parties who dominated the positions of power in the Senate at that time. Beginning with the 1958 election, more and more liberal Northern Democrats entered the Senate, and the conservative dominance began to break down.[7] Consequently, junior members had less incentive to observe the norm. Gradually, as these junior senators of the early 1960s became senior members, the expectations regarding the norm became less widely shared.

As the Senate returned to conservatism in the late 1970s and early 1980s, the continuing influx of junior members who made the ideological reversion possible had no interest whatsoever in restoring the norm that their earlier liberal brethren had helped abolish. Today junior members across the board neither want nor feel the need to serve an apprenticeship; furthermore, no senior members expect them to do so, as these statements from senators indicate:

> All the communications suggest "get involved, offer amendments, make speeches. The Senate has changed, we're all equals, you should act accordingly." [A junior Democrat]

> Well, that [apprenticeship] doesn't exist at all in the Senate. The senior Senators have made that very clear, both Democrats and Republicans. [A junior Republican]

> We now hope and expect and encourage the younger guys to dive right in to the middle of it. [A senior conservative Republican]

Thus, the Senate of the 1980s is a more egalitarian institution when considered along seniority lines than it used to be. Junior members now play an important role within the Senate, and this change in the informal rule structure of the body has contributed to several important changes in the formal rules.

For example, in 1970 a rule was adopted that limited members to service on only one of the Senate's four most prestigious committees: Appropriations, Armed Services, Finance, and Foreign Relations. This new rule prevented senior members from monopolizing these important committee posts and facilitated the appointment of relatively junior senators much earlier in their careers than would have been possible otherwise. In addition, both parties adopted rules limiting the role of seniority in the selection of committee chairmen. In 1973 the Republican Caucus agreed to a system whereby the Republican members of each committee would elect the ranking member. In 1975 the Democratic Caucus adopted a proposal by Dick Clark of Iowa (who had served only two years in the Senate) which permitted secret ballot votes by the caucus on any committee chairman if one-fifth of the Democratic senators requested it.

As junior members became more active, they began to feel more intensely the disparity of resources between themselves and the senior senators, particularly with regard to staff. Therefore, the junior members sponsored and aggressively pushed a resolution, S. Res. 60, which permitted them to hire additional legislative staff members to assist in their committee duties. The Senate adopted the resolution in 1975.

A number of the other reforms adopted by the Senate in the 1970s were not a direct consequence of the expanded role of newer senators vis-à-vis their more senior colleagues. Certainly the most publicized of these was the 1975 change in the Senate's rule for cutting off debate. Since the late 1950s, liberals had been seeking to alter the rule that required the vote of two-thirds of the members present and voting to end a filibuster. The new provision required the affirmative vote of only three-fifths of the entire Senate membership. If most members voted, cloture (the process by which debate can be ended in the Senate, other than by unanimous consent) would be easier to achieve under the new rule. Since the adoption of the rules change, cloture has proved somewhat easier to achieve, but filibusters continue to be important events in the Senate—including the more recent "filibuster by amendment" ploy used in the late 1970s by conservative Alabaman James Allen and by liberals Metzenbaum, James Abourezk (N.D.), and Lowell Weicker (Conn.). They have underscored the power of individual senators to stymie the legislative process.

A final set of reforms affected the openness of the Senate's conduct of its business. In 1975, almost three years after similar actions by the House, the Senate adopted rules that opened to the press and public most mark-up or bill-drafting sessions and conference committee meetings.

With the GOP takeover in 1981, there was no move to dismantle the changes wrought by junior members in earlier Senates or to return to a pattern of apprenticeship. It would not have been easy, if attempted; the Republican freshman class of 1980 was 16 strong or a full 30 percent of the Republican party, and half the majority was in its first term.

In sum, junior members have come to play an increasingly important role in Senate activity, and the expectations of senior members have gradually adapted to these changes. Partially as a consequence of this, the Senate has altered a number of its formal procedures. The overall effect of changes in the informal norms of conduct and written rules is that the Senate of the 1980s—for both parties—is a much more egalitarian and open institution in which the ability to affect policy is less dependent on a senator's formal position or seniority.

Leadership

The mid-1950s are remembered as an era of strong leaders in the Senate—Democrat Lyndon B. Johnson of Texas on the majority side and Republicans William Knowland (Calif.) and then Everett M. Dirksen (Ill.) on the minority. As Ralph Huitt, Donald Matthews, and others have noted, their leadership both contributed to the tight hierarchical structure of the institution and reinforced it.[8] But with the election of 1958, the ability of a leader to "strong-arm" the Senate declined dramatically. Johnson's last two years as Majority Leader, 1959 and 1960, were much more difficult for him than his earlier tenure because of the large number of assertive freshman Democrats.[9]

Johnson's successor, Mike Mansfield of Montana, was a much different figure. Easygoing and unwilling to accumulate personal power to exert leverage over his colleagues, Mansfield fit the changing institution he inherited—and he acted deliberately to accelerate the change. Mansfield served an unprecedented 16 years as Majority Leader, from 1961 to his retirement in 1976. When Mansfield left, the Senate was once again in the process of change—in some ways, as we have seen, back in the direction of an earlier era—and his successor, Robert C. Byrd of West Virginia, fit the pattern of his times. Byrd, like Mansfield, moved to the top leadership position after a stint as the number two leader, majority whip. Byrd had shifted over the years from a conservative to a moderate stance on most issues, thus becoming more like his colleagues in the late 1970s. And, while Byrd was no Lyndon Johnson, his somewhat more assertive leadership style compared with Mansfield's, especially in parliamentary management and strategy, satisfied senators who were increasingly uneasy with the burgeoning workload and unpredictable schedule of the Senate of the mid-1970s.

At the same time Byrd was ascending to the Majority Leader post, in January 1977, the minority Republicans had their own leadership change. On the opening day of the contest for the slot, Robert Griffin (Mich.), the minority whip since 1959, was edged out by Howard Baker (Tenn.) by a slim 19-18 margin. Baker had challenged his predecessor, Hugh Scott, twice previously but failed to win the position of Republican floor leader. Baker beat Griffin in 1977, not as a result of ideological differences but because a majority of the incoming Republican freshmen became convinced that he would make a stronger external spokesman and internal leader for their party. Four years later Baker became Majority Leader (he was unopposed after potential rivals such as Paul Laxalt of Nevada declined to run), and he showed even greater strength working with a narrow majority and his own party's president.

Before briefly assessing the effectiveness of floor leaders Byrd and Baker and looking to the future, we will provide some additional useful background information. From the early 1950s until 1977, only two Democrats, Johnson and Mansfield, served as floor leaders in the Senate. The Republicans, however, were led by four men: Robert Taft (Ohio, 1953), William Knowland (Calif., 1953-1958), Everett Dirksen (Ill., 1959-1969), and Hugh Scott (Pa., 1969-1976). The Democrats dominated the Senate in the 1960s and 1970s, and for most of this period the Senate Republican leadership was quite decentralized. With the major exception of Dirksen's rule, Republican leadership continued to be "more formalized, institutionalized, and decentralized" than its Democratic counterpart.[10]

Lyndon Johnson and Mike Mansfield

From 1955 through 1976, men with starkly contrasting personalities and leadership styles led the Democrats.[11] Johnson sought to centralize control over organizational and policy decisions in himself. Mansfield's objective, on the other hand, was to serve the Senate, to create and maintain a body that "permitted individual, coequal senators the opportunity to conduct their affairs in whatever ways they deemed appropriate." [12] One Democrat who served with both men summarized their differences this way:

> Johnson was aggressive and Mansfield is more the organizer, manager. I think he senses his primary duty is to insure the Senate moves in the conduct of its business in the most orderly fashion that we can. The result of our actions, while I'm sure he feels strongly on a lot of issues, he leaves up to each individual. Lyndon Johnson wanted to influence the outcome of every decision—not just to insure that we acted, but acted in a certain way.[13]

What can be concluded about the relative success of Majority Leaders Johnson and Mansfield? In his study of the last two Congresses under Johnson's direction and the first two Congresses under Mansfield's direction, John Stewart concluded:

> Despite the dispersal of many tasks of party leadership and the generally permissive if not at times passive attitude displayed by the majority leader (Mansfield) in managing the legislative program, the senatorial party in the Eighty-seventh and Eighty-eighth Congresses [1961-1964] functioned effectively, and its performance compared favorably with and often surpassed the record compiled by the Eighty-fifth and Eighty-sixth Congresses [1957-1960] under the driving and centralized leadership of Lyndon Johnson.[14]

Although greater historical perspective is needed to evaluate fully the relative effectiveness of these two leaders, they clearly exemplify the wide range of styles, given different environmental settings, allowable in effective Senate leadership. Mansfield's relaxed manner and his conscious attempts to bring junior members into Senate decisionmaking contributed to the diffusion of power and the opening of procedures that characterized the Senate in the 1970s. Byrd in the 95th Congress appeared to borrow techniques and strategies that seemed to work for his predecessors and to fuse them with his own personality and sense of the Senate. But with his abrupt shift to minority status in 1981, Byrd exercised less dynamic personal leadership of his party.

Robert Byrd

Byrd was first elected to Congress as a member of the House of Representatives in 1952 and then in 1958 as a senator from West Virginia. Thus, he gained firsthand knowledge of Johnson's leadership style and techniques. Moreover, Byrd had served under Mansfield's leadership for 10 years, first as secretary to the party conference and later as party whip. Given the enhanced independence of members and the breakdown of the apprenticeship norm, Byrd was well aware that he could not revert to a 1950s style of centralized command. Nor did he care to emulate many of Mansfield's more laissez-faire tactics. The result was a gradual consolidation of control over party instrumentalities such as the Policy Committee (which discusses issues and helps set the legislative agenda) and the Steering Committee (which makes committee assignments).

Byrd's relationships with the Carter White House were initially rather strained and testy. By the second session of the 95th Congress, however, the new Majority Leader had developed a reasonable working relationship with the Democratic administration, especially on important legislative items such as the ratification of the Panama Canal treaties, the Revenue Act, and the energy programs. Byrd's dogged devotion to detail, his mastery of Senate rules, his willingness to confront but also to compromise with key senators such as Russell Long (D-La.), Edmund Muskie (D-Maine), Republican leader Baker, and even his old antagonist, Edward Kennedy (D-Mass.), contributed to his reputation of effectiveness as Majority Leader.

As Minority Leader in the 1980s, however, Byrd was not viewed quite so positively by his colleagues. He retained his impressive work habits and parliamentary skill but lost some of his zest for legislative combat and strategic legerdemain. One of his colleagues noted midway through 1981:

> Byrd doesn't have his heart in it. He views the minority leadership as a demotion, and he's kind of withdrawn from any strong leadership role.

Byrd rebounded somewhat as the 1982 election approached. The Democrats in the Senate began to coalesce more as a minority—offering alternatives to President Ronald Reagan and Senate Republican policies and moving more aggressively to capture GOP seats in the election, and perhaps regain their majority status. While this goal proved fruitless, the Democrats under Byrd were more disciplined in 1983 and 1984 than they had been two years earlier, and the internal assessments of Byrd's leadership became cautiously positive.

Everett Dirksen and Hugh Scott

Until the stunning 1980 election, the Republicans had not been in the majority in the Senate since 1954. Unlike the Democratic party leadership, which is largely concentrated in the floor leader and whip, the Republicans elect different senators as floor leader, assistant floor leader or whip, chairman of the Republican Policy Committee, chairman of the Committee on Committees, and chairman of the Republican Conference. From the late 1950s through the 1960s, Minority Leader Everett Dirksen's leadership style approximated Johnson's, especially in terms of its centralizing tendencies. Dirksen's successor, Scott, in keeping with the changing membership and power structure of both the Democratic and Republican parties in the Senate, more closely paralleled Mansfield's lower keyed, shared leadership style.[15] The more open and relaxed leadership of both Scott and Mansfield was an important factor in the Senate's movement toward an egalitarian, decentralized form of decisionmaking.

Howard Baker

Just after Baker defeated Griffin in January 1977, he was asked what his relationship with incoming Democratic president Carter would be. The new Minority Leader replied that he "intended to hear him out" and act in the best interests of the country. "There is no longer a minority President, only a minority in Congress," he said. Following the presidencies of Richard Nixon and Gerald R. Ford, the Republican leaders in the Senate—Baker, newly elected whip Ted Stevens of Alaska, and holdover Policy Committee chairman John Tower of Texas—had to shift their roles. No longer did they endeavor to win passage of a Republican president's programs or uphold his vetoes. Instead they became responsible for voicing GOP alternatives in cooperation with the Republican House leadership and the Republican National Committee.

Everett Dirksen, Baker's father-in-law, had been especially adept at maximizing the role of the minority party in the Senate. Depending upon the issues, he either thwarted or cooperated with Democratic presidents. Baker followed in Dirksen's footsteps. Despite opposition from many GOP constituents, Baker supplied crucial support in favor of ratification of the Panama Canal treaties. He also played a critical role in support of Carter's Middle East jet package.

Baker's sometime support for the Democratic administration's policies and his centrist campaign for president in 1980 drew hostile fire from the conservative wing of the Republican party and led to speculation that he would be contested for the new position of Majority Leader in the 97th Congress—perhaps by President-elect Reagan's close friend and conservative ally, Senator Paul Laxalt. After surveying his colleagues, noting Baker's deep popularity, and counting the votes, Laxalt declined to run, preferring the less formal power of being known as "Reagan's best friend in the Senate." No other contestant came forward, and Baker became Majority Leader unopposed.

But leadership of his party would not be easy. The unprecedented influx of 16 freshman Republican senators, nearly all staunch conservatives, immediately confronted Baker with the problem of leading a large bloc of members who had no personal ties to him and often were not ideologically in tune with his views. The freshman group also split GOP ranks along generational lines, since more senior Republicans—for example, Lowell Weicker, Charles Mathias (Md.), Mark Hatfield (Ore.), and Robert Stafford (Vt.)—tended to be more moderate or even liberal.

However, Baker worked closely early in 1981 with key GOP committee chairmen Pete Domenici (N.M.) of Budget and Bob Dole (Kan.) of Finance to pass the Reagan economic package virtually intact, winning the kudos of the president and his conservative Senate colleagues. Throughout the 97th and 98th Congresses, Baker balanced loyal support for President Reagan with equally loyal attention to his Senate charges. He also balanced his attempt to accomplish policy goals on the Senate agenda with a sensitivity to the personal and policy demands, however impetuous, of his individual colleagues, from both left and right.

In the contemporary Senate, Baker was unable to twist arms or employ sanctions as had his late father-in-law, but his leadership by patience, savvy, and good humor was universally respected and admired. Said one colleague, "Baker's the best leader we've had in the Senate in a half-century." Baker also recognized that he could not rely for long on Republican party discipline, so he tailored his majority leadership to appeal to Democrats as well. For four years as Minority Leader, Baker had enjoyed a positive relationship with his majority counterpart Robert Byrd; in 1981 he took steps to cement that relationship. For example, the new Majority Leader diplomatically declined to take over the plush suite of offices occupied by Byrd, opting instead to stay in his old Minority Leader quarters and thus forestalling for Byrd the humiliation of a move.

Still, for all of Baker's skill, the leadership post proved increasingly frustrating. By 1982, the Senate schedule had become more uncontrollable, and Baker found himself buffeted between the demands of ultraconservatives such as Helms and East and the filibusters of liberals such as Weicker and Metzenbaum. In 1984, Baker announced that he would leave the Senate at the end of the year, with the objective of seeking the presidency in 1988 or later.

Several contenders immediately surfaced to succeed him, including Robert Dole of Kansas, James McClure of Idaho, Majority Whip Ted Stevens of Alaska, Richard Lugar of Indiana, and Pete Domenici of New Mexico. Each possessed distinct assets and liabilities, and the outcome awaited the 1984 elections and the 99th Congress.

Committees

From its earliest days, the U.S. Senate like the House of Representatives has used a division of labor into a committee system to organize its work. The committee system is the single most important feature affecting legislative outcomes in the Senate; not surprisingly, it has changed as other aspects of the Senate—workload, membership, power—have themselves been altered in the 1960s, 1970s, and 1980s.

Committee Assignments

Every senator is assigned to committees shortly after being sworn in. When a vacancy occurs on a more attractive committee, senators can and do switch assignments. The committee assignment process is crucial to the Senate because it often determines the policy orientation and activity of each committee. The Democratic and Republican parties handle their own members' assignments differently. Democrats use a 21-member Steering Committee chaired by the Majority Leader, while Republicans have an 18-member Committee on Committees with an elected chairman. In the 1940s and early 1950s, committee assignments reflected the norm of apprenticeship: freshmen were assigned only to minor committees, and senior members dominated prestigious committees such as Foreign Relations, Appropriations, Finance, and Armed Services.

When Lyndon Johnson became Majority Leader in 1955, he changed these procedures by instituting the "Johnson Rule," which guaranteed every Democrat, no matter how junior, a major committee assignment. However, as we have noted, Johnson ran the Steering Committee as a one-man show, and he handed out choice assignments very selectively. Senior, more conservative members continued to dominate the most prestigious committees.

Under Mike Mansfield, the Steering Committee operated more democratically, and assignments to all committees became more open to junior and liberal Democrats. This egalitarian pattern continued under Robert Byrd, although not entirely without controversy. Soon after Byrd's election as Majority Leader in 1977, junior liberal Democratic senators, led by John Culver of Iowa, forced an acrimonious debate in the Democratic Caucus to protest Byrd's choices to fill Steering Committee vacancies. The liberals won an agreement, still in effect, that future Steering Committee choices would be submitted in advance to the party membership. Republicans have made their assignments under a more automatic process based on a direct preference for seniority, but, in the 1970s—as important committees were enlarged, limits were imposed on the ability of senior members to "stockpile" assignments, and at the same time a large number of junior Republicans were entering the chamber—the GOP membership on committees also changed.

The combined effect of these changes in the mid- to late 1970s was that committees became more junior and more liberal. But in the 97th and 98th

Table 1-2 Mean Seniority in Years at Time of Appointment to Prestigious
Standing Committees

Committee	80th-84th Congresses*	94th Congress	96th Congress	98th Congress
Foreign Relations	8.1	4.0	3.5	4.8
Appropriations	5.8	2.0	4.0	4.4
Finance	3.0	2.7	1.1	2.6
Armed Services	2.1	1.2	0.0	2.7

* Figures taken from Donald R. Matthews, *U.S. Senators and Their World* (New York: Vintage Books, 1960), p. 153.

Congresses, patterns changed. Juniority became less important, despite the huge freshman class of 1980 (97th Congress figures are not far different from those of the 98th presented in Table 1-2), and the committees—continuing to reflect the Senate as a whole—shifted considerably to the right.

For many decades, Senate committee chairmanships have been selected through the process of seniority. While this procedure has been modified somewhat, as we have noted, its overall impact in recent years has served to dampen the overall trends in ideology and region that have affected both the Senate as a whole and its committee rosters. Thanks to the seniority process, the decline in the 1970s in the number of Southern Democrats in the Senate was reflected only partially in committee chairmanships. In 1975 southerners accounted for only 26 percent of Senate Democrats; however, they comprised 39 percent of committee chairmanships, including the leadership of powerful committees such as Appropriations, Finance, Armed Services, Foreign Relations, and Judiciary.

Seniority had a different effect on chairmanships when Republicans took over the Senate. Despite the strong conservative trend of the 1978 and 1980 elections, the more senior Republicans were more moderate than Senate Republicans as a whole; the top quartile in 1981 had an average conservative coalition voting ratio of 72, compared with an average of 88 for the other more junior three-fourths of Republicans. As a result, nearly one-half of the major committee chairmen in the Republican Senate were more liberal than their committee colleagues, including the chairmen of Appropriations and Foreign Relations.

The elections of 1980 and 1982 influenced the seniority distribution of the Democratic party as well. The departure, through defeat and retirement, of a number of post-1958 northern liberals was accomplished by the movement up the Democratic seniority ladder of several 1970s-vintage southerners. In the 98th Congress, nine of the Senate's 16 standing committees had Southern Democrats as ranking members, and 10 would be chairmen if the Senate reverted to the Democrats in 1985.

Committees and Workload

With a small legislative membership, the Senate is deeply affected by changes in its workload. The 1960s and 1970s saw that workload burgeon. There were five times as many roll call votes on the Senate floor in the 93rd Congress as there were in the 84th, and the more than 1,000 roll calls were accompanied by increases in the number of bills introduced and hearings held. In response to the increasing number and complexity of decisions senators had to make, the Senate expanded the committee system. In 1957 there were 15 standing committees with 118 subcommittees in the Senate. By 1975 there were 18 standing committees with 140 subcommittees; if special, select, and joint committees were included in the tally, it reached 31 committees and 174 subcommittees in all.

More importantly, perhaps, the Senate increased the sizes of many of its committees and subcommittees. Since the size of the Senate has increased by only four members since the admission to the union of Alaska and Hawaii in 1959, this meant more assignments for individual members. In 1957 each senator averaged 2.8 committee assignments and 6.3 subcommittee assignments, whereas by 1976 senators on the average served on 4 committees and 14 subcommittees.

Under pressure particularly from junior members, the Senate early in 1976 created the Temporary Select Committee to Study the Senate Committee System, a 12-member bipartisan panel chaired by Senator Adlai E. Stevenson (D-Ill.). After a year of extensive hearings and lively debate the Senate adopted a modified version of the Stevenson Committee plan, S. Res. 4, which eliminated three standing and five select and joint panels and transformed substantially four other committees: Energy and Natural Resources, Environment and Public Works, Governmental Affairs, and Human Resources. By placing strict limits on senators' subcommittee assignments and chairmanships, S. Res. 4 resulted in a dramatic drop in the number of subcommittees (from an overall total of 174 to 110) and in the number of assignments (the average dropped from 4 committees and 14 subcommittees to 3 committees and 7.5 subcommittees). However, in a trend typical for an individualized, democratized institution, committee and subcommittee assignments immediately began to expand again, well beyond the limits set by S. Res. 4. By the 98th Congress, the average number of assignments was up nearly to 12, and 40 senators had violated, in one way or another, the chamber rules on assignment limitations. Yet, despite the recent backsliding, the system remains more compact than in the past.

Even in today's more streamlined committee system, senators continue to be spread thin, with little time or attention to devote to any individual areas. To respond to this fragmentation, the Senate in the 1970s began to expand professional staffs. We have already mentioned S. Res. 60, a 1975 device to increase the number of legislative assistants available to senators. Committee staffs, as well as senators' personal staffs, have grown, from roughly 300 in the 85th Congress to well over 1,200 (including both permanent and investigative staff) by the 95th. With S. Res. 4 and the GOP takeover in 1981, staff numbers dropped slightly, and then stabilized in the early 1980s.

The expansion of staffs has allowed senators to cope more easily with their heavy workload and greater responsibilities. It has also distributed Senate resources broadly to junior as well as senior members. In recent years staffs have been allocated increasingly through subcommittees rather than full committees, which has accentuated the spread of power to junior senators and has correspondingly reduced the relative power of committee chairmen. Writing of the Senate in the 1950s, Donald Matthews commented, "Within certain limits, the [committee] chairman appoints and controls the committee staff." [16] Today, however, far more staff are appointed by subcommittee chairmen than by committee chairmen, who no longer maintain monopoly control over expertise and command unchallenged loyalty from staff. Expertise and staff are now widely dispersed throughout the Senate. Although the accession to committee chairmanships in the 97th Congress of aggressive GOP conservatives such as John Tower of Texas (Armed Services) and Jake Garn of Utah (Banking) resulted in a somewhat greater consolidation of power and initiative in some full committees and their chairmen, diffusion and decentralization remain the norm in the mid-1980s.

Along with expanding subcommittee chairmanships and expanding staffs, committee deliberations have become more open in recent years. All of these factors together have loosened the control that committee leaders once maintained over their committee members. Junior senators now have subcommittee bases from which to challenge the policy recommendations of committee chairmen. Moreover, senators who do not serve on a committee will have enough access to information to enable them to offer successful amendments on the floor to the committee's bills. Thus, committees have become less cohesive internally, and their bills have become more vulnerable to challenge on the Senate floor.

During the 1970s, legislation shifted from the committee rooms to the Senate floor, while the functions of agenda-setting and legislative oversight moved from the committees to the subcommittees. During the 1980s, legislative activity declined somewhat; the Senate considered fewer bills, took fewer roll call votes, and passed fewer laws than it had in the preceding several years. Nevertheless, the patterns of legislative initiation and the relative importance of Senate institutions remained the same. Committees continue to be highly important; all legislation is referred to them, as are all executive and judicial nominations, and they retain the authority either to kill or to report out the bills and nominations. But the Senate is a more open, fluid, and decentralized body now than it was in the 1950s. Power, resources, and decisionmaking authority have become more diffuse. The combined impact of changes in membership, norms, leadership, workload, and committees have produced a markedly different Senate in the 1980s.

The Senate as a Presidential Incubator

So far we have focused mainly on internal changes in Senate structures and behavior. But the Senate has not operated in a vacuum; it has been greatly affected by trends in the society and in the broader political system, and it has had, in turn, its own impact on American politics. Nowhere is this more true than in the area of presidential nominations. Although senators had actively contested for presidential nominations in past decades, in the period from 1960 to 1972 senators were dominant. During that 12-year span, the two parties relied exclusively upon either senators (Edward Kennedy, Barry Goldwater, and George McGovern) or former senators who became vice-presidents (Richard Nixon, Lyndon Johnson, and Hubert Humphrey) before obtaining their party's presidential nod.

The primaries and general election of 1976 were surprising on several counts. Former Georgia governor Jimmy Carter swept through the Democratic primaries and beat a number of congressional contenders to secure a first ballot nomination and eventually win the presidency. President Gerald Ford, a former House Republican leader, won his party's nomination but lost the election to Carter. However, both parties followed the predominant post-World War II pattern of selecting senators for vice-presidential candidates: Walter Mondale (D-Minn.) and Robert Dole (R-Kan.). Senators also competed actively, albeit unsuccessfully, for the presidency in the 1980 primaries (Howard Baker and Robert Dole for the Republican nomination and Edward Kennedy for the Democratic party choice) and in the Democratic race in 1984 (Gary Hart, John Glenn, Alan Cranston, Ernest Hollings).

There are numerous reasons for the string of successes by senatorial contenders from 1960 to 1972. The near revolutionary growth in media influence over politics, especially that of television, has focused public attention on Washington and on the Senate. Television has contributed to, and has been affected by, the increasing nationalization of party politics. A national attentiveness to foreign affairs has heightened the importance of the Senate with its well-defined constitutional role in foreign policy.

As the Senate opened up its proceedings, spread its resources, and decentralized its power, it became more attractive to potential presidential contenders. But the successful nomination efforts of Jimmy Carter and Ronald Reagan, combined with the lack of success of prominent and influential Senate leaders such as Baker, Dole, Glenn, and Cranston, have stripped some of the luster off the Senate as a base for presidential forays. Both Howard Baker and Robert Dole have asserted the near impossibility of running for president and serving in the Senate simultaneously. (Baker went further, leaving his Senate seat at the end of 1984.) Moreover, the public animosity toward Washington, the decline in legislative activity, and the move (with economic stagnation and deficits) toward unpopular, redistributive policies, have tarnished the appeal of the Senate for many first-rate politicians. In 1984, prominent governors such as Pete DuPont (R-Del.), Lamar Alexander (R-Tenn.), Richard Lamm (D-Colo.), Scott Matheson (D-Utah), and Ed Herschler (D-Wyo.) foreswore Senate contests to remain in their states.

The Senate, however, remains an institution that receives national and international attention and that contributes the lion's share of potential candidates and contenders for the White House. The effects upon the Senate of its members' presidential fever extend beyond those few legislators who obtain party nominations.[17] Many senators consider themselves presidential possibilities or are mentioned as such on television networks and in the polls. Senators tailor their behavior accordingly, spreading out their legislative interests beyond the concerns of their individual states, increasing their legislative activity and public visibility, and emphasizing media coverage over legislative craftsmanship. This preoccupation with presidential aspirations has contributed to violations of the norms of specialization and legislative work. It has also increased the pressure within the Senate to distribute resources and power to junior members.

Conclusion

As we have seen, the Senate since the 1950s has changed in varied and interrelated ways. The nature of its membership, its internal norms and rules, its leadership styles and effects, its committees, and its role as a breeding ground for presidential candidates have all evolved to make the Senate of the 1980s quite a different legislative institution.

The Senate has gone from a close partisan balance during the Truman and Eisenhower presidencies in the 1950s to dominant Democratic party control in the 1960s and 1970s to a narrow Republican majority in the early 1980s. A powerful Southern Democratic wing, which once maintained great power through the seniority system and a coalition with likeminded Republicans, gradually diminished in size and influence,[18] but is now making a comeback. Liberal northeastern and midwestern Democratic senators, from the 1958 election through the mid-1970s, experienced a corresponding growth in numbers and power only to diminish in numbers and power in 1978 and 1980. They in turn are looking to the 1984 and 1986 elections to replenish their numbers. Junior senators, once relegated to a position of apprenticeship and subservience, have found their importance enhanced in the contemporary Senate, even with the recent partisan and ideological shifts. With the active assistance of Majority Leader Mike Mansfield and the compliance of his successors, Democrat Robert Byrd and Republican Howard Baker, junior senators have won access to prestigious committee assignments and to legislative staff resources. Thus, they have carved out for themselves a highly significant role in the legislative process, one that is unlikely to change dramatically under Baker's successor.

Through these and other trends, the Senate has become more open, more decentralized, and more equal in its distribution of power. Throughout the seventies, it also became more overburdened with work. As senators' obligations and time commitments multiplied, their ability to deal with complex questions in an in-depth fashion diminished. The comprehensive committee system reorganization of 1977 helped the Senate to cope with these problems, as did the accession of more assertive leaders, especially Byrd and Baker. Changes continued through the 98th Congress. The overall work burden has declined roughly to the levels of the early 1970s, and Senate staffs are no longer expanding (and, indeed, under the Republicans, have been slightly reduced in number). But the Senate remains an institution dominated by its individual members. The forces of decentralization and democratization continue to be, pronounced. Although fewer bills are being processed in committees or on the floor, the less frenetic atmosphere has not returned the Senate to the leisurely, "clublike" atmosphere of the past or increased the role, level, or quality of debate.

Few members of the contemporary Senate are satisfied with its work or its outputs. Lawmakers are notorious for complaining about their institutions, but the frustrations of today's senators suggest genuine dissatisfaction with the uncertain role of today's Senate. Neither a great deliberative body nor an efficient processor of laws, the Senate, after years of dramatic and sometimes crosscutting change, is an institution in search of an identity. That search will produce even more change through the remainder of the 1980s.

NOTES

1. See the collection of articles by Huitt in *Congress: Two Decades of Analysis,* Ralph K. Huitt and Robert L. Peabody (New York: Harper & Row, 1969); and Donald R. Matthews, *U.S. Senators and Their World* (New York: Vintage Books, 1960).
2. See, for example, Michael Foley, *The New Senate* (New Haven: Yale University Press, 1980); Elizabeth Drew, *Senator* (New York: Simon & Schuster, 1979); Ross G. Baker, *Friend and Foe in the U.S. Senate* (New York: Free Press, 1980); Bernard Asbell, *The Senate Nobody Knows* (Baltimore: Johns Hopkins University Press, 1978).
3. Matthews, *U.S. Senators and Their World,* p. 92.
4. This essay is part of a broader study of the Senate conducted since 1973 by the authors with the help of a grant from the Russell Sage Foundation. In addition to legislative and electoral data, our analysis is based upon more than 60 semistructured, taped interviews with incumbent and former senators from 1973 to 1979, plus numerous other interviews and direct observations carried out since then.

5. For more on the Senate's move from a closed system to an open one, see Norman J. Ornstein, "The Open Congress Meets the President," in *Both Ends of the Avenue,* ed. Anthony King (Washington, D.C.: American Enterprise Institute for Public Policy Research, 1983).
6. Matthews, *U.S. Senators and Their World,* pp. 116-117.
7. For a discussion of the changes during the 1960s, see Randall B. Ripley, *Power in the Senate* (New York: St. Martin's Press, 1969).
8. See also Rowland Evans and Robert Novak, *Lyndon B. Johnson: The Exercise of Power* (New York: New American Library, 1966); Randall B. Ripley, *Majority Party Leadership in Congress* (Boston: Little, Brown & Co., 1969); and John G. Stewart, "Two Strategies of Leadership: Johnson and Mansfield," in *Congressional Behavior,* ed. Nelson W. Polsby (New York: Random House, 1971), pp. 61-92. Also see Neil MacNeil, *Dirksen: Portrait of a Public Man* (New York: World Publications, 1970); Jean Torcom Cronin, "Minority Leadership in the United States Senate: The Role and Style of Everett Dirksen" (Ph.D. diss., Johns Hopkins University, 1979); and Charles O. Jones, *The Minority Party in Congress* (Boston: Little, Brown & Co., 1970).
9. Evans and Novak, *Lyndon B. Johnson,* pp. 195-224.
10. Matthews, *U.S. Senators and Their World,* p. 124.
11. Stewart, "Two Strategies of Leadership"; and Robert L. Peabody, *Leadership in Congress: Stability, Succession and Change* (Boston: Little, Brown & Co., 1976), pp. 333-345.
12. Stewart, "Two Strategies of Leadership," p. 87.
13. David W. Rohde, Norman J. Ornstein, and Robert L. Peabody, "Political Change and Legislative Norms in the United States Senate" (a revised version of a paper delivered at the annual meeting of the American Political Science Association, Chicago, Illinois, August 29-September 2, 1974), p. 26.
14. Stewart, "Two Strategies of Leadership," p. 87.
15. Jones, *Minority Party.*
16. Matthews, *U.S. Senators and Their World,* p. 160.
17. For an extended treatment of the causes and impact of the Senate's role in presidential nominations, see Robert L. Peabody, Norman J. Ornstein, and David W. Rohde, "The United States Senate as a Presidential Incubator: Many Are Called But Few Are Chosen," *Political Science Quarterly* 91 (Summer 1976): 237-258.
18. One should not conclude that southern conservatives are now powerless. They still retain several important committee chairmanships. Moreover, a single dedicated senator with knowledge of the rules can have a tremendous impact on the legislative process. The late Senator James Allen of Alabama was one whose use of the filibuster and other techniques of parliamentary procedure delayed, killed, or significantly changed several pieces of major legislation in his last few years in the Senate.

2. THE HOUSE IN TRANSITION: PARTISANSHIP AND OPPOSITION

Lawrence C. Dodd and Bruce I. Oppenheimer

The 1980s have presented a distinct challenge to the House of Representatives. The landslide victory of Ronald Reagan in 1980 confronted the House not only with a president but also a Senate of the opposite party. The House, with its Democratic majority, thus was the center of "loyal opposition" to the government and the institution most likely to restrain the conservative juggernaut unleashed by Reagan's election. Yet House Democrats possessed only a small majority and were working in an institution that had experienced widespread changes during the previous decade. The Democrats thus had to refine and stabilize the new rules and procedures of the House while engaged in a highly partisan battle with a Republican president and Senate majority. This essay will describe the developments in more detail and assess how well the House has responded to these challenges.

Membership Change

In recent years the House has undergone significant membership turnover. At the start of the 92nd Congress, it could boast that a record 20 percent of its membership had been elected to at least 10 terms. But House "careerism," as Charles Bullock has called this condition, has declined significantly since then.[1] At the start of the 96th Congress, only 12.6 percent of House members met the 10-term criterion (the lowest since 1955). Careerists in both the 97th and 98th Congresses were slightly fewer than in the 96th but remained around 12 percent. As Figure 2-1 indicates, the drop in careerism has been accompanied by a growth in the number of new House members.[2] The 96th Congress had more junior members (those elected to three or fewer terms) than any Congress since 1937. The number of new members fell in the 97th and 98th Congresses but remained high by postwar standards. In each Congress there were 208 House members, nearly 48 percent of the entire membership, serving three or fewer terms.

Voluntary Retirement Trend

This increase in membership turnover in the House in the 1970s occurred for very different reasons than it did in past decades. In earlier

Figure 2-1 House Service: New Members (Three or Fewer Terms) and Careerists (Ten or More Terms), 1911-1983

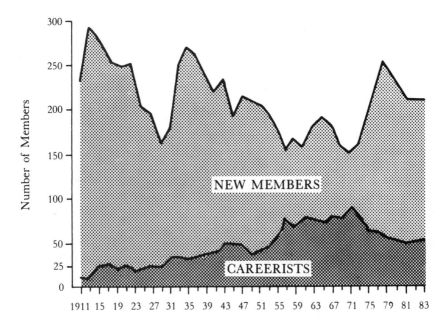

62nd - 98th Congresses

decades electoral defeat was usually responsible for much of the turnover. But with the exception of the 1974 defeat of Republican incumbents in the "Watergate" aftermath, House turnover in the 1970s was a function of retirement. In 1974, 1976, and 1978 the House set new post-World War II records for retirement. In 1978, 49 members announced that they would not seek an additional term in the House. By comparison, only 19 incumbents were defeated in the general election and 4 others in primaries.

In 1980, 1982, and 1984 the number of retirees declined somewhat from the record levels to 37, 31, and 22, respectively. And in 1982 and 1984 a majority of House retirees sought other elective offices. Turnover in 1980 and 1982, however, remained high because incumbents proved vulnerable. In 1980 six House incumbents lost primary contests, and another 31 met defeat in the general election—many of them Democratic victims of the Reagan landslide. In 1982 the Reagan recession as well as reapportionment and redistricting were seen as major factors contributing to the defeat of 33 House incumbents (4 in primaries and 29 in the general election). One important study convincingly argues that House incumbents are potentially quite vulnerable to electoral challenges, but the 1980 and 1982 elections did not provide sufficient evidence that this potential electoral vulnerability has, as yet, become a reality.[3]

Many explanations have been offered for the increase in voluntary House retirements. They include: (1) improved pensions for retired members; (2) the more demanding nature of the job of a House member; (3) frustration over the difficulties the House has in making policy; (4) increased visibility of House members that improves their ability to seek other offices; (5) the end of the great liberal-conservative fight over post-New Deal issues such as civil rights and aid to education; (6) House provisions limiting outside income, regulating campaigns, and requiring financial disclosure; and (7) change in the distribution of rewards for House service; those once given only to members with long tenure are available to many junior House members now. Retiring House members have generally cited one or more of these problems in explaining their exodus from the House. Although it is difficult to separate the public as opposed to the private reasons for retirement, it is fair to say that all of the above reasons have played a role.[4]

Of those retiring at the end of the 98th Congress, 13 did so in pursuit of another elective office. Others left out of frustration. In the case of Ray Kogovsek (D-Colo.), a three-term member, the frustration was personal. At age 42 Kogovsek claimed that he and his wife wanted time for themselves.[5] By comparison, Richard Ottinger (D-N.Y.) noted in his retirement announcement "the incredible frustration of being in Congress and still feeling as powerless as the average citizen to affect the great issues before the country."[6]

Whether members leave through retirement or defeat, of course, the result is in some ways the same. The House, criticized by Samuel Huntington in the 1960s for operating in isolation because it lacked "biennial infusion of new blood," received regular transfusions into the 1970s and 1980s.[7] Change in House membership means more than just new blood replacing old, however. The partisan, ideological, and sectional makeup of the institution has changed as well as the age, sex, and racial composition of its membership.

History of Democratic Control

Since 1955, and with the exception of only four years since 1931, the Democrats have been the majority party in the House. The size of that majority has fluctuated during the past 30 years with as small as a 30-seat margin in the 84th and 85th Congresses that left control of the House in the hands of a conservative coalition of Republicans and Southern Democrats. Following the 1958 landslide election, the Democratic seat total increased from 234 to 283, but conservatives were still able to hold their own. Only after the 1964 Goldwater debacle that gave Democrats a 295-140 House majority in the 89th Congress were many of the liberal policies enacted in the Kennedy-Johnson legislative program.

After the 89th Congress, Republicans reasserted their strength, forcing liberal Democrats to focus on saving the policy initiatives of the 89th Congress. Democrats failed again to gain overwhelming control of the House until the 94th and 95th Congresses; Democrats elected 291 and 292 respectively to these, giving them a sizable margin of control. The success Democrats have had in holding their open seats in this period, together with their ability to maintain control of the traditionally Republican seats won in 1974, allowed them to reach a high plateau of House control, surpassed in this century only by the New Deal Congresses of 1933 to 1939. Even in the wake of the Reagan landslide in 1980, the Democrats maintained control of the House and were able, in the 1982 elections, to rebuild from 243 seats after 1980 to 268 seats in the 98th Congress.

Ideological Changes

The majority the Democrats built up in the last 20 years is important because of the nature of its ideological makeup, as well as its size, particularly when contrasted to Congresses in the early postwar years. Table 2-1 compares the ideological composition of the House during the first sessions of the 86th and 98th Congresses and provides some insights into the nature of the change.

First, although Northern Democrats in the 98th were not as exclusively "liberals" as they were in the 86th (76 versus 82 percent), the number of

Table 2-1 Ideological Divisions in the House, 86th Congress, 1st Session (1959) and 98th Congress, 1st Session (1983)

	Northern Demo- crats	*Southern Demo- crats*	*All Demo- crats*	*Repub- licans*	*All Members*
86th Congress, 1st Session	*(N=171)*	*(N=110)*	*(N=281)*	*(N=153)*	*(N=434)*
Liberals	82% (140)	2% (2)	51% (142)	4% (6)	34% (148)
Moderates	13 (23)	13 (14)	13 (37)	15 (23)	14 (60)
Conservatives	5 (8)	85 (94)	36 (102)	81 (124)	52 (226)
98th Congress, 1st Session	*(N=177)*	*(N=90)*	*(N=267)*	*N=167)*	*(N=434)*
Liberals	76% (134)	4% (4)	52% (138)	2% (3)	32% (141)
Moderates	22 (39)	44 (40)	30 (79)	17 (28)	25 (102)
Conservatives	2 (4)	51 (46)	19 (50)	81 (136)	43 (186)

NOTE: The classification is based on a variation of the conservative coalition support scores published annually by Congressional Quarterly. The support score of a member was divided by the sum of his or her support and opposition scores, which removes the effect of absences. Members whose scores were 0-30 were classified as liberals, 31-70 as moderates, and 71-100 as conservatives. The number of members used to compute each percentage is shown in parentheses at the top of each column.

Northern Democratic liberals is nearly the same (134 versus 140) because their total number is higher (177 versus 171). The combined total of liberals and moderates has increased from 163 to 173. These differences resulted from Democrats winning seats held by Republicans. Since the Republicans were overwhelmingly conservative, the effect was to make the House more liberal. Second, there is a sizable decrease in the percentage of Southern Democrats classified as conservative and a corresponding increase in the moderate and liberal groupings of Southern Democrats between the two Congresses. Third, the Republicans, although fewer in number, remain very conservative.

Taken together, these changes indicate that the House is substantially less conservative than it was in the 86th Congress. True, the 97th and 98th Congresses were not as liberal as the 94th and 95th, but conservatives no longer comprised a House majority as they did in the 86th Congress. For more than a decade, moderates have held the balance of power in the House, with this change resulting in large part from the growth of moderates and liberals among the Southern Democratic delegation. This moderation in Southern Democratic representation is an outgrowth from the implementation of the Voting Rights Act of 1965 and the resulting enfranchisement of black voters in the South. The change has further decreased the influence of conservatives within the House Democratic party.

Table 2-1 does not reveal a related change among southern House members. This is the growth in the number of Southern Republicans who are almost uniformly conservative. In 1960 only seven Southern Republicans were elected to the House. This rose to a high of 34 following the Nixon landslide in 1972.[8] With declines in Republican party success following Watergate, the Southern Republican strength in the House dropped slightly to 31 members in the 96th Congress. The growth of Southern Republican House membership resumed in the 1980s with 42 serving in the 97th Congress and 39 in the 98th Congress.

Changes in Composition

There were other changes in House membership in the 1970s and 1980s. It should not be surprising, given the high turnover rate, to find that the average age of House members dropped. At the start of the 94th Congress in 1975, the average age of a House member was less than 50 for the first time since World War II, and it has continued to decline in succeeding Congresses, reaching a low of 45.5 in the 98th Congress.

The racial and sexual composition of the House has also changed. In 1983 there were 21 black House members, compared with only 5 in 1962. There were also 11 Hispanics, up from 7 in the 97th Congress. Corresponding to the increased activity of women in politics, more women are also serving in the House. In 1982, 21 women were elected to the House, an increase over the record 18 women members elected to the 94th and 95th Congresses.

Certainly these figures do not come close to being proportional to the size of these groups in the population, but, as with the growth of southern liberals and moderates, they do suggest trends toward membership diversification. Moreover, they demonstrate how the House, with narrower, more homogeneous constituencies, has a better capacity than the Senate to include southern liberals, northern conservatives, blacks, Hispanics, and women in its membership. The House provides a vital access point through which minorities can enter government and gain political power, as witnessed in the nomination of House member Geraldine Ferraro as the first woman vice-presidential candidate for a major political party. The openness and diversity of the House, however, also make it difficult to govern and increase its dependence on rules and procedures.

Rules and Procedures

Since the House is a much larger institution than the Senate—435 members as compared with 100 members—it must rely more on formal rules and explicit procedures than on norms. Norms do exist in the House: reciprocity, courtesy, hard work, expertise, and the most hallowed of all, seniority.[9] Nevertheless, the rules of the party caucuses, the rules of committees, and the rules of the House itself are primary guides to member behavior and are the centers of contention in struggles over power. Because there are so many new members in the House, it is difficult to socialize them rapidly to informal norms. As a result, formal rules have become even more important than they were in earlier decades; today formal rules are new members' primary guide to the legislative process in the House. In response to the reforms of the 1970s, the rules of the 1980s are different from the rules that most new members read about in the 1950s, 1960s, and early 1970s.

Beginning of Reform Movement

The reform movement of the 1970s began in the late 1950s with the creation of the Democratic Study Group (DSG), an organization of Democratic liberals committed to liberal legislation and liberal control of the House.[10] Throughout the 1960s the group pushed for changes in House procedures and party practice. Liberals' efforts in the 1960s to bring about formal changes in House rules resulted in the 1970 Legislative Reorganization Act. That act, passed by a coalition of House Republicans and liberal Democrats, primarily served to liberalize and formalize parliamentary procedure in committees and on the floor of the House.

During the late 1960s, just when these formal rules changes were approaching ratification, liberal Democrats fundamentally altered their strategy. Although they constituted the dominant faction of the House Democratic party in size, they did not dominate the positions of congressional power that are derived from party membership, particularly the chairmanships of key committees. The formal changes in House rules could not alter the distribution of power positions because those positions derive from the majority party. Formal changes in rules also could not ensure the procedural protection of House liberals (or Republicans) because the only real way to enforce the changes was through discipline of committee chairs and party leaders within the majority party. Few mechanisms of party discipline existed to encourage committee leaders to abide by the changes.

Revitalization of the Democratic Caucus

To widen the focus of congressional reforms and make committee chairs follow rules changes, liberals shifted their attention to reforms of the House Democratic party itself. In January 1969 the Democratic Caucus, which had been dormant for most of the century, was revitalized by the passage of a rule stating that a caucus meeting could be held each month if 50 members demanded the meeting in writing. Utilizing the party caucus, liberals throughout the early 1970s pushed for the creation of reform committees that would study the House and propose reforms of its structure and procedures.

Three reform committees were formed as a result of Democratic Caucus activity.[11] All were chaired by Representative Julia Butler Hansen (D-Wash.), and their proposals became known collectively as the Hansen Committee reforms. The proposals of Hansen I were debated and passed in January 1971, Hansen II in January 1973, and Hansen III in 1974. Another reform effort initiated by Speaker Carl Albert (D-Okla.) was the creation of a Select Committee on Committees headed by Representative Richard Bolling (D-Mo.). The Bolling Committee introduced its proposals in 1974, but they were defeated by the membership of the House, which chose instead to implement the proposals of Hansen III.[12]

Consequences of Reforms

These reform efforts had six particularly important consequences. First, they established a clear procedure whereby the Democratic Caucus could select committee chairs by secret ballot. This change in the traditional voting procedure provided a mechanism for defeating renominations of incumbent committee chairs, thereby bypassing the norm of committee seniority. Second, the reforms increased the number and strength of subcommittees. Third, in conjunction with these reform efforts the House moved to open to the public virtually all committee and subcommittee meetings. Fourth, the reforms increased the power of the Speaker of the House by giving him considerable control over the referral of legislation. A fifth change, which was not actually part of these caucus reforms but stemmed from the overall reform movement, was the creation in 1974 of a new congressional budget process and House Budget Committee.

Finally, the defeat of the Bolling Committee provisions restructuring committee jurisdictions left the maze of overlapping committee and subcommittee jurisdictions relatively untouched. In the 96th Congress the House created a new Select Committee on Committees to review jurisdictions and procedures. Chaired by Jerry Patterson (D-Cal.), this new committee approached the reform process differently than the Bolling Committee, presenting reforms in a piecemeal rather than package form. Nevertheless, this approach also faced considerable opposition.

Despite these failures, other reforms of the post-1973 period were adopted. In the 94th Congress House Democrats refined the procedure for nominating committee chairs and voted down several incumbents. The caucus also adopted a rule requiring nominees for Appropriations subcommittee chairs to be approved by similar procedures. This rule, which seemed in order because Appropriations subcommittees are in many cases more powerful than other standing committees, was employed in the 95th Congress to deny a subcommittee position to a member who had been censured in the previous Congress for financial misconduct, Representative Robert Sikes (D-Fla.).

The Ethics Issue

The Sikes case, as well as the sex and public payroll scandals involving Wayne Hays (D-Ohio) and the probe of South Korean influence-peddling on Capitol Hill, focused attention on the inadequacy of House ethics provisions. During the 95th Congress the House, following the recommendations of the bipartisan Commission on Administrative Review chaired by David Obey (D-Wis.), adopted a new code of ethics. The code required annual financial disclosure by House members, officers, and professional staff; prohibited gifts totaling $100 or more from a lobbyist or foreign national; prohibited unofficial office accounts; placed new restrictions on the use of the franking privilege; and limited members from receiving outside earned income in excess of 15 percent of their congressional salary.

This last provision was the most hotly debated. Some members claimed that it discriminated in favor of wealthier members since no restrictions were placed on unearned outside income from stocks, property, and other investments. Proponents claimed that there was no way the House could restrict unearned income and that the purpose of the provision was to limit the time members would devote to an outside job. (In 1981 the House increased the limit on outside earned income to 30 percent.) Although the ethics code contained a sweetener in the form of an increase in office expenses, it was a bitter pill for a number of House members.

The ethics code is one of the few reforms of the 1970s that placed serious constraints on the new levels of independence House members had reached. Some members threatened to quit because of the limitations on outside income, and in several instances the ethics code contributed to the decision of members to retire. Since passage of the ethics code in 1977, financial misconduct and other wrongdoings have continued to plague the House as seen in the scandals surrounding Daniel Flood (D-Pa.), Charles Diggs (D-Mich.), Charles Wilson (D-Calif.), George Hansen (R-Idaho), and those involving other House members implicated in the FBI Abscam bribery investigation.

In May 1982 the House responded to allegations that some of its members were engaging in sexual misconduct and drug usage with teenage congressional pages. It authorized its ethics committee, the Committee on Official Conduct, to investigate the charges. The committee found that two House members had engaged in questionable conduct and that the page system itself needed revision. In the aftermath of the investigation, on July 20, 1983, the House censured Daniel Crane (R-Ill.) and Gerry Studds (D-Mass.), the first members ever censured for sexual misconduct and only the fifth and sixth members censured in the twentieth century. The House also revised the page system and created a more centralized and coordinated management.

Conclusion

The foregoing changes in House rules and procedures in the 1970s and 1980s evidence two trends: the decentralization of power within committees and the centralization of authority in the party caucus, the Speaker, and a new budget committee. The move toward centralizing reform continued, although in a less extensive fashion, during the 98th Congress. Frustrated by efforts of minority members to stir up controversy and obstruct House business, the Democratic leaders tightened the rules of the House. The most controversial change was to restrict "riders"—amendments that are extraneous to the subject matter of a bill—to appropriations legislation. Conservative members were increasingly using riders to force roll call votes on controversial issues, such as school busing and abortion, and thereby bypass the authorizing committees with jurisdiction over these areas. The rules changes also increased the procedural authority of the Democratic leadership to avoid other types of "nuisance" votes.

The procedural reforms of the 98th Congress, together with those of the previous decade, indicate significant changes in the role of the congressional parties and their leaders. The overall nature and significance of these changes can best be seen by focusing separately on the House committee system and party leadership.

Committees

Party government began to decline in the early 1900s, and by the post-World War II era committee government dominated the House. The 1946 Legislative Reorganization Act contributed to the domination of the House by approximately 20 committee chairs. This era was characterized by brokerage politics in Congress—a politics in which committee chairs attempted to aggregate the numerous competing policy interests within their committee's jurisdictional domain through bargaining and compromise. The era was also characterized by a generally conservative bent to the policy process, since the norm of seniority tended to benefit conservative Democrats from safe one-party areas of the South.

As liberals began to dominate the Democratic party in the House during the 1950s and 1960s, opposition to the existing structure of committee government escalated. Aside from ideological considerations, the opposition was fueled by two environmental pressures on the House. First, the increase in both the number and complexity of federal concerns created the need for higher levels of legislative specialization, putting considerable pressure on the existing system and creating a demand for more meetings and investigations than could be handled easily by the standing committees. Second, the number of "careerists" in the House increased significantly during this period. As a consequence, numerous seasoned members of Congress experienced in legislative life and capable of undertaking serious legislative work were frozen out of the legislative process because there were not enough committee chairs to go around.

As reformers in the 1950s and 1960s looked for ways to weaken the power of conservative chairs, increase the workload potential of the House, and provide the growing number of careerists access to legislative power, they turned their attention to the strengthening of subcommittees within the standing committees. Their efforts resulted in the reforms of the 1970s, which had two major dimensions: the rise of subcommittee government and the decline of committee chairs. The reforms have also had consequences far beyond those ever envisioned by its creators.

The Rise of Subcommittee Government

During the early postwar years, most hearings, debates, and mark-up sessions were held at a committee level, and those that were not were subject to committee review and change. By the late 1970s policymaking activity was increasingly the province of the standing subcommittees.[13]

Subcommittee government exists when the basic responsibility for the bulk of legislative activity (hearings, debates, legislative mark-ups) occurs, not at a meeting of an entire standing committee, but at a meeting of a smaller subcommittee of the standing committee. The decisions of the subcommittee are then viewed as the authoritative decisions—decisions that are altered by the standing committee only when the subcommittee is seriously divided or when it is viewed as highly unrepresentative of the full committee.

One indicator of the growth of subcommittees is in their number and staff. As Table 2-2 indicates, at the start of the 84th Congress (1955-1956), when the Democrats began their current streak as the majority party in the House, there were 83 standing subcommittees in the House. By contrast, the

Table 2-2   Standing Subcommittees in the House of Representatives*

84th Congress	83	92nd Congress	114
86th Congress	113	94th Congress	139
88th Congress	105	96th Congress	139
90th Congress	108	98th Congress	135

* Budget committee task forces are not included in the count.

98th Congress had 135 subcommittees. Moreover, the chair and ranking minority members of each subcommittee were entitled to appoint at least one professional staff member. By comparison, in the 86th Congress, the first time the *Congressional Staff Directory* was published, only 57 of the 113 subcommittees were shown to have their own staffs.

Not only have the number and staff of subcommittees grown, but they have become increasingly independent from the standing committees and committee chairs.[14] The Subcommittee Bill of Rights passed in 1973 as part of the Hansen Committee's reforms, and various other rules changes of the 1970s, moved the selection of subcommittee chairs away from the respective committee chairs and gave this responsibility to the full committee caucus of the majority party. This arrangement enabled subcommittee chairs to develop personal constituencies and security independent of the full committee chairs. Subcommittees also gained control over their own budget and staff, and codified jurisdictions.

Finally, in an effort to spread subcommittee power more widely and break the hold of committee chairs on subcommittees, the reforms limited a member of the House to the chairmanship of only one committee. This significantly increased the number of House members who held a formal position in the committee system power structure. As Table 2-3 indicates, 102 different individuals held a committee or subcommittee chair in the 86th Congress; this number constituted slightly more than one-third of the Democratic Caucus. But by the late 1970s the number had reached nearly 140, with over half the members of the Democratic Caucus chairing a committee or subcommittee. And these levels have been sustained. This increase is all the more significant because the subcommittee positions held in the 96th Congress carried with them greater formal authority than those of the 1950s and 1960s.

With the rise of subcommittee government, committee decisionmaking responsibility flowed increasingly to subcommittees. One measure of this shift is the dramatic growth in the percentage of committee hearings held in subcommittee rather than in the full committee. During the late 1940s and early 1950s only 20 or 30 percent of committee hearings occurred in subcommittees, whereas by the first session of the 95th Congress, over 90

Table 2-3 Distribution of Committee and Subcommittee Chairs

	Number of Standing Subcommittees	Number of Standing Committees	Number of Individuals Holding at Least One Chair	Percent of Democrats Holding at Least One Chair
86th Congress	113	20	102	36.3
89th Congress	126	20	102	34.6
96th Congress	139	22	138	50.2
98th Congress	135	22	137	51.3

percent of all committee hearings took place in subcommittees.[15] Also indicative of the growth in subcommittee power is the increased number of floor managers for bills that are subcommittee chairs. As late as 1970, this responsibility was the exclusive province of committee chairs. Today this role is shifting to subcommittee chairs.

How then are subcommittee chairs selected since the rise of subcommittee government? Under the Subcommittee Bill of Rights, the majority members of each committee are allowed to bid in order of seniority for subcommittee chairs. The member bidding for a subcommittee chair is then either elected or defeated by majority vote of the committee's Democratic members. If defeated, another member can then bid for the chair. In recent years there have been several particularly heated chairmanship contests.

At the start of the 96th Congress, four senior members were defeated before the chair of a House Government Operations subcommittee was selected. Selection of a chair for the Health and Environment Subcommittee of the House Interstate and Foreign Commerce Committee was also controversial; a third-term member defeated a respected senior representative. In the 97th Congress contests arose for subcommittee chairs on the Foreign Affairs Committee. A liberal junior activist successfully challenged the incumbent chair of the Inter-American Affairs Subcommittee, and two senior members were passed over in filling the vacant Africa Subcommittee chair.

Some House members and observers criticize the selection process as a form of political cannibalism. Many of the challenges, they claim, are not based on merit but reflect instead the unrestrained ambitions of other members. Critics fear that the reactions to these contests may result in a return to strict seniority and that truly unworthy chairpersons will again be insulated from defeat.

The rise of subcommittee government, seen in these various quantitative indicators, is a qualitative change within the House. Basic legislative responsibility has shifted from approximately 20 standing committees to about 160 committees and subcommittees. Today most legislation is actually drafted and reviewed in very small subgroups within Congress. The jurisdiction of the subgroups is much narrower than the jurisdiction of the parent committees. Because of the numerous subcommittees and committees that meet simultaneously in the House and because of the press of other legislative business, often only a few members are present when a subcommittee meets, with primary responsibility falling on the subcommittee chair, the ranking minority member, and one or two other interested members. Since passage of sunshine legislation opening virtually all committee and subcommittee meetings to the press and the public, legislators have normally been far outnumbered by lobbyists who are present to push their special programs and perspectives. In response, support has grown for closing some committee and subcommittee sessions.

Once drafted in subcommittee, legislation goes for review to the standing committee, which acts as an appeals court where dissatisfied members can attempt to alter subcommittee decisions. Quite often legislation receives little meaningful alteration at a committee level and goes to the Rules Committee and the floor of the House for consideration largely as drafted in subcommittee.

The Decline of Committee Chairs' Powers

As subcommittees increased in importance during the postwar years, the influence of committee chairs waned. This decline can be explained with the same general variables that account for the rise of subcommittees: the opposition of liberals to conservative dominance in the House, the increasing workload of committees that inhibited the ability of chairs to control all facets of policymaking, and the pressure from careerists within committees to democratize committee activity and spread responsibility. In the face of these pressures, the chair positions of individual committees were progressively weakened throughout the late 1950s and 1960s—often immediately following the retirement of a particularly influential or arbitrary chairperson.[16] For this reason, powerful committee chairs had already become an endangered species in the House by the 1970s. The systematic and formal diminishing of their power as a group, however, came with the reforms later in the decade.

The first formal crack in the armor of the chairs occurred when House liberals established a procedure whereby the Democratic Caucus would elect standing committee chairs. The caucus adopted a Hansen Committee provision that allowed 10 members to demand a vote on a committee chair nomination, a procedure that clearly could threaten incumbent chairs. The threat was strengthened in 1973 when the caucus adopted the requirement of voting on every committee chair. Two years later, in the January 1975 meetings of the House Democratic Caucus, the rule was employed to defeat three sitting committee chairs in the bid for re-election. This "revolutionary" act went totally against the traditions of committee government and, by demonstrating the willingness of the majority caucus to discipline committee chairs, deprived them of their most potent weapon: their invulnerability to removal.

Changes in the procedures and traditions surrounding the selection of committee chairs, when combined with the other reforms of the early 1970s, clearly altered their status and authority. The chairs lost the right to determine the number, size, and majority party membership of subcommittees. They lost the power to appoint subcommittee chairs, to control referral of legislation to subcommittees, or to prevent their committees from meeting. Finally, as a result of the growth of subcommittee activity, many were forced to defer to their subcommittee chairs in the management of legislation.

It would be wrong to conclude from this analysis that committee chairs are devoid of power and that subcommittee government is all-encompassing. Despite the loss of formal powers, chairs generally remain influential. They still retain substantial control over the staff of the full committee and, to the degree that they do not abuse their powers, many maintain control over the agenda and the calling of meetings. Committee members still tend to defer to the judgment of the chair on questions about which they are unfamiliar or un-decided. Committee chairs with substantial policy expertise and/or political skill have the greatest potential for influence. In fact, the recent decline in the number of careerists in the House means that many subcommittee chairs will be younger and relatively inexperienced individuals whom an astute and experienced committee chair can seek to control or constrain through use of greater knowledge and legislative skill. John Dingell (D-Mich.), chairman of the Energy and Commerce Committee, and Richard Bolling, chairman of the Rules Committee until his retirement at the end of the 97th Congress, are two examples. Both men wielded influence reminiscent of chairs of the prereform period.

Although the majority caucus now has the ability to select the individuals it feels are best qualified to head House committees, it paradoxically has left those individuals with few sources of influence. The bulk of committee power has shifted to subcommittees and subcommittee chairs who, with the exception of the Appropriations Committee, are not selected by the full party caucus but rather by party caucuses within their committees. This shift toward subcommittee government and the related weakening of the parent committees and committee chairs (discussed more fully in Chapter 8) are changing substantially the character of committee decisionmaking.[17]

Committee Decisionmaking

Historically, so long as the basic responsibility for decisionmaking rested at a committee level, a large number of interests fell within the jurisdiction of a standing committee. This meant that committee decisionmaking tended toward brokerage politics; a particularized interest group could not dominate committee policymaking. As Richard Fenno demonstrated in *Congressmen in Committees*, variation did exist in the heterogeneity of committees' jurisdictional environments, with more homogeneous environments producing committee decisionmaking more likely to be clientele-dominated.[18] Nevertheless, committee jurisdictions by their very nature tend to be fairly broad so that a narrow single-interest group could seldom dominate the general decisions of a committee.

The Rise of Single-Interest Groups. As power has shifted from committees to subcommittees, committee decisionmaking has moved to work groups with far more homogeneous environments. In other words, when a committee jurisdiction is cut into a variety of segments and each subcommittee has one segment to review, that segment will include within it a fewer number of policy concerns. The placement of real responsibility for decisions in the discrete subcommittees has encouraged single-interest groups to disengage from umbrella lobby groups (that is, lobby groups that aggregate numerous interests in a policy domain into one lobby effort) and to concentrate their attention on the particular subcommittee determining the fate of their particularized interest. Concerned with only a few policy interests, these subcommittees are apt to become the captives of these clientele groups. The move to subcommittee government thus has fueled the rise of single-interest groups in Congress and augmented the power of particularized lobby groups, increasing the probability of clientele dominance of congressional policymaking.

This has affected not only the general pattern of decisionmaking, but also the nature of committee leadership and congressional careers. The era of committee government produced committee leaders who were basically brokers with broad policy interests. Within committees, individuals could specialize, but ultimately the decisive power to mold the overall pattern of a committee's decisions rested in the hands of the committee chair whose authority derived from responsibility over a broad range of policy jurisdictions. Because of the large number of interests within their authority, these committee chairs could maintain independence, if they so desired, from narrow interests and specific executive agencies.

Changes in Committee Leadership. The shift of power to subcommittee chairs, and single-interest groups' focus on them, have changed the nature of committee leadership. The power of subcommittee chairs rests not on their ability to balance numerous contending interests, but on their attention to a few specialized policy areas. As a result, there is considerable pressure for subcommittee chairs and members to be policy entrepreneurs who take a few narrow policy areas as their personal concerns, develop expertise in these areas, and build careers tied to narrow clientele groups.

Thus leadership within subcommittees is oriented less toward aggregating a broad range of interests and more toward articulating a few particularized interests. Over time, these subcommittee policy entrepreneurs are liable to identify their personal career interests with the success of their chosen clientele groups, becoming the captive of those interests psychologically as well as electorally. Moreover, the members of the subcommittees are not the only entrepreneurs. Subcommittee staff have a stake in developing activities for the members (hearings, legislation, amendments, speeches) as a way of proving their own worth and institutionalizing their positions.

Subcommittee members who wish to break out of the bind of specialized concerns must broaden the range of their policy interests and play a broader policy role. These efforts often produce a third pattern of change: the breakdown of jurisdictional alignments.

Committee Jurisdictions. As Fenno argues in *Congressmen in Committees,* House committee decisionmaking historically has tended to be "monolithic"; the committee given jurisdiction over a particular policy area guarded its authority in that area closely and opposed intervention by other committees. On the other hand, as Fenno points out, committee decision-making in the Senate was more permeable, with committees less jealous of their committee jurisdictions. This contrast existed largely because House members belonged to only one or two committees and were anxious to protect their power base, whereas senators, belonging to more committees and also having more national visibility, had a broader base of power and thus were less protective of their committee jurisdictions.

In many ways the rise of subcommittee government in the House creates a situation today somewhat analogous to the Senate described by Fenno. House members usually belong to a half dozen or more subcommittees. Since subcommittees are the real decision units in the House now, members have more diffuse loyalties. Unless a member is a subcommittee chair, he or she is normally torn between a number of different decision units and less tied to one subcommittee. Thus the desire to protect full committee jurisdictional boundaries that applied in an earlier era is less evident for most members except as it affects the jurisdiction of the subcommittees.

In addition, since most members today tend not to see the standing committees as the level at which they attain and exercise power, and since committee chairs lack the resources to protect committee jurisdictions that they once had, the capacity of committees to prevent encroachment on their jurisdictions by other committees has been considerably diminished. Moreover, the chaos created by the expansion of the number of House subcommittees makes it difficult to avoid overlapping jurisdictions. Finally, many current legislative issues cut across committee jurisdictions that have remained substantially unaltered since 1946. All of these factors orient the House today toward less monolithic committee decisionmaking. But the ultimate stimulus for a breakdown of committee jurisdictions is the motivation of the subcommittee chairs themselves.

At first glance it would appear that subcommittee chairs would be those most stringently committed to protecting the purity of committee and subcommittee jurisdictions. Since a House member can chair only one subcommittee, the power of subcommittee chairs seems tied closely to their subcommittee. Naturally, subcommittee chairs want to protect their jurisdictions. Thus, there is a pressure within a committee for subcommittees to honor each other's jurisdictional boundaries. Since subcommittee chairs are selected by the majority party caucus within a committee and can be disciplined if they fail to honor intracommittee and jurisdictional lines, such pressure has some success within committee. But control of jurisdictional raids into the policy areas of other standing committees is another matter.

As noted earlier, subcommittee chairs who seek to avoid being the captive of a narrow clientele group within their own subcommittee have a very natural desire to broaden the range of policy concerns under their authority. One way to do so in the long run is to move up a subcommittee hierarchy using committee seniority as a means to claim the chairs of more important subcommittees with broader policy domains. But in the short run, subcommittee chairs follow a very different strategy. Since most subcommittee chair positions rest on a vote of their committee caucuses, subcommittee chairs who want to broaden their policy domains cross into the jurisdictional boundaries of other committees that have related policy concerns. These other committees have few mechanisms to protect themselves and are often unaware of the encroachment at the time because of the general confusion in the highly decentralized House.

A case in point is the postwar growth in the number of subcommittees from different committees that hold hearings on the same general policy areas and executive departments.[19] Committee jurisdictional lines thus appear to be breaking apart, and committee decisionmaking to be taking on the permeable characteristics of the Senate.

As a result of the growth in congressional decentralization in the House, the rise of House members as policy entrepreneurs, and the increasing permeability of House committee decisionmaking, the House during the postwar years looks more and more like the Senate. Because of the basic structural and environmental differences between the two bodies, as the House comes in some ways to resemble the Senate, the ultimate decision calculus of House members and the decision processes of the House are driven farther from that of the Senate.

In the Senate, decentralization spreads power among relatively few members. Because senators serve constituencies that are normally quite heterogeneous (that is, states), they necessarily must focus eventually, not on a few particularized interests, but on balancing a range of interests. In addition, because there are fewer senators, the spreading of power positions among the members of the majority party still leaves each senator with a wide range of policy jurisdictions. In other words, even with decentralization of power there is a natural tendency on the part of senators to think about balancing and compromising various interests. Thus, decentralization helps senators aggregate and balance interests. By allowing them to become powerful in a number of different policy areas, decentralization gives senators the expertise and authority necessary to convince the different forces that press on them of the need to compromise. The permeability of Senate committees largely serves to augment the role of individual senators as interest aggregators.

The effects of decentralization in the House are quite different. Decentralization spreads power among a much larger number of members in the House, members that have under their jurisdiction a small number of legitimate policy domains. (No member chairs more than one subcommittee.) The particularized and narrow focus of House members is reinforced by their service of relatively homogeneous constituencies. Since House members serve homogeneous constituencies, the permeability of House committees does not serve the same function that permeability serves in the Senate. Instead of allowing broadly oriented legislators to balance numerous contending forces, it adds to the chaos of the House and to competition among members for the support of particularized single-interest groups.

The age of strong standing committees in the House tended to force members at least to recognize the existence and relevance of contending forces within a general policy domain. The standing committees, in fact, were the main elements of interest aggregation and compromise in the postwar House. The move to subcommittee government considerably lessens the aggregating role of the standing committees. The growth in the permeability and irrelevance of committees' jurisdictions lessens even more the ability of a standing committee to coalesce interests in its policy domain.

Summary

The rise of subcommittee government has altered considerably the character of House decisionmaking. It has brought more members into the policy process, opened the possibility of policy innovations by a wider range of members, and probably increased legislative expertise in the House. But subcommittee government has had its costs, too. Serious problems have been created that, if left unresolved, could cripple the legislative process in the House.

At its heart, subcommittee government creates a crisis of interest aggregation in the House. It largely removes committees as arenas in which interests will be compromised, brokered, and mediated. Subcommittee government has led to increased dominance of committee decisionmaking by clientele groups, particularly single-interest groups. If interests are to be checked and balanced, if the competing demands of different groups within a policy domain are to be weighed according to their relative merits, that action increasingly must occur, not within the committee system itself, but within the congressional parties and on the floor of the House. The responsibility for saving subcommittee government from itself—maintaining its benefits while offsetting its detriments—thus falls largely to the party and party leadership.

Strengthening Party Leadership

Throughout most of the postwar years, political parties in Congress have been weak, ineffectual organizations.[19] Power in Congress has rested in the committees or, increasingly, in the subcommittees. Although the party caucuses nominally have had the power to organize committees and select committee chairs, the norm of congressional or state delegation seniority has dominated committee assignments (though not exclusively), while committee seniority has dominated the selection of committee chairs.

In reality, throughout much of the past five decades Congress was governed by a conservative coalition composed of Southern Democrats and Republicans; their strength was particularly evident on the most powerful committees such as Appropriations, Ways and Means, and Rules. The primary function of party leaders was to assist in smoothing the flow of legislation and mediating conflict—not to provide policy leadership or coordination. The parties themselves—particularly the House Democratic party—were loose coalitions of convenience, not programmatic or cohesive organizations dedicated to enacting a specified set of policies. As one observer has written, political parties in the postwar Congress have been in many ways "phantoms" of scholarly imagination that perhaps should be exorcised from attempts to explain congressional organization, behavior, and process.[21]

Many of the 1970s reforms addressed the weaknesses of House parties, and to a degree they reinvigorated the parties and presented them with new, expanded roles in the operation of the House. However, while the reform process did evidence a short-term emergence of party activism, it has not produced thus far an institutionalized form of party government. An examination of the Democratic Caucus and the party leadership will indicate why the reforms leave the House far short of the party government model.

The Party Caucus

In the 1970s the Democratic party caucus came to the fore as a center of reform activity and political maneuvering. During this period the Hansen Committee expanded the powers of the caucus, particularly its power to approve the selection of committee chairs. Democrats also began to use the caucus to debate policy positions and nurture personal careers. The activism of the caucus led to cries from some Republicans and conservative Democrats that "King Caucus" was running the House and overriding the wishes of its total membership. These dissidents called for the opening of caucus meetings in the hope that this would cripple the effective operation of the caucus.

The eventual opening of the caucus, together with the election of a Democratic president, did undermine its effectiveness in the mid- to late 1970s. The Carter presidency in particular seemed to defuse the activism of the caucus by providing House Democrats with leadership and a program to support without extensive debate. The party caucus thus fell into disuse.

In the 1980s the role of the Democratic Caucus changed once again. The election of Reagan confronted Democrats with a Republican president and a conservative legislative program. In response, the chairman of the Democratic Caucus, Gillis Long of Louisiana, worked to regenerate the caucus. He created a Committee on Party Effectiveness to consider ways to strengthen the party. The caucus decided to meet in closed session and endeavored to reclaim its role as the center of party debate. In addition to holding pivotal discussions on the nation's budget, Central America, MX missiles, and the U.S. Marines in Lebanon, the caucus surveyed members' budget priorities in an attempt to shape the party's budget proposals.

The long-term fate of the rejuvenated caucus is uncertain. Thus far the caucus appears strong only when the opposite party controls the White House and when debates are held in private. The caucus, because of its size, may not be the best forum for handling problems of party strategy and making delicate decisions on party members. The Steering and Policy Committee may be the more natural arena for collective party leadership, and the Speaker remains the natural spokesperson for the party.

The Speaker

Throughout most of the twentieth century, parties in the House have been unwilling to invest power in their party leaders. This reticence stems from early in the century when Speaker "Uncle Joe" Cannon used the considerable authority of the Speaker to dominate House proceedings and relegate most members to a relatively insignificant status. After the 1910 insurgency against Cannon stripped the Speakership of all of its major powers except the constitutional role as presiding officer, members guarded their personal prerogatives and committee power assiduously against usurpation by the Speaker. Although the 1946 Legislative Reorganization Act attempted to resolve many problems of committee government, it did not include reforms strengthening the Speakership or party leaders.

In the early 1970s liberals in the House were willing to turn to the Speakership for a variety of reasons. First, the Speaker was Carl Albert, a man who supported, or at least did not oppose, many of the reform efforts of the caucus, including the strengthening of subcommittees and personal prerogatives of members on the floor. Albert had liberal leanings, at least for an Oklahoman. And because of his mild demeanor and consensual politics, he was not perceived by the members as a personal threat. A second factor, not to be underestimated, was the presence of Representative Richard Bolling, who strongly influenced reformers and Albert. Bolling studied the history and structure of the institution and developed reform proposals. As a result of his experience as a lieutenant to Speaker Rayburn and of his study of the House, Bolling became a staunch supporter of a strong Speakership and strong party leadership. He continually pushed his views, kept them alive, and added an element of legitimacy to them.

A third reason why House liberals in the 1970s looked to the Speaker for leadership was the existence of divided government and the presidency of Richard Nixon. As Nixon forced issues such as the Cambodia invasion and the impoundment of appropriated funds, Democrats needed some leadership and coherent strategy to thwart his efforts to undermine the role of Congress in public policy. A strong Speaker offered the possibility of leadership. Fourth, because the party caucus elected the Speaker by secret ballot, the Speaker should be more responsive to the caucus than committee chairs, protected by the seniority norm, had traditionally been. Finally, through procedural changes the party could strengthen the office of Speaker without investing in it all of the power Cannon had possessed. The three-day layover requirement governing consideration of conference reports and amendments, and electronic voting, limited the ability of the strengthened Speaker to arbitrarily control floor votes. In addition, the central power of the party could be divided between the Speaker and a Steering Committee in such a fashion as to keep the Speaker in bounds.

Reforms Strengthening Speaker. The move toward a strong Speakership came in two waves. First, the Hansen reforms of 1973 placed the Speaker, as well as the Majority Leader and caucus chair, on the Committee on Committees chaired by Wilbur Mills (D-Ark.), effectively curtailing his power. Simultaneously, they strengthened the Speaker, giving him a formal role in the selection of committee members and chairs. The 1973 reforms also replaced the dormant Steering Committee with a new Steering and Policy Committee consisting of 24 members: the Speaker, the Majority Leader, the chairman of the caucus, the majority whip, the chief deputy whip, the 3 deputy whips, 4 members appointed by the Speaker, and 12 members elected by regional caucuses within the House Democratic party. The role of the new committee was to help direct party strategy. The Speaker was made the chair of Steering and Policy and was given a dominant role in selecting its members. Not only would he appoint four members, but the five whips would also be indebted, since they are appointed by the Speaker in conjunction with the Majority Leader.

The second wave in strengthening the Speaker came at the end of 1974 and early 1975. The Hansen substitute for the Bolling plan gave the Speaker considerable control over the referral of bills. The early organizational caucuses of the 94th Congress further strengthened the Speaker by giving him the power to nominate the chair and Democratic members of the House Rules Committee, thus bringing that committee more clearly into the control of the Speaker and the party.[22] At the beginning of the 96th Congress, Speaker Tip O'Neill asserted this power when he refused to appoint Jerry Patterson (D-Calif.), the choice of California House Democrats to fill a Rules vacancy, and instead selected Anthony Beilenson, another Democratic representative from California.

Although the 1973 Hansen reforms made considerable headway in bolstering the power of the Speaker, 1975 brought even greater changes. The caucus in the 94th Congress took the Committee on Committees' power away from Ways and Means Democrats and placed it in the Steering and Policy Committee. This greatly increased the role of the party leadership, particularly the Speaker, in selecting committee members and committee chairs. Out of the committee of 24, the Speaker thus had 10 votes over which he should have considerable sway (his vote and those of his 4 appointees and the 5 whips). Subsequently, the Steering and Policy Committee was expanded to 29 members at the start of the 97th Congress and to 30 at the start of the 98th.

Two other changes took place in the 1970s that served to strengthen the Speaker. First, increases in the financial and staff resources of the party whip office and in the number of whips appointed by the party leadership resulted in a stronger and more active whip system at the disposal of the party leadership in efforts to pass legislation.[23] Second, the creation of the new budgetary process provided mechanisms through which a skillful party leadership could control the budgetary process and coordinate decisionmaking by House committees. The Speaker's potential control of the House budgetary process resulted from his appointment (in conjunction with the Senate's president pro tem) of the director of the Congressional Budget Office, the leadership's appointment of one of its lieutenants to the House Budget Committee, and the ability of the Speaker, as Steering and Policy chair, to oversee appointments of Democrats to the Budget Committee.

Consequences of Reforms. Taken together, all of these changes substantially increased the prerogatives of the Speaker. For the first time in decades, a Democratic Speaker now has a direct and significant role in committee nominations and the nominations of committee chairs. While he cannot make the decisions in a personal, arbitrary fashion (except in the case of Rules), the Speaker does chair the Committee on Committees and plays a dominant role in the selection of 9 of its members. Members of the party seeking committee positions or leadership roles now have far more reason to listen to and follow the Speaker than in the past, since this office, perhaps more than any other, is critical to successful candidacies.

Second, although the Speaker no longer chairs the Rules Committee (as was the case in Cannon's day) or is a member, he does choose its Democratic members, thereby lessening the likelihood that they will delay or block the scheduling of legislation desired by the party leadership. Third, as chair of the revitalized Steering and Policy Committee, the Speaker now has greater legitimacy as a policy representative of the party and greater opportunity to fashion and direct the party's legislative program. Fourth, the Speaker has regained some of the ground lost by Cannon concerning control over the referral of bills. Fifth, the Democratic Speaker now has a strengthened whip system to use in passing Democratic legislation. Finally, the Steering and

Policy Committee, together with the new budget process, provide tools that a Speaker can use to coordinate and direct major legislation.

Ironically, many of these reforms have created heightened expectations for leadership performance and resulted in members making new and increased demands on the leadership. However, the new powers are sufficiently modest that the expectations and demands are not easily satisfied, particularly in the context of decentralized, subcommittee government.

The one area in which the reforms of the 1970s do not seem to have significantly redressed the loss of ground after Cannon is the control of parliamentary procedures on the floor. Recorded votes on amendments and electronic voting (which has cut the time of roll call votes considerably and reduced leadership control over the pace of floor votes) have further reduced the Speaker's power as presiding officer and solidified the procedural protections of the average member. Nevertheless, the sum total of the changes constitutes a real resurgence of the Speakership and a move back toward the power of the era of Cannon. This movement is not uninhibited, however. It is constrained by the Subcommittee Bill of Rights and other rules changes that protect members' rights within committees and subcommittees, by the specification of fairly clear-cut procedural roles on the floor, and by the existence of the Steering and Policy Committee.

O'Neill's Leadership. In 1977 Speaker Tip O'Neill inherited these powers from Carl Albert. O'Neill is a more forceful, active, and visible leader than Albert. O'Neill's success in passing a controversial energy program during the early years of the Carter administration suggested to some that perhaps an era of strong party leadership had arrived. This optimism, however, proved premature. In fact, the leadership had to use its limited resources extensively to succeed with the energy package, and those resources once used were not easily replenished. Later in the 95th Congress when the leadership sought the support of Democratic members on other important legislation, some warded off persuasive efforts with the reminder of support they had given earlier on the energy program.

Subsequent defeats during the Carter years, as on common situs picketing legislation, indicated that even with strong personal leaders, increased substantive leadership powers, a president of the same party, and a two-to-one majority, the leadership could not overcome the independence of House members. The system of subcommittee government led to frequent jurisdictional disputes, and it was not feasible to create an ad hoc committee each time jurisdictions became entangled. Democrats on the Rules Committee, although generally supportive of the Speaker's wishes, balked occasionally. Members with their own fiefdoms were not only immune from leadership pressure but often possessed resources to attract the support of other members. Relations with the president did not always pay off, especially when issues like public works projects were involved. While the new leadership was more successful than its predecessors, it clearly lacked the recipe for party government; additional ingredients were still needed.

O'Neill's leadership problems increased substantially with the coming of the Reagan years. Although the more active party caucus provided him with a forum in which to seek support, he had a smaller majority to work with and faced a membership dispirited by the Reagan landslide in 1980. The president's victory was particularly impressive in the South and led some Southern Democrats—the "Boll Weevils"—to defect to the president and his policies. The voting alliance of Boll Weevils and House Republicans, who were almost perfectly cohesive, gave the Reagan administration the narrow majorities needed for passage of its budget resolution, reconciliation bill, and three-year tax cut program in 1981. Crucial to enactment of the Reagan economic program was the inability of the Democratic leadership to win important procedural votes setting the terms under which the House would consider the pieces of the program. In addition, the administration effectively used the budget process—designed to centralize House decisionmaking and increase *congressional* influence over taxing and spending—as a vehicle for its own leadership of the Congress.

The struggle over the Reagan economic program highlighted once again the limited resources of congressional leaders. O'Neill discovered at every turn that the president was simply able to outbid him in an effort to corral undecided House members. Only with the growing economic recession and the Democratic victories in the 1982 midterm elections was O'Neill able to fashion a reliable majority in the House.

Ironically, O'Neill's leadership in the 98th Congress was crippled by his own early support of the Reagan administration's foreign policy in Lebanon. This position led to a revolt within the Democratic Caucus. O'Neill's Speakership also was progressively hindered by the proliferation of small groups of members that used the open procedures of the House to engage in media politics and obstruct policymaking. One example is the debate on a nuclear policy resolution early in the 98th Congress. The leadership brought the resolution to the floor with an "open" rule that allowed members to amend it. The measure was then bombarded by amendments from critics who said they were "not trying to obstruct, but merely wanted to generate extended debate." The result was 42 hours of debate over a two-month period. The leadership was forced to cancel the open rule and impose a time limit on debate—a switch that had never occurred before.[24]

Another example of Speaker O'Neill's problems during the 98th Congress lies in the area of televised debates. Televised broadcasts of House sessions, begun in 1979, came of age in 1984 when junior Republicans began to reserve blocks of air time in the evening, when House business is over, to speak to the growing, prime-time television audience in the 17 million homes that receive the Cable Satellite Public Affairs Network (C-SPAN). The junior Republicans behaved as though the House chamber was full and proceeded to lambast Democratic colleagues and laud Republican policies.

Because the television cameras were focused solely on the speakers, the television audience could not tell that the chamber was empty.

The disparaging remarks of the junior Republicans and their deception of the viewing public incensed O'Neill. He made the unilateral decision to have the television cameras scan the chamber during these "special order" speeches to show viewers that the dramatic gestures and accusations were being made in a vacant room. The Republicans, uninformed of the change in camera policy, were embarrassed and embittered by the resulting telecasts. O'Neill justified his decision in harsh and pointed terms and angrily argued that the junior Republicans misused the television broadcasts. O'Neill was officially chastised for using derogatory words about a colleague, the first time for any Speaker.

Leading a highly partisan and fragmented House proved difficult for O'Neill and will challenge future Speakers in the 1980s. O'Neill's troubles during the Reagan administration illustrate the tensions on the Speaker as he attempts to lead a highly partisan and fragmented House. His actions also make clear the need for a group of advisers who can help restrain and guide the Speaker and serve as an intermediary between him and House members.

The Steering and Policy Committee

One key to closer party government may come from more active use of the Steering and Policy Committee. For party government to endure, caucus members must recognize that a cooperative effort is needed to fashion a widely accepted set of policies and strategies. The Steering and Policy Committee—a small committee composed of the Speaker's appointees and members selected by regional caucuses—provides the best arena in which the spirit of party cooperation and a representative direction to party efforts can be fashioned, while at the same time constraining and guiding the Speaker.

Ideally, the Steering and Policy Committee will become a representative body that keeps the Speaker in touch with the general sentiments of the party, provides healthy debate and innovative direction on public policy, gives guidance to committees and subcommittees, and spurs the party leadership into an articulate, persuasive policy role that reflects the dominant sentiment of the party. But since its creation in 1973, the committee only occasionally has given evidence of an ability to perform in these capacities.

Some recent developments, however, have demonstrated the Steering and Policy Committee's potential. Most encouraging has been the frequent use of Speaker's task forces, ad hoc groups which, working in coordination with the committee, have responsibility for the passage of a particular bill. These were used most effectively during the Carter administration on top priority legislation such as the energy package, Social Security tax increases, budget resolutions, and aid to Chrysler.[25]

The Steering and Policy Committee's role in making committee assignments, one of its most important functions, has been fairly consistent.

Overall, it has been a successful vehicle for assigning members to committees, but occasionally its decisions have been overturned. For example, at the start of the 96th Congress several of its assignment recommendations were contested in the party caucus; in two cases, the Steering and Policy Committee's choices were defeated.

In addition, there is some indication that O'Neill has expanded the role of the Steering and Policy Committee. Nevertheless, more direction still might have been given to the party legislative program by paying closer attention to long-range scheduling, and setting legislative priorities and goals for committees and subcommittees. These lofty goals for the Steering and Policy Committee often are neglected as the leadership finds itself under the day-to-day press of legislation.

The potential success of the leadership in making the Steering and Policy Committee a more useful instrument and in moving the House toward any semblance of party government requires that it clean up the jurisdictional nightmare among House committees and subcommittees. The current structure of committees and subcommittees invites jurisdictional disputes from those who see their influence threatened and from those who realize that such disputes can be used to delay and defeat legislation. In part for this reason, House Democrats in the 97th Congress started including on the Steering and Policy Committee the chairs of the Budget, Appropriations, Ways and Means, and Rules committees. The addition of these key chairs is designed to allow better coordination, but jurisdictional disputes are not likely to end.

In the last decade the leadership has relied on three primary weapons to confront jurisdictional disputes: the creation of ad hoc committees, the use of multiple referral of legislation combined with having the Rules Committee write complex rules of multiple-committee floor management, and persuasion. None of these is a long-term solution, and each has its drawbacks. The first, as mentioned earlier, can be used only occasionally. The second reinforces committees' desires to make jurisdictional claims and continues the piecemeal approach to complex policy problems. And the third uses time, energy, and resources that might better be applied elsewhere. Not until the problem of overlapping committee jurisdictions is thoroughly addressed and resolved will the House leadership, no matter how skilled, be able to provide the institution with clear policy direction. One thing is certain, however. Rearranging and clarifying committee jurisdictions is no easy task, as the Bolling and the Patterson committees discovered. Too many members and special interest groups have developed substantial personal stakes in the current committee structure.

The Future of Party Leadership

The direction of party leadership in the House in the mid- to late 1980s is tied in large part to who is Speaker. O'Neill announced his intention to retire by the end of the 99th Congress. Assuming that the Democrats maintain control of the House, Majority Leader Jim Wright of Texas is likely to succeed him. This would leave a wide-open contest among senior Democrats for the majority leadership.

Wright's move into the Speakership, should it come, will throw an element of uncertainty into the party. Wright is a more conservative legislator than O'Neill and somewhat to the right of the party's center in the House. As majority leader, he worked closely with O'Neill and pursued the Speaker's more liberal goals. Where he will lead once in office is less clear. Yet Wright is popular among the House Democrats, a far better orator and spokesman for the party than O'Neill, and an experienced legislative tactician. Furthermore, Wright's southwestern ties may help provide the regional balance and image of moderation that the Democratic party is seeking in the mid- to late 1980s.

The choice for majority leader is less clear cut, as Chapter 11 points out (see pp. 267-270). But whatever team emerges to lead the Democrats, one thing is certain: a period of significant leadership change is in the making.

Conclusion

Today the House of Representatives is experiencing a significant period of adjustment. As a result of the changes and reforms unleashed in the 1970s, the era of committee government that dominated the House for more than 60 years is gone. In its place is a reformed House in which power is shared by subcommittees, committees, and party leadership. This distribution of power among the distinct hierarchical levels of House organization is an uneasy arrangement. On the one hand, the career and power interests of individual members, together with specialized policy interests, generate support for a decentralized form of subcommittee government. On the other hand, subcommittee government lacks a means of generating support for interest aggregation and strong party leadership.

In the 1980s the House is confronting the tensions between these counteracting tendencies. Such a confrontation may end, of course, with a power structure and process much like the one that currently exists; such a resolution almost surely would require the emergence of new norms and structural/procedural supports that would rationalize and ameliorate the current tension, helping subcommittee government mesh more easily with party leadership. Alternatively, the House could slide decisively toward subcommittee government, react to the inadequacies of subcommittee government by implementing stronger party government, or return to a variant of committee government as a necessary compromise.

Many factors will influence the direction that the House takes. Chief among these are the quality and skill of party leaders, the role of the president in supporting party government, and the facility of subcommittee chairs at solidifying control of their policy arenas. Among all the various variables at work, however, one factor is probably overriding: the nature of membership change.

As the history of the House of Representatives demonstrates, turnover and careerism critically influence internal organizational dynamics.[26] Depending on the nature of turnover in the 1980s, several alternate organizational paths may develop within the House. A return to low turnover and careerism probably would solidify and increase preoccupation of members with personal power prerogatives, thereby lending support to an institutionalization of subcommittee government and a renewed weakening of the party leadership. By contrast, significant turnover, combined with a continuing drop in the number of careerists, might fuel support for strengthening party leadership. Such support could be gained in several ways: the large number of new members could create such chaos that strong leadership would be needed simply to maintain order in the House; the loss of a large pool of truly experienced members might deprive the House of the type of membership needed to provide rigorous support for the existence of subcommittee government; and a large number of inexperienced members could provide a group from whom an astute Speaker might build a supporting coalition. The existence of moderate levels of turnover, by contrast, might tilt the House toward committee government, with too few experienced members for full-fledged subcommittee government to work, yet too many careerists for a willing reliance on strong party leadership.

It is, of course, difficult to predict the patterns of turnover and careerism in the late 1980s. Much of the turnover in the last decade was voluntary in nature; many old-timers retired. With the coming of the 1980s, the large pool of careerists who fueled voluntary turnover particularly in the late 1970s is now largely gone. For voluntary turnover to continue, it must come increasingly from the newer members, members who may well have reason to leave more rapidly than their predecessors did at a similar stage in their careers. The financial constraints of service, the greater rigors of the job, and a more rapid rise to power positions that can serve as vehicles for advancement to higher office are factors that prompt members to leave the House.

Increased turnover could also come through defeat of incumbents. While the decline in competitiveness of congressional elections suggests that turnover probably will not occur because of defeat,[27] this situation might be reversed, at least temporarily, by a massive scandal, a new electoral realignment during a presidential election, the rise of single-interest groups, weariness with Democratic control, or fundamental campaign finance reforms that improved the resources of challengers in congressional campaigns. Involuntary turnover is more likely to produce partisan or at least ideological change in the House than voluntary turnover, with incumbents beaten in primaries by ideological opponents or in general elections by partisan opponents.

If the electorate continues to operate by traditional dynamics, we will witness in the 1980s neither high voluntary nor involuntary turnover, but rather a return to lower turnover and renewed careerism.[28] From this perspective, the turnover of the 1970s has served primarily to cleanse the House of an earlier generation and establish a new generation that now may stay for a significant length of time, attracted by the availability of power positions at a subcommittee level and buoyed by safe congressional seats. This vision of the future would suggest that turnover would be quite low in the late 1980s.

All three of these alternate models—high voluntary turnover, high involuntary turnover, or low turnover—have plausible supporting arguments. And it is possible to envision a number of permutations on them that would generate more complex dynamics. Whatever happens, it is clear that membership change in the 1980s is an important variable to watch as a key to the internal organizational dynamics of the House.

NOTES

1. Charles S. Bullock III, "House Careerists: Changing Patterns of Longevity and Attrition," *American Political Science Review* 66 (1972): 1295-1305. Bullock's operational definition of a House careerist is a member elected to 10 or more terms.
2. Much of the data on careerism was originally developed by Bullock with recent years updated here.
3. Thomas Mann, *Unsafe At Any Margin* (Washington, D.C.: American Enterprise Institute for Public Policy Research, 1978).
4. For an analysis of retirements, see Joseph Cooper and William West, "The Congressional Career in the 1970s," in *Congress Reconsidered,* 2nd ed., edited by Lawrence C. Dodd and Bruce I. Oppenheimer (Washington, D.C.: CQ Press, 1981).
5. *Congressional Quarterly Weekly Report,* February 4, 1984, p. 225.
6. Ibid., January 14, 1984, p. 60.
7. Samuel P. Huntington, "Congressional Responses to the Twentieth Century," in *The Congress and America's Future,* ed. David Truman (Englewood Cliffs, N.J.: Prentice-Hall, 1973), p. 9.
8. *Congressional Quarterly Almanac, 1974* (Washington, D.C.: Congressional Quarterly, 1975), p. 855.
9. See Herbert Asher, "The Learning of Legislative Norms," *American Political Science Review* 67 (1973): 499-513.
10. See Mark F. Ferber, "The Formation of the Democratic Study Group," in *Congressional Behavior,* ed. Nelson W. Polsby (New York: Random House, 1971), pp. 249-267; and Arthur G. Stevens, Jr., Arthur H. Miller, and Thomas E. Mann, "Mobilization of Liberal Strength in the House, 1955-1970: The Democratic Study Group," *American Political Science Review* 68 (1974): 667-681. For a discussion of the reform efforts in the House and the initial role of the DSG, see Norman J. Ornstein and David W. Rohde, "Congressional Reform

and Political Parties in the U.S. House of Representatives," in *Parties and Elections in an Anti-Party Age,* ed. Jeff Fishel (Bloomington, Ind.: Indiana University Press, 1976).

11. For a more extensive chronological discussion of the reform processes, see Lawrence C. Dodd and Bruce I. Oppenheimer, "The House in Transition," in *Congress Reconsidered,* 1st ed., edited by Dodd and Oppenheimer (New York: Praeger Publishers, 1977), pp. 27-32; see also Norman J. Ornstein and David W. Rohde, "Congressional Reform and Political Parties in the U.S. House of Representatives," in *Congress Reconsidered,* 1st ed.; and Leroy N. Rieselbach, *Congressional Reform in the Seventies* (Morristown, N.J.: General Learning Press, 1977).

12. For an excellent discussion of the Bolling Committee, see Roger H. Davidson, "Two Avenues of Change: House and Senate Committee Reorganization," in *Congress Reconsidered,* 2nd ed.; and Roger H. Davidson and Walter J. Oleszek, *Congress Against Itself* (Bloomington, Ind.: Indiana University Press, 1977).

13. On the growing importance of subcommittees, see Steven S. Smith and Christopher J. Deering, *Committees in Congress* (Washington, D.C.: CQ Press, 1984), pp. 194-198. See also their essay in this collection.

14. See David W. Rohde, "Committee Reform in the House of Representatives and the Subcommittee Bill of Rights," *The Annals* 411 (January 1974): 39-47; and Norman J. Ornstein, "Causes and Consequences of Congressional Change: Subcommittee Reforms in the House of Representatives, 1970-1973," in *Congress in Change,* ed. Ornstein (New York: Praeger Publishers, 1975), pp. 88-114.

15. See Lawrence C. Dodd and George C. Shipley, "Patterns of Committee Surveillance in the House of Representatives" (Paper delivered at the annual meeting of the American Political Science Association, San Francisco, California, September 2-5, 1975); and David E. Price, "Congressional Committees in the Policy Process," in this collection.

16. Neil MacNeil, *Forge of Democracy: The House of Representatives* (New York: David McKay Co., 1963), pp. 161-170; and James T. Murphy, "The House Public Works Committee" (Ph.D. diss., University of Rochester, 1969).

17. For case studies that demonstrate the legislative impact of committee change, see Norman J. Ornstein and David W. Rohde, "Shifting Forces, Changing Rules, and Political Outcomes: The Impact of Congressional Change on Four House Committees," in *New Perspectives on the House of Representatives,* ed. Robert L. Peabody and Nelson W. Polsby (Chicago: Rand McNally & Co., 1977). For a discussion of the impact of committee change on legislative oversight, see Lawrence C. Dodd and Richard L. Schott, *Congress and the Administrative State* (New York: John Wiley & Sons, 1979).

18. Richard F. Fenno, Jr., *Congressmen in Committees* (Boston: Little, Brown & Co., 1973).

19. For a study of committee hearings, see Lawrence C. Dodd, George C. Shipley, and Philip Diehl, "Patterns of Congressional Committee Surveillance, 1947-70" (Paper delivered at the annual meeting of the Midwest Political Science Association, Chicago, Illinois, April 1978).

20. See Robert L. Peabody, *Leadership in Congress: Stability, Succession and Change* (Boston: Little, Brown & Co., 1976), chap. 2.

21. David R. Mayhew, *Congress: The Electoral Connection* (New Haven: Yale University Press, 1974).

22. For a discussion of the Hansen substitute for the Bolling plan, see Davidson, "Two Avenues of Change." On the Rules Committee in earlier eras, see James A. Robinson, *The House Rules Committee* (Indianapolis: Bobbs-Merrill & Co., 1963); on the new Rules Committee, see Bruce I. Oppenheimer, "The Rules Committee: New Arm of Leadership in a Decentralized House," *Congress Reconsidered,* 1st ed., pp. 96-116.

23. On the whip system in an earlier era, see Randall B. Ripley, "The Party Whip Organizations in the U.S. House of Representatives," in *New Perspectives on the House of Representatives,* ed. Robert L. Peabody and Nelson W. Polsby (Chicago: Rand McNally & Co., 1969); on the new whip system, see Lawrence C. Dodd, "The Expanding Roles of the House Democratic Whip System," *Congressional Studies* 6 (Winter 1979).

24. Alan Ehrenhalt, "The House: Adopting the Senate's Bad Habits," *Congressional Quarterly Weekly Report,* October 15, 1983, pp. 2155.

25. For a detailed discussion and analysis of the task force operations, see Barbara Sinclair, *Majority Leadership in the U.S. House* (Baltimore: Johns Hopkins University Press, 1983), pp. 138-146.

26. For various discussions that indicate a linkage, see Nelson W. Polsby, "Institutionalization in the U.S. House of Representatives," *American Political Science Review* 62 (1968): 144-168; H. Douglas Price, "Congress and the Evolution of Legislative 'Professionalism,'" in *Congress in Change,* pp. 2-23; H. Douglas Price, "Careers and Committees in the American Congress: The Problem of Structural Change," in *The History of Parliamentary Behavior* (Princeton, N.J.: Princeton University Press, 1977).

27. For discussions of decline in competitiveness, see David R. Mayhew, "Congressional Elections: The Case of the Vanishing Marginals," *Polity* 6 (1974): 295-317; Morris P. Fiorina, *Congress: Keystone of the Washington Establishment* (New Haven: Yale University Press, 1977); Albert D. Cover and David R. Mayhew, "Congressional Dynamics and the Decline of Competitive Congressional Elections," in *Congress Reconsidered,* 2nd ed.

28. For a relevant discussion of the variables influencing turnover, see Morris P. Fiorina, David W. Rohde, and Peter Wissel, "Historical Change in House Turnover," in *Congress in Change,* pp. 24-57.

3. THE CHANGING CONGRESSIONAL CAREER

Charles S. Bullock III and
Burdett A. Loomis

Between 1900 and 1970 the House of Representatives evolved into a large and complex organization. From a transient body, populated by "revolving-door" members who stayed for a term or two, it matured into a professional legislature, where six or seven terms of service was the norm.[1] Indeed, the 92nd Congress (1971-1972) included 87 House members (20 percent of the body) whose tenure ran to 10 terms or more.[2] Congress was a place where most members sought a lengthy, somewhat leisurely career that would progress in measured and predictable stages. Young representatives initially would emphasize winning re-election; subsequently, they would devote attention to committee work; after four or five terms, they might chair a subcommittee or move to serve on a "power" committee (Appropriations, Rules, or Ways and Means). Entering the ranks of party leadership remained a future goal of these 10-year veterans.

The House service of Texas Democrat Sam Rayburn, from his initial election in 1912 to the end of his Speakership in 1961 when he died, serves as an archetype of this career pattern.[3] Over the course of five decades, Rayburn progressed from backbencher to ranking minority member of the Commerce Committee (after seven terms), to Majority Leader (after 12 terms), to Speaker (during his 13th term). His taciturn style and oft-repeated advice to younger members—"to get along, go along"—epitomized the tortuously slow, low profile approach to gaining power within both the committee system and the party leadership.

Not all of Rayburn's contemporaries followed this route to power, but deviations were sufficiently infrequent that such individuals, labeled "mavericks," remained outside the regular ladder of career progress and House respectability. In sum, House careers were lengthy, full of tedious committee work, and eminently predictable. The seniority system rewarded committee members who won re-election, and the parties chose loyalists from among this group for their leaders.[4]

Chuck Bullock would like to thank Brock Smith, his research assistant. Bird Loomis offers thanks to the Dirksen Center and the University of Kansas's Graduate Research Fund for continuing support of his research on congressional careers.

The House and Contemporary Political Careers

In the mid-1970s a young representative, appointed to the Appropriations Committee in his first term, was asked if he had considered that some day he might become chairman of that panel. His answer: "It's never crossed my mind." Similarly, in 1977 Representative Chris Dodd (D-Conn.) was recruited for a slot on the Rules Committee, a bastion of "inside" power in the House. Four years later Dodd won a Senate seat. He followed no set career pattern; rather, like many recently elected members, he created his own path. As we shall see, today's House member is less committed to a career in the chamber, less willing to wait patiently for the accrual of power through seniority, and more likely to aggressively seek influence and recognition early in his or her career. Before describing some of these developments, we will examine a few general changes in the congressional "structure of opportunities." [5]

Committees and Subcommittees

The nature of congressional committees and subcommittees changed dramatically during the early and mid-1970s as subcommittees became more powerful and the Democratic Caucus began electing committee chairs by secret ballot. After three chairmen were deposed in 1975, committee heads acted with increased deference and consideration toward their members. As Representative Carrol Hubbard (D-Ky.) observed, since 1975 "it's never been assumed by a committee or subcommittee chairman that they have a lock on the job." [6] Committees were also required to adopt written rules, which reduce the chair's arbitrary power and stipulate regular meetings so that the chair could not bottle up legislation that a majority favored. Especially significant was the limitation that no Democrat could chair more than one of the 130-plus legislative subcommittees, thus giving some second- or third-term members opportunities to chair subcommittees. Because subcommittee chairs ordinarily control some staff positions, this change further reduced the full committee chair's power. These (sub)committee reforms, which have served to democratize and decentralize power in the House, dictate that even a strong contemporary committee chair, such as Energy and Commerce's John Dingell (D-Mich.), must consult with colleagues. Otherwise, in the words of Representative Richard Ottinger (D-N.Y.), "[Dingell] knows that if he runs roughshod over them, the day of reckoning will come." [7]

The changing relative value of subcommittee and full committee chairs has reshaped the structure of committee-based opportunity. In the 1950s and 1960s such a structure could be characterized roughly as a sharply angled triangle with committee and Appropriations subcommittee chairs at the top, other subcommittee chairs in the middle, and the rank and file at the base. [8] (See Figure 3-1A.) This contrasts with the present configuration shown in Figure 3-1B. Committee chairs and Appropriations subcommittee chairs

Figure 3-1 The House Structure of Opportunities in Two Eras

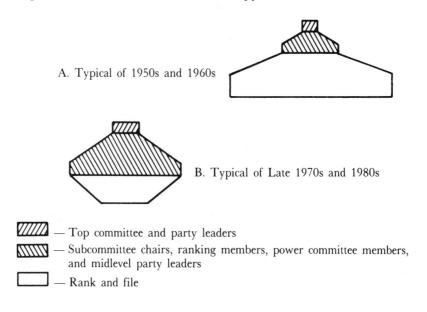

A. Typical of 1950s and 1960s

B. Typical of Late 1970s and 1980s

▨▨▨ — Top committee and party leaders
▧▧▧ — Subcommittee chairs, ranking members, power committee members, and midlevel party leaders
▭ — Rank and file

remain at the top of the opportunity structure, but their power—*relative* to other subcommittee chairs, other members of "power committees," and even backbenchers—has diminished considerably. In fact, today's pool of House backbenchers, who neither chair a (sub)committee, serve as a ranking member, nor sit on a power committee, is remarkably small. This is not to say that all subcommittee chairs or power committee seats are created equal; they are not. But few members must wait very long to obtain some important formal (sub)committee position.

Another change stems from the ability of members to play to other reference groups. In the past, when backbenchers commanded almost no attention from the public beyond their constituencies, they had little alternative to seeking rewards within the chamber. Now the intense coverage accorded Capitol Hill allows junior members to play to a national audience. A clever press aide and an ability to stake out a position on a hot issue may win a member a modicum of star status. Thus, members can obtain rewards that are not controlled by the chamber or party hierarchy. This is especially true for subcommittee chairs, who dictate much of the pace and content of the legislative process.

Party Leadership and Other Opportunities

Following on the heels of the expansion of subcommittee opportunities has come increased chances for junior legislators to participate within the party leadership.[9] Over one-third of each party's members hold some policy-oriented leadership position, such as a whip or a member of the Rules or Budget committee. When the congressional campaign committees are included, this rises to approximately half the members of the House. Many of these so-called "leadership" slots confer no real power, but both parties have addressed the requirements of operating in a democratized House by seeking to include as many members as possible in the ranks of the leadership. Regardless of the actual power parceled out, this inclusive approach to leadership has opened up the parties' structures of opportunities, at least at the lower entry levels.

Expansion of the subcommittee and leadership structures of opportunity has been accompanied by the development of two new avenues for influencing policy. Since the early 1970s a number of caucuses and ad hoc partisan task forces dealing with specific pieces of legislation have developed. Caucuses and task forces allow junior members to lead, publicize issues, build coalitions, and generate personal visibility. While serving as chair of the Northeast-Midwest Economic Advancement Coalition/Institute, in his third term, Representative Bob Edgar (D-Pa.) directed a staff of 20, sought and obtained outside funding for the organization, and helped to produce a wide range of issue papers that attracted substantial attention. Representative David Bonior (D-Mich.) with the Vietnam Veterans' Caucus, Representative Charlie Rose (D-N.C.) with the Congressional Clearinghouse on the Future, and members with other congressional groups, such as the Black Caucus, Steel Caucus, and Arts Caucus, have achieved similar results.

Unlike many major caucuses, which are often bipartisan and are becoming long-term House fixtures, task forces are temporary, partisan groupings organized around a single piece of legislation.[10] The party leadership appoints task force chairs and members. In so doing, it creates resources (opportunities to help shape strategy and legislation) and bestows them mostly on junior legislators. As a side benefit, task force performance allows leaders to judge the coalition-building talents of promising younger members. For example, Richard Gephardt (D-Md.) and Tim Wirth (D-Colo.), potential top Democratic leaders of the future, headed task forces early in their House careers. Given their ad hoc nature, task forces permit party leaders to experiment with their appointments. "Mistakes" in task force choices do not return to haunt the party leadership as do longer term commitments, such as the committee assignments given Texas conservatives Phil Gramm (Budget) and Kent Hance (Ways and Means), who subsequently worked diligently against the Democratic leadership and for all the Reagan administration's budget and tax initiatives in 1981 and 1982.

In the 98th Congress, newly elected Democrats combined the caucus and task force formats. The new members' caucus created task forces on issues ranging from employment to defense to the budget. Of special significance has been their activity on deficit reduction, where the budget group has coordinated substantial efforts to cut federal spending—both by encouraging the first-termers to vote as a bloc and by maintaining private and public pressures on the party leadership to hold down deficits.

In sum, many institutional possibilities exist for members to build careers in, and beyond, the House. Some old verities do remain. Developing expertise in a subject area is important, but committee work no longer represents the sole, or perhaps even major, path to influence. Hard work is expected, but members need not apply themselves only to re-election efforts and committee work. Re-election is still a central goal of younger members, but with greater office resources, as well as expanded caucus, subcommittee, and leadership opportunities, the road to re-election may not be simply that of serving constituents and generating local publicity. In fact, many members run for re-election as increasingly prominent national politicians.[11]

A reincarnated Sam Rayburn, gone less than 25 years, might have great difficulty making sense of new patterns.[12] The dominant, almost unchallenged career pattern of his era has given way to a variety of opportunities, which can be grasped early in a representative's tenure and which are often well supported with staff and other resources.

Traditional Career Patterns

With the institutionalization of House careers, between 1900 and 1950, came longer average tenure for members and a seniority system for allocating leadership positions in committees.[13] Selection of committee chairs and ranking minority members on the basis of seniority replaced the authority exercised by institutionally powerful Speakers, circa 1900, who could reshuffle committee rosters and elevate new chairs to reward friends and punish opponents. Full implementation of a seniority system placed a premium on members getting assigned to the committees they wanted early in their careers. They then edged their ways to the top as more senior members died, retired, or lost public support.

A cursory review of the careers of top leaders during the last half century indicates that power has generally come slowly. Of those who have served as Speaker, the most rapid advancement came to William Bankhead (D-Ala.), who achieved the office after "only" 19 years. At the other extreme, John Mc-Cormack (D-Mass.) waited 33 years. Jim Wright (D-Texas), heir apparent to the current Speaker, Tip O'Neill (D-Mass.), will have 32 years of service if he becomes Speaker in 1987. (O'Neill has announced his plans not to seek re-election in 1986.)

The slow progress of party leaders Wright and McCormack was more than matched by Representative Jamie Whitten (D-Miss.), who served 38 years before chairing the Appropriations Committee. The chairmen of the Rules and Ways and Means committees in the 98th Congress, Claude Pepper (D-Fla.) and Dan Rostenkowski (D-Ill.), respectively, each spent a generation in the House before achieving their positions. During the last 50 years only rarely has a member risen to chair one of the top three committees with less than two decades of House service.

Changes in career patterns and the high voluntary turnover of the 1970s have not yet had a visible impact on the gestation period for chairs of major committees. Even though the proportion of members who had 20 years or more of service was almost halved during the 1970s,[14] the chamber's most powerful positions are still reserved for the very senior members. It remains to be seen whether the decline in the number of careerists that began in 1973 will at some point substantially shorten the waiting time. The present lack of effect may be due to lower turnover rates among Democrats than Republicans. Should the GOP suddenly win control of the House, the new committee chairs would have much less seniority than their Democratic predecessors.

Career Development for Five Classes

To get a perspective on the changes in House careers, we will briefly trace what happens to the members of five postwar classes of freshmen from the 80th (elected 1946), 86th (elected 1958), 89th (elected 1964), 92nd (elected 1970), and 94th Congresses (elected 1974).[15] These are all sizable classes, and only the class elected in 1970 came to the House in a year when one party did not enjoy a marked advantage in the electorate. Republicans made up 70 percent of the 1946 freshmen, while Democrats constituted 76, 78, and 82 percent of the freshmen chosen in 1958, 1964, and 1974, respectively. The 1970 class had a partisan distribution much like the full chamber—58 percent Democratic. We chose to follow these relatively large classes because a fair number of members remained in the chamber after several terms.

The initial reading on what happens to each class comes three terms after their first election. For all but the freshmen elected in 1974, there is a full second reading after five terms, and for the three earlier classes a third measure is taken after seven terms. We consider three aspects of career development.

First we look at whether members remain in the House, pursue alternatives, or must leave the chamber due to forces beyond their control. The second and third considerations are membership on the three most prestigious committees and the frequency with which members achieve positions of leadership.

Career Development

House seats have become increasingly safe. (See Table 3-1.) In the Class of 1946, almost half the members left the House within three terms due to electoral defeat. In the next two classes early career losses were down to a third of the class, and for the Class of 1970 defeat wiped out only 13 percent of the members during the first three terms. The Class of 1974 was more vul-

Table 3-1 Career Development for Selected Classes of House Members (all figures are cumulative)

Classes	After 3 Terms %	(N)	After 5 Terms %	(N)	After 7 Terms %	(N)
1946 (80th Congress, N = 90)						
In House	37	(33)	28	(25)	17	(15)
Ran for Senate	7	(6)	9	(8)	10	(9)
Governor	2	(2)	2	(2)	2	(2)
Other	0	(0)	1	(1)	1	(1)
Defeated in House Re-election	48	(43)	51	(46)	58	(52)
Retired/Resigned	4	(4)	7	(6)	9	(8)
Died	2	(2)	3	(2)	3	(3)
1958 (86th Congress, N = 79)						
In House	51	(40)	46	(36)	30	(24)
Ran for Senate	5	(4)	5	(4)	6	(5)
Governor	1	(1)	1	(1)	4	(3)
Other	1	(1)	3	(2)	3	(2)
Defeated in House Re-election	32	(25)	34	(27)	41	(32)
Retired/Resigned	6	(5)	8	(6)	13	(10)
Died	4	(3)	4	(3)	4	(3)
1964 (89th Congress, N = 83)						
In House	46	(38)	34	(28)	25	(21)
Ran for Senate	8	(7)	11	(9)	12	(10)
Governor	2	(2)	2	(2)	2	(2)
Other	1	(1)	1	(1)	2	(2)
Defeated in House Re-election	34	(28)	41	(34)	43	(36)
Retired/Resigned	6	(5)	8	(7)	13	(10)
Died	2	(2)	2	(2)	2	(2)
1970 (92nd Congress, N = 48)						
In House	58	(28)	35	(17)	29	(14)
Ran for Senate	15	(7)	17	(8)	17	(8)
Governor	6	(3)	8	(4)	8	(4)
Other	0	(0)	0	(0)	0	(0)
Defeated in House Re-election	13	(6)	17	(8)	17	(8)
Retired/Resigned	6	(3)	15	(7)	19	(9)
Died	2	(1)	8	(4)	10	(5)
1974 (94th Congress, N = 86)						
In House	65	(56)	41	(35)		
Ran for Senate	9	(8)	20	(17)		
Governor	1	(1)	2	(2)		
Other	0	(0)	0	(0)		
Defeated in House Re-election	22	(19)	29	(25)		
Retired/Resigned	3	(3)	8	(7)		
Died	0	(0)	1	(1)		

nerable; a quarter of its members were defeated. Our analysis of five postwar classes conforms with the research of Mayhew,[16] Fiorina[17] and others who have observed that members of the House have made themselves less susceptible to defeat. Insulation against defeat distinguishes only junior members of recent years from junior members in the past. There is much less difference in the rates at which incumbents lose *after* winning three elections. In the fourth and fifth election bids the proportion of the classes that lost ranges from 2 percent (1958) to 7 percent (1964).

The incidence of progressive ambition (that is, seeking an office other than representative) was fairly constant for the first three classes, but rose for the latter two. A larger share of the members of the Class of 1970 campaigned for a Senate seat than ran for all other positions in previous classes. The Class of 1970 also had an unusually large incidence of gubernatorial aspirants. The tendency of ambitious representatives to make their move early has remained constant; most bids for higher office come during the first three terms. After three terms, members may feel that they have too much invested in their House career to try to win some other position. An alternative and perhaps more likely explanation is that the most ambitious individuals see the House as a steppingstone to their ultimate goal. Regarding House service as a means, not an end, they hurry on to the next stage in their careers.

This pattern of early decisions to seek higher office may be changing with the Class of 1974. Four of its members, all subcommittee chairs, sought Senate seats in their fifth terms, and another, Bob Edgar (D-Pa.), plans a Senate candidacy in 1986. The 1974 group has already nurtured the largest number of Senate candidacies of any single class in the post-1945 House. Within their first 10 years of congressional service, 20 sitting members (23 percent) of this group had made at least one run at higher office. This far exceeds the other classes in absolute numbers, and it approaches the 1970 group in percentage terms. Thus, the 1974 Class, like its 1970 counterpart, exhibits a great deal of ambition. The latter group, however, has broken the pattern of "settling down" after three House terms.

Departure from the House as a result of retirement, resignation, or death was not unusual for the Class of 1970. During its first five terms, almost a quarter of this group left via one of these routes. This proportion is twice as great as in the comparable period for the four other classes. The higher incidence of retirements and resignations in the Class of 1970 is in line with the numerous voluntary departures from the House during the mid-1970s. But no general trend is emerging. Of the 87 original members of the 1974 group, only five have voluntarily retired.

The rate of voluntary departures combines with the greater electoral security of contemporary House members to produce overall turnover rates that are lower during the first three terms than for earlier classes. Survival rates beyond three terms ranged from 37 to 51 percent for the first three classes but are 58 and 65 percent for the last two classes. By the sixth term, however, the retention level in the 89th and 92nd classes were below that of the 86th Congress.

Power Committees

Since World War II the number of seats on the more desirable committees have been increased as the leadership has coined new currency with which to bargain for support. This expansion has produced additional opportunities for service on exclusive House committees.[18] These three "power" committees, traditionally the chamber's most attractive panels, are Appropriations, Rules, and Ways and Means.[19]

We test two expectations in this section. First, the availability of more seats on power committees should enable a larger share of the members of recent classes to obtain one of these coveted assignments. Second, the undermining of the apprenticeship norm[20] and the unity and demands of the same recent classes should make it easier for representatives to achieve power committee assignments earlier in their careers.

Data on success in obtaining power committee seats appears in Table 3-2. There has not been a consistent increase in the frequency with which class members are placed on these committees. After controlling for seniority, we see that the Class of 1964 was less successful at each stage in getting seats on power committees than was the Class of 1958. Indeed, the Class of 1964 fared even worse than the Class of 1946.

The Class of 1970 was the most successful in getting seats on power committees. A third of the Class of 1970 that was still in the House after three terms had a seat on one of the top three committees. After five terms, this fig-

Table 3-2　Assignments to Power Committees

Class Elected in	Appro-priations	Rules	Ways & Means	Total	%
1948, after 3 terms	3	0	1	4	12
after 5 terms	6	0	2	8	32
after 7 terms	2	1	1	4	27
1958, after 3 terms	8	0	2	10	25
after 5 terms	8	1	2	11	31
after 7 terms	6	1	3	9	38
1964, after 3 terms	4	1	2	7	18
after 5 terms	3	0	3	6	21
after 7 terms	2	0	2	4	19
1970, after 3 terms	4	1	4	9	32
after 5 terms	3	0	4	7	41
1974, after 3 terms	6	2	7	15	27

ure had risen to 41 percent, which was twice as large as for the Class of 1964 after five terms. The success rate for the Class of 1970 after five terms exceeded that of earlier classes after seven terms. These data support the expectation that recently elected junior members can more rapidly acquire seats on prestigious committees.

The Class of 1974 poses a bit of an anomaly. Although it has produced large absolute numbers of power committee members, its percentages of such slots is not especially high. This reflects two changes in the House. First, there are fewer transfers of members to the power committees, largely because many would-be switchers now chair subcommittees, positions they are loath to give up. Second, a new power committee, Budget, has been created; members can serve temporarily on this committee without surrendering their other committee seats. Beyond these changes, there remain only a limited number of power committee slots. An especially large class, like the 1974 group, will suffer in percentage comparisons due to its very size.

Some changes have occurred in the distribution of legislators across committees. Power committee members of earlier classes, particularly those elected in 1964, clustered on Appropriations. More recently, the fortunate who acquire these key assignments are divided evenly between Appropriations and Ways and Means. This suggests that Ways and Means has become more accessible. Two explanations seem appropriate. First, in 1975, Ways and Means expanded from 25 to 37 members. Second, Democrats on Ways and Means lost the authority to make assignments to House standing committees. Once Ways and Means was deprived of this authority, veteran Democrats may have been unwilling to give up the seniority they had accrued on other committees in exchange for Ways and Means. This in turn would have opened the way for relatively junior members. To support this speculation, members of the classes under study here have been divided about equally between Ways and Means and Appropriations since the fifth term of the Class of 1964. This again would be 1975, which was the year that Democrats transferred the committee assignment function from Ways and Means to the Steering and Policy Committee.

For all classes, assignment to the relatively small Rules Committee has been infrequent. As the Speaker has come to exert authority over Rules, it has ceased to be an independent force in shaping the House agenda. In addition, Rules requires exclusive service, offers few subcommittee opportunities, and attracts relatively little attention from political action committees. Finally, the committee's small size partially accounts for the absence of any surge in junior appointments, although some individual exceptions have occurred (for example, the 1983 selection of first-term member Alan Wheat (D-Mo.).

Leadership Positions

The number of committee leadership positions has been expanded. Reforms of the 1970s restricted each member to chairing a single committee and subcommittee. This rule, in combination with the increase in subcommittees, greatly enlarged the number of individuals who were entitled to wield a gavel. A similar growth has come in the number of party leadership positions.[21] Additional members have been incorporated into the whip organizations and consequently assigned some responsibility for helping the parties achieve their policy objectives. The increased number of leadership opportunities makes comparisons from earlier to later classes difficult except in the case of committee chairs or ranking minority members, since there has been little change in the number of standing committees.

Table 3-3 reveals no clear trend for legislators to become their party's most senior member on a committee earlier in their careers. It is impossible to determine if the success of the Class of 1970 portends more rapid advancement for contemporary representatives. Although the Class of 1970 had more committee leaders after three and five terms than any other class, the inability of anyone in the Class of 1974 to reach the top of a committee ladder raises the possibility that freshmen elected in 1970 were uniquely fortunate. The rate at which the Class of 1970 had become chairs or ranking minority members after five terms was slightly greater than that for the Class of 1964 after seven terms (24 percent) and twice as great as the success of the Class of 1958 after seven terms (13 percent).

Table 3-3   Incidence of Attainment of Leadership Positions

Class Elected in	Chair/ Ranking Minority Member of Committee %	N	Chair/ Ranking Minority Member of Subcommittee %	N	Party Leadership %	N	Total	%
1948, after 3 terms	Not Available							
after 5 terms	20	(3)	53	(8)	Not Available			
after 7 terms	20	(3)	53	(8)	Not Available			
1958, after 3 terms	3	(1)	33	(13)				
after 5 terms	6	(2)	67	(24)	17	(6)	32	89
after 7 terms	13	(3)	50	(12)	33	(8)	23	96
1964, after 3 terms	0	(0)	39	(15)	8	(3)	18	47
after 5 terms	11	(3)	82	(23)	21	(6)	32	114
after 7 terms	24	(5)	76	(16)	33	(7)	28	133
1970, after 3 terms	7	(2)	54	(15)	18	(5)	22	79
after 5 terms	29	(5)	53	(9)	24	(4)	18	106
1974, after 3 terms	0	(0)	67	(37)	13	(7)	44	80

Note: Percentages are the proportions of the members of the class who were still in Congress.

Recent classes very quickly became chairs or ranking minority members on subcommittees. Attainment of subcommittee leadership positions came most rapidly to the Class of 1974, two-thirds of whose members were chairs or ranking minority members. However, the survivors of earlier classes were more likely to be senior members of subcommittees after five terms than were the representatives elected in 1970, who succeeded in moving to the power committees, albeit with junior status.

Since members now can chair only one committee or legislative subcommittee, we coded only one chair per person even in the earlier period to maintain comparability. When classes are compared in terms of the proportion of their members who chair a committee or a subcommittee, the most recent two classes were the most successful after three terms. After five terms, the Class of 1964 was most successful with 94 percent holding chairs, compared with 82 percent in the Class of 1970. After seven terms, all those who survived from the Class of 1964 chaired a committee or a subcommittee. This is substantially higher than in the earlier classes after seven terms.

Positions in the party hierarchies are the third dimension of leadership we will consider. There has been less variation in the rate at which legislators have moved into party leadership positions. After five terms, the proportion of survivors who were party leaders ranged from 17 percent in the Class of 1958 to 24 percent in the Class of 1970.

Finally, Table 3-3 presents figures on the share of each class's survivors who hold a chair or a party leadership position. Since chairing a committee or subcommittee and participating in party leadership are not mutually exclusive, the number of chairs or leadership jobs held may exceed the number of survivors. Largely due to earlier accession to subcommittee chairs, recent classes had more members in leadership positions after three terms than did the Class of 1964—the only one of the three earlier classes for which full information was available. The Class of 1970 did not enjoy a marked advantage over earlier classes once five terms had elapsed.

Although the overall pattern has been for recent classes to advance more rapidly than did their predecessors, there is no consistency across all three dimensions. The Class of 1970 had more chairs and ranking minority members of full committees after five terms than did previous classes. However, the Classes of 1958 and 1964 had more subcommittee leaders than did the Class of 1970 after five terms. The reforms of recent years that opened opportunities to members earlier in their careers appear to have given more members leadership opportunities during their first three terms. Early access to power did not deter members of the Class of 1970 from leaving the House in record numbers to pursue other interests in and out of politics. Voluntary turnover in the Class of 1974 is comparable to that of the first three classes— an indication that while the reforms of the 1970s did not create incentives sufficient to make the House more attractive than it had been 10 or even 30 years earlier, neither was the House so difficult or frustrating as to push many members back to private life.

The statistical description of these classes provides only the skeleton for analysis. We will now move to put some flesh on these bones by examining the emerging career patterns of members elected since 1974. New styles have developed, and partisan differences in a Democratically controlled House are significant.

Members in the Postreform House: Some Sketches

Many members of the House have taken on the role of "policy entrepreneur";[22] that is, they aggressively mix policy goals with personal drives for power within the House, advancement, and re-election. These members generally feel comfortable seeking publicity for both themselves and their ideas; they are often not content to remain insiders or, especially, "backbenchers," a term borrowed from parliamentary systems that denotes a party's rank-and-file membership. Indeed, few true backbenchers remain in the House.[23] This does not alter the fact that most members have become adept at melding policy initiatives into their own career development. Without attempting to catalog all the career possibilities, we can offer a few brief examples of contemporary policy entrepreneurs. These politicians have remained in the House; two are Republicans, two Democrats, and they have served, as of the 98th Congress, between three and five terms. All are in their early forties and have adopted political styles that combine policy goals and personal ambition.

Policy, Party, and Publicity: Richard Gephardt

No single member can typify the contemporary congressional career, and Representative Richard Gephardt (D-Mo.) is no typical member. But his visibility on key policy issues and advancement within the ranks of House Democratic leaders do illustrate how one member can integrate policy initiatives with personal career goals. As one of four appointed deputy whips, Gephardt occupied an important formal leadership post in his third term. By then he had also won committee slots on Ways and Means and Budget, where he served as a key Democratic spokesman both inside the House and out.

Like his GOP colleague, Jack Kemp of New York, Gephardt has received substantial attention for his tax reform package, coauthored with Senator Bill Bradley (D-N.J.). They seek to create a modestly progressive tax structure that would be simpler and more equitable than the current system. Although this proposal has become a major part of the debate on tax changes, Gephardt is not a single-issue entrepreneur. Rather, like many of his junior Democratic colleagues, his policy approach centers on problem solving, not the furtherance of a broad and consistent liberal ideology. Gephardt has been active in shaping policy alternatives on an array of economic issues, which range from encouraging competition to reducing medical costs to developing, with fellow policy activist Tim Wirth (D-Colo.), a Democratic Caucus-sponsored industrial policy. In a legislative body where majority coalitons are difficult to build, Gephardt and other entrepreneurs often take the lead, sometimes officially, sometimes not, in defining party positions. One leadership staff aide notes:

> Members like Leon Panetta [D-Calif.] and Dick Gephardt are highly valued by the leadership because they're bright and hardworking and do what they say they'll do. Even though there is some reluctance to acknowledge them as a group defining the party, they're popular as individuals in any case.[24]

In 1984 Gephardt faced an important career choice: to run for the Senate seat vacated by Democrat Thomas Eagleton, who announced he would not seek re-election in 1986, or to remain in the House, as chair of the Democratic Caucus, as of 1985, and a strong candidate for the Whip's position in the post-O'Neill leadership structure. Regardless of the ultimate outcome, he will continue to play a central, visible role in attempting to weave together the often disparate interests of issue activists and party leaders.

The Modified Traditional Career: Phil Sharp

Indiana's Phil Sharp won his initial election to the House in the post-Watergate Democratic sweep of 1974. Sharp took advantage of Watergate's repercussions to defeat the Republican incumbent, after having run twice previously to lay the groundwork for his 1974 success. Such hard work is a trademark of many junior members, both in their electioneering and legislative capacities. Given a very competitive district and a cautious nature, Sharp's House career has proceeded in more conventional and less visible ways than has that of the more activist Gephardt.

Sharp's strength in Congress lies in his expertise on energy policy and, more importantly, in his forum—the chairmanship of the Energy and Commerce Subcommittee on Fossil and Synthetic Fuels. Like most of his colleagues in the Class of 1974, Sharp became a subcommittee chair by his third term, joining fellow "classmates" James Florio (Transportation), Henry Waxman (Health and Environment), and Wirth (Telecommunications) as chairs of Energy and Commerce subcommittees that influence broad segments of American society. A subcommittee chairmanship offers great opportunities for policy activists. "It isn't," one aide pointed out, "just the subcommittee chair. Rather, it's what you can do with it."

Some subcommittee chairmen, such as Wirth on the breakup of ATT, have used their positions aggressively to promote both themselves and their policy alternatives. Sharp has followed a more traditional path, often waiting as long as possible before adopting a position on an issue. "He had always been cautious and slow to make up his mind, weighing all the alternatives," said one committee staff member. "We tried to convince him to exercise a little more leadership once he became chairman. But he just won't do it." This does not mean that Sharp has not acted as a leader on several crucial energy issues. Rather, his pace and actions demonstrate that a quieter style of leadership, which may harken back to an earlier era, can be undertaken in an institution that increasingly allows policy entrepreneurs to seek visibility for themselves and their issues, regardless of whether good legislation is forthcoming.

A Party Divided on Style and Substance: Republicans Richard Cheney and Newt Gingrich

Several years ago a senior Republican leadership aide was asked to name a couple of his party's most able young legislators. Without hesitation, he chose Arkansas's Ed Bethune and Georgia's Newt Gingrich. Bethune he praised as an energetic team player, who was conservative and independent yet willing to compromise. Gingrich, on the other hand, was characterized as a continual thorn in the leadership's side, who sought publicity for himself and a variety of far right ideas. (In 1984 Bethune ran for the Senate and was defeated.) The retirement of several senior GOP moderates, such as Barber Conable (N.Y.) and Joel Pritchard (Wash.), has, if anything, intensified the battle between hard-line conservatives and those who emphasize coalition building and legislation. Two of the central players in this struggle are Gingrich and Wyoming's Richard Cheney, the chairman of the House Republican Policy Committee, both of whom face the special difficulties the minority must confront in the House.

Building a House career has traditionally been more frustrating and difficult for Republicans than for Democrats. The explanation is simple. Since 1933, the GOP has controlled the House for only four years. The last time was in the 83rd Congress (1953-1954). Save for a couple of Democratic defectors, no current Republican House member has ever served as part of the majority. Republicans face a continuing dilemma of whether to seek policy accommodation with the majority Democrats (or some of them) or to oppose energetically all Democratic initiatives, even if that means abandoning any hope of exercising short-term influence. This dilemma becomes more sharply defined when a Republican occupies the White House, and it was further honed after 1980, with the GOP's capture of the Senate.

Dick Cheney, former chief of staff to President Gerald Ford, won his policy-committee position in only his second House term. Although his conservative credentials are intact (he was Reagan's most consistent supporter in 97th Congress votes),[25] Cheney has emphasized coalition-building in pursuit of legislation much more than his more vocal colleagues. Newt Gingrich, on the other hand, sees his role largely as a conservative agenda-setter and partisan position-taker. Budget politics illustrate the differences in the Cheney and Gingrich styles. Cheney, as a pragmatist and party leader, looks for ways to pass budget legislation, while Gingrich is much less willing to consider compromise or accommodation, observing that

> The best Republican strategy is to recognize that the Democrats run the House and will do all they can to butcher the [Reagan] budget. We should point out their obstruction until November . . . [Minority Leader] Bob Michel should relax . . . and refuse to take up the burden of being Speaker himself.[26]

Gingrich and several other conservative Republicans have adopted a highly visible and confrontational strategy to bring home their philosophy. Knowing that roughly 200,000 people watch the cable coverage of the House by C-SPAN, a small band of Republicans, calling themselves the Conservative Opportunity Society, have sought to slow down the legislative process and to create a series of debates on controversial subjects such as abortion and school prayer. These tactics of harassment and delay win Gingrich and his allies few in-House friends, but they are driven by a conservative policy agenda, not by the desire to construct congressional careers as legislators.[27]

Cheney, on the other hand, takes a much longer view, seeking to alienate neither Republicans nor Democrats, even though they may have profound policy disagreements. If Gingrich's chosen medium is live television, Cheney's is more traditional and literary; he has written a historical treatment of the Speakership,[28] which might offer some hints of his long-term plans. Cheney sees the need for a return to a House that values strong leadership, while Gingrich takes full advantage of a body that allows each member to head off on his or her own, with little concern for the institution as a whole.

All legislative bodies encourage members to choose among various career options. For contemporary Republicans, one choice—institutional cooperation or obstructionism—affects the general attractiveness of the body to all its members.

Career Patterns and Institutional Implications

> It's a giant smorgasbord. If you measure the job satisfaction in terms of having this fantastic variety of things you can do if you want to, issues you can get involved in, or styles of operation on the floor, in committee, or with constituents, then the opportunities are endless. If, on the other hand, you measure it in terms of the extent to which the process produces the ultimate result you think it ought to produce . . . then it can be terribly frustrating.[29]

In many ways it is the best of times and the worst of times for House members. The average member controls staff, information, and communication resources that would stagger a Sam Rayburn. Junior representatives can frequently move important items onto the national agenda, as Jack Kemp and Richard Gephardt have done on tax policy. Members garner considerable media attention through the expanding news coverage of the networks, cable television, and public broadcasting.

Obtaining substantial press coverage is central to the public styles adopted by many junior members. Media attention also reflects their influence within the policy process. On key issues, midcareer subcommittee chairmen, such as Representatives Henry Waxman (health and environment), Michael Barnes (Latin America), and Bill Hefner (military construction) exercise leverage in the development and enactment of broad policy agendas. Their subcommittees hold the key hearings, mark up the legislation, and they, as chairmen, manage the bills on the House floor. Even subcommittee chairs with modest policy responsibilities become crucially important at times. In addition, members such as Gephardt and Cheney have risen quickly into important positions of party leadership, while many others have used unofficial caucuses to bolster their institutional clout. The House is indeed a smorgasbord of opportunities, awaiting the hungry junior members.

As almost everyone discovers, however, smorgasbords have their drawbacks; they encourage overindulgence and ordinarily possess no theme. The House smorgasbord is no exception. Members run from policy breakfast to subcommittee sessions to caucus meeting to greeting constituents, with staff aides trailing along. The temptations are great to take on too much work, tackle too many issues, and make too many promises. These individual-level problems, while real, pale beside the difficulties faced by the House as an institution. With large numbers of members holding valuable pieces of "turf," policymaking, already made complex by the nature of many contemporary problems, has become even more difficult. "Followership" has all but disappeared, save in extraordinary situations such as the 1981 tax and budget cuts or the 1983 Social Security package, where tremendous political pressures arose to overcome the normal fragmentation of the legislative process.

More opportunities for participation often translate into more opportunities for delay. Junior members who in the past would have watched the struggle of the congressional titans now crowd forward to grab a tasty morsel for their constituents, a piece of the spotlight for themselves, or a debating point for their conception of good public policy.

Dispersal of power to numerous subcommittees has had several consequences. First, it has made the fashioning of coalitions more difficult and time-consuming. A generation ago, committee chairs often quashed dissent among their partisans on the committees so that there were fewer experts to offer competing views during floor debates. Chairs could also "logroll" with one another, bargaining and trading favors to pass legislation.

Second, increasing the number of important players has reduced the predictability of the deliberative process. Predictability is further decreased by the accession of many inexperienced members to positions of influence. Some young subcommittee chairs have lost on the floor when they failed to line up votes or master the chamber's intricate procedures.[30] Had the legislation been handled by the more experienced full committee chairs, some of these setbacks could have been avoided.

Junior members may also be less willing to compromise. After observing numerous floor fights and handling several pieces of legislation, a representative may gain a clearer understanding of the limits of the possible. Another important lesson may be learned from repeated re-elections. Survival at the polls under varying conditions may teach legislators that they have more latitude in how they vote than they had initially expected. Discovering that few issues are important enough to determine the outcome of an election, representatives may feel less constrained in negotiating compromises.

Congressional careers will continue to change, as the institution and its environment evolve. For the rest of the 1980s, House careerism may increase as the relatively young members remain in office. Policymaking successes, however, are not likely to come any more easily than they have in the past, and the costs of service, whether personal, financial, or political, probably will continue to rise. We do not know what happens when a generation of policy activists begins to move through the contemporary House. Ironically, the reforms of the 1970s that made the House a more attractive place for new members may have rendered it more frustrating for career-building. The high incidence of retirements from the Class of 1970 raises doubts about how many of today's members will find the rewards of House service sufficient to want a career there. But some incentives surely remain. "The old joke," notes Representative Norm Mineta (D-Calif.), "is that the longer you're here, the better seniority looks." [31] If policy activists and agenda-setters of the 1970s can become the effective legislators and coalition-builders of the 1980s, Congress will again encourage longer careers and the marriage of expertise with the requirements of representative government.

NOTES

1. H. Douglas Price, "The Congressional Career: Then and Now," in *Congressional Behavior*, ed. Nelson W. Polsby (New York: Random House, 1971), pp. 14-27; and Robert J. Brookshire and Dean F. Duncan III, "Congressional Career Patterns and Party Systems," *Legislative Studies Quarterly* 8 (February 1983): 65-78.
2. *Roll Call,* March 1, 1984; also see Charles S. Bullock III, "House Careerists: Changing Patterns of Longevity and Attrition," *American Political Science Review* 66 (1972): 1295-1305.
3. Much of this comes from Robert A. Caro, *The Path to Power* (New York: Knopf, 1982), p. 306ff. Rayburn, we might note, was not as patient as he later counseled others to be.

4. See Joe Martin, *My First Fifty Years in Politics* (New York: McGraw-Hill, 1960).
5. This term comes from Joseph Schlesinger, *Ambition and Politics* (Chicago: Rand McNally, 1966).
6. Diane Granat, "Whatever Happened to the Watergate Babies?" *Congressional Quarterly Weekly Report,* March 3, 1984, p. 503.
7. Granat, "Watergate Babies," p. 503.
8. This discussion explicitly covers only the majority party, but a similar description, using ranking members, would apply to the minority. Although some full committee ranking members have enjoyed substantial power, ranking status at the subcommittee level has generally been less important. The minority thus has a disproportionate share of backbenchers.
9. See Burdett A. Loomis, "Congressional Careers and Party Leadership in the Contemporary House of Representatives," *American Journal of Political Science* 28 (February 1984): 180-203.
10. See Barbara Sinclair, "The Speaker's Task Force in the Post-Reform House of Representatives," *American Political Science Review* 75 (June 1981): 397-410. More generally, see Sinclair, *Majority Leadership in the U.S. House* (Baltimore: Johns Hopkins, 1983).
11. For example, in *Congressional Quarterly Weekly Report,* March 19, 1984, Diane Granat notes that most congressional members of the Democratic platform committee come from the ranks of post-Watergate classes (pp. 630-631).
12. Norman Ornstein conjures up this image in "The Open Congress Meets the President," in *Both Ends of the Avenue,* ed. Anthony King (Washington, D.C.: American Enterprise Institute for Public Policy Research, 1983), p. 185ff.
13. Nelson W. Polsby, "The Institutionalization of the U.S. House of Representatives," *American Political Science Review* 62 (March 1968): 144-168.
14. Joseph Cooper and William West, "The Congressional Career in the 1970s," in *Congress Reconsidered,* 2nd ed., edited by Lawrence C. Dodd and Bruce I. Oppenheimer (Washington, D.C.: CQ Press, 1981), p. 94.
15. For our purposes a freshman class is composed of those individuals whose first House service begins on January 3 of an odd-numbered year. We exclude members who have had previous House service, who win special elections, or who immediately fill a vacancy after a November election.
16. David R. Mayhew, *The Electoral Connection* (New Haven: Yale, 1974).
17. Morris P. Fiorina, *Congress: Keystone of the Washington Establishment* (New Haven: Yale, 1977).
18. The number of slots on power committees increased from 80 to 105 between 1947 and 1983.
19. Malcolm E. Jewell and Chu Chi-hung, "Membership Movement and Committee Attractiveness in the U.S. House of Representatives, 1963-1971," *American Journal of Political Science* 18 (May 1974): 433-441. See also Bruce Ray, "Committee Attractiveness in the U.S. House, 1963-1981," *American Journal of Political Science* (August 1982): 609-613.
20. Herbert B. Asher, "The Learning of Legislative Norms," *American Political Science Review* 67 (June 1973): 499-513.
21. Loomis, "Congressional Careers," p. 186.
22. For the genesis of this term, see David Price, *Who Makes the Laws?* (Cambridge, Mass.: Schenkman, 1972); and Eric Uslaner, "Policy Entrepreneurs and Ama-

teur Democrats in the House of Representatives: Toward a More Party-Oriented Congress?" *Legislative Reform,* ed. Leroy Rieselbach (Lexington, Mass.: Lexington, 1978), pp. 105-116.

23. On former representative John Fary, a classic Chicago machine representative, see Alan Ehrenhalt, ed., *Politics in America: Members of Congress in Washington and at Home, 1984* (Washington, D.C.: CQ Press, 1983), p. 6.

24. Richard Cohen, "Strains Appear as 'New Breed' Democrats Move to Control Party in the House," *National Journal,* June 25, 1983, p. 1330.

25. Ehrenhalt, *Politics in America, 1984,* p. 1681.

26. Richard Cohen, "His Troops Restless over the Budget, GOP Leader Michel Is on the Spot," *National Journal,* February 20, 1983, p. 319.

27. Gingrich and his cohorts did succeed in angering Speaker O'Neill, who responded to their attacks by televising the empty House chamber during their remarks. The vocal GOP conservatives were defended by all House Republicans, including Cheney and Minority Leader Michel. See T. R. Reid, "Outburst," *Washington Post,* May 16, 1984, p. A1.

28. Richard Cheney and Lynne Cheney, *Kings of the Hill* (New York: Continuum, 1983).

29. Anonymous House member. See John Bibby, ed., *Congress Off the Record* (Washington, D.C.: American Enterprise Institute for Public Policy Research, 1983), p. 50.

30. Bruce I. Oppenheimer, "Subcommittee Government and Congressional Reform: Perspectives for Studying the House of Representatives," *DEA News* (Summer 1976): 8-11.

31. Granat, "Watergate Babies," p. 503.

Part II

ELECTIONS AND CONSTITUENCIES

4. VOTERS, CANDIDATES, AND ISSUES IN CONGRESSIONAL ELECTIONS

Robert S. Erikson and
Gerald C. Wright

Elections for the U.S. House of Representatives fascinate observers of American politics almost as much as presidential elections do. Unlike Senate elections with staggered six-year terms and gubernatorial elections with an irregular electoral cycle that varies from state to state, House elections provide a biennial measure of the national electoral pulse. Interest in House elections generally centers on the partisan balance of House seats and the mood of the electorate that underlies this partisan verdict.

Still another source of fascination with House elections is that there are so many of them. Every two years, the composition of the new U.S. House is the result of 435 separate contests for 435 separate House seats. In part, the results are determined by national electoral forces. But to a larger extent, they are determined by the candidates in these contests and the conduct of their individual campaigns.

Before focusing on the role of candidates in individual House contests, we will examine the national forces in House elections and their influence on the partisan divisions in votes and in House seats.

The National Verdict in House Elections

The national result of House elections can be represented either as the partisan division of seats won or as the partisan division of the national vote. Although the partisan seat division generally gets the most attention at election time, it is largely determined by the partisan vote division in the 435 districts. Figure 4-1 shows the pattern of the two-party vote and the two-party seat division over a 30-year period. Between 1952 and 1982, the seat division varied from about an even split between Republicans and Democrats to a Democratic edge of more than two-thirds of the seats. This major movement

This research was partially supported by the National Science Foundation, grant SES 83-10443. The authors thank Kathleen Frankovic, Warren Mitofsky, and Elda Vale of CBS News for making available the CBS News/*New York Times* 1982 congressional candidates poll. We offer special thanks to Kathleen Knight and James Stimson for their assistance .

is a response to far smaller vote variations, from about 50 percent to about 58 percent Democratic.

How many seats does a party gain for each percentage point gain in its vote? This quantity—often called the swing ratio—has been variously estimated at 1.90 and 2.14 over recent decades.[1] Conveniently, these estimates average out to about an even 2.0. Changes in the national two-party vote have an exaggerated impact on seat gains: a party wins an additional 2 percent of the seats for every 1 percent of the vote that it gains. Each of the 435 individual House contests is won by the candidate who wins the most votes, or a plurality. In practice, this almost always means that the winner is the major-party candidate with the majority of the two-party vote. The swing ratio is about 2.0 because each party is generally 1 percentage point short of victory in about 2 percent of the districts. Thus, when the party gains an additional 1 percent of the national vote (and if this vote swing is reasonably uniform across districts), the party wins this additional 2 percent of the seats that it otherwise would have lost.

The general rule of a swing ratio of about two has many irregularities. The seats gained from any vote gain depends on the geographic location of the additional votes. A few votes gained or lost can have a major impact in close district elections, but the same votes would be of no consequence if they were distributed in districts with one-sided contests.

In recent years, incumbents of both parties have held increasingly safe seats that insulate them from partisan tides. The relatively strong Republican vote gain in 1980 produced a relatively small Republican gain in seats because very few Democratic-held districts were sufficiently marginal to tip Republican with the addition of a few percentage points more Republican votes. For similar reasons the Democrats gained few new seats when the tide turned back in their favor in 1982. A few decades earlier, vote shifts on the order found in 1980 and 1982 would have brought far more massive changes in the partisan division of House seats.

The Normal Vote

Figure 4-1 shows clearly that the Democratic party does far better than the Republicans in House elections. This Democratic dominance at the congressional level—so unlike the recent dominance of the presidency by the Republican party—is one clear manifestation of the Democrats' numerical edge over the Republicans within the electorate. Since World War II, the distribution of party identification within the American electorate has been relatively stable: the percentage of the electorate calling themselves Democrats remains generally in the low forties and Republicans in the twenties. (The remainder are mainly Independents.) If most partisans were to vote for their party's candidate and the Independents were to split about 50-50, the outcome of a national election would be about 54 percent Democratic and 46 percent Republican. Such an outcome where the election is decided on a party line vote is called the "normal vote." [2] Observe in Figure 4-1 how the the national House vote approximates the "normal vote," with relatively small oscillations around the baseline of about 54 percent Democratic.

Election outcomes that depart from the normal vote are due to short-term defections by partisans and to the temporary vote movement by Independents. These temporary deviations from the normal vote are due to "short-term partisan forces" of the campaign. At a national level, short-term partisan forces intrude only lightly in House elections. Nevertheless, the small national deviations from the normal vote are not random. As we have seen, even small perturbations in the vote can have major consequences in terms of party seats.

Presidential Election Years

In presidential years, the short-term forces of the presidential election and the short-term forces of the House election are in the same partisan direction: the party that does better than the normal vote for president does better than the normal vote in the congressional vote. Whether this happens because the House vote and the presidential vote are influenced by the same national issues, or because people decide their congressional vote on the basis of their partisan choice for president, is not clear. But whatever the cause, this phenomenon is called the "coattail effect." Some House candidates are seemingly carried into office by riding the coattails of their party's popular presidential candidate. Democratic coattails were at their strongest in 1964, when President Lyndon Johnson's landslide victory created an overwhelming 295-140 Democratic majority in the House of Representatives. Similarly, some of the best Republican years in recent House elections were with the strong Republican presidential victories in 1972 and 1980.

The size of the coattail effect is decidedly irregular. One statistical estimate of the size over recent decades puts it at .31 congressional votes nationally for every percent of the vote gained by the party at the presidential level.[3] Put another way, every added percent of the vote gained by a presidential candidate also adds almost one-third of a percent of the vote to the presidential candidate's congressional running mates. Prior to World War II, presidential coattails appeared to be stronger than they are today; the national presidential vote and the national congressional vote marched more in lock-step. One consequence of the weakening of the coattail effect is the increase in split-party control of government, with one party controlling the presidency and the other party controlling at least one house of Congress.

Midterm Years

One regular pattern of House elections is that the party that wins the presidency suffers a net loss of votes and seats in the following midterm

Figure 4-1 House Seats and Votes Over Time, 1952-1982

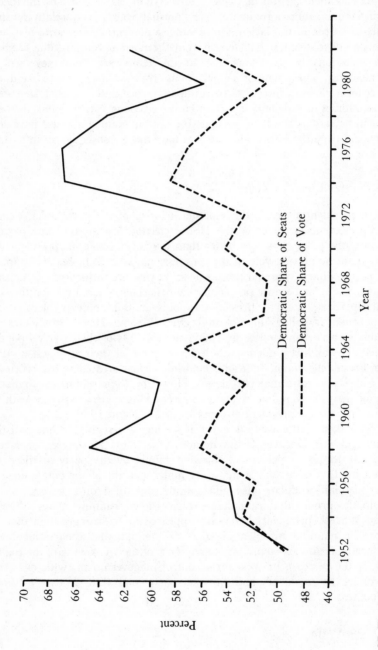

SOURCE: The data are from Norman J. Ornstein, Thomas E. Mann, Michael J. Malbin, and John F. Bibby, *Vital Statistics on Congress, 1982* (Washington, D.C.: American Enterprise Institute for Public Policy Research, 1982), p. 38.

election. Republican losses in the 1982 midterm election followed this routine pattern. Midterm losses for the president's party were once thought to result from some sort of inevitable erosion of support for the president and his party as the president's term of office evolved. We see now a simpler explanation. The president's party loses the advantage of the president's coattails. In presidential years, the congressional vote for the president's party is inflated by presidential coattails. In the following year, the congressional vote reverts to something close to normal. Thus, the key to the midterm decline for the president's party is not the midterm vote but instead the artificially strong beginning in the presidential year.[4]

Fluctuations of the midterm election vote also follow a predictable pattern. The more popular the president and the more the economy is improving (or the less the economy is deteriorating), the stronger will be the president's party at midterm. For example, the worst post-World War II midterm showing for the Republican party was the post-Watergate election of 1974. The second worst Republican vote at midterm was in 1982 during the Reagan recession.

The Economy and the Congressional Vote

Congressional elections are responsive to short-term changes in economic conditions. According to one estimate, .622 percent of the vote shifts for every percent change in per capita real personal income over the year preceding the election.[5] When per capita income increases, the vote shift favors the president's party; when per capita income declines, the vote shift favors the opposition party. An interesting question is why this is so. Is it because voters hold the president's party responsible for their personal economic circumstances and vote accordingly? We call this "pocketbook voting." Or is it because a sufficient number of voters evaluate the competence of the president's party on the basis of momentary economic performance irrespective of their personal economic circumstances? This behavior has been labeled "sociotropic voting."

If pocketbook voting were widespread, newly prosperous voters would vote disproportionately for the "in" party while their unfortunate opposites skidding down the economic ladder would vote disproportionately for the "out" party. Numerous surveys have sought evidence of this, but with surprisingly slim success.[6]

By elimination, then, it appears that sociotropic voting explains the effect of economic conditions on the vote. It remains possible, however, that evidence of pocketbook voting simply eludes our attention because it is difficult to measure. Even a major change in the national vote involves only a few percentage points—say from 54 percent Democratic to 59 percent Democratic. In such a case it is difficult for a survey to isolate the small percentage of the respondents who are in the set of voters whose response creates the electoral change and the reasons for their behavior.

Still a third explanation of economic voting is Gary Jacobson and Samuell Kernell's "strategic politicians" theory.[7] The key to this explanation is that potential candidates for Congress *believe* that economic conditions affect the vote. Strong prospective candidates tend to decide to run when the economy appears to favor their party's chances. They decide to wait for a better electoral opportunity when economic conditions work against their party's chances. Moreover, active candidates run more serious, better financed campaigns when the state of the economy (good for the "ins," bad for the "outs") fosters political optimism for the candidate's party. Note that this explanation requires that candidates and their supporters only *believe* that voters respond directly to economic conditions but not that voters actually do so. In this way, the "strategic politicians" explanation represents a possible self-fulfilling prophecy.

Jacobson and Kernell find some intriguing evidence for their thesis. Over several elections, the party helped electorally by the economy has the stronger set of candidates as reflected by indicators such as their background of political officeholding. (The disadvantaged party runs more novice politicians, for example, who tend to run weaker races.) Similarly, each party's candidates tend to be better financed when the economy appears to favor its chances.

The "strategic politicians" explanation only partly explains economic voting. Politicians' anticipation of economic voting helps determine the vigor of Democratic and Republican campaigns. But more than the anticipation of economic voting is involved in the responsiveness of elections to economic conditions. Movement by a few voters in response to economic conditions can create, in the aggregate, a major partisan surge. This movement is a response to personal economic conditions as well as general economic conditions, for which the affected voters hold the president's party responsible.

Electoral Change as Policy Direction

We have seen that the electorate may respond to economic conditions when it casts its collective congressional vote. But does the electorate also respond to broader political issues? More specifically, when the electorate collectively creates a change in the party composition of Congress, does it intend a specific policy purpose?

Democratic congressional gains signify that the electorate wants more liberalism; Republican gains signify that the electorate wants more conservatism. This is the popular view, often promoted by pundits around election time, but public opinion research finds little evidence to support it. During the two years between congressional elections, public opinion rarely changes on specific issues of public policy or in terms of general orientation to liberalism and conservatism.[8]

As we have seen, changes in the national congressional vote reflect rewards and punishment for the president's party on the basis of the economy and other aspects of presidential performance. In presidential years, the coattail effects of presidential races carry over into congressional elections, but even these generally lack a strong basis in policy preference. For instance, popular reports of how Ronald Reagan's 1980 victory (and the corollary Republican congressional gains) represented a strong public mandate for a rightward move in the conservative direction were greatly exaggerated. Earlier Democratic victories, most notably the Johnson landslide of 1964, were similarly misinterpreted as signifying a public desire for change in the liberal direction.

The reason why electoral shifts should not be taken as policy directives is that public opinion rarely takes abrupt liberal or conservative turns. The reason is not that the public is incapable of giving policy direction. As we will see, the two parties offer the electorate a policy choice, and individual constituencies respond to the menu of policy choices their candidates provide, with the candidates' party affiliations serving as a major cue.

Policy Consequences of Electoral Change

Even if it is not the collective intent of the national electorate, the policy consequences of changes in the party composition of Congress can be substantial. When Republicans replace Democrats in the House, conservatives almost always replace liberals. Similarly, when Democrats replace Republicans, liberals almost always replace conservatives.

The 1982 CBS News/*New York Times* poll of congressional candidates illustrates these party differences. Taken during the campaign but before the 1982 general election, this poll focuses on the candidates' stands on 10 issues judged to have been important in the preceding Congress or which were likely to come before the new Congress.

Table 4-1 displays the patterns of responses for the pair of major-party candidates in each of the 371 district elections that were contested by both major parties. Column I shows, for each issue, the percent of the districts in which the Republican took the liberal position and the Democrat took the conservative position. As the table makes clear, this pattern was rare. Columns II and III show patterns of agreement—either both conservative or both liberal—on the 10 issues. Levels of candidate agreement vary considerably. On some issues, such as a balanced budget amendment, agreement was quite low. On others, such as cutting military spending, the candidates generally agreed—in this case to slow down spending on arms. Column IV shows the extent to which the Democratic candidate held the liberal position and the Republican opponent held the conservative view. This expected pattern of liberal Democrats and conservative Republicans is very frequent, particularly for those issues emphasized by the Reagan administration and its critics: the balanced budget amendment, the nuclear freeze, tax cuts, and domestic spending cuts.

Table 4-1 Candidates' Positions on 10 Issues, 1982 Contested House Elections

	Candidates' Positions			
	I	II	III	IV
Republican:	Liberal	Conservative	Liberal	Conservative
Democrat:	Conservative	Conservative	Liberal	Liberal
Constitutional Amendments				
1. States prohibit abortion	6.3%	15.8%	33.2%	44.6%
2. Prayer in public schools	4.5	13.2	28.2	54.1
3. For balanced budget	1.1	22.2	9.5	67.3
4. Equal Rights Amendment	1.8	7.9	40.6	49.6
Issues				
5. Nuclear freeze with Soviets	2.6	13.2	22.4	61.7
6. Domestic content, foreign cars sold in U.S.	6.3	17.7	28.2	47.8
7. Cancel July 1983 tax cut	1.8	18.7	7.1	72.3
8. Cut military spending increases	3.2	7.7	54.9	34.3
9. Reduce domestic social programs	2.4	15.3	20.1	62.3
10. Increase regulation of air pollution	5.5	56.7	4.7	33.0

SOURCE: The data are from the CBS News/*New York Times* 1982 poll of congressional candidates.

Generally, a congressional voter in 1982 had an easy decision rule for casting a partisan ballot: to help elect the more conservative candidate, vote Republican; to help elect the more liberal candidate, vote Democratic. In fact, if we score each candidate from 0 to 10 on the basis of his or her number of conservative positions on the 10 issues (extreme liberals score 0, extreme conservatives score 10), the Republican is the most conservative candidate in 92.8 percent of the districts, the Democrat is the most conservative in only 3.2 percent, and in 4.0 percent the two candidates find themselves in a net tie on the ideological spectrum. This result is not unique to the 1982 election. A similar pattern has been found in studies of the 1966, 1974, and 1978 House elections.[9]

The overall differences between Republican and Democratic candidates can be seen most clearly if we cumulate their issue or ideology scores on the 0-to-10 scale and compare all Republican candidates with all Democratic candidates. The comparison, which is shown in Figure 4-2, is striking. The vast majority of Democratic candidates are clumped well to the left with only a few moderates and conservatives. On the other hand, the Republican candidates are markedly to the right on this scale. Clearly, the centers of gravity of the two parties are quite different. As a result, election of Democrats leads to a different policy mix than election of Republicans.

District-Level Outcomes in House Elections

So far we have discussed congressional candidates almost solely in terms of their party affiliation, as if all Democrats were alike and all Republicans were alike. Similarly, we have discussed the electorate's choice as if it were solely between the national Democratic party and the national Republican party. In actuality, of course, candidates within each party differ considerably. Candidates often take positions on issues that depart from their party's norm,

Figure 4-2   Distributions of Candidate Ideology, 1982 House Elections

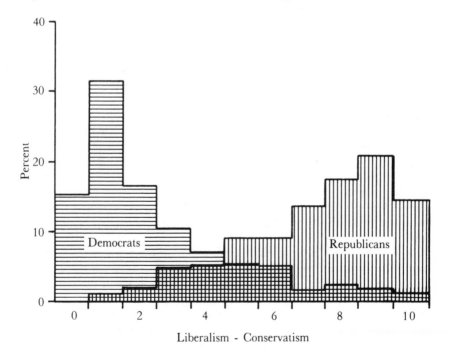

Liberalism - Conservatism

SOURCE: Liberalism-conservatism is measured by an index constructed from the 1982 CBS News/*New York Times* poll of congressional candidates.

perhaps because they see it as electorally necessary. And whether by posturing on issues or in other ways, local candidates do have considerable effect on district election outcomes. Local candidates can do more than watch helplessly while constituency partisanship and the national partisan trend determine whether they are elected or defeated. Although constituencies tend to vote according to their partisanship (the local "normal vote") and the national partisan trend, constituencies also vote according to the capabilities they see in their local Democratic and Republican candidates.

When voters cast their ballots in congressional elections, they have two sets of cues: the candidates' party affiliations plus whatever they have learned about the candidates themselves. At first glance it would seem that voters generally possess insufficient information about their local candidates to vote on more than a simple partisan basis. Consider some evidence from surveys: Only about one-half of the voting electorate can name their U.S. representative and slightly less claim to have "read or heard" something about their representative. The content of this information is generally vague (for example, "He is a good man." "He knows the job.") and rarely touches on policy issues or roll calls. Only by the generous criterion of *recognition* of the representative's name does the electorate perform well. Over 90 percent claim to recognize their representative's name when supplied with it.

Candidates for open seats (with no incumbent running) are less visible, and challengers trying to defeat incumbent representatives are the least visible of all. Only about 20 percent of the voting electorate can recall their representative's name or recall anything about the representative. Only about one-half of the electorate can even recognize the name of their representative.[10]

Just because voters generally are not well informed about their local House candidates is insufficient reason to infer that the candidates have little impact on election outcomes. Recall the analogous situation regarding economic voting. Surveys show that very few voters respond directly to economic conditions, yet economic conditions clearly drive the national vote. It takes few voters to create this movement. Similarly, movement by relatively few voters in a constituency can create a major surge toward or against a candidate.

How large are these candidate effects? One way of demonstrating the importance of candidates is to show the relationship between the local vote in one election and the local vote in the next election when the two major-party candidates change. For example, Figure 4-3 shows the relationship between the Republican share of the two-party vote in 1978 and the Republican share of the two-party vote in 1980, for the set of constituencies where both parties changed their candidates from one election to the next. The inertial effect of district partisanship allows some correlation across elections, but with new candidates the 1980 outcomes were not easy to forecast from 1978 results.

Figure 4-3 Vote in 1980 by Vote in 1978, for Districts with Different Major-Party Candidates Running in the Two Elections

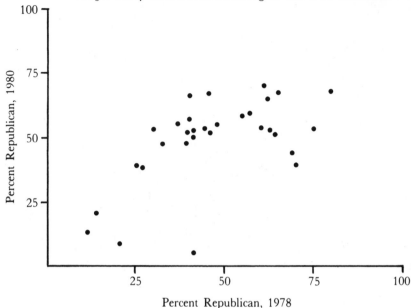

SOURCE: The data are from *America Votes, 1982: A Handbook of Contemporary American Election Statistics,* compiled and edited by Richard M. Scammon and Alice V. McGillivray (Washington, D.C.: Elections Research Center and Congressional Quarterly, 1983).

The Value of Incumbency

House incumbents almost always win re-election. More than 90 percent of all House members seek re-election in a typical year, and of these more than 90 percent win. Thus, from one election to the next, more than 80 percent of the House membership will be the same.

There are three reasons why incumbents generally win re-election. First, many constituencies persistently vote for the same party election after election. Second and more important, incumbency status adds to a candidate's vote margin. Third and most obvious, strong candidates tend to win. Apart from constituency partisanship and the national trend, elections are determined by whether the Democratic candidate or the Republican candidate has the stronger vote appeal. The stronger of the two candidates is more likely to obtain incumbency status. But in this instance, candidate popularity creates the incumbency status rather than the other way around.

Figure 4-4 provides useful insight on incumbency. It shows the relationship between the 1980 presidential vote and the 1982 House vote

Figure 4-4 House Vote with Reagan Support by Incumbency Status

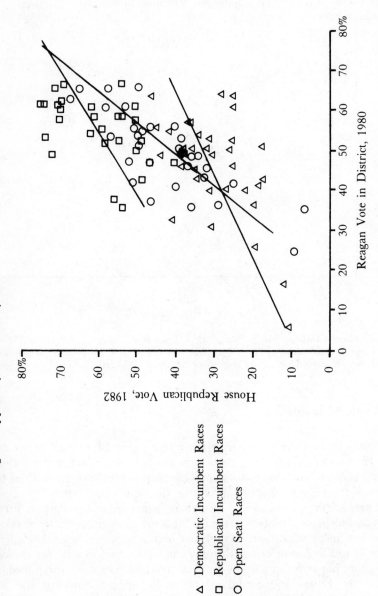

△ Democratic Incumbent Races
□ Republican Incumbent Races
○ Open Seat Races

SOURCE: The data are from *Politics in America: Members of Congress in Washington and at Home, 1984*, ed. Alan Ehrenhalt (Washington, D.C.: Congressional Quarterly, 1983).

(both as the percent Republican). Three kinds of districts are represented: those with a Democratic incumbent running, those with a Republican incumbent running, and open seats. Figure 4-4 shows the positive but hardly binding relationship between district partisanship as measured by the 1980 Reagan vote and the 1982 congressional vote. Of special interest are the differences among the three types of districts.

For open seats, the relationship is strong with a steep slope. Open seat outcomes are closely tied to district partisanship. Incumbents of both parties perform very well compared with their party's local showing in the 1980 presidential contest. With a Democratic incumbent in the race, the Republican vote in 1982 tends to be far below Reagan's 1980 showing. Meanwhile, Republican incumbents generally perform far better than Reagan had two years before.[11]

We can see more clearly why incumbents generally win. First, most but not all incumbents represent constituencies that favor their party: Democratic-held districts generally were weak for Reagan while Republican-held districts were strong for Reagan. Second, incumbents tend to run well compared with the local showing of their presidential ticket. Incumbents run ahead of their party for two reasons: because, as we discussed earlier, they must be strong candidates to win, and because incumbency gives them an advantage.

How large is the incumbency advantage? The best way to measure it is to observe the size of the "sophomore surge," the added percentage of the vote that candidates gain from their first victory to their first re-election attempt. Averaged across freshman incumbents and adjusted for the national partisan trend, the sophomore surge is a simple but accurate measure of the vote share gained from incumbency.

Since about 1966, the sophomore surge has averaged about 6 percent of the vote.[12] This incumbency advantage of about 6 percentage points helps protect incumbents from adverse electoral developments. For instance, suppose a newly elected House member wins with 51 percent of the vote, aided by a national vote trend that averages 4 percentage points in favor of the candidate's party. Without an incumbency advantage, our candidate would expect to lose when the partisan tide returns to normal:

$$51\% - 4\% = 47\% \text{ of the two-party vote.}$$

However, if we add the 6 percent incumbency bonus, our hypothetical House member would expect to win:

$$47\% + 6\% = 53\% \text{ of the vote.}$$

Of course, an adverse partisan tide, a popular challenger, or some decline in the candidate's own popularity could easily change a probable 53 − 47% win into a defeat. But even when the reason for a candidate's first election to Congress is some temporary benefit, such as an unpopular opponent or a favorable partisan tide, a 6 percent incumbency advantage may be sufficient to keep the new incumbent in Congress for a long time.

Interestingly, the size of the incumbency advantage has increased over time. In the 1950s and the early 1960s, the sophomore surge—and therefore the incumbency advantage—averaged under 2 percentage points. The sudden increase to an advantage of 6 percentage points or so in the mid-1960s had the immediate impact of insulating the Democratic class of 1964. An unusually high number of freshman Democrats were elected in the Democratic tide of 1964 (on President Johnson's coattails), and the increased incumbency advantage helped keep a surprisingly high proportion of them in office for several years. Since then, the growth in the incumbency advantage has helped protect incumbents of both parties from adverse partisan swings. But why do incumbents have an electoral advantage, and why has this advantage grown? Three explanations seem plausible.

Decline of Party. Beginning in the mid-1960s when the electoral advantage of incumbency began to increase, the American electorate suddenly became less partisan in terms of its party identification. The proportion of voters who called themselves Independents dramatically increased. Without partisan attachments, Independents are likely to respond to the available cue of incumbency and select the candidate already in office. In this way the decline of partisanship may be responsible for the growth of the incumbency advantage.

Perquisites of Office. Congressional incumbents benefit from the perquisites of office such as the frank (or free mailing privilege), a generous travel allowance for visits home to the district, and money to maintain district offices. During the 1960s at about the same time as the increase in the electoral advantage of incumbents, Congress bestowed upon its members many generous increases in its perks. Plausibly, these increased benefits generated sufficient positive publicity for incumbents to account for the increase in the incumbency advantage.

Strategic Politicians. Earlier we used a "strategic politicians" explanation to account for economic effects on the vote. Recall the argument that strong potential candidates choose to run for Congress only when economic conditions enhance their party's prospects, thereby reinforcing the economy's impact on the national vote. Strategic political decisions also can help account for the incumbency advantage. Prospective candidates prefer to run for open seats or against an unusually vulnerable incumbent. These races therefore attract strong candidates. Winners of such races appear strong and invulnerable, thereby drawing weak opponents in subsequent races. In this way weak challengers contribute to the sophomore surge and reinforce the appearance of an incumbency advantage.[13]

Conclusion. Each of these explanations of the growing incumbency advantage has its weakness. Contrary to prediction, even partisan voters have become more attracted to incumbent candidates. Like the decline of party explanation, the perquisites of office theory has its flaw: surveys do not show increased voter awareness of incumbents.[14] The strategic politicians explanation at best would seem to offer a reinforcement of an incumbency advantage generated from other sources. And it is not apparent how this explanation can account for a growth in the incumbency advantage. Thus, incumbency advantage remains a puzzle with no clear resolution.

Candidates, Issues, and the Vote

Other features about candidates than just incumbency influence voters in House elections. Money also is important, particularly for challengers. Nonincumbent candidates gain the most from the money they spend, since heavy spending is necessary to give them credibility and attention. Once elected, however, a member of Congress is about as well known as he or she will get and additional campaign spending helps little.[15]

Some scholars see constituency service as a major source of candidate popularity. The House member who promptly responds to constituents' requests and stays in the local political spotlight probably makes a stronger candidate than his or her counterpart who downplays constituency service.

Candidates' election chances also are influenced by their ideological position on major issues. As noted earlier, Republican candidates tend to be conservative and Democratic candidates liberal. Although the potential constituents hold a wide variety of views, the *average* constituent will locate between the two candidates on the ideological map. If voters are responsive at all to ideology and issues, candidates can gain votes by moving away from their party's norm toward the center of the spectrum. In principle, each candidate would maximize his or her votes by moving in the direction of the opponent. If both candidates do so, they will meet in the center of the local ideological spectrum.[16]

Of course, candidates do not converge at the local center of the spectrum. The countervailing forces of their own liberal or conservative beliefs and those of their strong supporters work against such a tendency. Still, within each party the candidates do vary in their ideological positions. And the degree to which they moderate their stands by moving toward the opponents does influence the vote.[17]

The effect of candidate positions on the 1982 vote can be estimated by using the CBS News/*New York Times* candidate survey. Ideological positions are measured as the number of conservative positions (from 0 to 10) that the candidate supports on the 10 issues listed in Table 4-1.

Electoral effects of candidate ideology are estimated using multiple regression analysis, with the results shown in Table 4-2. Separate regression equations were generated to predict the Republican congressional vote for districts with Democratic incumbent candidates, districts with Republican incumbent candidates, and open seats. Coefficients are shown for the estimated effects of three predictor variables, the Reagan vote in the district (as a control), the Democratic candidate's ideology, and the Republican candidate's ideology.

Moderate candidates are the best vote getters; both conservative Democrats and conservative Republicans hurt the Republican vote. Thus we expect negative coefficients for both Democratic and Republican candidate ideology. All six coefficients for candidate ideology in Table 4-2 are negative, as expected. The strongest effects of candidate positions are for incumbents. For both Democratic and Republican incumbents, the coefficient for candidate ideology is about −.80 and statistically significant. A coefficient of this size means that, on the average, each digit moved toward the center on the 10-point scale is worth about .80 of a percent of the vote. For example, a Republican in the center of the scale at 5 should win about 4 percent more of the vote than an extreme conservative at 10.

The coefficients for Republican and Democratic challengers and for both Democrats and Republican candidates for open seats are all in the appropriate negative direction but are not statistically significant. This corresponds to the findings of a similar study of the 1974 election.[18] Possibly, nonincumbent

Table 4-2   Regression of the House Vote on Candidate and District Ideology by Incumbency

	Democratic Incumbent	*Type of District* *Republican Incumbent*	*Open Seat*
Reagan Vote	0.556*	0.760*	1.223*
(standard error)	(.066)	(.099)	(.139)
Democratic Ideology	−0.852*	−0.428	−0.376
(standard error)	(.296)	(.372)	(.541)
Republican Ideology	−0.068	−0.752*	−0.825
(standard error)	(.304)	(.308)	(.660)
Constant	7.962	24.340	−10.659
R	0.568	0.540	0.800
R̄²	0.310	0.277	0.620
Number of Districts	163	152	56

* Statistically significant, regression coefficient is twice its standard error.

candidates' positions are insufficiently visible to have much impact but take on electoral relevance when the candidate gains the notoriety of incumbency.

Candidate Responsiveness to the Constituency

Constituencies tend to reward and punish incumbents (and possibly challengers) on the basis of their policy positions. A second source of control is the candidates' expectations of these electoral sanctions. A candidate who expects that an extreme ideological position would produce electoral damage can move toward the center of the spectrum. The degree of adjustment will depend on the electoral security of the district plus the district's mean position on the liberal-conservative spectrum. As a result, each party's most conservative candidates tend to be in the most conservative and Republican congressional districts and their most liberal candidates in the most liberal and Democratic districts.

We can observe these tendencies among the candidates surveyed for the CBS News/*New York Times* poll. Figure 4-5, parts A, B, and C, show candidate positions as a function of the Reagan vote for each party when an incumbent Republican runs, when a Democratic incumbent runs, and for open seats. Each line represents the statistical regression of candidate conservativism on the Reagan vote. Note in particular the steep slopes for the two sets of incumbents. For them, 10 percentage points difference in the Reagan vote appears to create a difference of about 2 points on the ideology scale.

Candidate responsiveness is less and unstable across the nonincumbent groups. Democratic challengers tended to be very liberal no matter how strong the Reagan vote. Curiously, Democratic contenders for open seats were somewhat more conservative overall than were Democratic challengers, but they too displayed the same ideological tendency for each level of the Reagan vote. Among nonincumbents, only Republican challengers and Republican contenders for open seats varied their position in response to the Reagan vote.[19]

For many elections, scholars have reported strong relationships between the positions of each party's incumbents (usually measured from roll call votes in Congress) and the presidential vote.[20] Actually, this relationship may not depend entirely on attempts by members to adjust their public positions for electoral considerations. For instance, the member may seem to follow the district because the member and the district share the same policy interests. Or, over time, the representative and the constituency may grow to become alike in their views because the representative educates the constituency rather than the reverse. Still, the tendency for each party's incumbents to take positions in ideological accord with the district's presidential voting certainly reflects that House members respond in advance to the threat of electoral sanctions.

Figure 4-5 Candidate Conservatism and Reagan Vote, 1982 Contests

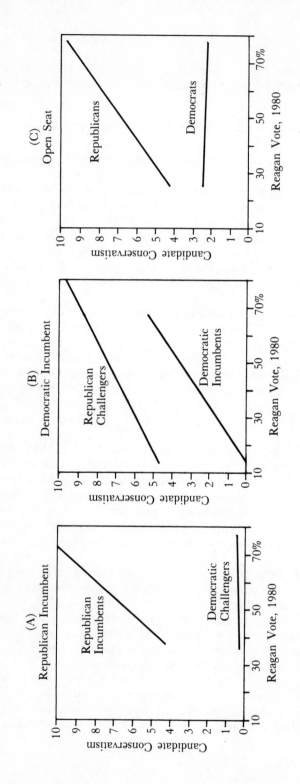

SOURCE: Conservatism is measured by an index constructed from the 1982 CBS News/*New York Times* poll of congressional candidates.

Congressional Elections and Representation

The political parties and the candidates themselves provide the mechanisms by which constituencies can electorally determine the policy views of their representatives in Congress. First, consider the role of political parties. Democratic and Republican congressional candidates are sufficiently divergent from each other on the liberal-conservative spectrum to provide their constituencies with a clear choice. Liberal districts generally vote Democratic and thereby elect liberals while conservative districts generally vote Republican and thereby elect conservatives.

Second, consider the role of the individual candidates. Candidates for Congress sometimes deviate from their party's ideological orthodoxy. By moving toward a more moderate position, one that is closer to the constituency's prevailing view, the candidate enhances his or her electoral chances and by doing so can enhance the representation of constituency views. The candidate who is more ideologically extreme runs the risk of enhancing representation by suffering electoral defeat.

As Figure 4-6 indicates, the net result is a clear pattern whereby the most liberal House members represent the most liberal districts and the most conservative House members represent the most conservative districts. The horizontal axis represents constituency conservatism as measured by the 1980 Reagan vote. The vertical axis represents policy conservatism as measured by the CBS News/*New York Times* 10-item scale. The upward moving line representing the regression for winning candidates; the downward moving line represents the regression line for losing candidates. Clearly, constituencies elect candidates who are ideologically compatible and reject those who are not.

But what about changes in the ideological composition of the House of Representatives at the national level? Ideological changes follow changes in the House's party composition, but, as we have seen, the forces behind these partisan changes are presidential popularity and the condition of the economy—not any collective public desire for an ideological shift of direction. Still, by responding to presidential popularity and economic conditions, the electorate does affect policy by its endorsement or rejection of existing policy. A popular president who is widely perceived to be doing a good job with the economy and his other responsibilities will be rewarded at election time with new House members who support his policies; an unpopular president will find fewer House supporters. For example, the net loss of 26 House Republicans in 1982 following the Reagan recession clearly resulted in a House less accepting of the Reagan initiatives and slowed the progress of the administration's program. In general, then, although the public may not explicitly desire a given policy direction, it does make presidential programs easier or more difficult to enact when it registers its judgment of the president and the economy in House elections.

Normally, the American electorate is rather static in its collective position on the ideological scale. But if the national electorate were to shift

Figure 4-6   Candidate Conservatism and Reagan Vote, Winners and Losers, 1982

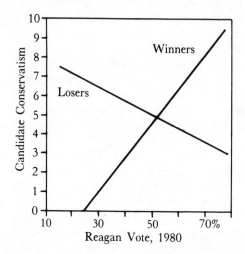

SOURCE: Conservatism is measured by an index constructed from the 1982 CBS News/*New York Times* poll of congressional candidates.

ideologically, could it get the House of Representatives to change with it? The likely answer is yes. The same forces that work at the constituency level to create representation would work at the national level to make the House responsive to a true ideological shift in the national mood. Since constituencies generally elect the candidate from the party most ideologically compatible with their views, an ideologically changed national electorate would elect a greater proportion of members from the more ideologically compatible party. Since local candidates tend to modify their ideological positions when the local constituency changes, candidates generally would tend to move in response to a national ideological drift. And since local candidates who are out of ideological step with their constituencies are the most likely to lose, candidates who are out of step with a national ideological movement would be more likely to lose. All these processes would ensure that an ideologically changed electorate would get an ideologically changed Congress.

Voters, Candidates, and Issues 107

NOTES

1. Gary C. Jacobson and Samuel Kernell, "Strategy and Choice in the 1982 Congressional Elections," *PS*, 15 (Summer 1982): 426; John A. Ferejohn and Randall L. Calvert, "Presidential Coattails in Historical Perspective," *American Journal of Political Science* 28 (February 1984): 131.
2. Philip E. Converse, "The Concept of the Normal Vote," in *Elections and the Political Order*, ed. Angus Campbell, Philip E. Converse, Warren E. Miller, and Donald E. Stokes (New York: John Wiley & Sons, 1966), pp. 9-39.
3. Ferejohn and Calvert, "Presidential Coattails."
4. Angus Campbell, "Surge and Decline: A Study of Electoral Change," in *Elections and the Political Order*.
5. Edward R. Tufte, *Political Control of the Economy* (Princeton, N.J.: Princeton University Press, 1978), p. 112. This estimate is an update of Tufte's earlier work, "Determinants of the Outcome of Midterm Congressional Elections," *American Political Science Review* 68 (September 1975): 812-826. The estimate is based on midterm elections only. Tufte's estimate of the economic effect on the congressional vote in presidential years is 1.06 percent of the vote for the presidential party for every percentage point gain in income in the year before the election (p. 112).
6. Donald R. Kinder and D. Roderick Kiewiet, "Sociotropic Politics: The American Case," *British Journal of Political Science* 11 (1981): 129-161.
7. Gary C. Jacobson and Samuel Kernell, *Strategy and Choice in Congressional Elections* (New Haven: Yale University Press, 1981).
8. Robert S. Erikson, Norman R. Luttbeg, and Kent L. Tedin, *American Public Opinion: Its Origins, Content, and Impact*, 2nd ed. (New York: John Wiley & Sons, 1980), chap. 2.
9. John L. Sullivan and Robert E. O'Connor, "Electoral Choice and Popular Control of Public Policy: The Case of the 1966 House Elections," *American Political Science Review* 66 (December 1972): 1256-1268; Gerald C. Wright, "Elections and the Potential for Policy Change in Congress," in Gerald C. Wright and Leroy Rieselbach, *Congress and Policy Change* (New York: Agathon Press, 1985).
10. On voter awareness of candidates, see Thomas E. Mann, *Unsafe at Any Margin: Interpreting Congressional Elections* (Washington, D.C.: American Enterprise Institute for Public Policy Research, 1978); Donald E. Stokes and Warren E. Miller, "Party Government and the Salience of Congress," *Public Opinion Quarterly* 26 (Winter 1962): 531-546; and Barbara Hinckley, *Congressional Elections* (Washington, D.C.: CQ Press, 1981), chap. 2.
11. To avoid clutter, Figure 4-4 is based on only a sample of the contested House races in 1982. Thirty-two cases were randomly selected for each of the three incumbency situations. The three regression lines, however, are based on the full set of contested races.
12. For various estimates, see Robert S. Erikson, "Malapportionment, Gerrymandering, and Party Fortunes in Congressional Elections, *American Political Science Review* 66 (December 1972): 1234-1245; David Mayhew, "Congressional Elections: The Case of the Vanishing Marginals," *Policy* 6 (Spring 1973): 295-318; and Albert D. Cover and David R. Mayhew, "Congressional Dynamics and the Decline of Competitive Congressional Elections," *Congress Reconsidered,* 2nd

ed., edited by Lawrence C. Dodd and Bruce I. Oppenheimer (Washington, D.C.: CQ Press, 1981), pp. 62-82.

13. Jacobson and Kernell, *Strategy and Choice in Congressional Elections.*
14. Cover and Mayhew, "Congressional Dynamics"; John A. Ferejohn, "On the Decline of Competition in Congressional Elections," *American Political Science Review* 71 (1977): 166-176.
15. Gary C. Jacobson, "The Effects of Campaign Spending in Congressional Elections," *American Political Science Review* 72 (June 1978): 469-491.
16. Anthony Downs, *An Economic Theory of Democracy* (New York: Harper & Row, 1957), chap. 8.
17. Robert S. Erikson, "The Electoral Impact of Congressional Roll Call Voting," *American Political Science Review* 65 (December 1971): 1018-1032; Gerald C. Wright, Jr., "Candidates' Policy Positions and Voting in U.S. House Elections, *Legislative Studies Quarterly* 3 (1978): 445-464; Robert S. Erikson and Gerald C. Wright, Jr., "Policy Representation of Constituency Interests," *Political Behavior* 1 (1980): 91-106.
18. Erikson and Wright, "Policy Representation."
19. Ibid. Very similar patterns were found for 1974.
20. John E. Schwarz and Barton Fenmore, "Congressional Election Results and Congressional Roll Call Behavior: The Case of 1964, 1968, and 1972," *Legislative Studies Quarterly* 2 (1977): 409-422; Erikson, "The Electoral Impact"; Erikson and Wright, "Policy Representation."

5. CONSTITUENCY SERVICE IN THE UNITED STATES AND GREAT BRITAIN

Bruce Cain, John Ferejohn, and Morris Fiorina

The empirical study of representation has focused largely on the extent to which roll call votes cast by representatives comport with the policy preferences of their constituents.[1] But of late, a steady stream of revisionist work has developed the argument that modern representation involves a great deal more than simply voting in a manner consistent with one's constituents' desires.[2] In particular, constituents appear to attach greater importance to what Heinz Eulau and Paul Karps term "service responsiveness" and "allocation responsiveness" than do academics who traditionally have been preoccupied by "policy responsiveness" or "congruence." To be sure, policy congruence is an important matter, but "exclusive emphasis on the policy aspects of responsiveness may give a one-sided view."[3] As Fenno remarks:

> The point is not that policy preferences are not a crucial basis for the representational relationship. They are. The point is that we should not start our studies of representation by assuming they are the only basis for a representational relationship. They are not.[4]

Survey data drawn from recent elections support such judgments. Although constituents attach great importance to policy congruence in the abstract, only a few respondents in the surveys evaluate their representative primarily on the basis of national policy or ideological considerations. They are much more likely to evaluate their representative on the basis of constituent assistance and district service considerations.[5] While policy/programmatic considerations undoubtedly are important, "service responsiveness" and "allocation responsiveness" deserve more attention than the scholarly literature on representative-constituency relations has heretofore accorded them. Until recently, the literature has viewed such aspects of representation as more primitive or lower forms of political behavior—belonging to a category ranging from baby kissing to bribery—best kept out of serious academic discussion.

Recent work, however, has begun to draw attention to the more mundane side of representative-constituency relations. The *American Political Science Review* has even published an article on baby books.[6] In this spirit the present chapter will immerse the reader in some of the less exalted aspects of representative-constituency relations. We will describe the constituency services offered by representatives, looking at these from the standpoint of both constituents and representatives. The term "representative" in this chapter refers both to U.S. congressmen and British members of Parliament (MPs). The chapter is drawn from a larger study of representative-constituency relations in the United States and Great Britain, and we think the reader will find the comparative focus enlightening. British MPs, of course, do not have the individual importance and independence of American members of Congress (MCs), but in both countries members have distinct districts to which they are electorally responsible. Moreover, in both countries members have long traditions of providing services to individuals and groups in their districts. And, as will be seen, in both countries members behave in similar fashion in the realm of service responsiveness.

Constituency Service:
The View from the Constituency

Taking first things first, what do we mean by constituency service? Our usage is similar to Fenno's:

> Many activities can be incorporated under the rubric of "district service," or "constituent service," but the core activity is providing help to individuals, groups, and localities in coping with the federal government. Individuals need someone to intercede with the bureaucracies handling their veterans' benefits, social security checks, military status, civil service pension, immigration proceedings, and the like. Private groups and local governments need assistance in pursuing federal funds for water and sewer projects, highways, dams, buildings, planning, research and development, small business loans, and so forth. Sometimes service benefiting individuals is known as "casework" and service having larger numbers of benefactors [sic] is called "project assistance." Sometimes both are lumped together as casework.[7]

Responding to the increased interest in constituency service, the 1978 and 1980 National Election Studies/Center for Political Studies surveys asked respondents:

> Have you (or anyone in your family living here) ever contacted Representative (name) or anyone in his/her office?

> (If yes) Was it to:
> Express an opinion?
> Seek information?
> Seek help on a problem you had?

> Did you get a response?

> How satisfied were you with the response: very satisfied, somewhat satisfied, not very satisfied, or not at all satisfied?

The respondent then was asked whether he or she knew of anyone else who had contacted the representative, and if so whether they had received a response, and their degree of satisfaction with the response. No differentiation by purpose of contact (opinion, information, help) was made, however. Constituents also were asked the following less personal question:

> Do you happen to remember anything special that your U.S. representative (name) has done for this district or for the people in this district while (he/she) has been in Congress?

Up to two responses per respondent were coded. We took the preceding items and modified them in the obvious ways for use in a 1979 survey in Great Britain. (See Table 5-1.)

Table 5-1 Constituent Communications/Requests, United States and Great Britain

		U.S. 1978	U.S. 1980	G.B. 1979
Citizen-Initiated Contacts		15%	16%	8%
Express Opinion		6	6	2
Seek Information		6	6	1
Seek Help		5	9	5
Response:				
	Opinion	10	4	17
None	Information	4	6	5
	Help	6	6	9
	Opinion	52	49	31
Very Satisfied	Information	61	64	47
	Help	65	61	54
	Opinion	13	20	12
*Not Satisfied	Information	7	8	19
	Help	10	16	18
Secondhand C-I Contacts		19	20	6
Response:				
None		4	3	—
Satisfied		69	62	—
Unsatisfied		6	6	—
District Service		29	18	13
Particularized		10	9	—
Pork Barrel		8	8	—

* The two least positive coding categories were collapsed.

As a perusal of Table 5-1 makes clear, the 1978 and 1980 U.S. figures are very similar. About one-sixth of the American sample reports having gotten in touch with the MC or his or her office. The communications or requests are fairly evenly distributed across the three categories of purposes, with perhaps a slight plurality for seeking help with a problem. In Britain fewer people report having contacted their MP, with most of them specifying that the contact involved a request for help.

The citizens of both countries overwhelmingly report that their requests and communications are handled satisfactorily. Ninety percent or more report receiving a response, nearly half in Great Britain and more than half in the United States are highly satisfied with the response, and only small minorities in both countries are unhappy with the response they receive. The slight variations in these figures seem common-sensical enough. Those who write or call to express opinions are the most likely to be ignored in Great Britain and also in the 1978 (but not 1980) American data. They also are somewhat more likely to express dissatisfaction with their response in the United States, but not in Britain. We would expect, of course, that representatives would have most difficulty satisfying those who communicate strong policy disagreements or crank positions, and in some cases might just choose to ignore the communication. The flip side of the preceding variations are the relatively higher levels of satisfaction expressed by those requesting information or seeking help. Note, however, that in Britain "information" and "help" requests result in more highly satisfied *and* more dissatisfied respondents than do expressions of opinion. In general, the help and information responses are sufficiently similar that we have combined them into a single "casework" variable.[8]

In addition to personal and familial communications, constituents hear about the experiences of others who communicate with representatives. About one-fifth of the American sample and a much smaller proportion of the British sample have such secondhand experiences. These too are highly positive.[9] Secondhand communications are not differentiated by opinion, information, and help topics, but it seems most probable that constituents would hear about the aid representatives have provided their friends and coworkers. Thus, we will treat the secondhand citizen-initiated contact data as secondhand casework data, although this may overestimate the latter somewhat.

Finally, about one-fifth of the American respondents and one-eighth of the British claim to "recall something special" the incumbent has done for the district. This item was intended to tap "allocation responsiveness." It did that and more in the United States. Follow-up probes indicate that about half of the individuals who recall something special mean a particularized benefit of some sort, with slightly fewer specifically mentioning a local project or program. In Britain most of those responding positively to the item refer to a clearly local matter when probed.

The figures in Table 5-1 show that only small minorities of constituents have personally received assistance from their representatives. Of course, the proportions are somewhat larger among voters, especially in the United States. Also, in the United States but not in Britain, the probability of voting increases with the satisfaction of the casework experience. The direction of causality is unclear. Possibly those more "connected" to political affairs are both more likely to vote and to contact their representative, or alternatively, the communication may stimulate participation, or, of course, some of both. But at any rate the figures in Table 5-1 are noticeably higher when nonvoters are removed.

The sheer number of constituents who have personally received assistance from their representative may not be the crucial consideration. Because of differences in their sociodemographic composition, some constituencies may have a much greater basic demand for assistance than others, but lower demand constituencies may still believe that, *should the need arise,* their representative would be there to help. Such possibilities are raised by Fenno in *Home Style,* a rich discussion of representative-constituency relations. According to Fenno, MCs attempt to create generalized beliefs that they are accessible to constituents, that they would be helpful in appropriate situations, in short, that they are trustworthy.

The 1978 NES/CPS survey included a new item intended to tap such beliefs. Variously dubbed the "expectation of access" or "expectation of helpfulness" item, it reads:

> If you had a problem that Representative (your MP) [name] could do something about, do you think he/she would be very helpful, somewhat helpful, or not very helpful to you?

The item refers to an expectation rather than an experience, and the expectation presumably would be a function of the *reputation* of the representative. This reputation would naturally reflect the efforts of the representative on behalf of his or her constituents. It also would have the potential to affect the behavior of numerous constituents who had not had personal dealings with the member. The effect could work in either direction, incidentally: a representative with a poor reputation could be evaluated negatively by constituents who had not had negative personal experiences with him.

In both countries, however, representatives enjoy positive reputations. As Table 5-2 shows, about a quarter of British and American constituents expect their member to be "very helpful" if a problem arose, and only about 10 percent expect that he or she would not be helpful. The distributions are highly similar in the two countries; the only difference is a slight relative preference for the contingent "depends" answer by the British respondents.

Of course, items like "expectation of helpfulness" raise suspicions. Perhaps constituents simply expect incumbents of their party to be helpful and those of another party not to be. Or perhaps constituents are naturally prone to optimism and respond in a positive manner. Table 5-3 contains some indication that constituent expectations have real content and are neither

Table 5-2   Expectation of Helpfulness, United States and Great Britain

	U.S. 1978	U.S. 1980	G.B.
Representative (MP) Would Be:			
Very Helpful	27%	26%	28%
Somewhat Helpful	34	40	28
Not Very Helpful	10	11	11
Don't Know	25	21	24
Depends	4	3	10

purely random nor purely rationalization. The statistical estimates are for models that presume that incumbent reputations depend positively on visibility and on the actual provision of assistance to constituents. Additionally, the models admit the possibility that constituents may have more positive expectations about an incumbent who shares their party affiliation. On the other side of the ledger, a visible challenger might dim the luster of the incumbent given that the former may attack the incumbent's record or character as part of his or her campaign. Such suggestions are no more than common sense, and as seen, all are reflected in the data.

The British and American equations are quite similar. MPs may get more political mileage out of personal contacts than MCs, and MCs perhaps more out of secondhand contacts.[10] After taking contacts into account, name recall appears to have little or no effect in Great Britain or in the United States in 1980, but significant effects in the expected direction are evident in the United States in 1978. Partisanship is somewhat more important, *ceteris paribus,* in Britain; the small group of minor party identifiers has by far the lowest expectations of the MP, while identifiers with the incumbent's party naturally are the most sanguine about the likelihood that he or she would help in a pinch.[11] Finally, in the United States tenure in office yields inconsistent results. In 1978 new incumbents are expected to be more helpful than more senior ones, but in 1980 the relationship is just the opposite. No relationship at all is apparent in Britain.

The largest coefficients in Table 5-3, however, are those that reflect the incumbent's previous efforts. Satisfied constituents are highly positive about the incumbent's future potential, and dissatisfied constituents (rare) are highly negative.[12] Those who claim to recall something already done for the constituency are likewise very positive. These figures unsurprisingly suggest that incumbent representatives can perform services that enhance their constituents' images of them, and that suggestion holds for MPs as much as for MCs.

To be sure, the preceding analysis relies exclusively on survey data, all of which is potentially subject to rationalization and misreporting. Thus, we will preview data of a more objective nature.[13] Across our samples, respondents in

Table 5-3 Expectation of Access Equations, United States and Great Britain

	U.S. 1978 (n=1135)	U.S. 1980 (n=811)	G.B. (n=821)
Contact			
Personal	.13*	.36**	.56**
Media	.36**	.39**	.23**
Secondhand	.32**	.24*	−.02
Casework			
Very Satisfied	.90**	1.07**	.92**
Somewhat Satisfied	−.32*	.17**	−.60*
Not Satisfied	−1.18**	−1.22**	−1.39**
Secondhand Casework			
Satisfied	.36**	.66**	⎫
Somewhat Satisfied	.40*	.02	⎬ .57**
Not Satisfied	−1.22	−.67*	⎭
District Service	.53**	.38**	.55**
Party Identification			
Independent	.04	.02	—
Minor Party ID	—	—	−.44*
No Party ID	—	—	.24*
Same Party ID	.30**	.19*	.41**
Recall Incumbent	.30**	.16†	.05
Recall Challenger	−.49**	−.05	−.02
Year Elected	.01*	−.01*	.01
Constant	−2.55	1.25**	.14
R²	.33	.36	.29

* p<.05
** p<.01
† p<.10

different congressional and parliamentary districts show considerable variation in their expectations, from more than three-quarters "very helpful" to none "very helpful." Such cross-district variation relates positively and significantly to independently obtained reports of incumbent activities and allocation of resources. Thus, some degree of rationalization probably does underlie the relationship in Table 5-3, but the additional data demonstrate that the table reflects reality as well.

Constituent Service:
From the Vantage Point of the Representative

The preceding section considers constituency service from the vantage point of the citizen only. In the remainder of this chapter we will take a detailed look at constituency service from the vantage point of members of Congress and Parliament. What do they do to help constituents with their problems? What are typical problems? Do MCs and MPs merely respond to exogenous demands for constituency service, or do they contribute to these demands?

The Demand for Constituency Service

The attempt to secure projects for the district applies almost exclusively to the MC; hence, we will not discuss "allocation responsiveness" (for example, pork barrel activities) in this chapter. For present purposes the crucial component of constituency service is casework, which we define as the provision of information and/or assistance to constituents who have problems. The range of matters that constituents bring to the attention of members is enormous, encompassing both egregious injustices and trivial inconveniences. Sometimes even the representatives are surprised by what they are asked to do. Consider the experience of one MP:

> My wife was going through some old correspondence the other day and she came across a letter that said: "Dear Mr. Tuck, I want to thank you for all the help you have given me the past few weeks. My toaster has never worked better." I can't for the life of me remember the details of the case, but I must have helped her get her appliance fixed.

More typically, however, cases arise from disagreements between the constituent and some governmental body. Consider the following graphic example from the United States:

> A shipyard worker had been severely crippled in an on-the-job accident. Because of technicalities in his former employment status, he had been three times ruled ineligible for disability compensation. A "Catch 22" interpretation also made welfare unavailable. By the time the constituent sought help at his Congressman's field office the situation was desperate. He had been unable to work for several years, medical and other bills had piled up, the family budget was in shambles, home utilities were about to be shut off, the family car had been repossessed and a bank was about to foreclose on the home mortgage.
> Resolving this case required several months and more than a hundred caseworker manhours. Eventually the shipyard (federal agency) was persuaded to reclassify the former employee. That enabled the constituent to qualify (following more appeals by the caseworker) for disability compensation (state agency) as well as for welfare (county agency—more appeals).

Meanwhile, the caseworker and the AA [administrative assistant] used their patron's good offices to persuade the constituent's banker (private), automobile credit agency (private), hospital (county) and utility company (city) to accept delayed debt-repayment schedules. Finally, the caseworker went to the constituent's home to give advice on home economics and family budgeting.[14]

Another example comes from the newsletter of a young British MP:

> For five years—ever since he was first elected to represent Walsall South—Bruce George had campaigned to get the barriers for people whose lives were made miserable by the din of six lanes of motorway traffic roaring past day and night. The trouble was that some civil service types had said that only motorways built after a certain date could have barriers. This led to the ridiculous situation where the M6 south of the Bescot junction could have noise barriers, but north of the junction it could not.
>
> But just a few weeks ago, Bruce's patient years of campaigning paid off. It was announced that the so-called cut-off date for noise barriers had been scrapped—meaning that barriers can be installed wherever motorways pass close to housing.[15]

As these examples demonstrate, casework frequently provides an opportunity for elected representatives to help constituents challenge the decisions of bureaucrats. This is reflected in the kinds of cases that members of Congress and Parliament typically receive. In the United States, about 90 percent of all congressional offices in 1978 reported social security and military/veterans' benefits problems as among their most common types of cases. Immigration problems were mentioned next, and unemployment benefits, disputes with the IRS, health care problems, civil service issues, housing, and black lung cases finished the list. Like their American counterparts, British MPs also receive cases that concern pensions and social security, taxes, immigration, health care, and military problems. However, there are some notable cross-national differences. In Britain, more requests deal with education, planning permits, and various public utilities. Moreover, the most common type of case in Britain (85 percent of the MPs) involves housing, a type which is minor in the United States. These differences obviously mirror differences in the kinds of services offered by the two governments. For instance, the large size of the public housing stock in Great Britain partly explains the many hours MPs spend investigating unrepaired windows, acts of vandalism, and the expedition of housing transfers. As British local councils have assumed the role of landlord, MPs have become, in effect, the tenants' defenders.

As the shipyard worker example illustrates, handling cases often means that members and their staffs work with officials at several levels of government. A complex case in the United States might involve federal, state, and local agencies, as well as the private sector. British MPs also must work with borough, county, and national civil service officials. But even when the cases are not complex, they often fall outside what reasonably could be assumed to be the natural jurisdiction of a congressman or MP. This presents a dilemma. Rejecting a constituent's request for assistance can alienate a potential vote, but at the same time representatives and their staffs often feel uncomfortable about non-national cases.

Housing in Great Britain is illustrative since it concerns the local borough council and not the national government. Complaints about the waiting list for houses or the lack of repairs in council flats really should be referred to the local housing officer in the first instance, and then to the local councillor. In fact, many constituents take their housing complaints directly to the MP in the not unfounded belief that the MP's greater influence will increase the chances of successful resolution. Different MPs handle housing cases in different ways. Some discourage housing cases and routinely refer them to local councillors while others handle all or a large number of them directly. But on the whole, MPs are somewhat less likely to observe local versus national distinctions than their congressional counterparts. Whereas 54 percent of the congressional offices regularly refer state or local cases to the appropriate state or local authority, only 17 percent of the MPs said that they declined local authority cases. Even so, one-third of the MPs said that although they assisted on local cases, they did so reluctantly. As one MP put it, "There are actually two levels of government, but people don't understand this. For many people, the MP is the only one they know. People see us as the way to deal with the system. You have to help them." Another complained that "periodically I tell people that housing is a local councillor responsibility, but they persist. I am no more effective than a local councillor in dealing with housing: in fact, I take care not to be more effective."

One explanation for why MPs feel more compelled to handle local cases outside their natural jurisdiction is that in Britain there are fewer elected officials who can provide such services. In the United States, assemblymen, state senators, mayors, and a variety of elected county and city officials have their own offices and staff to deal with citizen complaints.[16] By comparison, British local councillors are less visible, have fewer resources, and are not usually career officials. Thus, MPs often explain their involvement in local affairs by the twin facts that councillors cannot be trusted to do the job right and that mishandled complaints can reflect negatively on the MP.

Although the nature of constituent work is fairly similar in the United States and Great Britain, the resources available to representatives certainly are not.[17] This simple fact helps to explain a number of cross-national differences in constituency service practices. Above all, there is a crucial difference in the amount of staff support. Compared with congressmen, MPs get very little assistance. In addition to their administrative and legislative aides, research assistants, receptionists, community representatives, and project workers, MCs have on average between four and five full-time caseworkers who work exclusively on constituent service problems. Many of these caseworkers (75 percent) work in the district offices. One-eighth of the offices in our sample even bring their services to the district by means of a mobile van.

District offices play a crucial role in the casework process. Many representatives maintain more than one district office to maximize the accessibility of their staff to constituents: 60 percent of those surveyed had at least two district offices, and 27 percent had three or more. Typically, these offices are open five days a week; in a few instances, they are open every day. Usually, the district offices are administered by a district representative (47 percent) or by an administrative assistant in Washington (24 percent), but sometimes the authority is completely decentralized (17 percent). Only rarely (5 percent) do the MCs administer the district offices themselves. In most cases the district and Washington offices closely coordinate their activities: in only 10 percent of the offices is there little or no daily contact between the two. The distribution of the casework burden varies widely. In one-third of the sample, the Washington office handles 10 percent or less of the cases, and at the other extreme, in 10 percent of the sample, the Washington office handles all of it. Most fall between these extremes, with the number of instances where the Washington office handles more cases than the district offices being less (n=40) than the number where the district offices handle more (n=51).

About one-quarter of the administrative assistants surveyed thought that cases were generally handled better in Washington, but most felt that it depended on the kind of case under consideration. For example, some said that the Washington office was better able to handle complex and delicate cases. Others felt that military and immigration problems were better handled in Washington, whereas social security and veterans' benefits were better handled in district offices, which are generally closer to regional social security and veterans' department offices. In general, district offices tend to deal with constituents in a more personalized manner than the Washington office does. District offices rely heavily on personal contact and phone calls, whereas the Washington office handles casework primarily by mail.

Although the pattern of working relationships between the Washington and district offices varies from member to member, one feature seems to be pretty much constant across all the offices: casework in the United States is primarily a staff activity. In sharp contrast, MPs labor with almost no assistance from staff and have a more direct hand in their constituent affairs. Most MPs have a part-time secretary to assist them with their constituent work. Nearly three-quarters of the secretaries do more than handle the clerical work associated with casework such as answering phone calls and typing letters (even so, a few MPs proudly told us that they answer many letters in longhand). When questioned about the amount of autonomy their secretaries had in dealing with cases, half the MPs insisted that they directly supervise each case themselves and that their secretaries have no autonomy in such matters. Another third said that their secretaries sometimes handle cases without their direct supervision, and less than 10 percent said that their secretaries deal with cases autonomously.

In addition to secretarial support, MPs sometimes receive help from the local party agent. Although the agent's primary tasks are to maintain the organization of the local party and to assist in the running of constituency election campaigns, some are also responsible for screening cases during the week and arranging appointments for the weekend surgeries, the designated time when the MP meets with constituents to hear their complaints. The amount of the agent's casework involvement often depends upon his personal relationship with the MP since it is not a formal duty: agents are technically employees of the party and not of the members.

All things considered, the substantial personal involvement of the MP differs greatly from the more bureaucratic approach of most congressional offices. When asked to estimate the amount of time the congressman personally spends on casework, 47 percent of our sample said that the congressman rarely spends any time on casework, and only 9 percent said that the congressman spends more than 10 percent of his or her time on casework. In contrast, 37 percent of the MPs said that they spend between 50 and 60 percent of their time on constituency service, and another 10 percent gave no specific estimate but said "most" or "a good deal" of their time. Only 5 percent of the sample said that they spend 10 percent or less of their time on constituent affairs.

A consequence of the bureaucratized approach that congressional offices take toward casework is that there is little or no correlation in the United States between the importance the member assigns to casework and his or her personal involvement. Most congressmen and MPs take casework very seriously: about 75 percent of the respondents in both countries rated casework as "very important." Thirty percent of the congressional sample even said that casework was their top priority. Yet it was not unusual to get comments like the following: "It matters a lot for staff, but not much personally. That is, the Congressman himself spends little time on casework, but he thinks that it's important and wants his staff to do it well." Or, "it matters a lot. Nothing hurts him more than when people come to him because the staff couldn't help him. Then we have failed in our job." In short, the key to the congressman's casework commitment is the effectiveness of his or her organization; the key to the MP's casework commitment is the personal time and effort he or she is willing to devote to constituency service.

Not surprisingly, some MPs are concerned about the strain that casework puts upon their time and energies. In fact, two-thirds of those interviewed felt that it was important that MPs be given larger staff allotments. Fifteen percent (usually the older members and the Conservatives) said that they wanted the staff for legislative purposes only, but 43 percent (especially the younger members and the Labourites) indicated that they would use the staff to lessen their casework burden. Those who opposed the expansion of the MP's staff offered several reasons for their position. By far the most common was that Britain is a small country lacking the resources and wealth of the United States, and that it therefore was not reasonable for the MP to have staff support comparable to their congressional counterparts. MPs also noted that British constituencies are about one-fifth the size of congressional districts.[18] Some MPs, especially ministers and Conservatives, felt that adding staff would only further the professionalization of the MP's role, ruining the personal touch and adding to the growth of the government sector. As they perceived it, the library adequately provided basic information; if members were given staff for legislative purposes, it would make it easier for them to avoid thinking about issues and to shirk their policy responsibilities.

The Generation of Demand

The investment of staff resources and personal time are not merely passive responses to exogenously arising demands. Members may work actively to stimulate demand inasmuch as an image of helpfulness can be fostered by the aggressive solicitation of new cases, whereas a more passive approach can signal indifference or remoteness from the affairs of constituents. Of course, complaints will come to representatives even when their services are not advertised at all; however, advertising will raise the caseload level, and by so doing increase contacts with individual citizens.

Most MPs (64 percent) and congressmen (85 percent) advertise their casework services in some way. The exceptions offer two main reasons for not doing so. A few claim that they have enough cases already. This does not necessarily mean that they are inattentive to their constituents' problems. An older representative with high name recognition and a well-established reputation for constituency service, for instance, may not feel that he has to remind voters of his services, particularly if there is a high rate of repeat business. Others do not advertise because they find casework distasteful. One congressional office even put out a comprehensive listing of government services in a special newsletter in order "to tell people where to go so that they wouldn't come to their Congressman." This is an example of negative advertising designed to discourage the flow of casework. We hasten to add that such examples are not common.

In the United States the methods of casework advertisement are diverse. By far the most common (44 percent) is the newsletter or district mailing. The latter often will describe the services available and list the phone number of the office and the hours when the staff are on call. Sometimes, it will also include examples of cases so that people can get a better idea of what is being offered. Some offices add supplementary mailings and questionnaires. There are also more personal methods of generating cases such as sending the staff out "shopping for cases" or tying casework into the congressman's regular district tours (9 percent). A few congressmen even hold formal "workshops" or "town halls" where cases are taken personally in the manner of the British surgery. In many instances, just having good relationships with key groups in the district fosters cases. One office reported that it made a point of keeping up good ties with senior citizen organizations because "they will recommend to us people with social security and Veterans' Administration problems."

In Britain advertising casework often involves highly personalized methods such as touring neighborhoods, picking up cases at political and social functions, getting referrals through local party activists, and even knocking on doors to call on constituents individually. A good, if slightly extreme example of the personal efforts of some young MPs to promote casework is that of Mr. G.:

> Mr. G. is deeply involved in all sorts of community affairs. He holds surgeries every week at two locations for two hours each. He actively solicits cases by advertising his surgeries in the local paper and by walking through the town on weekends and letting people approach him on the street with their problems. As Mr. G. explains, this serves the dual purpose of picking up cases from people who could not attend the surgery as well as making him visible to his constituents. As we walked through the town market and through the complexes of council homes, people would come up to Mr. G. to tell him their problems. Mr. G. recorded the person's request in a notebook and promised to get back to them shortly. Some of the people we saw invited Mr. G. in to have a quick cup of coffee while they complained about the vandalism of neighborhood kids or the neglect the local council had shown toward the repair of their homes. . . . The immigration cases are a very important bridge to the immigrant community for Mr. G. He has no trouble developing ties with the white, working class community, but the immigrants tend to maintain separate religious and cultural ties. Thus, Mr. G. took us to a local immigrant bar-brothel where he nonchalantly collected cases and heard complaints while we looked on in slightly embarrassed discomfort.[19]

Approximately 70 percent of the MPs sampled advertised their surgeries (often in the newspapers) or sent out circulars about their casework services— what many referred to as their "may I help you" letters. Members commonly concentrate their mailings on eighteen-year-olds just entering the electorate and on areas of "new estates" where many constituents do not yet know their member and his or her agent or assistant. In addition, 27 percent of the MPs solicited cases by knocking on doors or by directly writing to a constituent when they read or heard about a problem that the constituent had. As one member told us, "The process of electioneering is seeking out cases. I wrote letters to people seeking cases. I carried a notebook and went to see people at their own homes when I was campaigning." Other casework practices seem to be uniquely British. Several MPs told us that they advertised their services through local council publications or enlisted the aid of local councillors in drumming up new problems. Again, this is less likely to occur in the United States where many of the state and local elected officials handle cases themselves. Many candidates for seats will take up residence in the constituency upon their nomination and begin to do casework before the election. The usual explanation is that some constituents feel uncomfortable about bringing their problems to an incumbent from the "other party." It goes without saying that this practice also gives the challenger a chance to show his or her commitment to interests of the constituency.

One peculiarly British institution for generating cases deserves special mention. The *surgery*—so named because it resembles a doctor's office hours—provides an opportunity for citizens to meet with the MP to discuss their problems and complaints. Usually the MP is assisted by an agent, party volunteer, or secretary who takes the names of those who are waiting and determines the order in which the MP will see them. Sometimes the MP writes down the details of the case himself, and in other instances, the member circulates around the room while those assisting him take down the necessary information. Many of those who show up have attended before, and not infrequently, about the same matter.

Surgeries have been used in the past as a rough indicator of an MP's constituency effort, but there are reasons to be suspicious of this measure by itself. MPs in rural constituencies maintain that surgeries are more useful in densely populated areas than in sparsely populated areas because of the greater difficulty constituents experience in getting to a designated area. A rural MP may be just as dedicated to his constituency as an urban counterpart but hold fewer surgeries. Bearing this in mind, we cautiously report the frequency with which MPs hold surgeries. Only 9 percent of our sample said that they hold no surgeries or hold surgery only irregularly and infrequently. Eighty-nine percent of the sample hold surgeries at least every month, and 58 percent said that they hold them every two weeks or more.

The preceding figures, incidentally, present a notable contrast to those reported in 1963 by Dowse based on a mail survey of 69 MPs.[20] More than one-third of Dowse's respondents claimed to hold no regular surgery, a number that dwindles to a corporal's guard in our survey. At the other extreme, only one-third of Dowse's respondents held surgery at least every two weeks, whereas our survey produced a figure well over one-half. Assuming both surveys elicited representative data, it appears that in the span of two decades surgery has become a much larger part of the MP's professional life.

Dealing with Cases

The first component of an aggressive casework strategy is generating cases. A representative who wishes to increase the number of contacts he or she has with constituents will advertise widely and take the initiative to drum up business. There is no point in soliciting cases, however, if they are not handled well. Thus, a second component of an aggressive strategy is the expeditious handling of cases. This means (1) taking quick action to deal with cases and (2) achieving a satisfactory result.

With respect to the first, we have seen already that some MCs and MPs regularly refer cases outside their national jurisdiction to local and state officials. Nevertheless, nearly all those interviewed in the United States and Great Britain felt that it was important to give a prompt and courteous answer to every request that came to them whether the case was referred or not. It was common for them to say things such as "I always try to give a sympathetic reply," "I always listen to them," or "we try to handle all calls courteously." Inevitably, however, some proportion of the cases sent to members are hopeless or fabricated, so problems naturally arise. A few members bravely inform their constituents that the case is unworthy of attention. Said one retiring MP, "I tried to let it be known that I would handle good cases only." Most, however, will go through the motions of handling the case anyway. As one member lamented, "I tried to explain early in my career that I couldn't help people on certain matters. But I decided that I couldn't afford the appearance of indifference and now I go through the formalities in all cases."

Several members and staff in both countries suggested that they had developed an informal signalling system with the officials they had to deal with most frequently so that they could subtly indicate when they felt that a case was important and when they wanted only a formal reply to show the constituent. As one put it, "we pursue some cases more vigorously than others." The important thing is to show the constituent that the member cares about the problem and has done all that can be done. Even if there is nothing to be done, there may still be credit to claim if the member and staff can show that their effort was sincere. Consider the case of one MP, Sir H.:

> As he explains it, the very fact that a man of his stature in the community takes the time to listen to some average fellow's problems in itself creates good will and electoral reward. To illustrate his point, he gave us the example of some fellow in a pub complaining about a problem he has with the government. His friends tell him that he has been wronged and suggest that he see Sir H. So the fellow calls or writes Sir H. who dutifully sends off a letter to the constituent informing him of his actions and one to the relevant minister to please enquire into the matter. The minister writes back a reply—in many cases, unable to help—and Sir H. sends a photocopy of the minister's letter to the constituent. The constituent's problem often does not get solved, says Sir H., but at least the constituent can take the letter with him to the pub "happy in the knowledge his case has received attention at the highest levels." Sir H. in return acquires the reputation of being a good constituency man who cares about his constituents.[21]

Sympathy and courtesy are all well and good, but the clearest example of a successful case is one resolved in the constituent's favor. Estimates of the cases that are resolved successfully in this sense are highly disparate. In the United States, where administrative assistants were willing to give a numerical estimate, the figures ranged from 10 percent to 90 percent, but a majority felt that cases were successfully resolved more often than not: 44 of the 64 who gave percentage estimates thought that the results were favorable in 50 percent or more of the instances. Of those who did not want to give numerical estimates, 15 out of 20 said most of the cases and one said all. Few MPs ventured to give us numerical estimates, but when they did, they too were usually over the 50 percent level. Several MPs maintained that the success rate was really lower and that their colleagues were deluding themselves about their impact on the outcome. Much appears to depend on the nature of the case. For instance, when MPs try to get repairs for council property they are extremely effective, but they have much less success when people ask them to assist in getting transfers because the housing lists are set by a uniform point system.

Of course, legislators may claim credit for actions that would have occurred—albeit at a later date—had they not interceded. Most members feel, however, that their intervention forces bureaucrats to give a case special attention. As one A.A. put it:

> He was merely a statistic in some bureaucrat's in-basket without our help. Once we started making inquiries he became a "problem" for the agencies. By the time we were through, he had become an individual person—instead of a statistic or problem.[22]

When the British civil servants themselves were asked about the handling and significance of MP's requests they seemed to confirm such judgments:

> We asked several local officials why, and in what ways, they paid attention to the Member's requests. The Housing director told us that a complaint from an MP did not get special attention per se: if the complaint was unjustified, there would be no special circumstances applied to it. However, the MP's enquiry was usually given a higher priority in the sense that where the normal time for a reply was about four months, the department would handle the MP's request in a matter of days.
>
> As for why the MP's request received a higher priority, there were two responses. One, already mentioned, was that while it was not a "duty" or "right," the MP was entitled to a prompt reply as a matter of "courtesy." But in addition, it was based on a wariness of the consequences of not responding properly. As one official frankly admitted, an MP's letter was viewed with apprehension since in most cases, if the letter got that far, it indicated that the complaint was important. When asked what would happen if they did not respond, we were told that the MP could cause a great deal of trouble by giving the department bad publicity. The fear of a messy, public row formed a strong incentive to comply. Thus, the MP's influence in these matters derives both from the courtesy of good working relations with permanent officials and from the implicit threat of public exposure of departmental or individual incompetence.[23]

Are members hurt in some way when they fail to resolve cases successfully? A majority (60 percent) in the U.S. sample felt unsuccessful cases did not hurt them so long as the office acted promptly and could demonstrate effort. About 10 percent felt that they hurt the member no matter what. The British respondents also felt that much depended on how the cases were handled. Most (63 of 68) emphasized the importance of promptness and competence and the need to prevent overly high expectations; their rule was never promise more than can be delivered. In short, most members and staff in both countries think that casework can be politically beneficial whatever the outcome so long as it is handled properly. This corresponds with our earlier finding that most citizens who contact their member for help or information tend to find the incumbent's response satisfactory and evaluate the incumbent positively.

Publicizing Casework

Solicitation and resolution of cases are the first two elements of an aggressive casework strategy. But these may contribute little to the representative's reputation if a third element is not present: publicity. To some extent, incumbents can count on word of mouth to inform people of what they have done for constituents who have contacted them. In addition, a degree of attention from the media may occur as a matter of course. Some incumbents, however, publicize their casework accomplishments to build their reputations more quickly. Almost all MPs and congressmen try to get publicity for projects that benefit the constituency as a whole or some significant segment of it, but an entrepreneurial representative may extend credit claiming to successful individual cases as well. Many, however, feel that publicizing individual cases is unnecessary and improper. Sixty-eight percent of the congressmen and 51 percent of the MPs we sampled took this position. Some of those who publicize cases in the United States (11 of 27) try to preserve the anonymity of the person who was helped unless they have secured that person's permission to use his or her name. Moreover, all but a handful restricted their casework publicity to newsletters only. The British, by comparison, tend to use newspapers to publicize their casework. Many MPs actually write their own press releases and, if the local press is not hostile, may regularly place stories in the local paper about individual or constituency-wide causes they have assisted.

About one-third of the sample do not advertise their surgeries or publicize their casework services in any way. Some feel that doing so is undignified. Said one member, "you shouldn't thrust yourself upon your constituents." Others added that "success breeds success" and "people tell their friends" when a case gets resolved successfully. A few actually feel that negative consequences might arise from an overly aggressive approach to casework, particularly cases involving local officials. One young MP told us that older members had warned him not "to step on the toes of local officials."

A study of the relationship between an MP who did a lot of local casework and the public officials in his community suggests that indeed there may be a real basis for such fears. When interviewed some local officials did complain about the member and felt that he was excessively quick to try to embarrass them with adverse publicity to facilitate a case.[24]

The Volume of Casework

Most MPs and MCs seek to generate casework, resolve it, and publicize it, but how much casework do they actually do? In posing this question we tried to get the respondent to distinguish ongoing cases from the number of pieces of mail he or she received in a given week, since the mail *per se* could contain multiple letters on the same case or expressions of constituent opinion as opposed to requests for assistance. Not all respondents were willing or able to give numerical estimates of their case volume, either because they did not know or for some reason did not want to tell us. The figures that were obtained are displayed in Table 5-4. In absolute number, of course, congressmen and their staffs have larger caseloads than MPs. The average number of cases per week was 71 in the United States and 36 in Great Britain. A smaller percentage of congressmen than MPs fall into the 0-to-20 range, and many more fall into the 100+ range. In per capita terms, however, the caseload of the MP is higher, given that the average parliamentary constituency is approximately one-quarter to one-fifth of the population of the average congressional district. The comparison is all the more remarkable when one considers the paucity of the MPs' staff support.

Summary

To sum up, our surveys suggest several tentative conclusions. First, constituent problems are generally similar in the United States and Great Britain, with specific differences in types of cases reflecting the nature of state services in the two countries. Second, MPs have only a small fraction of the support services of MCs, but they devote a greater portion of their personal time and effort to constituent service than do MCs. Third, in both countries members encourage demand for their services. Fourth, members in both countries feel they are quite successful in handling the cases that come to

Table 5-4 Number of Cases Handled Per Week

	Congressmen	*MPs*
<20	9%	23%
21-40	28%	23%
41-60	18%	14%
61-80	6%	10%
81-100	14%	8%
100+	16%	3%
MV	10%	19%
n	102	101

them. And finally, the level of casework is higher in absolute terms in the United States and in per capita terms in Britain.

Viewed more broadly, our findings help to flesh out the general theme of the revisionist works cited earlier. Representation in modern democracies involves a great deal more than demonstrating fealty to the policy preferences of constituents. Of course, one could argue that the complex of activities we have described does not constitute representation, but that would be to claim that much of what representatives do is not representation and that much of what constituents want is not representation. Along with Fenno and Eulau and Karps, we argue that academics generally take too narrow a view. As is their wont, university intellectuals show a penchant for the intangible and the distal, while ordinary constituents attach relatively greater importance to the tangible and the proximal.

NOTES

1. For the classic study, see Warren Miller and Donald Stokes, "Constituency Influences in Congress," *American Political Science Review* 57 (1963): 45-56. For later examples of the genre, see John Sullivan and Robert O'Connor, "Electoral Choice and Popular Control of Public Policy: The Case of the 1966 House Elections," *American Political Science Review* 66 (1972): 1256-1268; and Walter Stone, "The Dynamics of Constituency Electoral Control in the House," *American Politics Quarterly* (1980): 399-424.
2. For the principal arguments to this effect, see David Mayhew, *Congress: The Electoral Connection* (New Haven: Yale University Press, 1974); Morris Fiorina, *Congress: Keystone of the Washington Establishment* (New Haven: Yale University Press, 1977); and Richard Fenno, *Home Style: House Members in Their Districts* (Boston: Little, Brown & Co., 1978).
3. Heinz Eulau and Paul D. Karps, "The Puzzle of Representation: Specifying Components of Responsiveness," in *The Politics of Representation,* ed. Heinz Eulau et al. (Beverly Hills, Calif.: Sage Publications, 1978), p. 63.
4. Fenno, *Home Style,* p. 241.
5. The basis of these assertions is the analysis of open-ended questions about what constituents like and dislike about their representative and about why they approve or disapprove of their representative's performance. See Glenn R. Parker, "The Advantage of Incumbency in House Elections," *American Politics Quarterly* 8 (1980): 449-464; Morris Fiorina, "Congressmen and Their Constituents: 1958 and 1978," in *Proceedings of the Thomas P. O'Neill, Jr., Symposium on the U.S. Congress,* ed. Dennis Hale (Boston: Eusey Press, 1982), pp. 33-64; and Glenn Parker and Roger Davidson, "Why Do Americans Love Their Congressman So Much More Than Their Congress?" *Legislative Studies Quarterly* 4 (1979): 53-62.
6. Albert D. Cover and Bruce S. Brumberg, "Baby Books and Ballots: The Impact of Congressional Mail on Constituent Opinion," *American Political Science Review* 76 (1982): 347-359.

7. Fenno, *Home Style,* p. 101.
8. As discussed by Fiorina in "Congressmen and Their Constituents," the percentage of respondents who report making an information or help request in the United States approximately tripled between 1958 and 1978.
9. In the British sample only the fact of such secondhand experience was obtained; satisfaction levels were not available.
10. The contact variables are created by collapsing the contact battery. Based on Glenn Parker's analysis in "Interpreting Candidate Awareness in U.S. Congressional Elections," *Legislative Studies Quarterly* 6 (1981): 219-234, the responses were used to create two dummy variables: *personal contact* (met the incumbent, heard him/her at a meeting, talked to staff, agent, secretary or other employee), and *media contact* (newspaper/magazine, mail, radio, TV). The collapsing is necessary to reduce collinearity and to keep the number of variables in the analysis to a manageable number.
11. Party affiliations are coded as follows. In the American sample all respondents fall into mutually exclusive classes: same party as incumbent (51 percent), independent (14 percent), opposite party from incumbent (35 percent). In the British sample 38 percent share the incumbent's affiliation, and 17 percent admit to no party affiliation. The opposite party category includes adherents of any party whose MP is not of that party—45 percent. To capture any additional differences between national and minor party identifiers, an additional dummy variable, minor party ID, is included. This variable takes on a value of one for those 2.5 percent of the respondents who report an identification with other than the Conservative, Labour, or Liberal parties. To avoid statistical degeneracy in the analyses, one category, opposite party ID, is omitted from each equation reported in Table 5-3.
12. The omitted reference category for these sets of dummy variables consists of those who report no casework experience. As noted in note 9, we do not have a clean measure of satisfaction with secondhand casework experience in Britain. Thus, the dummy variable takes on a value of one for all who report knowledge of friend, relative, or coworker experience. The large and highly significant coefficient suggests that the effects of satisfactory secondhand experience are very strong, given that the estimate in Table 5-3 is watered down by inclusion of a presumed minority who recall unsatisfactory experiences.
13. Our data is from a larger study of which this essay is only a part.
14. John D. Macartney, "Political Staffing: A View from the District" (Ph.D. diss., University of California, Los Angeles, 1975), pp. 113-114.
15. Bruce George, *The Bruce George Report* (undated campaign newsletter), p. 1.
16. Macartney, "Political Staffing."
17. Austin Ranney, "The Working Conditions of Members of Parliament and Congress: Changing the Tools Changes the Job," in *The Role of the Legislature in Western Democracies,* ed. Norman Ornstein (Washington, D.C.: American Enterprise Institute for Public Policy Research, 1981).
18. MPs get free train travel to their districts. We have found no relationships between distance of the constituency from London and various indicators of constituency attentiveness.
19. Bruce Cain, John Ferejohn, and Morris Fiorina, "The House Is Not a Home: British MPs in Their Constituencies," *Legislative Studies Quarterly* 4 (1979): 509-510.

20. R. E. Dowse, "The MP and His Surgery," *Political Studies* 2 (1963): 333-341.
21. Cain, Ferejohn, and Fiorina, "The House Is Not a Home," p. 506.
22. Macartney, "Political Staffing," p. 114.
23. Bruce E. Cain and David B. Ritchie, "Assessing Constituency Involvement: The Hemel Hempstead Experience," *Parliamentary Affairs*, vol. 35, no. 1 (Winter 1982): 75-76.
24. Ibid., p. 75.

6. PARTIES AND PACS IN CONGRESSIONAL ELECTIONS

Gary C. Jacobson

In the political market place no less than in the economic market place, competition is the mother of invention. Electoral politics offer enduring incentives for people to find new ways to win and hold political office. Every election produces losers trying to figure out how to become winners and winners looking for ways to hang on to what they have won.

At no time has electoral ingenuity been more apparent than in the last two decades. During the 1960s, declining partisanship among voters, greater ease of travel and communication, augmented resources for serving constituents, and expanded government programs combined to offer new ways for members of Congress to please constituents and win votes. Members soon became expert practitioners of the candidate-centered politics these political and technological changes encouraged. Among the evident consequences were a notable increase in the electoral value of congressional incumbency and greater insulation of congressional elections from national political trends.[1] This naturally helped the Democrats, whose good fortune it was to be the majority party at the time.

But congressional incumbents were not left alone for long to enjoy the fruits of innovation. During the 1970s, other participants in electoral politics began figuring out how to operate in the new political environment. They were unintentionally helped by changes in the campaign finance laws, which eventually produced two major new forces in federal elections: revitalized national party campaign committees and nonparty political action committees (PACs).[2] Together, parties and PACs are restructuring electoral politics yet again, and by no means to the advantage of either incumbents in general or Democrats in particular. In this essay I try to explain how and why this has been happening and how these new electoral institutions are changing congressional politics.

Origins

National party involvement in congressional campaigns is nothing new.[3] Political action committees, especially those run by organized labor, also have a notable history. Nor are corporations newcomers to campaign finance; the legal ban on direct corporate contributions enacted in 1907 was routinely circumvented.[4] But the new rules coming into force in the early 1970s with the Federal Election Campaign Act (FECA) and its amendments drastically altered the legal environment of campaign financing, setting conditions that invited both national party committees and PACs to flourish. The result has been a qualitative as well as quantitative change in their campaign roles.

The rules governing PACs evolved from a series of decisions by Congress, the Federal Election Commission (FEC), and the Supreme Court. In brief, these decisions clarified the ambiguous legal status of PACs and legally acknowledged their financial role in campaigns.[5] Organizations of all kinds may establish committees to solicit funds to contribute to candidates for federal office. If organized by a labor union or corporation, the parent organization may pay the overhead but not contribute directly to the committee. To qualify as a multicandidate committee, a PAC must raise money from at least 50 people and contribute to at least five candidates. The maximum contribution is $5,000 per candidate per campaign (which means, in effect, $10,000; that is, $5,000 each in the primary and general campaigns). PACs may also give up to $15,000 to a national party committee and $5,000 to any other political committee. There is no limit to the total amount a PAC may contribute to all candidates. The law thus gives PACs two significant advantages over private persons: individuals may give no more than $1,000 per candidate per campaign and may contribute no more than $25,000 in total to candidates or committees in any calendar year.

Most of the regulations governing PACs were worked out in Congress, sometimes in response to administrative and court decisions that had upset previous arrangements. The main political constraint was the need to balance the opportunities of organized labor (financial allies of the Democrats) with those of business corporations (that favored Republicans). The Democratic majority could not impose rules favoring labor because Republicans held the White House. This balancing act ultimately failed, although not for want of trying. But one major decision was imposed by the Supreme Court quite against the desire of either party. The FECA, passed in 1971, had imposed a limit of $1,000 on how much people or groups could spend independently of candidates' official campaigns. The Court declared five years later in *Buckley* v. *Valeo* that this was an infringement on First Amendment rights and hence void.[6] PACs and individuals are thus free to spend as much as they can on independent campaigns for or against federal candidates.

The establishment of clear rules governing PACs gave them a solid institutional role in financing campaigns. Their activities are thoroughly regulated, but compliance is not difficult, and the independent spending route is available to any group that feels overly constrained. This is one instance where regulation, rather than discouraging entrepreneurial activity, has made it more attractive.

Incentives for building national party organizations were also greatly strengthened by the FECA. The experience of most members of Congress was that parties were of little electoral help, financially or otherwise,[7] and their first inclination was to treat party committees as no different from any other political group. Hence the FECA Amendments of 1974 subjected national and local party organizations to the same direct contribution limits as PACs. But the special character of parties could hardly be denied, and most members did not want campaign finance regulation to weaken what were already ailing institutions. So state and national party organizations were allowed to spend additional money on behalf of their candidates. The opportunity to spend money for candidates opened the way for national party organizations to become major participants in congressional election politics for the first time.

Coordinated party spending, as it is called, is also limited, but the ceilings are higher and, unlike contribution ceilings, rise with inflation. The original limit for a House campaign was $10,000; by 1984, inflation had pushed it up to $20,200. The ceiling for Senate campaigns varies with the population of the state ($.02 times the voting age population, adjusted for inflation since 1974, with a minimum of $20,000, also adjusted). For the 1984 elections, it ranged from $40,400 (in the five least populous states) to $752,409 (in California). The Senate limit also applies to House candidates in those states with a single House seat.[8]

State parties may also spend up to this ceiling for federal candidates, but almost no state party has the money to do it. Republican party officials have exploited this situation to double, in effect, the amount the national party may spend for its candidates. The national party committee simply contracts with each state party to act as its agent for raising and spending the money. The Democrats challenged the legality of this ploy but failed to persuade the Supreme Court.[9]

National party committees thus can legally put quite respectable amounts of money into congressional campaigns. In 1984, for example, a House candidate could receive as much as $70,400 in assistance directly or indirectly from national party sources (direct contributions of $5,000 in both the primary and general election from the party's national committee, the congressional campaign committee, and the state party committee, plus twice $20,200 in coordinated spending). For Senate candidates the ceiling varied from $108,300 in the least populous states to more than $1.5 million in California, which did not, as it happens, have a Senate election that year.

Of course, before national party committees can spend any of this money on candidates they have to raise it. And Republican party committees have done a much better job of fund raising than have their Democratic counterparts. Republicans have also far surpassed the Democrats in building organizations capable of distributing party resources efficiently and using them effectively. Not surprisingly, the minority party, facing a system of electoral politics extraordinarily favorable to incumbents, has shown the greater knack for institutional innovation.

In addition to regulatory changes, two other developments have contributed to the institutional flowering of parties and PACs: technological innovation and the expansion of the federal government's role in economic and social life. Both the national party committees and PACs are creatures of new technologies for raising and spending campaign money. The exponential growth in computer capabilities, combined with the continued development of electronic mass media, offered new ways of storing, retrieving, and exchanging information of all kinds. Avenues of communication in every direction—among candidates, political activists, contributors, and voters—have multiplied. For example, computerized direct mail technology allows money to be raised efficiently through small donations from millions of individuals scattered around the country, tapping resources previously inaccessible on a large scale to political organizers. Republican party committees and conservative ideological PACs have been quickest to take advantage of it. Ideological entrepreneurs with a mission, and on occasion an eye to profiting from selling services to the PAC,[10] have been the most persistent direct mail innovators. The major independent campaigns are financed largely through direct mail solicitations. Direct mail is also used, of course, for campaigning itself. Indeed, the line between fund raising and campaigning frequently disappears in direct mail, since every solicitation contains a message, and most messages include pleas for money.

Technological advances have made polling much more sophisticated and useful, allowed more careful targeting of campaign messages, and permitted greater central coordination of campaign activities; centralization is stimulated by major economies to scale. The new technologies are expensive to use, so they raise the cost of campaigning and, therefore, the demand for the kinds of help PACs and parties offer. Technological changes have contributed to both the supply of, and demand for, the services parties and PACs provide.

The federal government's expanded role in American life has also encouraged the growth of PACs. The greater the impact Congress has on the distribution of economic goods and social values, the greater the incentives for people and groups to engage in political action.[11] When government policy has a major influence on the balance sheet, it is simply good business to invest in politics. When Congress decides whose social values are to prevail, it is no surprise to find people passionately committed to a particular vision of the social good using whatever resources they can muster to influence elections and policies. The growth of political institutions in the private sector is a predictable consequence of a spreading public sector.

It is no small irony that the FECA's principal goals included putting a lid on campaign expenditures and reducing the financial role of special interests. The first goal was stymied by the Court, which found spending limits unconstitutional. This, along with the expensive new campaign technology, increased incentives for putting money into politics, and a decade of inflation, made it impossible to achieve the second goal. As campaign spending has continued to grow, candidates in search of ever larger campaign war chests have naturally turned to PACs, now flourishing under their firmly established legal status. The relative efficiency of soliciting groups that could give as much as $10,000 rather than individuals who could give no more than $2,000 became harder to overlook as inflation cut the real value of a dollar. But inflation also enhanced the position of party committees, whose coordinated spending limits are indexed. And despite many instances of cooperation, parties and PACs remain, fundamentally, as we shall see, natural rivals.

Growth

Party and PAC entrepreneurs wasted little time in responding to the new rules of the campaign finance game, and their campaign activities have expanded rapidly. But institutional development has proceeded unevenly among different kinds of PACs and between the two parties. Thus the enlarged financial role of these organizations has redistributed electoral advantages and political influence.

The term "political action committee" encompasses an enormously diverse set of organizations. The FEC's categories—labor, corporate, trade/membership/health, nonconnected, cooperative, and corporation without stock—only begin to suggest the variety. Within, not to mention between, each of these categories, PACs differ widely. Some are little more than an entrepreneur with a mailing list; others are adjuncts of large corporations or labor organizations. In some, all contribution decisions are made centrally by one or a few individuals; others encourage extensive input from members and contributors. The goals of some are immediate, narrow, and self-interested; others pursue long-term objectives involving widely shared values or other collective goods. Most PACs only give money, but a few of them also supply campaign volunteers, work to get out the vote, produce media advertising, advise on campaign strategy and tactics, and recruit and train candidates. Some participate in coalitions of PACs or cooperate with one of the parties; others make completely independent decisions. Indeed, variety is such that virtually everything said at one time or another about PACs is true of some PAC.[12] Caution is always necessary when generalizing about them.

The proliferation of PACs since 1974 is a familiar story to any observer of American politics. Between 1974 and early 1984, the number of political action committees registered with the Federal Election Commission grew from 608 to 3,525.[13] Corporate and nonconnected PACs (PACs that are independent, self-sustaining organizations without any sponsoring body) have multiplied most rapidly over this period. PAC contributions to congressional candidates have shown a parallel increase. Adjusted for inflation, these contributions more than tripled over the decade. Impressive as it is, the overall growth of PAC contributions is less significant than the shift in the relative financial importance of different kinds of PACs. Labor PACs, which once accounted for one-half of all PAC contributions, now supply less than one-quarter. They were surpassed by corporate PACs in 1980 and by trade/

membership/health PACs in 1982. From a very low starting point in 1974, nonconnected PACs, largely ideological organizations, have doubled their contributions every succeeding election cycle. These groups are also responsible for a major share of independent campaign expenditures, which have increased sharply from $.3 million in 1977-1978 to $5.7 million in 1981-1982. Their financial role has been expanding rapidly. These changes are important because, as we shall see, different sorts of PACs have different contribution strategies and favor different sorts of candidates.

The figures on increased PAC spending have been used, on occasion, to argue that PACs are swamping the electoral process. Therefore, it is important to place them in context. As the data in Table 6-1 show, contributions from private individuals continue to be the most important source of direct contributions by a wide margin. The share of funds supplied by PACs has grown, but it still amounts to less than one-third of House candidates' money and only about one-fifth of Senate candidates' money. Party donations comprise only a small proportion of *direct* contributions to congressional candidates, but most party assistance comes in the form of coordinated spending, which is not included in these data.

National party committee activities have grown just as explosively as PAC activities, at least on the Republican side. Table 6-2 documents the growth of national party receipts between 1976 and 1982. The table actually understates Republican superiority because it does not include money officially credited to the state and local parties although actually raised by national party "agents." If state and local money is included, Republican party committees raised a total of $215 million in 1981-1982—*more than was raised by all PACs combined* ($199 million) during that election cycle.

Not all of this money goes to congressional candidates directly or as coordinated spending, to be sure, but plenty of it does. Coordinated party spending has been concentrated disproportionately in Senate races, reflecting the much higher legal spending ceilings for these contests as well as strategic considerations (Senate incumbents are more often thought to be vulnerable). Republican House candidates now get from the party about 10 percent of their money; Senate candidates get more than 15 percent. The equivalent figures for Democratic candidates are 2 percent and 4 percent, respectively. In 1982, half of the Republican Senate candidates received more than $200,000 worth of assistance from national party sources; Pete Wilson of California topped the list with more than $1.3 million. Only one Democratic Senate candidate got more than $200,000 worth of help.

Why do Republican committees raise so much more money than Democratic committees do? There are several reasons. One is that they have spent years expanding and perfecting their direct mail fund raising systems; more than 80 percent of their funds are raised in small sums (averaging less than $30) solicited through the mail. Democratic committees, in contrast, still rely heavily on large individual and PAC donations. Another reason is that congressional Republicans have spent most of the last several decades as the

Table 6-1 Sources of Campaign Contributions to Major Party House and Senate General Election Candidates, 1974-1982

	1974	1976	1978	1980	1982
House Elections					
Average contribution:	$ 61,084	$ 79,421	$111,232	$ 148,268	$ 222,620
Percentage from:					
individuals	73	59	61	67[a]	63[a]
parties[b]	4	8	5	4	6
PACs	17	23	25	29	31
candidates[c]	6	9	9	—	—
Senate Elections					
Average contribution:	$455,515	$624,094	$951,390	$1,079,346	$1,771,167
Percentage from:					
individuals	76	69	76	78[a]	81[a]
parties[b]	6	4	2	2	1
PACs	11	15	14	21	18
candidates[c]	1	12	8	—	—
unknown	6	—	—	—	—

[a] Includes candidates' contributions to their own campaigns, loans, transfers, and other items.
[b] Does not include party expenditures on behalf of candidates.
[c] Includes candidates' loans unrepaid at time of filing.

SOURCE: Gary C. Jacobson, "Money in the 1980 and 1982 Congressional Elections," in *Money and Politics in the United States,* ed. Michael J. Malbin (Washington, D.C.: American Enterprise Institute for Public Policy Research and Chatham House Publishers, 1984), p. 39. Used with permission.

Table 6-2 National Party Receipts, 1976-1982 (in millions)

	Democrats	•	Republicans
1976	$18.2		$ 45.7
1978	17.6		63.5
1980	28.1		127.4
1982	31.7		191.0

SOURCE: Compiled from Michael J. Malbin and Thomas W. Skladony, "Appendix: Selected Campaign Finance Data, 1974-1982," in *Money and Politics in the United States,* ed. Michael J. Malbin (Washington, D.C.: American Enterprise Institute for Public Policy Research and Chatham House Publishers, 1984), Table A.9, pp. 292-293. Used with permission.

opposition party, an advantage because direct mail appeals are most effective when they can play on emotions of frustration, fear, and anger, and it is easier to arouse people in opposition to politicians and policies than in support of them. A third is that Republicans appeal to a more affluent constituency; even a small donation is likely to be missed by a large proportion of Democratic supporters. Finally, Republicans are much more ideologically homogeneous; it matters little to contributors which candidate ultimately gets the money, so it is reasonable to let the party decide. Contributors to Democrats have much more reason to care about which Democrat gets the money (a Boll Weevil or an urban liberal?) and so keep that decision for themselves.

Abundant money has allowed Republican party officials to build an extensive organization and to pursue a wide range of party-building and electoral activities. The national party maintains a bureaucracy of 600 and supports a flock of outside pollsters, media specialists, stationers, direct mail outfits, computer vendors, and advertising professionals.[14] It conducts sophisticated voter registration drives, mounts national advertising campaigns, trains party workers, teaches fund raising, and coordinates contribution strategies of cooperative PACs.[15] It even maintains a staff of caseworkers who help campaign contributors deal with government agencies[16]—a function members of Congress no doubt would prefer to monopolize themselves. All of this is in addition to the primary task of helping candidates win elections:

> Its cash and resources equip the GOP to nurture candidates through the entire electoral process: initial ticket selection, preliminary organization, training, fund-raising, polling, hiring of consultants, analysis of the opposition, manipulation of the media, computerized phone banks, advertising, direct mail and last-minute get-out-the-vote drives.[17]

Democrats try to offer many of the same services, although necessarily at much lower levels. They simply lack the money to begin to match Republican efforts. In 1980, the Democratic National Committee (DNC) was still trying to pay off debts from the 1968 election.[18] Party officials have worked to expand their direct mail operation, but it takes time before this kind of investment pays off; most of the take has to be plowed back into fund raising and therefore is not available to candidates. Democrats lag far behind organizationally as well as financially, putting them at an increasingly serious electoral disadvantage.

Parties vs. PACs

National party committees (especially on the Republican side) and PACs have both thrived in the new legal and technological environment. Sometimes they cooperate with one another. Many Republican-oriented corporate PACs, for example, take cues from the National Republican Congressional Committee (NRCC) and the National Republican Senatorial Committee (NRSC) when deciding where to contribute their funds, and labor

PACs often look after the collective interests of congressional Democrats. But in a very basic sense, as noted earlier, parties and PACs are natural rivals. They pursue conflicting goals and so follow conflicting strategies both in elections and in Congress.

Viewed as a collective entity, a party's primary electoral goal is to win as many seats as possible.[19] In the abstract, it makes little difference to the party which individual candidates win, only that as many as possible do. The party's individual candidates, on the other hand, care very much who wins. Losers do not share the collective benefits of the party's victory. Although one can imagine a situation in which winning is of little value unless one is part of a majority (and thus in which candidates would be willing to take considerable electoral risks to improve their party's chances), this is emphatically not true of congressional election politics. The fruits of victory by no means go exclusively to the majority. The primary interest of candidates, then, lies in maximizing their own likelihood of winning. The party's collective interests are decidedly secondary.

Parties and candidates thus have different preferences about the distribution of campaign resources. The party would prefer to deploy resources in a way that promises to maximize the number of seats it wins. It would redirect resources of campaigns of its stronger candidates to the campaigns of weaker candidates up to the point where the expected marginal gains in seats among the latter are matched by the expected marginal losses among the former. Individual candidates, on the other hand, would resist giving up resources if this would increase the risk of defeat; the size of the party's cohort is, after all, a collective good, and one which candidates would not even share were they not themselves winners.

The outcome of this conflict depends on who controls resources and what goals they can pursue. The greater the share controlled by the party and the freer its officials are to pursue collective ends, the more efficiently the party will deploy campaign resources, and therefore the more seats it should win. The more resources controlled by the party's stronger candidates, the less efficient and collectively successful it should be. In congressional elections, the key practical issues are the amounts of money controlled by national party campaign committees and the extent to which these committees avoid domination by the party's incumbents.

With few exceptions, PACs pursue objectives that readily lead them to subvert collective party goals. Although all PACs intend to influence public policy, they differ in how broadly or narrowly policy objectives are conceived and in the strategies they use to reach them. To many business corporations, labor unions, and trade associations, the PAC is simply an aid to traditional lobbying for narrowly focused economic interests. Policy goals are specific and immediate: a tax break, regulatory relief, a higher price support subsidy, a loan guarantee. Money is given not so much to affect the outcome of an election as to gain access and curry favor with whomever winds up in a position to serve or damage immediate economic interests. Already holding office and very likely to retain it, incumbents naturally benefit. PACs with narrow economic objectives contribute to sure winners who do not need the money, to members of both parties sitting on committees dealing with legislation they care about, and to newly elected members *after* the election. The popularity of this approach explains why PAC contributions as a whole strongly favor congressional incumbents. (Illustrative data are presented later in Tables 6-3 and 6-4.) Money spent on incumbents almost certain to win or on other candidates after they have won is, from the party's collective perspective, almost entirely wasted.

At the opposite end of the spectrum lie PACs with broad ideological agendas. Like parties, they aim to maximize the number of seats held by members of Congress who share the correct views. The idea is to change policies by changing members rather than by persuading members to change policies. So they support promising nonincumbent candidates and concentrate their resources in close races, where they are most likely to make a difference. This makes conservative PACs natural allies of Republicans and liberal PACs of Democrats, but it does not prevent ideological PACs from subverting collective party interests when their objectives conflict with the party's simple goal of winning the seat. In an extreme example, the 1984 election found the National Conservative Political Action Committee (NCPAC) supporting liberal Democratic Senate candidate Paul Simon over Republican incumbent Charles Percy of Illinois. Percy, a moderate, was chairman of the Foreign Relations Committee; next in line for the chairmanship was Jesse Helms, a favorite of the New Right. NCPAC's position was that "the prospects are far less of Paul Simon, as a freshman Democrat, doing damage to the Western World than Chuck Percy as chairman of the Foreign Relations Committee." [20]

Parties are more commonly troubled by passionate single-issue PACs who care only about an individual's position on their issue. Democrats must contend with peace groups, feminists, gay rights activists, and radical environmentalists; Republicans with anti-abortionists, school prayer advocates, and tax-cut activists. Although such groups often provide valuable support for the more congenial party, they also promote the nomination of more extreme, hence weaker, candidates and introduce campaign issues that the candidates would be better off ignoring.

Between the extremes are PACs that pursue both short- and long-term political goals. Many business-oriented PACs, for example, support incumbent Democrats when it seems certain that they will win re-election but switch to nonincumbent Republicans when their chances look unusually promising. Thus, for example, corporate PACs gave 39 percent of their funds to nonincumbent Republicans in 1980 but only 22 percent in 1982, reflecting different assessments of Republican prospects in the two elections. Their behavior thus contributes to the party's collective performance in good years but weakens it in bad years. The common corporate preoccupation with short-term policy at the expense of the long-term political climate has frustrated Republican party officials for years.[21] But they have had only limited success in persuading business PACs that they would be better served by working to elect more right-thinking Republicans than by keeping their access to incumbent Democrats. Many business corporations treat the question of who to support as a variant of the familiar collective good problem: why risk the individual costs of offending Democratic officeholders to pursue the collective good of a more Republican Congress?

This is fine for Democratic incumbents, but it does little to help the party collectively. It contributes to a remarkably inefficient distribution of Democratic campaign resources. This was most obvious in 1982, when millions of PAC dollars went to Democratic incumbents who did not need it, while a number of promising challengers remained seriously underfunded.[22] The problem was compounded by the relative poverty of Democratic party committees; they spent a major portion of their funds on challengers and other candidates in close races, but the sums they had to spend were so small as to be nearly imperceptible. Democrats have about as much campaign money as Republicans overall, but because so little of it flows through the party, it is apportioned much less efficiently.

Democrats vs. Republicans

The expansion of both party and PAC involvement in congressional elections thus has favored Republicans over Democrats. This is clearest in the case of party development because Republican committees are so much wealthier and better organized. Republican candidates can count on more help from the party, and party resources are concentrated where they are most likely to make a difference. By 1982 no Republican candidate with any reasonable chance of winning was inadequately funded. Although it is not so obvious from aggregate data, PAC development has also favored Republicans. Democratic candidates have continued to receive more PAC money, but their advantage has decreased over time. A decade ago they routinely received about two-thirds of PAC money; now they get little more than half. This advantage remains only because they have kept their House majority. The connection between Democrats and most corporate and trade association PACs is a marriage of convenience only, not a love match, and does not extend to nonincumbent Democrats; it will dissolve if the Republicans ever take over the House. The Democrats' problems here are evident from Tables 6-3 and 6-4, which show the distribution of PAC contributions, by source, to House and Senate candidates in the 1980 and 1982 election cycles. Democratic incumbents enjoy adequate support from PACs of all kinds. But except for labor and, in 1982, some new liberal nonconnected PACs, PACs virtually ignore nonincumbent Democrats. Business-related PACs in particular have no reason to help candidates who are neither in office nor preferred on ideological or partisan grounds. And these are the PACs whose participation has grown most rapidly in recent years. Notice that only nonconnected PACs

Table 6-3   PAC Contributions to House Candidates, by Candidates' Status, 1979-1980 and 1981-1982 (in percentages)

Committee Type	Amount Contributed	Incumbent Dem.	Incumbent Rep.	Challenger Dem.	Challenger Rep.	Open Seat Dem.	Open Seat Rep.
1979-1980							
Distribution of candidates	(N=738)	34	19	13	23	6	5
Labor	$ 8,883,834	69	4	16	0	10	0
Corporate	11,662,361	36	32	1	20	1	9
Nonconnected	2,831,209	21	15	5	41	4	12
Trade/membership/ health	11,215,269	39	32	2	17	3	8
Cooperative	985,177	59	26	2	3	3	7
Corporations without stock	387,740	47	30	2	11	2	7
Total	$35,965,590	45	24	5	15	4	7
1981-1982							
Distribution of candidates	(N=830)	26	20	20	21	6	6
Labor	$14,557,589	53	4	28	0	14	1
Corporate	18,136,407	32	45	1	9	3	9
Nonconnected	6,886,695	29	19	16	18	8	10
Trade/membership/ health	15,901,781	34	42	4	8	4	8
Cooperative	1,650,239	52	33	4	1	6	3
Corporations without stock	771,847	51	32	5	3	5	4
Total	$57,904,558	39	30	11	7	7	7

NOTE: General election candidates only are represented in the table. Percentages may not add to 100 because of rounding; nonconnected PACs in 1979-1980 also gave more than 1 percent of their House contributions to challengers who were neither Democrats nor Republicans.

SOURCE: Compiled from Michael J. Malbin and Thomas W. Skladony, "Appendix: Selected Campaign Finance Data, 1974-1982," in *Money and Politics in the United States*, ed. Michael J. Malbin (Washington, D.C.: American Enterprise Institute for Public Policy Research and Chatham House Publishers, 1984), Tables A.17 and A.18, pp. 301-302. Used with permission.

routinely give a substantial proportion of their funds to nonincumbents, evidence that this category is composed largely of ideological groups bent on changing the makeup of Congress.

Tables 6-3 and 6-4 also show the sensitivity of PACs to the prevailing political winds. In 1980, which promised to be a good year for Republicans,

Table 6-4 PAC Contributions to Senate Candidates, by Candidates' Status, 1979-1980 and 1981-1982 (in percentages)

Committee Type	Amount Contributed	Incumbent		Challenger		Open Seat	
		Dem.	*Rep.*	*Dem.*	*Rep.*	*Dem.*	*Rep.*
1979-1980							
Distribution of candidates	(N = 66)	27	9	9	27	14	14
Labor	$ 3,428,404	65	9	14	1	11	1
Corporate	6,445,566	25	14	1	47	2	11
Nonconnected	1,690,574	22	6	2	53	2	14
Trade/membership/ health	3,816,424	37	17	3	32	5	7
Cooperative	325,050	65	11	1	11	6	6
Corporations without stock	214,853	40	18	3	27	5	7
Total	$15,920,871	37	13	4	33	5	8
1981-1982							
Distribution of candidates	(N = 66)	29	17	17	29	5	5
Labor	$ 4,830,051	56	7	27	0	9	1
Corporate	8,275,630	26	41	1	17	1	14
Nonconnected	3,150,309	28	20	15	23	6	7
Trade/membership/ health	4,857,841	37	39	4	10	2	8
Cooperative	427,526	52	19	12	2	1	14
Corporations without stock	262,140	45	33	3	6	2	11
Total	$21,803,497	36	29	10	12	4	9

NOTE: General election candidates only are represented in the table. Percentages may not add to 100 because of rounding.

SOURCE: Compiled from Michael J. Malbin and Thomas W. Skladony, "Appendix: Selected Campaign Finance Data, 1974-1982," in *Money and Politics in the United States,* ed. Michael J. Malbin (Washington, D.C.: American Enterprise Institute for Public Policy Research and Chatham House Publishers, 1984), Tables A.20 and A.21, pp. 304-305. Used with permission.

more money went to Republican challengers and Democratic incumbents. Republican-oriented PACs pursued an offensive strategy designed to take advantage of favorable trends (especially in Senate races); Democratic contributors responded with a defensive campaign (stimulated by the greater demand for money by nervous Democratic incumbents). In 1982, the deep recession altered the political climate to favor Democrats. Democratic challengers got a larger share of PAC funds (labor was not so concerned with defending incumbents), and Republican contributors concentrated on defending incumbents. But the pattern of contributions from corporate and trade association PACs indicates that nonincumbent Republican candidates will be in a much better position to take advantage of favorable political conditions.

Democrats thus have two major problems with PACs. First, PAC contributions to Democrats are distributed very inefficiently. Only Democratic incumbents get generous support from most kinds of PACs; the candidates least in need of PAC money for their campaigns are the best funded. Second, the kinds of PACs that, other things being equal, prefer Republicans, have far outstripped those favoring Democrats in the overall expansion of PAC activity. Moreover, these PACs are willing to help Republican challengers and candidates for open seats, so Republican PAC funds are deployed more efficiently as well.

The Republicans' institutional advantage in contemporary electoral politics served them well in the 1980 and 1982 elections. Both the national party committees and Republican-oriented PACs contributed to the Republican sweep in 1980. Among the Democratic victims were eight House members who had served more than nine terms, including five committee chairmen and the majority whip. Many of them had been shrewdly targeted by party officials in Washington despite the fact that years of weak opposition had given them an illusion of invulnerability. Republicans also took nine Senate seats from incumbent Democrats—several by very narrow margins— to emerge with their first Senate majority in almost 30 years. Not coincidentally, Republican party committees and independent PACs had concentrated their efforts in these races.[23]

Although aggregate election results make it less obvious, superior organization served Republicans at least as well in 1982. Republicans lost 26 House seats in 1982 while breaking even in the Senate. But given the recession and the Reagan administration's waning popularity at the time of the election, they should have done much worse.[24] Republican party officials used their centralized control over information and resources to adjust quickly to the deteriorating political environment, thereby rescuing a number of endangered incumbents. The Democrats' decentralized campaign finance system kept them from fully exploiting the opportunity handed them by the faltering economy. They were without institutional means to redistribute resources from campaigns where they were no longer needed to campaigns where they might have put a competitive challenger over the top.

Challengers vs. Incumbents

The expanded activities of PACs and national party committees have created new electoral difficulties for incumbents as well as for Democrats (the categories overlap, of course). It is often argued that because PACs give three times as much money to incumbents as to challengers, their growing role in congressional campaign finance can only benefit officeholders.[25] This would be true only if campaign money were equally valuable to incumbents and challengers. It is not. The marginal returns on campaign spending are much greater for challengers than for incumbents. Statistically, in fact, incumbent spending is totally unrelated to election results.

The more a challenger spends, on the other hand, the larger his or her share of the vote on election day.[26] This is why most contributions to incumbents are, from the parties' collective perspective, a waste of money. It also means that any increase in the amount of money available to help both challengers and incumbents will favor the challengers—even if in absolute terms the incumbent enjoys the greater increase. A further corollary is that it matters much less to incumbents what PACs and parties give them than what they give to their opponents.

PACs and parties could make electoral life more difficult for incumbents just by making more money available to everyone. But their threat to incumbents goes much deeper than this, for they restructure electoral politics in ways designed to frustrate incumbents' favorite re-election strategies. During the late 1960s and early 1970s, members of Congress exploited political and technological changes to strengthen their personal hold on constituencies.[27] They gave themselves greater resources for travel, communication, and casework, and used them to establish more independent, less partisan, political identities. Candidate-centered electoral politics were also encouraged by diminishing partisanship among voters and new communication technologies. Incumbents who took advantage of the new opportunities prospered.

The prosperity of incumbents was contingent, however. It depended on their ability to control the information about themselves going to the district, to define electoral issues, and, most of all, to scare off vigorous opposition. A lot of it was simple bluff. Members remained unbeatable by convincing potentially formidable opponents that they were unbeatable, thus avoiding strong opposition.[28]

Strong national parties and PACs threaten all of these conditions. They are institutionally adapted to the very same political environment that gave incumbents their initial advantage. They, too, have learned to play candidate-centered electoral politics. For example, national party officials (with Republicans, as usual, taking the lead) have recognized that winning elections depends on fielding strong individual candidates. Therefore they have invested heavily in recruiting and training promising challengers. Some PACs, notably on the New Right, have done the same thing. The skills they teach are the same as those mastered by incumbents.

Parties and PACs have also learned to make imaginative use of new communication technologies. A prominent example is the Republicans' centralized polling operation, which enables them to probe the real strength of any Democratic incumbent to detect signs of weakness not evident in vote margins against feeble opposition. The Republicans are also able to monitor individual campaigns, using tracking polls to tell them when and where the party's campaign resources can be used to greatest advantage—a major contribution to efficiency. Direct mail is another example of a new communication technology that is skillfully used by parties and PACs. Given enough money, a PAC or party can eliminate whatever advantage the franking privilege confers on incumbents. Centralized media production is a third example; the Republican party produces highly professional, carefully pretested television spots for its candidates. The list could go on. The point is that national party campaign committees and PACs have evolved into organizations as well suited to the present-day electoral environment as the most sophisticated incumbent.

This affects incumbents in several ways. It intensifies their sense of electoral insecurity. A lot more resources are available to be mobilized against a member, and, through coordination among PACs and parties, resources can be mobilized quickly. Career-minded members, notoriously risk-averse, like to be prepared for the worst possible case. Their demand for campaign funds has increased dramatically quite apart from the actual level of opposition they face. Incumbents are spending ever increasing amounts of money regardless of what their opponents are doing. In 1972, an incumbent would have spent, on average, $76,000 (in constant dollars, 1982=1.00), if the challenger spent nothing; the comparable figure for 1982 was $183,000.[29] Parties and to an even greater extent PACs are responsible; they have increased both the supply of and demand for campaign money among congressional incumbents.

Members of Congress also have more to fear because increased party and PAC activity destroys their ability to control the content of campaigns. Incumbents thrive on campaigns that center around personal performance, experience, and services. Few members are vulnerable if they can persuade voters that this is what the contest is about; even losing incumbents get high marks on these dimensions.[30] Trouble comes when campaign issues are framed in a way that makes them less relevant. This is what PACs and parties try to do. PACs with specific policy agendas naturally try to inject them into campaigns. Indeed, a basic aim of single-issue groups, such as anti-abortionists or nuclear freeze proponents, is to make sure that their issue enters the campaign even if both candidates would prefer to ignore it. The idea is to give one or the other a weapon too useful to refuse. If both cave in to the group's demands, so much the better. The greater the number of divisive and controversial issues introduced into the campaign, the more likely it is that an incumbent would face something like a Downsian coalition of minorities, which, at least in theory, ensures defeat.[31]

The most extensive and prominent work to weaken incumbents by raising new issues designed to make them look bad has been carried out by conservative PACs in independent campaigns. The distribution of independent expenditures in House and Senate elections in the 1980 and 1982 election cycles is shown in Table 6-5. The largest share of the independent spending by far has gone for negative campaigns against Senate Democrats. Democratic leaders in the House were also targeted in 1982. Most of these negative campaigns were not intended to help any particular challenger. Indeed, much of the money was spent long before anyone knew who the challenger would be. Rather, the campaigns were intended to soften up the incumbent for whomever eventually entered the fray. The strategy looked effective; four of the six liberal Democrats targeted by NCPAC and other conservative groups in 1980 lost their Senate seats. (There are, of course, alternative explanations for all of these defeats.) But by 1982 the independent campaigns themselves had become the issue. Terry Dolan, chairman of NCPAC, in a moment of candor had acknowledged one advantage of

Table 6-5 Independent Expenditures in Congressional Campaigns, 1979-1980 and 1981-1982

Campaign	For Candidate	Against Candidate
1979-1980		
Senate		
Democrats	$127,381	$1,282,613
Republicans	261,678	12,430
Total	389,059	1,295,043
House		
Democrats	190,615	38,023
Republicans	410,478	45,132
Total	601,093	83,155
1981-1982		
Senate		
Democrats	142,512	3,119,593
Republicans	291,325	493,326
Total	433,837	3,612,919
House		
Democrats	229,477	825,524
Republicans	492,170	97,089
Total	722,187	922,613

NOTE: Independent expenditures are those made without communication or coordination with any candidate's campaign. Some of the money reported during any election cycle may reflect bills paid from the previous election cycle.

SOURCE: For 1979-1980, Federal Election Commission, "FEC Study Shows Independent Expenditures Top $16 Million," press release, November 29, 1981. For 1981-1982, Federal Election Commission, "Independent Spending Increases," press release, March 22, 1983.

independent campaigning: "A group like ours could lie through its teeth and the candidate it helps stays clean." [32] Democrats targeted in 1982 responded by reminding voters of Dolan's admission and working, with some success, to make NCPAC's activities, rather than its charges, the main issue.[33]

The $5.7 million spent on independent campaigns in 1981-1982 amounts to only 2 percent of the money spent on campaigns in that election cycle; had it not been concentrated in a few contests it would scarcely have been noticed. At present, independent PAC spending is more important for what it portends for the future than for any consequence it has had so far. As PACs continue to raise greater amounts of money, the ceiling on contributions to candidates is bound to seem more limiting and the independent spending route more attractive. The richest PACs will be perfectly capable of mounting full-scale campaigns of their own, and they will have strong organizational incentives to do so, if only to justify their continued expansion. Incumbents are likely to suffer on two grounds from expanded independent campaigning: they are its favorite targets, and even when they are not themselves targets, independent campaigns deprive them of control over the content of the campaign.

The growing institutional capabilities of PACs clearly make many members of Congress uneasy. One common complaint about them is especially revealing. PACs are criticized for bringing outside influences to bear on what should be purely local electoral decisions. National funding sources force national issues onto the local agenda; candidates find it necessary to campaign on issues that may be of marginal interest or relevance to their constituents but are of deep concern to groups outside the state or district.[34] A neutral observer might ask, so what? It is common in modern democracies for national issues to dominate campaigns for national legislatures. Because members of Congress make policy for the whole country, outsiders naturally try to influence local decisions.

Members are inclined to assume, on the contrary, that they should be beholden to no one but their own constituents, that representation should be strictly territorial. Although dated as political theory, it is easy to understand the appeal of this view to members whose political careers rest on diligent personal cultivation of constituencies.[35] A career strategy of this sort crucially depends on maintaining *autonomy,* the freedom to maneuver as an independent political entrepreneur. The expansion of PAC organization and activity threatens autonomy and, fundamentally, the strategic basis of many congressional careers.

The development of vigorous national party organizations carries the same implications. Although sensitive to the need to tailor local campaigns to local conditions, national party officials inevitably inject a national component into local campaigns. Sometimes this is done deliberately. The Republican National Committee spent $9 million in 1980 on a nationwide television campaign urging people to "vote Republican—for a change." In 1982, it spent another $14 million urging them to "stay the course." Democrats countered with some nationally produced ads of their own that ridiculed "trickle-down" economics and other "unfair" Republican policies. National campaigns with common themes seem destined to become regular features of federal elections. The problem for incumbents is that national campaigns may disrupt individual re-election strategies. They make it harder for incumbents to separate themselves from an administration or party when this seems prudent. For example, "stay the course" reminded voters of the national economy in a year when Republican incumbents might have been better off ignoring national issues and running on their own performance.[36]

Parties clearly have succeeded in putting national issues on the local electoral agenda. Compare 1982 to 1978. In the 1978 midterm election, Jimmy Carter and his policies were not an important focus of either party's campaigns, so evaluations of the Carter administration had virtually no influence on House voting decisions.[37] Ronald Reagan and his programs, by contrast, were the subject of major national campaigns by both parties in the 1982 midterm; as a result, evaluations of Reagan's performance and expectations about the future success or failure of his economic policies had a strong influence on individual voting decisions.[38] The vote was, to an important degree, a decision about whether or not to "stay the course" despite the deep recession, because that is what voters had been led to think the election was about.

National party activities undermine members' autonomy in other ways as well. Coordinated campaign expenditures are controlled, by law, by the party not the candidate. The party decides what to spend the money on, and candidates who want the party's help have to take what the party offers. This gives party officials considerable influence over campaign strategies and messages even if they do not consciously try to impose a uniform approach. Training schools for candidates have a similar effect, as does the party's reliance on a common pool of outside campaign professionals.

More ominous for members who have learned to thrive on independence is the inherent possibility that party leaders will use control over major campaign assets to impose party discipline. An incident in September 1982 brought this home. Republican National Committee (RNC) officials and White House political operatives threatened to withhold party resources from Republican representatives who voted against the Reagan administration's "revenue enhancement" legislation.[39] This and a couple of other examples are inevitably mentioned whenever proposals are made to allow parties an even larger role in congressional campaign finance. Democrats are particularly prone to envision the imminent resurrection of Boss Tweed.[40] Much of this is pure politics; Democrats are not about to unleash the parties while the Republicans are so much stronger. But it is by no means entirely insincere. Parties no less than PACs may obligate them to interests outside the district, limiting the autonomy that is essential to their career strategies.[41]

If it is true that the expansion of party and PAC activities has favored challengers, congressional incumbents should be more vulnerable to defeat.

There is some evidence that this is now the case. Senate incumbents have certainly been at greater risk recently than they were in the 1960s. During that decade, 90 percent of the Senate incumbents seeking re-election were successful. Since then their re-election rate has dropped to 78 percent; for the four most recent elections it has been lower still, 64 percent. Senate seats have been the main targets of national party efforts and independent PAC campaigns, so we have at least circumstantial evidence that these new institutional forces have altered the electoral environment to the detriment of incumbent senators. Certainly the losers have reason to think of themselves as victims of a new kind of electoral politics.

House incumbents continue to win re-election at about the same rate as they have for 30 years (approximately 92 percent, on average), and the proportion of marginal victories has not changed since decreasing sharply in the mid-1960s. On the other hand, travel to the district, franked mail, staff, district offices, and most of the other official perks members use to pursue re-election have continued to increase, in some cases steeply, without any further increase in incumbent security whatsoever. Incumbents have been doing more of what is supposed to keep them safe without becoming any safer.[42] They appear to be running ever harder just to stay in the same place. House incumbents' campaign spending practices are consistent with this view; in this and other ways, members' behavior suggests that at least subjective feelings of electoral insecurity have grown. This naturally has consequences for what they do in office. How parties and PACs are changing congressional politics is the subject of the final section.

Effects on Congress

The workings of Congress are profoundly affected by how its members win and hold office.[43] It follows that new electoral institutions and practices will alter the internal politics of Congress. How have PACs and renascent national party organizations changed congressional life?

One change is undeniable: members now spend a lot more time thinking about, and pursuing, campaign money.[44] PACs and parties have contributed to this in at least three ways. By tapping new sources of contributions, and old sources more efficiently, they have increased the supply of campaign funds. By expanding the pool of resources that could be mobilized against incumbents, they have increased their demand for campaign funds (the demand among nonincumbents has always far outstripped the supply). And by introducing expensive, sophisticated technology, they have raised the cost of campaigning.

PACs, in particular, have been singled out for their part in making campaigns more expensive. PAC critics always include this in their lists of "horribles," [45] and they get a sympathetic hearing from a public convinced that too much money is spent on campaigns.[46] But, in fact, the great majority of congressional campaigns suffer from too little rather than too much money;

levels of popular familiarity with the candidates show this plainly.[47] Candidate-centered electoral politics is unavoidably expensive. There is no real contest unless both candidates can reach voters with their messages, and for any candidate not blessed with the advantages of incumbency or celebrity, reaching voters normally costs a great deal of money.

Accepting the value of well-financed campaigns does not, by itself, lay to rest the central question of how members' anxiety about campaign money might be influencing congressional decisions. For some observers, the answer here is simple. PACs are corrupting the entire political process, turning fund raising into an obsession that exposes members of Congress to the destructive influence of selfish special interests. Put most starkly, the argument is that PACs buy votes and policy, period. The evidence offered for this claim is typically anecdotal and circumstantial. Common Cause or an enterprising reporter shows that members supporting legislation desired by some group— milk producers, used-car dealers, doctors, and the shipping industry are recent examples—get more campaign money from PACs representing the group than do members who oppose the legislation.[48] Note is also taken of incidents where members are bullied by lobbyists whose PACs have contributed to their campaigns; stories are told of unnamed members who admit to voting with a group because they received money from it.[49]

There is no reason to dismiss this kind of evidence out of hand, but it is hardly conclusive. Recipients of PAC contributions invariably argue, at least in public, that the PACs are merely helping out those members who have the wisdom to agree with their own quite defensible view of the public interest. For example, liberal Democrats do not support labor's interests because labor PACs have contributed to their campaigns; rather, labor contributes to their campaigns because labor shares their notions of what constitutes good public policy. It would be bizarre to expect *no* relationship between contributions and behavior; PACs do not distribute money randomly. Any simple cross-sectional comparison of contributions and roll call votes is necessarily inconclusive because the direction of causality is indeterminate.

A few more careful studies have tried in various ways to untangle the complicated causal links between PAC contributions and roll call votes. Severe technical problems preclude definitive conclusions, but clearly PACs support members whose votes they like (no one ever doubted this). Evidence that PAC contributions affect individual votes is much more limited and, on methodological grounds, open to question. At least some members on some issues (those drawing little public or district attention) seem to vote in a way that reflects prior PAC contributions independent of ideology, partisanship, or local interests.[50] The effects of prior contributions are usually dwarfed by other factors in these studies, but they remain statistically significant.

Roll call votes may also be influenced by the expectation of *future* contributions. And because the most effective re-election strategy is to avoid strong opposition, behavior may be affected by members' reluctance to stir up groups that might finance their opponents. For example, a consultant who worked on Environmental Action's campaigns to target the "Dirty Dozen" representatives with the worst (by its standards) environmental records claimed that the tactic "was very effective at making congressmen think twice about certain votes. There were numerous examples of members or their staffs calling and saying, 'Is the congressman close to being on the list?' or 'Is this vote going to be used to determine the list?' " [51] Needless to say, efforts of this sort, involving influence by anticipated response, are extraordinarily difficult to measure systematically.

So far only a few PACs have been thoroughly studied, and only in limited ways for restricted periods of time. Much more work is needed before we can have a clear idea of how commonly PAC contributions influence congressional behavior. But it would be surprising to find that they have no effect at all; otherwise, why would interest groups be putting so much time, energy, and money into PAC activities? Irrationality on this scale would be difficult to explain. Officials of PACs that openly pursue narrow policy goals usually claim that PACs buy not votes but access, a necessary if not sufficient condition for successful lobbying. A contribution ensures a polite hearing when their lobbyist wants to make a pitch. To their most vehement critics, this alone makes PACs a corrupting influence, for it gives them an insider's edge in legislative politics.[52] Members of Congress freely admit to giving access to their contributors but quickly add that they also hear out people and groups who have given them nothing, particularly if they are connected to their state or district.[53]

Members must handle the question of contributors' influence delicately. Those who contend that PAC money is corrupting imply that at least some of their colleagues have been corrupted. They are challenged to provide specifics: Have they themselves been corrupted? Who has been bought? Since members do not lightly attack one another's integrity (in public, anyway), the problem is redefined as the *appearance* of corruption and the loss of public approbation it engenders. Proponents of the corruption thesis are at a serious rhetorical disadvantage because they can make their case only by impugning the honesty of members of Congress.

Assuming that PAC contributions do influence congressional decisions, at least on occasion, the question remains whether this represents any real change in congressional behavior. Congress has always practiced distributive politics, conferring narrow, particularized benefits that impose diffuse costs even when the costs plainly outweigh the benefits. Distributive politics involving groups are not new, nor are they inherently different from, or more objectionable than, distributive politics involving localities—the classic pork barrel. In this and many other ways, much of what PACs do is little more than a continuation of familiar political practices. Indeed, Michael Malbin points out that only a small fraction of the money spent on lobbying takes the form of contributions to candidates. When it comes to lobbying, PACs are the tail, not the dog.[54]

Still, PACs (and parties) have visibly altered congressional politics. Consider lobbying. The classic study of lobbying a generation ago by Raymond Bauer, Ithiel de Sola Pool, and Lewis Dexter depicted a process dominated by insiders. It was largely a matter of friends talking to friends. Lobbyists worked through friends and allies in Congress, encouraging them to take on projects they were already inclined to pursue by providing organizational backup. Lobbyists persuaded members to help them out by helping members to look good when they did. Opponents were ignored; pressure tactics in the insulated social world of Congress were considered imprudent. Small wonder that members regarded lobbying as basically helpful and benign and lobbyists as a resource to be exploited.[55]

Few members would take such a sanguine view today. Insiders still lobby in the old way, although most of them now supplement their work with outside activities. Not a few PACs have been created at the behest of Washington representatives who see this as a way of making their inside work more effective.[56] But they have been joined by a host of activists and organizations working to influence Congress from the outside. Dozens of groups now rate roll call votes, target opponents, stimulate mail and phone calls, and mobilize campaign volunteers—in addition, of course, to raising and distributing campaign funds. An effective outside strategy does not depend on maintaining friendly relations with incumbents, so outsiders are free to use pressure tactics. Single-issue and ideological PACs have no compunction about threatening to withdraw support from—or to support opponents of—members who oppose them. For many of them, this is the whole point of having a PAC.

PACs have thus contributed to the shift in focus of congressional politics from the inside to the outside. More time and attention is devoted to politics outside the institution; outside influences on internal politics have become stronger and more pervasive. PACs are by no means the only reason for this shift. They form only one part of a broader syndrome that includes changes in formal rules (creating a more decentralized, fragmented, and permeable legislative system far more exposed to public scrutiny) and in informal modes of behavior (aggressively independent entrepreneurial politics in and out of Congress). But PACs have furthered these developments by giving institutional form to activities designed to exploit the new avenues of influence opened by changing patterns of congressional politics.

PACs, and the proliferation of external demands on Congress they reflect and reinforce, are thus commonly blamed for Congress's inability to deal with tough, divisive national problems. A fragmented Congress that is overly responsive to too many conflicting demands is susceptible to stalemate; it cannot make the hard choices that impose concentrated costs on organized groups to achieve widely shared benefits.[57] PACs are also responsible for forcing zero-sum redistributive issues onto the political agenda. Moral issues take this form; the abortion question is a prominent example. Congress has particular difficulty dealing with such issues because normal politics—

compromise, side payments, logrolling, and the other common methods of coalition-building—do not work. Internal congressional politics thrives on deals, on compromise; a focus on external politics promotes posturing and intransigence.

Structural fragmentation, the multitude of outside pressures, and aggressive individualism have all raised new impediments to effective leadership in Congress. Congressional leaders are the quintessential insiders, and their traditional methods of persuasion and coalition-building are best suited to internal politicking. Effective presidential leadership has also traditionally depended on combining public activity with a skillful insider's game. But even leaders have begun to exploit the outside approach. During the Carter administration, House Speaker Tip O'Neill occasionally worked through influential groups (primarily labor organizations) in the districts of members whose votes the party needed; he had local leaders calling on them to back the party's position.[58] The Reagan administration also recognized the possibilities of grass-roots lobbying and used it effectively in its battles to cut taxes and spending. Administration strategists mobilized groups around the country that had supported Reagan's presidential bid to rally in support of his programs. For example, people and PACs that had given to both the Reagan campaign and to Southern Democrats in 1980 were identified by computer and asked to lobby the "Boll Weevils" to support the administration's bills.[59] The avalanche of letters and telephone calls that followed was instrumental in persuading some reluctant Democrats to cooperate.[60]

Parties, however, remain the principal instruments of congressional leadership and coalition-building. Thus observers who worry about the excessive fragmentation reinforced by PACs and other interest groups, and see no legitimate way to suppress them, often propose to strengthen the parties. If party committees are allowed to do more for congressional candidates, members will be less reliant on PACs for essential electoral resources and thus less subject to their influence (or the appearance of it). The more money that passes through the parties' hands, the broader the interests represented by the campaign finance system.[61] Republicans naturally think this is a terrific idea; with so much money coming in, their main problem is figuring out new ways to spend it legally for their candidates. Democrats remain too poor to be bothered by the present ceilings. Still, even some Democratic leaders envision a day—to arrive after they have caught up—when parties are unleashed to counteract PACs.[62]

Although this solution is appealing to congressional leaders, many members are not so sure. Remember that parties, no less than PACs, may diminish autonomy and so undermine the arrangements that keep members in office. The ghost of Boss Tweed invoked by Democrats every time the issue is raised is probably more than a figment of partisan rhetoric. And members can hardly welcome rival providers of casework services. Still, strengthening the parties is the only solution in sight to many of the problems raised by PACs. Aside from political difficulties (Republicans are not about to give up the advantages they enjoy under the present law), legislation to restrict PAC contributions to candidates will only push PACs into independent spending. The costs of organization have already been paid; the simple desire of PAC officials to maintain their organizations and keep their jobs would drive them to independent campaigning if other avenues of participation were closed off. And as Malbin points out, the PACs whose overhead is covered by large parent organizations (major corporations and unions) would do this most readily and so would gain an additional advantage.[63] If the institutional flowering of PACs cannot be reversed, the only option left is further development and expansion of countervailing institutions: the parties. No matter what happens, the environments of congressional elections and congressional politics are bound to become less conducive to political careers founded on independence and autonomy. No wonder many members of Congress elected in the late 1960s and early 1970s are disturbed by what they see happening; their new politics is becoming the old politics.

NOTES

1. For a short account of the extensive literature on this phenomenon, see Gary C. Jacobson, *The Politics of Congressional Elections* (Boston: Little, Brown & Co., 1983), pp. 25-37.
2. The revitalized national party campaign committees are the Republican National Committee (RNC), the National Republican Congressional Committee (NRCC), the National Republican Senatorial Committee (NRSC), the Democratic National Committee (DNC), the Democratic Congressional Campaign Committee (DCCC), and the Democratic Senatorial Campaign Committee (DSCC).
3. For a fascinating account of the role of the parties in congressional campaign finance in an earlier era, see Robert Caro, *The Years of Lyndon Johnson: The Path to Power* (New York: Knopf, 1982), chap. 31.
4. Joseph E. Cantor, *Political Action Committees: Their Evolution and Growth and Their Implications for the Political System* (Report No. 81-246 of the U.S. Library of Congress, Congressional Research Service, November 6, 1981), pp. 28-35.
5. For the details see ibid., pp. 35-54.
6. 424 U.S. 1 (1976).
7. Charles L. Clapp, *The Congressman: His Work as He Sees It* (Washington, D.C.: Brookings Institution, 1963), p. 397; Richard F. Fenno, Jr., *Home Style: House Members in Their Districts* (Boston: Little, Brown & Co., 1978), p. 113.
8. *Federal Election Commission Record* 10 (March 1984): 1-2.
9. *Federal Election Commission* v. *Democratic Senatorial Campaign Committee,* 454 U.S. 27 (1981).
10. Michael J. Malbin, "Looking Back at the Future of Campaign Finance Reform," in *Money and Politics in the United States,* ed. Michael J. Malbin

(Washington, D.C.: American Enterprise Institute for Public Policy Research and Chatham House Publishers, 1984), p. 257.

11. The closer the relationship between an industry and the federal government, the more likely its firms are to have PACs. See Edwin M. Epstein, "Business and Labor under the Federal Election Campaign Act of 1971," in *Parties, Interest Groups and Campaign Finance Laws,* ed. Michael J. Malbin (Washington, D.C.: American Enterprise Institute for Public Policy Research, 1980), p. 133.

12. For a diverse collection of claims about PACs, see U.S. Congress, House of Representatives, Committee on House Administration, Task Force on Elections, *Campaign Finance Reform,* hearings June 9, 16, 21, 23; July 8; August 22, 23; and October 12, 1983.

13. *FEC Record* 10 (March 1984): 10.

14. Thomas B. Edsall, "The GOP Money Machine," *Washington Post,* national weekly edition, July 2, 1984, p. 7.

15. Gary C. Jacobson, "Congressional Campaign Finance and the Revival of the Republican Party," in *The United States Congress,* ed. Dennis Hale (New Brunswick, N.J.: Transaction Books, 1983), pp. 313-330; David Adamany, "Political Parties in the 1980s," in *Money and Politics in the United States,* pp. 70-121.

16. Thomas B. Edsall and Helen Dewar, "The GOP Aims to Please," *Washington Post,* national weekly edition, June 4, 1984, p. 12.

17. Edsall, "GOP Money Machine," p. 7.

18. Adamany, "Parties in the 1980s," p. 77.

19. The idea that rational politicians would pursue a "minimum winning coalition" does not apply; see Gary C. Jacobson, "Party Organization and the Efficient Distribution of Congressional Campaign Resources: Republicans and Democrats in 1982," *Political Science Quarterly,* forthcoming.

20. Bill Peterson, "Strange Bedfellows in Illinois," *Washington Post,* national weekly edition, June 11, 1984, p. 13.

21. Edward Handler and John R. Mulkern, *Business in Politics* (Lexington, Mass.: Lexington Books, 1982), pp. 8-9.

22. Jacobson, "Congressional Campaign Resources."

23. Gary C. Jacobson and Samuel Kernell, *Strategy and Choice in Congressional Elections,* 2nd ed. (New Haven: Yale University Press, 1983), pp. 76-84.

24. See Gary C. Jacobson, "Reagan, Reaganomics, and Strategic Politics in 1982: A Test of Alternative Theories of Midterm Congressional Elections" (Paper delivered at the annual meeting of the American Political Science Association, Chicago, Illinois, September 1-4, 1983); Jacobson, "Congressional Campaign Resources."

25. See, for example, the testimony of Archibald Cox, chairman of Common Cause, in U.S. Congress, House, *Campaign Finance Reform,* p. 506.

26. Gary C. Jacobson, "Money and Votes Reconsidered: Congressional Elections, 1972-1982" (Paper delivered at the Carnegie-Mellon Conference on Political Economy, Carnegie-Mellon University, Pittsburgh, Pennsylvania, June 22-23, 1984), pp. 8-21.

27. A summary of the literature on these changes can be found in Jacobson, *Politics of Congressional Elections,* pp. 26-37.

28. Ibid., pp. 37-47.

29. Jacobson, "Money and Votes Reconsidered," pp. 14-15; see also Gary C. Jacobson, *Money in Congressional Elections* (New Haven: Yale University Press, 1980), pp. 113-122.

30. Jacobson, *Politics of Congressional Elections,* pp. 114-119; Gary C. Jacobson, "Running Scared: Elections and Congressional Politics in the 1980s," in *Theories on Congress: The New Institutionalism,* ed. Mathew McCubbins and Terry Sullivan (Lexington, Mass.: D. C. Heath, 1985).

31. Anthony Downs, *An Economic Theory of Democracy* (New York: Harper & Row, 1957), pp. 55-60.

32. *Dollar Politics,* 3rd ed. (Washington, D.C.: Congressional Quarterly, 1982), p. 88; originally quoted in the *Washington Post,* August 10, 1980.

33. Rhodes Cook, "Senate Elections: A Dull Affair Compared to 1980's Upheaval," *Congressional Quarterly Weekly Report,* November 6, 1982, p. 2792.

34. See U.S. Congress, House, *Campaign Finance Reform,* pp. 52 and 143.

35. See Fenno, *Home Style,* for a detailed account of the various ways in which members do this.

36. Jacobson, "Strategic Politics in 1982," pp. 11-12.

37. Gary C. Jacobson, "The Case of the Vanishing Challengers," in *Congressional Elections,* ed. Louis Sandy Maisel and Joseph Cooper (Beverly Hills: Sage Publications, 1981), p. 238.

38. Jacobson, "Strategic Politics in 1982," p. 16.

39. Dennis Farney, Leonard M. Apcar, and Rich Jaroslovsky, "How Reaganites Push Reluctant Republicans to Back Tax-Rise Bill," *Wall Street Journal,* September 9, 1982, p. 1.

40. See comment by Task Force Chairman Al Swift in U.S. Congress, House, *Campaign Finance Reform,* p. 658.

41. See comment by Rep. Coehlo, chairman of the DCCC, in ibid., pp. 632-633.

42. Jacobson, "Running Scared."

43. See Mayhew's convincing analysis in Chapter 2 of *Congress: The Electoral Connection.*

44. Albert Hunt, "An Inside Look at Politicians Hustling PACs," *Wall Street Journal,* October 1, 1982, p. 1; U.S. Congress, House, *Campaign Finance Reform,* pp. 204, 610.

45. U.S. Congress, House, *Campaign Finance Reform,* pp. 105-106, 139, 142.

46. Ibid., p. 164.

47. Jacobson, *Politics of Congressional Elections,* pp. 86-89.

48. See, for example, the testimony of Joan Claybrook, president of Public Citizen (one of Ralph Nader's operations), in U.S. Congress, House, *Campaign Finance Reform,* pp. 538-547; see also Elizabeth Drew, *Politics and Money: The New Road to Corruption* (New York: Macmillan, 1983).

49. See, for examples, Drew, *Politics and Money,* pp. 44-45, 96; U.S. Congress, House, *Campaign Finance Reform,* pp. 49 and 533; Brooks Jackson and John J. Fialka, "New Congressmen Get Many Offers of Money to Cut Campaign Debt," *Wall Street Journal,* April 21, 1983, p. 1.

50. James Kau and Paul Rubin, *Congressmen, Constituents, and Contributors* (Boston: Martinus Nijhoff, 1982); Diana Evans Yiannakis, "PAC Contributions and House Voting on Conflictual and Consensual Issues: The Windfall Profits Tax and the Chrysler Loan Guarantee" (Paper delivered at the annual meeting of the American Political Science Association, Chicago, Illinois, September 1-4,

1983); John P. Frendreis and Richard W. Waterman, "PAC Contributions and Legislative Behavior: Senate Voting on Trucking Deregulation" (Paper delivered at the annual meeting of the Midwest Political Science Association, Chicago, Illinois, April 20-22, 1983); Candice J. Nelson, "Counting the Cash: PAC Contributions to Members of the House of Representatives" (Paper delivered at the annual meeting of the American Political Science Association, Denver, Colorado, September 2-5, 1982); Henry W. Chappell, Jr., "Campaign Contributions and Voting on the Cargo Preference Bill: A Comparison of Simultaneous Models," *Public Choice* 36 (1981): 301-312, and "Campaign Contributions and Congressional Voting: A Simultaneous Probit-Tobit Model," *Review of Economics and Statistics* 64 (1982): 77-83; William P. Welch, "Campaign Contributions and Voting: Milk Money and Dairy Price Supports," *Western Political Quarterly* 25 (1982): 478-495; and Kirk F. Brown, "Campaign Contributions and Congressional Voting" (Paper delivered at the annual meeting of the American Political Science Association, Chicago, Illinois, September 1-4, 1983).
51. "The Trail of the 'Dirty Dozen,'" *Congressional Quarterly Weekly Report,* March 21, 1981, p. 510.
52. *Dollar Politics,* 3rd ed., p. 57.
53. See remarks of Rep. Ferraro, U.S. Congress, House, *Campaign Finance Reform,* pp. 211-212.
54. Malbin, "Future of Campaign Finance Reform," pp. 249-251.
55. Raymond A. Bauer, Ithiel de Sola Pool, and Lewis Anthony Dexter, *American Business and Public Policy* (New York: Atherton, 1968).
56. Theodore J. Eismeier and Philip H. Pollock III, "Political Action Committees: Varieties of Organization and Strategy," in *Money and Politics,* pp. 124-126.
57. Malbin, "Future of Campaign Finance Reform," pp. 267-268.
58. Lawrence Dodd and Terry Sullivan, "House Leadership Success in the Vote Gathering Process: A Comparative Analysis" (Paper delivered at the annual meeting of the Midwest Political Science Association, Chicago, Illinois, April 24-26, 1980).
59. Edsall, "GOP Money Machine," p. 7.
60. Elizabeth Wehr, "White House's Lobbying Apparatus Produces Impressive Tax Victory," *Congressional Quarterly Weekly Report,* August 1, 1981, pp. 1372-1373.
61. Malbin, "Future of Campaign Finance Reform," pp. 269-270.
62. U.S. Congress, House, Campaign Finance Reform, p. 171; Brooks Jackson, "The Problem with PACs," *Wall Street Journal,* November 17, 1982, p. 30.
63. Malbin, "Future of Campaign Finance Reform," p. 255.

Part III

COMMITTEE AND SUBCOMMITTEE
POLITICS

7. CONGRESSIONAL COMMITTEES
IN THE POLICY PROCESS

David E. Price

Levels of executive-congressional conflict during the presidencies of Jimmy Carter and Ronald Reagan have been relatively high, despite circumstances that at first seemed to promise increased cooperation. Carter's election in 1976 brought unified party control to the White House and to both houses of Congress for the first time since Lyndon Johnson's administration, and the foreign policy questions that had fractured the majority party during his presidency had largely passed from the scene. The Reagan election of 1980 brought Republican control to the Senate and produced sufficient political momentum to enable the president to pass through Congress an ambitious package of taxing and spending reductions during his first year in office. But in both the Carter and Reagan administrations, Congress and the president developed contrasting approaches to legislation and frequently sparred in a wide range of policy areas—from energy and education to agriculture and public works.

Attempts to explain these persistent patterns of conflict sometimes give contrasting pictures of Congress as a policymaking institution. We hear, on the one hand, of congressional resurgence: Congress has emerged from the Vietnam and Watergate years more assertive, better equipped and more inclined to make policy on its own terms and in its own way. On the other hand, Congress is often portrayed as an "obstacle course," immobilized by conflict, susceptible to obstruction by determined minorities, resistant to presidential initiatives yet incapable of developing its own coherent alternatives.

These accounts are not as contradictory as they at first appear. Congress tends to balk at what presidents request in some areas and to push them farther than they want to go in others. Obviously, presidential objectives will vary greatly depending upon the individual in office. But certain patterns of congressional-executive interaction transcend these personal and partisan differences. Congress has resisted or modified the initiatives of Democratic and Republican presidents alike on numerous matters of national scope that have involved painful conflicts of value and interest (for example, energy, urban assistance, welfare, tax reform). But on less conflictful issues pushed by groups and constituencies that are firmly based in a bloc of congressional

161

districts, it is the Congress that has often resisted presidential constraints. For example, Congress took the lead during both the Carter and Reagan administrations in designing generous programs of agricultural price supports and in expanding the president's preferred list of water projects.

Although the way in which (and the ease with which) Congress handles policy questions differ considerably from area to area, the picture of congressional organization and responsiveness that emerges from a range of cases is fairly consistent. First, the policymaking process in Congress is decentralized and fragmented. Conflict among committees in the House and Senate slowed passage of both Gerald Ford's and Jimmy Carter's energy bills. The legislation no doubt would have passed with great difficulty in any case, but congressional fragmentation complicated the process considerably and provided checkpoints for those who were determined to oppose one provision or another.[1] No less fragmentation is usually visible on farm and public works bills, although here the element of competition between committees is missing. Congress parcels out decisionmaking authority and, as Woodrow Wilson wrote in 1885, usually meets "to sanction the conclusions of its committees as rapidly as possible." [2]

These episodes reveal, secondly, what might be termed congressional "particularism." Protagonists in energy debates frequently speak for energy-producing areas favoring deregulation or for high-consuming states seeking continued price controls. Opposition to President Carter's welfare reform package came from Agriculture Committee spokesmen who saw replacing food stamps with cash payments as detrimental to farm interests, while many of those working to salvage the bill were mainly concerned with giving hard-pressed state and local governments financial relief. Safeguarding district water projects or agricultural commodity programs is often a higher priority of legislators than identifying with the broader fiscal-management or con-sumer-protection objectives that presidents articulate. This is not to say that members of Congress are incapable of taking broad-gauged policy initiatives. Indeed, as we shall see below, they are increasingly motivated to gain stature in nationally visible policy areas. Nevertheless, a general tendency exists in Congress to give priority to constituency-based interests, to aggregate the demands of groups and constituencies in such a way as to minimize tradeoffs and conflict among them, and thus to reject or modify presidential proposals that are aimed at redistributive or other "universalistic" objectives. Congress, in Theodore Lowi's phrase, displays a penchant for "distributive" politics.[3]

This leads us to a third generalization: congressional policymaking is committee-centered. Congressional fragmentation and particularism are insti-tutionalized in the committee system. It is this realization that furnishes the point of departure for this chapter. My purpose is to give a general account of the legislative process, keeping, as one must, the committee system in central focus. What capacities, disabilities, and biases does Congress display by virtue of the central place of committees in its life? How have committees come to occupy the place they do in our national legislature, and is their continuing pre-eminence assured? How do committees differ in their legislative roles, and what does one need to know about a committee to understand its role? Exploring such questions should take us beyond the contrasting stereotypes of Congress as the "broken branch" or as the last best hope of American government, and help us understand the kind of public policy we get from Congress and what kind of performance it is reasonable to expect.

Congressional Strengths and Weaknesses

As we have seen, Congress acts more readily and easily on distributive issues that are responsive to discrete constituencies than it does on broader and more conflictful problems. And the same organizational characteristics that often encourage both dependence on and defiance of the executive on policies of national scope may facilitate congressional leadership on matters like agricultural price supports, public works, and transportation subsidies. The decentralization of decisionmaking authority invites vetoes by determined minorities in areas such as energy, but on matters like tobacco or cotton supports it gives the partisans who have worked their way onto the relevant subcommittees a chance to write their preferences into law and—given the norms of reciprocity and mutual deference that have developed among members working in low-conflict, distributive policy areas—to have their decisions ratified by their peers. This is not to say that Congress or the president makes "better" policy of one type or the other. That is a separate question, impossible to answer in general terms. Certainly, one cannot simply assume that "more is better"; the constraints exercised by presidents on congressional activism in the area of public works, for example, might be quite efficacious. On occasion, thwarting initiatives may be as important as taking them. The point is simply that Congress is willing and able to assume policy leadership on certain *types of issues* more than on others. These capacities and inclinations are related as both cause and effect to the legislature's organizational fragmentation and particularism as institutional-ized in the committee system.

Similarly, an estimate of Congress's strengths and weaknesses might depend on the *stage of the policymaking process* being discussed. Too many accounts of presidential-congressional conflict portray policymaking as an undifferentiated process: it is not. Issues occasionally arise overnight in response to a catastrophe or crisis, but more often they are deliberately articulated and publicized by leaders in or out of government. Once a matter is identified as an issue, specific remedies must be formulated, further information gathered, and the range of relevant interests sought out and accommodated. Finally, sufficient political force must be mobilized to hammer out a definitive legislative compromise and secure its enactment. Publicizing, formulating, gathering information, aggregating interests, mobi-lizing, refining and modifying—all are important and complementary aspects of the development and enactment of new policies.[4] Only rarely does any single actor in the process possess sufficient skills and resources to perform all of these functions with equal success or in isolation. Legislative case histories typically reveal a division of labor—within Congress and between Congress and the executive—in which elements of cooperation and conflict are present and by virtue of which responsibility for the policy product is shared.

Recognition of the multifaceted and cooperative character of policymaking undermines simplistic generalizations about congressional or executive domination of the process in general. But just as Congress displays a penchant for certain types of policy, so does it have an easier time with some stages of policymaking than it does with others. One's estimate of Congress's capacities is likely to be more favorable, in short, if one is looking at the *early* stages of policy formation—the generating of issues, the gathering of information, the floating of new ideas, the development of the policy agenda. One interested in the capacity to forge difficult compromises and push them through to enactment is apt to be less impressed.

Again, it is important to avoid oversimplification. Obviously, the president has a tremendous capacity, at least for the top few items on his agenda, to publicize an issue and to influence the terms of subsequent debate. Nor is mobilization a problem for Congress in many of the distributive, low-conflict areas in which it specializes. But if one were to look only at the early stages of policymaking, the case for congressional preoccupation with distributive policy would seem far less strong. In fact, members are often quite anxious to publicize problems and abuses and to float legislative remedies in controversial areas of broad national scope. Most of the items in President Johnson's aid-to-education, Medicare, antipoverty, and other Great Society proposals had been kicking around Congress in one form or another for years. The same was true of most of the major legislative initiatives of the Carter administration and of Reagan's vaunted "supply side" economic proposals. The problem is that all too often Congress's "germination" function amounts to no more than that. On high-conflict issues, Congress often needs a strong push from the executive or a swelling of popular opinion if its scattered initiatives are to bear fruit.

Congress's penchant for publicizing and issue-generating, like its proclivity for distributive politics, is closely tied to its organizational characteristics. And again, what spells weakness at one point may provide strength at another. In fact, Congress's decentralized, committee-centered decision structure is ideally suited to the early stages of legislative initiative. Committee and subcommittee members, as they establish their claim to a piece of policy turf and seek the approval of interested groups and constituencies, have every reason to cajole the executive, to seek out the views of concerned parties in hearings, and to establish a position of policy leadership.

A case in point is airline deregulation, which came to legislative fruition in 1978. The issue first hit the headlines in 1974 when Senator Edward Kennedy (D-Mass.) used his Judiciary Subcommittee on Administrative Practice and Procedure to attack the Civil Aeronautics Board's approval of fare increases and its other anticompetitive regulatory practices. Howard Cannon (D-Nev.), chairman of the Commerce Subcommittee on Aviation that had jurisdiction over the CAB, had already reported a bill dealing with the narrower question of CAB restriction of charter airlines. While Kennedy's intrusion annoyed Cannon, it also stimulated him to increase his efforts and strengthen his own proposals in the area of airline deregulation, a matter both senators felt to be increasing in its potential salience and appeal to the public. The fact that each man had the resources of a subcommittee at his disposal and that jurisdictional overlaps created competition between them clearly made for heightened congressional activity at the publicizing, information-gathering, and formulation stages.

Congressional fragmentation threatened to have a contrary effect later on, however. The chairman of the full Commerce Committee, closely tied to the major commercial airlines (who opposed deregulation), was skeptical of Cannon's initial efforts—to say nothing of Kennedy's. The limited jurisdiction of the Judiciary Subcommittee over the CAB prevented Kennedy from moving beyond the hearing stage. And Cannon's counterparts in the House were not sympathetic. As it turned out, the impact of anticompetitive regulation on the economy caught on as a consumer issue, and Presidents Ford and Carter took up the deregulation cause. The seeds sown by Kennedy and Cannon thus bore fruit in the 95th Congress. But the case shows how congressional decentralization could heighten the senators' visibility and leverage at one legislative stage even as it complicated their prospects for success at another.

Committees as a Reflection of Congressional Individualism

As we have seen, the congressional committee system both derives from and reinforces the fragmentation of power in Congress and the particularistic policy orientations of its members. The system is well suited to the publicizing of issues and the development of the policy agenda, and it facilitates congressional leadership in distributive, constituency-related policy areas. By the same token, however, Congress is often difficult to mobilize, particularly on high-conflict issues of broad scope.

How has a system with these legislative strengths and weaknesses evolved? A comparison with the most familiar alternative model—the parliamentary system as it is found in Britain and most Commonwealth countries—points up important elements of constitutional structure and political history. The separation of powers at the federal level has removed the president and cabinet heads from any decisive control of the legislative process. And strong and cohesive parties have not emerged to bridge the gap. Party divisions in the United States, by virtue of the country's ideological inheritance and social structure, coincide neither with basic divisions in society nor with distinctive philosophical outlooks. Organizationally and ideologically diffuse, American parties have displayed only a limited capacity to bind together the branches of the federal government—and disparate elements within the legislature—in the pursuit of well-defined policy goals.

There have been historical variations in the allegiance party has commanded in the electorate and among officeholders. Relatively strong party and/or executive leadership has characterized a number of state legislatures and, at certain periods, the U.S. Congress itself. But the general pattern is clear: while their parliamentary counterparts have seen adherence to party discipline as the most promising pathway both to electoral security and to power and preferment within the government, members of Congress have seen it as one alternative among many and by no means always the most promising one. The looseness of the party tie in the electorate and within government, and the vagueness of the parties' ideological and programmatic appeals, have made it possible for members to respond to a broad range of cues and to develop alternative bases of electoral support and political leverage.

Thus to an appreciable extent, members of Congress seeking election and re-election are "on their own." [5] They face electorates increasingly disinclined to vote for them on partisan grounds alone and a public largely unconcerned about their party loyalty once in office. Members are generally nominated in direct primaries—not by party caucuses or conventions—and few party organizations retain the power to influence decisively the nomination process. Most members must raise their own funds and build their own organizations at the primary and general election stages, although the national parties, especially the GOP, have recently begun to contribute far more substantially to congressional campaigns.

Even in areas where local or state parties are cohesive and well organized, their members are likely to be only sporadically interested in the party's national endeavors and to offer their congressional representatives only limited inducements toward teamsmanship in Washington. National partisan swings have become less and less determinative of election outcomes in most districts, and ticket splitting has become endemic. Understandably, members are inclined to see constituent service and visibility in their districts as more crucial to their electoral fortunes than whatever advantages they might gain from high presidential and partisan support scores in Congress. It is hardly surprising that when they perceive a conflict between party cues and district interests, members of the U.S. Congress, in contrast to their parliamentary counterparts, frequently defect from their party.

The maintenance of electoral strength involves more than "voting the district" on critical issues, however. David Mayhew has developed a typology of the electorally rewarding activities of American legislators. They *advertise,* building name familiarity and a favorable image through newsletters, newspaper and radio reports to the district, and huge volumes of mail. They *claim credit,* performing thousands of favors for constituents, facilitating their dealings with government agencies, and publicizing the member's role in securing projects and allocations of funds for the district. And they *take positions,* making speeches, introducing bills, publicizing their roll call votes, assuming postures designed for maximum electoral appeal.[6] This list of congressional activities is not exhaustive; few members can be viewed purely and simply as seekers after re-election. But the collective portrayal in many respects rings true. Elections take place in single-member districts often remote from national electoral trends. Party organizations are decentralized and frequently in a weakened state. This leaves American legislators on their own electorally and leads them to advertising, credit-claiming, and position-taking as strategies for staying in office.

It is important to recognize how congressional policymaking—characterized as it is by fragmented power, particularism, and the domination of committees—fits into this broader picture. Often electorally minded members see little reason to defer to presidential or party leadership but have strong incentives to secure needed benefits for their districts, to exert leverage on critical federal agencies, and to take visible policy stands. The committee system is admirably equipped to help in this regard. Committees like Agriculture, Interior, Public Works, and Merchant Marine enable members to have a hand in the formulation of legislation crucial to their districts and to claim credit for it. Membership on Appropriations, Public Works, Armed Services, Commerce, and other committees gives members an inside track with relevant federal agencies as they plan their activities, administer projects, and allocate funds. Although most committees offer a forum for position-taking and the staff resources to underwrite policy advocacy, some, like the Foreign Relations and Government Operations Committees in both houses, have become particularly noteworthy as arenas for the exposure of alleged abuses and the publicizing of policy stances.

Members seek not only electoral security but also power, prestige, and preferment within Congress and the governmental establishment. These desires give party and executive leaders some leverage with members, but here, too, the committee system has a great deal to offer. Legendary Senate power broker Robert Kerr (D-Okla.), as chairman of the Public Works Subcommittee on Rivers and Harbors and a key member of the Finance Committee, needed and wanted no additional institutional base, least of all the party leadership; he could bargain for virtually anything he wanted with his fellow members and the Kennedy administration. More recently, the policy role assumed by House Democrats of modest seniority—such as Philip Sharp (Ind.) in energy policy, Leon Panetta (Calif.) in budget policy, and Charlie Rose (N.C.) in agriculture—would scarcely have been conceivable without the prior parceling out of power and authority through the committee-subcommittee system.[7] Committees give members expertise, a voice in policy formation, and bargaining leverage with their peers and the executive that only a few leaders would enjoy in a more hierarchical system.

Recent years have seen a heightening of the electoral and power stakes that members have perceived in the committee system and some altering of that system in the process. Government has grown, policies and programs have proliferated, and the ties that bind citizens and localities to federal agencies have become more numerous and more complicated. Thus it has become increasingly important for the legislator who would be "effective" to be in a position to influence policy formulation and to intervene effectively on behalf of persons, groups, and governments with a stake in various programs. At the same time, party identifications have faded in the electorate, party organizations have eroded, districts have grown in size and heterogeneity, and television has become a dominant campaign medium. Highly visible position-taking, credit-claiming, and policy leadership have become far more important electoral techniques than they were in the days of friends-and-neighbors and clubhouse politics.

All of this has made members more anxious to gain the visibility and resources that come with committee and subcommittee leadership and at an earlier point in their careers. New members are less willing to defer to their party and committee elders or to adhere to the norms of apprenticeship that formerly kept junior members "in their place." On virtually every House and Senate committee there have been strong pressures over the past three decades to create more subcommittees, to give them more authority, and to spread the leadership around. For a number of years virtually every majority-party senator, including most freshmen, has been assured of a subcommittee chairmanship. Rules changes and pressures from the membership have made subcommittee chairmanships available to almost half of the House Democrats as well.

Further changes in rules and practice have made desirable committee and subcommittee assignments more widely available, have increased and dispersed staff resources, and, by increasing the autonomy and authority of subcommittees, have greatly enhanced their value as mechanisms for issue and policy development. In short, the congressional committee system, characterized by particularism and fragmented power, in recent years has become *more* fragmented but in ways that are highly serviceable to individual members desiring a base for self-promotion and a piece of policy "turf." How serviceable the trend is for the policymaking capacities of Congress as a whole is, however, a more complicated question.

Committees as a Corrective to Congressional Individualism

As we have seen, congressional committees fill the policymaking vacuum left by the absence of strong, cohesive parties. Moreover, the dominance of congressional committees in policymaking well suits the electoral and power needs of individual members. From the first, however, committees have been regarded not simply as organizational forms appropriate to large and diffuse assemblies such as the U.S. House and Senate, but as a means of overcoming some of the decisionmaking difficulties such assemblies experience.

Henry Clay, Speaker intermittently from 1811 to 1825, first brought committees to a dominant role in the conduct of House business. Although he was constrained by the necessity of including spokesmen for numerous blocs on key committees, his delegation of decisionmaking to these sublegislatures still represented "a functional adaptation to the early Congress's incapacity to organize itself for effective policymaking by majorities."[8] Although the committee system reflects congressional decentralization and the aspirations of individual members, it also represents a corrective to congressional individualism. The committee system is a means of bringing expertise and attention to bear on congressional tasks in a more concerted fashion than the free enterprise of scattered members could ever accomplish.

As one observes legislators scrambling for subcommittee chairs and liberalizing the rules of participation, it is easy to assume that they want as much policymaking "action" as they can get and that the committee-subcommittee system simply accommodates their desires. This assumption, however, seriously underestimates the independent impact the committee system has on their priorities and their behavior. As Mayhew has pointed out, the quest for re-election often leads members to no more than superficial stabs at policymaking; a desire to "claim credit" will awaken interest only in those few measures most directly related to the constituency, while "position-taking" generally requires only the publicizing of an issue rather than any serious attempt to do anything about it.[9] In other words, members often will need incentives beyond the desire for public approval and electoral success if they are to undertake the arduous tasks of policy development and oversight of the executive. One House freshman made clear that one of the reasons for his extensive labors on the Commerce Subcommittee on Oversight was *not* the electoral payoff: "My work hasn't gotten much play back in the district."[10] Even in a highly visible issue like health, the electoral rewards are slim. As another member noted: "Very few people back in the district know anything about the work I do on that [Health] subcommittee."

Why, then, do members engage in serious legislative work? Many, in fact, do not. Congress contains many members who concentrate on constituent service, self-promotion, and the taking of well-publicized stands on issues—what Speaker Sam Rayburn liked to call "show horse" behavior. Such members may be re-elected by large margins, but they are unlikely to gain that power and prestige within the governmental establishment that many legislators covet.[11] This desire for a reputation in the Washington community provides a crucial motivation for purposefully addressing policy problems. The committee system channels these desires for leverage and status into activity that serves the institution's needs and builds its policymaking capacities. Members who do not pull their weight are apt to feel the disapproval of fellow committee members, and most members understand quite well that to slough off as a subcommittee chairman is to gain an unfavorable reputation as a lightweight.

In other systems legislators are induced to do serious work by the prospect of promotion and preferment within the party or the government. In the American setting, where these structures have less to offer, the committee system represents an alternative incentive-producing mechanism indigenous to the legislature. Without committees, American legislators would have many fewer inducements to, and opportunities for, serious legislative and oversight activities. Committees thus provide an important corrective to what analysts like Mayhew regard as the natural tendencies of the system. Members who wish to influence the direction of policy and/or to enhance their standing and leverage in Washington find in committee work the prescribed and often quite promising means to these objectives.

Although committees stimulate legislative efforts, those efforts are still likely to reflect the fragmentation and particularism discussed earlier. Committees and subcommittees are generally populated by members with a particular stake in the programs they are authorizing. They are often able to write bills without paying much attention to conflicting objectives or broader impacts. Thus the aggregate congressional output is apt to appear uncoordinated, unbalanced (in favor of those interests that have a firm footing in the committee system), extravagant (since each committee is authorizing programs it favors with little attention to overall spending levels), and vulnerable to delay and obstruction in areas of conflict.

These characteristics of congressional policymaking are often at the root of legislative-executive conflict. Because rampant particularism is apt to lead to successful challenges by the executive, concern in Congress is excited as well. Hence the need arises for a second "corrective," not only to the undisciplined impulses of individual members, but also to the policy they produce once in harness. The committees, the major element of the "solution" in the first instance, become part of the problem in the second.

It is common to contrast the "centrifugal" force represented by congressional committees to the "centripetal" force of party leadership.[12] Indeed, the parties and executive leadership are critically important in setting priorities, resolving conflicts, overcoming procedural obstacles, and mobilizing majorities—all functions that a particularistic, fragmented assembly is likely to find problematic. But here, too, committees comprise part of the solution.

'Control' Committees

Congressional committees vary considerably in their power and prestige. Of particular importance are those Mayhew describes as "control committees," whose members are "paid in internal currency for engaging in institutionally protective activities."[13] Three House committees—Appropriations, Ways and Means, and Rules—perform important functions of coordination and control, although their roles have shifted considerably in recent years. And of course the Budget Committees in both houses must now be added to the list.

Appropriations and Budget Committees

The House and Senate formed their modern appropriations committees in the early 1920s, reversing a process whereby jurisdiction over key funding bills had been parceled out to numerous legislative committees. Since then, any program authorized by these committees has had to undergo a second examination by the appropriations panels to determine at what level it will be funded. The power and reach of the appropriations committees have made them highly sought after by members who wish to ensure adequate funding for favored programs and who value the bargaining leverage such a position provides. But the appropriations committees, especially in the House, have also played key institutional roles as guardians of the budget and protectors of Congress against its own (and the executive's) enthusiasms.

Richard Fenno found one key "strategic premise" to dominate House Appropriations deliberations in the 1960s: "reduce executive budget requests." [14] Committee members were socialized to adhere to this norm of fiscal austerity; those who kept their particularism in check tended to fare better on the committee. Most House members felt that they had a collective stake in the power and fiscal control exercised by the committee. But they viewed the committee with some ambivalence: members naturally felt less strongly about the House's collective stake when it was *their* programs that were being cut. Fenno thus found Appropriations members holding a second strategic premise in tension with the first: "provide adequate funding for executive programs." In view of their own political interests and the expectations of their colleagues, Appropriations members could not push their budget-tightening, control functions too far. Nevertheless, they still saw themselves as protecting Congress's institutional credibility and the coherence of its policy product—and most members, in granting the Appropriations Committee extraordinary deference, proved willing to underwrite such a role.

The limitations of appropriations as a control device became increasingly evident in the 1970s. At best, appropriations covered only half of the fiscal picture; the intake side was controlled by separate revenue committees— Ways and Means in the House and Finance in the Senate—thus complicating the coordination of taxing and spending policy. "Backdoor spending" techniques, such as the granting of fixed entitlements to individuals and groups by law and the delegation of contract and borrowing authority, further limited the appropriations committees' control. By fiscal 1974 only 44 percent of the budget could be directly controlled by the appropriations committees on an annual basis.

The appropriations committees were also influenced by changes in the congressional environment. Legislators became less inclined to defer to prestigious committees and demanded a greater measure of responsiveness from them. The tension Fenno identified on House Appropriations between providing "adequate" funding and exerting fiscal control began to tilt in the direction of particularism in a number of policy areas. This tendency was reinforced by certain reform measures. Opening hearings and meetings to the public, for example, made it more difficult for committee members to resist the demands of colleagues and interest groups. Rules adopted in 1975 provided for the selection of House Appropriations subcommittee chairs by the full House Democratic Caucus, thus giving these chairs powerful incentives to cater to the policy interests of their peers. And Appropriations Committee members, formerly appointed to subcommittees by the chair, were now allowed to "bid" for these slots. This often brought members to the subcommittees who were more interested in protecting pet programs and less ready to exercise overall fiscal constraint.[15]

The deficiencies of appropriations as a control device—as well as the immediate challenge of President Richard Nixon's impoundments and his accusations that Congress was irresponsible and free-spending—led Congress to pass the Budget and Impoundment Control Act of 1974. New House and Senate budget committees were given authority to set binding overall limits to guide other committees as they passed individual authorization, appropriations, and tax bills. A Congressional Budget Office was also established to give Congress a capacity for budget and policy analysis comparable to that of the executive branch.

The budget process has substantially increased the capacity of Congress to achieve fiscal coordination and control. The budget committees still operate in a context of fragmented power: they lack specific budget and tax-writing authority, and the House has taken steps to limit its Budget Committee's independence and continuity of membership.[16] But while the targets and limits set by the budget committees have sometimes provoked defiance by one committee or another, "for every confrontation there have been dozens of legislative decisions routinely made with fidelity to the budget process." [17]

During the first year of Ronald Reagan's presidency, the concentration of budgetary power reached new heights, albeit under conditions that enhanced presidential rather than congressional control of spending. In 1980 Congress had experimented with moving the budget act's "reconciliation" procedures—originally designed to bring congressional spending decisions into line with the final budget resolution—from the end to near the beginning of the budget cycle. This change was firmly established in 1981. The reconciliation bill then became, in effect, a set of authoritative instructions to Congress as it went about its work, greatly increasing the constraints the budget process placed on the authorizing committees and on entitlement programs.

The Reagan administration exploited the reconciliation process—and political momentum from the 1980 elections—to push through more than $100 billion in multiyear cutbacks in 1981. That feat was not matched by the administration in subsequent years. Shifts in the political climate induced by the economic recession weakened the president's hand. The budget committees found themselves torn between presidential and congressional demands, and appropriations and legislative committees began to reassert themselves.[18] But while the capacities of the budget committees may wax and wane, there can be no doubt that the budget process has decisively altered the congressional landscape. Amid strong decentralizing trends, this "reform" has strengthened centripetal forces in Congress by providing a mechanism that party leaders and presidents may use to enhance their own control and by setting up new control committees alongside the traditional ones.

Rules and Ways and Means Committees

Two additional House committees, Rules and Ways and Means, have also performed important control functions, although neither operates as independently as it did before the 1970s. The Rules Committee, which schedules and structures the consideration of measures on the House floor, was controlled by the Speaker in the period of strong party leadership that preceded the revolt against Speaker Joseph Cannon in 1910. The committee subsequently emerged as a power in its own right. After Conservative Coalition members gained a majority on the committee in the late thirties, it frequently exercised its control functions in a way that conflicted with the Democratic party leadership. Recent years have seen major turnovers in Rules Committee membership and leadership, and rules changes have returned to the Speaker the power to name the committee's Democratic members. As a result, Rules has emerged as an "arm of the Speaker," critically important to party efforts at coordination and control. The committee frequently uses its gate-keeping powers to force the resolution of jurisdictional disputes between committees, to provide feedback to the committees and an inducement to trim their sails, and to hold measures back until key Democrats can agree on them. "Under (committee chairman Richard) Bolling, Rules brought a good deal of discipline to the committees," observed one member in 1982. "It made them more particular on bills, getting them in shape, both politically and substantively, to go to the floor." [19] Even with Bolling's retirement these functions have continued, although not with the same level of attention and skill.

The Ways and Means Committee has traditionally ranked with Appropriations and Rules in power and prestige and, like them, has been deferred to by the membership as a guardian of the House's institutional interests. Mayhew in 1974 described Ways and Means as, in effect, "hired to put a damper on particularism in tax and tariff matters and to protect what members call the 'actuarial soundness' of the social security program." [20] This deference has not been rooted merely in the desire of members to protect the House's place in the system; Ways and Means, after all, writes the law in areas that are important to every representative, and from 1911 until 1974 Ways and Means Democrats also controlled their party's committee assignments in the House. In recent years, as members have become less convinced that the power and autonomy of Ways and Means serve their interests, they have proved willing to weaken its control functions for the sake of greater openness and responsiveness. Emboldened by Chairman Wilbur Mills's involvement in a sex-alcohol scandal, the Democratic Caucus proceeded in the 94th Congress to enlarge the committee from 25 to 37 members and to shift Democratic committee-assignment functions to the party's Steering and Policy Committee. These and earlier rules changes, together with membership turnover and the accession of less authoritative chairmen, have made Ways and Means a more diverse and accessible committee, but they have also reduced the committee's capability to develop a united front and to keep its bills intact on the floor.

The powerful role that the old Ways and Means Committee played in mobilizing the House was dramatically demonstrated in 1970 and 1971 as it steered the Nixon administration's controversial welfare reform bills to passage. (Both bills died in the Senate Finance Committee, where conflict was sharper and less controlled.) It would be too simple to blame the failure of the Carter administration's analogous bill in the House in 1978 on the Ways and Means Committee's weakened powers, but this much can be said: the support and the clout of Ways and Means were major assets for the Nixon administration, assets that the Carter administration would have found immensely valuable in its welfare and energy battles had they been available eight years later.

Ways and Means's reduced capacity was not limited to isolated instances. While committee bills were subjected to an average of 25 roll calls in the 91st to 93rd Congresses, the average figure jumped to 96 in the 94th and 95th Congresses. Floor votes went against the chairman's preferences only six times in the 1969-1974 period (8 percent of all votes), but the chairman was reversed 33 times between 1975 and 1978 (17 percent of all votes). Ways and Means, compared with other committees, still commands considerable deference. But the trend is unmistakable: challenges to Ways and Means have become more frequent and more often successful. Given the committee's past role, this represents a decline in the House's capacity to counter particularism and the fragmentation of power.

Summary

This overview of the control committees suggests that while the committee system mirrors congressional fragmentation, particularism, and individualism, it also represents a corrective of sorts to these organizational characteristics. The corrective mechanisms are themselves rather dispersed and subject to centrifugal pressures. And they are not effective to a degree that would satisfy an advocate of parliamentary or party government. But committees represent not only a device for spreading power and serving the needs of members, but also a means by which Congress partially overcomes its policymaking disabilities. Attempts to increase the coherence of Congress's policy product must not simply look to strengthened party or executive leadership, but must explore ways of increasing the integrative capacities of the committee system as well. Attempts in recent years to recast and rationalize jurisdictional boundaries and Speaker Tip O'Neill's occasional appointment of intercommittee ad hoc groups to process complex legislation represent two not altogether auspicious attempts in this direction.

Differences Among Committees: The Policy Impact

Thus far we have explored the reasons for the persistence of committees as the dominant organizational form in Congress and have asked how these structures are related to the institution's general ability to make public policy. As Richard Fenno has stressed, however, congressional committees not only *matter;* they also *differ* in ways that have a considerable impact on the decisions they make and the authority they are able to muster.[21] Any account of congressional policymaking that attains any degree of specificity is bound to explore not only the effects of a committee-centered organizational structure in general, but also the dimensions along which committees and their policy roles systematically vary. Our task in the space remaining is to indicate which aspects of committee life should be examined if we want to understand the kind of policy they produce.

Committees are collections of individuals who bring different goals, values, identifications, and skills to their committee roles; the performance of a committee may be seen in part as a function of these characteristics of its membership. According to Fenno, one of three broad "member goals" predominates on many House committees and shapes their respective policy roles: gaining influence in the House, helping constituents and thereby ensuring re-election, and making good public policy. For example, the Appropriations Committee's determination to guard the power of the purse may be explained in terms of its members' orientation toward power in the House; the Interior Committee's determination "to secure House passage of all constituency-supported, member-sponsored bills" is rooted, by contrast, in the predominance of constituent-service orientations among its membership.[22]

While such goals undoubtedly influence members' initial choice of a committee and continue to influence their behavior after they are seated, they are often too general to explain many of the policymaking tendencies and trends that committees display. For example, Ways and Means's recent tendency to report more, and more controversial, legislation may reflect a shift in emphasis from the cultivation of power in the House to the making of "good public policy." But both goals have been important all along; more decisive may have been shifts in membership views of what constitutes "good public policy" and in preferred strategies for accommodating the parent chamber. Changes in the performance of oversight by the House Government Operations Committee, "more aggressive and wider in scope than previously," are more plausibly explained by the increased liberalism and activism of its members than by any turnabout in general member goals.[23] The Senate Commerce Committee is also impossible to categorize in terms of any one dominant member objective; the dampening of consumer and environmental protection initiatives on the committee in the late 1970s was less indicative of any shift in its eclectic mix of member goals than of the replacement of several of its liberal activists with more conservative members.

These examples point up the difficulty of pigeonholing committees according to Fenno's criteria. A richer account of member characteristics is needed to account for legislative performance. Clearly important is ideology, the members' beliefs about the proper role of government and desirable goals for public policy. Equally decisive can be the members' legislative orientations—the degrees of initiative and activism they are willing to undertake or support. Members' ties and identifications can exert a powerful influence on both the frequency and content of their policymaking efforts. Finally, the particular purposes and skills of individual members and groups of members must be taken into account as a critical determinant of what committees undertake. These multifarious member characteristics are not as elusive or as difficult to generalize about as it might seem. Often committees attract members with similar constituency ties or ideological inclinations, and committee life itself can foster common goals and orientations.

The characteristics of committee and subcommittee leaders have a particularly important policy impact. The dispersion of power in Congress and the degree of autonomy enjoyed by committee and subcommittee chairs place a great many people in a position to translate their objectives more or less directly into policy proposals and public law. This autonomy, to be sure, is not what it once was. Recent congressional history contains numerous examples of leaders who were deposed and prospective leaders who were denied their slots because they were judged hostile to the interests of a caucus or committee majority. The recent denial of subcommittee chairs to several senior representatives suggests, in fact, that members are becoming more willing to violate seniority not simply in cases of extreme autocracy or misconduct but also where "one candidate's views are closer to them than the others." [24] Still, most committee and subcommittee leaders can be expected to retain their slots and to enjoy a great deal of latitude in implementing their own priorities and preferences. Several examples of leader-induced change leave little doubt that much of what is done on committees is a function of their leaders' goals and skills. Senate Commerce Committee activism was reduced upon Howard Cannon's accession to the chairmanship in the 95th Congress, and a broadening of the Judiciary Committee's agenda came with Edward Kennedy's chairmanship in the 96th. Fernand St. Germain's assumption of the House Banking, Finance, and Urban Affairs chair in 1981 brought with it a marked tilt toward the interests of small banks and savings and loan associations.[25]

At the subcommittee level the effect can be even more profound. For example, in 1975 House Commerce Democrats replaced Harley Staggers (D-W.Va.) with John Moss (D-Calif.), an unusually active and aggressive member, as chairman of the Oversight and Investigations Subcommittee. A series of major alterations in the subcommittee's product and performance, including heightened levels of activity and increased attention to highly controversial health and energy issues, followed this leadership change:

> By far the most important factor in altering the [subcommittee's] role was the selection of John Moss as chairman. Rules changes made it possible for committee Democrats to make a deliberate choice for the position, and they increased the autonomy and resources Moss enjoyed after he won. But the "reforms" themselves would have had little impact on performance had the swing vote on that seventh ballot gone to Staggers.[26]

The characteristics of a committee's staff also significantly affect its policy role. Many of the disparities that once existed in the size and expertise of committee staffs have disappeared. As recently as 1964, Harry Byrd ran the Senate Finance Committee with one professional staff member, but those days are gone forever. In 1960 all congressional committees and subcommittees employed fewer than 1,000 persons. This figure tripled by the mid-1970s and in 1984 exceeded 3,600.[27] Committee aides today are more likely to have specialized experience and training and less likely to be purely patronage appointees.

With respect to the distribution of staff resources within committees, more significant differences remain. Here, too, some of the disparities have been reduced. Changes in House rules have generally assured subcommittees of sizable staffs and of independence from the full committee chairmen in appointing them and directing their work. Senate rules provide junior members with personal aides to cover their committee responsibilities. But despite these changes, the Senate still has several committees where the chairman virtually monopolizes staff resources, and in both houses staff have sometimes become so decentralized as to make an efficient division of labor impossible and the full committee practically bereft of expertise.

Staffs also vary in their partisanship, which affects their accessibility and the kind of services they render. Although most committees have established the separate majority and minority staffs authorized by the Legislative Reorganization Act of 1970, the degree of cooperation between them varies widely. And the appropriations and budget committees in the House and the armed services and ethics committee in both the House and Senate have maintained the tradition of a "nonpolitical" bipartisan staff.

Finally, the orientations of committee aides toward their work influence the number and kinds of projects their committees undertake. While these orientations are often prescribed by committee leaders, and their impact is dependent on the members' receptivity to staff efforts, in many cases staff have considerable discretion in the handling of issues. How they define their job has an independent impact on what their mentors are able or inclined to do. This is all the more true as staffs get larger and the legislative workload increases. Staff orientations often approximate what might be termed "professional" and "entrepreneurial" syndromes, the former stressing the "neutral" provision of expertise, the latter the active stimulation of initiatives.[28] The activist role of the Senate Commerce Committee in consumer affairs from 1965 to 1976 is a classic example of the impact a politically skilled entrepreneurial staff can have, while the Joint Committee on Taxation staff, which serves the revenue committees in both houses, demonstrates the kind of credibility and clout—albeit with some limits on policy innovation—a group of experts adhering to the norms of "neutral competence" can provide. The continuing debate over how assertive and "political" the Congressional Budget Office staff should be suggests that, while such orientations will rarely be found in unmixed form, very real policymaking strengths and liabilities can come with a tilt in either direction.

Organizational Variations

In exploring the policy impact of various characteristics of a committee's members and staff, we have already encountered the committee as an organization. We need to know, not simply person-for-person who wants or aspires to what, but how roles are distributed, resources deployed, and decision-making controlled. Only then will we understand whose goals and preferences are likely to matter and what kind of policy leadership the committee as a whole will be able to muster. In this section two of the most important organizational variables will be considered: the degree and style of partisanship and the way power and resources are allocated via the subcommittee system.

Partisanship

The level of partisan cooperation on a committee depends on a number of factors: the ideological complexion and range of identifications of the membership, the extent to which policies under the committee's jurisdiction are the objects of partisan conflict, and the styles and preferences of the full committee and subcommittee chairmen and ranking minority members.[29] Partisan cooperation generally has some advantages for both sides. For the majority it means a reduced likelihood of sniping or obstruction in committee and on the floor; for the minority, a chance to contribute to key decisions at an earlier point. In areas of sharp partisan division, however, the costs of cooperation may be judged too high—the possibility of a restricted agenda or diluted policy content for the majority, or of co-optation or the pre-empting of campaign issues for the minority. Trade-offs in committee may develop between the "strength" of policy content and the probability of consensual approval; both are likely to be influenced by the extent and character of the committee's partisanship.

Subcommittee Government

Congressional reform has focused on the subcommittee system, as the following chapter discusses in further detail. The proliferation of subcommittees has widened the distribution of authority, visibility, and resources in both chambers. By the mid-1970s the major legislative committees had spawned an average of nine subunits. In the Senate, however, proliferation occurred later, was less formalized and standardized by rules changes, and resulted in greater scheduling conflicts and a more burdensome workload. With 100 members populating 174 Senate and joint committee subunits, the average senator in 1976 served on 14.3 subcommittees. Amendments reorganizing the Senate committee system in 1977 effected a modest retrenchment, reducing the 31 Senate and joint committees to 25, marginally adjusting jurisdictions, prohibiting any senator from chairing more than three committees and subcommittees, and limiting senators to eight subcommittee memberships (three on any one committee).

Senate committees responded to these changes in various ways. Commerce and Judiciary, for example, consolidated several subcommittees, while Human Resources, Banking, and Judiciary reduced the size of the subunits and/or forced members to choose among them. In some instances—Labor and Human Resources, for example—the reorganization gave renewed importance to proceedings at the full committee level: members who had to drop subcommittee slots came to value full committee hearings and mark-ups as the only place where they could get a crack at many of their former policy areas.

In recent years the number of subcommittees has begun to creep back up, and some one-third of the Senate's members are now in violation of the 1977 limits.[30] After party control of the Senate shifted in 1981, Republicans, long deprived of the leadership positions that come with majority status, renewed pressures for more subcommittees. Most members, despite their complaints about being thinly spread, still have an important stake in the wide dispersal of committee authority and resources.

During the 98th Congress (1983-1984), some 154 House and joint committee subunits were available to House members (compared with 113 subunits in the Senate at that time). Less thinly spread and more dependent on subcommittee positions for visibility and leverage, members of the House have been less inclined than senators to try to limit the proliferation of subcommittees. But in 1981 the House Democratic Caucus, which earlier had established a rule requiring committees to form at least five subcommittees, made the decision to cap the number of subcommittees on most committees at eight.

Figure 7-1 gives a comparative picture of the rate and degree of decentralization on selected House and Senate committees since the mid-1960s. The indicator chosen, the percentage of committee hearings held at the subcommittee level, gives a more extreme picture of committee decentralization than would a tally of committee meetings at the mark-up and modification stage.[31] But it provides a roughly accurate gauge of House-Senate and intercommittee differences. House committees, which displayed considerable diversity 15 years ago, have become more uniformly decentralized. This is attributable in large part to the adoption of rules by the chamber and by the Democratic Caucus that have mandated the creation of subcommittees and guaranteed them a great deal of autonomy. Because the chairman and most committee members on Ways and Means are reluctant to delegate responsibility for major tax bills, these crucial items continue to be handled at the full committee level. But on most House committees the presumption in favor of referring all bills to subcommittees and taking them through at least an initial mark-up at that level is quite strong.

Subcommittee roles vary more in the Senate. Chamber rules and members' attitudes give Senate chairmen more flexibility than their House counterparts in determining their committees' working arrangements. As Figure 7-1 suggests, the degree of decentralization on Senate committees continues to fluctuate. A decisive chairman still can effect a partial reversal of the parceling out of committee functions, as William Proxmire (D-Wis.) showed upon taking the Banking, Housing, and Urban Affairs helm in the 94th Congress and as Edward Kennedy (D-Mass.) demonstrated upon assuming the Judiciary chair in the 96th.[32] A number of Senate committees still mark up all legislation at the full committee level.

Committees thus continue to differ, particularly in the Senate, in their degree of centralization, and these differences influence policymaking. Decentralization usually increases the number of members who are able to play a substantial policy role and heightens the committee's overall quantity of activity. After the Ways and Means Committee formed subcommittees in 1974, the number of hearings held jumped by 148 percent, from 103 days in the 93rd Congress to 255 in the 94th. Increases at the later legislative stages were smaller but nonetheless impressive: from 45 to 96 committee reports (a 113 percent increase compared with 8 percent in the House as a whole) and from 34 to 49 public laws enacted (a 44 percent increase compared with a 10 percent decrease in the House).

Decentralization also influences policy content: subcommittee autonomy normally reinforces the tendency of committees, such as Interior and Agriculture, to cater to clientele groups, and it permits enthusiasts of various sorts to write their single-minded preferences into Congress's working drafts. The extent to which their particularism is modified, or their "strong" bills are diluted, will partially depend on the kind of review that is exercised at the full committee level. Such a retention of full committee authority can also increase a committee's capacity to bring a refined and credible proposal to the floor.

One House Energy and Commerce member, reflecting in 1978 on the consolidation of subcommittee prerogatives after some resistance from full committee chairman Harley Staggers, made it clear that, on balance, the

Figure 7-1 Percentage of Days of Hearings* Held at Subcommittee Level, Selected Committees, 89th-97th Congresses (1965-1982)

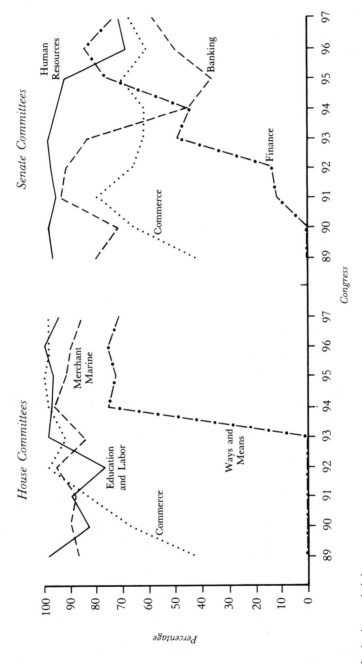

* Nominations excluded

SOURCE: Computed from legislative calendars.

assumption of responsibility by subcommittee heads for managing legislation had increased the committee's effectiveness. But he added:

> The right chairman could play an important role in coordinating and refining what the subcommittees produce. There's also a need for a tempering role, so we don't waste lots of time coming out with something that the subcommittee members are all excited about but which really doesn't have a chance. I think a number of members would welcome such a role; we're pretty frustrated with the slipshod ways things are handled in full committee now.

When John Dingell inherited the Energy and Commerce chair in 1981, he attempted to build up the full committee staff and to exert more control over the committee's policy output. But because of serious policy disagreements and a reluctance to have their powers weakened, Commerce's subcommittee chairs were willing to underwrite a more assertive role for the full committee only up to a point. The system that Dingell had helped build when he was a rebellious subcommittee chairman proved resistant to change. "John inherited the boundaries he helped create," an aide remarked. "Once you've let the quicksilver out of the thermometer you'll never get it all back in." [33]

It is impossible to predict the substantive policy effects of decentralization in a given situation without knowing who will receive the authority and resources. Decentralization could actually mean a dampening of initiative, as House Commerce Democrats recognized in 1977 when they denied the Consumer Affairs subcommittee chair to hardline conservative David Satterfield (D-Va.). But the House's Select Committee on Committees was correct when it suggested in 1974 that the designation of separate oversight subcommittees would ordinarily have a stimulative effect; members would be given tools and incentives, in terms of their desire for reputation and leverage, to build up an active oversight operation. Here, too, the Commerce Committee furnishes a pertinent example. The mere existence of resources and authority at the subcommittee level had only limited effect as long as Harley Staggers chaired the oversight subcommittee; it remained for John Moss to take full advantage of the entrepreneurial opportunities the situation offered.[34] Although the intentions and ties of congressional members and leaders are the major factors influencing Congress's policy product, committee organization plays a crucial role in facilitating or deflecting, stimulating or discouraging, their efforts.

The Policymaking Environment

Policy is influenced not only by the patterns of a committee's internal life but by the external forces that impinge on its operation. The committee's "sociology" shapes the pursuits of its members in many ways; the legislator must become a part of ongoing, institutionalized processes, and the gaining of acceptance and effectiveness requires a measure of cooperation and conformity. But committees, even the prestigious control committees of the House, can hardly be seen as insulated, self-contained organizations. They are buffeted continually by organized interests, governmental agencies, and other political forces, and their roles are often determined by how the politicians that comprise them respond to the opportunities and perils that the environment offers.

Fenno has examined four clusters of "outsiders"—members of the parent chamber, the executive branch, clientele groups, and the political parties—who are likely to have "an interest in committee behavior coupled with a capacity to influence such behavior." [35] Different outside influences predominate on different committees and are reflected in their respective policy roles. For example, the House Foreign Affairs Committee, which operates in an area where the executive traditionally dominates and the Senate tends to monopolize congressional prerogatives, has generally displayed a reactive policy role and only limited independence. Education and Labor, by contrast, is a committee that various and contending elements— groups, party, executive, congressional—seek to influence. The prominence of organized labor and educational groups has influenced who seeks membership on the committee and how they direct their efforts once they get there. But environmental crossfire makes many such undertakings vulnerable; both the content and the success rate of Education and Labor bills are very sensitive to presidential support and to the number of liberal Democrats in the House.[36]

One can also think of the environmental influences of a committee as a set of incentives and constraints that derive from the character of the policy the committee handles. Exactly which cluster of outsiders is able to command the attention of a committee may be less important than certain characteristics of the policy that make involvement appear profitable or costly to the prospective policymaker. Committees seldom exploit their jurisdictional possibilities with equal enthusiasm. While our emphasis thus far has been on how certain characteristics of a congressional committee may standardize its behavior across a range of policy areas, it is also true that a single committee may construe its responsibilities differently in different areas. The Commerce committees, for example, have staked out an innovative role and advanced positions in areas like consumer protection and major disease research, while in surface transportation and communications regulation they have traditionally assumed policy leadership reluctantly and with difficulty. To account for such differences within and between committees, one needs to understand how the policy environment looks to committee members and leaders. What is it that attracts, discourages, or constrains their involvement? [37]

Table 7-1 illustrates how several policy areas within the jurisdiction of the House and/or Senate Commerce Committees can be classified on two critical dimensions: the degree of conflict they entail and the public salience members perceive them to possess. Members wishing to gain visibility and a

Table 7-1 Policy Areas Handled by the House and Senate Commerce Committees, Categorized According to Their Perceived Levels of Public Salience and Conflict

| *Public* | *Level of Conflict* | | |
Salience	High	Medium	Low
High	health care delivery; environmental protection	most consumer protection measures	medical research
Medium	aviation regulation; telephone regulation	AMTRAK; coastal zone development	tourism promotion
Low	broadcasting regulation	merchant marine subsidies; aviation promotion	oceanographic and fisheries research

reputation for policy leadership find issues in the high-salience, low-conflict cells uniquely attractive, while they ordinarily avoid as unrewarding and perilous those issues that tend toward the lower left-hand cells (low-salience, high-conflict).

Other areas offer more ambiguous incentives. As constituency-servers, legislators are drawn to those distributive policies that fall, by and large, under the low-conflict, low-salience designation, but they are increasingly unlikely to see such service as greatly enhancing their public or in-house reputation. The lure of public salience may overcome the perils of conflict, leading members into high-salience, high-conflict areas like health care delivery and environmental protection. The result, however, can be politically costly. The difficulties that an assembly structured like the Congress presents to such broad-gauged initiatives represent an added disincentive to serious effort.

Thus far we have identified some of the environmental conditions that influence the propensity of committees to take up particular policy questions. These conditions also influence the *content* of a committee's policy moves. The presence of public salience, for example, may dampen particularism (that is, the tendency to defer to the best-organized clientele groups) even as it enhances an issue's attractiveness. As airline deregulation and the cost of telephone service have become more salient issues, members have become more inclined to get "out in front" on those issues and less inclined to take their cues solely from the established carriers. Similarly, the presence of conflict may trigger the often-noted congressional tendency to recast redistributive and regulatory measures in some sort of positive-sum form. The comprehensive "rewrite" of the Communications Act of 1934 put forward by

Communications Subcommittee Chairman Lionel Van Deerlin (D-Calif.) in the 95th and 96th Congresses contained numerous plums—unlimited license terms for local stations, for example, and a development fund for public broadcasting—designed (vainly, as it turned out) to head off the crossfire among contending interests that otherwise was sure to sink the proposal.

These examples also show that the situational conditions a committee confronts are not immutable; unpromising issues can become more attractive, and vice versa. The court-ordered breakup of the American Telephone and Telegraph Co., for example, has greatly increased the salience of telephone regulation. "Many members now feel compelled to get involved," a House Commerce aide reports. But members do not merely react; their actions often enhance the attractiveness of an issue. Policy entrepreneurship is not simply a matter of responding to favorable conditions. It also involves the active building of salience and tempering of conflict. Of course, members are not absolutely bound by these conditions; their purposes and interests may lead them to idiosyncratic applications of the profit calculations we have imputed to them or to the abandonment of such calculations altogether. The delineation of the incentives and constraints offered by the policy environment does not offer a determinate picture of committee behavior. It merely shows, given the normal desires for re-election and political influence, what sorts of issues are likely to attract committee attention most readily.

Conclusion

The impact of committees on the congressional policy process can be examined at two levels. The committee system as a whole both reflects and reinforces congressional particularism and fragmentation; its persistence can be understood in terms of the weakness of alternative organizational forces and the "fit" between the committee system and the re-election and power needs of individual members. Committee government gives Congress important strengths in policymaking. It ensures attention to constituency-based needs and interests and provides a forum for the publicizing of a wide assortment of problems and proposals, converting the energies and ambitions of its members into institutionally useful activities. On the other hand, committee government often makes it more difficult for Congress to act in high-conflict areas and to achieve overall fiscal and policy coordination.

The power granted to the control committees, the reliance on the president for priority-setting and political mobilization, and the strengthening of party leadership and caucus authority can all be seen as correctives, not always compatible with one another, to the shortcomings and excesses of committee government. But other "reforms" have reinforced the system's basic fragmentation and particularism. A large-scale organizational reversal seems unlikely because most members have a strong stake in continuing the present system, whatever its shortcomings from an institutional perspective.

To this general view must be added an examination of committees in their particularity, for Congress's policy product reflects not only the strengths, weaknesses, and biases imparted by the system as a whole, but also the differences that individual committees display as they develop lives of their own. Of prime importance are the purposes, ideologies, and identifications that members bring to the committee and the nature of the policy environment they face—the threats of opposition or pre-emption from influential groups and agencies, the prospects for support and alliance, the profits and costs of involvement as determined by levels of conflict and public salience. To this basic delineation of member and environmental characteristics must be added an understanding of the committee as an organization with its own ethos, leadership style, level and style of partisanship, and internal allocation of authority and resources. It is these factors that mediate and shape the efforts of individual members and thus help determine what the committee as a collectivity finally produces.

NOTES

1. Bruce I. Oppenheimer, "Congress and the New Obstructionism: Developing an Energy Program," in *Congress Reconsidered,* 2nd ed., edited by Lawrence C. Dodd and Bruce I. Oppenheimer (Washington, D.C.: CQ Press, 1981), chap. 12.
2. Woodrow Wilson, *Congressional Government* (New York: Houghton Mifflin Co., 1913), p. 78.
3. "Distributive policies are characterized by the ease with which they can be disaggregated and dispensed unit by small unit, each unit more or less in isolation from other units and from any general rule." Theodore Lowi, "American Business, Public Policy, Case-Studies, and Political Theory," *World Politics* 16 (July 1964): 690.
4. See David E. Price, *Who Makes the Laws?* (Cambridge: Schenkman Publishing Co., 1972), pp. 2-6. For a summary account of the division of labor on 13 major bills, see pp. 289-297.
5. See the discussion in David E. Price, *Bringing Back the Parties* (Washington, D.C.: CQ Press, 1984), pp. 56-60.
6. David R. Mayhew, *Congress: The Electoral Connection* (New Haven: Yale University Press, 1974), pp. 49-77.
7. See "A New Old Guard Has Come Forward in the House," *National Journal,* August 13, 1977, pp. 1264-1269; and "Freshmen in the Senate Being Seen—and Heard," *National Journal,* March 17, 1979, pp. 439-443.
8. James Sterling Young, *The Washington Community, 1800-1828* (New York: Harcourt, Brace & World, 1966), pp. 132-133, 151.
9. Mayhew, *Congress,* pp. 110-125.
10. This and subsequent quotations are from personal interviews with members of the House Committee on Energy and Commerce.

11. For some cases in point see Albert R. Hunt, "The 'Show Horse': Rep. Pressler Works Hard to Create Image, Not to Create Laws," *Wall Street Journal,* May 20, 1977, p. 1; and Hunt, " 'Popsicle Brigade': New GOP Legislators Impress Their Seniors, Though Not Favorably," *Wall Street Journal,* December 14, 1981, p. 1. For an empirical validation of the show horse-work horse typology, see James L. Payne, "Show Horses and Work Horses in the United States House of Representatives," *Polity* 12 (Spring 1980): 428-456.

12. Stephen K. Bailey, *Congress in the Seventies* (New York: St. Martin's Press, 1970), chaps. 4-5.

13. Mayhew, *Congress,* p. 146.

14. Richard F. Fenno, Jr., *Congressmen in Committees* (Boston: Little, Brown & Co., 1973), pp. 48-49.

15. See Timothy B. Clark, "Appropriations Committees Losing Their Grip on Spending," *National Journal,* July 22, 1978, 1169-1174; Diane Granat, "House Appropriations Panel Doles Out Cold Federal Cash, Chafes at Budget Procedures," *Congressional Quarterly Weekly Report,* June 18, 1983, pp. 1209-1215; and Steven S. Smith and Christopher J. Deering, *Committees in Congress* (Washington, D.C.: CQ Press, 1984), pp. 93-95.

16. Five of the House Budget Committee's members must come from Appropriations, 5 from Ways and Means, and 17 from other committees. No member may serve on Budget for more than 6 years out of a 10-year period.

17. Allen Shick, *Congress and Money* (Washington, D.C.: The Urban Institute, 1980), p. 361; see also Joel Havemann, *Congress and the Budget* (Bloomington: Indiana University Press, 1978), pp. 131-133, 163-173.

18. See Allen Schick, *Reconciliation and the Congressional Budget Process* (Washington, D.C.: American Enterprise Institute for Public Policy Research, 1981); and Schick, "The Budget as an Instrument of Presidential Policy," in *The Reagan Presidency and the Governing of America,* ed. Lester M. Salamon and Michael S. Lund (Washington, D.C.: The Urban Institute, 1985).

19. Andy Plattner, "New Rules Committee Head Expected to Carry Forward in Tradition of Rep. Bolling," *Congressional Quarterly Weekly Report,* November 6, 1982, p. 2802. See also Smith and Deering, *Committees in Congress,* 91-93.

20. Mayhew, *Congress,* pp. 154-155.

21. Fenno, *Congressmen in Committees,* pp. xiii-xv.

22. Ibid., pp. 1-14, 47-49, 57-59.

23. See Norman J. Ornstein and David W. Rohde, "Shifting Forces, Changing Roles, and Political Outcomes: The Impact of Congressional Change on Four House Committees," in *New Perspectives on the House of Representatives,* 3rd ed., edited by Robert L. Peabody and Nelson W. Polsby (Chicago: Rand McNally & Co., 1977), pp. 198, 249.

24. "New Setbacks for House Seniority System," *Congressional Quarterly Weekly Report,* February 3, 1979, p. 183; and "House Liberals Retain Clout on Foreign Affairs Panel," *Congressional Quarterly Weekly Report,* February 7, 1981, p. 263.

25. See Linda E. Demkovich, "The Cautious Approach of Cannon's Commerce Committee," *National Journal,* May 27, 1978, pp. 846-850; Nadine Cohodas, "Kennedy and Rodino: How Two Very Different Chairmen Run Their Panels," *Congressional Quarterly Weekly Report,* February 2, 1980, pp. 267-271; and

Jacqueline Calmes, "Fernand St. Germain's Banking Committee," *Congressional Quarterly Weekly Report*, September 8, 1984, pp. 2198-2205.

26. David E. Price, "The Impact of Reform: The House Commerce Subcommittee on Oversight and Investigations," in *Legislative Reform: The Policy Impact*, ed. Leroy N. Rieselbach (Lexington, Mass.: Lexington Press, 1978), pp. 153-154.

27. Susan Webb Hammond, "Congressional Change and Reform: Staffing the Congress," in *Legislative Reform*, p. 185. Figures for 1984 were furnished by William McW. Cochrane, Democratic Staff Director, Senate Committee on Rules and Administration.

28. See David E. Price, "Professionals and 'Entrepreneurs': Staff Orientations and Policymaking on Three Senate Committees," *Journal of Politics* 33 (May 1971): 316-336. On the political role of staff more generally, see Michael J. Malbin, *Unelected Representatives* (New York: Basic Books, 1980).

29. For a discussion of the factors making for overall similarities and marginal (but consequential) differences in partisanship between House-Senate counterpart committees in two instances—Commerce, and Education and Labor/Labor and Public Welfare, see David E. Price et al., *The Commerce Committees* (New York: Grossman, 1975), pp. 50-55; Price, *Who Makes the Laws?*, pp. 261-264, 273-277; and Fenno, *Congressmen in Committees*, pp. 83-87, 174-177.

30. Smith and Deering, *Committees in Congress*, pp. 128-130.

31. Ibid., pp. 131-137, 149-153.

32. Note, however, the resistance Judiciary's subcommittee leaders offered to the centralizing moves of both Kennedy and Strom Thurmond (R-S.C.), who became chairman in 1981. Cohodas, "Kennedy and Rodino"; and Nadine Cohodas, "Senate Judiciary's Tenor Shows Dramatic Shift," *Congressional Quarterly Weekly Report*, January 24, 1981, pp. 184-185.

33. David Maraniss, "Powerful Energy Panel Turns on Big John's Axis," *Washington Post*, May 15, 1983; Maraniss, "Power Struggle Splits Democrats on Energy Panel," *Washington Post*, May 17, 1983; and Andy Plattner, "Scrappy House Energy Panel Provides High Pressure Arena for Wrangling Over Regulation," *Congressional Quarterly Weekly Report*, March 12, 1983, pp. 501-508.

34. Price, "Impact of Reform," pp. 133, 153-155.

35. Fenno, *Congressmen in Committees*, p. 15.

36. Ibid., pp. 30-35, 226-242. See also Helen Dewar, "Twilight of the House Education and Labor Committee," *Washington Post*, national weekly edition, October 1, 1984, p. 13.

37. This discussion is adapted from David E. Price, *Policymaking in Congressional Committees: The Impact of "Environmental" Factors* (Tucson: University of Arizona Press, 1979).

8. SUBCOMMITTEES IN CONGRESS

Christopher J. Deering and Steven S. Smith

For well over a century, committees have been regarded as the primary work groups in Congress.[1] Throughout that time most committees created subcommittees to assist in their work, but these subcommittees attracted little attention. Indeed, until 1972, subcommittees were not even listed in the *Congressional Directory*. Today, scholars and practitioners increasingly argue that Congress in its subcommittees is Congress at work.[2] Some have gone so far as to characterize the congressional system as "subcommittee government."[3]

If true, this shift from committee to subcommittee dominance is one of the major changes in Congress during the past two or three decades. The purpose of this chapter is to examine that proposition. Does subcommittee government—that is, the making of public policy by autonomous subcommittees—accurately describe the modern Congress? The core of this chapter examines changes in the behavior of congressional committees from the late 1960s to the 1980s, highlighting the relationship between committees and their subcommittees.[4] The analysis demonstrates that Congress has moved in the *direction* of subcommittee government over the past two decades, but the *degree* to which subcommittees now dominate Congress is another matter. The House has moved toward subcommittee government far more rapidly than the Senate, and in both chambers standing committees retain considerable power.

These arguments highlight both the growing importance of subcommittees and the very different roles that subcommittees play within the various committees and the two chambers. The chapter proceeds by focusing on the growth of subcommittees, their legislative roles, and the variation in those roles among standing committees.[5]

The Growth of Subcommittees

The emergence of subcommittees began in the nineteenth century when standing committees would occasionally divide their members into different policy groups in order to manage committee workloads. By 1915 about 35 House committees and 27 Senate committees used formal subcommittees on a regular basis. About half of those committees had permanent or standing subcommittees.[6] These subcommittees varied greatly in size, jurisdiction, resources, and influence.[7] By the late 1940s each chamber had approximately 60 subcommittees.[8] The number of subcommittees gradually increased during the 1950s and 1960s, reaching more than 120 in both the House and Senate by 1970.

The growing number of subcommittees had roots in the practical problems involved in managing larger and more complex workloads, in the desire of larger numbers of senior members for positions of leadership, and in isolated efforts within individual committees to loosen the tight control of committee activity by full committee chairs.[9] In some cases the chairs of less important committees—especially in the Senate where members held at least two full committee assignments—tried to induce committee members to become more active on their panels by offering them the opportunity to chair a subcommittee.

Subcommittees normally served as important political tools of the full committee chairs, who determined the subcommittee structure and membership. In a few instances, chairs withheld clear policy assignments from their subcommittees, allowing them to refer legislation to subcommittees that would act in closest accord with their own views. By chairing a subcommittee as well as directing full committee affairs, a committee chair and a small group of friendly colleagues could completely dominate a committee's consideration of legislation. And a few chairs, most notably those of the Senate Finance and House Ways and Means committees, refused to establish (or abolished existing) subcommittees in order to retain personal control of all legislation at the full committee level.

By the mid-1970s, full committee chairs' stranglehold on subcommittee decisionmaking loosened considerably. A series of reforms adopted by the House Democratic Caucus severely limited the formal powers and resources of full committee chairs in that chamber. These reforms deprived them of the power to create and appoint subcommittees, determine their jurisdictions, and set their agendas. Moreover, under a new House rule most committees were required to create at least four subcommittees. In turn, committee members were allowed to select their own subcommittee assignments, and subcommittee chairs were guaranteed staff, funding, written jurisdictions, referral of all appropriate legislation, and a chance to manage that legislation on the floor.

Jointly, these changes (many of which were part of the 1973 "Subcommittee Bill of Rights") represented, at least on paper, a significant shift in power away from full committee chairs and toward subcommittee chairs.[10] An additional rule change allowed each member of the majority party to chair only one legislative subcommittee, thereby distributing positions of power more widely than ever. In the Senate, no comparable reform of the role of full committee chairs or subcommittees was achieved during this period, although the number of subcommittee assignments senators could hold was limited in 1977.

Despite the addition of many new panels in the mid-1970s, the House has managed to halt the proliferation of subcommittees in recent Congresses—and on three committees it actually trimmed the number of subcommittees. In fact, if the subcommittees of Ways and Means, which had no subcommittees for 16 years prior to the reforms, and the two new standing committees are excluded, the number of subcommittees of the remaining House committees actually fell marginally from 120 to 118 between 1973 and 1984. This decline is partly the result of a cap on subcommittees adopted by House Democrats in 1981.[11] Consequently, no House committee increased the number of its subcommittees at the start of the 97th or 98th Congress, the first Congresses since 1947 in which that happened. And the average number of subcommittee assignments per member dropped back to about 3.5 after exceeding four subcommittees per member in 1975-1976.[12] The House, then, has an effective floor set by chamber rules and a ceiling set by majority party caucus rules on the number of subcommittees.

The number of Senate subcommittees on standing committees fell from 127 to 90 between 1973 and 1979 as a result of limits placed on subcommittee assignments and chairs in 1977. The mean number of subcommittee assignments per senator also dropped from nearly ten to just under seven. Nevertheless, when Republicans gained control of the Senate in 1981, they increased the number of subcommittees by two on Judiciary and by one on Commerce. Two years later, Commerce and Small Business each added a subcommittee, and Banking added two subcommittees, increasing its number of subcommittees to more than at any time since 1949. The average number of subcommittees per senator also began to creep back up. In 1977, nearly 80 percent of the Senate had between six and eight subcommittee assignments on standing committees. By 1983, senators were regularly ignoring these limits. In fact, the number of senators with more than eight subcommittees nearly tripled to 32 by 1983.[13]

The Senate retains far greater variation in committee structure than does the House because of the absence of an explicit floor or ceiling for Senate subcommittees. The Senate has had more committees with numerous subcommittees and more committees with few subcommittees than the House. In the 98th Congress, for example, the average number of subcommittees per committee is nearly identical for the two chambers, but the Senate has five committees with nine or more subcommittees and three with no subcommittees, while the House has only one committee with more than nine subcommittees and one with no subcommittees.

Variation in committee structure also means variation in the distribution of the positions of power. Not surprisingly, as the number of formal positions of power expanded, so did the number of members holding such positions. From 1955 to 1968 the proportion of House majority party members chairing at least one committee or subcommittee increased from 27.2 percent to 44.9 percent.[14] By 1979, with the help of the reforms between 1971 and 1975, more than half the majority members (52.1 percent) chaired at least one committee or subcommittee. As with the increase in total subcommittees, positions of power in the House had been widely distributed by the 90th Congress, but the reforms served as an additional impetus to decentralize the committee system.

In the Senate, small numbers of majority members and large numbers of positions combine to create widespread participation. Even so, the proportion of majority party members holding at least one chair increased from 85.9 percent in the 90th Congress to 98.3 percent in the 96th Congress. Thus, even with the cutback in subcommittees forced by the 1977 reforms, Senate committee leadership positions are distributed nearly universally among majority party members.

Similar effects may be seen within the minority parties of the House and Senate. In the 96th Congress, for example, all Republican senators and 80 percent of Republican representatives were ranking minority members of committees or subcommittees. Similar distributions of ranking committee positions were present in the 97th and 98th Congresses.

The Role of Subcommittees

The presence of numerous subcommittees and chairs, even when bolstered by rules that grant subcommittees some independence from parent committees, does not guarantee a decisionmaking pattern that is properly labeled "subcommittee government." Independence in activity does not necessarily provide autonomy in decisionmaking, although independence in activity is probably a precondition for autonomy. The simple fact is that subcommittees remain the creatures of parent committees that may ignore or amend their recommendations.

Committees have developed a variety of roles for their subcommittees; thus, simple characterizations of committees as centralized or decentralized do not capture the rich diversity of orientations that have evolved in standing committees. To explore this variety, four important aspects of subcommittee activities and resources are examined: the amount of *legislation reported to the floor* that was considered by subcommittees, the number of *meetings and hearings* held by subcommittees, patterns of *bill management,* and the level of subcommittee *staff resources.*

Reported Legislation

Virtually every piece of legislation passed by Congress is first referred to a committee, where hearings are held, final language is drafted (marked up), and a vote is taken to report it to the floor. As subcommittees have expanded their roles, a similar process has been carried out increasingly at the subcommittee level *prior* to full committee action. This means that, in many cases, subcommittees assume the initial responsibility for discussing and drafting major legislation. And, in the absence of full committee review, these decisions may determine the legislative fate of many bills. In order to examine how, or whether, these responsibilities have shifted, the amount of legislation referred to and reported from subcommittees and the number of hearings and meetings held by subcommittees were tabulated for the 91st Congress (1969-1970), prior to the reforms, and the 96th Congress (1979-1980).

The percentage of legislation referred to House subcommittees more than doubled between the 91st Congress and the 96th Congress. (See Table 8-1.) Until the 1970s, many full committee chairs did not bother to refer legislation to subcommittee if it was not likely to be taken up by the full committee. This meant, of course, that full committee chairs could retain control of legislation they did not support. But since 1975, when the 1973 Subcommittee Bill of Rights was implemented in most House committees, subcommittees have become the dungeons in which most legislation dies in the House.

More importantly, there is much less change in the path of legislation eventually reported to the House floor. Even in the late 1960s, most legislation brought to the floor had been referred to subcommittee at least at some point in committee deliberations, if only for a hearing. Since the reforms, several House committees have adopted rules to keep certain types of legislation at the full committee. For example, the House Ways and Means Committee keeps legislation amending the Internal Revenue Code at the full committee. And several House committees hold completed Senate bills at the full committee, especially late in a congressional session when there is no

Table 8-1 Legislation Referred to and Reported from Standing Committees That Was Referred to Subcommittee or Was the Subject of a Subcommittee Hearing (in percent)

	Congress	
	91st	*96th*
House		
Referred	35.7	79.8
Reported	75.4	80.0
Senate		
Referred	41.5	41.1
Reported	40.0	44.8

NOTE: Excludes House and Senate Appropriations committees and House Rules Committee because they do not publish comparable committee calendars. Excludes matters related to executive nominations.

SOURCE: House and Senate committee calendars.

chance of further action or when similar legislation already has been reported to the floor. Thus, not all referred or reported legislation is sent to subcommittee.

In contrast, the aggregate Senate pattern remains unchanged. A majority of both referred and reported legislation is not sent to subcommittee. The Senate retains a far more committee-oriented process than does the House: all committee senators can participate fully in shaping major legislation.

Subcommittee Meetings

The pattern of committee and subcommittee meetings and hearings confirms the chamber differences. The percentage of House meetings and hearings held by subcommittees increased greatly during the 1970s. (See Table 8-2.) Today, nearly all House hearings are held by subcommittees. Subcommittee chairs usually control the timing and content of their hearings, and full committee chairs pursue most of their own interests through the subcommittees they chair rather than by using the full committee.

The key change is that a majority of meetings at which substantive policy decisions are made ("mark-ups") are now held by subcommittees in the House. The reforms had a clear effect, as is suggested by the presence of greater change in the 1970s than in the 1960s. Subcommittees gained the authority and resources with which to make substantive policy decisions. And yet the figures also demonstrate that full committee meetings are still not greatly outnumbered by subcommittee meetings, even though House full committees are outnumbered by subcommittees by more than 6-to-1. The

Table 8-2   Standing Committee Meetings and Hearings Held by Subcommittees (in percent)

	Congress		
	86th	*91st*	*96th*
House			
Meetings	45.6	47.9	56.1
Hearings	72.3	77.0	90.7
Senate			
Meetings	27.1	30.6	19.1
Hearings	77.7	79.6	65.2

NOTE: The House Appropriations Committee is excluded because it does not report its meetings in the *Daily Digest*. The table excludes meetings and hearings on nominations.

SOURCE: *Congressional Record, Daily Digest.*

pattern of meetings indicates, therefore, that while the House has clearly moved toward subcommittee government, committee activities still represent a mixed pattern of subcommittee and full committee involvement. The most common decisionmaking pattern has three stages: subcommittee hearings, subcommittee mark-up, and full committee mark-up.

Full committee activity continues to be significant in House members' daily routines. A study of their allocation of time in 1977, based upon daily logs kept by appointment secretaries, indicated that House Democrats spent 53 percent of their time on full committee activities.[15] While only 37 percent of the time spent in hearings was in full committee hearings, 64 percent of the time spent by Democrats in mark-up was at the full committee level. Similar allocations of time were found for Republican representatives. A survey conducted in 1976 disclosed that 82 percent of the responding House members rated their work "in subcommittees to develop legislation" as "very important," while 71 percent considered their full committee work to develop legislation very important.[16] Again, the appropriate interpretation is that the most common House decisionmaking pattern is one of mixed committee and subcommittee participation.

In the Senate, the longstanding pattern of subcommittee hearings and full committee mark-up remains. (See Table 8-2.) Most Senate committees operate on the assumption that subcommittee mark-ups are an inefficient use of senators' scarce time when the effort will often be repeated at the full committee anyway. As one Senate committee staff director explained:

> We tried a subcommittee mark-up a couple of years ago, but we could only get two senators to show. They just decided to get together over lunch and make some recommendations to the committee without taking formal action. We haven't tried it since.[17]

Despite the Senate's propensity to create new subcommittees, the pattern of meetings and hearings shows no discernible movement toward subcommittee government. Indeed, the percentage of Senate meetings held in subcommittee in recent Congresses is still lower than the House percentage of 25 years ago.

An examination of committee-specific patterns shows that House committees have generally moved in the direction suggested by the aggregate patterns, some quite dramatically, although several committees (for example, Education and Labor, and Interior) had active, independent subcommittees in the 1960s. In the Senate, on the other hand, several committees have substantially weakened the role of their subcommittees. For example, the Commerce and Energy committees discontinued the use of subcommittees to mark up legislation in the 1970s. In the case of Commerce, the change was made abruptly when Nevada's Howard Cannon became chair. The shift away from subcommittees was more gradual in the case of Energy and Natural Resources and was associated with a change in the committee's agenda and subcommittee attendance problems.

Bill Management

Each bill coming to the House or Senate floor is "managed" by a member who assumes the responsibility of gaining passage for the legislation. A "bill manager" or "floor manager" sometimes must work hard to build a majority for the legislation and to protect it against potentially crippling amendments. The skills of the bill manager can be decisive. At other times, managing legislation is merely an administrative duty. But even then, bill management can have great symbolic importance, indicating who should take credit for the legislation and providing an opportunity for a member to gain additional visibility inside and outside of Congress.[18]

Since 1971, the Democratic Caucus in the House has directed committee chairs to allow subcommittee chairs to manage bills on the floor whenever possible.[19] For most full committee chairs, this rule change presented no problem. For example, upon taking over the Interior Committee in 1973, James A. Haley expressed his willingness to have subcommittee chairs manage their own bills on the floor:

> I want the chairmen of the subcommittees who hear the testimony and . . .
> have the responsibility of writing the bill to take it to the floor and explain
> it. I'll be glad to help them out when I can but I don't want to stand in the
> way of . . . the man who has done the work [so] I take all the bows. . . . If
> it's a good bill, fine, let him take the credit. If it's a bad bill, let him take
> that.[20]

There has been no need for such a rule change in the more open Senate, where members have traditionally managed their own legislation on the floor.

House subcommittee chairs, rather than the chairs of the full committees, now manage most of the bills that reach the floor. (See Table 8-3.) Despite this shift, the full committee chairs still manage legislation out of proportion to their numbers. In the 95th Congress, for example, 18 full committee chairs managed more than 28 percent of the bills in the House. The remaining 72 percent of the bills were managed by 104 different members. Therefore, when compared with what the average subcommittee chair manages, most full committee chairs remain very active participants, although subcommittee chairs in the House are much more active than they were prior to the reforms.

Most of the change in the overall pattern of House bill management is accounted for by four policy-oriented committees (Banking, Commerce, Education and Labor, Judiciary) and by Armed Services, Interior, and Ways and Means. The number of bills managed by the full committee chairs dropped significantly in all of these committees. The two constituency-oriented committees, Armed Services and Interior, have always had broad participation by subcommittee chairs, even though they have evolved to even lower levels of full committee chair management. In contrast, three of the four policy committees and Ways and Means have all had periods of full committee chair dominance. There are few exceptions to this overall trend

Table 8-3 House and Senate Bill Managers by Position, Selected Congresses (in percent)

Position	*Congress* 86th	89th	91st	92nd	93rd	94th	95th
House							
Full Committee Chairs	54.1	48.3	40.0	39.4	35.7	30.8	28.4
Subcommittee Chairs	30.3	41.8	49.0	49.4	53.1	63.3	66.9
Others	15.6	10.0	11.1	11.2	11.1	5.9	4.9
Total Number of Bills	492	603	588	587	652	707	796
Senate							
Full Committee Chairs	15.3		14.3				13.6
Subcommittee Chairs	30.6		26.8				21.9
Majority Leader	12.7		23.2				45.2
Others	41.4		35.7				19.4
Total Number of Bills	353		414				640

SOURCE: *Congressional Record.*

toward management of bills by subcommittee chairs. The activist Rep. Jack Brooks has markedly increased the management of bills by the full committee chair on Government Operations. And the chairs of the Veterans' Affairs Committee generally manage most of that committee's few bills.

In the Senate, a large portion of the routine floor business is now managed by the Majority Leader. During the 86th Congress, the Majority Leader managed only 12.7 percent of the bills that reached the floor, but with the burgeoning Senate workload this responsibility expanded dramatically. By the 95th Congress, the Majority Leader, Democrat Robert Byrd, managed 45.2 percent of the bills that reached the floor. Virtually all of them passed on a voice vote and without debate. Of the remaining bills, 21.9 percent were handled by subcommittee chairs, 19.4 percent by members who did not chair the subcommittee, and 13.6 percent by the full committee chairs. The major change represented in Table 8-3 is the shift away from the "other" category and toward the routine handling of business by the Majority Leader. This has been an efficiency mechanism used to speed the handling of minor legislation on the floor.

Unlike the House, subcommittee chairs in the Senate actually managed a smaller portion (but a larger absolute number) of the bills that reached the floor in the 95th Congress than in either the 91st or the 86th Congress. In the Senate, virtually all bills are managed by the bill's sponsor (or by the Majority Leader in the sponsor's absence), so participation is tied more closely to individual initiative than to subcommittee government. In the 95th Congress, 75 different senators (including 19 minority party Republicans) managed at least one bill on the floor. In contrast, almost all of the 122 bill managers in the House held a majority committee leadership position.

Staffing Patterns

The final indicator of subcommittee orientation is the use of committee staff. For many years the two chambers followed roughly parallel tracks in the use and development of committee staff. Committee staff for both the House and Senate was provided by the Legislative Reorganization Act of 1946. In both chambers, the staffs were typically small (by today's standards), centralized, and controlled by the full committee chair. This remained true in 1970 when a new Legislative Reorganization Act authorized a major boost in committee staff levels and provided staff assistance for the minority party for the first time. Since then, the House and Senate have followed distinctly different tracks, although both have increased overall staff levels. The House, as a result of Democratic Caucus rule changes, has moved toward increasingly independent subcommittee staffing—a move that is consistent with the subcommittee government thesis. The Senate generally has retained centralized committee staffing while increasing the staff resources of individual members—a move that is consistent with a characterization of the Senate as individualistic rather than decentralized.

As a result of the 1970 act and subsequent funding increases, House and Senate committee staffs increased in size over the next decade. (See Table 8-4.) House committee and subcommittee staff more than tripled between the 91st and 96th Congresses (1969-1980). Senate committee and subcommittee staffs increased by about 80 percent. The different rates of increase for the House and Senate can be attributed to the centralization of most Senate committee staffs under the control of committee chairs and their staff directors. Senate full committee staffs have increased in both absolute and relative terms since 1970 while Senate subcommittee staffs have grown at a much slower rate than their House counterparts. Indeed, half of all subcommittee staff in the Senate in 1970 belonged to a single committee—Judiciary. By 1980, the Judiciary and Government Affairs committees, which had grown steadily during the period, employed 228 of the 312 subcommittee staff in the Senate. Thus, a better understanding of these shifts requires a look at committee specific patterns of staffing.

In 1970, 12 House committees had no subcommittee staff. Of the seven committees with staff at the subcommittee level, only Appropriations and Government Operations had clearly decentralized modes of operation. By 1980, nearly all House committees (the exceptions being Armed Services, District of Columbia, and Veterans' Affairs) had formally created separate

Table 8-4   Distribution of Senate and House Standing Committee and Subcommittee Staff, 91st-97th Congress (in percent)*

	Congress						
	91st	*92nd*	*93rd*	*94th*	*95th*	*96th*	*97th*
House							
Full Committee	76.8	72.3	63.6	67.2	61.2	57.0	60.2
Subcommittee	23.2	27.7	36.4	32.8	38.8	43.0	39.8
Total Number of Staff	461	575	664	1,083	1,250	1,608	1,507
Senate							
Full Committee	57.9**	55.4	59.5	67.9	72.3	65.4	67.5
Subcommittee	42.1	44.6	40.5	32.1	27.7	34.5	32.5
Total Number of Staff	504	635	775	859	869	902	906

* Excludes select and special committees.
** Without the Senate Judiciary Committee the figures for full and subcommittee staff are 78.2 and 21.8, respectively. Judiciary similarly affects the figures throughout the period.
SOURCE: *Congressional Staff Directory.*

subcommittee staffs. On seven committees total subcommittee staff equaled or exceeded that at the full committee and on only two other committees did it fail to reach at least 30 percent. But, overall, subcommittee staff still represent less than half of all committee staff.

Staffing patterns in the Senate remained much more stable during the 1970s. In fact, while total subcommittee staff increased by 100, the proportion of subcommittee staff actually declined. The number of committees employing separate subcommittee staff also declined by one. This may be a bit misleading, however, in that only two committees, Judiciary and Government Operations, employed subcommittee staff of any consequence in 1970.[21] By 1979, three committees had well-developed subcommittee staffs—Appropriations having been added to the group when Senator Warren Magnuson became the chair. Nonetheless, committee staff in the Senate, relative to the House, have been and remain highly centralized—additional evidence that subcommittee government has yet to take hold in that chamber.

Patterns of Subcommittee Orientation

The preceding analysis indicates that committees vary considerably in the extent to which they have become more subcommittee oriented and that the two chambers differ dramatically in this regard. In this section, the overall shift toward subcommittees and specific patterns of subcommittee orientations are evaluated for the 91st and 96th Congresses.

Change in Subcommittee Orientation

Overall, House committees have become more subcommittee oriented than Senate committees. This is clearly visible in a composite measure of "subcommittee orientation" calculated as the average of the percentage of reported legislation receiving subcommittee consideration, the percentage of meetings held at the subcommittee level, the percentage of bills managed by subcommittee chairs, and the percentage of total committee staff employed by the subcommittees in the 91st and the 96th Congresses.[22] The findings are straightforward.

Based on these four indicators, House committees had an average "subcommittee orientation" of 47 percent in 1969-1970 and of 62 percent in 1979-1980. In contrast, Senate committees became (very marginally) more full committee oriented by 1980—dropping from 26 to 25 percent. Thirteen of the 17 House committees examined became more subcommittee oriented while 8 of the 13 Senate committees included became more full committee oriented.

The House move toward more active subcommittees was related at least partially to members' goals.[23] Over the years, observers of congressional committees have found it useful to categorize House committees according to the dominant political goals of the members who serve on those committees. Some committees, they found, attract members primarily concerned about the pursuit of personal policy interests. Other committees seem to attract members primarily concerned with re-election and serving constituency interests. Still other committees have attracted members because of their importance within the chambers and the power and prestige they confer. Similar distinctions can be made for Senate committees, although senators appear to hold these goals less intensely than do representatives. For each of these categories, different decisionmaking processes have been identified that are related to the goals of the members. These same goals also are related to the role of subcommittees within House committees, with no consistent relationship in the Senate.

In the 91st Congress, policy-oriented committees and constituency-oriented committees in the House had almost identical averages on the subcommittee orientation index—48.5 and 47.5, respectively. But by the 96th Congress, the policy committees became decidedly more subcommittee oriented on average than constituency committees—70.3 and 59.3, respectively. Thus, within the House the policy committees accounted for the lion's share of the move toward greater subcommittee activity and resources during the 1970s.

Part of the explanation for this lies in the move by policy-oriented members—on Banking, Commerce, Education and Labor, Foreign Affairs, and Judiciary—to seize the opportunity presented by new procedures and resources to pursue their personal policy interests. Subcommittees provided a very attractive vehicle for this. In contrast, the constituency committees, which depend more upon consensus or, perhaps more accurately, mutual noninterference in their operations, proved to be less intent on exploiting the new procedures and resources. The Post Office and Civil Service Committee, with major increases in subcommittee staff and bill management by subcommittee chairs, and the Public Works Committee, with major increases in hearings on reported legislation and bill management, are the most dramatic exceptions to this trend.

No similar differences between type of committees appear in the Senate. In large part this is because senators, who have more committee assignments and a traditionally more open process, are less dependent upon committee assignments to pursue personal goals. Senators also have greater personal resources at their disposal than do members of the House. As a result, subcommittees have been less vital to personal goal achievement in the Senate.

Types of Subcommittee Orientation

What is the overall orientation of committees toward their subcommittees? Do they allow subcommittees a substantial share of their resources and activities? A positive response would be a strong indicator of subcommittee government. Do they retain a large share of their resources and perform most of their work themselves, suggesting the predominance of committee government? Or do committees rely on some mixture of the two?

To answer these questions, the committees have been classified as high or low on each of the indicators, with 50 percent and up as high and 49 percent and below as low. With four indicators, there are 16 possible approaches to subcommittee usage, ranging from committees that are high across all four indicators to those that are low on all. Most committees fall into one of five types. These types, presented at the top of Table 8-5, characterize 23 of the 30 committees examined in the 91st Congress (1969-1970) and 24 of the 30 committees examined in the 96th (1979-1980). The remaining committees have patterns that are very similar to one of the five dominant types.[24] The distribution of committees across these five types and alterations in the distribution tell a great deal about the changing role of subcommittees. Before discussing the five committee patterns individually, two general observations must be mentioned.

First, as Table 8-5 makes clear, interchamber differences, noted earlier, appear once again. On balance, House committees have been and remain more subcommittee-oriented than Senate committees. In the 91st Congress the chambers are much less distinct—as the greater intermixture of House and Senate committees listed under each type demonstrates—than in the 96th Congress. The overall shift is accounted for primarily by House committees moving into the more subcommittee-oriented categories.

Table 8-5 Typology of Subcommittee Orientations, 91st and 96th Congresses

Indicators	Type				
	I	II	III	IV	V
Reported Legislation	High	High	High	High	Low
Bill Management	High	High	High	Low	Low
Meetings	High	High	Low	Low	Low
Subcommittee Staff	High	Low	Low	Low	Low

91st Congress Committees

I	II	III	IV	V
H-Gov't. Operations	H-House Admin.	H-Education & Labor	S-Interior	S-P.O. & Civil Service
S-Labor & Public Welfare	H-Judiciary	H-Interstate & Foreign Commerce	H-P.O. & Civil Service	S-Armed Services
	H-Merchant Marine & Fisheries	H-Veterans' Affairs	S-Agriculture & Forestry	S-Banking & Currency
	H-District of Col.	(S-Commerce)	S-District of Col.	S-Finance
	H-Armed Services			H-Banking & Currency
	H-Agriculture			S-Rules & Admin.
	(H-Interior & Insular Affairs)			S-Foreign Relations
	(H-Science & Astronautics)			H-Ways & Means
				(S-Public Works)

Indicators

Type

I	II	III	IV	V

96th Congress Committees

I	II	III	IV	V
H-Interstate & Foreign Commerce	H-Public Works & Transportation	H-P.O. & Civil Service	H-Veterans' Affairs	S-Banking, Housing & Urban Affairs
H-Judiciary	H-Interior & Insular Affairs	H-Foreign Affairs	S-Armed Services	S-Foreign Relations
H-Banking, Finance & Urban Affairs	H-House Admin.	H-Ways & Means	S-Energy & Nat. Resources	S-Finance
H-Science & Tech.	H-Armed Services	S-Labor & Human Resources	S-Comm., Science & Transportation	S-Veterans' Affairs
(H-Education & Labor)	H-Agriculture	S-Agriculture, Nutrition & Forestry	S-Gov't. Affairs	S-Rules & Admin.
(H-Merchant Marine & Fisheries)	H-District of Col.			(S-Environ. & Public Works)
(H-Gov't. Operations)				(S-Judiciary)

NOTE: Committees in parentheses are listed under the closest type. Committees where data for only three of the indicators were available are excluded: House Appropriations, Senate Appropriations, House Budget, Senate Budget, House Small Business, Senate Small Business, and Senate Aeronautical and Space Sciences. Four committees in the 91st Congress—Senate Government Operations, Senate Judiciary, House Public Works, and House Foreign Affairs—are not included because they are not sufficiently close to any of the categories.

Second, the patterns indicate that by the 96th Congress the 50 percent mark for referral of reported legislation to subcommittee is the easiest threshold for committees to achieve; 23 of the 30 committees fall into the high category on this indicator. Bill management follows with 20 of the 30 committees falling in the high category. Thus, a majority of the committees—decidedly more in the House than in the Senate, however—achieve this minimal level of emphasis on subcommittees.[25] In contrast, only 12 of the 30 committees have more meetings at the subcommittee level than at the full committee level and only 9 of the 30 have more staff at the subcommittee level. A scant four committees fall into the high category on all four indicators; in the 91st Congress only two committees fall into the high category on all four.

On the surface, Type I committees appear to be the most "decentralized," but appearances may be deceiving in this case. A more accurate statement would be that Type I committees have the most *active* subcommittees. In general, they feature independent, active, policy-oriented subcommittees. Nevertheless, these committees are not necessarily the prototypes of "subcommittee government." Part of the explanation for this is that five of the seven Type I committees are policy committees. Challenges to decisions made by Type I subcommittees are frequent at the full committee level, especially on the five policy committees. Thus, while the Type I subcommittees are active and independent, they are not necessarily autonomous.

Subcommittees on Type II committees demonstrate much greater autonomy than on Type I committees; all but the staff indicator falls into the high category. And yet the relative lack of staff on Type II committees actually reveals an important characteristic about them. In contrast to the Type I committees, four of the six Type II committees are constituency committees. Therefore, subcommittees on these panels tend to be differentiated along clientele-related lines. Unlike policy committees, constituency committees usually operate with an eye toward securing benefits for constituents rather than pursuing policy interests. As noted earlier, this yields a decisionmaking process characterized by mutual noninterference. On constituency committees, independent subcommittee staff, used on policy committees to serve the subcommittee chairs' needs and to fight battles at the full committee and on the floor, becomes much less desirable. And the full committee seems much more likely to "rubber stamp" the actions of Type II subcommittees than of Type I subcommittees. Hence, despite the lack of staff, these are actually better examples of subcommittee government than are Type I subcommittees.

Type III committees have subcommittees that are fairly active but less independent or autonomous than on either Type I or II committees. On at least four of these six committees—House Foreign Affairs, House Ways and Means, Senate Agriculture, and Senate Labor—the most important bills are usually reserved for the full committee. Thus, the percentage of subcommittee mark-ups on these committees is comparatively low, as is subcommittee staff, even though the percentage of subcommittee hearings tends to be high and subcommitee chairs tend to manage legislation referred to the subcommittees. These are clearly mixed cases, but certainly not examples of subcommittee government.

The remaining committees are essentially full committee oriented. Subcommittees on Type IV committees hold many hearings, but virtually all mark-ups are held in full committee. Type V committees are decidedly full committee oriented with subcommittees used primarily for limited hearings. With a single exception, House Veterans' Affairs, all of the Type IV and V committees are from the Senate; without exception, Type I and II committees· are from the House. This reflects the difference between the two chambers noted earlier.

Based on the evidence examined here, generalizations about subcommittee government should be tempered. A move toward more active, independent, and sometimes autonomous subcommittees is undeniable, and undeniably important, in the House. But committees differ considerably in this regard, as indicated by the typology of subcommittee orientation. In the Senate, virtually no move has been made toward subcommittee government. Indeed, some retrenchment may have occurred over the last five to ten years. The Senate continues to be a highly individualistic, rather than truly decentralized, legislative body.

The Significance of Subcommittees

Not surprisingly, the importance of subcommittees varies between the chambers. In the Senate, subcommittees are a component of an individualistic and flexible decisionmaking process. For individual senators—who have large personal staffs, many committee and subcommittee assignments, and greater national visibility than representatives—membership on a subcommittee, or the opportunity to chair it, is merely one resource among many. Indeed, in 1984 all but five majority party Republicans chaired at least two committees or subcommittees. Many chaired three or more. Compared with the typical representative, therefore, the typical senator is less dependent on any one subcommittee or subcommittee chair. And the legislative burdens associated with more assignments, larger constituencies, and national prestige make senators less likely to insist that their subcommittees be active, effective decisionmaking units. Few senators could tolerate such a burden on their daily schedules. Nevertheless, the staff, the opportunities to be associated with certain issues and causes, and the authority to call hearings continue to make subcommittees a valued resource.

In contrast, House subcommittees have developed a more thoroughly institutionalized role. This role is established not only in the rules of the House and the Democratic Caucus, but also in the interests of individual representatives. Although more representatives chair subcommittees in the

1980s than in the 1960s, still only about half of the majority party members are chairs of either committees or subcommittees. Representatives who do chair a subcommittee ordinarily chair only one. And this is usually the representative's major avenue of effective participation in the legislative process. House subcommittee chairs therefore have a greater incentive to take full advantage of their positions than do their Senate counterparts.

The independence acquired by House subcommittees and subcommittee chairs during the past two decades has had some negative consequences for rank-and-file members, full committee chairs, party leaders, and the policy process.[26] The number of meetings and hearings House members must attend has increased, approaching but not yet matching senators' workloads. There is a widespread feeling among representatives that they lack control over their own legislative schedules. Now they are less able to concentrate on only a few topics at a time or to specialize as they have in the past. They have become more dependent on staff and somewhat less dependent on close working relationships with colleagues.

The independence of House subcommittees and their chairs has increased at the expense of full committee chairs. On most House committees, full committee chairs can do very little to block a determined subcommittee chair's effort to hold hearings or write legislation. Accommodating the demands of committee colleagues is now the chairs' central activity. The net effect has been to create a more unpredictable, more unmanageable environment for full committee chairs. In fact, House chairs often find themselves in a more precarious position than many Senate chairs because of the explicit constraints on their authority. Senate full committee chairs often retain firm control of the flow of legislation to subcommittees, of the committee staff, and of the committee agenda, control that has been limited in the House by the reforms of the 1970s. House full committee chairs are now far more dependent on personal skills and resources to lead their committees.

For majority party leaders in the House, the rise of independent subcommittees has been a mixed blessing. No longer faced with committee chairs who maintain dictatorial control over committee business, party leaders now have more avenues of access to committee members and more ways to influence their decisions. There are more opportunities for party leaders, but there are also more opportunities for rank-and-file members, especially subcommittee chairs, to place demands on them. Party leaders now must consult and accommodate more members, which by itself makes leaders' jobs more difficult. Some subcommittee chairs, especially those who have served only two or three terms in the House, are not well known by party leaders, which makes chairs' demands and support less predictable.

In addition, it is important to recognize that subcommittee chairs are not true substitutes for the once dominant full committee chairs in the decisionmaking process of the House. On major issues, subcommittee chairs are in no position to guarantee party leaders that certain legislation will be reported to the floor in a particular form at a particular time. Many full committee chairs could do so in the 1950s and 1960s. Subcommittee chairs must coordinate their actions with the full committee chairs, work with full committee staff, and find majority support at the full committee even if they can steer their subcommittees as they wish. On balance, independent subcommittees have made the job of central party leaders more difficult by extending and multiplying the lines of communication for leaders and by increasing the number of effective participants placing demands on them.

Perhaps even more significantly, the nature of the policymaking process in the House has been altered in many areas as a result of having subcommittees assigned initial responsibility for writing legislation. First, less continuity exists in subcommittee membership than in full committee membership, limiting the "institutional memory" of subcommittees. Second, small size and narrow jurisdictions often narrow the political interests represented on the units with the initial responsibility to write legislation. And finally, independent subcommittees add obstacles to the legislative process by adding at least one more stage to an already complex process and by increasing the likelihood of jurisdictional fights between the more active subcommittees. In fact, some members and observers have blamed subcommittees for the immobilism they see in congressional decisionmaking.

These negative consequences of independent subcommittees should be kept in perspective. The Senate has not experienced a systematic trend toward more independent subcommittees during the last two decades. Even in the House, the role of subcommittees varies widely. Clientelism may be strengthened by independent subcommittees, but many interests that were locked out of congressional decisionmaking by powerful House full committee chairs now have several avenues of access through subcommittee chairs, members, and staff. Moreover, the problems of clientelism are less severe than they could be because full committees carefully review the work of subcommittees handling the most important, salient, and divisive issues. In addition, despite the recognition that subcommittees have made legislative work more demanding, most House members do not believe that their circumstances are less desirable today than in the 1960s. To the contrary, few rank-and-file members, especially majority party Democrats, would give up the enhanced role in policymaking that subcommittee independence has provided them.

In sum, congressional action is more circuitous with independent subcommittees, which may reinforce the effects of factionalism in Congress. But seldom is an intransigent subcommittee chair the cause of congressional inaction in the face of clear chamber majorities. Subcommittees play an increasingly strong role in Congress, but they do not govern the institution as completely as committees did at the height of their power.

NOTES

1. Woodrow Wilson, *Congressional Government* (Gloucester, Mass.: Peter Smith, 1885, 1923).
2. Roger H. Davidson, "Subcommittee Government: New Channels for Policy Making," in *The New Congress,* ed. Thomas E. Mann and Norman J. Ornstein (Washington, D.C.: American Enterprise Institute for Public Policy Research, 1981), pp. 99-133; Steven Haeberle, "The Institutionalization of Subcommittees in the U.S. House of Representatives," 40 *Journal of Politics* (1978): 1054-1065; Barbara Sinclair, "Majority Party Leadership Strategies for Coping with the New U.S. House," in *Understanding Congressional Leadership,* ed. Frank Mackaman (Washington, D.C.: CQ Press, 1981), pp. 181-206; Christopher J. Deering and Steven S. Smith, "Majority Party Leadership and the New House Subcommittee System," in *Understanding Congressional Leadership,* pp. 261-292; and Christopher J. Deering, "Subcommittee Government in the U.S. House: An Analysis of Bill Management," 7 *Legislative Studies Quarterly* (November 1982): 533-546. See also Chapter 2 in this collection.
3. For example, Dodd and Schott have argued that "by the mid-1970s, Congress had institutionalized subcommittee government." See Lawrence C. Dodd and Richard L. Schott, *Congress and the Administrative State* (New York: John Wiley & Sons, 1979), p. 124.
4. See also Norman J. Ornstein and David W. Rohde, "Shifting Forces, Changing Rules, and Political Outcomes: The Impact of Congressional Change on Four House Committees," in *New Perspectives on the House of Representatives,* 3rd ed., edited by Robert L. Peabody and Nelson W. Polsby (Chicago: Rand McNally, 1977), pp. 186-269.
5. For a more detailed discussion of the issues and data presented in this essay, see Steven S. Smith and Christopher J. Deering, *Committees in Congress* (Washington, D.C.: CQ Press, 1984).
6. Burton K. French, "Subcommittees of Congress," *American Political Science Review* (February 1915): 68-92.
7. George Goodwin, Jr., *The Little Legislatures: Committees of Congress* (Amherst: University of Massachusetts Press, 1970); and Charles O. Jones, "Representation in Congress: The Case of the House Agriculture Committee," 55 *American Political Science Review* (June 1961): 358-367.
8. George B. Galloway, *The Legislative Process in Congress* (New York: Thomas Y. Crowell Co., 1953), p. 594.
9. Lawrence C. Dodd and Bruce I. Oppenheimer, "The House in Transition: Change and Consolidation," in *Congress Reconsidered,* 1st ed., edited by Lawrence C. Dodd and Bruce I. Oppenheimer (New York: Praeger Publishers, 1977), pp. 33-34.
10. Details of the Subcommittee Bill of Rights and other reforms are discussed in Chapter 2 of this book. See also Deering and Smith, "Majority Party Leadership," pp. 26-40.
11. The caucus rule provides that, with the exception of Appropriations, standing committees are limited to eight subcommittees; committees with more than 35 members and fewer than six subcommittees may increase the number to six or, with Steering and Policy Committee approval, may have seven subcommittees. In response, Agriculture and Banking reduced the number of their subcommittees to

meet the eight subcommittee limit. Education and Labor was forced to disband its Task Force on Welfare and Pension Plans to comply with the limit because the rule explicitly counted task forces and other special subunits as subcommittees. No incumbent subcommittee chair was forced to give up a chair, although three members in line for a chair could not assume one.

12. Data on assignments in this and the following paragraphs for the 98th Congress are by the authors. For the earlier periods, see Sula P. Richardson and Susan Schjelderup, "Standing Committee Structure and Assignments: House and Senate," Congressional Research Service, Report No. 82-42 Gov., March 12, 1982.

13. This situation may yet be reversed. On June 6, 1984, the Senate voted to create a new Temporary Select Committee to Study the Senate Committee System. The panel was given a mandate to study the size, jurisdiction, rules, and procedures of Senate committees. In practice, the committee, which had a reporting deadline of December 15, 1984, was expected to achieve few, if any, significant changes in the Senate committee system. Nonetheless, a stricter limitation on committee and subcommittee assignments (perhaps at the levels originally set in 1977) was being considered actively by panel members.

14. See Norman J. Ornstein, Thomas E. Mann, Michael J. Malbin, John F. Bibby, *Vital Statistics on Congress, 1982* (Washington, D.C.: American Enterprise Institute for Public Policy Research, 1982), pp. 101-102.

15. The following figures were calculated from Thomas J. O'Donnell, "Controlling Legislative Time," in *The House at Work,* ed. Joseph Cooper and G. Calvin Mackenzie (Austin: University of Texas Press, 1981), Table 5.2, p. 131.

16. Cited in U.S. Congress, House Select Committee on Committees, *Final Report,* H. Rept. No. 96-866, 96th Cong., 2d sess., p. 198.

17. Interview conducted by the authors.

18. See Deering, "Subcommittee Government in the U.S. House," for an account of the bill management data collection. Data on the Senate were collected in the same fashion.

19. The Democratic Caucus rule (No. 39) reads: "The chairmen of full committees shall, insofar as practicable, permit the subcommittee chairmen to handle on the floor legislation from their respective subcommittees."

20. "New Chairman Of House Interior Plans To Share Power," *Congressional Quarterly Weekly Report,* January 27, 1973, p. 134.

21. While Armed Services has a high proportion (50 percent) of subcommittee staff, the absolute number (9) is low and they were on a single subcommittee. The use of a separate subcommittee staff on the one subcommittee in this instance was a short-lived exception on Armed Services.

22. The reader is reminded that bill management data are from the 95th Congress for the second period in the discussion that follows. Data for the other three indicators are from the 96th Congress.

23. On members' goals see Steven S. Smith and Christopher J. Deering, "Changing Motives for Committee Preferences of New Members of the U.S. House," 8 *Legislative Studies Quarterly* (May 1983): 271-282; Smith and Deering, *Committees in Congress,* pp. 83-124; and Charles S. Bullock III, "Motivations for U.S. Congressional Committee Preferences: Freshmen of the 92nd Congress," *Legislative Studies Quarterly* 1 (May 1976): 201-212. The theoretical relevance of members' goals was established by Richard F. Fenno in *Congressmen in*

Committees (Boston: Little, Brown & Co., 1973). The categories referred to here are the same as those used by Smith and Deering. Policy committees: Banking, Foreign Affairs, Energy and Commerce, Judiciary, Education and Labor, and Government Operations. Constituency (or district) committees: Agriculture, Armed Services, Interior, Merchant Marine and Fisheries, Public Works, Science and Technology, Small Business, and Veterans' Affairs. Prestige committees: Appropriations, Budget, Rules, Ways and Means. And undesired committees: District of Columbia, House Administration, Post Office and Civil Service, and Standards of Official Conduct.

24. In both the 91st and 96th Congresses, committees that differ on only one of the characteristics and for which that one characteristic approaches the high/low breakpoint have been categorized with the nearest type. In the 91st Congress, four committees—Senate Government Operations, Senate Judiciary, House Public Works, and House Foreign Affairs—do not readily fall into any of the patterns and none of the indicators falls close enough to the breakpoint to allow even provisional categorization.

25. It should be reiterated that House Democratic Caucus rules force at least this minimal level of decentralization.

26. On these topics see Davidson, "Subcommittee Government," pp. 108-134; and Norman J. Ornstein, "The House and Senate in a New Congress," in *The New Congress*, pp. 367-369.

9. FISCAL RESPONSIBILITY AND THE REVENUE COMMITTEES

Catherine E. Rudder

Despite congressional reforms of the early 1970s that shook the foundations of the House Committee on Ways and Means, the revenue committees remain the most powerful committees on Capitol Hill. From the standpoint of their vast jurisdiction and their pivotal role in the pre-eminent policy debate of the nation—federal fiscal policy—it would be difficult to identify congressional committees more important than Ways and Means and the Senate Finance Committee, whose jurisdictions cover not only all federal taxation but 40 percent of all direct federal spending.

Shifts in Direction

The last decade, however, has been one of transition for the tax committees. The way they operate, the degree of autonomy they enjoy, their environment, and their chairmen have changed. As a result, the kind of policy these committees produce is quite different from that of the past. Most notably, the tax policy has been unusually erratic over the last decade, the growth of revenues has slowed considerably, and large deficits in the range of $200 billion annually are anticipated through the 1980s primarily as a result of tax policy decisions.[1]

Tax Bill Turnabouts

The erratic shifts in policy are evidenced in the major tax bills enacted in the last decade. The Tax Reform Act of 1976 was in fact hailed as a major tax reform measure in that it broadened the income tax base by reducing tax expenditures (special tax breaks for groups of taxpayers) by $8 billion and maintained the mildly progressive structure of the personal income tax (the higher one's income, the greater the proportion paid in taxes). The Revenue Act of 1978 was an abrupt reversal. Tax expenditures were expanded in the interest of encouraging capital formation, and the progressiveness of the tax structure was dampened.

Joyce Murdoch and John Gist provided useful assistance on an earlier draft of this chapter. The author is also indebted to Constance Barnes for her expert clerical help.

Reagan Administration Tax Cuts. By 1981, the concern for capital formation had been translated into "supply-side economics," which argued for greatly reduced marginal rates of taxation as a work incentive and for further reductions in taxation on capital to promote saving and investment. As the highest priority of the new Reagan administration, principles of supply-side economics were enacted into law in the Economic Recovery Tax Act (ERTA) of 1981. The act included major individual tax rate reductions over a three-year period and a number of other reductions, most notably in the number of years over which businesses and individuals could depreciate assets for tax purposes. The staggering revenue loss from this legislation—$1.5 trillion through this decade—has resulted in structural deficits and a consequent fiscal crisis.[2] Economists have predicted a range of dire consequences of this legislation (which was not accompanied by comparable spending cuts) including higher to much higher interest rates, a slowdown in the economic recovery, a recession, substantial inflation, and great uncertainty in financial markets. Further, with the enactment of ERTA and the Revenue Act of 1978 many of the revenue-raising reforms of 1976 were reversed.[3] The overall effect of supply-side taxation was to lower corporate taxes, greatly reduce taxes on capital gains income (which is earned disproportionately by the economically well off), and increase the relative tax burden of the low-income taxpayer.[4]

Efforts Toward Deficit Reduction. The 1981 act, the largest tax cut in U.S. history, was followed immediately by the largest peacetime tax increase. Many of the tax advantages incorporated in ERTA were modified by the Tax Equity and Fiscal Responsibility Act (TEFRA) of 1982 in an effort to reduce anticipated deficits. Tax expenditures were reduced by 13 provisions of the act, including two—the alternative minimum tax for individuals and the reduction in business preference items—that lowered the overall benefits of tax expenditures. The net effect of TEFRA was to reduce revenue losses from tax expenditures by $100 billion from fiscal years 1983 through 1987.[5] All told, by increasing revenues by $283 billion from 1983 through 1989, the 1982 act recouped a substantial portion of the loss entailed in the 1981 act.

Subsequent Tax Hikes. The approach of raising revenues by increasing the tax base was followed again in 1984, after a similar attempt to raise taxes failed in 1983. Common political wisdom was turned on its head when taxes were raised in an election year for the second time in a row. Ways and Means and Senate Finance agreed on $50 billion worth of tax increases for the three fiscal years of 1985-1987. In order to avoid a presidential veto, the Deficit Reduction Act of 1984, like the 1982 bill, did not raise tax rates directly nor was the three-year tax cut of 1981 or the indexing of tax rates to inflation altered. Even though the 1984 act entailed substantial benefits to particular groups, the net effect was a considerable revenue gain fueled by concern for anticipated deficits.

Control of Tax Policy

What has led to this erratic, largely unpredictable pattern of tax policy? The loss of Ways and Means as a control committee has contributed to this result. The Ways and Means Committee was a small, elite body operating behind closed doors and without subcommittees. It brought bills to the floor under closed rules that permit no amendment, thereby ensuring that compromises shaped in committee could not be torn apart on the floor of the House. The committee was composed of relatively senior House members with safe seats, led by a knowledgeable, respected and consensus-building chairman, Wilbur Mills (D-Ark.), and composed of members who followed norms of restrained partisanship, "responsible" legislating, and apprenticeship. The committee was able to enforce its will on the House—demonstrated by the fact that Mills rarely lost votes on the floor—and had a substantial restraining influence on the Senate.

Congressional Reforms

The reforms of the 1970s severely undercut the ability of Ways and Means to operate as a control committee. Expansion of the committee by almost 50 percent, the establishment of subcommittees, the requirement that meetings be held in public unless the committee chose in a roll call vote to close them, the loss by Democratic members of the committee of the role of assigning fellow Democrats to other House committees, the requirement that the chairman serve at the pleasure of the Democratic Caucus of the House, modification in the use of the closed rule for tax legislation on the House floor, and other changes all weakened the chairman's ability to lead. They also undermined the committee's ability to hold legislative packages intact on the House floor, to bargain effectively with Senate Finance in conference, and to withstand pressure from other members and interest groups. The committee's autonomy was curtailed as members outside Ways and Means not only challenged Ways and Means bills on the floor but also circumvented the committee altogether, for example by attaching legislative language affecting tax policy to appropriations bills.

Prior to the reforms it was much more difficult to hold members accountable individually for specific provisions of tax legislation. Instead, bills were a collective, privately forged committee product that was presented to the House in a take-it-or-leave-it manner. Consequently, voters back home had virtually no way of knowing what members were doing in committee.

Furthermore, because committee members had safe seats, they did not feel the need to respond seriously to every person or group making a claim. In the House itself, Democratic members not serving on Ways and Means felt somewhat beholden to Democratic committee members for their committee assignments and realized that opposition to a Ways and Means bill could affect adversely their chances to obtain a more desirable committee assignment. Thus, bills crafted by Ways and Means met little meaningful opposition on the House floor.

With the congressional reforms the balance of power shifted. In order to retain their seats in Congress and to win House approval of committee bills, Ways and Means members had to be more responsive to requests from constituents, organized interests, and fellow members of the House. These new pressures were intensified by the sunlight of open meetings. Ways and Means members could now be held individually accountable for their positions on every provision that made up a tax package. In short, the Ways and Means Committee was more penetrable particularly by organized interests and much less autonomous as a result of the reforms.

Given this turn of events, one might expect the tax policy depicted in the previous section: unstable, unpredictable, and responsive to claimants. Especially in 1981, the committee appeared to be vulnerable to virtually every substantial economic interest group in Washington. The normal process of developing legislation broke down completely and turned into an "unprecedented bidding war" between the White House and the Democrats, led by Ways and Means Committee Chairman Dan Rostenkowski (D-Ill.), to attract floor votes for their two versions of the legislation—each upping the ante with new tax privileges.[6] There seemed to be little concern for the quality of the bill or the integrity of the tax code.

The reforms that led to the loss of Ways and Means as a control committee do explain *some* of the legislative outcomes in recent years. Rostenkowski, like his predecessor Al Ullman (D-Ore.), has been much less successful in controlling his committee and persuading members on the House floor to follow his lead. Even after the auction for votes that characterized the drafting of the 1981 Ways and Means bill and the Republican/Reagan administration alternative, Rostenkowski and the Democrats lost on the House floor to the alternative, which was tendered by a junior Democratic member of the Ways and Means Committee, Kent Hance (D-Texas), and the ranking Republican on Ways and Means, Barber Conable (R-N.Y.).[7]

Changes in Approach to Tax Policymaking

Concomitant with the reforms have been two other factors that have contributed to the difficulty of making tax policy in a consistent and restrained manner so that the integrity of the tax code is preserved. One of these factors is the prevalence of *ad hoc* policymaking on tax matters so that members often make decisions more on the basis of ahistorical, *prima facie* arguments than on well-reasoned philosophical grounds or in a historical context. The confusion surrounding the application of economic theories has augmented this phenomenon of *ad hoc* policymaking. Stagflation of the 1970s left Keynesian economics in some disrepute and opened the way for supply-side economics, which in turn has led to historically high deficits. Partly as a result, tax policymakers have little to lean on when making important decisions affecting fiscal policy other than the prevailing arguments of the moment.[8]

The second factor is the increasing use of the tax code for nontax purposes. For example, to encourage preservation of historic buildings, a rehabilitation tax credit is offered rather than a direct subsidy. This practice gives the revenue committees virtually unlimited jurisdiction and increases greatly the demands on the tax committees, which have few tools at their disposal to withstand effective lobbying, especially in the postreform era.

The decentralizing reforms, the prevalence of *ad hoc* policymaking, and the opening of the tax code for virtually any policy purpose (not just raising revenues and stabilizing the economy) all point in the same direction: a very manipulable environment open to exploitation by effective lobbyists with surface arguments and strong grass-roots backing (so that members will see the electoral connection between the policy advocated and their re-election efforts). Nevertheless, the 1982 and 1984 tax cuts shifted tax policy back on an unexpected course: tax expenditures were reduced and revenues raised. This feat is especially remarkable because President Ronald Reagan initially opposed the tax increases and had to be persuaded to support the tax packages. The 1982 and 1984 bills demonstrated that the reforms affecting the Ways and Means Committee have not left Congress unable to enact politically difficult and fiscally disciplined legislation. Examining how Congress—and the tax committees in particular—managed to pass such legislation is instructive in understanding the tax legislative process and its impact on policy outcomes, and also provides clues as to whether a pattern of more consistent, fiscally responsible policymaking is emerging.

The Deficit Crisis and the Emergence of Leadership

Rostenkowski and Republican Senator Robert J. Dole of Kansas assumed the chairmanship of their respective committees after the 1980 elections but under very different circumstances. The Democrats had sustained a stunning blow in the landslide election of Ronald Reagan and the loss of their Senate majority. As if to underscore the Democrats' loss, the Ways and Means chairmanship was open because Ullman was defeated in his re-election bid.[9] In contrast, Dole, a Republican, took the helm of Senate Finance after his party won the White House and because it had gained a Senate majority (for the first time in 26 years).

The first year of Reagan's presidency saw the passage of his economic program, including his tax proposals. Rostenkowski and the Democrats could not muster a majority in the House where they nominally constituted the majority. Subsequently, when it became clear that the unprecedented tax cuts of 1981, coupled with other revenue-depressing factors such as the recession, would require large tax increases, it was Dole who took the lead in addressing those deficits.[10]

Congress passed the first concurrent resolution on the budget, in this case a Republican measure, on June 17, 1982, and set the parameters for a tax increase. Under the reconciliation instructions of the resolution, the tax committees were told to increase revenues by an estimated $98.3 billion and cut health and welfare spending under their jurisdiction by $17 billion for fiscal years 1983-1985. In other words, Ways and Means and Senate Finance alone were responsible for producing one-half of the deficit reduction under the three-year budget agreement. Ways and Means was to report its reconciliation legislation by August 1, and Senate Finance by July 12.

The impending deficits and the worries about their potentially devastating effects on the economy provided the impetus for action. Yet it was a touch-and-go matter from the start. Although worried about the effect of deficits on their re-election bids, members were generally unenthusiastic about raising taxes in an election year. This reluctance was especially evident among House Democrats who did not want to be saddled with the blame for a tax increase that they believed Republican tax cuts the previous year had made necessary. Moreover, no help came from the White House initially. Reagan was unwilling to sign any bill that reduced the personal tax cuts enacted in ERTA in 1981, and Treasury Secretary Donald Regan was unwilling to suggest ways to increase taxes sufficiently to meet the reconciliation instructions. Initiative would have to come from Congress, but Rostenkowski refused to take the lead as Ways and Means normally would have done on behalf of the House as the originator of tax legislation under the Constitution.

Senate Finance Takes Charge

Dole, however, was willing to act. To compound the difficulty of reporting tax hikes, half of his committee—including six of its twelve Republicans—were up for re-election.[11] Nevertheless, Dole produced all the deficit reductions called for in the first budget resolution, and he did so ten days before the deadline. The reconciliation bill was reported out of committee on a straight partisan vote that reflected Dole's technique: the entire bill had been written in closed caucuses involving only the committee's Republicans and then, in effect, was ratified in committee. This reversal of the spirit of the open-meetings reform that extended to most congressional deliberations may have been indispensable in producing the legislation.

On the Senate floor, Dole was again aided by the Budget Act of 1974, which limits debate and amendments on reconciliation bills. When the Senate adopted an amendment—to ease depreciation rules for real estate—that lopped off $2.8 billion in revenues necessary to fulfill reconciliation instructions, Dole demonstrated legislative creativity by offering a successful alternative proposal—to restrict the rehabilitation tax credit enjoyed by the real estate industry—that recouped the loss. He threatened even greater tax increases if the Senate insisted on weakening the bill. He mustered a 50 to 47 majority, again a primarily party-line vote.

In contrast, Rostenkowski was unable to unite the House Democrats on his committee. In the absence of a presidential proposal, he offered his own tax package. It was rejected soundly by Ways and Means Democrats, however, and the committee instead agreed to go directly to conference without a House bill. The House assented to this decision and in so doing broke the constitutionally derived tradition of the House having the lead in tax bills. The constitutional problem was circumvented by attaching the Senate's bill to a minor House-passed tax measure unrelated to deficit reduction.

Explaining Success

Despite predictions that no agreement would be reached in conference, the conferees, particularly Dole, were committed to producing a conference report. By the time the conference was under way, President Reagan was campaigning vigorously for this legislation. A conference report was produced. When it reached the House, "the legislative machinery of both parties ... was effective and essential" to its passage.[12]

Despite opposition from the Business Roundtable, the U.S. Chamber of Commerce, and other influential business interests, and with the 1982 election only two months away, this major tax increase bill was enacted. The key factors were: first, the use of the Budget Act, which structured the situation, set a timetable for action, and supplied strict germaneness rules on the Senate floor (where tax bills ordinarily are subject to numerous amendments sometimes far afield from the subject of the legislation); second, the sense of fiscal crisis stemming from projected budget deficits that led to the realization that doing nothing could be more damaging to re-election chances than voting for tax increases; third, Dole's leadership, including his techniques of using party caucuses and closing meetings; and, finally, the eventual team work of the administration, the revenue committees, and congressional party leaders in shaping successful legislation and securing final passage.

Deficit Reduction Revisited

As projected deficits were again revised upward in 1983 and early 1984, Congress was faced once more with the prospect of raising revenues and lowering spending. By 1983 Rostenkowski had begun to exert leadership in deficit reduction. The jurisdiction of his committee had been strengthened early that year by several changes in House rules at the beginning of the 98th Congress, including a rule making more difficult the practice of attaching legislative riders to appropriations bills and a rule allowing Ways and Means to raise a point of order to prevent bills with tax or trade restrictions from coming to the floor if they have not been approved by Ways and Means.[13]

Even with these changes, however, Ways and Means was circumvented in the successful effort to repeal a provision in the 1982 bill to establish withholding on dividends and interest. Despite the vigorous opposition of

Rostenkowski and Dole, withholding was repealed. Norman D'Amours (D-N.H.) successfully used a discharge petition to force House action on the bill, which Rostenkowski had bottled up in his committee. Robert Kasten (R-Wis.) forced the Senate Finance Committee to act by threatening to attach the repeal amendment to a crucial bill to increase the debt limit. The repeal effort demonstrated the powerlessness of the tax committee chairmen in the face of an extraordinarily strong, well-organized, grass-roots lobbying campaign.

Although Rostenkowski was able to exert some leadership on the major Social Security financing bill enacted in 1983 and on a bill to limit the third-year tax cut that passed the House but not the Senate, he faced a major defeat as the House turned down the rule permitting consideration of the Ways and Means deficit-reduction bill. This legislation conformed to the reconciliation instructions of the budget resolution, whose provisions to raise $12 billion for fiscal 1984 and $73 billion for fiscal 1984-1986 were not met before the close of Congress in 1983.

New Tactics for Ways and Means

Rostenkowski and Ways and Means did, however, devise methods of operating that were to characterize the more successful work of the committee in 1984. First, he closed Ways and Means markups, even on uncontroversial bills. Second, he continued to make frequent use of Democratic caucuses in the committee (just as Dole did with the Republicans on Senate Finance) to develop partisan majorities on the committee. Third, like Mills before him, he developed consensus "by molding legislation as much as possible to meet the major concerns of each member of the caucus." [14] Fourth, like Dole, he floated deficit-reduction packages to assess the strength of interest group opposition and the likelihood of passage. Fifth, like Dole, he worked for a package of tax increases that would be acceptable to the House and the president; this entailed two related elements: considering legislation on the House floor under a closed rule so that legislative compromises could not be picked apart by forceful lobbying efforts and developing a package with enough "sweeteners" (benefits to particular interests that members care about) so that the total package could win a majority even though many specific provisions might not if voted on separately.

Explaining Failure

In 1983 Dole had even less success than Rostenkowski, as the factors present in 1982 did not converge in 1983. Specifically, the sense of urgency had dissipated. Congress had just passed its largest peacetime tax bill in history, and because the 1983 budget resolution provided for a three-year deficit reduction, Congress could always enact a reconciliation bill in 1984 to cover the relevant three fiscal years, 1984-1986. Also, in 1983 there was no cooperation (even late in the year) from the administration, which preferred a stand-by tax to be triggered, if necessary, in fiscal 1986 to reduce deficits. In addition, certain interest groups, especially those working to protect the tax value of industrial development bonds, were sufficiently strong to prevent action.

The failure to enact deficit-reduction legislation in 1983 suggests that the budget process, consensus-building leadership—in this case by both chairmen—and closed meetings are insufficient to enact deficit-reduction bills. Missing were administration support, proposals that could withstand the onslaught of interest group opposition, and, most importantly, the will to act.

Doing the Impossible

In many ways 1984 was a replay of 1982. The dire effects of upwardly revised deficit projections were discussed widely, and there was a general belief that Congress would be unable to reduce the deficits. The administration not only did not cooperate with initial efforts to raise taxes, it again threatened vetoes if certain measures were passed (thereby reducing the options of the tax committees) and proposed in its budget costly new tax expenditures—including tax breaks for urban enterprise zones, individual retirement accounts for nonworking spouses, and tuition tax credits for parents who send their children to private schools—none of which was enacted.

As in 1982, much of the deficit reduction would have to emanate from the revenue committees. Once again Dole insisted from the beginning of the year that deficits had to be addressed even though short-run expediency might favor inaction. He took the lead by directing the Finance Committee staff to prepare a package of proposals that could be attached to the reconciliation bill that had not been enacted in 1983.

A Strengthened House

The primary difference in 1984 compared with 1982 was the leadership of Rostenkowski and the ability of his committee and the House to produce a deficit-reduction package. The techniques Rostenkowski had used in 1983, coupled with the sense of urgency and the desire to get credit for deficit reduction, were key factors in the passage of a Democratic deficit-reduction bill in the House.

Ways and Means met behind closed doors to combine the previous year's unpassed reconciliation bill with provisions to close tax shelters and improve compliance. By a wide margin the House Rules Committee agreed to a closed rule and to allow the House to vote separately on almost $1 billion worth of cuts in Medicare, as opposition to the health spending cuts threatened to defeat the deficit-reduction package. On April 12, by a lopsided vote of 318 to 97, the House passed the deficit-reduction bill and on the following day defeated the Medicare cuts.

A Contentious Senate

In the Senate, Dole had rough going, in part because of the voting procedure used by the Finance Committee whereby votes on individual provisions remain open until work on the entire package is completed. "The lobbyists are changing votes faster than I can," Dole complained.[15] One proposal in particular that was eliminated in committee (but reinstated on the Senate floor) because of this procedure was to limit the deduction allowed for the purchase of luxury automobiles for business use. Even with the open-ended procedure, Senate Finance did manage to fend off a number of lobbying efforts to dilute the committee bill, including an all-out effort by the real estate industry to maintain a depreciation provision enacted in 1981 that encouraged investment in real estate. Although cutting the deficit was the overriding concern, the bill as passed by the Senate included $8 billion in new tax breaks, including the president's proposal for enterprise zones and an expansion of individual retirement accounts. Part of the Senate bill, in particular major changes in taxation of the insurance industry, had been forged by Ways and Means and then adopted by Senate Finance, thereby partly renewing the pre-1981 pattern of Ways and Means writing tax bills and Senate Finance amending them.

In both the House and Senate, deficit reduction was the overriding concern, and the budget and tax committees were operating in tandem on this matter. Because by 1984 the Republican Senate and Democratic House were in a race to produce deficit-reduction legislation first and thereby get credit for being the most fiscally responsible party, tax legislation preceded House-Senate agreement on a budget resolution. However, the budget process did provide the structure for action in 1984.

A Successful Conference

In conference, both chairmen were committed to producing a conference report under the imperative of reducing the deficit. Negotiations were held in secret. Treasury Department officials and Office of Management and Budget (OMB) Director David Stockman were actively involved in them. The conference lasted for almost three weeks, the end of which was capped by a marathon session beginning at 8:30 a.m. and ending a little over 20 hours later at 5:15 a.m. The conference adjourned for hours while the conferees from each house caucused in private, and messages were sent back and forth between the groups. The most difficult items were postponed until the end of the conference. The final product included $50 billion in new taxes and $13 billion in reduced spending, along with a number of new tax breaks.

The Future

Common political wisdom has proved of little use in understanding the making of tax policy in recent years. Not only can taxes be raised in an election year, there can be more pressure to raise taxes (to reduce deficits) when elections are impending than when they are not. Tax policy can change radically and quickly. Moreover, not only can Congress initiate fiscally responsible legislation, it can do so in the face of initial presidential opposition and divided party government. Finally, Congress can make politically difficult decisions necessary for the long-term health of the economy.

While the decentralizing congressional reforms of the 1970s have left the Ways and Means Committee, in particular, more permeable, more susceptible to the influence of interest groups (especially those that can generate apparent grass-roots activity), less autonomous, and harder to lead, the revenue committees have adapted to a new internal and external environment. Recent rules changes in the House have restored some Ways and Means control over the tax product. Tax committee chairmen Dole and Rostenkowski have developed effective techniques—some of which negate the 1970s reforms—to produce successful legislation: using party caucuses within their committees, consulting widely on legislation, developing a salable product, using rules to keep packages intact on the floor, working closely with party leadership, closing meetings, and bargaining flexibly. Their leadership is especially notable in light of the absence of formal coercive powers available to them and the great difficulty members of Congress, including members of tax committees, have in saying "no" to claimants.

The legislative successes of 1982 and 1984 can be attributed to the felicitous convergence of leadership (first Dole, then Rostenkowski and Dole), the mechanisms of the budget process, an eventual uniting of both parties and the administration to enact deficit reductions, and a fiscal crisis. The sense of an impending economic downturn, if not disaster, defined the overall legislative situation, just as the perceived need to improve economic performance through tax incentives defined it in 1978 and 1981. If the fiscal pressure remains strong, one might expect Congress to continue in its 1982 and 1984 path of a net reduction in tax expenditures, all other things being equal. Both projected deficits and the indexing of income tax rates to inflation may help keep that pressure on and prevent a redefinition of the situation that could lead to quite different tax policies. Alternatively, however, tax policy may shift markedly again as it did in 1981 in the face of other forces redefining the issues and potential solutions.

In the tax policy area, Congress is unmoored intellectually and structurally. Another erratic policy shift should surprise no one.

NOTES

1. There has also been a continued shift in the sources of revenue. While individual income taxes as a percent of total revenues have ranged between 40 and 50 percent since 1960, payroll taxes (which fall most heavily on those with low incomes) have doubled from 16 percent of revenues in 1960 to 35 percent in 1983.

Estate and gift taxes (which fall almost exclusively on upper income taxpayers) also have been substantially reduced, and corporate income taxes have sharply declined from 23 percent in 1960 to 6 percent in 1983. See Congressional Budget Office, *Reducing the Deficit: Spending and Revenue Options* (Washington, D.C.: U.S. Government Printing Office, 1984), pp. 184-185.

2. A deficit is the amount by which expenditures exceed revenues in a given fiscal year. A structural deficit is the projected amount by which expenditures would exceed revenues when the economy is operating at its full capacity. Sizable structural deficits are worrisome because they cannot be overcome even by excellent economic performance and are therefore "mortgaging the future."

3. Congress also enacted the Windfall Profits Tax Act of 1980, which raised taxes on oil companies but also included several new tax breaks.

4. Supply-side policies also contributed to the slowdown in the growth of federal revenues. Between 1980 and 1983, federal revenues grew at half the rate for the previous three-year period. At the same time, revenues declined as a percent of Gross National Product (GNP) from 20.1 percent in 1980 to 18.6 percent in 1983. See Congressional Budget Office, *Reducing the Deficit,* p. 184.

5. Tax expenditures were reduced further by the Social Security Amendments of 1983, which provided for the taxation of some Social Security and railroad retirement benefits.

6. *Washington Post,* August 2, 1981.

7. There are many reasons for the success of the 1981 bill, the most important of which was that President Reagan had an effective majority in the House and Senate although nominally the Democrats controlled the House. It also might be noted that the Democrats, led by Rostenkowski, were bidding for votes just as the Republicans were. Not only was the Ways and Means chairman unable to control the process, he was contributing to the raiding of the Treasury.

8. For further discussion of *ad hoc* policymaking, see Catherine E. Rudder, "Tax Policy: Structure and Choice," in *Making Economic Policy in Congress,* ed. Allen Schick (Washington, D.C.: American Enterprise Institute for Public Policy Research, 1983), pp. 208-210.

9. Even though the power of the chairman had been diluted, Rostenkowski chose to become chairman rather than accept the position of House Democratic party whip, the third ranking Democrat in the House.

10. One might wonder why Dole took it upon himself to lead the tax increase battle and risk being known by his constituents as a tax increaser and face what then seemed to be probable defeat on the issue rather than wait for public pressure to build until Reagan was forced to act and take the blame for increasing taxes. While it is difficult to attribute motives accurately, it is fair to say that by proposing to close tax loopholes, Dole was pre-empting the Democrats' position and was also transforming himself into a respected national political leader.

11. All were re-elected in 1982, a fact that surely was not lost on members when faced with the prospect of raising taxes in the next election year.

12. *Congressional Quarterly Weekly Report,* August 28, 1982, p. 2121.

13. Now Ways and Means can also raise a point of order if Senate amendments attached to a House-passed bill that are within the jurisdiction of Ways and Means but have not been approved by Ways and Means are brought to the House.

14. *Congressional Quarterly Weekly Report,* January 29, 1983, p. 194.

15. *Congressional Quarterly Weekly Report,* March 10, 1984, p. 536.

Part IV

CONGRESSIONAL LEADERSHIP
AND PARTY POLITICS

10. SENATE LEADERS:
JANITORS FOR AN UNTIDY CHAMBER?

Roger H. Davidson

*Father in heaven, we are here under duress, but we
have imposed this upon ourselves.*
Rev. Richard C. Halverson
Chaplain of the Senate
October 9, 1984

Fact number one about Senate leaders: they are the first to arrive for chamber sessions and the last to leave. Aside from the presiding officer, the majority and minority floor leaders are often the only ones present to hear the chaplain's prayer that opens each day's session. The end of the day's business usually finds the two leaders again at their posts, swapping information on future scheduling and propounding unanimous consent requests governing upcoming debates. Majority Leader Howard H. Baker, Jr. (R-Tenn.) wondered aloud whether "the principal duty of the leadership is janitorial." [1]

Other Senate leaders have voiced frustration with their jobs. Former majority leader Robert C. Byrd (D-W.Va.) once said that if anyone asked his occupation he would put down "slave." His predecessor, Mike Mansfield (D-Mont.), wryly observed that "you don't organize chaos." Even the legendary Everett Dirksen (R-Ill.), a fearful force in his day, lamented that "there are 100 diverse personalities in the U.S. Senate. O Great God, what an amazing and dissonant 100 personalities they are! What an amazing thing it is to harmonize them. What a job it is." [2]

These expressions of self-pity may be exaggerated. Yet the underlying issue is whether Senate leaders are mere caretakers in an era of rampant individualism—one in which senators are preoccupied with tending their own careers and ministering to their constituencies. Are the leaders' jobs merely glorified clerkships, to borrow political scientist Richard Neustadt's suggestive label for the presidency? [3] Given the pluralism and fragmentation of the

The views expressed in this chapter are those of the author and not necessarily those of the Congressional Research Service. The author wishes to thank Mary Etta Cook and Mary Dunkley for their assistance.

political process, individual senators resist being led, herded, or managed. They expect leaders to run the Senate with minimum fuss and maximum deference to their differing goals and schedules. In such a setting, what is the state of leadership in the Senate?

Historical Evolution

The origin of formal Senate party leadership is something of a puzzle. For one thing, it happened relatively recently. In the House of Representatives, strong partisan leadership dates from the era of Speaker Henry Clay, in the early decades of our nation's history. Yet identifiable Senate leadership dates only from the late nineteenth century, and in modern form from Woodrow Wilson's day. Moreover, the processes by which this leadership arose are not well understood.[4]

The Senate has no lack of presiding officers, but these are not its leaders. The constitutional president of the Senate is the vice president of the United States. Early vice presidents, such as John Adams, took an active part in floor debates; today's vice presidents are prohibited from speaking unless granted permission by the body. Except for ceremonial occasions, they seldom preside over the Senate and can vote only to break a tie. The Constitution also provides for a president *pro tempore* to preside in the vice president's absence. In modern practice, the president pro tem is the most senior majority-party senator. Occupants are apt to chair a key committee and be influential figures in their own right; their influence does not flow from the post itself, which is mainly ceremonial. Usually the Senate's presiding officer is a junior majority member, serving brief stints in the chair each day, so the Senate has no official comparable to the House Speaker, who combines political and parliamentary duties.

During its first century, the Senate was a smallish body whose members were chosen indirectly by their state legislatures. Some senators were kingpins in their own right, controlling statewide political machines and blocs of delegates to national party conventions. Others were agents for dominant interests in their states. In contrast, the caucus chairmen who emerged as distinct leaders in the 1890s were not necessarily powerful figures outside the Senate—often they were simply the most senior party members. But their Senate duties, even though shared with others, were not insignificant: making committee assignments, scheduling and managing legislation on the floor, and occasionally applying party discipline.

In the first two decades of the twentieth century, an invigorated office— called floor leader—emerged from the caucus chairmanship. Perhaps, as one scholar suggests, the advent of activist presidents such as Woodrow Wilson and Franklin D. Roosevelt demanded Senate leaders who could confer with the White House and manage the president's legislation.[5] However, the activist presidency developed fitfully until the FDR era, and activist presidents even before Wilson had found ways of dealing effectively with key senators. Another explanation is that the Seventeenth Amendment's provision for direct election of senators in 1913 forced senators to function as individual political entrepreneurs, so they needed efficient leaders to take care of "housekeeping" matters and, incidentally, adjust the Senate's schedule and workload to serve their own political schedules and goals. From the vantage point of the 1980s, these two functions—dealing with the White House and serving individual senators' needs—are at the core of the floor leaders' jobs.

Even so, personal characteristics and skills have always exerted a powerful force on floor leadership, and leaders differ considerably in approaching their duties. In other words, the posts are not yet entirely institutionalized; rather, they fluctuate according to individual leaders' definitions of their jobs, and their personal talents or limitations.

The floor leader's job has not always been held in high esteem. "The office is one that requires no gifts of a high order," proclaimed so astute an observer as Richard Rovere in 1953. "It has generally been held as a reward for enterprising mediocrity." [6] In the late 1940s and early 1950s, several floor leaders faced criticism and even rejection at the polls as a result of their duties. Prevented by conservatives from trying to enact President Harry S Truman's "Fair Deal" programs, Democratic Leader Scott Lucas lasted only two years until Illinois voters ended his political career in 1950. His successor, Arizona's Ernest McFarland, also failed re-election after only two years in the job. William Knowland (Calif.), the GOP Leader during the 1950s, was a stronger figure but often found himself at odds with the Eisenhower administration over foreign policy.

At the same time, a strong party leadership precedent had been established, even if not always followed. Democratic Leaders such as John Worth Kern (1913-1917), Joseph T. Robinson (1933-1937), and Alben W. Barkley (1937-1947) were influential both within the chamber and in working with activist Democratic presidents. And while Republican presidents of that period had more modest legislative agendas, GOP Senate leaders were upon occasion distinguished figures.

The post surely came of age in 1953. In that year, Robert A. Taft of Ohio, "Mr. Republican," took over as Majority Leader after nearly a decade of being GOP Leader in everything but name. Across the aisle, the Democrats, temporarily in the minority, chose as their floor leader a senator elected only four years earlier. Two years later that senator, Lyndon B. Johnson of Texas, became Majority Leader. Taft in his brief tenure revitalized the floor leader's job; Johnson wholly remade it.

The Democrats

The Democrats controlled the Senate from 1955 to 1981. Initially razor-thin, their majority swelled after 1959, peaking at 68 in the 89th Congress (1965-1967). Republicans took control in 1981. Floor leadership innovations took place more often, and more dramatically, under the Democrats.

Surprisingly, however, changes tended to affect both parties' floor leaders. The parties' leaders and margins of seats are shown in Table 10-1.

The Johnson Senate

The pliability of the floor leadership was shown dramatically when Lyndon B. Johnson took over as the Democrats' floor leader. As Americans were soon to learn, Johnson was not just another politician; he was a protean force. "He doesn't have the best mind on the Democratic side," conceded Richard B. Russell of Georgia, leader of the southern wing. "He isn't the best orator; he isn't the best parliamentarian. But he's the best combination of all those qualities." [7]

Johnson gathered together all the strands of power associated with the office and exercised them to the utmost. To these he added persuasive powers and attention to every detail of Senate business. As political scientist John G. Stewart summarized, "He set for himself no less an objective than *running* the Senate, in fact as well as in theory, by wielding decisive influence in generating majority support for the issues he permitted to come before the Senate for decision." [8]

Although Johnson mastered virtually all phases of the Senate's business—including strategy, tactics, and parliamentary procedure—he was most noted for one-on-one persuasion. No one subjected to the "Johnson treatment" ever forgot it. When reporter Stewart Alsop published an article containing a couple of mildly critical sentences about LBJ's defense record, he was summoned that very day for a two-hour session with the Majority Leader:

> By gradual stages the relaxed, friendly, and reminiscent mood gave way to something rather like a human hurricane. Johnson was up, striding about his office, talking without pause, occasionally leaning over, his nose almost touching the mesmerized reporter's, to shake the reporter's shoulder or grab his knee. Secretaries were rung for. Memoranda appeared and then more memoranda, as well as letters, newspaper articles, and unidentifiable scraps of paper, which were proffered in quick succession and then snatched away. Appeals were made, to the Almighty, to the shades of the departed great, to the reporter's finer instincts and better nature, while the reporter, unable to get a word in edgewise, sat collapsed upon a leather sofa, eyes glazed, mouth half open. [9]

The "treatment" was the hallmark of Johnson's dominating *persona,* not only during his Senate years but in the White House and to the very end of his life.

Johnson's Senate was a joyless place to work, if one were a senator or staff member outside the Johnson circle. Rarely did he call all Democratic senators together: only five conferences of the chamber's Democrats were held during his first six years, although under pressure from liberals he held six conferences in his last two years. The Policy and Steering committees, which he chaired, usually ratified his decisions. In the Capitol, Johnson was

Table 10-1 Senate Parties and Their Leaders

Congress	Years	Democratic Leaders	Party Seats			Republican Leaders
			D	R	Other	
83rd	1953-1954	Lyndon B. Johnson (Texas)	47	48	1	Robert A. Taft (Ohio), 1953; William Knowland (Calif.), 1953-1954
84th	1955-1956	Johnson	48	47	1	Knowland
85th	1957-1958	Johnson	49	47	—	Knowland
86th	1959-1960	Johnson	65	35	—	Everett M. Dirksen (Ill.)
87th	1961-1962	Mike Mansfield (Mont.)	65	35	—	Dirksen
88th	1963-1964	Mansfield	67	33	—	Dirksen
89th	1965-1966	Mansfield	68	32	—	Dirksen
90th	1967-1968	Mansfield	64	36	—	Dirksen
91st	1969-1970	Mansfield	57	43	—	Dirksen, 1969; Hugh Scott (Pa.), 1969-1970
92nd	1971-1972	Mansfield	54	44	2	Scott
93rd	1973-1974	Mansfield	56	42	2	Scott
94th	1975-1976	Mansfield	60	37	2	Scott
95th	1977-1978	Robert C. Byrd (W.Va.)	61	38	1	Howard H. Baker, Jr. (Tenn.)
96th	1979-1980	Byrd	58	41	1	Baker
97th	1981-1982	Byrd	46	53	1	Baker
98th	1983-1984	Byrd	45	55	—	Baker
99th	1985-1986	Byrd	47	53	—	Robert Dole (Kan.)

☐ Democratic Control ▧ Republican Control

omnipresent: he roamed the floor and cloakrooms, talking to senators and staff members, listening, questioning, and cajoling.

Johnson brought extraordinary personal qualities to his duties, but he also profited from two factors unique to the 1950s. First, his tenure coincided with the presidency of Eisenhower, a singularly popular figure with a modest legislative agenda. Until 1959, moreover, Johnson's majority in the Senate was no more than two. Thus, Johnson's main strategy was a holding action: "responsible opposition" and accommodation (Johnson used to whip from his pocket newspaper clippings showing how much he had contributed to passing Eisenhower's legislation). To do this he had to expose his left flank—the small band of liberal senators who wanted to push farther than Johnson was prepared to go. These senators—including Paul H. Douglas (Ill.), Hubert Humphrey (Minn.), and Joseph S. Clark (Pa.)—were thwarted and frustrated, complaining bitterly of the "Senate establishment." Yet as the Eisenhower administration aged, and especially in election years, Johnson tolerated bolder Democratic counterplans—most of which he knew the president would veto. By 1960, therefore, an extensive body of proposals, all introduced and refined by the liberal activist bloc, was ready to be sponsored and implemented by an activist Democratic president.[10]

A second factor was that Johnson represented the center of gravity of the Senate Democratic party, if not the national party. The Senate was still dominated by southern and border-state senators who, in concert with conservative Republicans from the Midwest and West, kept the institution on a conservative course. It was the southerners' leader, Russell, who decided in 1953 that Johnson should be a party leader. And it was Russell and his allies to whom Johnson turned repeatedly for advice. Johnson probably could have behaved no differently even if he had wanted to. Observers of the 1950s Senate (and the House as well) agree that the conservative coalition—often termed an "unholy alliance" between Democrats and their counterparts across the aisle—dictated the course of action on Capitol Hill. Their control was buttressed by a bipartisan "inner club" of influential senior senators, and by a series of norms, or "folkways," that encouraged new senators to defer to the establishment.[11]

In short, whatever Johnson's shortcomings, his tightly controlled leadership satisfied certain partisan and institutional needs. His leadership style, Stewart concludes,

> met the clear need of reducing the Democrats' penchant for factionalism and intraparty strife as they assumed responsibility for organizing the Congress in six of Eisenhower's eight years as president.[12]

Johnson provided his party with an identifiable spokesman and a rallying point during the Eisenhower years. (Each year, he issued his own "State of the Union" report.) In doing so, he proved a faithful agent of the conservative coalition of Republicans and southern Democrats who dominated the congressional scene.

Pressures for a new leadership style eventually accelerated, however. For one thing, Johnson's centralized control of the senatorial program limited the junior senators' chances to participate and reap the benefits of legislative activism. Gradually the Johnson style exacted its toll in senators' patience, goodwill, and loyalty. "After eight years of Lyndon Johnson," one observer remarked, "a lot of senators were just worn out." [13] Restlessness grew after the 1958 elections, which boosted the Democrats' margin from two to thirty seats and augmented the party's liberal wing with the addition of Eugene McCarthy of Minnesota, Philip Hart of Michigan, Edmund Muskie of Maine, Harrison Williams of New Jersey, and others.

It was then that Johnson stepped up party conferences and invited three freshman senators to sit on the Policy Committee. Finally, as the Eisenhower years drew to a close, Democrats assumed a more aggressive stance, developing legislative alternatives and preparing for the 1960 campaign season.

The Mansfield "Revolution"

When the leadership shift occurred, it was sudden and sweeping. Johnson accepted John F. Kennedy's invitation to join the national ticket as the vice-presidential nominee; after their election, Johnson resigned from the Senate to become its constitutional presiding officer. In 1961 Mike Mansfield of Montana, the party whip (a post of little significance under Johnson), was chosen Democratic Leader without opposition. A liberal, Mansfield was nonetheless respected by conservatives and universally praised for fairness and deference to his colleagues.

Mansfield had little taste for heavy-handed leadership. "We've had a dispersal of responsibility," he conceded. "I'm not the leader, really. They don't do what I tell them. I do what they tell me." [14] Nor did he hold to "folkways" that dictated, for example, that junior senators defer to senior colleagues and refrain from speaking out on issues. "Senators realize that they are treated as I'd like to be treated—as mature people. Their independence is not infringed upon. They know that everything is on the table. They know all about our moves ahead of time. There are no surprises." [15]

Mansfield deliberately abandoned many of the tools Johnson had used so vigorously. He dispersed leadership responsibilities, encouraged broad participation, and consulted widely before making assignments or appointments. Conferences were held more frequently. Conference bodies, most notably the Policy Committee, were more representative and met more often. The Majority Leader himself typically stayed in the background, serving as a neutral arbitrator and executor of decisions when they were finally reached. Mansfield's style, it seemed, was almost a photographic negative of Johnson's.

The Mansfield revolution did not occur without controversy. Some criticized his leadership as weak or aimless. The conservative hard-liners— old, increasingly outnumbered, and overcome by such issues as civil rights—

suffered relative deprivation, inasmuch as their seniority posts no longer protected them against younger senators. However, most senators flourished under Mansfield's regime, for its very looseness gave them the leeway they needed to pursue their increasingly diverse legislative and career goals. The liberal outsiders were naturally pleased. Clark of Pennsylvania, one of the most vocal liberals, concluded: "The old times have changed. The old Senate establishment is gone. Democracy is now pretty much the rule in the Senate." [16]

Just as Johnson enjoyed fortunate circumstances in the 1950s, Mansfield held enormous advantages in leading the Senate during the 1960s. First, Kennedy and later Johnson were activist Democratic presidents with ambitious legislative programs. Second, a wide range of legislative proposals had gained momentum since the late 1950s in the hands of liberal Democrats. Finally, the Democrats boasted a two-to-one Senate margin throughout this period.

The Democratic leadership strategy survived into the GOP era of Nixon and Ford (1969-1976). With substantial majorities, Democrats continued to generate and enact lengthy legislative agendas. Despite the hostility between Nixon and the liberal wing, senators were free to negotiate with the administration to gain support for their proposals. A surprisingly large body of environmental, consumer, and welfare legislation, pushed by Senate liberals with bipartisan support, was enacted into law: the National Environmental Policy Act (NEPA) of 1969, clean air and water bills, the Occupational Safety and Health Act (OSHA) of 1970, the Consumer Products Safety Act of 1972, and the Comprehensive Employment and Training Act (CETA) of 1972, not to mention voting rights extension, the 18-year-old vote, and ratification of nuclear nonproliferation and Strategic Arms Limitation Talks (SALT) treaties.

Like his predecessor, Mansfield responded to political conditions inside and outside the Senate. The 1961 transition had, to be sure, been sudden, but long-term forces were rendering the Johnson leadership style obsolete. Johnson's reliance on the conservative coalition could not have survived as the party's center of gravity shifted leftward in the 1958-1978 period. Moreover, the increasingly independent careers pursued by senators (whether running for re-election or for the White House) demanded active participation and public exposure. Mansfield's permissive leadership allowed his colleagues to advance their career goals through activism within the chamber.

Byrd, the Master Mechanic

Mansfield's successor, Robert C. Byrd of West Virginia, added another ingredient to Senate leadership: meticulous attention to the details of floor procedure. Byrd was the quintessential Senate insider; his climb up the leadership ladder was literally built on housekeeping chores—innumerable favors performed for colleagues and countless hours of presiding over the

Senate. Neither Mansfield nor his whips, Russell Long of Louisiana (1965-1969) and Edward M. Kennedy of Massachusetts (1969-1971), enjoyed remaining on the floor for long stretches of time. So Byrd made himself available on the floor, keeping a pocket notebook in which he jotted down requests from colleagues, for example, informing them when matters of interest came up or scheduling debates for their convenience. When Byrd challenged Kennedy for the whip's post in January 1971, his record of service paid off and he won the conference vote, 31 to 24 (one of his votes was a proxy from the dying Russell).

As whip and (since 1977) Democratic Leader, Byrd continued to devote his time to floor proceedings and to stress procedural and scheduling matters. He instituted reforms to help the Senate conduct its business more efficiently. The legislative work-year was rearranged to permit scheduled recesses ("nonlegislative work periods"). He perfected Mansfield's "track" system in which noncontroversial measures could be disposed of while controversial ones, even those being filibustered, could be debated. Byrd also was involved in altering Senate rules, and his interest in procedure remained keen even after the Democrats lost their majority in 1981.

Byrd's leadership thus was as service-oriented as Mansfield's if not more so. Senatorial independence had become so ingrained that forceful leadership would undoubtedly be resisted. Moreover, Democrats were becoming more fractious and less aggressive as the nation veered on a conservative course. Accordingly, Byrd built his leadership upon parliamentary adroitness and even-handed assistance to colleagues. Senators who differed with him on issues nonetheless respected his skills and service in the Senate chamber.

The Republicans

Senate GOP leadership followed a pattern roughly parallel to that of the Democrats. The similarity is in fact remarkable in view of partisan differences such as composition and ideological mix, relationships to the White House, and the personalities and styles of individual leaders.

The Old Style: Taft through Dirksen

Robert A. Taft installed a centralized leadership when he became Republican floor leader in 1953. Denied his ultimate ambition of the White House and at odds with many in the Eisenhower camp, Taft threw himself into his duties with his usual force and intelligence during the few months before cancer claimed his life. This activist style continued under successors William Knowland of California (1953-1958) and Everett M. Dirksen of Illinois (1959-1969). Both leaders dominated their party's policymaking bodies and played an active role in scheduling and floor strategy. In other respects, however, their leadership styles were rather different. Knowland's leadership drew controversial reviews because of his inability to rein in the reckless "Red-baiting" of Senator Joseph McCarthy (R-Wis.), his frequent foreign-policy quarrels with the Eisenhower administration, his preoccupation with defending Taiwan, and his humorless, unbending personal demeanor. In contrast, Dirksen was generally regarded as singularly effective.

Dirksen was one of the Senate's most colorful figures, perhaps the last member of that body who could draw crowds to the floor and the galleries by dint of his rhetorical flourishes. It was no accident that he was dubbed "the wizard of ooze." One reporter wrote, not entirely flatteringly, that

> his flamboyance and theatricality make him a conspicuous figure of fun. In chronic poor health, he rumbles around the Senate like a skeleton in oversize clothes. His throaty baritone and arm-flinging oratorical style are a burlesque of the 19th-century superpatriot.[17]

Beyond his theatrics, however, Dirksen was well placed to lead his party. A fervent Taft supporter and last-ditch defender of McCarthy, he could not be accused of heresy by "old-guard" Republicans; yet his flexibility on issues was so marked that some called him "the great chameleon." The *Chicago Sun-Times,* examining Dirksen's voting record, once reported that he had changed his stance 70 times on farm policy, 62 times on foreign relations, 31 times on military affairs, and had shifted between isolationism and internationalism as circumstances dictated.[18] His very unpredictability was part of his effectiveness; it also reflected a flair for bargaining and compromise that enabled him to construct coalitions on both sides of the aisle. "I am not a moralist," he announced to a group of ministers. "I am a legislator." Or, according to his most famous aphorism: "The oilcan is mightier than the sword."

Most of Dirksen's leadership years were spent in opposition, and his approach to the White House was reminiscent of Lyndon Johnson's in the Eisenhower period. Although no lover of the Democrats' social or economic agenda, he provided support at dramatic moments. His most celebrated maneuver was an elaborately staged retreat on the landmark Civil Rights Act of 1964, featuring a dramatic late entrance on the stage, haggling over a series of amendments, and finally an eloquent embrace of the bill as "an idea whose time has come." (This performance made him a national celebrity, a lovable curiosity who even made a hit recording.) In foreign policy, he supported President Kennedy on the United Nations loan bill of 1962 and the Nuclear Test Ban Treaty of 1963. More important, he stood by his good friend Lyndon Johnson throughout the Vietnam War, a role that tended to mute Capitol Hill opposition to the war and angered Republican liberals.

The New Style: Scott and Baker

When Dirksen succumbed to lung cancer in September 1969, there was no designated successor. Earlier that year, however, liberal Hugh Scott (Pa.) had bested conservative Roman Hruska (Neb.), Dirksen's choice, for the

GOP whip's job. Scott found himself shut out of major decisions, a frustrating situation that won his colleagues' sympathy. With Dirksen gone, Scott won the floor leader's post by three votes over Dirksen's son-in-law, Howard Baker of Tennessee. In 1971, he won by five votes. (The Nixon White House opposed him both times.)

Although regarded as a liberal, Scott (a former law professor who read six languages and quoted Shakespeare) was as flexible on the issues as Dirksen had been. The 1974 *Almanac of American Politics* called him "a shameless practitioner of ... serpentine twisting and turning, a form of behavior that he justifies with the same urbane aplomb with which he appraises Chinese vases." [19] He took pains to support the Nixon administration, despite his coolness toward Vice President Spiro Agnew and members of the White House's "palace guard." As GOP Leader, he stood up for Nixon during Watergate until the White House tapes undercut the president's credibility.

Within the Senate, Scott instituted an open leadership that looked very much like that of his counterpart, Mike Mansfield. His personal style of dealing with colleagues, quiet and gentle, was indeed congenial to Mansfield's. He shared leadership tasks, and toward the end of his tenure delegated many floor duties to his whip, Robert Griffin of Michigan.

Although personally more forceful, Baker—Scott's successor—continued the low-key, collegial style. In January 1977, Baker decided at the last moment to challenge Griffin for the post, winning by a single vote. His colleagues apparently thought that his ability to articulate issues would serve the "loyal opposition" better than Griffin's acknowledged parliamentary skills.[20] Perhaps, too, they felt more comfortable with Baker's easy congeniality than with Griffin's hard-charging style.

Baker steered a middle course, aiding the Carter administration at crucial moments, most notably the Panama Canal treaties of 1978. As Majority Leader (1981-1984), Baker gained national stature as the pivotal figure of the first Reagan administration. However, his leadership fully respected the decentralized character of the Senate. Especially after 1981, the chamber's idiosyncrasies took their toll upon Baker's leadership.

In short, the collegial leadership instituted by Mansfield and imitated by Scott remains the order of the day. The wide distribution of power, a trend that began in the 1950s and came to full fruition in the 1960s and 1970s, has remained intact. Today's floor leadership is thus a complex and frustrating enterprise that requires a variety of formal and informal roles.

The Leaders' Duties

Floor leadership is primarily a product of custom. It is not a creature of the Senate rules, even though the rules confer upon the leaders certain powers. For example, the Majority and Minority Leaders jointly can waive the requirement that standing committees not meet while the Senate is in session (Rule XXVI); they can temporarily increase standing committees' size to ensure that the majority party has a majority of seats (Rule XXV); move that a measure be referred to two or more committees (Rule XVII); and waive the rule requiring that reports be available for at least three calendar days before floor action (Rule XVII). In addition, the leaders (along with the Committee on Rules and Administration) are directed to review the Senate's committee system on a continuing basis.[21] It is significant that all these powers are conferred jointly on the leaders of the two parties.

But the Senate rules give little hint of the scope of leaders' duties in managing the chamber. The leaders, operating in tandem, represent their colleagues' interests in planning and conducting the work of the Senate. The floor leaders' jobs now embrace the following responsibilities: (1) managing the affairs of the senatorial party; (2) scheduling Senate floor business in accord with workload needs and individual senators' desires; (3) monitoring floor deliberations, which includes seeking unanimous consent agreements governing debates and votes; (4) serving as a conduit between the Senate, the White House, and the House; and (5) acting as a public voice of the Senate through the media. Not all leaders stress all of these duties; few leaders do all of them equally well. But they add up to responsibilities that far transcend the "tedious and unpleasant job" of the 1950s.[22]

Leader of the Party

Partisan leadership is the most obvious aspect of the leaders' jobs. Some leaders are, or become, national figures in their own right—for example, Robert Taft, Everett Dirksen, Lyndon Johnson, or Howard Baker. Others are chosen because their ideological stance or personal qualities make them ideal bridges among party factions—for example, Mike Mansfield or Hugh Scott. Even if they come from one of the party's ideological tributaries, leaders are expected to swim in the party's mainstream, and most try to do so.

The two parties distribute their formal posts differently. Senate Democrats permit their floor leader to chair the Policy Committee, the Steering Committee (which recommends committee assignments), and the Conference. Senate Republicans give these posts to different members.

Lyndon Johnson used his powers to advance allies and to exclude others. He and his chief staff aide, Bobby Baker, weighed senators' competing claims for assignments and made the initial designations, which were usually ratified by the Steering Committee. All factors were weighed, not the least of which was loyalty to the floor leader. Other perquisites—office space, campaign contributions, banquet speakers, added staff assistance, or overseas travel funding—were meted out with an eye to the degree of cooperation a senator had given or might be expected to give in the future. Stewart writes that

> scarcely any aspect of senatorial life, however routine and seemingly removed from the formulation of national policy, escaped Johnson's

watchful eye or his uncanny talent for translating these activities into resources which could be used in running the Senate according to the Johnson formula.[23]

No one exploited perquisites quite as assiduously as Lyndon Johnson did; but other leaders of that era, most notably Taft and Dirksen, actively employed them.

The first year he was leader, Johnson decided to guarantee one major committee assignment to every party member regardless of seniority. The original purpose of this so-called "Johnson rule" was apparently to expand the leader's bargaining chips, inasmuch as he retained tight control of the process.[24] But the long-term effect was to disperse desirable committee seats more widely. Later, rules were passed that spread out committee leadership posts as well. In the 98th Congress (1983-1984), for instance, two-thirds of all senators served on Appropriations, Finance, or Foreign Relations. The average senator had 3.4 committee and 7.7 subcommittee seats, for a total of more than 11 assignments. Every senator either chaired or served as ranking minority member of a committee or subcommittee.

Today's Senate leaders do little more than oversee a selection process within the Steering Committee that is designed to be as accommodating as possible. The majority or minority secretary (a staff post) receives applications from all new senators and returning senators who want to shift committees. These are combined, and the Steering Committee tries to satisfy as many requests as possible. Many senators get their first-choice committees; nearly all receive their second or third choices. That is not to say that the leader's word is not heeded, nor that of other influential members; but there is less room than there once was to reward friends or punish enemies.

Leaders influence their party also by choosing other party leaders and appointing party committees. Again, the range of discretion is not unlimited, for various factions and interests must be included in the party's councils. In 1981 Democratic Leader Byrd appointed nine task forces to help develop party alternatives in such fields as industrial policy and tax reform. He also appointed a Democratic Leadership Council to "analyze what went wrong in the election and plan strategy and raise funds for the midterm elections of 1982." [25] These panels did in fact help rally Senate Democrats and, perhaps more important, helped unify the party in the chamber.

Party leaders sometimes need to resort to coaching psychology to foster a team spirit. This may go beyond the weekly meetings and private consultations that leaders routinely hold. In 1981 Senate Democrats were in disarray, reeling from a string of Reagan triumphs and still trying to adjust to their first minority status in a generation. Toward the session's end, Byrd held a private retreat for his colleagues at a West Virginia state park. It was there that Senate Democrats decided to make a stand against the alleged unfairness of Reagan's programs. Even more significantly, the retreat permitted them to become better acquainted with one another. Surrounded by staffs and driven by their schedules, today's senators have few opportunities to get to know their colleagues really well.

Chief Scheduler

Describing the leader's job, Byrd explained: "He facilitates, he constructs, he programs, he schedules, he takes an active part in the development of legislation, he steps in at crucial moments on the floor, offers amendments, speaks on behalf of legislation and helps to shape the outcome of the legislation." [26] Of all of these various duties, scheduling probably consumes the most time and energy while the Senate is in session. And it is undoubtedly the function that colleagues find most useful. Scheduling can be frustrating because it depends on factors that are largely out of the leader's control: the pace of committee deliberations and the vagaries of individual senators' schedules, not to mention such external events as presidential requests or nominations and national crises.

The experience of Howard Baker illustrates scheduling resources and limitations. When he became Majority Leader in January 1981, Baker vowed to schedule floor activities in advance and cut down on late-night sessions, Saturday sessions, and roll-call votes. As a result, the average Senate day during Baker's regime was shorter than it had been previously.[27] Senators of both parties—not to mention their families and appointment secretaries—were grateful for shorter, more predictable Senate sessions.

Coordinating the activities of the Senate's scattered committees is, however, a tougher task. Baker approached it with characteristic thoroughness. Each Tuesday morning, he met with the committee chairmen, just before the weekly lunch of all Republican senators. Early in his tenure, he had his staff canvass all committee leaders to obtain their plans; a large chart was prepared outlining the proposed schedule for floor debates. Although the schedule could not be carried out totally, key parts of it were fulfilled over the spring and summer of 1981. After that, scheduling became looser.

A major cause of Baker's initial success was President Reagan's decision to limit his first-year agenda to economic issues. Although the decision was Reagan's, it had been urged on him by Baker and Budget Committee Chairman Pete V. Domenici (R-N.M.). When Baker sensed the agreement was endangered, he requested—and obtained—a statement from the president reaffirming the need to emphasize economic issues, mainly tax and budget matters. But other agenda items were pressing for action, and by mid-1981 Baker realized they could no longer be contained. "The dam is breaking on this stuff and [Baker] admitted as much to the members at yesterday's policy luncheon," one staff aide reported.[28] Economics continued to play a large part in the Senate's agenda, but other issues such as the conservatives' "social agenda" involving school prayer, abortion, crime, and the balanced-budget amendment took more and more floor time.

Even more difficult has been adjusting daily floor business to senators' peripatetic schedules, both in and out of Washington. By tradition, senators have the right to be informed when major matters that concern them are taken up, and to be present if at all possible. Their concerns are communicated through, and coordinated by, the respective floor leaders. In the Johnson-Dirksen days, such courtesies were selectively extended. William S. White wrote:

> I have seen one member, say a Lehman of New York, confined by niggling and almost brutal Senate action to the most literal inhibitions of the least important of all the rules. And again I have seen a vital Senate roll call held off by all sorts of openly dawdling time-killing for hours, in spite of the fact that supposedly it is not possible to interrupt a roll call once it is in motion, for the simple purpose of seeing that a delayed aircraft has opportunity to land at Washington Airport so that a motorcycle escort can bring, say a Humphrey of Minnesota in to be recorded.[29]

Since the Mansfield era, however, procedures have been applied more evenhandedly.

Senators harboring substantive objections to measures, treaties, or nominations may place "holds" on them. This is an informal practice nowhere mentioned in the rules and carried out through the two floor leaders. The effect is to delay Senate action on the pending matter. In his first two years as Majority Leader, Baker scrupulously observed holds for indefinite periods of time. In 1983, however, he and Byrd announced that they would no longer regard holds as sacrosanct orders preventing floor deliberation. Rather, senators would simply be notified when the bill would come up so they could come and object.[30]

Every senator's right to come to the floor and object is significant because of the Senate's habit of doing business through complex unanimous consent agreements. These set the guidelines for floor consideration of specific major bills. Usually proposed orally by the two leaders, such agreements often are worked out in advance through negotiations with key senators. Once approved, they are transmitted in writing to all senators. "The fundamental objective of unanimous consent agreements," legislative analyst Walter J. Oleszek notes, "is to limit the time it takes to dispose of controversial issues in an institution noted for unlimited debate."[31] For this reason they are often called "time agreements."

The leader's job is to forestall objections to such agreements by ensuring that everyone's interests are protected. "If the majority leader wants to take up a bill," observed Dan Quayle (R-Ind.), "all 100 senators basically have to agree."[32] Because every issue potentially can be delayed by a single senator— a delay that can be prolonged if several senators are opposed—the Senate continually flirts with breakdowns in its schedule. While senators repeatedly deplore the system, few are willing to yield their own rights under it. What keeps the Senate from recurring breakdown is the floor leaders' skill in negotiating with their colleagues, as well as the (usually unstated) premise that the institution's work must go on.

Two techniques for handling the Senate's unpredictable schedule are *quorum calls* and *vote stacking*. Quorum calls are used to buy time for behind-the-scenes bargaining, to wait for senators to get to the floor, or to stall between consideration of different pieces of legislation. Stacked votes are those that are grouped together for the convenience of senators, usually following long weekends. Because of senators' insistence, the Senate is normally on a three-day work schedule. As Senator Alan K. Simpson (R-Wyo.) put it, "It's like children lining up in the elementary school classroom asking when they can go to the bathroom. 'Howard, I've got to be in Cheyenne tonight.' Or 'I've got a fund-raiser in Dubuque. Can you move up the vote?' "[33] Leaders often voice exasperation at having to resort to such tactics. In his third year as Majority Leader, Baker not only clamped down on holds but announced he was no longer going to stack votes. At the same time he repeatedly lamented the Senate's plight, sometimes drawing lessons from the chaplain's opening prayers. Needless to add, few of his colleagues were on hand to refute him.

However impressive the leaders' skill, scheduling can collapse in the face of concerted opposition. Often there is nothing to be done but plunge ahead, allowing a filibuster to take place. As Oleszek is fond of saying, the Senate operates under one of two rules: unanimous consent or exhaustion. If a compromise cannot be negotiated, then cloture can be invoked. The floor leaders usually support cloture as a courtesy to the bill's authors and as a means of getting Senate business back on track. However, the extent to which leaders lobby for the cloture motion varies with the individual leader and the issue involved. In recent years, several divisive issues, including abortion and school prayer amendments, have come to a halt on the Senate floor when filibusters against them could not be broken. Historically, filibusters were mounted on major issues of conscience or public policy. Increasingly, however, they are invoked for lesser issues. "The trivialization of the Senate" is Senator Quayle's phrase for the development. "The first time cloture was ever invoked was in 1919 on the Treaty of Versailles," he noted with irony in 1984. "The last time cloture was invoked was Monday, September 11, on a procedural motion to proceed on the banking deregulation bill." [34] In the last two weeks of the 1984 session, cloture was invoked five times, as often as in the 1919-1926 period (whose issues included the Versailles Treaty and the World Court) and more than during the civil rights debates of the 1960s.

Monitor of Floor Debate

Senate leaders, unlike those in the House, lack strong rules and procedures by which they can structure debate and limit the time devoted to specific measures. This places a premium on the leaders' skill and patience. It is not surprising, therefore, that leaders take an active interest in what might be called "institutional maintenance"—reviewing or revising the chamber's rules and procedures. Mansfield, Byrd, and Baker all took on structural or procedural questions of consequence: for example, filibusters, committee realignment, and televising the Senate.

In the case of "extended debate," leaders' stakes in expediting floor deliberation have led them to devise innovations. Costs as well as stakes are high. In the late 1940s, Majority Leader Scott W. Lucas (D-Ill.) tried to change the rules to make it easier to end filibusters and pass pending civil rights bills. Caught in a crossfire between southern patriarchs angry at any assault on their prerogatives and liberals who charged he was not pressing hard enough, Lucas lost the fight and spent three weeks in the hospital recovering from exhaustion.[35] Nearly a decade passed before major civil rights legislation overcame the barrier of the filibuster.

The practice of extended debate continues to tax leaders' ability to produce timely votes on controversial measures. While he was majority whip in 1975, Robert Byrd helped liberalize the cloture rule to require three-fifths rather than two-thirds of the senators to shut off debate on all issues except proposed rules changes, where the old two-thirds requirement still applied. Senators such as James Allen (D-Ala.) soon sidestepped cloture by perfecting the "postcloture filibuster"—dilatory amendments not subject to the 100-hour debate limit under cloture. Byrd unsuccessfully sought to cut off this tactic in 1977. The following year, a pair of liberal senators tied up debate on a natural gas pricing bill for nine days after cloture had been invoked. Rulings by Vice President Walter Mondale, under instructions from Byrd, curtailed the filibuster but provoked an emotional floor reaction.

When the Senate convened in 1979, Byrd was ready with a new plan to close off postcloture filibusters. The core of the plan (S. Res. 61, 95th Congress) was to make all Senate actions after cloture subject to the 100-hour limit. Many senators, including then-minority leader Baker, balked at limiting the minority's freedom of debate; six weeks after Byrd unveiled his proposal, however, a scaled-down version passed the Senate by a 78 to 16 vote. Byrd gained his main objective, the 100-hour cap, by promising to jettison other aspects of his proposal.[36]

When he became Majority Leader in 1981, Baker decided to propose televising Senate debates (S. Res. 20, 96th Congress) as a way of stimulating changes. "Turning on the cameras to let the people see us as we really are," he told his colleagues, "can help bring a beginning of respect for public service and public servants again." He argued that TV coverage of selected debates was "an opportunity for the Senate to actually become the great deliberative body which it was thought to be when it was created, as it has sometimes been in the past, and that we would all like for it to be every day." [37]

The TV cameras, in Baker's view, would do more than focus public attention on the body; they could also force major changes in the way the Senate conducted its business. Instituting "town meeting" sessions on major issues, he reasoned, could lead to other innovations, including greater regularity in floor sessions, streamlined procedures for disposing of routine business, briefer sessions over the calendar year, and perhaps even a thorough rewriting of the Senate's rules. Baker's intentions were not fulfilled. The Rules and Administration Committee held hearings and reported a resolution (S. Res. 66, 98th Congress) governing possible radio and TV broadcasting. But it was not to be. Many senators were implacably opposed to the idea, some because it was expensive but most because they feared grandstanding or playing to the TV cameras. When Baker finally called up the resolution in September 1984, several senators began a filibuster, and the cloture vote failed by a 37-44 vote. Conceding defeat, Baker remarked that "it is clear to me that this is an idea whose time has not come. I regret that, but I face reality when I find it." [38] His sponsorship of the idea, and its linkage to leadership duties, was nonetheless significant.

In other instances, Senate leaders serve as brokers for procedural changes desired by groups of members. Such was the case in the committee realignment effort of 1976-1977. Complaints about the Senate committee system mounted through the mid-1970s, when Senators Adlai Stevenson (D-Ill.) and Bill Brock (R-Tenn.) gained 55 cosponsors for their proposal that a temporary select committee study the situation. The proposal languished until early 1976 when Byrd—by this time a candidate to succeed Mansfield as Majority Leader—suddenly brought it before his Rules and Administration subcommittee, where it was reported out and subsequently approved by the Senate.

The select committee, chaired by Stevenson, worked throughout 1976 to draft a broad committee realignment plan. Mansfield and Byrd remained in the background, relaying advice and suggestions. Mansfield inserted key material into the *Congressional Record,* and Byrd engineered a series of unanimous consent agreements that ensured that the resulting plan would be handled expeditiously in the Rules and Administration Committee and on the floor. In the final bargaining over the plan within the Rules panel, Byrd exerted his influence. He met with committee chairmen to shape a consensus and decided how far to accommodate various interests. When the compromise plan (S. Res. 4, 95th Congress) was reported unanimously by the committee and passed 89 to 1 on the floor, it was in large part due to Byrd's role as an "honest broker" among various senators. [39]

Participation in floor deliberations—framing strategies, coordinating the efforts of sponsors, taking part in debate, and soliciting votes—varies with the individual floor leader, and with the issue at hand. As usual, Lyndon Johnson stands at the activist end of the continuum. An observer summarizes his impact:

> . . . Since [Johnson] worked longer and harder than anyone else at the business of running the Senate, he became a legend in his time, a man who allegedly never made a move until he had the votes, a man who clearly established himself as the most crucial single factor in deciding what the Senate accomplished. [40]

Johnson actively participated in nearly every major issue that came to the Senate floor. And, as we have already noted, few measures got to the floor without his approval. Priding himself on legislative products, Johnson wanted to be sure a bill could be passed before taking it up; he compiled estimates of votes, consulted with key senators, and, if needed, devised compromises that would attract sufficient votes. (Sometimes these deals involved the Majority Leader's assurances on other measures.) Once the bill was taken up, Johnson regulated the timing and pace of the floor debate, whenever possible crafting unanimous consent agreements to limit debate. Then he would bargain for senators' votes, on the theory that every bill was a test of his leadership. As with other aspects of Johnson's leadership, his floor domination began to wear thin, especially in his last two years. It restricted other senators' chances to participate in the floor debate. And his tendency to seek any and all compromises that would ensure passage vexed the increasingly numerous liberals, who wanted to pass stronger bills even at the risk of presidential vetoes.

Recent leaders have assumed floor generalship selectively. Some have not specialized in floor procedure, preferring to delegate those chores to others or defer to committee leaders and bill sponsors. Issues have become simply too numerous and conflictual for leaders to invest in them all. Slade Gorton (R-Wash.), then a first-year senator, once came upon Majority Leader Baker sitting peacefully at his desk in the chamber while an intense debate was raging around him. When Gorton wondered aloud why the Majority Leader was sitting out the debate, Baker replied with a homey epigram: "Ain't got no dog in this fight." [41]

Whatever their style, floor leaders jump in to handle emergencies. Some are recognized policy experts—for example, Johnson on the space program, Scott on legal issues, and Mansfield on the Far East. And all are active on issues important to their state or region, their party, or the incumbent president.

Senators do not relinquish local concerns when taking on leadership duties; indeed, they are better positioned to help their state or region. Democratic Leader Byrd, for instance, once used his privilege of recognition to help West Virginia coal producers modify a strip mining provision. Traditionally, floor leaders are recognized by the chair whenever they wish to speak. By controlling the floor, Byrd was able to prevent other senators from offering amendments, eventually forcing them to accept his own amendment. An opponent, Senator Howard Metzenbaum (D-Ohio), complained: "I do feel very strongly that a member of this body should not be precluded by parliamentary procedures which favor the Majority Leader . . . so far as gaining recognition is concerned." [42] Other leaders have acted similarly. Howard Baker was prominent (although not always successful) in advancing projects for his home state of Tennessee, for example the Clinch River breeder reactor, the Tennessee-Tombigbee waterway, and various Tennessee Valley Authority (TVA) measures.

Partisan issues also engage leaders' skills. An early test of the Reagan-GOP Senate alliance was a 1981 vote raising the debt limit. Republican senators faced, many of them for the first time, the question of supporting their own president's call for raising the debt ceiling in order to fund government operations. Majority Leader Baker held a meeting of all GOP senators, calling upon President Pro Tem Strom Thurmond (S.C.) for an emotional appeal. When the bill reached the floor, Democratic Leader Byrd engineered a steady stream of "no" votes from his side of the aisle until the Republicans (many of whom had campaigned against debt-ceiling hikes) mustered enough votes to pass the proposal. Three years later, Democrats again withheld their votes—this time the deficit was indisputably Reagan's—forcing 16 GOP senators who had departed for campaigning to scurry back (four of them aboard Air Force jets) to pass the debt-ceiling extension.

Not all measures engage the party leaders so directly. Especially in today's Senate, with its multiplicity of power centers and activist members, it is unwise to take on every controversy. As Byrd explained, "The Senate usually works its will on legislation before [floor deliberation], and these chairmen, who are acting as managers of the bills, are able to work the things out themselves. It's better for a Majority Leader in that kind of a situation to stay in the background." [43]

Like their colleagues, Majority and Minority Leaders cherish their freedom to vote their own conscience or constituency needs. Not infrequently leaders schedule legislation, even overseeing negotiations among interested parties, when they themselves vote against the measure. However, most leaders are "middle people" standing near the center of the party and acceptable to most of its factions.[44] They are products of a peer review process that starts as soon as they arrive in the Senate. Not only must they gain familiarity with chamber matters but—more important—they must win the confidence of their colleagues. Patience and fairness are the qualities most mentioned by senators in connection with successful leaders.

Despite personal and temporal variations, Senate leaders do tend to be party loyalists in their voting. Figures 10-1 and 10-2 compare "party unity" scores of Majority/Minority Leaders with average scores for the party. ("Party unity" votes are those in which a majority of Democrats are opposed to a majority of Republicans. A senator's "party unity score" is the proportion of times he or she goes with the party on "party unity" votes.) Only three times have Democratic Leaders dipped below their party's norm: Lyndon Johnson in his first and fifth years as leader, and Robert Byrd in his first year. On only one of these occasions (Byrd in 1977) did the leader's party control the White House. GOP Leaders' records are somewhat more variable, due mainly to Hugh Scott's straying from the party fold during the mid-1970s Watergate era. Dirksen fell below his party average in 1964, the first year his friend Johnson was in the White House. Baker, too, was below the party average in 1978-1979, when he drew criticism for supporting the administration on issues such as the Panama Canal treaties. Most of the time, however, leaders are paragons of party loyalty.

Emissary to/from the White House

Maintaining a firm relationship with the incumbent president is an important facet of senatorial leadership. For one thing, leaders are expected to handle presidential requests and initiatives. This expectation is underscored when the president and the leader are of the same party, or when a crisis arises that threatens the nation's security. For another thing, the leader's access to the White House provides extra leverage for dealing with colleagues. Knowledge of the president's intentions and the ability to get the president's ear are valuable attributes that set leaders apart from most of their colleagues most of the time and help them build coalitions in the Senate chamber.

Presidents have consulted informally with prominent senators ever since the first Congress, and regular meetings have been held since Theodore Roosevelt's time. Some historians, as we noted, believe that modern leadership posts emerged around the turn of the present century in response to the need for a regular channel of communication between the White House and the Senate. One historian writes that

> since 1900, a tradition has developed that a principal function of a Senate majority leader is to serve as a link with the chief executive. The growth of the power and scope of the presidency has created the expectation that presidents will formulate and actively promote a legislative program.[45]

Even when of the opposing party, leaders may feel obligated to assist with the president's program, as Johnson, Dirksen, and Baker often did. Alben W. Barkley, who was Majority and Minority Leader and then Truman's vice president (1949-1953), even declared that "by and large, no matter what party is in power—no matter who is President—the Majority Leader of the Senate is expected to be the legislative spokesman of the administration."[46]

Modern leaders take a more independent stance. They view themselves as two-way conduits, not only informing lawmakers of executive plans, but also communicating legislative views to the president. As Baker described his role during the Reagan administration,

> The majority leadership of this body has a special obligation to see to it that the president's initiatives are accorded full and fair hearing on Capitol Hill. By the same token, we have a special duty to advise the president and his counselors concerning parliamentary strategy and tactics.[47]

Robert Byrd, who struggled often to uphold Carter administration initiatives, put it more bluntly: "I'm the president's friend, I'm not the president's man."[48]

Loyalty to the president in the fullest sense was illustrated by Baker's role in President Reagan's decision to sell Saudi Arabia an arms package

Figure 10-1 Party Unity of Senate Democrats and Their Leaders, 1947-1983

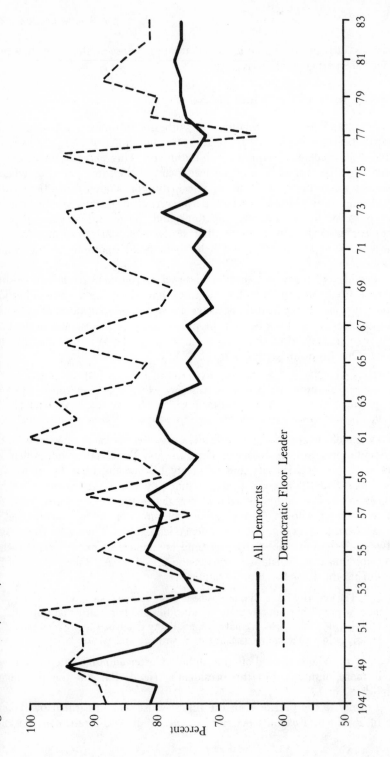

SOURCE: *Congressional Quarterly Almanac.* Scores recomputed to eliminate the effect of absences.

Figure 10-2 Party Unity of Senate Republicans and Their Leaders, 1947–1983

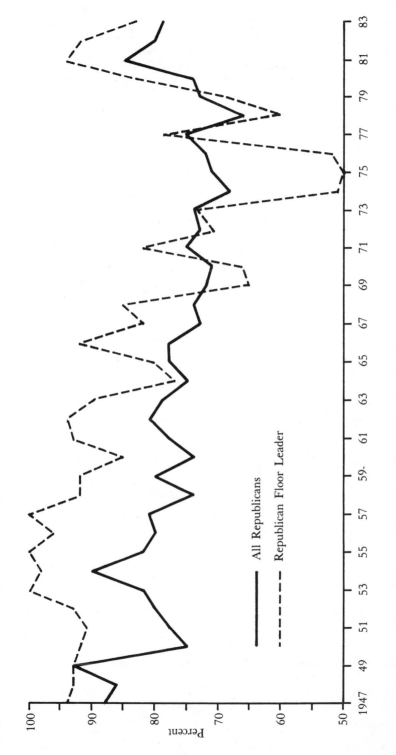

SOURCE: *Congressional Quarterly Almanac.* Scores recomputed to eliminate the effect of absences.

including Airborne Warning and Control System (AWACS) radar planes. When the deal was first announced in March 1981, Baker advised the administration to go slowly, predicting that the Senate would defeat the plan if it was submitted immediately. Five months later, the outlook was more favorable. Baker endorsed the plan, worked to win senators' votes, and was widely credited with providing Reagan with an impressive victory.

While leaders render advice and assistance to presidents, they do not owe them unswerving support. No recent Senate leader has gone as far as William Knowland, who left his desk and moved to the rear of the chamber when speaking against President Eisenhower's foreign policies. But sooner or later all leaders part company with their presidents. Byrd differed with Carter on many occasions, starting with the president's assault on water projects popular with western senators. Baker's role with the Reagan administration went through several phases. Initially, when Reagan's programs seemed invincible, Baker was a faithful lieutenant, commanding the GOP forces and helping to keep the troops in line. After 1981, however, he found himself more often informing and admonishing the White House, staking out a middle ground between the president and the Democratic House and quietly seeking alliances to seize the initiative when the president declined to take it.

Like all politicians, Senate floor leaders pay attention to presidential popularity in charting their course of action. Popular presidents, such as Eisenhower, Johnson in his heyday, and Reagan in 1981, are given wide berth, even by opposition leaders. When presidents falter or lose touch with public opinion, however, leaders display greater independence, as did Scott after Watergate and Baker after 1981. In short, while leaders are expected to work with the president, they retain their independence. Of equal importance, their colleagues expect them to represent the Senate as an institution in dealing with the White House.

When congressional control is divided, Senate leaders hold increased leverage. In all three twentieth-century cases in which the Senate and House have been in opposite hands, Republicans have controlled the Senate and the White House. This enhances the Senate leaders' role, because that chamber's support is essential for the president and provides leverage for dealing with the other body.

Media Voice

Like it or not, Senate leaders often become public figures and media spokesmen. The leader's relationship with the White House is critical. A strong, activist president of the same party tends to reduce the visibility of the Senate leader. Although charged with managing the president's legislation in the Senate, leaders in this position take a back seat in initiating policy proposals. An exception of sorts was Baker, who early in the Reagan administration was credited with masterminding the strategy of concentrating on economic programs.

Senate leaders opposing the president usually have greater visibility. They are expected to challenge the president's proposals and propose alternatives. This was part of the attention accorded Dirksen and Johnson. There is some evidence that Howard Baker was chosen as Minority Leader in 1977 in part because he was deemed a better public spokesman than his rival.

Some leaders gain great visibility through their press exposure. In the 1950s, Lyndon Johnson—who systematically cultivated the press—became the voice of moderate Democrats. He worked tirelessly to promote the notion that he was the only figure who could bind the party's warring factions together and get legislative results. Running for president in 1960, Johnson persisted in reciting his Senate victories while other candidates talked about broad issues. In the 1960s, Dirksen was the voice of "the loyal opposition," opposing the Democrats' liberal thrusts but coming to their rescue at dramatic moments. The "Ev and Charlie Show"—press conferences featuring Dirksen and House Minority Leader Charles Halleck (Ind.)—was amply publicized if often derided. In recent years only Howard Baker has commanded equivalent attention. As elsewhere, the leader's role here rests largely on personal characteristics and skills.

Summary

Senate leadership in the 1980s remains an unformed commodity. Despite certain imperatives, the post still depends largely on the personality and priorities of the individual occupant. None of the recent leaders has been a carbon copy of his predecessor. Mansfield turned the Johnson office almost completely on its head. Later, asked whether he modeled himself upon his predecessors, Byrd denied it emphatically: "I haven't modeled myself. I'm the Robert C. Byrd model, and as Popeye used to say, 'I yam what I yam and that's all I yam.' I can't be someone else." [49] Republican Leaders have been equally varied in style and performance. Taft and Knowland shared similar policy preferences, but their personal styles were very different—Taft's intellectualism contrasted with Knowland's dogged orthodoxy. Then there was Dirksen's flamboyant flexibility, followed by Scott's liberal permissiveness and Baker's middle-of-the-road bargaining mastery. In sum, leadership positions have shifted in accord with personal skills, preferences, and styles; they are not yet institutionalized, in the sense that incumbents have to conform to rigorous models or sets of expectations.

This fluidity extends to other positions—the majority and minority whips and chairs of key party committees. Some floor leaders, such as Scott and Mansfield, delegate floor work to their whips. Others ignore them and work independently. Flexibility also marks the operation of party committees. Although Democratic Leaders chair all these committees, they have approached them quite differently. Johnson and Byrd, for example, shifted gears when changing political fortunes dictated it. Republicans distribute these offices to different senators, and on occasion they operate quite independently. For example, in the 1980s the Republican Conference under Senator James McClure (Idaho) developed an elaborate campaign to publicize the achievements of the GOP majority.

Despite all this fluidity, the hard core of Senate leadership today is its stewardship—some would say subservience—to the scattered goals and schedules of the Senate's 100 members and to the Senate as an institution. Johnson, Taft, and Dirksen of the post-World War II generation could command loyalty and threaten reprisals; but today's leaders have far less firepower. The contemporary Senate, with its widely dispersed prerogatives, requires a more restrained leadership—one that relies not on forceful commandeering but on fairness, camaraderie, and accommodation. In this respect, the U.S. Senate accurately reflects the political system as a whole: it stubbornly resists being led.

NOTES

1. U.S. Congress, Senate, *Congressional Record,* 98th Cong., 2d sess., 1984, p. S4877.
2. *Time,* March 20, 1964, p. 22.
3. Richard E. Neustadt, *Presidential Power: The Politics of Leadership from FDR to Carter* (New York: John Wiley & Sons, 1980), p. 7.
4. See David J. Rothman, *Politics and Power: The United States Senate 1869-1901* (Cambridge, Mass.: Harvard University Press, 1966), and Margaret Munk, "Origin and Development of the Party Floor Leadership in the United States Senate," *Capitol Studies* (Winter 1974): 23-41.
5. Munk, "Party Floor Leadership," p. 24 and following.
6. Richard Rovere, "What Course for the Powerful Mr. Taft?" *New York Times Magazine,* March 22, 1953, p. 34.
7. Robert L. Peabody, *Leadership in Congress* (Boston: Little, Brown & Co., 1976), p. 323.
8. John G. Stewart, "Two Strategies of Leadership: Johnson and Mansfield," in *Congressional Behavior,* ed. Nelson W. Polsby (New York: Random House, 1971), pp. 61-92.
9. Stewart Alsop, "Lyndon Johnson: How Does He Do It?" *Saturday Evening Post,* January 24, 1955, p. 43.
10. James L. Sundquist, *Politics and Policy: The Eisenhower, Kennedy, and Johnson Years* (Washington, D.C.: The Brookings Institution, 1968), pp. 396-402.
11. See William S. White, *Citadel: The Story of the U.S. Senate* (New York: Harper and Brothers, 1967); and Donald R. Matthews, *The U.S. Senators and Their World* (Chapel Hill, N.C.: University of North Carolina Press, 1960), chapter 5.
12. Stewart, "Two Strategies of Leadership," p. 70.
13. Ibid.
14. *New York Times,* July 17, 1961, p. 11.

15. Andrew J. Glass, "Mansfield Reforms Spark 'Quiet Revolution' in Senate," *National Journal,* March 6, 1971, p. 509.
16. U.S. Congress, Senate, *Congressional Record,* 89th Cong., 1st sess., 1965, p. 23495.
17. Edward S. Gilbreth, "Dirksen: The President's Chameleon," *The Nation,* February 5, 1968, p. 168.
18. Cited in Lloyd Shearer, "The Wizard of Ooze—72 and Still Going Strong," *Parade,* April 7, 1968, p. 4.
19. Michael Barone, Grant Ujifusa, and Douglas Matthews, *Almanac of American Politics 1974* (Boston: Gambit Press, 1973), p. 851.
20. Michael J. Malbin, "The Senate Republican Leaders—Life Without a President," *National Journal,* May 21, 1977, pp. 776-780.
21. S. Res. 4, adopted February 4, 1977.
22. Rovere, "What Course?"
23. Stewart, "Two Strategies of Leadership," p. 66.
24. Ibid., p. 82.
25. Richard E. Cohen, "Minority Status Seems to Have Enhanced Byrd's Position Among Fellow Democrats," *National Journal,* May 7, 1983, pp. 958-960.
26. Richard E. Cohen, "Byrd of West Virginia: A New Job, A New Image," *National Journal,* August 20, 1977, p. 1294.
27. Irwin B. Arieff, "Under Baker's Leadership Senate Republicans Maintain Unprecedented Voting Unity," *Congressional Quarterly Weekly Report,* September 12, 1981, p. 1747.
28. Francis X. Clines, "Baker Ends Effort to Bar Social Issues," *New York Times,* June 18, 1981, p. B12.
29. White, *Citadel,* p. 83.
30. U.S. Congress, Senate, *Congressional Record,* 97th Cong., 2d sess., 1982.
31. Walter J. Oleszek, *Congressional Procedures and the Policy Process,* 2d ed. (Washington, D.C.: CQ Press, 1983), p. 157.
32. U.S. Congress, Senate, *Congressional Record,* 98th Cong., 2d sess., 1984, p. S0957.
33. Diane Granat, "Ruling Rambunctious Senate Proves to Be Thorny Problem for Republican Leader Baker," *Congressional Quarterly Weekly Report,* July 16, 1983, p. 1429.
34. U.S. Congress, Senate, *Congressional Record,* 98th Cong., 2d sess., 1984, pp. S 10957-10958.
35. William S. White, "Rugged Days for the Majority Leader," *New York Times Magazine,* July 3, 1949, p. 14.
36. Ann Cooper, "Senate Limits Post-Cloture Filibusters," *Congressional Quarterly Weekly Report,* February 24, 1979, pp. 319-320.
37. U.S. Congress, Senate, Committee on Rules and Administration, *Television and Coverage of Proceedings on the Senate Chamber,* 97th Cong., 1st sess., 1981, committee print, p. 5.
38. U.S. Congress, Senate, *Congressional Record,* 98th Cong., 2d sess., 1984, p. S 11675.
39. The committee realignment case is recounted in the author's "Two Avenues of Change: House and Senate Committee Reorganization," in the 2d edition of this volume (Washington, D.C.: CQ Press, 1981), pp. 107-133.
40. Stewart, "Two Strategies of Leadership," p. 68.

41. Martin Tolchin, "Howard Baker: Trying to Tame an Unruly Senate," *New York Times Magazine,* March 28, 1982, p. 70.
42. Lance T. LeLoup, *The Fiscal Congress* (Westport, Conn.: Greenwood Press), p. 71.
43. Cohen, "Byrd of West Virginia," p. 1294.
44. Peabody, *Leadership in Congress,* p. 470.
45. Munk, "Party Floor Leadership," p. 41.
46. Simeon S. Wallis et al., *The Process of Government* (Lexington, Ky.: University of Kentucky Bureau of Government Research, 1949), p. 46.
47. U.S. Congress, Senate, *Congressional Record,* 97th Cong., 2d sess., 1982, p. S 16115.
48. Cohen, "Byrd of West Virginia," p. 1295.
49. Ibid., p. 1294.

11. HOUSE PARTY LEADERSHIP: STABILITY AND CHANGE

Robert L. Peabody

Every two years, but especially in a presidential election year, partisan rhetoric heats up in the U.S. Congress. Because Speaker Thomas P. "Tip" O'Neill, Jr., of Massachusetts is the principal elected spokesman for the Democratic party in the House and the nation, it is not surprising that his press conferences during the 98th Congress (1983-1984) became a prime vehicle for criticism of President Ronald Reagan's policies.

Under normal circumstances O'Neill and House Minority Leader Robert H. Michel (R-Ill.) are friendly opponents who agree to disagree on many public issues but almost always maintain a spirit of comity (even on the golf course). They have known and worked with each other for more than two decades, but especially after they both became party whips—O'Neill in 1971 and Michel in 1974.[1] Events in the spring and summer of 1984, however, conspired to polarize their formal relationships. Spurred on by their supporters, both enlarged the scope and intensity of their partisan activities.

Although the Republican party regained the White House and controlled the Senate as a result of the 1980 election, the House of Representatives has remained in Democratic hands since the 84th Congress (1955-1956). Unable to break out of minority status, House Republicans have grown increasingly frustrated over the years, especially during the late 1970s and early 1980s with the new crop of Republican activists in Congress.

Michel has had to exercise more assertive leadership to deal with this disgruntlement (and even the potential threat of revolt). A group of junior dissidents, led by Newt Gingrich (R-Ga.) and Robert S. Walker (R-Pa.), have formed a loose coalition of some 30 to 40 Republican members who call themselves the "Conservative Opportunity Society" (COS). Normally supportive of their own leadership, these Republicans have been loud and vocal in their criticism of Speaker O'Neill in particular and of the policies and voting stances of moderate-to-liberal House Democratic members in general. Still, Michel cannot afford to rest on his laurels. As recently as 1959 and 1965, Republicans have ousted incumbent Republican floor leaders.

Conflict between House Democrats and Republicans came to a boiling point (one of several) in mid-May 1984. Gingrich, Walker, and their colleagues had taken a series of "special orders"—a congressional procedure

253

by which a member may speak for up to an hour, usually before an empty hall, after the day's legislative business has been concluded. The purpose of these speeches was to roundly denounce the House Democratic leadership and the voting records of other House Democrats. The Republicans' "targets of opportunity" were an estimated 200,000 viewers who regularly follow the gavel-to-gavel coverage of House floor proceedings on C-SPAN (the Cable Satellite Public Affairs Network).

Since almost everything done by Congress may have partisan implications, it is hardly surprising to find Democrats and Republicans squabbling over the manner and mode by which House floor proceedings are covered. (The Senate has found the implications so profound, it has yet to initiate television coverage of its floor proceedings. The House began TV coverage in 1979.) As Speaker, O'Neill is responsible for the buildings and operations on the House side of the Capitol, including the rules governing television coverage. He took two steps designed to thwart the impact of the Republicans' "special order" speeches. First, he changed the cameramen's directions. No longer did they have to confine their filming to "head shots" of the representative who was speaking. Instead, they could, from time to time, scan the floor with wide-angle lenses, designed to show the empty seats at the end of the day. Second, O'Neill called for a caption running along the bottom of the screen every two minutes informing viewers that "the House has completed its scheduled legislative program . . . and is now proceeding with special orders."

House Republicans, from Minority Leader Michel to the lowliest freshman, were outraged. Not so much by what O'Neill had ordered—which made some sense—but because he had refused to consult with them on such a delicate matter. For nearly a week the House angrily debated the rules governing television. On May 15, 1984, Gingrich rose to address the House on "a point of personal privilege"—a rarely used parliamentary procedure under Rule IX, whereby a member may obtain one hour of time "to respond to criticism of his integrity or conduct in a representative capacity." [2] In the midst of the Gingrich tirade against the House leadership, Speaker O'Neill, who had stepped down as presiding officer, hurried to a microphone, angrily calling to Gingrich: "Will the gentleman yield?" Gingrich, who up to this point had refused to give up the floor to Majority Leader Jim Wright (Texas) and other upset Democrats, yielded to O'Neill. Shaking his finger at Gingrich, O'Neill accused him and his Republican colleagues of misuse of the special order proceedings. "You deliberately stood in that well before an empty House and challenged these people [Democrats] when you knew they would not be here," shouted O'Neill. "And you challenged their Americanism," he continued. "It is the lowest thing that I have ever seen in my 32 years in Congress."

Immediately, Trent Lott of Mississippi, the Republican whip, was on his feet, challenging O'Neill's last sentence as contrary to the rules of the House. Ironically, Representative John J. Moakley (D-Mass.), one of the

Speaker's closest friends, was in the chair, presiding as Speaker pro tempore. Based on earlier precedents and on advice of the parliamentarian, Moakley was forced to rule that O'Neill's use of the word "lowest" was, indeed, out of order. For the first time in nearly 200 years, a Speaker, speaking from the floor, was forced to suspend.

While Republicans cheered en masse, O'Neill temporarily took his seat. Later, in a calmer mood, he acknowledged that the ruling was correct. "I was doing my best to control my temper," the Speaker admitted. "Much harsher thoughts were in my mind." [3]

What can be learned about House party leadership from this example of political "infighting" in an election year? First, although intensely involved, the key actors were not only interacting with each other, but also appealing to the television audience—a relatively new and potent force in House debate. In effect, the House galleries have been greatly enlarged and extended. Some criticize House television as a political "soap opera" for the masses, but it is much in keeping with a basic tenet of participatory democracy—the quest for an informed if not always enlightened electorate.

Second, although the Speaker is normally the most powerful legislative leader in the House, he is not omnipresent nor all powerful. It is no longer the case, if it ever was, that "the Speaker has but one Superior and no peers." [4] He must appeal to other members for their support primarily by means of persuasion like every other member; but he must also abide by the rules and traditions of the House.

Third, despite a rather steady erosion of party discipline over the years, identification with party remains a strong voting cue. Members continue to see themselves primarily as either "Democrats" or "Republicans." They continue to select their leaders, such as Speaker O'Neill and Minority Leader Michel, in party caucuses or conferences. Much of the partisan rhetoric and assertiveness characteristic of the 98th Congress can be traced to the renewed hope and sense of momentum the Republicans have felt as they endeavored to become the majority party in the House in the 1980s.

All of these themes will be amplified further in the pages to follow. This essay has four principal objectives: (1) to describe briefly the historical evolution of the most important leadership positions and the growth of parties in the House; (2) to examine the contemporary patterns of leadership recruitment and performance among Democrats and Republicans; (3) to comment on modifications in party organization and personnel over the past several Congresses; and (4) to speculate about developments in party leadership among the Democrats and Republicans in future Congresses.

The Influence of Historical Traditions

The organizational complexity of the House of Representatives, in general, and its patterns of party leadership, more specifically, reflect many interacting forces. Among the most important are the continuing influence of historical traditions on the operations of this nearly 200-year-old institution; the development and maintenance of a controlling, if necessarily decentralized, two-party system; and the ways in which the characteristic functions of the House as a representative and lawmaking body set limits on party leadership.

The operations of the contemporary House are nested in preceding Congresses stretching back to the first U.S. Congress (1789-1790) and before then to the shortcomings of the Congresses of the Confederation, to the experiences of the American colonial legislatures, and to the long-range influences of prior centuries of British parliamentary traditions. The continuing impact of these meaningful historical traditions is reflected in the major leadership position in the House: the Speakership. Its origins can be traced back to fourteenth-century English parliamentary practices. Sir Thomas Hungerford, in 1377, was the first individual to be assigned the title of Speaker in the British House of Commons. In the British experience the Speaker's role is limited to that of an impartial presiding officer. The American Speakership, however, has had a strong partisan leadership component almost from the beginning.[5]

The Speakership is the only House office specifically mandated by the Constitution. Article I, section 2, specifies that "the House of Representatives shall chuse their Speaker and other Officers." All other party positions, such as the floor leaders and whips, grew out of increasing demands for leadership as the House increased in size and complexity. Among the rules adopted by the first House, which convened in New York in April 1789, was one that defined the limited powers of the Speaker. The first rule of each successive compilation of the *Rules of the House of Representatives* has continued to set forth the "duties of the Speaker," although these duties have undergone considerable expansion over time. Moreover, every Speaker since the first, Frederick Muhlenberg of Pennsylvania, has been guided by precedents evolved from rulings of the chair (such as the one discussed earlier) and have also helped to establish and support new ones. Gradually, these precedents form a body of rulings that guide and constrain House deliberations.

Neither the colonial experiences, nor the formal language of the Constitution, nor the initial rules of the House of Representatives anticipated a very active role for political parties in the legislative process. But the American Revolution experience of pro- and anti-British sentiment, differing East Coast and frontier perspectives, and northern and southern alignments gradually crystallized into Federalist versus anti-Federalist divisions in the country. These, in turn, led to the formation of political parties in the House. Initially, the various factions coalesced around New York's Alexander Hamilton, the first secretary of the treasury, and his principal opponents within the Cabinet and the House, Virginians Thomas Jefferson and James Madison.

The development of political parties in the House was further enhanced by the need to elect a Speaker at the beginning of each new Congress. By the early 1800s, members were taking sides for or against candidates for Speaker. As the Speaker became more powerful, he began to solidify his position by appointing loyal lieutenants as chairmen of the key legislative committees. Within the first several decades of the House, the standing committee system also emerged. Party-identified chairmen began to expand their roles in committee deliberations and as floor managers of legislation.

Perhaps the high-water marks of partisan control in the House were reached under two strong Republican Speakers, Thomas B. Reed of Maine (1889-1891, 1895-1899) and Joseph G. Cannon of Illinois (1903-1911), both of whom had a deep appreciation of the rules of the House and did not hesitate to discipline recalcitrant members. From 1911 to 1915, House Democrats revitalized the party caucus as a means of shaping legislation under the leadership of Majority Leader Oscar Underwood of Alabama and Speaker Champ Clark of Missouri.

Party allegiance to leaders appears to have reached a high point in the late nineteenth and early twentieth centuries. Despite a rather steady erosion since then, political party affiliation remains the single most reliable factor in predicting and explaining voting patterns in the House. That is to say, if one was restricted to a single piece of information about a given member's propensity to vote "yes" or "no" on a legislative issue, party identification— Democrat or Republican—would tell one the most about his or her voting propensities. But in the contemporary House, party remains a "weak" signal. Aside from the opening roll call vote on the Speakership, few roll call votes in the House will find all Democrats united on one side, all Republicans in agreement on the other. A wide range of crosscutting influences frequently enter into voting: a member's personality, ethnicity, and ideology; district forces; presidential and interest group pressures; and the advice of party leaders and fellow colleagues.[6]

From a national perspective, a representative can be seen as part of a greatly decentralized but nevertheless reasonably cohesive community: the House of Representatives. But from another perspective, each representative controls one of 435 separate fiefdoms, only loosely coordinated and tied together by personal, committee, regional, and party ties. Given the centripetal pressures from the diverse constituencies and the weakened effect of party, members of the House have become more dependent on their contemporary leaders, and the organizational machinery they have available to them, in order to carry out their legislative and representative tasks.

House Party Leaders

The Speakership is the only constitutionally designated position in the House. All the other major leadership positions—floor leaders, whips, and the chairmen of various party organizations such as the caucus or conference— have evolved rather slowly and informally. Indeed, both parties did not have active, elected floor leaders until the turn of the nineteenth century.[7] As the legislative workload grew more complex, party whips and chairmen of policy or steering committees came into being. Major House party leadership positions and the individuals who held them in the early 1980s are evaluated in this section.

The Speaker

As Figure 11-1 indicates, the incumbent of this constitutional office sits at the apex of the formal hierarchy of the House. He ranks second in the line of presidential succession just behind the vice-president. The Speaker has a number of important responsibilities. He is (1) presiding officer of the House; (2) leader of his party; (3) chief administrative officer of the House; (4) chief ceremonial officer, as well as; (5) a member of the House with the same obligations as the other 434 members.

As chief presiding officer of the House, the Speaker opens each daily session, rules on parliamentary questions, decides which members will be recognized to speak or offer amendments, determines voice and division (standing) votes, and refers bills to committees (with the advice of the parliamentarian). One of the Speaker's most important responsibilities is appointing the chairman of the Committee of the Whole, the parliamentary mechanism through which the House considers most legislation. In all of these activities, the Speaker is expected to carry out his responsibilities in a fair and impartial manner, looking after the rights of minority as well as majority members.

The Speaker is also leader of the majority party, and it is his responsibility to try to implement his party's legislative program. If the president is of the same party as his own, then the objective becomes to adopt the administration's program. Skilled legislative leaders, such as Presidents John F. Kennedy and Lyndon B. Johnson, will make every effort to consult closely with the Speaker and other party and committee leaders of the House and Senate *before* major legislation reaches the priority-setting and implementation stages. Generally, the top party leaders will breakfast with a president of their own party each Tuesday morning to go over the legislative schedule for that and upcoming weeks. Even with a president of the opposite party, such as President Ronald Reagan, a Democratic Speaker will have occasional meetings, at least until a campaign year forces them apart.

One of the most powerful tools of a Speaker for accomplishing his legislative leadership is his control of his party's policy committee. Under Speakers Carl Albert (D-Okla., 1971-1976) and O'Neill (1977-), Democrats have revitalized their Democratic Steering and Policy Committee. Of the 30 members on the committee, 12 are selected by region, and 18 are made up of House leaders, major committee chairmen or members appointed by the Speaker. Under O'Neill's direction, the committee has met several times a month during the legislative session to discuss forthcoming legislation and what the Democratic stance should be.

Figure 11-1 Organization of the House of Representatives, 98th Congress (1983-1984)

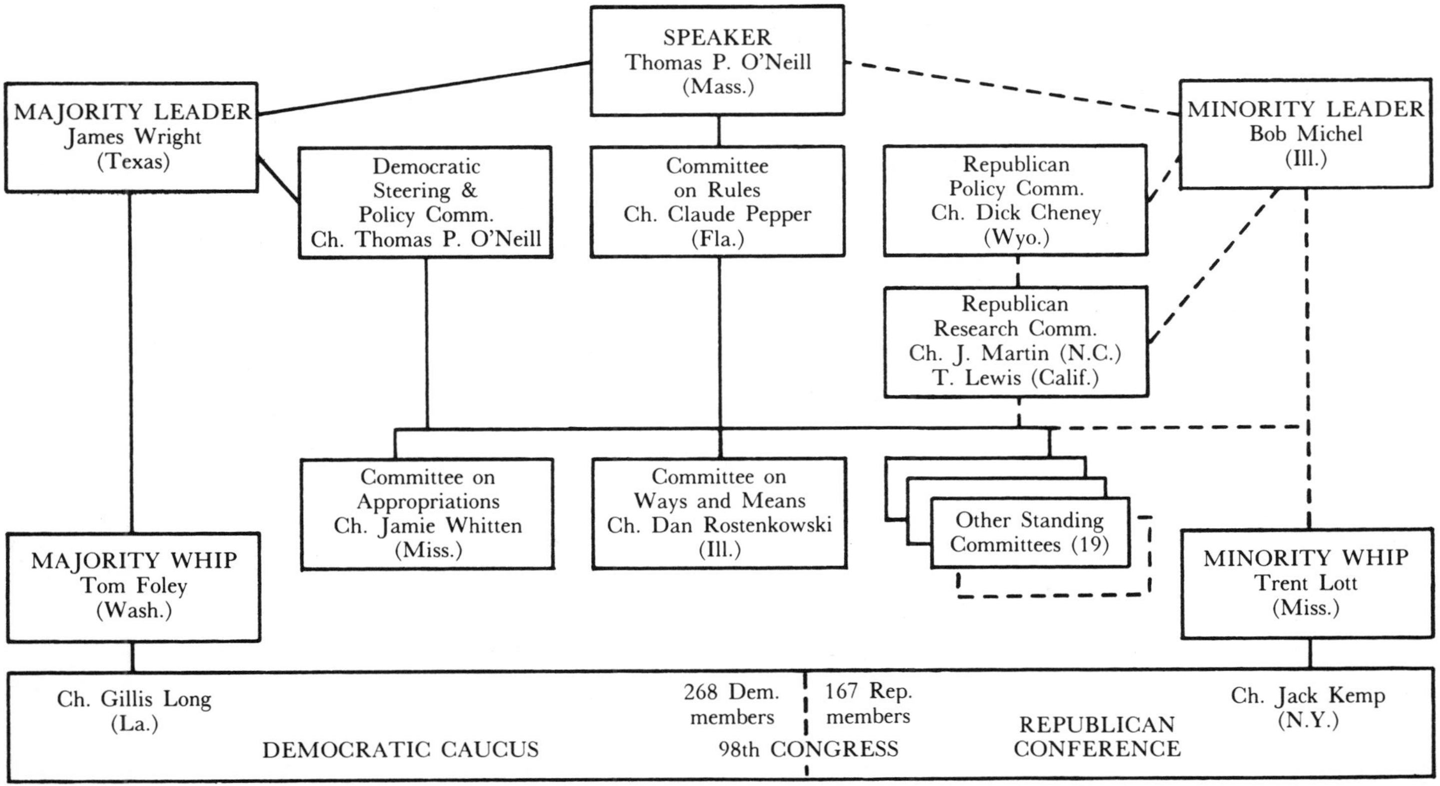

MINORITY LEADER
Bob Michel
(Ill.)

MINORITY WHIP
Trent Lott
(Miss.)

Ch. Jack Kemp
(N.Y.)

Republican
Policy Comm.
Ch. Dick Cheney
(Wyo.)

Republican
Research Comm.
Ch. J. Martin (N.C.)
T. Lewis (Calif.)

Other Standing
Committees (19)

REPUBLICAN
CONFERENCE

SPEAKER
Thomas P. O'Neill
(Mass.)

Committee
on Rules
Ch. Claude Pepper
(Fla.)

Committee on
Ways and Means
Ch. Dan Rostenkowski
(Ill.)

Democratic
Steering &
Policy Comm.
Ch. Thomas P. O'Neill

Committee on
Appropriations
Ch. Jamie Whitten
(Miss.)

MAJORITY LEADER
James Wright
(Texas)

MAJORITY WHIP
Tom Foley
(Wash.)

Ch. Gillis Long
(La.)

DEMOCRATIC CAUCUS

167 Rep.
members

268 Dem.
members
98th CONGRESS

The other main responsibility of the Steering and Policy Committee is to make committee assignments. At the beginning of each new Congress, the committee receives requests for preferred committees from each entering Democratic freshman. More senior members who wish to transfer from one committee to another also submit their requests. In the process of overseeing committee assignments, a Speaker has one of his best opportunities to reward the party faithful and to build credit toward future legislative needs.

The Speaker also assigns members to conference committees, usually following the advice of his committee chairmen, and appoints the members of special and select committees and commissions. Since 1974, the Speaker has had the power to nominate members of the House Committee on Rules, subject to Democratic Caucus approval. A Speaker's administrative and ceremonial responsibilities—looking after the Capitol building and grounds, greeting foreign dignitaries—may not be as major as presiding over the House or leading his party, but they can be very time-consuming. A senior member with office space in the Capitol dies. Who is to inherit his space? The Speaker must decide usually, but not always, according to the dictates of seniority. In any given session of Congress, two dozen or more heads of state will come to Washington, and many will wish to address a joint session of Congress. It is up to the Speaker and his staff to decide how the request will be met and to make the necessary arrangements.

Although several Senate Majority Leaders have suffered electoral defeat in past decades, no incumbent Speaker has been defeated at the polls in the twentieth century. In part, this is because the office is highly respected and reflects well upon the people back home. But it is also because Speakers are members of the House, and they and their staffs work hard at representing their home district as well as serving as a national leader.

"Tip" O'Neill has represented the eighth district of Massachusetts (Cambridge and parts of Boston) since 1953. A former Speaker of the Massachusetts House of Representatives, he first won his congressional seat when John F. Kennedy left the House to become a senator. A heavyset Irishman, six feet two inches tall, with a genial temperament and a facility for telling stories with a message, O'Neill was quickly assimilated into Democratic leadership circles. John McCormack of Massachusetts, then Majority Leader and later Speaker (1962-1971), became his mentor. O'Neill was placed on the Committee on Rules only one term after he came to the House.

In 1971, after Majority Leader Carl Albert advanced to the Speakership and Majority Whip Hale Boggs of Louisiana was elected Majority Leader, they appointed O'Neill as whip. Two years later when Boggs was killed in an Alaskan airplane crash, O'Neill moved up to Majority Leader.

By 1984, O'Neill was serving his eighth year as Speaker. Some observers have judged him to be the strongest, most persuasive Speaker since Sam Rayburn (D-Texas, 1940-1947, 1949-1953, 1955-1961). A committed national Democrat, O'Neill continues to look after his people back home. "All politics," he has observed, "is local politics."

Floor Leaders

The primary responsibility of floor leaders— majority and minority—is to marshall their party's forces to develop winning coalitions on key amendments and on final passage. If the president is of the same party, it is generally the "administration's program" that the floor leader attempts to implement. If the president is of the opposite party, then floor leaders try to defeat the president's program and develop alternative legislative proposals.

Working closely with the Speaker, the Majority Leader prepares the weekly schedule of legislation coming to the floor. In a typical week the schedule may go through more than 10 revisions as decisions are made about timing and the amount of support a given bill may have. Above all, a Majority Leader waits, watches, and builds support for the time when there will be a vacancy in the Speakership. By tradition, he is the leading candidate to succeed the Speaker.

The Minority Leader plays a role similar to the Majority Leader's. At the beginning of each new Congress, he is nominated by his party for the Speakership, a contest he will inevitably lose on a strict party-line vote. Thereafter, he works as closely as possible with his Senate counterpart, either to assist the legislative programs of a president of his own party or to modify or thwart the bills of a president of the opposite party. Republican congressional leaders generally cooperated with Presidents Richard Nixon (1969-1974), Gerald R. Ford (1974-1976), and Ronald Reagan (1981-) but usually opposed President Jimmy Carter's legislative objectives in the 95th (1977-1978) and 96th (1979-1980) Congresses.

All floor leaders—Democratic or Republican, majority or minority—are involved almost continuously in five broad areas of policymaking: (1) monitoring internal party organization, especially maintaining relationships with committee and other party leaders; (2) formulating and implementing legislative agendas; (3) keeping in touch with other House members, especially from their own state delegations and regions; (4) overseeing the activities of key staff; and (5) developing outside contacts, especially with White House and executive branch officials, interest group representatives, and media personnel.

James Wright has served as Majority Leader since the 95th Congress. The position of Minority Leader was held by John Rhodes (R-Ariz.) from 1973 until 1981 when Michel took over. Wright was first elected to the House in 1954, ran unsuccessfully for the Senate in 1961, and was about to become chairman of the House Public Works Committee when he decided to run for Majority Leader in 1976. A former deputy whip, Wright hop-scotched over three other candidates for Majority Leader, defeating Representative Phil Burton (D-Calif.) in the final run-off by one vote.[8]

Rhodes entered the House in 1953 and, once appointed, rose steadily through the ranks of minority members on the Appropriations Committee.

He became chairman of the House Republican Policy Committee in 1965. When Minority Leader Gerald Ford was selected by President Nixon as his vice-president, Rhodes advanced to Minority Leader with only token opposition. After his initial election to the House in 1956, Michel became chairman of the National Republican Congressional (Campaign) Committee in 1973 and then minority whip in December 1974. He was elected Republican Minority Leader in December 1980. His major competition came from Representative Guy Vander Jagt (R-Mich.), first elected to the House in 1966, and later the chairman of the National Republican Congressional (Campaign) Committee.

Party Whips

The whip is generally viewed as the third-ranking leader in the House majority party and the second-ranking official in the minority party. By tradition, the leaders of the Democratic party appoint their whips. They are usually the Speaker's choice, but floor leaders may have a strong voice in the decision. The choice of a whip can determine future party selection for a decade or more, since the whip often, but not always, is elevated to Majority Leader. Republicans, in contrast, elect their whip, usually at their biennial party conferences.

The tasks of whips, regardless of party, are essentially twofold: (1) to communicate constantly with their party colleagues—on the floor, in the corridors, by telephone, and through whip notices and advisories; and (2) to help their leaders obtain the most up-to-date and sensitive information concerning how their colleagues feel about forthcoming legislation, especially key floor amendments. Often on major legislation the party whip organizations will poll their members, that is, sound them out on how they regard the forthcoming votes. Are they in favor, opposed, or undecided? Both party whip systems are elaborately organized by regional and state (or assistant) whips to facilitate these processes. Whips circulate on the floor, confiding in their colleagues, arguing the merits of the legislation.

As the pace of legislation increases, a number of polls may be going almost simultaneously. Frequently, the regular House polls are supplemented by same-party White House assessments and information obtained from friendly or involved interest groups.

Thomas S. Foley (D-Wash.) was appointed majority whip by Speaker O'Neill and Majority Leader Wright in December 1980. A former chairman of the Democratic Caucus and of the House Agriculture Committee, Foley was first elected to the House in 1964.

Trent Lott had served in the House for only eight years when he bested another four-term member, Bud Shuster (R-Pa.), by a vote of 96 to 90 in the December 1980 contest for minority whip.

Other Party Offices

Democrats and Republicans have created other party offices of which the most important are the chairmen of their respective party caucuses and policy committees. In past Congresses, meetings of all incoming party members were generally confined to an opening-day session designed to select nominees for the Speakership. But from the mid-1960s on, both parties began to hold meetings almost every month to discuss party and committee reforms and other legislative matters. As a consequence, the chairmen of the Democratic Caucus and the Republican Conference began to emerge as important party leaders who no longer served as mere party functionaries.

Both parties also have reactivated "policy committees" in the 1960s and 1970s for the purpose of discussing and taking party positions on major legislation. Republicans have made consistent use of this party mechanism for about two decades; Democrats, only since 1974. As long as the Democrats continue in the majority, their Speaker will preside over their Steering and Policy Committee. As already noted, in addition to evaluating party positions, this group makes committee assignments. Republicans assign committee positions through a separate committee, called a "Committee on Committees," mainly controlled by the heads of large state delegations through a weighted voting system (one vote for each Republican member in their delegation).[9]

Organizational Reforms

Both parties in the House undertook sweeping organizational reforms in the 1960s and 1970s. Major Democratic reforms can be dated from the creation of the Democratic Study Group (DSG) in the late 1950s. Increasingly, junior members, railing against the seniority system and other hallowed House norms, were able to help organize and vote through committee and caucus reforms, especially in the 1970s.

One of the most critical developments for party leadership and reform activities in both parties has been the reactivation of party caucuses or conferences. For Republicans, their renewed emphasis dates from the election of Gerald Ford to the chairmanship of the Republican Conference in 1963. Although Ford's reform contribution was modest, he used the position as a springboard for the ousting of Minority Leader Charles Halleck of Indiana two years later. As chairman, Ford was able to call and organize a mid-December Republican Conference in Washington in 1964. Following upon substantial election losses in the House, dissident Republicans hostile to Minority Leader Halleck capitalized upon this change-oriented climate to replace him with Ford. Decentralizing modifications in House GOP party and committee structure followed.[10]

Under reform procedures adopted in the 93rd Congress, members of both parties are directed to return to Washington about a month before a new

Congress convenes in January. These early caucuses have had crosscutting consequences. An entrenched leadership can use the time to indoctrinate an incoming freshman class, which was primarily the goal for the House Democratic party after the 1978, 1980, 1982, and 1984 elections. But such caucuses also provide party reformers—leaders or nonleaders—additional time and an appropriate climate within which to bring about change.

The net effects of the House Democratic party reforms of the 1970s and early 1980s are still being evaluated, but several preliminary conclusions can be advanced. Although committee chairmen lost some ground to the leadership, individual members gained greater autonomy. In the pendulum shifts characteristic of House reforms, more contemporary moods appear to call for further changes designed to strengthen the party and committee leadership.[11]

House Leadership in the 97th and 98th Congresses

Each Congress has its unique characteristics, its perennial as well as new issues, its distinctive place in history. But every Congress also shares many political and organizational aspects in common with its predecessors. Thus any given Congress is most likely to approximate the Congress immediately before it, and its characteristics and accomplishments, in turn, will bear heavily on the Congress to follow.

One major reason for these approximations is overlapping personnel. In recent elections more than 300—sometimes close to 400—House members have sought re-election. So powerful are the advantages of incumbency that proportionately more than 90 percent of all these members who run will find themselves re-elected to the next Congress.[12] Except for those rare Congresses with relatively high turnover—a fifth or more of their members—stability in personnel and practices is almost guaranteed. Moreover, as already noted, leadership continuity rather than change is traditional with the House of Representatives. Leaders typically reach high office after two decades or more of service in the House. Innovative leadership is the exception rather than the rule. Nevertheless, the circumstances and pace at which the House operates can be altered substantially: through membership change, leadership turnover, and/or external events.

In the 95th and 96th Congresses (1977-1980), Democrats had controlled the White House and both chambers of Congress. But the election of 1980 brought about dramatic changes. Ronald Reagan defeated President Carter, and Republicans regained control of the Senate for the first time in 26 years. With a net gain of 12 seats, the ratio became 53 to 47. As a direct consequence, Senate floor leaders Robert Byrd (D-W.Va.) and Howard H. Baker, Jr. (R-Tenn.) reversed their majority-minority roles and all the committee chairs became Republican.

Democrats continued to organize the House, but a pronounced shift to the right among the nation's electorate resulted in a net gain of 33 Republican representatives in 1980—a combination of 37 victories in previously held Democratic districts with only four losses of Republican seats to incoming Democrats. Among the Democrats who lost were Majority Whip John Brademas (Ind.), and House committee chairmen Al Ullman (Ore., Ways and Means), Harold T. Johnson (Calif., Public Works and Transportation), and James C. Corman (Calif.), head of the Democratic Congressional Campaign Committee.)

On the defensive for most of the 97th Congress, House Democratic leaders regained much of the ground they had lost as a consequence of a 26-seat net gain in 1982. Retirements, redistricting, and recession produced a large class of incoming freshmen—57 Democrats and 24 Republicans. In contrast, Senate membership remained surprisingly stable. The party ratio of 54 Republicans and 46 Democrats remained the same. Of the 30 incumbents seeking re-election, all but two—Harrison Schmitt (R-N.M.) and Howard W. Cannon (D-Nev.)—returned.

House Democratic Leadership

For the most part, House Democratic leadership has remained remarkably stable during the 95th through 98th Congresses (1977-1984). In 1976 Carl Albert retired after 30 years in Congress, the last six as Speaker (1971-1976). "Tip" O'Neill, his successor, has proven to be a strong Speaker. Born in 1912, O'Neill is almost as old as President Reagan. The two national leaders have many traits in common. Both are Irish politicians who grew up in relative poverty and worked their way through school and college. Both enjoy sports and excel in story-telling. And both prefer to keep an eye on the larger picture, leaving details to be carried out by subordinates.[13]

In the 16 times from 1952 to 1982 that O'Neill has run for the House from his Cambridge, North Boston district, his margin of victory never dropped below 69 percent of the two-party vote. In five elections (1960, 1964-1970) he ran unopposed.[14]

O'Neill's gruff, hearty style has endeared him to almost all of his Democratic colleagues in the House. There has never been a threat of a challenge to his leadership since he became Majority Leader in 1973 and then Speaker in 1977. He has given the Democratic party strong, effective, and consistent leadership. O'Neill is at his best in one-to-one interactions or in small groups. His press conferences, which meet in his Capitol office just off the floor of the House 10 minutes before the House is to convene, are always crowded and often entertaining as the Speaker outlines the day's program and engages in one-liners and banter with TV and press media representatives. Seldom a man for detail, O'Neill leaves the bulk of day-to-day scheduling operations to Majority Leader Wright and Majority Whip Foley. House

Democratic leadership is a team operation, but no one, principals or staff, forgets who calls the plays.[15]

Jim Wright is the potential Speaker-in-waiting; he drafts the House schedule, assists committee chairmen and other bill managers in floor strategy and the rounding up of votes, and frequently criticizes the opposition downtown and in the Congress. He also plays an active role in fund raising on behalf of incumbents and would-be Democratic candidates. When Speaker O'Neill decides to retire, possibly in 1986, Wright will be among the first to know. He is widely assumed to be the heir apparent.[16] (The last 10 Speakers previously were Majority or Minority Leaders.)[17]

Wright's election as Majority Leader was one of the most dramatic leadership contests the House has experienced. For more than seven months in 1976 the four candidates for the position—Wright, John McFall and Phil Burton of California, and Richard Bolling of Missouri—worked to secure commitments from their fellow Democrats. Finally, on December 6, 1976, the Democratic Caucus elected Wright after three secret ballots. Democratic Whip McFall, losing support because of possible involvement in a Koreagate lobbying scandal, was the first to drop out. On the next ballot, Wright edged Bolling by two votes for the right to contest Burton, the front-runner. On the final ballot, Wright, the most conservative candidate, edged Burton, the most liberal candidate, by one vote, 148 to 147. Although there were more liberals than conservatives among House Democrats, Wright's lower keyed, less abrasive personality helped to carry the day. Bolling's supporters, on the whole moderate to liberal, would have been expected in most circumstances to support Burton, a fellow liberal. Yet they split about three to two in favor of Wright. With just one more vote, Burton, not Wright, would have become Majority Leader and the heir apparent to the Speakership.[18]

Later in the week O'Neill picked John Brademas of Indiana as majority whip; Dan Rostenkowski of Illinois became deputy whip. Rostenkowski, who had campaigned extensively for Wright for Majority Leader, had been Wright's first choice for whip, but O'Neill's preference for Brademas carried the greater weight. Tom Foley, the newly elected chairman of the caucus, rounded out the Democratic leadership for the 95th and 96th Congresses.

Although deprived of a position of formal party leadership (he had previously served as chairman of the Democratic Caucus), Burton remained an influential force in the House until his death from a heart attack on April 12, 1983. His hopes for a return match with Wright for the Majority Leadership never materialized.

Their impressive 33-seat net gain in the House in 1980 won the Republicans a working control of the chamber but not enough seats to become a formal majority. With the support of conservative Southern Democrats, however, House GOP leaders were in a favorable position to promote President Reagan's legislative programs. As already noted, Majority Whip Brademas was one of the casualties. His position in the Democratic leadership was taken by Tom Foley. Gillis Long of Louisiana won the chairmanship of the Democratic Caucus.

House Republican Leadership

Riding the crest of a conservative tide in 1980, Republicans undertook a wholesale change of leadership. Robert Michel, the Republican whip, advanced to Minority Leader, defeating Guy Vander Jagt, the party's campaign chairman, by a 103-87 vote. Vander Jagt, the keynote speaker at the 1980 Republican National Convention, appealed to a majority of the 52 incoming Republican freshmen, but Michel remained popular with a majority of the 140 returning incumbents, most of whom felt he had earned a promotion.[19]

In contested elections for other leadership posts, Republicans selected Trent Lott as whip, Richard Cheney (Wyo.) as chairman of the Policy Committee, and Jack Kemp (N.Y.) as chairman of the Republican Conference. All of them were re-elected at the beginning of the 98th Congress.

Traditionally, the party not in control of the White House picks up seats in the midterm election. The election of 1982 was no exception. Democrats made a net gain of 26 seats to place the party ratios in the House at 267 Democrats, 168 Republicans.

The retirement of numerous senior members of both parties coupled with large incoming freshman classes made the 97th and 98th Houses relatively youthful and open to change. Junior members, especially active on the Republican side, also made life interesting for party and committee leaders on both sides of the aisle. For example, conservative Democrats Phil Gramm (Texas) and Andy Ireland (Fla.) changed parties. Both were "Boll Weevils"—Southern Democrats who supported President Reagan's tax and budget programs in the 97th Congress (1981-1982). Gramm left the House in January 1983 after he was ousted from the Budget Committee. In a special election the next month, he was re-elected to the House as a Republican. Subsequently, Gramm won the Republican nomination for retiring John Tower's Senate seat. Ireland changed his party registration and then decided to seek re-election as a Republican in 1984.[20] In November 1984 Gramm won his Senate race and Ireland was returned to the House.

Future Developments in Party Leadership

What lies ahead? Intense competition for major leadership positions in both parties can be expected. As long as O'Neill remains Speaker, the Democratic leadership will remain fairly stable. "Once the Speaker announces he's going to leave, it's like a stone thrown in water," said Representative George Miller (D-Calif.). "There's no end to the plots." [21] In the fall of 1984, O'Neill announced his plans to retire at the end of the next Congress, the 99th (1985-1986).

What happens when a vacancy occurs in the Speakership? Historical patterns of leadership succession suggest that the most probable scenario would be the advancement of the Democratic Majority Leader up the ladder, probably without a contest. With four Congresses as his party's floor leader already behind him, Jim Wright has become the strong favorite to be elected to the Speakership. Ten years younger than O'Neill, he has been a faithful lieutenant and O'Neill supporter. In 1980 he survived the strongest Republican challenge to his Fort Worth seat in years. He won by 62 percent of the vote, even though his district was targeted by the National Republican Congressional (Campaign) Committee. Traditionally, the marginal seats in the Democratic party have been held by liberals. Thus severe election losses almost inevitably result in a more conservative House Democratic party. It would take an unusually large bloc of incoming Democratic freshmen, on the order of the classes of 1964 or 1974, for any liberal challenger for the Speakership to have a chance against Wright, who has become a centrist among House Democrats in terms of voting patterns.

Majority Whip Tom Foley has set his sights on advancement to the position of Majority Leader. Born in 1929, he can afford to bide his time. Among the top leaders, he is considered to be the most effective television performer. A moderate like Wright, Foley appeals to all but the most conservative or liberal members of the party. But because the Majority Leadership is the principal hurdle before the Speakership, he is more likely to be challenged than Wright.

Another respected House leader, Ways and Means Committee Chairman Dan Rostenkowski, was first elected to the House in 1958, two years after Wright and six years before Foley. He is occasionally mentioned as a possible challenger to either Wright or Foley, but his options are somewhat more limited. A principal supporter of Wright in the 1976 Majority Leader contest, Rostenkowski would think twice before opposing his colleague. Another impediment to his advancement in the party may be his leadership style. Rostenkowski has sometimes antagonized other members with his brusque manner and propensity to contest the more controversial issues—taxes, Social Security, tariffs—that come before his committee.

Other House Democrats who were mentioned before the election as possible contenders are Gillis Long, the former chairman of the Democratic Caucus; James Jones (Okla.), the outgoing chairman of the Budget Committee; John Dingell (Mich.), the chairman of the Energy and Commerce Committee; David Obey (Wis.), a reform spokesman; and Bill Alexander (Ark.), the chief deputy whip.

In the coming years more junior members, especially those from the Classes of 1974, 1976, and 1978, will be seeking greater involvement in party matters. Two of the most promising of these possible future contenders are Richard Gephardt (Mo.), the leading candidate to become chairman of the Democratic Caucus in 1984; and Tony Coelho (Calif.), who effectively discharged his responsibilities as chairman of the Democratic Congressional

(Campaign) Committee from 1981 to 1984. Geraldine Ferraro (N.Y.), another member of the Class of 1978, served as secretary of the Democratic Caucus before she became the Democratic nominee for vice-president in 1984.

With Speaker O'Neill and the House majority as a common unifying target, House Republicans were united behind their leadership for most of the 97th and 98th Congresses. Despite some private unrest, they exhibited strong public support for their leaders. With a Republican in the White House for 12 of the 16 years between 1968 and 1984, and the Senate under Republican control since 1980, there were high hopes, particularly among junior members, that they too could obtain majority status. After the election setback of 1982 and the general prospects for 1984, few GOP leaders expected that their party would soon or easily gain control of the House. The main problem concerns the advantages incumbents enjoy—at least a million dollar head start in terms of staff, free trips home, and favorable publicity.

Over the past two decades, House Republicans have gone from a low of 140 seats in the 89th Congress, to a high of 192 seats in the 91st and 93rd Congresses. In 1984 they hoped to avoid a repeat of 1972 when the popular incumbent president, Richard Nixon, swept all but one state yet only 11 new Republican members rode into the House on his coattails. As usual, during the 1984 campaign season the GOP planned aggressive and well-funded efforts in support of its objectives—a net gain of 20 to 30 House seats. Minority Whip Trent Lott, who chaired the Republican platform committee, was even more hopeful: "We can have a great shift in numbers if Reagan runs on the issues. If we can break out of the mold, we can gain 30-40 seats." [22] As long as the Mondale-Ferraro ticket trailed Reagan-Bush, the vast majority of House Democratic incumbents looked for ways to distance themselves and to run instead on the strengths of their incumbency. Despite President Reagan's overwhelming re-election, House Republicans were held to a net gain of 14 seats.

Party leadership selection in the 99th (1985-1986) and future Congresses will be worth watching for several reasons. First, contests, whenever they occur, are fascinating for their parallels and contrasts in the personalities and the backgrounds of the candidates—a Ford vs. a Halleck, a Wright vs. a Burton— in the ideological beliefs of their supporters—liberal, moderate, and conservative—and in the regional patterns of allegiance that develop.

Second, the outcomes of leadership choices have important consequences for other members in terms of leadership careers, internal influence, and committee control. For example, the compromise choice of O'Neill as whip by Speaker Albert and Majority Leader Boggs was the first and most crucial step on his path to the Speakership. What choices will the winners of 1984 or 1986 leadership contests in either party make that might influence the choice of a future Speaker?

Finally, those House and Senate leaders who are selected will play a major role interacting with the president and the executive branch. Most importantly, they will play decisive roles in controlling the substance, and especially the timing, of legislative policy in the years ahead.

POSTSCRIPT: On December 3, 1984, House Democrats renominated Tip O'Neill to be Speaker for what is anticipated to be his last Congress. A threatened challenge from Charles W. Stenholm (Texas), a "Boll Weevil" leader, failed to materialize. Jim Wright was re-elected Majority Leader, and retiring caucus chairman Gillis Long was replaced by Richard A. Gephardt (Mo.), a leader of a growing group of younger, more junior House Democrats. Tom Foley, a prior caucus chairman and the Majority Whip since 1981, seemed likely to become the last *appointed* whip. The Democratic Caucus moved to make that post an *elective* office, following the appointment of the whip for the 99th Congress. House Republicans re-elected a full slate of leaders headed by Bob Michel, Minority Leader, and Trent Lott, Minority Whip. The 99th Congress consists of 253 Democrats and 182 Republicans.

NOTES

1. In the 98th Congress, O'Neill was the 7th (tied) most senior Democrat in the House. First elected in 1952, he had served 16 consecutive terms. (Appropriations Committee Chairman Jamie L. Whitten of Mississippi was the "dean" of House Democrats; he was first elected in 1941.) Michel, first elected in 1956, was tied with William S. Broomfield (Mich.) as the most senior Republican with 14 consecutive terms. *Congressional Directory*, 98th Cong. (Washington, D.C.: U.S. Government Printing Office, 1983), p. 254.

2. Under Rule IX of the House, one member cannot criticize another and may be subject to "a point of personal privilege." A member may take up to one hour "to respond to criticism of his integrity or conduct in a representative capacity." See *Procedures in the U.S. House of Representatives,* 4th ed., by Lewis Deschler, the House parliamentarian for many years, and William Holmes Brown, now serving in that office (Washington, D.C.: U.S. Government Printing Office, 1982), p. 114.

3. Richard E. Cohen, "Frustrated House Republicans Seek More Aggressive Strategy for 1984 and Beyond," *National Journal,* March 3, 1984, pp. 413-417; Cohen, "Wide-Angle Coverage," *National Journal,* May 19, 1984, p. 997; T. R. Reid, "O'Neill, Colleagues Trade Static," *The Washington Post,* May 15, 1984, p. A2; Reid, "Outburst: Speaker O'Neill and Republicans Clash Fiercely in House Debate," *The Washington Post,* May 16, 1984, pp. A1-A6. For a transcript of the debate, see U.S. Congress, House, *Congressional Record,* daily ed., 98th Cong., 2nd sess., May 15, 1984, pp. H 3840-3855.

4. *Congressional Quarterly Weekly Report,* November 17, 1961, pp. 1847-1854. Speaker Thomas B. Reed made this observation while presiding over the House. He and his Republican successor, Joseph G. Cannon, were referred to as "czars" because of their effective use of concentrated powers.

5. M. P. Follett, *The Speaker of the House of Representatives* (New York: Longmans, Green, 1896), p. 3.

6. John W. Kingdon, *Congressmen's Voting Decisions* (New York: Harper & Row, 1973); Donald R. Matthews and James Stimson, *Yeas and Nays: Normal Decision-Making in the U.S. House of Representatives* (New York: John Wiley & Sons, 1975).

7. Randall B. Ripley, *Party Leaders in the House of Representatives* (Washington, D.C.: Brookings Institution, 1967).

8. Bruce I. Oppenheimer and Robert L. Peabody, "How the Race for House Majority Leader Was Won—By One Vote," *The Washington Monthly* 9 (November 1977): 46-56.

9. Robert L. Peabody, *Leadership in Congress* (Boston: Little, Brown & Co., 1976), pp. 28-39.

10. Robert L. Peabody, "Political Parties: House Republican Leadership," in *American Political Institutions and Public Policy,* ed. Allan P. Sindler (Boston: Little, Brown & Co., 1969), pp. 180-229.

11. See *Changing Congress: The Committee System,* ed. Norman J. Ornstein (Philadelphia: The Annals of the American Society of Political and Social Science, 1974); *Congress in Change,* ed. Ornstein (New York: Praeger Publishers, 1975); and *Congress Reconsidered,* 2nd ed., edited by Lawrence C. Dodd and Bruce I. Oppenheimer (Washington, D.C.: CQ Press, 1981), chap. 2.

12. See Milton C. Cummings, Jr., *Congressmen and the Electorate* (New York: Free Press, 1966); Thomas E. Mann, *Unsafe at Any Margin* (Washington, D.C.: American Enterprise Institute, 1978); and Albert D. Cover and David R. Mayhew, "Congressional Dynamics and the Decline of Competitive Congressional Elections," in *Congress Reconsidered,* 2nd ed., pp. 62-82.

13. "The Speaker calls the President 'the most political man I've ever seen in the White House.' To Mr. Reagan and most who know Mr. O'Neill, there is no more political man on Capitol Hill than Thomas P. O'Neill, Jr. And both men are doubly political in a campaign season." Martin Tolchin, "After Three Years, Kindred Enemies," *The New York Times,* October 7, 1983, p. B9. See also Paul Clancy and Shirley Elder, *Tip: A Biography of Thomas O'Neill, Speaker of the House* (New York: Macmillan, 1980); Lou Cannon, *Reagan* (New York: Putnam, 1982); and Ronnie Dugger, *On Reagan: The Man and His Presidency* (New York: McGraw-Hill, 1983).

14. See *Guide to U.S. Elections* (Washington, D.C.: Congressional Quarterly, 1976) and the *Congressional Directories* for the 97th and 98th Congresses.

15. Many profiles of O'Neill exist, especially since 1977, when he became Speaker. On his rise to power, see Peabody, *Leadership in Congress*; on his legislative skills, see Clancy and Elder, *Tip*; for a sensitive film treatment, see PBS-WGBH (Boston), "Mr. Speaker: A Portrait of Tip O'Neill," July 19, 1978.

16. See Diane Granat, "Jim Wright: On the Road to Being Speaker," *Congressional Quarterly Weekly Report,* April 7, 1984, pp. 775-779; Richard E. Cohen, "Presidential Election Could Determine Shape of House Democratic Leadership," *National Journal,* June 2, 1984, pp. 1076-1081.

17. Peabody, *Leadership in Congress,* p. 31.

18. Oppenheimer and Peabody, "How the Race for Majority Leader Was Won."

19. "My job is to orchestrate your many talents. I know some of you prefer to speak quietly, like woodwinds, and some loudly, as brass and percussion. But our measure of success is how well we harmonize," Michel asserted in his acceptance speech. Margaret Hornblower and Richard L. Lyons, "House GOP Picks Michel as Leader," *The Washington Post,* December 9, 1980, pp. A1, A4.

20. Dale Tate, "Gramm: An Unrepentant Weevil Bolts Party," *Congressional Quarterly Weekly Report,* January 8, 1983, p. 5; George F. Will, "A Democrat Quietly Departs the Party," *The Washington Post,* August 2, 1984, p. A19.

21. Cohen, "Presidential Election," p. 1076.

22. Cohen, "Frustrated House Republicans," p. 417.

12. THE DECLINE OF PARTISAN VOTING COALITIONS IN THE HOUSE OF REPRESENTATIVES

Melissa P. Collie and David W. Brady

For more than a decade, analysts of American politics have heralded the demise of the contemporary party system. Although the extent and impact of its erosion remain unclear and controversial, few would argue that the character of American politics in the 1980s bears more than a faint resemblance to the 1930s when the bases of the contemporary Democratic and Republican parties were established. Despite the considerable attention devoted to party decline, remarkably few analyses have examined its contours in the Congress. As a result, the nature of party decline remains incomplete and our understanding of its dynamics inhibited.

The major purpose of this chapter is to show the weakening importance of party as a basis of cleavage in congressional voting coalitions. The chapter is divided into three sections. In the first section, we outline the conceptual parameters of party in the American political system and in the Congress in particular. This discussion suggests the multifaceted and interrelated profile of party decline. In the second section, the voting coalitions in the House of Representatives during the 1930s, the 1950s, and the 1970s are examined. The results indicate the declining importance of the partisan cleavage to the overall or aggregate character of voting alignments as well as its declining importance to the voting alignments associated with broad areas of public policy. In the last section, we discuss the possible causes and consequences of the decay of partisan voting coalitions in the House.

The Parameters of Party Decline

As Frank Sorauf has argued, the American political party resembles a tripartite social structure composed of party in the electorate, party as organization, and party in government.[1] Party in the electorate comprises the individuals who affiliate with it and are the "regular consumers of the party's candidates and appeals."[2] Party as organization comprises the network of leaders and followers that constitute the national and local components of the party bureaucracy. Finally, party in government encompasses the set of individuals in each party that have captured elective office.

The significance of this threefold profile lies not only in its recognition of the multibased character of the American political parties but also in its implications for the interrelationship among the three facets of party. Sorauf's analysis reminds us that in examining legislative voting coalitions we are examining only one facet of party relations. In addition, his analysis suggests that changes observed for party relations in the government are linked to those that have occurred in its constituent and organizational bases. In the latter regard, Sorauf's threefold profile of the American political party provides us with a general analytic framework for considering a variety of analyses on how political parties have fared in recent decades.

Party in the Electorate

The character of recent research on party in the electorate suggests two criteria by which the salience of party may be gauged. The first criterion is compositional and concerns the proportion of individuals in the electorate who identify with one of the two major political parties. The second criterion is behavioral and concerns the degree to which partisan identification determines individual voting decisions.

With regard to the compositional profile of the electorate, analysis has shown that the proportion of partisans in the electorate has declined and the proportion of Independents has risen over the last few decades.[3] Moreover, attitudinal research has attributed the decline to a reduction in the salience of parties in the political process rather than to an increase in dissatisfaction with party performance.[4] From this perspective, the two parties have become less meaningful to voters rather than more disdained by them.

The shift in the compositional profile has paralleled a shift in voting patterns. Both split-ticket voting and partisan defection in congressional races have increased.[5] In addition, analysis on the determinants of voter decisionmaking in recent congressional elections has shown that voters' evaluations of candidates exert a substantial impact on their choice, separate from party identification and candidate visibility.[6] These findings introduce a perspective on congressional voting that differs markedly from the one emerging from early research which maintained that voters' decisions were primarily a function of party identification and candidate visibility.[7]

Therefore, in terms of both compositional and behavioral criteria, evidence suggests that the salience of party in the electorate has weakened in the last few decades. Not only has the proportion of partisans in the electorate decreased, the strength of party as a determinant of voting appears to have diminished.

Party as Organization

Longitudinal analysis of party as organization has been sparse. Consequently, evidence on the declining salience of party as organization is less straightforward. Indeed, one recent study has concluded that party organizational strength, as indicated by levels of bureaucratization and programmatic activity, has increased since the early 1960s.[8] This evidence notwithstanding, the central if not overriding purpose of the party bureaucracy conventionally has been to grease the electoral wheels of the party's candidates for public office. Therefore, the strength or importance of party as organization may be evaluated alternatively by the extent of its role in electoral politics. In this respect, several factors suggest its declining salience.

One of the key features of the changing landscape of electoral politics has been the erratic but ongoing development of candidate-centered campaign organizations.[9] Recent research has concluded that individual candidates seeking congressional office increasingly rely on their personal organization as primary rather than supplementary to local party organizations.[10] Also challenging the impact of the party bureaucracy in congressional electoral politics has been the proliferation and increasing activity of myriad political action committees (PACs). For example, recent statistics indicate that PAC contributions to winning House candidates have risen with each election over the period from 1976 to 1982.[11] Therefore, while party-based congressional campaign committees have shown signs of revitalization, their influence in electoral politics remains far from singular.

Perhaps most indicative of the declining salience of the party bureaucracy in electoral politics is that remarkably few of the recent studies on the mobilization and maintenance of district support in congressional elections make any mention of the role of local party organizations and their activities at all. Emphasized instead is the advantage incumbents retain in generating positive impressions in the district through information management and "home styles" of communication and interaction tailored to constituency profiles.[12] Other research has emphasized that the advantage of incumbency is mitigated by the well-financed and accordingly well-publicized challenger.[13] Therefore, the character of these studies suggests generally that congressional races are now viewed by voters and scholars more as contests between incumbents and challengers than as contests between Democrats and Republicans.

This is not to say that party as organization has atrophied. Still, it appears to have become less of a force in its most crucial role. Rather than party products, candidates for office have become primarily "self-starters" and, in view of recent research, "self-maintainers."

Party in Government

Our primary concern in this chapter is with party in government. Regarding the Congress, research suggests that two separate but interrelated components of party constitute party in government.[14] The first is institutional and reflects the capacity of party to serve as a source of institutional authority. The second component is behavioral and reflects the capacity of party to serve as a basis of voting coalitions. The institutional strength of party rests on the degree to which party encompasses and overrides other modes of institutional authority. The behavioral strength of party rests on the degree to which party blocs represent the primary basis of cleavage in the legislature. Since our focus in this chapter is on the behavioral strength of party, we shall restrict our attention in this section to the institutional strength of party.

From an institutional perspective, the apex of party strength in the House occurred during the period from 1903 to 1910 when Republican Joseph Cannon of Illinois served as Speaker.[15] For most of this era, the Speaker enjoyed substantial latitude in shaping the party program and imposing party discipline on the rank-and-file membership. Moreover, party leaders served as chairmen of key committees such as Rules, Ways and Means, and Appropriations. Thus, the party and committee systems in the House were meshed, which reinforced the influence of party in the development and direction of policy at the committee stage.

Since that time, the institutional strength of party in the House has declined substantially. As a result of the 1910-1911 revolt against "Boss" Cannon, the Speaker lost considerable powers. The direction of party policy then rested for some years in the caucus; however, factions that soon developed within the caucus prevented any approximation of the Speaker's ironclad rule exhibited during the Cannon years. By the 1950s, caucus activity had all but disappeared. It was in fact discouraged by Democrat Sam Rayburn of Texas during his Speakership (1940-1947, 1949-1953, 1955-1961). Rather than partisanship, Rayburn fostered conflict reduction between the parties and brokerage politics among the relatively autonomous committee chairmen. In a 50-year span, then, the House had moved from "party government" to "committee government."[16]

The 1970s were characterized by an augmentation of the Speaker's powers and avenues of influence as well as by a revitalization of the party caucus and other party mechanisms such as the Democratic Steering and Policy Committee. However, in the literature on the institutional character of the recent House, few scholars have discussed the significance of party. Rather, attention has focused on the dispersal of power among an increasingly important but disjointed network of subcommittees.[17] The 1970s also has seen a proliferation of issue-oriented informal groups and caucuses whose formation, almost by definition, challenges any consolidative trend activated by the party caucuses.[18] Therefore, while the institutional prerogatives associated with party have been strengthened in recent years, the larger character of the House is one of greater decentralization vis-à-vis two decades ago when significant pull rested in the hands of a few committee chairmen. In short, the renewed institutional strength of party in the House has been more than counterbalanced by the trend toward fragmentation and dispersal of power.

Summary

In this section we have considered recent research on party in the electorate, party as organization, and party in government. In each case the central implication is that the salience of party has declined. There are fewer partisans in the electorate and there is less partisan voting behavior. Party organizations appear to play a role in electoral politics secondary to candidates' personal electoral "machines." Finally, the institutional authority of party in the Congress has eroded in the face of a highly decentralized system of subcommittees. If, as we have argued here, patterns in the three components or bases of party are interrelated, we would expect that the importance of party as a basis of cleavage in House voting alignments has declined as well.

Voting Alignments and Partisan Cleavages

To analyze the importance of the partisan voting cleavage in the House, we will examine nine Congresses in the 1930s, 1950s, and 1970s. During the span of these decades, the political agenda underwent substantial flux.[19] Propelled by Franklin Roosevelt's election in 1932, the Democrats established themselves as the party whose national program represented a federal response to the severe economic crisis that had engulfed the nation. By the 1950s, the country had weathered the Second World War and with the resolution of the Korean conflict witnessed both peace and growing affluence. During the 1960s, black civil rights issues intensified as did conflict over America's increasing involvement in Vietnam. By most accounts, the 1970s brought a new complex of issues—concerning the environment, energy resources, consumer protection, women's rights, and national commitment abroad—that challenged traditional loyalties inside and outside the Congress. While acknowledging the varying contours of the political agenda, most scholars would agree that there has been no major realignment of the political parties during the last four decades. Therefore, in comparing voting alignments of the three periods, we may address change and stability within an era.

We approach our analysis of the importance of the partisan cleavage from two perspectives. First, we examine the aggregate profile of voting alignments to determine what proportion of the total number of votes in each of the nine Congresses reveals a strong partisan cleavage. Second, we explore the relationship between the partisan cleavage and broad areas of public policy.

To assess this relationship, we have classified votes in each House into five broad policy domains: government management, social welfare, agricultural assistance, civil liberties, and international involvement.[20] The government management policy domain includes legislation concerning the economy and the nation's resources. Examples include business regulation, energy and environmental policy, and fiscal and monetary policy. The social welfare policy domain includes legislation that deals more directly with the general welfare of the individual. Examples include relief programs, minimum wage and labor legislation, and educational and medical programs. The agricultural assistance policy domain concerns legislation that aids the farming community, such as farmer credit programs and commodity subsidies. The civil liberties policy domain includes legislation dealing with the legal rights and immunities of the citizenry. Examples include black civil rights legislation, subversive activities regulation, and ERA ratification. Last, the international involvement policy domain includes legislation dealing with nondomestic policy questions such as those concerning military and economic aid, trade policy, and national defense.

Once votes have been classified, unidimensional clusters of votes, or "policy dimensions," have been obtained for the votes within each policy domain. We examine partisan cleavages on the largest policy dimension within each policy domain.[21]

The strength or salience of the partisan cleavage rests on the degree to which the congressional parties represent cohesive *and* conflictual blocs.[22] To detect change in the strength of the partisan cleavage, it is necessary to monitor levels of intraparty cohesion and interparty conflict. A decline in either or both indicates a decline in the behavioral strength or importance of party. Therefore, in examining the aggregate profile of voting alignments as well as the voting alignments associated with each policy domain, we present results on levels of intraparty cohesion and interparty conflict.

The Aggregate Profile

The results in Table 12-1 provide information on the strength of partisan cleavages in the House from an aggregate perspective. The party vote scores are the proportion of recorded votes in each Congress on which party majorities opposed each other. The average party unity scores reflect the average level of party cohesion across votes on which there was interparty conflict.

In general, the results indicate the variable contours of voting alignments in the American Congress. Interparty conflict was most frequent in the 76th Congress. Even then, party majorities opposed each other on only 71.4 percent of the votes. In a similar vein, party unity scores indicate that levels of intraparty cohesion in the House have been far from absolute in any of the three periods. These results reiterate the conclusion drawn frequently in crossnational comparisons: Party cohesion and party conflict in the American setting are seldom as strong as that found in most non-American legislatures.

Nonetheless, the results presented in Table 12-1 indicate a relatively clear-cut decline in the behavioral strength of party in the House. During the 1930s, party majorities voted against each other almost two-thirds of the time. By the 1950s, they opposed each other less than half of the time, with a fur-

Table 12-1   Party Cohesion and Conflict in the House in the 74th-76th
(1935-1940), 84th-86th (1955-1960), and 94th-96th (1975-
1980) Congresses

Congress	Average Party Unity Score		Party Vote Score 50% v. 50%
	Democratic	Republican	
74th	83.5%	85.8%	59.9%
75th	80.4	87.0	63.9
76th	83.1	87.6	71.4
Mean	87.3	86.8	65.1
84th	80.1	77.7	42.3
85th	77.8	74.5	49.2
86th	80.1	80.8	52.8
Mean	79.3	77.7	48.1
94th	74.5	76.0	42.1
95th	72.7	76.3	37.9
96th	76.2	79.0	42.8
Mean	74.5	77.1	40.9

SOURCE: Results on the 74th-76th and 84th-86th Congresses are from Joseph Cooper, David W. Brady, and Patricia A. Hurley, "The Electoral Basis of Party Voting: Patterns and Trends in the U.S. House of Representatives," in *The Impact of the Electoral Process,* ed. Louis Maisel and Joseph Cooper (Beverly Hills: Sage, 1977), pp. 133-166. Results on the 94th-96th Congresses are from Melissa P. Collie, *Party Voting and Policy Dimensional Perspectives of Alignments in the U.S. House of Representatives During the Post-New Deal Period* (Ph.D. diss., Rice University, 1984).

ther decrease evident for the 1970s. With each period, then, the overall level of interparty conflict declined.

Intraparty cohesion, like interparty conflict, was highest during the 1930s. The mean party unity score for each period shows that the average level of Democratic cohesion on interparty conflict votes dropped successively across the three periods. While Republican cohesion was lower in the 1950s than in the 1930s, no substantial difference distinguished the 1950s from the 1970s.

During the 1970s, majorities of the congressional parties were far more likely to agree with each other than they were to disagree. Moreover, when party majorities opposed each other, each party lost, on the average, roughly one-quarter of its membership to the opposing side. In terms of both intraparty cohesion and interparty conflict, the degree to which party serves as a basis of cleavage in the House has declined in the post-New Deal period.

The Policy Profile

We shall now examine the voting alignments associated with the five areas of public policy described earlier. Again, we are interested in levels of intraparty cohesion and interparty conflict, which together reflect the salience of the partisan cleavage in voting alignments. Table 12-2 presents party vote scores that have been tabulated across the votes in the largest policy dimension in each policy domain for the nine Congresses.

During the 1930s, voting on four of the five policy dimensions was characterized by high interparty conflict, the exception being the civil liberties policy dimension. During the 1950s, the level of interparty conflict had declined on the four. The decrease was especially drastic on the international involvement dimension where interparty conflict declined from an average of 91.0 percent during the 1930s to an average of 10.8 percent during the 1950s. While a decline vis-à-vis the 1930s was evident in voting on the other three dimensions—government management, social welfare, and agricultural assistance—interparty conflict remained relatively high. Moreover, interparty

Table 12-2 Party Vote Scores on Policy Dimensions in the House in the 74th-76th (1935-1940), 84th-86th (1955-1960), and 94th-96th (1975-1980) Congresses

Congress	Government Management	Social Welfare	Agricultural Assistance	Civil Liberties	International Involvement
74th	100.0%	100.0%	100.0%	—	91.7%
75th	93.8	100.0	100.0	0.0	85.7
76th	100.0	100.0	100.0	20.0	95.7
Mean	97.9	100.0	100.0	10.0	91.0
84th	84.0	100.0	81.8	25.0	14.3
85th	91.7	84.6	100.0	21.4	18.2
86th	100.0	92.3	88.9	30.8	0.0
Mean	91.9	92.3	90.2	25.7	10.8
94th	84.2	84.5	70.0	63.6	43.5
95th	88.7	77.3	42.9	65.1	70.0
96th	95.5	84.0	66.7	52.0	87.9
Mean	89.5	81.9	59.9	60.2	67.1

NOTE: The percentages reflect the number of votes within the dominant policy dimension on which a majority of the total Democratic membership opposed a majority of the total Republican membership.

SOURCE: Collie, *Party Voting and Policy Dimensional Perspectives.*

conflict on the civil liberties dimension increased slightly to an average of 25.7 percent. Still, party conflict remained consistently low during the 1950s on both the civil liberties and the international involvement dimensions.

During the 1970s, the level of interparty conflict on the government management dimension showed little change. However, it declined on the social welfare dimension and even more so on the agricultural assistance dimension. In contrast, interparty conflict increased on both the civil liberties and the international involvement dimensions.

In sum, the voting alignments during the 1930s associated with different policy areas were, with one exception (civil liberties), characterized by high interparty conflict, which was not the case in either the 1950s or 1970s. During both the latter periods, levels of interparty conflict were lower and began to vary with policy areas. While interparty conflict increased during the 1970s on two of the dimensions, the larger profile of voting alignments resembled the 1950s far more than did it the 1930s.

Table 12-3 presents the average level of cohesion in the two parties across votes in the largest policy dimension in each policy domain. During the 1930s, intraparty cohesion was relatively high in both parties across policy dimensions, with the exception of the Democratic party on the civil liberties dimension. Therefore, combining the results on interparty conflict and intraparty cohesion, we may conclude that the congressional parties were relatively cohesive and opposed across four of the five policy areas during this period.

Vis-à-vis the 1930s, Republicans were less cohesive on each of the five policy dimensions during the 1950s. Democratic cohesion was higher on the government management and agricultural assistance dimensions but lower on the other three. Thus, while both the government management and social welfare dimensions were still characterized by relatively high levels of interparty conflict during the 1950s, voting on the two policy dimensions was distinguishable by the lower level of intraparty cohesion in both parties on the social welfare dimension. No substantial difference in cohesion levels distinguished voting on government management from voting on agricultural assistance.

The civil liberties dimension found the Democratic party fragmented and the Republican party relatively cohesive whereas both parties were relatively fragmented on the international involvement dimension. With the party vote scores, these results indicate that on the civil liberties dimension a relatively fragmented Democratic majority usually voted with a relatively cohesive Republican majority. This was in contrast to voting on the international involvement dimension, which found relatively fragmented majorities of both parties voting together. In short, during the 1950s, the partisan cleavage remained strong only in voting alignments associated with the government management and agricultural assistance policy areas.

During the 1970s, party cohesion declined in both parties, although more so in the Democratic party, on the government management dimension.

Table 12-3 Party Cohesion Scores on Policy Dimensions in the House in the 74th-76th (1935-1940), 84th-86th (1955-1960), and 94th-96th (1975-1980) Congresses

Congress	Government Management		Social Welfare		Agricultural Assistance		Civil Liberties		International Involvement	
	Dem.	Rep.	Dem.	Rep.	Dem.	Rep.	Dem.	Rep.	Dem.	Rep.
74th	91.4	92.6	91.9	93.6	85.5	92.0	—	—	89.8	87.3
75th	77.7	94.8	88.5	93.1	79.7	92.6	58.8	84.6	79.9	77.4
76th	87.0	91.0	83.0	90.7	78.8	88.1	74.4	97.7	89.9	91.9
Mean	85.4	92.8	87.8	92.5	81.3	90.9	66.6	91.2	86.5	85.3
84th	89.7	85.4	76.6	67.2	90.4	86.8	56.0	85.9	79.2	63.8
85th	89.1	86.5	67.0	73.5	84.6	75.6	57.9	85.3	66.9	61.1
86th	89.5	89.1	78.9	79.9	83.7	87.6	62.7	82.4	69.5	63.2
Mean	89.4	87.0	74.2	73.5	86.2	83.3	58.9	84.5	71.9	62.7
94th	77.8	80.5	81.0	79.9	69.9	75.6	66.7	70.2	69.1	82.1
95th	82.9	85.5	76.3	77.5	62.0	74.0	71.5	79.6	69.0	77.6
96th	83.1	90.3	85.0	84.8	66.9	79.0	75.6	77.7	73.9	85.4
Mean	81.3	85.4	80.8	80.7	66.3	76.2	71.3	75.8	70.7	81.7

NOTE: Cohesion scores are the mean percentage of the Democratic and Republican House membership, respectively, that voted together on votes within the dominant policy dimension in each policy domain.

SOURCE: Collie, *Party Voting and Policy Dimensional Perspectives.*

In contrast, cohesion rose in both parties on the social welfare dimension. The salience of the partisan cleavage on agricultural assistance evident during the 1950s disappeared during the 1970s: Intraparty cohesion dropped as did interparty conflict. Moreover, while interparty conflict rose during the 1970s on the civil liberties and international involvement dimensions, both parties were on the average rather fragmented on both dimensions. Therefore, although party majorities conflicted more often during the 1970s in these policy areas, they were fragmented rather than cohesive in their opposition. In general, an increase in interparty conflict on one dimension during the 1970s was compensated by a decrease in intraparty cohesion on another. Furthermore, while the partisan cleavage remained salient during the 1950s on both the government management and agricultural assistance dimensions, its salience declined during the 1970s in these two policy areas.

The results qualify the 1930s as the period in which the partisan cleavage was strongest. During the 1930s, intraparty cohesion and interparty conflict were high in four of the five policy areas. By the 1950s, high levels of cohesion and conflict characterized voting in only two of the policy areas.

Finally, while interparty conflict increased in two policy areas during the 1970s, intraparty cohesion and interparty conflict decreased in others, further eroding the already weakened partisan cleavage of the 1950s.

Summary

Our results on the aggregate and the policy profile of voting alignments in the House have indicated that the salience of the partisan cleavage declined in the 1950s and again in the 1970s. Indeed, as the aggregate profile of party cleavages implies, any increases during this period in interparty conflict or intraparty cohesion in specific policy areas were more than overshadowed by the general decline in both. With the 1950s, "policy coalitions" that cut across the partisan cleavage in a manner varying with particular policy areas became evident. With the 1970s, they became the norm. Thus the decline in the salience of party in the electorate and in party as organization has appeared for party in government from both an institutional and a behavioral perspective.

Causes and Consequences

An explanation of the declining importance of partisan voting coalitions in the House plausibly rests on a number of factors. As discussed in the first section, their decay has coincided with other changes in the character of the American political parties, such as the decline in partisan identification and partisan voting behavior in the electorate, the rise of candidate-centered congressional campaign organizations, and the weakening of institutional authority of party leaders and mechanisms within the Congress. In addition, the last 20 years have been marked by the rise of primary elections as the central conduit through which congressional candidates are nominated and by an increase in the tendency and efficiency of incumbents to provide nonpartisan constituent services. Finally, changes in the policy agenda during the last few decades may have rendered the traditional bases of Democratic and Republican unity and conflict less relevant.

The coincidence of these changes implies that the decline of partisan voting coalitions in the House is closely related to changes that have occurred inside as well as outside the Congress. In the literature, the theoretical and empirical specification of the linkages or cause-and-effect relationships among these changes remains tenuous at best. Nevertheless, it is important to recognize that the decay of partisan voting coalitions in the House is a function of factors internal and external to the Congress. Our position is that the character of House voting coalitions is electorally and institutionally generated.

Consider the voting behavior of legislative parties in other Western democracies. Even in the heyday of party voting in the House under "Boss" Cannon, the congressional parties never demonstrated the consistently high levels of unity and opposition observed in most European parliaments. In these legislatures, political parties conventionally have been characterized as voting blocs representing distinct points on a socioeconomic continuum. Party rules additionally provide the party leadership with an array of sanctions with which to discipline dissident members.[23] Thus, in European parliaments, the legislative parties' distinct and electorally based ideological viewpoints, and leaders' ability to sanction party members who vote the "wrong" way, combine to account for high levels of intraparty unity and interparty conflict. In short, external and internal variables combine to affect party behavior.

Evidence on the historical Congress also suggests the interplay of both external and internal forces. The high point of party voting in the House was in the 1890-1910 period when roughly half of all votes were characterized by high intraparty cohesion and interparty conflict (that is, 90 percent of one party voting against 90 percent of the other party). On about 80 percent of the votes, party majorities opposed each other. From an electoral perspective, this period featured political parties with distinct centers of gravity. The Republicans in Congress represented northern industrial concerns; the Democrats represented southern and border state agricultural interests. From an institutional perspective, strong party leadership centralized control in the Speaker of the House.

Thus, at the turn of the century, the political parties represented distinct and polarized components of the electorate. Institutional authority derived from party leaders and mechanisms within the House.[24] As has generally been the case in European parliaments, the U.S. House of Representatives during the 1890-1910 period marked the confluence of clear differences in the electoral bases of the legislative parties, institutionally based party strength within the Congress, and high levels of party unity and opposition. Further substantiating the role of both electoral and institutional determinants, analysis of American state legislatures has shown that levels of party voting are higher in states with polarized parties and strong Speakers than in states without these characteristics.[25]

Our argument maintains that salient partisan voting coalitions result from an electorate that votes for parties rather than for individual personalities and from an institutional arrangement that vests party leaders with an authority recognized by the rank-and-file party membership in the Congress. At the turn of the century, the electoral and the institutional environment converged to induce strong partisan voting coalitions. The revolt against the Speaker in 1910 and 1911 reduced the House leadership's power; however, partisanship in the electorate remained relatively high. The New Deal realignment of the 1930s increased partisan voting behavior in the electorate. Therefore, the relative salience in our analysis of the party voting coalitions evident in the 1930s period was, for the most part, electorally or externally driven. Democrats, for example, voted with the president and with their party because they correctly perceived that their electoral fate was linked to their president's and party's fate.

The strength of the electoral sanction remained high at least through the 1950s. (Recall the "coattail effect" in 1952 when Republican majorities were elected in the House and Senate on the strength of Dwight Eisenhower's popularity.[26]) The American electorate became less partisan in the 1960s, and by the 1970s the "average" Democrat or Republican in the House was not encumbered by either electoral or institutional sanctions.

In recent years the impact of party on individuals' electoral and legislative experience has become decidedly more obscure. Candidates for congressional office in the 1980s obtain their party's nomination in a direct primary election. Their primary campaign is fueled and staffed by an organization largely independent of the local or state party bureaucracy. In the general election, candidates confront a less partisan electorate or one in which, by most accounts, partisan identification is a less dependable source of electoral support.

Once elected, representatives find themselves in a highly decentralized institution. Even junior members have considerable opportunity to forge their own power base, and senior party leaders are likely to punish only the most egregious behavior. (For example, in the 98th Congress the House Democratic party leadership removed Phil Gramm (D-Texas) from the prestigious House Budget Committee for his activity on the Reagan administration's budget package. Gramm then ran for Congress as a Republican, was re-elected, and was rewarded by the Republican party leadership with an excellent committee assignment.) Members' partisan affiliation is with congressional parties that encompass diverse sets of interests, particularly in the case of the Democrats, rather than with homogeneous and polarized blocs. Moreover, confronted with the numerous caucuses and informal groups now active in the House, members' loyalties are less likely to be confined to their party.

Overall, neither the electoral nor the legislative scenario in which recent House members operate is conducive to strong partisan voting coalitions. Due to both the electoral and legislative circumstances of the contemporary House, members have the opportunity and incentive to act independently.

The central consequence of the decay of partisan voting coalitions is that the character or composition of legislative majorities becomes more uncertain. From a historical perspective, the congressional parties have proved the broadest and most stable basis of coalition formation in the Congress. In this respect, the congressional party has served as the primary mechanism for the integration of diverse interests and the consolidation of support and opposition across policy areas.[27] In the absence of strong partisan voting coalitions, the tendency in a legislative body such as the U.S. House of Representatives is for majorities to form and reform around particular policy questions. Hence, legislative majorities tend to vary from policy to policy, majority building becomes less predictable, and the general character of voting coalitions becomes more fragmented. These developments have several policy-related ramifications.

First, legislative proposals are more likely to be watered down or compromised during the legislative process. A prime example is the debilitation of the Carter administration's energy package.[28] President Jimmy Carter presented the 95th Congress with legislation strongly oriented toward energy conservation. As a whole, the energy package drew the attention of numerous factions within the House, each of which was primarily interested in amending a particular facet of the legislation. To secure a coalition sizable enough to pass any form of energy legislation, the House leadership was forced to incorporate many of these demands, the ultimate outcome being a weakened, patchwork version of the initial Carter legislation.

A second ramification of weak partisan voting coalitions is that policy "contradictions" are more likely to occur. In a legislative body where substantively organized committees shape the initial parameters of public policy and where party fails to integrate legislative decisions across substantive areas, federal policy in one area may contradict that in another. Thus, it becomes possible for the Congress to find itself in a position where, for example, it supports the antismoking admonitions of the National Institute of Health at the same time it heavily subsidizes the tobacco industry.[29]

A third ramification is that the legislative logroll becomes the hallmark of the legislative process. In the absence of strong partisan coalitions that act to mesh disparate interests into coherent policy wholes, policy outcomes are more likely to be the conglomerates of highly individualized concerns. Federal land use policy, for example, is characterized by the satisfaction of timber, grazing, and mining interests. In the classic logroll, each interest supports the discrete concerns of the others, thereby accommodating all via omnibus legislation.[30]

In general, the decay of partisan voting coalitions likely marks changes in the character of the legislative process and the character of public policy itself. To be sure, the consequences of this decay are at least as interrelated and complex as its causes. Nonetheless, a more refined understanding of the determinants and implications of the variations in partisan voting coalitions shall provide insight into the shifting contours of American electoral and legislative politics in the 1980s.

NOTES

1. Frank J. Sorauf, *Party Politics in America,* 3rd ed. (Boston: Little, Brown & Co., 1976), pp. 9-12.
2. Ibid., p. 12.
3. For example, see Barbara Hinckley, *Congressional Elections* (Washington, D.C.: CQ Press, 1981), p. 63.
4. Martin P. Wattenberg, "The Decline of Political Partisanship in the United States: Negativity or Neutrality?" *American Political Science Review* 75 (1981):

941-950; and Arthur H. Miller and Martin P. Wattenberg, "Measuring Party Identification: Independent or No Partisan Preference?" *American Journal of Political Science* 27 (1983): 106-121.

5. On split-ticket voting, see Walter DeVries and V. Lance Tarrance, *The Ticket-Splitter* (Grand Rapids, Mich.: Erdmans, 1972). On partisan defection, see Thomas E. Mann and Raymond Wolfinger, "Candidates and Parties in Congressional Elections," *American Political Science Review* 74 (1980): 617-632.

6. See, for example, Thomas E. Mann, *Unsafe at Any Margin* (Washington, D.C.: American Enterprise Institute for Public Policy Research, 1978); Alan I. Abramowitz, "A Comparison of Voting for U.S. Senator and Representative in 1978," *American Political Science Review* 74 (1980): 633-640; and Barbara Hinckley, "The American Voter in Congressional Elections," *American Political Science Review* 74 (1980): 641-650.

7. Donald E. Stokes and Warren E. Miller, "Party Government and the Saliency of Congress," *Public Opinion Quarterly* 26 (1962): 531-546.

8. James L. Gibson et al., "Assessing Party Organizational Strength," *American Journal of Political Science* 27 (1983): 193-222.

9. Sorauf, *Party Politics,* p. 84.

10. Thomas E. Mann, "Congressional Elections," in *The New Congress,* ed. Thomas E. Mann and Norman J. Ornstein (Washington, D.C.: American Enterprise Institute for Public Policy Research, 1981), pp. 32-54.

11. Brooks Jackson, "More Incumbents Turn to PACs," *The Wall Street Journal,* May 1, 1984, p. 60. See also J. David Gopian, "What Makes PACs Tick? An Analysis of the Allocation Patterns of Economic Interest Groups," *American Journal of Political Science* 28 (1984): 259-281.

12. See Richard Fenno, *Home Style: Congressmen in Their Districts* (Boston: Little, Brown & Co., 1978); Hinckley, "The American Voter in Congressional Elections"; and Glenn Parker, "Incumbent Popularity and Electoral Success," in *Congressional Elections,* ed. Louis Maisel and Joseph Cooper (Beverly Hills: Sage, 1981), pp. 249-279.

13. Gary Jacobson, *Money in Congressional Elections* (New Haven: Yale University Press, 1980).

14. See Joseph Cooper, "Congress in Organizational Perspective," in *Congress Reconsidered,* 1st ed., edited by Lawrence C. Dodd and Bruce I. Oppenheimer (New York: Praeger, 1977), pp. 140-159.

15. See Joseph Cooper and David W. Brady, "Institutional Context and Leadership Style: The House from Cannon to Rayburn," *American Political Science Review* 75 (1981): 411-426; David W. Brady, *Congressional Voting in a Partisan Era* (Lawrence: University of Kansas, 1973); and Charles O. Jones, "Joseph G. Cannon and Howard W. Smith: An Essay on the Limits of Leadership in the House of Representatives," *Journal of Politics* 30 (1968): 6-25.

16. See Cooper and Brady, "Institutional Context and Leadership Style"; and Lawrence C. Dodd and Richard L. Schott, *Congress and the Administrative State* (New York: John Wiley, 1979), pp. 58-105.

17. See Norman J. Ornstein, "Causes and Consequences of Congressional Change: Subcommittee Reforms in the House of Representatives, 1970-1973," in *Congress in Change,* ed. Norman J. Ornstein (New York: Praeger, 1975); and Roger H. Davidson and Walter J. Oleszek, *Congress Against Itself* (Bloomington: Indiana University Press, 1977).

18. Susan W. Hammond, Daniel P. Mulhollan, and Arthur G. Stevens, "The Institutionalization of Interests in Congress: An Organizational Perspective on Informal Groups" (Paper presented at the annual meeting of the Southwestern Political Science Association, Dallas, Texas, 1981).

19. See Barbara Sinclair, *Congressional Realignment, 1925-1978* (Austin: University of Texas Press, 1982).

20. These are the policy categories developed in Aage Clausen, *How Congressmen Decide* (New York: St. Martin's, 1973). Also see Sinclair, *Congressional Realignment, 1925-1978.*

21. A matrix of the absolute values of Yule's Q coefficients has been generated for the voters within each policy domain in each House. With .6 as the cutoff value, a complete linkage hierarchical clustering procedure has yielded one or more unidimensional clusters of votes for each policy domain. For a more detailed description of the methodology, see Melissa P. Collie, "Policy Dimensional Analysis and the Structure of Voting Patterns: The U.S. House of Representatives in Three Periods" (Paper presented at the annual meeting of the American Political Science Association, Chicago, Illinois, 1983).

22. See Joseph Cooper, David W. Brady, and Patricia A. Hurley, "The Electoral Basis of Party Voting: Patterns and Trends in the U.S. House of Representatives," in *The Impact of the Electoral Process,* ed. Louis Maisel and Joseph Cooper (Beverly Hills: Sage, 1977), pp. 133-166.

23. For a comparative perspective on party behavior in American and non-American legislatures, see Leon D. Epstein, *Political Parties in Western Democracies* (New Brunswick, N.J.: Transaction Books, 1979); and Michael L. Mezey, *Comparative Legislatures* (Durham, N.C.: Duke University Press, 1979).

24. See David W. Brady and Phillip Althoff, "Party Voting in the U.S. House of Representatives, 1890-1910: Elements of a Responsible Party System," *Journal of Politics* 36 (1974): 753-775.

25. See Duncan MacRae, Jr., "The Relation Between Roll-Call Votes and Constituencies in the Massachusetts House of Representatives," *American Political Science Review* 46 (1952): 1046-1055; and Hugh Le Blanc, "Voting in State Senates: Party and Constituency Influences," *Midwest Journal of Political Science* 13 (1969): 33-57.

26. For a recent analysis of presidential coattail effects in congressional elections, see John A. Ferejohn and Randall L. Calvert, "Presidential Coattails in Historical Perspective," *American Journal of Political Science* 28 (1984): 127-146.

27. Cooper, "Congress in Organizational Perspective."

28. See Bruce I. Oppenheimer, "Congress and the New Obstructionism: Developing an Energy Program," in *Congress Reconsidered,* 2nd ed., edited by Lawrence C. Dodd and Bruce I. Oppenheimer (Washington, D.C.: CQ Press, 1981); and Charles O. Jones, "Congress and the Making of Energy Policy," in *New Dimensions to Energy Policy,* ed. Robert Lawrence (Lexington, Mass.: Lexington Books, D. C. Heath & Co., 1979).

29. For other examples, see Dodd and Schott, *Congress and the Administrative State.*

30. See Richard F. Fenno, Jr., *Congressmen in Committees* (Boston: Little, Brown & Co., 1973).

Part V

CONGRESS, THE EXECUTIVE,
AND PUBLIC POLICY

13. AGENDA, POLICY, AND ALIGNMENT CHANGE FROM COOLIDGE TO REAGAN

Barbara Sinclair

Although congressional voting behavior has been studied extensively, the emphasis has been static rather than dynamic; that is, research has shown us "snapshots" of one policy area at one point in time, rather than change over time.[1] This study examines three aspects of change: change in political agenda, change in policy outputs, and alignment change. Our purpose is to describe such change over the half century from 1925 through 1982.

By the political agenda, we mean the set of problems and policy proposals being seriously debated by the attentive public and by policymakers and the terms of that debate. *Agenda change* can be said to have occurred when new problems are perceived, when new solutions to existing problems are proposed, or when the terms of the debate, that is, the basis of the division between the "sides," change significantly.

Policy change occurs during every Congress but is usually incremental; it is aimed at a problem on which a previous body of legislation exists, and its approach to the problem is similar to that embodied in existing legislation. Occasionally, however, Congress will pass legislation dealing with a major problem on which the federal government has not acted previously or legislation that approaches an old problem in a radically new way. It is such nonincremental legislation that represents true policy change.

In this study *voting alignments* are characterized in terms of party and region. Analyses of recent Congresses have shown these variables to be of major importance in describing members' voting behavior. We are interested in whether the influence of these factors varies over time.

The Issue Domains

To discuss congressional alignments over a half-century period, a schema for classifying votes into a limited number of issue categories is needed. It would be impossible to study individually the thousands of roll calls taken. We shall use an issue categorization developed by Aage Clausen in his work on the Congresses of the 1950s and early 1960s.[2]

The four policy domains of Clausen's that will be used here are government management of the economy, social welfare, civil liberties, and international involvement. The government management category centers on legislation dealing with the economy and the nation's resources. Examples are business regulation, public works, conservation and environmental legislation, monetary and fiscal policy, and the overall level of governmental spending. In contrast, the social welfare domain includes legislation designed to aid the individual more directly. Aid to education, public housing, and labor legislation are examples. The civil liberties category includes civil rights for blacks and issues such as subversive activities regulation and federal criminal justice procedures. The international involvement domain includes all nondomestic policy questions.

For an issue classification to be useful, it not only must make substantive sense, but the votes included in a given category must evoke similar voting alignments. After roll calls were categorized into the issue domains, a procedure to select those that evoked similar alignments was employed.[3] Usually a large proportion of the roll calls met the test for inclusion into the resulting issue scale or dimension. Each member of the House was then given a score on each issue dimension in each of the Congresses in which he or she served. The score is simply the percentage of the roll calls included in the dimension on which the member took a position that would popularly be called liberal. For example, a high score on the social welfare dimension indicates the member voted in favor of establishing and expanding various social welfare programs.

The Great Depression and the Transformation of the Political Agenda, 1925-1938

In 1925 the Republicans had been the majority party in the country for several generations. This dominance was reflected in a Republican president, Calvin Coolidge, and a heavily Republican Congress. In the House of Representatives elected in 1936, however, Democrats outnumbered Republicans by more than three to one. By the late 1930s the Democrats had become the nation's majority party. Franklin Roosevelt had twice been elected to the presidency by landslide margins, and Democrats had controlled the House since 1931.

Government Management

The Great Depression precipitated this party realignment and led to a transformation in the policy agenda. Only one of the four issue dimensions—government management—was found in the pre-depression Congresses. It appears in each of the Congresses from 1925 through 1938, and in each case voting is along party lines.

Although alignments remained stable, the content of the dimension and the terms of the debate changed radically with the coming of the New Deal. In the pre-New Deal Congresses the extent of pro- or anti-big business sentiment to some extent distinguished the parties, but neither party advocated an activist federal role in regulating or managing the economy. With the 73rd Congress (1933-1934) the government management dimension became a New Deal dimension. A high score on the 73rd, 74th, and 75th government management scales indicates the representative voted for the creation of the Tennessee Valley Authority (TVA), the invalidation of the gold standards clause, Roosevelt's "soak the rich" tax bill, and the regulation of public utility holding companies.

By and large, the bills included in the dimension during the New Deal represent an activist federal government philosophy. But while the content of the measures included in the government management dimension changed, representatives' voting behavior remained highly partisan. A much greater ideological distance between the parties resulted. The Democrats clearly supported an activist position. As Table 13-1 indicates, the average Democrat's support for the party position on the government management dimension is higher after 1930 than in the less ideologically charged preceding years.

Despite the strong relationship between party and vote on the government management dimension, certain regional differences within the parties appear.[4] Southern Democrats tend to be more supportive of the party position than their northeastern party colleagues, although the differences are slight after 1930. Within the Republican party the progressive heritage of many representatives from the West North Central area shows up in their willingness to defect from the party position, while northeasterners are the conservative mainstay of the Republican party.

Table 13-1 Government Management and Social Welfare Support Scores, 1925-1938 (In Percentages)

| | Democrats | | | Republicans | | |
	All	*North-east*	*Solid South*	*All*	*North-east*	*West North Central*
Government Management						
1925-1930	84.8	75.6	88.6	9.9	4.0	14.8
1931-1938	91.3	90.3	94.2	10.1	4.6	23.3
Social Welfare						
1929-1938	91.0	93.3	92.9	8.9	4.3	13.7
1938 Fair Labor Standards Act	77.8	99.0	39.2	43.5	46.1	39.8

Social Welfare

The origins of the welfare state are popularly associated with the New Deal. Prior to the depression, legislation designed to help the individual relatively directly was not completely without precedent in American history. Some labor legislation was on the books; veterans' pensions and other social services for certain classes of veterans had a relatively long history; and, in the early 1920s, legislation concerning maternal and infant health needs was passed. Nevertheless, direct help to individuals was generally not considered within the province of legitimate federal action at that time.

During the 1925-1938 period the social welfare dimension first appears in the 71st Congress (1929-1930). Roll calls on a veterans' pension bill and on providing additional hospital facilities for veterans are included. More clearly related to the depression are roll calls on taking a census of unemployment and on the use of federal funds for relief. Firmly opposed to a federal "dole," President Herbert Hoover favored relying upon private charity to alleviate the misery caused by widespread unemployment. The Democrats read their gains in the 1930 election as a mandate, and in the 72nd Congress Speaker John Nance Garner proposed a several billion dollar relief bill. Democratic control of the House and Hoover's statement that the bill was "the most gigantic pork barrel ever proposed ... an unexampled raid on the public treasury,"[5] helped ensure that the measure would be perceived in partisan terms. The struggle over relief spending continues to dominate the social welfare dimension during the New Deal 73rd to 75th Congresses. While in the 71st and 72nd, debate centered around whether the federal government should provide direct relief, in the later Congresses the controversy concerned the dollar level.

Most of the relief programs were temporary, but the 74th Congress (1935-1936) passed two major permanent programs: the Social Security Act and the Wagner Labor Relations Act. In terms of the expansion of federal responsibility for the welfare of the individual, the bills represented truly nonincremental change, yet both passed with relative ease. During the 75th Congress two more clearly nonincremental programs were passed: the Housing Act of 1937, which committed the federal government for the first time to a long-range program of public housing for low-income families, and the Fair Labor Standards Act, the first federal wages and hours bill. Passage of the second act was especially difficult because it evoked a very different alignment from that characteristic of the major social welfare dimension.

As Table 13-1 shows, voting on the major social welfare dimension was partisan at its inception in the 71st Congress and remained so through 1938. Democrats were highly supportive; there is little regional variation and no tendency for the South to be less supportive than other segments of the party. While the average support level of Republicans is low, support does vary along regional lines with West North Central Republicans being the most consistently deviant regional grouping.

The roll calls on the Fair Labor Standards Act did not evoke the same alignments as the major social welfare dimension. The bill divided the Democrats along North-South lines; Southern Democrats were much less supportive of the party position than their northern colleagues. This split had an economic foundation. Southerners feared that a nationwide minimum wage would nullify their region's advantage in attracting industry. (For the same reason, some usually very conservative northeastern Republicans supported the bill.) Thus, the first beginnings of the Democrats' regional split, so pronounced in later years, was evident by the 75th Congress (1937-1938).

Clearly, the new agenda was the product of the Great Depression. Faced with economic collapse and widespread misery, the public demanded government action. When President Hoover did not respond, a Democratic president and Congress were swept into office by landslide margins. In attempting to cope with the emergency, Congress passed numerous innovative bills that immensely expanded the scope of government responsibility. Voting on most of this legislation was heavily partisan. Consequently, interparty membership replacement was crucial for policy change.

Expansion of the Political Agenda:
Civil Liberties and International Involvement, 1937-1952

The late 1930s saw the development of two new issue dimensions: civil liberties and international involvement. The origins of both can be traced to changes in the political environment.

Civil Liberties

Because the Democratic coalition that emerged from the New Deal realignment included northern blacks, civil rights inevitably entered the political agenda. Roosevelt, keenly aware of the party-splitting potential of the issue, kept his distance from civil rights legislative proposals, but Democratic representatives from the Northeast felt no such compunction.[6] Blacks were now a part of their voting constituency, and a modicum of attention had to be paid to their demands.

Civil liberties becomes an element of the House agenda in the 75th Congress (1937-1938) when an antilynching bill passed the House. The 76th House again passed an antilynching bill, and from 1942 through 1949 the House passed five bills barring the poll tax as a voting requirement. None of this legislation survived the Senate; the filibuster proved to be an insurmountable barrier for civil rights forces to overcome.[7] Although civil rights was the dominant component of the civil liberties dimension, also included were roll calls on subversive activities legislation.

Table 13-2　Civil Liberties Support Scores, 1937-1950 (In Percentages)

Democrats			Republicans
All	*North*	*Solid South*	*All*
49.1	84.8	6.4	80.3

Southern Democrats were bitterly opposed to civil rights legislation, and the dimension deeply divided the Democratic party. In contrast, Republicans were highly cohesive and supportive, as Table 13-2 indicates.

International Involvement

During most of the 1930s the United States was preoccupied with domestic concerns. Not until the 76th Congress (1939-1940) does a substantial cluster of roll calls appear that warrants the international involvement designation. This scale consists mostly of roll calls on the Neutrality Act but also includes several roll calls on the draft and on defense appropriations. From 1939 on, international involvement is a continuing element of the House agenda. In content, the 77th scale is similar to that found in the 76th but also includes lend-lease. The 78th and 79th scales include, as a major component, roll calls on funds for the United Nations Relief and Rehabilitation Administration. From the 80th through the 82nd, the scales are dominated by roll calls on the Marshall Plan, aid to Greece and Turkey, mutual security legislation, and aid to Korea.

As Table 13-3 shows, the level of Republican support for international involvement varies, but the party is always deeply split along coastal versus interior lines. A secular change in Democratic voting alignments is evident. Democrats from the Solid South, the most supportive regional grouping in the 1939-1942 period, move to being distinctly the least supportive grouping from 1949 on.

The origin and development of the international involvement dimension in the 1939-1952 period clearly reflects the impact of world events. The dimension developed in response to the situation in Europe. During most of the 1930s Congress concentrated its time and attention on the domestic scene; large majorities supported a hands-off policy toward Europe. Not until 1939 did a majority become convinced that the conflict in Europe required a change in U.S. policy. Even then the majorities were party-based and were frequently very narrow. Not until the Japanese attacked Pearl Harbor on December 7, 1941, did a consensus develop.

During the war years, party differences on foreign policy issues were few and much less deep. Although Democrats provided greater support than

Table 13-3 International Involvement Support Scores, 1939-1952 (In Percentages)

	Democrats				Republicans			
	All	*North*	*Solid South*		*All*	*North-east*	*Pacific*	*Interior*
1939-1942	87.9	79.7	96.7		24.9	40.5	41.1	11.7
1943-1948	90.4	88.4	90.3		61.3	84.4	79.7	43.4
1949-1952	84.9	94.0	72.1		33.2	49.8	41.4	19.6

Republicans for the administration's aid program, most measures drew support from Republican majorities. A hot war did not seem the time to oppose the president's foreign policy. Bipartisanship in foreign policy voting continued during the 80th Congress. The Cold War was taking shape, and the first Republican congressional majority since the 1920s was not inclined to defeat President Truman's foreign policy proposals and thereby risk winning a reputation for irresponsibility. When the Democrats regained control in the 81st Congress, the influence of party on foreign policy voting increased. By then, a bipartisan consensus on the containment policy and on presidential supremacy in the foreign policy area was firmly established. Congressional conflict had been largely narrowed to the details of the foreign aid program.

Constituency attitudes, in addition to world events and partisan control of the Congress, seem to have influenced voting on the international involvement dimension. Regional culture—the greater parochialism and isolation from world events of the small town and rural people of the interior regions—has frequently been offered as an explanation for the coastal-interior split within the Republican party.[8] Certainly its persistence suggests that it is rooted in constituency differences. During the pre-Pearl Harbor period southerners were consistently most favorable toward the adoption by the United States of an activist role in helping the allies; the public in the Midwest and Great Plains was least favorable.[9] This pattern of opinion was roughly reflected in congressional voting in the prewar period. Southern Democrats were most supportive of international involvement; interior Republicans the least.

How is the decline in southern Democratic support on international involvement to be explained? It can be argued that, from the point of view of southern representatives and quite likely of their constituency elites, the issues changed. Charles Lerche contends that southerners always have supported a strong national defense, believed the United States should pursue clear-cut victory in wars, cold or hot; and opposed "giveaways" to countries not sufficiently grateful and subservient.[10] By the early 1950s the foreign aid program began to look less and less like a temporary emergency measure; to many southerners, it began to appear increasingly like a giveaway for which the United States received no real return.

The political agenda expanded further in the late 1930s. Unlike the issues that dominated the earlier part of the decade, the new issues deeply split the parties along regional lines. The cohesive party-line voting of the New Deal era was not extended to the new issues that activated intraparty constituency differences.

Return to Normal Politics:
Government Management and Social Welfare, 1939-1952

The sense of urgency that had fueled the New Deal had largely dissipated by the late 1930s. Numerous reforms had been passed; the economy, while still not fully recovered, was no longer in danger of total collapse. After Pearl Harbor the war overshadowed all other problems. War production brought prosperity and thus eroded any remaining impetus toward further domestic reform.

Although the Democrats were clearly the majority party during the 1939-1952 period, the huge congressional majorities of the New Deal were a thing of the past. Republicans made big gains in House seats in the 1938 and 1942 elections and in 1946 won control. The conditions for further nonincremental policy change were absent, and a return to normal politics was to be expected.

From 1939 to 1952 there were no significant agenda changes in the social welfare or government management areas. Controversy centered primarily around the issues that had come to the fore during the New Deal, and policy change was incremental. The permanence of the New Deal reforms became clear when the Republican-controlled 80th Congress made no real attempt to repeal them. A number of New Deal programs were expanded during this period, but no new departures were made.

Although the policy agenda remained stable, voting alignments changed. On both the social welfare and the government management dimensions, a North-South split developed within the Democratic party. Democrats from the Solid South, who had been the most supportive segment of their party during the New Deal, became by the mid-1940s the least supportive group by far. Republican voting patterns also changed. On government management, West North Central Republicans no longer defected from the party position, and party cohesion increased. On social welfare, northeasterners, the most conservative regional grouping within the Republican party in the late 1920s and 1930s, became the most supportive group by the early 1950s. West North Central Republicans followed the opposite path, and, as Table 13-4 indicates, by the late 1940s the once insurgent Midwest had become the center of Republican orthodoxy.

Table 13-4   Government Management and Social Welfare Support Scores, 1939-1952 (In Percentages)

	Democrats			Republicans		
	All	North	Solid South	All	North-east	West North Central
Government Management						
1939-1942	89.0	88.6	89.5	10.2	12.3	9.6
1943-1952	78.8	88.0	69.1	12.7	7.4	14.0
Social Welfare						
1939-1944*	86.7	93.9	80.9	10.6	9.7	13.3
1945-1952	67.0	87.0	45.6	17.1	21.2	13.8

*The 77th Congress dimension is excluded from the means because it evoked a deviant alignment pattern.

The North-South split in the Democratic party is so familiar to political scientists that they have largely been blind to the need to explain it. The reasons for the development of the split, however, are far from self-evident. Southern representatives' high support for New Deal programs in the 1930s was consonant with public opinion in the South. Opinion surveys from the 1930s and early 1940s show southerners to be the regional grouping most supportive of New Deal programs.[11] If, during the late 1940s and early 1950s, southern public opinion had swung sharply right, the increased conservatism of southern representatives could be explained as a response to constituency opinion change. Surveys indicate, however, that, except on race, there were no significant regional attitude differences on domestic issues during those years.

The explanation seems to lie in the change in political atmosphere generally and in a change in the southern economy coupled with the special character of southern politics. Public opinion polls show an overall decline in support for further policy departures in the late 1930s.[12] Many people, mass as well as elite, perceived the emergency to be over and believed additional change to be unnecessary. When the war brought prosperity, those whose support for the New Deal rested upon the emergency argument could see little rationale for further policy innovation. Equally important, prosperity probably brought a decline in the saliency of domestic politics.

In the postwar years the South began to industrialize. Industrializing elites tend to be strongly opposed to government intervention of the sort supported by liberals in the post-New Deal years.[13] When the forces of industrialization were added to the older agrarian conservatism, the remnants of agrarian radicalism in the South were largely extinguished. Southern elites in the postwar years had a heavily conservative cast.

If these developments are considered in the light of the special character of southern politics, an explanation for the North-South split begins to emerge. The low level of political participation in the South gave elites in the area greater influence than in the rest of the country. When the saliency of politics to the mass public drops, elite influence should be further magnified. The lack of a rich organizational life in the South—particularly the absence of unions—limited the avenues of expression for those opposed to the economic elite. In many northern districts a supportive coalition could be based upon blue collar workers and union leaders. In the South this was not possible.

The difference in interest between agrarian and industrializing areas on the one hand and industrialized areas on the other may explain the changing alignments within the Republican party. The key factor according to Everett Ladd is "the essential harmony between the thrust of the New Deal and the conditions of advanced industrialism."[14] By the late 1940s northeastern Republicans seem to have realized that the New Deal's social welfare programs were a force for stability in their heavily industrialized area, and their opposition softened. Northeasterners then became the most deviant section of the Republican party on social welfare.

As the aftershocks of realignment gave way to a period of normal politics, policy change became incremental once again, and the high party cohesion characteristic of the height of the New Deal was replaced with party fragmentation along regional lines. By the early 1950s the pre-realignment voting patterns had been completely transformed.

From Political Quiescence to Policy Activism: Domestic Policy Change, 1953–1968

The 1952 elections ended 20 years of uninterrupted Democratic control of the presidency and Congress. The shift in partisan control did not signal, however, a basic change in policy direction. In the fight for the presidential nomination, the moderate wing of the Republican party had emerged victorious. Republican majorities in the House and Senate were narrow. If dreams of "repealing" the New Deal still lurked in some Republican hearts, political reality militated against their expression.

When Democrats regained control of the Congress in the 1954 elections, the Democratic party was divided fairly evenly between an increasingly conservative southern wing and the northern liberals. Not until the recession sharply increased the Democratic majority in the 1958 elections did the northern wing gain a clear numerical preponderance. Even then, their committee positions gave southerners power out of proportion to their still very considerable numbers.

The 1950s saw few burning issues that involved large numbers of people. Two wars followed by general prosperity led to a period of low saliency politics. By the mid-1950s the Cold War had become routine. Public pressure for domestic policy departures was minimal. In only one area—civil rights—did a popular movement demanding change emerge.

Democratic presidential candidate John Kennedy promised to "get the country moving again," and with his election in 1960 eight years of divided control ended. Although Kennedy's winning margin was small and the Democrats lost seats in the Congress, their majority was nevertheless substantial. The president himself and the northern wing of the party were committed to change. Signs that the political quiescence of the 1950s was a thing of the past became increasingly evident. The civil rights movement gained momentum and attracted widespread public notice. In late 1960, 46 percent of a national sample said that the new president and Congress should "do more to end segregation."[15]

The assassination of Kennedy brought into office the first southern president since the Civil War. Lyndon Baines Johnson soon made it clear that his dedication to civil rights was at least equal to that of his predecessor. When the right wing of the Republican party captured the presidential nomination in 1964, a Democratic landslide followed. Barry Goldwater did make inroads in the South, however. Several Deep South states elected Republicans to the House for the first time.

Civil Liberties

Civil liberties was the first of the issue areas to change significantly. When the Supreme Court in 1954 outlawed school segregation, a grass-roots civil rights movement began to develop, and the Congress came under increasing pressure to pass civil rights legislation. The House passed a civil rights bill in 1956, but it was not until 1957 that Congress enacted the first civil rights legislation since the post-Civil War Reconstruction period. In 1960 a second bill was passed. Although important symbolically, this legislation was quite weak. During the Johnson administration three much stronger bills were enacted: the 1964 Civil Rights Act, the 1965 Voting Rights Act, and the 1968 Open Housing Act. In terms of the problems attacked, the remedies proposed, and their social and political impact, these bills represented truly nonincremental policy change.

As Table 13-5 shows, from 1953 to 1968 the civil liberties dimension continued to split the Democrats deeply along North-South lines. Republican support on the dimension decreased, and the party divided along regional lines. The first drop in Republican support occurred in the mid-1950s, and it was not due to defections on civil rights. Also included in the dimension during the late 1950s are votes on bills attempting to curb the power of the

Table 13-5   Domestic Policy Support Scores, 1953-1968 (In Percentages)

| | Democrats | | | Republicans | | |
	All	North	Solid South	All	North- east	Other*
Civil Liberties						
1955-1956	53.1	98.1	.7	89.0	94.4	91.0
1957-1964	54.8	86.3	9.2	50.9	62.5	46.4
1965-1968	51.9	73.1	10.5	33.9	50.6	32.1
Social Welfare						
1953-1960	71.5	93.5	42.2	32.7	43.4	27.1
1961-1968	76.6	95.4	33.6**	33.3	55.0	22.6
Government Management						
1953-1960	85.3	91.7	77.1	13.2	13.0	12.9
1961-1964	85.5	92.1	73.5	19.3	25.5	16.0
1965-1968	84.2	92.0	65.3	15.3	25.6	11.7

*Republicans from the Solid South are excluded from mean civil liberties scores.
**The 88th Congress score is excluded as it is atypically high and obscures the pattern.

Supreme Court; many Republicans joined the Southern Democrats on these roll calls. As the antiwar movement became prominent during the mid-1960s, bills aimed at curbing such protests drew heavy support from Republicans, but Republican support for civil rights legislation also decreased. Open housing and school busing were matters directly affecting Republicans' white, middle-class constituents, and the mail from home was sharply opposed. Thus, as the thrust of the civil rights bills changed, so did the Republican voting response.

Social Welfare

The quiescent 1950s were followed in the 1960s by a burst of nonincremental policy change in the social welfare area as well. Aid to education was finally enacted in 1965, and Medicare, long a dream of liberals, was passed. The passage of the antipoverty program in 1964 signaled an even more significant departure. Social welfare programs from the New Deal through the early 1960s were aimed at helping the non-rich majority. In the mid-1960s the emphasis shifted to programs intended to aid the poor minority.

The new issues gave rise to high intensity politics. The regional split within each party, dating back to the 1940s and continuing during the 1950s, intensified in the 1960s. Northeastern Republicans provided higher support for social welfare than did Democrats from the Solid South.

Government Management

When compared with the policy innovation that occurred in the civil rights and social welfare areas, activity in the government management area during the Kennedy-Johnson administrations is much less dramatic. Although a number of new programs were enacted—most notably area redevelopment—most of the issues debated had been around since the 1940s and 1950s: federal spending levels, the pros and cons of deficit spending as an antirecession measure, the role of the federal government in power facilities development, and the structure of the tax code.

Although the political agenda remained stable from the 1950s to the 1960s, voting alignments changed. The North-South split within the Democratic party, which had moderated during the 1950s, intensified, especially in the 89th and 90th Congresses (1965-1966, 1967-1968). During the 1950s the Republican party was quite cohesive on the government management dimension. In the 1960s the party began to split along regional lines; by the mid-1960s northeasterners were considerably more supportive than Republicans from other areas.

The Activist Sixties

Peace, growing affluence, and the lack of dramatic issues led to low saliency politics in the 1950s. The early 1960s saw an increase in political interest.[16] The civil rights movement and the Kennedy personality both seem to have contributed to the increase. The trauma of John Kennedy's assassination probably focused public attention on Washington even more.

The 1964 presidential election campaign further transformed the complexion of American politics. Not only was Republican candidate Goldwater perceived as trigger-happy and opposed to federal action on civil rights, but he also questioned the post-New Deal consensus on domestic policy.[17] Offered clear alternatives, the electorate made its choice unmistakably clear. A Democratic landslide of a magnitude unequaled since the New Deal was the result.

These changes in the political environment were conducive to policy change. The more attentive public clearly favored civil rights legislation and social welfare programs such as aid to education and Medicare.[18] To the extent data are available, they indicate that such preferences do not represent a major change in attitudes since the 1950s. What did change was the extent to which politics was salient to the average voter. If members of Congress perceive their constituents to be attentive, they are more likely to feel constrained by constituency preferences.

The events of the early 1960s did not, however, affect the North and the South in the same way. Southerners became more conservative relative to the rest of the country on domestic social and economic issues.[19] In the 1950s they held distinctive attitudes only on race-related questions, but during the following decade the region began to diverge from the North across the whole spectrum of domestic issues. While southerners were becoming more conservative, northeasterners were becoming more liberal. Polls from the 1940s and 1950s show northeasterners to be more tolerant on civil liberties issues than the public as a whole. In the 1960s they continued to be the most liberal section on civil rights and became more liberal than the inhabitants of other sections on social and economic policy issues as well.[20] The constituency signals that eastern Republicans received were more likely than previously to point toward support for at least some of the measures proposed by Kennedy and Johnson.

The changes in voting behavior during the 1960s are consonant with changes in public opinion in the Northeast and the South. Especially in a period of high intensity politics, members of Congress will reflect the general thrust of constituency opinion in their voting behavior.

International Involvement, 1952-1976

From 1952 to 1968, foreign aid dominated the international involvement agenda in the House. Although the foreign policy consensus that had kept other issues off the voting agenda began to break down in the mid-1960s, the House leadership during the Johnson presidency kept most anti-Vietnam War measures from coming to the floor.

From 1969 to 1976, two distinct clusters of international involvement roll calls appear in each Congress. One set, very similar in content to the international involvement dimension found in earlier Congresses, consists mostly of roll calls on foreign aid bills. The other includes numerous votes directly related to the Vietnam War as well as roll calls on cutting Department of Defense appropriations, on cutting funds for a wide variety of weapons systems (the antiballistic missile, nerve gas, and the B-1 bomber, for example), on barring aid to Chile and other dictatorships, on overseas troop cuts, on prohibiting the importation of Rhodesian chrome, and on barring the Ford administration from becoming involved in Angola. This dimension will be labeled foreign and defense policy reorientation.[21] Certainly those members who supported these departures were challenging basic precepts of American foreign and defense policy.

The House displayed limited enthusiasm for a thorough reorientation of U.S. foreign and defense policy. As Table 13-6 indicates, no segment of the Republican party showed much support, although northeasterners were somewhat less opposed than members from other areas. Solid South Democrats also were firmly opposed, and Northern Democrats were split.

Table 13-6 Foreign and Defense Policy Reorientation Support Scores, 1969-1976 (In Percentages)

All Members	Democrats			Republicans			
	All	*North*	*Solid South*	*All*	*North-east*	*Pacific*	*Interior**
36.7	49.3	66.3	18.1	18.4	29.0	15.8	17.4

*Republicans from the Solid South are excluded.

The overwhelming Republican opposition and the divisions within the Democratic party account for the failure of many of the proposals aimed at a basic reorientation of foreign and defense policy. The defeat of many of the more drastic proposals does not, however, mean that policy remained unchanged. The change in agenda was followed by policy change. Funds for the Indochina war were eventually cut off, some cuts in defense spending were made, and Congress refused to let the Ford administration get involved in Angola.

On the reorientation dimension, congressional voting behavior roughly corresponded to constituency opinion. In the population, Democrats after 1968 were somewhat more likely to be doves than Republicans; northeasterners were distinctly more dovish than inhabitants of other sections. On questions concerning defense spending and U.S. relations with communist countries, southerners were especially inclined to take a hard line.[22]

Public opinion was, however, ambivalent. Americans wanted to get out of Vietnam, but to do so with honor; as a result, public opinion swung erratically from dovish to hawkish and back again.[23] Not until 1971 did a stable majority in favor of relatively rapid withdrawal develop.

Certainly, the general public's growing disillusionment with the war in Southeast Asia had an important effect on policy decisions. In terms of support for a more general reorientation of foreign and defense policy, however, it seems likely that the representatives' own attitudes and those of their active supporters were the primary voting cues. The antiwar movement that favored such a reorientation was predominantly liberal, middle-class, and urban in composition. Members of the House who represented districts in which these elements were important and who themselves shared these characteristics were most likely to favor a reorientation of American foreign and defense policy.

On the traditional international involvement dimension, Democrats continued to split along North-South lines and Republicans along coastal versus interior lines. The only secular change apparent is the increased opposition of Republicans from the Pacific states.

Table 13-7   Presidential Influence on International Involvement Support Scores, 1949-1976 (In Percentages)

| President | Democrats | | | Republicans | | | |
	All	North	Solid South	All	North-east	Pacific	Interior*
Truman, 1949-1952	84.9	94.0	72.1	33.2	49.8	41.4	19.6
Eisenhower, 1953-1960	69.0	88.3	41.2	60.8	87.3	74.3	41.0
Kennedy-Johnson, 1961-1968	77.1	92.2	47.2	39.6	63.5	39.4	29.4
Nixon-Ford, 1969-1976	63.9	78.9	36.2	51.8	73.4	52.6	49.5

*Republicans from the Solid South are excluded.

Although the form of the alignment remained stable, support levels varied depending upon the party affiliation of the president. As the support scores for the 1949-1976 period depicted in Table 13-7 indicate, members of each party gave higher support to a president of their own party than to one from the opposition. On foreign aid—a program without a domestic constituency yet one not highly salient to most constituents—the president does influence voting behavior.

Domestic Politics in a Time of Turmoil, 1969-1976

When the public sends a strong and clear signal, the Congress usually responds. During the 1969-1976 period the public's signals, as indicated by opinion polls and election returns, lacked that clear thrust. In 1968 the Republican candidate Richard Nixon was elected president, and American Independent George Wallace received 13.5 percent of the popular vote; in 1972 Nixon was re-elected by a landslide. Yet the elections of 1968 through 1974 returned heavily Democratic majorities to the Congress.

The concerns of the public were not difficult to discern—Vietnam, crime and lawlessness, race, pollution, inflation, and unemployment.[24] But on many of these issues both liberals and conservatives could claim, with equal justification or lack of it, a mandate for their approach. Under such circumstances one would expect policy change also to lack a clear thrust.

Neither the civil liberties nor the social welfare agenda changed significantly during these years. By and large, controversy, which was frequently intense, centered around the issues that came to the fore during the 1960s, and congressional liberals concentrated on preserving previous gains against attacks from conservative presidents.

Table 13-8   Domestic Policy Support Scores, 1969-1976 (In Percentages)

| | Democrats | | | Republicans | | |
	All	North	Solid South	All	North-east	Other*
Civil Liberties						
1969-1972	54.6	75.5	15.3	27.2	39.2	26.9
1973-1976	63.6	78.1	33.3	31.3	45.3	32.9
Social Welfare						
1969-1972	79.4	94.8	46.7	33.3	50.0	28.3
1973-1976	79.6	91.0	55.0	32.4	52.2	26.2
Government Management						
1969-1976	70.5	83.1	45.3	24.6	39.2	19.5

*Republicans from the Solid South are excluded from mean civil liberties scores.

Table 13-8 shows that on both dimensions Republicans from the Northeast continued to be more supportive than their party colleagues from other areas. Within the Democratic party the familiar North-South split narrowed somewhat after 1972. To a considerable extent this narrowing was due to membership replacement. The large southern Democratic freshman classes elected in 1972 and 1974 were much more supportive on civil liberties and social welfare than their more senior regional colleagues. As the race issue declined in salience in the South, districts that were similar demographically to those represented by Northern Democrats began to elect representatives who voted more like Northern Democrats.

Stagflation, the Arab oil embargo, and the environmental and consumer movements did bring about a major change in the government management agenda. But only in the environmental area were public signals both strong and clear, and only in that area was agenda change accompanied by nonincremental policy change. The 1970 Clean Air Act, the single most important piece of environmental legislation during this period, not only attempted to attain its goals through regulation (rather than through the subsidies that had been the primary mechanism in earlier environmental legislation), but also contained "technology-forcing" provisions, provisions that set standards above what was thought to be feasible with present technology. The Arab oil embargo, however, ended the period of easy victories. Attention shifted to the need for increased energy production, and environmentalists were forced onto the defensive.

As the focus of government management legislation shifted, so did voting alignments. The distance between the parties decreased as the support of

Solid South Democrats plummeted and that of northeastern Republicans increased. This change in alignments can be linked to constituency interests. Environmental and consumer protection legislation had its greatest appeal to the affluent in the industrialized areas.[25] In industrializing areas, however, elites and often the general population as well objected to such regulations as a barrier to growth. Energy policy pitted producer against consumer interests. Thus, northeastern Republicans representing affluent constituents in a heavily industrialized and non-oil-producing area moved toward the Democratic pole on the government management dimension, and Solid South Democrats representing an oil-producing and a still industrializing area moved to the Republican pole.

Congressional Alignments Under Carter, 1977-1980

Jimmy Carter's election to the presidency did not coincide with a change in political agenda. The state of the economy continued to be the problem of primary concern to most Americans. The Carter administration emphasized the passage of an energy program as its top domestic priority.

Domestic policy change was incremental. In response to the high unemployment rate, Congress passed an economic stimulus program. Strip mining legislation and an Alaska lands bill were finally enacted. After a long struggle, an energy program passed, but it had little relationship to the one originally requested by Carter. Neither labor nor blacks—two important components of the Democratic coalition—fared well. Common situs picketing legislation and labor law reform were defeated. The Humphrey-Hawkins full employment bill was watered down to the point of meaninglessness. A strengthened fair housing bill passed the House but died in the Senate.

As Table 13-9 shows, voting alignments were very similar to those characteristic of the Nixon-Ford years. In the domestic area the only significant change is the splitting of the government management dimension into two scales. One is dominated by roll calls on energy and environmental legislation and is clearly a continuation of the government management dimension of the 1970s. The second scale includes roll calls on economic stimulus programs, debt limit increases, budget resolutions, and, in the 95th Congress, the Humphrey-Hawkins bill.

The parties were much less regionally split on this economic policy scale than on the other government management scales of the 1970s. Alignments were, in fact, quite similar to those characterizing the government management dimension of the 1960s. The greater partisanship was probably due to the recapture of the presidency by the Democratic party. With a fellow partisan in the White House, Democrats from all regions seemed to be more willing to follow party lines on those issues that the congressional leadership and the president considered to be crucial to the party program—so long as constituency interests were not fundamentally compromised. Unfortunately

Table 13-9   Policy Support Scores, 1977-1980 (In Percentages)

	Democrats			Republicans		
	All	*North*	*Solid South*	*All*	*North-east*	*Other*
Social Welfare	79.2	88.9	56.6	26.7	44.8	21.6
Civil Liberties	65.5	77.0	39.6	23.5	38.5	21.8*
Government Management:						
Environment	69.6	81.5	43.7	24.1	41.9	19.0
Economic	80.5	86.9	65.7	16.4	27.6	13.1
International Involvement:						
Aid	71.1	83.7	45.6	37.4	62.8	30.3
Reorientation	49.9	63.5	20.8	16.0	28.9	12.3
Hard-line	66.7	78.1	42.4	22.8	36.8	18.7

*Republicans from the Solid South are excluded.

for the president and the leadership, this condition excluded many of the most crucial issues (energy, for example); on those, Democrats from the South, and to a less extent from border and mountain states, continued to defect massively from the party position.

In the international involvement area a new scale also appeared. The reorientation dimension represented a challenge from the left to the hard-line foreign and defense policy of Republican presidents, so some change in the debate could be anticipated with the advent of the Carter presidency. Carter attempted to incorporate elements of the new perspective into his foreign policy. His human rights convictions led him, in selected instances, to cut off or diminish aid to right-wing dictatorships. His somewhat tougher stance requiring the military to justify expensive new weapons systems led to the decision against production of the B-1 bomber. Carter's initiatives in foreign affairs infuriated congressional hard-liners but did not go far enough to satisfy those committed to a true reorientation of U.S. foreign and defense policy.

The new scale represents a hard-line challenge to Carter's foreign policy. Prominent are votes on measures aimed at restricting the president's discretion with respect to foreign aid, the pull-out of U.S. troops from Korea, and policy toward Rhodesia, Taiwan, and the Panama Canal. As Table 13-9 shows, the level of support on this scale is quite different from that on the foreign aid scale. Northeastern Republicans as a group were a part of the right-wing attack on the Carter policy; Northern Democrats' support of Carter's policies against attack from the right was considerably lower than their support on the foreign aid scale, which itself was significantly below the support Northern Democrats gave Kennedy and Johnson on foreign aid.

Thus, Carter's complaint about the difficulty of building majority coalitions in the foreign and defense policy area was founded on reality. Foreign and defense policy is no longer beyond debate; consequently presidential dominance has been reduced. Furthermore, unlike his Republican predecessors, Carter faced challenges from both the left and the right.

The Reagan Revolution

The 1980 elections, many members of Congress believed, carried a mandate for policy change. Spiraling inflation and interest rates had doomed Carter's reelection bid. Ronald Reagan did not, however, simply promise to do better; he campaigned on a platform of massive cuts in taxes and domestic spending. Not only did Reagan defeat an incumbent president by 10 percentage points; Republicans gained 33 seats in the House and took control of the Senate for the first time in a quarter century.

In 1981 the new administration was remarkably successful in enacting its economic program—a program that did entail a significant change in policy. The budget process was used to make major cuts in many social programs all at once; a huge tax cut bill was passed. All of the House roll calls critical to passage of the Reagan administration's program fall into the government management domain, and all are part of the economic policy scale. In fact, scores on that scale for 1981 can be interpreted as Reagan policy opposition scores.[26] The administration's success, as Table 13-10 shows, was the result of extraordinarily high Republican support and considerable backing from Southern Democrats. The Reagan forces fully exploited the perception that the 1980 elections carried a mandate for the president's proposals and cleverly employed the congressional budget process to present members with a simple up or down vote on Reagan's economic program.

As the economy worsened, the perception of a mandate began to fade. In 1982 the administration had less success in pushing its policy initiatives through Congress. The 1982 economic policy scale shows an increase in support for the liberal position. No longer was the attention of the House confined almost exclusively to Reagan's economic policy proposals. Environmental issues reappeared on the agenda, and the House often opposed the administration's anticonservationist stances.[27] It returned to making social welfare decisions on a program-by-program basis rather than making them wholesale.[28] The result was House decisions much less favorable to the administration. The Congress in 1982 did not fundamentally reverse the policy decisions of 1981. But, by 1982, congressional policymaking in the government management and social welfare domains became once again largely incremental.

New Right groups interpreted the 1980 elections as a mandate for action on abortion, busing, and school prayer. Although the elections did increase the

Table 13-10   Policy Support Scores, 1981-1982 (In Percentages)

	Democrats			Republicans		
	All	*North*	*Solid South*	*All*	*North-east*	*Other*
Government Management: Economic						
1981	78.9	89.1	55.9	9.1	16.9	6.6
1982	82.1	89.8	65.0	24.9	40.1	19.9
Environment	78.1	88.0	58.1	33.5	59.6	24.7
Social Welfare	85.2	93.1	67.2	32.1	51.9	25.6
Civil Liberties	65.1	76.9	39.2	22.3	38.2	19.1
International Involvement:						
Aid	65.4	75.9	46.0	61.7	80.4	55.5
Reorientation	53.7	70.0	21.2	18.6	31.1	14.5

number of members of Congress sympathetic to New Right views on those so-cial and civil liberties issues, poll results disputed the mandate interpretation, and the new administration concentrated instead on changing economic policy. When Reagan did address civil liberties issues, he was unsuccessful in bringing about policy change. For example, the administration initially advocated severely weakening the Voting Rights Act, but the Congress refused to go along. Despite New Right hopes and civil libertarian fears, the 97th Congress did not make significant changes in the civil liberties area.

Defense and foreign policy hard-liners had sounder grounds for claiming a mandate for their views. Reagan had campaigned on a platform of higher defense spending and a tougher stance toward the Soviets; polls showed that a majority believed the United States should spend more for defense.

In 1981 the large increase in defense spending that Reagan requested was approved by Congress. It also gave him essentially all the specific weapons systems he wanted. By 1982, however, the public at large and many members had become wary of further huge increases. Congress cut Reagan's defense proposals but, with a few exceptions, approved the weapons systems the administration requested. In sum, although the 97th Congress was not willing to go quite as far on defense spending as Reagan proposed, the policy change it approved in this area did go beyond the incremental.

In the international involvement domain, Reagan's presidency brought about changes in dimensional structure and alignments. The hard-line scale disappeared. A hard-liner himself, Reagan was not subject to systematic attacks from the right as Carter had been. In the late 1970s defense issues had become an increasingly important component of the reorientation dimension. During the 97th Congress the level of defense spending and the procurement of various weapons systems completely dominated the reorientation scale. As Table 13-10 shows, Northern Democrats as a group opposed Reagan's defense buildup; Southern Democrats and Republicans supported it. The change in partisan control of the White House brought the expected change in alignments on foreign aid; Democrats decreased their support while Republicans' support increased. In fact, Reagan received considerably more backing from Republicans than Nixon or Ford had. Republican control of the Senate may have increased House Republicans' sense that their party was responsible for governing and that may account for their higher support for a no more popular program.

Conclusion

Significant change in the political agenda usually can be traced to a change in the broader, politically relevant environment. Such change is not generated within the Congress. For example, the Great Depression led to a fundamental change in the domestic policy agenda; the change in the composition of the Democratic party during the New Deal thrust civil rights onto the agenda in the late 1930s; and the environmental and consumer movements of the 1970s and the Arab oil embargo strongly influenced the domestic policy agenda. In foreign affairs, the worsening situation in Europe in the late 1930s centered national attention on foreign policy, and during the 1960s the Vietnam War led to a major change in the foreign policy agenda.

How the political agenda is set explains why significant agenda change requires an environmental stimuli of considerable magnitude. The competition to place items on the agenda is intense; there are always more problems that someone perceives to be important than the government can possibly handle. At any given point in time, the agenda consists of the problems considered important by those with enough political clout to persuade a considerable number of decisionmakers to share their concerns. For the agenda to change, such powerful groups must alter their priorities, or new groups must become sufficiently potent to influence the agenda. Only a real change in the politically relevant environment is likely to produce such alterations.

Because the barriers are even greater, truly nonincremental policy change is rarer than agenda change. In the domestic area, two clusters of clearly nonincremental policy change occurred during the half century under study. Although change was not of the same magnitude as during the New Deal Congresses and the 89th Congress (1965-1966), the first Congress of the Reagan presidency also saw a significant change in policy direction. All three instances were preceded by landslide elections that produced heavy interparty membership turnover, and in each case the majorities that passed the policy changes were primarily party-based. Nevertheless, landslide elections do not necessarily lead to nonincremental policy change. The environmental stimulus must be present and, if it is, policy change may occur without a massive change in party balance. Thus, the 1964 Civil Rights Act and the antipoverty program were passed before the 1964 election. Enactment of the major environmental legislation of the early 1970s cannot be attributed to a landslide election that replaced unsympathetic with sympathetic members.

If, as seems to be the case, the single most important factor influencing how a representative votes is his or her constituency, congressional alignments will change when the signals the representative receives from the constituency change. It seems likely, however, that it is not the whole geographical constituency to which the member attends but that segment that supports him or her electorally. Party voting, at least in part, is due to similar interests among the supportive constituencies of members of the same party. Thus, Democratic unity during the New Deal was due to the common plight of the members' districts and the resulting clear need to do something about the depression. When Southern Democrats during the post-World War II years saw continuation of the New Deal thrust as a threat to rapid industrialization in the South, the party split. Conversely, many eastern Republicans began to defect from their party's conservative position on social welfare as it became clear that some of these programs were in the interest of their supportive constituencies. The high saliency issues of the 1960s further divided the regional groupings within each party. The increasing conservatism of the southern populace and the growing liberalism of northeasterners were reflected in congressional voting alignments. The 1970s saw some of the highly divisive civil rights and social welfare issues fade in saliency, and as a result the Democratic split on these issues narrowed. The newly prominent energy and environmental legislation, however, pitted industrialized against industrializing areas and split both parties.

The 97th Congress clearly illustrates these complex relationships. High inflation thrust economic policy questions to the center of the agenda in 1980. The Republican landslide was interpreted by many members—Southern Democrats as well as Republicans—as a mandate for Reagan's economic program; that is, a majority of House members perceived a change in constituency signals. They responded by quickly passing the Reagan program, a program that involved a very significant change in the direction of the U.S. domestic policy.

NOTES

1. See Herbert Asher and Herbert Weisberg, "Voting Change in Congress," *American Journal of Political Science* 22 (May 1978): 391-425.
2. Aage Clausen, *How Congressmen Decide* (New York: St. Martin's Press, 1973). Clausen's agricultural assistance domain is not discussed here for lack of space.
3. For a description of the methodology and a much more extensive analysis, see Barbara Sinclair, *Congressional Realignment 1925-1978* (Austin: University of Texas Press, 1982).

4. The regional categorization used is that of the Survey Research Center.
5. E. Pendleton Herring, "First Session of the 72nd Congress," *American Political Science Review* 26 (October 1932): 869-872.
6. Frank Freidel, *F.D.R. and the South* (Baton Rouge: Louisiana State University Press, 1965), pp. 71-102.
7. No civil rights legislation got to the floor of the House in either the 82nd or 83rd Congress, and the civil liberties dimension did not appear in either Congress.
8. Leroy Rieselbach, *The Roots of Isolationism* (Indianapolis: Bobbs-Merrill Co., 1966), pp. 16-17.
9. Alfred Hero, *The Southerner and World Affairs* (Baton Rouge: Louisiana State University Press, 1965), pp. 91-103.
10. Charles Lerche, *The Uncertain South* (Chicago: Quadrangle, 1964), p. 262.
11. Everett Ladd and Charles Hadley, *Transformations of the American Party System* (New York: W. W. Norton & Co., 1975), pp. 131-132.
12. Hadley Cantril, ed., *Public Opinion, 1935-1946* (Princeton: Princeton University Press, 1951), pp. 978-979.
13. Ladd and Hadley, *American Party System*, pp. 138-139.
14. Ibid., p. 141.
15. George Gallup, *The Gallup Poll: Public Opinion, 1935-1971*, vol. 3 (New York: Random House, 1972), p. 1700.
16. Norman Nie, Sidney Verba, and John Petrocik, *The Changing American Voter* (Cambridge: Harvard University Press, 1976), pp. 271-273.
17. Ibid., especially chaps. 8 and 10.
18. James L. Sundquist, *Politics and Policy* (Washington, D.C.: The Brookings Institution, 1968), pp. 441-452, 484-489.
19. Ladd and Hadley, *American Party System*, p. 168.
20. Ibid., pp. 168-172.
21. See Aage Clausen and Carl Van Horn, "The Congressional Response to a Decade of Change: 1963-1972," *Journal of Politics* 39 (August 1977): 624-666.
22. Gallup, *Public Opinion, 1935-1971*, pp. 2125, 2223 and Ladd and Hadley, *American Party System*, p. 170.
23. William Watts and Lloyd Free, *State of the Nation* (New York: Universe Books, 1972), pp. 194-198.
24. Nie, Verba, and Petrocik, *Changing American Voter*, p. 103 and Gallup Opinion Index, 1973-1976.
25. Louis Harris, *The Anguish of Change* (New York: W. W. Norton & Co., 1973), pp. 99-118.
26. The economic policy roll calls in 1981 and 1982 form one scale; separate scales for the two years were constructed to allow a comparison of support levels.
27. This scale is based on roll calls from the entire Congress but, in fact, there were few environment roll calls in 1981 and many in 1982. Almost 87 percent of the votes in the scale were taken in 1982.
28. The scale is based on roll calls from the entire Congress, but almost 80 percent of those in the scale were taken in 1982.

14. THE GREAT EXCEPTION: THE CONGRESSIONAL BUDGET PROCESS IN AN AGE OF DECENTRALIZATION

John W. Ellwood

The procedures used by Congress to make economic and budget policy since 1974 are the great exception in an overall trend toward congressional decentralization. During the same era when congressional scholars pointed to the decline of political parties, the seniority system, the power of committee chairmen, and such guardians of the federal purse as the House Appropriations Committee and to the rise of subcommittee government and autonomous legislators, the Congressional Budget and Impoundment Control Act of 1974 created new procedures and institutions that reflected a more centralized and integrated decisionmaking process than previously had been used to make economic and budget policy.

This essay examines what happens when a policymaking process that is predicated on centralization and the aggregation of interests is created in an environment where all the other forces are moving in the opposite direction. To place this phenomenon in perspective we will first describe how Congress made economic and budget policy prior to the 1974 act and then examine the new budgetary procedures and institutions. We will then turn to the heart of the matter—the effects of the new budget process.

The Changing Nature of Congressional Budgeting

The outcome of any public sector budget process is the result of the interaction of three factors: the economic conditions in which the budget is made; the policy desires of decisionmakers (and, in a representative system, of the electorate); and the procedures that govern the decisionmaking process. The quarter-century prior to the passage of the Congressional Budget and Impoundment Control Act of 1974 (hereafter called the Congressional Budget Act) was a period of fairly vigorous economic growth. Partly as a result of this growth, the public and their representatives in government supported an expansion of the federal sector. This, in turn, caused an increase in the rate of growth of federal spending and tax expenditures.[1] Until the mid-1960s, the decisionmaking procedures governing congressional budgeting were characterized by the model of disjointed incrementalism so well described by

Aaron Wildavsky in *The Politics of the Budget Process* and by Richard Fenno in *The Power of the Purse*.[2] Looking back at this period Wildavsky referred to it as an "idyllic" age.

> When I was writing *The Politics of the Budgetary Process* in the early 1960s, . . . the federal budget process appeared to be a marvelous example of coordination without a coordinator. Without central direction, expenditures were close to revenues, evidencing a slow and gentle rise that could be accelerated or reversed in incremental steps without too much trouble. What was remarkable, it seemed to me, was that the games the participants played fell within well-defined boundaries, compensating for their crudities and inefficiencies by keeping within the rules.
>
> In retrospect, it all seems idyllic. Suddenly the mechanisms of coordination—belief in a balanced budget, national political parties, Congressional cohesion, a slow rate of development permitting programs and their finances to grow together—all disappeared or were weakened.[3]

Changing Economic Conditions

Budgeting is an exercise that is required only in an environment of scarcity. The degree of scarcity necessarily affects the nature of the budgeting exercise. During periods of rapid economic growth, budgeting does not dominate the congressional year the way it does during periods of stagnation, recession, or depression. Higher levels of growth provide greater revenues that allow public officials to increase public sector spending without increasing the relative share of the economy devoted to the public sector.[4]

The interplay of the rate of economic growth and the ability to increase federal expenditures (hereafter referred to as outlays) without increasing the size of the public sector as a proportion of the economy is illustrated in Table 14-1. The table divides the last three decades into four periods: the post-Korean War years of the 1950s, the 1960s, the six years prior to the implementation of the Congressional Budget Act (1970-1975), and the first eight years under the new budgetary procedures (1976-1983).[5] For each period the table shows the average annual growth rates of the real (measured in constant 1972 dollars) Gross National Product (GNP), real personal income, and real federal expenditures (outlays). The average annual deficit and outlays as a percentage of GNP also are included.

The constraining effect of slower economic growth is illustrated by the following example. Imagine that all federal revenues are collected from personal income and wage taxes.[6] Suppose further that the tax rates in force at the beginning of each period in Table 14-1 are not changed during that period. Finally, assume that individuals are not forced into higher marginal tax brackets through the effect of inflation on their incomes. In such a world members of Congress could avoid a zero-sum decision—one that we will refer to as a redistributive decision—as long as a growing economy and the

Table 14-1   Economic and Budget Growth, 1952-1983

	1952-1959	*1960-1969*	*1970-1975*	*1976-1983*
Growth (annual percentage increase in real GNP)	2.7	4.4	2.6	2.4
Income (annual percentage increase in real personal income)	3.3	4.4	3.1	2.7
Federal Expenditures (annual increase in real federal outlays)*	1.2	4.9	3.4	3.7
Federal Outlays as Percentage of GNP (average over period)	18.9	19.4	20.3	22.5
Federal Budget Deficit as Percentage of GNP (average over period)	0.6	0.8	1.5	3.0
The Difference Between the Growth Rates of Real GNP and Real Outlays (real GNP minus real outlays)	1.5	−0.5	−0.8	−1.3
Difference Between the Growth Rates of Real GNP and Real Personal Income (real GNP minus real personal income)	2.1	−0.5	−0.3	−0.1

* Federal outlays are measured in fiscal years while the economic indicators are measured in calendar years.

SOURCE: Averages calculated from data in the *Economic Report of the President, 1984,* and from the Office of Management and Budget, "Federal Government Finances: 1985 Budget Data," February 1984.

resulting growth in personal income provided enough revenues to pay for the growth of federal expenditures.

Such a scenario occurred during the 1950s and well into the 1960s. As the figures in the bottom two rows of Table 14-1 show, real GNP during the 1950s grew at an average annual rate of 1.5 percentage points faster than did real outlays. Personal income grew at an even faster rate, outpacing the growth in federal outlays by an average of 2.1 percentage points per year. In the 1950s, therefore, a fairly slow rate of economic growth provided enough additional revenues for the desired increases in expenditures because of the lower demands for federal support or because of the ability of those in power to withstand those demands, or a combination of both reasons. This was Wildavsky's idyllic world.

In the 1960s, very high rates of sustained growth by historical standards provided almost enough additional revenue to pay for a dramatic increase in federal expenditures, with the growth rate of real federal outlays being only an average 0.5 percentage points higher than the growth rates of real GNP and real personal income. Unfortunately, as the 1970s progressed the rate of economic growth declined. Although the rate of outlay growth also declined—from 4.9 percent per year in the 1960s to 3.4 percent for the 1970-1975 period to 3.7 for the 1976-1983 period—this decline occurred at a slower rate than that of the economy. Thus, during the first half of the 1970s the gap between the growth rates of real GNP and real outlays increased to 0.8 percentage points per year and then further widened to an annual average of 1.3 percentage points for the 1976-1983 period.

In such a deteriorating environment, decisionmakers were faced with two unpleasant choices: they could reduce the growth rate of expenditures by reducing existing commitments and denying new ones, or they could increase the size of the federal sector at the expense of the private sector (either by increasing taxes, accepting higher deficits, or both). In practice, the Congress did a little of each: the growth rate of nondefense, noninterest federal expenditures was constrained, particularly after fiscal year 1977; the burden of federal taxation was increased from an average of 18.3 percent of GNP during the 1952-1959 period to an average of 19.5 percent during the 1976-1983 period; and federal deficits were allowed to grow from an average of 0.6 percent of GNP between 1952 and 1959 to 3.0 percent of GNP between 1976 and 1983. But the need to face such choices makes for neither low levels of conflict nor happy politicians.

The Political Environment:
From Distributive to Redistributive Politics

In the previously cited tax rate example we assumed that the public's desire for federal subsidies remained constant regardless of economic conditions. But in the real world this is not the case. During the 1970s, as the rate of economic growth declined and the rates of unemployment and inflation rose, the public (in many cases through groups) came to the federal government for relief with greater frequency.[7] The number of lobbyists registering with the Clerk of the House rose from an annual average of 282 in the 1960s to 1,507 in 1981; the number of political action committees (PACs) rose from 608 in 1975 to 3,371 in 1983; and the percentage of trade associations located in Washington, D.C., increased from 19 percent in 1971 to 30 percent in 1983.

Thus, at the very time when slower economic growth constrained the growth of federal revenues (in other words, limited the "fiscal dividend"), the problems created by the slowdown in growth increased the pressure on legislators. Those with power—large business and labor unions, for example—sought to use that power to guarantee that they would hold their own in the more constrained environment. The legislator of the 1970s and 1980s—an entrepreneur who, unlike his predecessors in Congress, is not shielded by strong committee chairmen or strong political parties—has had to face this pressure alone.

Naturally, members of Congress, being politicians, like to please voters. Although they hold their own views on policy questions and seek to benefit interests outside of their districts and states, their fundamental imperative is to get re-elected.[8] Responding to this imperative, legislators try to create the impression that the decisonmaking system is dispensing benefits without creating losers. It does not matter if a given policy creates winners at the expense of losers as long as the politics of the process creates the impression that winners are created without losers. In politics, perception is reality. Even those who seek higher office with a wider constituency will try to maximize the number of favorable reactions and minimize the number of unfavorable reactions.

This is the world of distributive politics.[9] It is the pattern that has traditionally dominated the making of economic and budget policy. During the New Deal, President Franklin Roosevelt sought to lift up the poor, not to redistribute income and wealth from the top 10 percent of the population to the bottom half. The landmark programs of the New Deal and the Great Society were not presented as redistributive programs although they have had redistributive effects. President Ronald Reagan has gone out of his way to deny studies that have shown that his spending reductions and tax cuts have benefited those in the upper income brackets at the expense of the working poor (those who are employed but whose income falls below 150 percent of the poverty line) and the poor. Instead he and his administration stress the positive effects of economic growth on all classes and their commitment to maintain the "safety net" of programs for the poor.

In the world of redistributive politics, issues are presented, debated, and decided in a manner that highlights the losers as well as the winners. Although legislators seek to avoid such a political environment, many of the forces affecting the legislative process in the 1970s made their task harder. First, as we have pointed out, as the rate of economic growth declined the ability to increase federal subsidies for some groups without making compensating expenditure reductions for other groups or without shifting additional private sector resources to the public sector became more and more difficult. Second, the creation of the autonomous legislator backed up by technical staff and more sophisticated analytical support working for interested parties made it much more difficult to ignore the negative effects of program options. Increasingly, each interested party in a policymaking arena had the analytical support necessary to make sure that its constituents were not hurt by the final decision.

Not only did Congress find it more difficult to engage in distributive politics in the 1970s because of the economic and political environment, but it also moved, through the passage of the Congressional Budget Act, from procedures reflecting the fragmented approach of disjointed incrementalism toward the comprehensive approach long advocated by students of public finance. It is to this topic that we now turn.

Congressional Budget Procedures Prior to 1975

Prior to the enactment of the Congressional Budget Act, the procedures employed by the Congress to make economic and budgetary decisions facilitated, or at least were compatible with, the disjointed incrementalist model of decisionmaking.[10] Associated with the work of Charles Lindblom, disjointed incrementalism departs from the typical assumptions of classical economics and rational planning models; that is, that the rational actor first lays out all the alternatives, then attaches a set of consequences to each, then rank orders the alternatives based on some preference (or utility) function, and then selects the alternative that would produce the preferred result. Disjointed incrementalism—a behavioral theory taking into account the inevitability of uncertainty and complexity in decisionmaking—is based on quite different assumptions:

- Decisionmakers concentrate on marginal changes from the status quo, rather than undertake a comprehensive analysis of policy issues.
- Decisionmakers restrict their activity to analyzing a few consequences of a limited number of options, rather than analyzing all the consequences of all the options.
- Decisionmakers often allow *ends* to be readjusted and altered to *means* as the policy process develops, because in many cases it is impossible to state or concentrate analysis on a specific policy problem.
- Decisionmakers tend to develop policies by addressing aspects of a problem rather than by attempting a single comprehensive solution.
- Decisionmakers usually use analysis to avoid bad results rather than to move toward a set of goals.
- Finally, decisionmaking and the analysis that supports it tend to be done disjointedly at multiple points and levels.[11]

The congressional budget process prior to 1975 was compatible with these assumptions. Comprehensive treatment of policies was almost impossible. Since before the Civil War a distinction has been made between programmatic legislation and the appropriations necessary to fund those programs. By the 1970s the distinction had progressed to the point that the members and staff of the legislative committees that framed the programmatic legislation (authorizations) had no idea of the funding levels (appropriation of budget authority) that applied to the various programs within their committees' jurisdiction.

The average program required a two-step process: first the enactment of an authorization and then a yearly appropriation. In the extreme case, legislators could please those who wanted program expansion by liberalizing the program's authorization through the legislative process while pleasing those who desired fiscal constraint by voting to reduce the appropriation for the budget account that funded the program.

Following the establishment of the Appropriations Committees after the Civil War, tax rates and the raising of revenues were handled by separate committees and were not formally related to expenditures. The Congress never formally considered the fiscal policy effects of its decisions.

Advantages

This system provided a number of aids to calculation that helped members of Congress deal with the uncertainty and complexity of their world. By operating off a base—either the previous year's funding level or the president's recommendation—legislators could limit the scope of their decision. Rather than having to analyze an entire program (as in zero-base budgeting), legislators could limit their activity to a few options affecting a limited proportion of the program (its base). In addition, by separating the programmatic function from the funding process, they could maintain the fiction that the prime goal of the budget (appropriations) process would be programmatic efficiency (whether money was being wasted), leaving to the legislative process the decision of whether and how a given programmatic activity should be undertaken.

Although inefficient, these procedures overcame the defects that Lindblom and others had identified with the comprehensive approach.[12] They were adapted to man's limited problem-solving capacities. They allowed for the inevitable inadequacy of information and avoided the costs and failures that traditionally have been associated with trying to construct a satisfactory method of evaluating alternatives. The procedures took into account the observed relationships between fact and value in policymaking and reflected the openness of the decisionmaking system. Decisionmakers were able to consider the strategic consequences of their moves and the analysis that was presented to support those moves. The multiple layers were able to handle the diverse forms and timing associated with how and when problems arise. Most important, the procedures facilitated what Lindblom calls *partisan mutual adjustment,* the process that allows rational actors with different values to achieve ad hoc accommodations without changing those values.[13]

Costs

The old process for making economic and budget decisions thus limited the extent and scope of political conflict. It also provided an ideal environment for the carrying out of distributive politics. But these advantages were obtained at some cost. The aggregate effects of the many decisions made at multiple levels were rarely understood and almost never explicitly debated except in reaction to presidential initiatives. This fact and the need for some coordinating force were major factors in the abrogation of much of the power of the purse to the executive branch and especially to the president and his budget officers.

The old system was also not very efficient from a managerial standpoint. In four of the eight years prior to the passage of the Congressional Budget Act (fiscal years 1970, 1971, 1974, and 1976), Congress failed to pass a single appropriations bill before the start of the fiscal year; its best record was in fiscal 1972 and 1973 when it enacted three out of the 13 appropriations bills. On average it took three months after the start of the fiscal year for Congress to complete action on the 13 major appropriations bills.

Particularly for conservatives, the old procedures also appeared to have failed to control the growth of federal spending and deficits. Although lower than the 4.4 percent annual rate of the 1960s, the 3.4 rate of real outlay growth during the first half of the 1970s was almost three times the rate experienced in the 1950s. As indicated in Table 14-1, federal budget outlays that had averaged 18.0 percent of GNP during the 1950s, and which had grown to an annual average of 19.4 percent during the 1960s, rose to an annual average of 20.3 percent of GNP in the six fiscal years prior to the implementation of the Congressional Budget Act. The frequency and size of deficits also increased. Federal budget deficits had averaged 0.6 percent of GNP during the 1950s. This figure grew to 0.8 percent during the 1960s and then rose further to 1.5 percent in the six fiscal years prior to the implementation of the new procedures.

Finally, it appeared that Congress could no longer manage its internal conflict over economic and budget issues by using its pre-1975 budgetary procedures. As we have indicated, the level of conflict rose and the practice of distributive politics became more difficult as the rate of economic growth declined in the 1970s. But conflict also became more difficult to manage as the nature and purpose of federal expenditures shifted from the provision of goods and services to the provision of transfer payments and as the control of these transfer payments was shifted from the appropriations to the legislative committees.

Prior to the 1960s, most federal activity involved the direct provision of goods and services. The national government provided for the national defense, built dams, ran its own public works projects, and hired experts to help farmers, the merchant marine, airlines, and other industries. The limited number of programs that provided direct payments to individuals or to state and local governments—Social Security, unemployment insurance, the federal retirement program, and federal highway aid—were funded through separate trust funds that, until 1969, were separated from the government's administrative (operating) budget. The programs that provided goods and services were funded in most part through an annual appropriations process. As the previously cited Wildavsky quote indicated, the nature of the programs allowed Congress to increase or decrease funding as necessary.

But as the 1960s progressed, the nature of federal activity shifted from the direct provision of goods and services to the provision of transfer payments to individuals, either through direct federal payments or through state and local governments. The funding levels of these new programs—Medicare and Medicaid, Aid to Families with Dependent Children (AFDC), food stamps, and supplemental security assistance for the elderly poor (SSI)—were determined not through an annual appropriation but rather through the interaction of economic and demographic conditions and the programs' funding formulas that were contained in their authorization statutes. The formulas were so designed as to make the programs countercyclical; that is, to have higher levels of funding as economic conditions worsened and to adjust the funding levels to changes in the price level. Eligibility for a program was determined in most cases by a "means test" contained in the formula found within the program's authorization. (The major exceptions were Social Security and Medicare, which used an age test, and unemployment insurance and federal pensions, which used a payment into a trust fund test.) During economic downturns, more individuals would qualify for the programs and their funding levels would rise. By the mid-1970s just about all the formulas were designed so that their funding levels would be tied to a measure of inflation, most frequently the Consumer Price Index (CPI). Thus, as the rate of inflation rose in the 1970s, the size of the transfer payments from these programs was driven upward at the same pace.

In fiscal year 1967, expenditures for these "entitlement" programs represented 28 percent of noninterest federal budget outlays. By the last fiscal year under Congress's old budget procedures—fiscal year 1974—they accounted for 44 percent of noninterest federal budget outlays. This pattern has continued. In fiscal year 1983, spending for entitlement transfers made up 50 percent of noninterest federal budget outlays.

In the jargon of federal budgeting, this type of funding is classified as "relatively uncontrollable under current law." The notion of uncontrollability is a confusion; Congress can control any spending that has not been obligated. What is really meant by uncontrollability is that these expenditures are not controllable through the annual appropriations process.[14]

Thus, the real message of the rise in the percentage of federal expenditures that are classified as uncontrollable is the decline in the power and influence of the appropriations process and its committees. It is true that most budget accounts are still funded through the annual appropriations process (77 percent in fiscal year 1983). But these accounts now fund a minority of federal expenditures (46 percent of all federal expenditures). Moreover, it is the accounts outside the jurisdiction of the appropriations committees that have funded most of the growth in federal spending during the last decade. Between fiscal years 1970 and 1983, the 23 percent of budget accounts not under the direct jurisdiction of the appropriations committees accounted for 60 percent of the total growth in noninterest federal outlays. (If interest outlays were included, these accounts would account for a higher percentage of the growth in spending, since the net interest account, one of the fast growing parts of the federal budget, is under the jurisdiction of the Ways and Means and Finance committees.)

Increasingly, therefore, the disjointed nature of Congress's incremental decisionmaking budget system disappeared. The same set of actors decided on programmatic and budget questions. Moreover, the structure and design of entitlements worked against an incremental control process. In the traditional funding model, the separation of programmatic from funding values facilitated the partisan mutual adjustment process at the heart of incrementalism. In other words, the multistage process increased the access points for various interests. The final shape of the budget resulted from bargaining within and across committee jurisdictions.

As entitlements began to dominate the budget, program design had to be changed in order to change funding levels. Moreover, members of Congress had to take positive action to reduce spending levels. For budget accounts funded by the annual appropriations process, those desiring higher levels of spending had to achieve a positive act: Congress had to pass a higher level of budget authority. Those who wanted to lower a program's funding level could always threaten inaction, thus eliminating all funding. But the situation for entitlements was reversed. The funding levels for these programs were determined by the rules contained in their authorizations, and these authorizations were either permanent (as with Social Security and Medicare) or multiyear (as with food stamps). In these cases, therefore, the burden of action fell on those who wanted to reduce expenditure levels.

The initial reaction in Congress was to reject the implications of the new funding patterns by claiming that the work of the authorization process was programmatic rather than budgetary. The introduction of the concept of uncontrollability reflected this trend. When criticized for their inability to control spending, members of Congress frequently would point out that each year the appropriations process granted less budget authority than requested in the president's budget. Failure to control existing entitlement spending, the liberalization of existing rules, and the creation of new ones could be ignored because these actions were not part of the budget process.

But such avoidance behavior could not last forever. As the revenue burden and deficits rose, public pressure for expenditure control grew. During Richard Nixon's administration, budget wars between the president and Congress became commonplace. As the pressure to do something about the growth in entitlement outlays grew, conflict increased among the three classes of congressional committees: appropriations, revenue, and legislative or authorizing committees. Congress was less able to manage its internal conflict. The appropriations committees sought to regain their control over these budget accounts that were responsible for the growth of federal spending. The authorizing committees wanted to improve coordination between program design and funding. And the revenue committees were pulled in both directions. They tended to accept the conservative norms associated with actors in the budget process, but they also had jurisdiction over the major entitlements such as Social Security, Medicare, and unemployment compensation.

The Congressional Budget Act of 1974 was an attempt to deal with each of these problems. Its authors had four main goals: (1) to re-establish Congress's historic "power of the purse"; (2) to build Congress's managerial efficiency by requiring it to meet its budget deadlines and pass spending and legislation before the beginning of the fiscal year; (3) to help Congress manage internal conflict over budget issues; and (4) to curb the growth of federal spending, the federal revenue burden, and the frequency and size of federal budget deficits. The new procedures failed to achieve their intended goals. As a result they have been modified in practice. In the next section we will address these changes.

The Congressional Budget Act's Procedures

Allen Schick has called the Congressional Budget and Impoundment Control Act of 1974 a treaty among the warring groups within Congress and between Congress and the executive branch.[15] The treaty, he claims, reflects seven principles: (1) that the new procedures should be neutral concerning the appropriate levels of spending, taxing, and resulting fiscal policy; (2) that Congress should be allowed to act according to its own budgetary preferences; (3) that information, rather than formal control mechanisms, should be used to change congressional behavior and enforce budget deadlines; (4) that all interested parties should be represented and should participate in the process; (5) that Congress should recapture the responsibility for budget and fiscal policy decisions from the executive branch; (6) that the power of existing interests in Congress should be protected; and (7) that the new process should benefit all of the major participants—appropriations, revenue, and legislative committees—in Congress.[16]

These principles were in line with the values and norms underlying other congressional "reforms" of the early 1970s. If the new budget procedures had continued to reflect them, they would have enhanced the power of the autonomous legislator and would have been compatible with the dispersion of power from committees to subcommittees and from committee chairmen and ranking members to individual representatives. They would have been compatible with the practice of distributive politics.

Unfortunately, the new budget procedures did not operate in practice as they were expected to on paper. Many of the principles had to be abandoned, several new ones added, and the process modified in a manner that went against the incrementalist model. The modified procedures increased the power of central leaders and adopted many of the approaches of top-down comprehensive planning. We will first examine the process as it was supposed to work and then consider what actually happened.

The New Procedures on Paper

At the heart of the new process were a set of new procedures and two new committees to oversee those procedures. Congress would be forced for the first time to vote on budget aggregates and the appropriate fiscal policy through the enactment of at least two concurrent resolutions on the budget. The first concurrent resolution was to be reported out of committee by April 15 of each year and be fully enacted by both houses by May 15. It would contain five aggregate targets: total budget authority, total outlays, total revenues, and the resulting surplus or deficit, and public debt. In addition to these five aggregate numbers, the resolution also would contain targets for budget authority and outlays for each of the budget's functions.

The second concurrent resolution on the budget was to be enacted by September 15. The aggregate numbers in the second resolution were to be binding; once the fiscal year began on October 1 (the start of the fiscal year had been shifted ahead three months to give Congress more time to pass its money bills), any bill coming to the floor of either house that would cause aggregate budget authority or outlays to exceed the aggregate levels in the resolution, or would cause total revenues to fall below the aggregate level of the resolution, would be considered out of order until compensating changes had been made or until Congress passed a new resolution.

The new procedures did recapture the "power of the purse." By adopting a resolution, Congress was forced for the first time to vote on a budget. As time progressed the impact of the president's budget receded as Congress turned to other sources for its budget information.

But Schick was correct in pointing out that information rather than control was at the heart of this process. The new procedures (as rules of each chamber) could be modified or waived by simple majorities. Their real power resulted from the fact that they forced members to go on record for higher deficits, higher spending, or higher taxes if Congress could not live within its budget.

The information criteria also applied to the new procedures for improving the management of budget activity. To guarantee (supposedly) that Congress would complete all of its budget activity prior to the beginning of the fiscal year affected by that activity, the Congressional Budget Act contained the following series of deadlines. The president's budget was to be sent to Congress no later than 15 days after Congress convened; by March 15 each committee was to inform the budget committee of its chamber of how much new budget authority it believed was necessary to fund the programs within its jurisdiction; the budget committees were to report out a first concurrent resolution on the budget by April 15; all congressional action on that resolution was to be completed by May 15; all new authorizations affecting the upcoming fiscal year were to be reported to the floor by May 15 so that the appropriations committees would know what they had to fund; all spending (including appropriations) and revenue bills were to be enacted by 7 calendar days after Labor Day; all action on the second concurrent resolution on the budget was to be completed by September 15; and where the second resolution differed from the actual pattern of enacted money bills, a reconciliation bill to reduce budget authority or outlays or raise revenues was to be enacted by September 25.

Congress could ignore these deadlines. Only the power of information—the embarrassment of setting the new procedures aside—would keep Congress in line. The deadlines were also crucial to maintaining the balance of power and to limiting conflict among the three types of committees. It was assumed that the focus of the House and Senate budget committees would be on the budget's aggregates, on fiscal policy, and on the trade-offs among different types of spending. Once the aggregate targets had been set, it was assumed that the appropriations, revenue, and legislative committees would then make specific decisions within the targets. To bring this about, Congress again relied on information. For the first time the authorizing committees were informed of the funding levels of the programs within their jurisdictions. Once the first resolution was enacted, the budget authority and outlay targets were allocated to the various committees and to the various subcommittees of the appropriations committees.

The multiple steps of the new procedures attempted to include all the major players in the decisionmaking process. One can think of the process as the interplay of a series of information cues. The president was represented by his budget; last year's "base" was represented by a current services or current policy budget projection that was produced initially by the Office of Management and Budget (OMB) and then by both OMB and the Congressional Budget Office (CBO); and the views of the appropriations, revenue, and legislative committees were entered through the submission of their March 15th reports to the budget committees. In line with an incremental system, issues were not settled by a single vote. They would have to surmount a series of hurdles: inclusion in the president's budget, inclusion in the March 15th vote, inclusion in the first budget resolution, inclusion in an authorization bill (where appropriate), inclusion in an appropriations bill (where appropriate), inclusion in a second budget resolution, and sometimes inclusion in a reconciliation bill.

The New Procedures in Practice: Stage 1

The principles of the new system could not be maintained. With all the other committees acting as claimants for federal subsidies, neutral coordinating budget committees did not provide enough of a counterweight to the system to fulfill their function of institutional maintenance. The provision of information embarrassed members without changing their behavior.

In practice, the power of information to control congressional behavior was soon dismissed. Although there is general agreement that the new procedures recaptured the power of the purse from the executive branch, the other three goals—meeting budget deadlines, managing internal conflict, and curbing the growth of spending, taxes, and deficits—were not achieved.

After some initial success, Congress soon reverted to its inability to meet its own deadlines. With increasing regularity, provisions of the Congressional Budget Act were waived. In the eight years after the implementation of the new procedures (1976-1983), Congress took about the same number of days (102) after the start of the fiscal year to enact all of its major appropriations bills as it did between 1968 and 1975, the eight years prior to the act's implementation (101 days).

The hopes that the new procedures would reduce the growth rate of federal spending or the number and size of budget deficits also were not fulfilled. During the seven years before the implementation of the new procedures, high-employment federal outlays in constant dollars (so as to control for economic cycles and inflation) grew at an average rate of 2.8 percent per year. During the next seven years under the act, they rose at an annual average rate of 3.6 percent.

The same pattern occurred with deficits. In the seven years before the Congressional Budget Act's implementation, there was a budget deficit in all but one year; but there has been a deficit in every year since 1975. Moreover, the deficits have been getting larger. Even when measured on a high-employment basis as a percentage of high-employment GNP, federal deficits rose from an annual average of 0.6 percent during the 1969-1975 period to 1.2 percent during the following seven years.

Nor did the new procedures help Congress manage its internal conflict. If anything, they increased conflict. Constraints on federal resources grew after 1975. (As shown in Table 14-1, the annual growth rate of real personal income declined from 3.1 percent in the 1970-1975 period to 2.7 percent from 1976 through 1983.) Moreover, the information effect of making votes on total spending and deficits visible to the electorate worsened the problem. The new procedures appeared to add more steps to the budget process without reducing conflict or improving the chance of a policy resolution. By the 1980s, members of Congress were quick to criticize the new procedures.[17]

The New Procedures in Practice: Stage 2

During the first stage of the development of the new procedures (1975 through 1979), both budget committees, and especially the House Budget Committee, acted as brokers for the claimants within each chamber. Their budget resolutions frequently reflected a balance among the wants of the various committees, the party leaders, and the president. In this role the committees were traffic cops of a bottom-up (that is, from the subcommittees and committees) incremental budget process.

Over time, however, the budget committees became budget guardians because they alone were in a position to add up the effects of the incremental requests and actions of the other committees. The appropriations committees had abandoned their role as guardians of the purse and had become claimants for federal money. The budget committees were able to build their power to the extent that they could work their will on the budget process.

The guardian role was first advanced by the leaders of the Senate Budget Committee, Chairman Edmund Muskie of Maine and ranking minority member Henry Bellmon of Oklahoma. Because their power in the Senate would increase as the Budget Committee became more powerful, it was in their interest to expand the committee's jurisdiction and power vis-à-vis the other committees of the chamber. Their first action was to attempt to get the Senate to accept the notion that spending could not be controlled (a budget function) unless authorization limits also were controlled (traditionally seen as a program function). During the next few years—1976 through 1978—they sought to introduce multiyear projections and targets into budget resolutions, to place limits on federal credit activity, to interpret widely the provisions of the Congressional Budget Act, and to invoke reconciliation with the second budget resolution. In 1979, they sought to hold enacted appropriations bills at the desk (that is, prevent their being sent to the president for his signature) until all 13 regular appropriations bills were passed. In this way the Senate could determine whether the ceilings of the second resolution (for fiscal year 1980) had been breached.

The limited tenure and mandated membership of the House Budget Committee led its membership to be much more tentative, lest the committee "break faith" with the other committees of the House. (Originally, no member of the committee could serve for more than 4 out of a 10-year period. Two members had to hold party leadership posts. Three members also had to serve on House Appropriations and three members on Ways and Means.) By calendar year 1980, however, following a series of failures to achieve "legislative savings" through agreements with the other committees of the House, Chairman Robert Giaimo (D-Conn.), supported by his junior members, was ready to assume a more active guardian role.

Reconciliation and Top-down Budgeting

The critical transformation in the budget committees from brokers in an information-controlled system to guardians of the federal purse occurred in 1980. For the first time they invoked the Congressional Budget Act's reconciliation procedures in connection with the first rather than the second budget resolution. Thus they became the chief actors in a process that attempted to use central control to mandate actions to the various committees of each chamber.

Between 1974 and 1980, as the budget committees gained experience with the structure of the federal budget, it became obvious that the growth of federal outlays could not be controlled through the appropriations process. Budget growth was driven by entitlements, and the act's provisions were not very effective in controlling their growth, much less in bringing about reductions. As we have seen, the only way to limit the growth of entitlement spending is to change program rules and formulas that are part of the program's authorization. Since the authorizations of entitlements are either permanent or multiyear, the budget committees needed a mechanism to force the legislative committees to act.

The budget resolutions were not effective tools to force action. Through inaction, members of Congress who wanted to maintain the funding level of an entitlement could ignore the budget process. The budget committees were then obliged to either maintain their aggregate spending levels by forcing the annual appropriations process to make compensating cuts or to increase the aggregate levels in the subsequent budget resolutions for that fiscal year.

Nor was the reconciliation process as written into the act very effective in dealing with entitlements. Changing entitlement rules takes time, particularly if the programmatic as well as the funding effects of the changes are addressed. Reconciliation was associated with the second budget resolution, and the process allowed committees only a 10-day period (September 15 through 25) to make any changes. Under these conditions, efforts to alter entitlements were bound to be resisted.

From 1976 through 1979 a pattern was established whereby entitlement changes were assumed in each first concurrent resolution. In almost all cases, the legislative committees failed to report out such changes. When they did, as with hospital cost containment in 1979, the changes were frequently rejected on the floor. In 1979, for example, the first concurrent resolution for fiscal year 1980 assumed the enactment of approximately $6 billion in savings. The House Budget Committee negotiated agreements with the committees of the House to bring the necessary legislation to the floor. When the session ended, however, only changes reducing fiscal year 1980 outlays by $200 million had been enacted.

In response to this failure the Senate Budget Committee included reconciliation instructions along with its second concurrent resolution for fiscal year 1980. Adopted by the Senate but rejected by the House as coming too late in the session to be workable, these instructions would have required seven committees in each chamber to report legislation lowering fiscal year 1980 budget authority by $3.2 billion and fiscal year 1980 outlays by $4.0 billion. Following the failure of their "legislative savings" strategy, the members of the House Budget Committee were willing by the spring of 1980 to adopt a more aggressive stance than they had in the past. The Senate Budget Committee members had already reached this stage.

The key change was to shift the reconciliation process from the second to the first resolution. As set out in the act, reconciliation is a process and a bill. The process involves a set of instructions that are recommended by the budget committees and voted on by each chamber. The instructions have two key components. They instruct each committee to report out legislation (1) by a certain date that will (2) affect the budget by a certain dollar amount. Once the committees report out their legislation, the budget committees group the changes into a single bill that is called a reconciliation bill. The bill is then considered by each chamber in the standard manner (with the key exception that debate is limited in the Senate).

In the spring of 1980 President Jimmy Carter, in response to the negative reaction of the credit markets to his budget, sought to revise his recommendations in order to achieve a balanced budget. As his budget staff met with members of the budget committees it became obvious that the only way to guarantee that the necessary legislative changes actually would occur was to use the reconciliation process as part of the first budget resolution.

When the reconciliation instructions were included in the first concurrent resolution in the House, 18 committee chairmen signed a letter to their colleagues claiming that the use of reconciliation as part of the first resolution was counter to the spirit of the Congressional Budget Act. In this they were correct, for by shifting reconciliation to the first resolution the budget committees shifted the budget process from one in which information would provide control to one in which central direction in the form of reconciliation instructions would control the committees and subcommittees.

In every session since 1980, Congress has enacted a set of reconciliation instructions and one or more reconciliation bills. Table 14-2 contains a summary of the budget effects of these measures. Most observers have focused on the large reductions achieved by the Reagan administration through the reconciliation process in 1981. This is a mistake. In the long run what is important is that Congress has institutionalized a procedure for bringing about changes in entitlements and revenues. As can be seen from the data, the new procedures can be used to raise or lower taxes or to increase or decrease spending. The reconciliation process, therefore, is neutral as to the direction of change but not neutral as to the locus of power; it has shifted power from committees and subcommittees to the budget committees, to the party leadership, and to each chamber as a whole.

The budget process that has emerged since 1980 is a more top-down and comprehensive process than was intended by the framers of the Congressional Budget Act. It is top-down in three respects.[18] First, the needs of fiscal policy and decisions concerning the proper size of the budget have become more important in determining the size of individual budget accounts. Traditionally, budgeting has involved a war between the parts and the whole. Prior to 1980, particularly in the congressional setting, the sum of the parts tended to drive the whole rather than the other way around.

Second, policy initiatives that had come from executive branch agencies and the various subcommittees of Congress now tend to come from the White House and the Office of Management and Budget in the executive branch and from the budget process in Congress. Finally, the system has become top-down in its power relationships. Power has shifted from the agencies to OMB in the executive branch and from the appropriations, revenue, and legislative committees to the budget committees and to the party leadership in Congress.

Table 14-2   Budget Effects of Reconciliation and Tax Bills Required by Reconciliation Instructions (in billions of dollars)

	First-Year Effect	Three-Year Effect
1980		
Omnibus Reconciliation Act of 1980		
Budget Authority	−2.8	NA
Outlays	−4.6	NA
Revenues	+3.6	NA
1981		
Omnibus Reconciliation Act of 1981		
and Economic Recovery Tax Act of 1981		
Budget Authority	−53.2	−172.3
Outlays	−35.2	−130.9
Revenues	−26.9	−114.7
1982		
Omnibus Reconciliation Act of 1982		
and Tax Equity and Fiscal		
Responsibility Act of 1982		
Budget Authority	−3.4	−14.9
Outlays	−6.9	−29.9
Revenues	+18.0	+98.3
1983		
Omnibus Reconciliation Act of 1983		
(enacted on April 18, 1984)		
Budget Authority	+2.0	+2.3
Outlays	−0.4	−1.8
Revenues	0.0	0.0
1984		
Deficit Reduction Act of 1984		
Budget Authority	−0.9	−7.2
Outlays	−3.9	−12.2
Revenues	+10.5	+50.0

NOTE: Cost and revenue estimates were prepared by the Congressional Budget Office and the Joint Tax Committee when the various measures were passed. Changing economic conditions have affected the actual savings or losses.

The process also became more comprehensive. During the first years of the new process, budget committee members frequently acted as ambassadors or representatives from their other committees or from their constituents. Line-item amendments to budget resolutions were a frequent occurrence. But since 1980, packages have replaced amendments. Previously the budget committees would mark up resolutions by going through the budget's functions and debating and voting on options affecting the main policy issues in each function. Today this detailed review has almost disappeared. Instead the committees discuss and debate a series of comprehensive alternatives. In 1984, for example, the Senate Budget Committee confined its discussion and voting to five comprehensive packages.

A similar pattern characterizes the mark-ups of the House Budget Committee and the floor debate of resolutions and reconciliation bills in both the House and the Senate. A series of amendments to the House Budget Committee's resolution are not taken up. Instead, the typical pattern of House floor action in the 1980s has been to debate and vote on the committee's resolution, a liberal Democratic alternative, and a conservative coalition alternative reflecting the views of the Reagan administration.

The movement away from disjointed incrementalism toward a more centrally coordinated top-down decisionmaking process has been caused by four factors: the desire of the budget committees to gain power within Congress; the need to achieve budget reductions; the new system of strategic budgeting that has dominated the executive branch since the appointment of David Stockman as OMB director in 1981; and the rising influence of economists and policy analysts in the budget process. We have already discussed the first factor. The adoption of coordinated, top-down budgeting is bound to increase the power of the coordinator, thus increasing the power of the budget committees. But top-down budgeting also increases the power of all the central leaders of Congress. It thus can be a powerful mechanism for the party leadership.

A coordinated, top-down decisionmaking system can help those who want to reduce the growth of expenditures and revenues because it is capable of overcoming the public choice logic of concentrated benefits and dispersed costs that normally creates a system bias toward ever greater spending. As long as programs (or budget accounts) are taken up, debated, and voted on one at a time, their beneficiaries are likely to work very hard for the programs' passage while the average taxpayer is not hurt enough to complain.

Consider this hypothetical subsidy of $100,000.00 to each of the 1,000 companies that make widgets. The total cost to the government of this subsidy will be $100 million. Because each widget firm is receiving a good deal of money it will work actively to secure passage. No doubt it will be in a widget firm's self-interest to create a PAC to make contributions to the chairmen and ranking minority members of the committees and subcommittees with jurisdiction over the widget bill. The subsidy will cost the average taxpayer only an additional dollar in taxes. It is unlikely, therefore, that taxpayers will work against the subsidy or vote for a member of Congress because of his active opposition. The average taxpayer will become upset, however, when he learns that Congress has enacted 99 other new subsidies, for now his tax bill will go up by $100.

Top-down budgeting helps control expenditures to the extent that it shifts attention from the benefits of the parts to those of the whole. This is the great virtue of the reconciliation process. It also explains the movement away from amendments toward substitutes in the budget process. The key votes on the Reagan budget cuts in 1981 were the adoption of rules that limited voting to substitutes, thus forcing the House to vote on the merits of entire packages rather than the merits of individual programs.

The growth of a coordinated, top-down budget process was also fostered by a change in the budget procedures used by the president and the Office of Management and Budget. In the past, the president and his budget advisers concentrated their efforts on putting together a budget that would reflect the views of his administration. Because the process was bottom-up, most of the effort was directed at examining the proposals generated from bureaus within executive agencies. Little thought was given to what would happen to the budget once it went to Congress.

Stockman's appointment as OMB director fundamentally changed how OMB approached the budget.[19] The appointment of Stockman—a U.S. representative (R-Mich.)—also reflected Congress's regained power of the purse. Stockman understood that as a plan the president's budget was useful only if it could be enacted. To accomplish this, Stockman introduced coordinated, top-down budgeting within the executive branch. Initiatives began to be put together within OMB rather than within the agencies. The budget's aggregates controlled its parts. And, most important, the budget was shaped strategically to improve its chances of being passed by Congress. Stockman, who served in Congress from 1977 until his OMB appointment in 1981, understood the budget act's procedures and knew how to use them— particularly the reconciliation process—to the administration's advantage.

The final force behind the movement toward a more coordinated, top-down process was sociological—the increasing influence of staff trained in economics. As early as 1961, Charles Lindblom contrasted the incrementalist reality of federal decisionmaking on expenditures and taxation with the norms of economists.[20] Drawing from the work of Arthur Smithies, Lindblom pointed out the economists' assumptions that the ideal decisionmaking procedure would be synoptic rather than incremental. Although Lindblom and other political scientists spent the next two decades showing that such a system was not compatible with the reality of decisionmaking in the public sector, economists continued to hold the same view of the ideal decisionmaking process. At times they have tried to change the decisionmaking system to reflect their view—usually unsuccessfully, as with the Planning, Programming, Budgeting System (PPBS) of the 1960s.

Many of the PPBS staff went on to develop the congressional budget procedures. Although no attempt was made to introduce the formal structure of PPBS, the norms of the economic and policy analysis staff were reflected in the movement toward a more coordinated, top-down budget process. A multiyear planning approach was advocated in place of the traditional historical one that used last year's base to determine next year's budget. The difficult economic conditions of the 1970s focused debate on fiscal policy. This, in turn, reinforced the tendency of economists to start with macroeconomic options and then analyze individual programs. As early as 1978, for example, the Congressional Budget Office, in its annual report to the budget committees, created four aggregate budgets each of which would achieve a different macro goal—a smaller federal sector with lower economic growth, a slightly smaller federal sector with vigorous economic growth, and a larger federal sector with rapid economic growth. Individual program decisions were then seen as trade-offs within the budget spaces that had been created.[21]

The Effects of the New Budget Procedures

What happens when a centralized, coordinated decisionmaking system is imposed on an institution that tends to operate incrementally? An advantage of the incremental process is that it controls the level of conflict by creating a market mechanism that allows decisionmakers with different values to make ad hoc accommodations without changing those values. One would predict, then, that a movement toward greater centralization and coordination would increase conflict. This is exactly what has occurred under the new budget process.

Our measure of conflict is the degree to which partisanship characterized voting on budget questions versus other types of issues. Table 14-3 shows what percent of all roll call votes in the House and Senate between 1975 and 1983 were "party unity" votes; that is, recorded votes that split the parties, a majority of voting Democrats opposing a majority of voting Republicans. Two patterns are evident. Since the implementation of the new budget procedures in 1975, votes on budget resolutions and reconciliation bills have been much more partisan than other votes. In the House, for example, 71 percent of the roll calls on budget resolutions and reconciliation bills were party unity votes while only 41 percent of all roll calls fell into this category. A similar, though less dramatic pattern occurred in the Senate, where 44 percent of all roll calls were party unity votes while 59 percent of the roll calls on budget resolutions and reconciliation bills fell into this category. Second, it appears that the level of conflict for budget resolutions and reconciliation bills was higher than for other budget related voting. Thus, only 49 percent of House and 47 percent of Senate roll calls on appropriations bills were party unity votes.

The degree of conflict across types of issues can be seen by examining the pattern of Rice Cohesion Index scores for the party unity votes. A Rice Index score of zero means that the members of the party split evenly on the vote, a score of 50 means that 75 percent of the party members voted one way while 25 percent voted the opposite way, and a score of 100 means that all party members voted the same way.

Table 14-4 presents the average Rice Cohesion Index score for party unity roll call votes on appropriations bills and on budget resolutions and reconciliation bills from 1975 to 1984. Once again, voting on budget resolutions and reconciliation bills is more partisan than voting on appropriations measures. Between 1975 and 1984, on the House floor, the average Rice

Table 14-3 Party Unity Votes as a Percent of Total Roll Call Votes

Year	*House*			*Senate*		
	All Votes	Appro- priations	Budget & Reconciliation	All Votes	Appro- priations	Budget & Reconciliation
1975	48	50	92	48	53	13
1976	36	40	86	37	25	36
1977	42	52	64	42	35	50
1978	33	38	73	45	41	51
1979	47	44	76	47	51	56
1980	38	52	75	46	50	44
1981	37	58	68	47	64	66
1982	36	47	61	44	46	72
1983	57	66	83	44	42	69
Weighted Average 1975-1983	41	49	71	44	47	59

SOURCE: Measures of party unity for all roll calls are from annual editions of the *Congressional Quarterly Almanac.* Party unity measures for appropriations and budget and reconciliation roll calls were calculated by the author.

Cohesion Index for roll calls on budget resolutions and reconciliation bills was 14 points higher than the average for appropriations bills. The same pattern occurred in Senate voting, where roll calls for budget resolutions and reconciliation bills averaged 15 points above the Rice Index for appropriations bills.

The pattern of the cohesion scores in Table 14-4 also indicates that the level of partisan conflict was much higher during the second stage of the development of the new procedures than during the first stage. In the House, for example, the average cohesion score for budget resolution and reconciliation bill roll call voting·increased from 60 during the 1975-1979 period to 69 during the following five years. Average cohesion scores for appropriations bills increased more, rising from 43 to 53. The increase in partisanship was even more dramatic in the Senate, where the average cohesion score for budget resolutions and reconciliation bills rose from 40 to 61 between the two periods. The rise of the average appropriations score was almost as great, from 33 to 52.

Most of this increase in partisanship can be explained by the nature of the Reagan administration's budget proposals and by the desire of the newly elected majority of Republicans in the Senate to support the newly elected president of their party. The retirement of the bipartisan leadership of the

Table 14-4 Average Rice Cohesion Index Scores for Floor Roll Calls of Appropriations Bills and Budget Resolutions and Reconciliation Bills, 1975-1984

	House		*Senate*	
Year	Appropriations	Budget and Reconciliation	Appropriations	Budget and Reconciliation
1975	39	63	30	45
1976	42	59	27	38
1977	44	62	37	39
1978	42	59	36	32
1979	44	59	35	44
1980	49	72	45	47
1981	51	67	61	63
1982	58	57	50	72
1983	56	78	47	61
1984*	55	71	55	62
Weighted Averages				
1975-1984	48	62	45	60
1975-1979	43	60	33	40
1980-1984	54	69	52	61

* Includes roll calls through September 15, 1984.

SOURCE: Calculated by author from recorded votes published by Congressional Quarterly.

Senate Budget Committee, Senators Muskie and Bellmon, does not appear to have been the significant factor since the same rise in partisanship is evidenced in the appropriations process as in the voting on budget resolutions and reconciliation bills.

Why is partisanship (conflict) consistently higher on budget resolutions and reconciliation bills than on appropriations bills? One explanation is the movement toward a coordinated, top-down decisionmaking process. In the appropriations process, members have conflicting interests. They have an individual and party commitment to increases or decreases in expenditures, revenues, and deficits; but they also want to serve their constituencies and interest groups. Faced with such cross-pressures, they are more likely to abandon their ideological and party positions.

In the coordinated, top-down world of budget resolutions and reconciliation bills the weight of the argument has been shifted from the parts to the whole, and the issues of the whole are more likely to be determined by ideology and party loyalty. One test of this hypothesis is to compare the budget resolution and reconciliation bill index scores for votes on line-item amendments (the parts) to those for votes on substitutes and final passage (the whole). The votes on the substitutes and final passage should be more partisan, and they are. In the House, for example, the 1975-1984 average index score for votes on substitutes and final passage of budget resolutions is 69 while the average for the roll calls on line-item amendments to budget resolutions is only 52.

Conclusion

Decisionmaking in the U.S. Congress traditionally has been explained by Charles Lindblom's theory of disjointed incrementalism. Over the last two decades congressional "reforms" have increased the incremental nature of congressional decisionmaking by dispersing power from central leaders and institutions to autonomous legislators working in subcommittees. As the number of actors (subcommittee chairmen, staff, organized interests) have increased, partisan mutual adjustment has become more crucial. In this environment a centralized budget process has been the great exception.

Lindblom readily admits that incrementalism and partisan mutual adjustment are not always superior to more coordinated decisionmaking systems. He recognizes that "questions about the merits of alternative methods [of decisionmaking] arise in various specific contexts; hence it is in these contexts that one needs finally to evaluate them." [22]

Expanding on Lindblom's notion, Ian Lustick has suggested that there are certain cases where more coordinated decisionmaking systems are superior to incrementalism as strategies for coping with uncertainty.[23] More centralized and coordinated decisionmaking processes make sense, he contends, for organizations that must operate in an environment of scarcity and lack extra resources to meet their goals. He cites the work of Alfred Chandler who found that "sustained losses and dangerously low profit margins led corporate executives to disregard incremental, disjointed, and highly decentralized administrative procedures, in favor of heavier reliance on a priori analysis and comprehensive reorganizational schemes."[24]

For political and economic reasons, Congress since 1965 has had to make macroeconomic and budget decisions in an environment of low profit margins and sustained losses. A slower growing economy has made the practice of distributive politics more difficult. Changes in the makeup of the budget and the design of programs have weakened the power of the appropriations committees. The demise of the seniority system and the rise of the autonomous legislator have made it harder to aggregate interests.

In such an environment, it is not surprising that the congressional system has moved toward a more coordinated centralized process. But can such a process be maintained in an organization such as Congress? So far, the new procedures have facilitated dramatic budget changes: the shift from domestic to defense spending that began in 1978, the large domestic budget reductions of 1981, and a series of very large tax cuts and increases. The price of these changes has been high. Conflict is up. Budgeting now dominates the congressional agenda, much to the displeasure of many members.[25] So far, at least, Congress is having great difficulty coping with the increasing complexity and uncertainty of its environment.

The scholars of incrementalism are not very specific about what happens when a centralized and coordinated decisionmaking system is imposed on an organization that requires partisan mutual adjustment to avoid unacceptable levels of conflict or stasis. Lindblom implies that since synoptic decisionmaking systems do not facilitate partisan mutual adjustment they will be rejected or abandoned by political decisionmakers. This train of thought was adopted by Allen Schick and Aaron Wildavsky to explain the failure of PPBS in the 1960s.

One possibility, therefore, is that Congress will abandon the new budget process and the use of reconciliation to control entitlement spending growth and to mandate tax changes. Such a move probably would decrease internal conflict in the short run. But given America's economic problems, it is doubtful whether it would solve the current budget dilemma of very large deficits into the foreseeable future unless Congress once again relinquished its power of the purse to the executive branch.

More important, the abandoning of reconciliation would not help to solve Congress's fundamental problem—the dispersal of power within the institution. The transformation of the budget committees into the new guardians of the purse as well as into institutional maintenance committees was bound to take place once the traditional guardians abandoned their roles.

The more centralized and coordinated decisionmaking process of reconciliation is only one of the alternatives that is being tried to overcome the inability of a Congress dominated by subcommittee government to deal with an environment of scarce resources. In the last three years, informal "gangs" of legislators have been put together to deal with specific problems. There has been an increasing tendency to create nonpartisan commissions to bargain out compromises on those issues (Social Security and the MX missile) that subcommittee government cannot resolve.

Seen in this light, the recent development and future of the congressional budget process is but one example of the more important problems facing Congress: How can it reach policy decisions in an environment of scarcity when it is in the interest of individual members to disperse power? In the case of the budget process, Congress has chosen to move toward greater centralization. What is still unclear is whether it will be willing to live with the side effects of such a system.

NOTES

1. The standard definition of tax expenditures is "provisions of the federal tax code that give special incentives for particular kinds of activities or that give selective tax relief to certain groups of tax payers." In normal parlance, tax expenditures are referred to as "loop holes," except, of course, when they apply to the groups that one is a member of, in which case they are needed provisions. The same public choice argument (or forces) that political scientists and economists use to explain the growth of direct spending are applicable to the growth of tax expenditures.

2. Aaron Wildavsky, *The Politics of the Budget Process*, 4th ed. (Boston: Little, Brown & Co., 1984); and Richard F. Fenno, *The Power of the Purse: Appropriations Politics in Congress* (Boston: Little, Brown & Co., 1966).

3. Aaron Wildavsky, *How to Limit Government Spending* (Berkeley: University of California Press, 1980), p. 56.

4. Although the data is interpreted slightly differently, the following section follows Allen Schick's argument in "The Distributive Congress," in *Making Economic Policy in Congress*, ed. Allen Schick (Washington, D.C.: American Enterprise Institute for Public Policy Research, 1983), pp. 257-273.

5. The years 1950 and 1951 were excluded because of the dramatic buildup associated with the Korean War. Federal budget outlays accounted for 14.6 percent of GNP in fiscal year 1951 and 20.0 percent of GNP in fiscal year 1952. All of this growth was associated with the need for military expenditures.

6. In fiscal year 1983 the individual income tax and the wage taxes associated with social insurance accounted for 82.9 percent of all federal revenues.

7. John W. Ellwood, "Budget Control in a Redistributive Environment," in *Making Economic Policy in Congress*, pp. 69-99. See also James Annable, *The Dual Wage Theory: The Role of Wages in Business Cycles and Economic Growth* (Lexington, Mass.: D. C. Heath, 1983). During the 1970s the variation of wage increases granted by the 116 industries used by the Bureau of Labor Statistics to compile its monthly establishment survey increased dramatically as the rate of inflation rose. Larger firms and firms with labor unions granted larger wage increases than did smaller firms and nonunion firms.

8. David Mayhew, *Congress: The Electoral Connection* (New Haven: Yale University Press, 1974).

9. The notion of distributive and redistributive politics was first put forth by Theodore J. Lowi in "American Business, Public Policy, Case Studies, and Political Theory," *World Politics* 16 (July 1964): 677-715. For the most useful extension of Lowi's work in this area, see Michael T. Hayes, "The Semi-Sovereign Pressure Groups: A Critique of Current Theory and an Alternative Typology," *Journal of Politics* 40 (1978): 134-161.

10. In applying incrementalism to the making of economic and budget decisions in Congress, I have relied on two major sources: Charles E. Lindblom, "Decision-Making in Taxation and Expenditure," in *Public Finances: Needs, Sources, Utilization: A Conference of the Universities—National Committee for Economic Research* (Princeton, N.J.: Princeton University Press and National Bureau of Economic Research, 1961), pp. 295-336; and John F. Witte, *The Politics and Development of the Federal Income Tax* (Madison, Wis.: University of Wisconsin Press, forthcoming), chap. 1.

11. This list is a paraphrase of a list found in Charles E. Lindblom, *The Intelligence of Democracy* (New York: Free Press, 1965), pp. 144-152; and in Witte, *The Politics and Development of the Federal Income Tax*, chap. 1.

12. The main critique of the comprehensive approach, labeled by Lindblom the synoptic approach, is found in David Braybrooke and Charles E. Lindblom, *A Strategy of Decision* (New York: Free Press, 1963), p. 38. See also Witte, *The Politics and Development of the Federal Income Tax*, chap. 1. In "Decision-Making in Taxation and Expenditures," Lindblom has applied the critique to the congressional budget process as it existed in 1960.

13. See Lindblom, *The Intelligence of Democracy*, pp. 28-29, quoted in Witte, *The Politics and Development of the Federal Income Tax*, chap. 1. Partisan mutual adjustment is the term given by Lindblom to a series of methods that are used to achieve coordination among partisan decisionmakers. Partisan decisionmakers are defined as follows: "In a group of decisionmakers, a decisionmaker is partisan with respect to the others if (a) he does not assume that there exists some knowable criteria acceptable to him and all the other decisionmakers that is sufficient, if applied, to govern adjustments among them; and (b) he therefore does not move toward coordination by a cooperative and deliberate search for and/or application of such criteria or by an appeal for adjudication to those who do so search and apply."

14. The category of "relatively uncontrollable under current law" includes two other types of spending: open-ended programs and fixed costs (such as net interest on the public debt, general revenue sharing, and farm price supports) and outlays resulting from budget authority enacted in prior fiscal years. In fiscal year 1983, expenditures for all relatively uncontrollable programs accounted for 74.6 percent of all federal outlays. Congress does not directly control federal outlays. Rather it grants budget authority. Such authority allows the executive branch to enter into contracts or *obligations*. When these contracts are fulfilled, the Treasury makes payments. The sum of these payments over a fiscal year equal *total federal outlays*. Thus, once the executive branch "obligates" the budget authority, Congress cannot withdraw that authority. (In some cases, provisions are written into the contracts that allow such cancellation but with a penalty payment.) Congress can, however, rescind unobligated budget authority.

15. Allen Schick, *Congress and Money: Budgeting, Spending and Taxing* (Washington, D.C.: The Urban Institute Press, 1980), pp. 51-81.

16. Schick, *Congress and Money*, pp. 71-79.

17. Complaints about the process are extensively covered in U.S. Senate, Committee on the Budget, *Proposed Improvements in the Congressional Budget Act of 1974*, 97th Cong., 2nd sess., September 14, 16, 21, 23, 1982; and U.S. House of Representatives, Committee on Rules, Task Force on Budget Process, *Congressional Budget Process*, 97th Cong., 2nd sess., September 15, 17, 23, 29, 1983.

18. For a discussion of top-down versus bottom-up budgeting, see Barry Bozeman and Jeffrey D. Straussman, "Shrinking Budgets and the Shrinkage of Budget Theory," *Public Administration Review* (November/December 1982): 509-515.

19. For the effects on the budget process of David Stockman's OMB appointment, see Bruce E. Johnson, "From Analyst to Negotiator: OMB's New Role," *Journal of Policy Analysis and Management*, 3 (1984): 501-515.

20. Lindblom, "Decision-Making in Taxation and Expenditures," pp. 295-298.

21. Congressional Budget Office, *Budgetary Strategies for Fiscal Years 1979-1983* (Washington, D.C.: Congressional Budget Office, February 1983).
22. Lindblom, *The Intelligence of Democracy,* pp. 293-294. Quoted in Ian Lustick, "Explaining the Variable Utility of Disjointed Incrementalism: Four Propositions," *American Political Science Review,* 74 (June 1980), p. 342.
23. Ian Lustick, "Explaining the Variable Utility of Disjointed Incrementalism," 342-353.
24. Ibid, p. 349.
25. During the 1960s less than 20 percent of floor votes in the House and the Senate were on money and revenue bills (appropriations, tax bills, debt ceiling resolutions, budget resolutions, and reconciliation bills). By the 1980s these matters account for about half of the floor votes in the Senate and more than 30 percent of the roll calls in the House.

15. EXECUTIVE-CONGRESSIONAL CONFLICT IN FOREIGN POLICY: EXPLAINING IT, COPING WITH IT

I. M. Destler

Throughout most of the postwar period, the general attitude of foreign policy-minded Americans toward congressional influence could be summarized in four words: "the less, the better." As one careful critique of the academic literature put it, presidents were seen as "formulating bold and forward-looking new policies for the nation, while an unimaginative Congress . . . appeared to be hindering those efforts and defending parochial interests." [1] Practitioners shared this attitude. Even the Chairman of the Senate Foreign Relations Committee, J. William Fulbright (D-Ariz.), wondered in 1961 whether congressional influence on foreign policy was not greater than the country could afford. He found it

> highly unlikely that we can successfully execute a long-range program for the taming, or containing, of today's aggressive revolutionary forces by continuing to leave vast and vital decision-making powers in the hands of a decentralized, independent-minded, and largely parochial-minded body of legislators. The Congress, as Woodrow Wilson put it, is a "disintegrated ministry," a jealous center of power with a built-in antagonism for the Executive. [2]

After all this of course came Vietnam. Beginning around 1965, senators like Fulbright led the foreign policy community to a rediscovery of the value of checks on executive power. [3] After Richard Nixon ordered U.S. troops into Cambodia in 1970, 13 executive-oriented Harvard scholars made a pilgrimage to Capitol Hill to endorse congressional actions against the president, expressing what one of them termed a "dramatic shift in views I have held long and deeply with regard to the efficacy of Congressional action designed to restrain presidential discretion in national security affairs." [4] Years of struggle led to action in 1973: the War Powers Resolution establishing a more explicit congressional role in the commitment of American troops overseas; the prohibition on further U.S. bombing of Indochina. Then hard upon Vietnam came Watergate, where millions of Americans again looked to the Congress to deliver them from what executive power had wrought. Building on this momentum, the Congress of the mid-seventies moved effectively into a range of issues—linking improved U.S.-Soviet trade relations to free emigration of Soviet Jews; embargoing arms aid to Turkey after its invasion of Cyprus; prohibiting clandestine U.S. involvement in Angola. And Congress also established new procedural vehicles for policy influence, including the right of legislative veto on executive arms sales and import relief decisions.[5]

Yet even before the decade ended, much of the bloom had left the congressional rose.[6] It took an enormous Carter administration effort to get the "parochial-minded" Senate to ratify the Panama Canal treaties in 1978 and to get the even more parochial House to pass implementing legislation. In 1979 the Congress approved the comprehensive multilateral trade agreements submitted by the president, but his strategic arms limitation treaty (known as SALT II) never made it to the Senate floor, even though it (like the trade package) was the product of seven years of negotiation, most of it under the Nixon and Ford administrations.[7] Once again, the question was whether the United States could operate effectively in the international arena if its legislature tied the executive's hand or rewrote painfully negotiated accords. And following the Soviet invasion of Afghanistan in December 1979, Congress in fact eased certain restrictions on presidential flexibility. But the political-military aggressiveness of the Reagan administration triggered yet another reaction, as Congress sought to constrain its Central American operations and to soften its arms control posture vis-à-vis Moscow.

In significant part, this flowing and ebbing of congressional standing is a function of two factors: substantive preferences and the presence or absence of crisis. Many who write on such matters are moderate liberals in orientation; hence some shift back to an executive orientation was predictable once Vietnam was behind us and the White House returned to Democratic hands. Conversely, Senator Barry Goldwater (R-Ariz.)—who opposed the War Powers Resolution as an intrusion on needed presidential authority—argued vainly in court that it was unconstitutional for President Carter to withdraw the United States from its security treaty with Taiwan without congressional assent. The second factor, crisis, usually reinforces presidential power and the argument that the president needs the flexibility to respond.

But the deeper cause of executive-congressional conflict is a core political-procedural dilemma. Americans want two things that often prove incompatible in practice: *democratic government* (involving ongoing competition among a range of U.S. interests and perspectives) and *effective foreign policy* (which requires settling on specific goals and pursuing them consistently). To reconcile these competing needs insofar as they can be reconciled, the framers of the Constitution established, in Richard Neustadt's apt phrase, a government of "separated institutions sharing powers."[8]

It is an oversimplification to say that the executive represents policy coherence in any pure sense, or that the legislature is a pure decentralized democracy. The Congress, or portions thereof, can take purposive decisions, as happened on Indochina and Watergate in 1973 and 1974. And the executive is typically divided in opinion and interest. Moreover, most foreign policy issues do not involve a simple, two-sided struggle between the executive and Congress; the typical pattern is rather one of policy advocates in one branch working with allies in the other against executive and legislative officials with opposing views. But the executive and the Congress are "separated institutions." These two primary decision arenas in American foreign policy have distinct characters.

In general, the genius of Congress is democracy, diversity, debate. Often Congress nurtures creativity. Nelson Polsby describes the Senate as "a great incubator of policy innovation in the American system," and Alton Frye emphasizes the "policy entrepreneurship" role.[9] The executive, by contrast, offers the hierarchy and concentrated formal authority that make coherent policy execution at least possible. What Alexander Hamilton called "energy in the executive" is particularly important to the conduct of foreign policy.[10] In periods when the United States is conducting an activist foreign policy— the case since 1940—there is a need for "decision, activity, secrecy, and despatch" which only the president and his senior advisers can supply.[11]

Because executive-congressional conflict reflects a deep tension among core values, it has no simple solution. Yet it demands deeper analysis, both for those seeking to understand conflict and those responsible for coping with it in the executive-legislative arena. The place to begin, of course, is the Constitution, which gives both the president and the Congress authorities that influence policy on particular issues. Conflict results from differing views about policy goals or means and efforts to advance those views by employing these authorities. The two branches do not come to the battle equally armed, however. The executive generally has the initiative. One reason is that the president has particular constitutional powers in foreign policy: to negotiate treaties, to command the armed forces, and to appoint and receive ambassadors. Conflict arises when senators and representatives seek to use congressional powers—over appropriations, general legislation, treaties, appointments—to control or constrain the president and the executive in their exercise of foreign policy discretion.

Sources of Conflict

But when and why do members do this? Why does conflict arise at some times and not others, on some issues and not others? For insights one must examine what motivates members of Congress and executive officials in their dealings with each other. Such an examination should also shed light on some common prescriptions for conflict management. Executive-congressional consultation, for example, can help prepare the way on issues likely to involve congressional action. But how consistent is such consultation with other demands on those at both ends of Pennsylvania Avenue? Similarly, while strengthening the foreign policy staffs of members of Congress may enhance expertise and raise the level of executive-congressional dialogue, it also adds new actors to the foreign policy process, actors with their own interests in policy engagement.

To analyze congressional (and executive) motivations, it is useful to consider four overlapping sources of foreign policy conflict on current issues: (1) *persistent substantive orientations* on Capitol Hill that diverge from those of the president and his senior advisers; (2) the *electoral political interests* of individual senators and representatives; (3) the *institutional characteristics of Congress;* and (4) the *expansion and proliferation of congressional staffs.*

Substantive Differences

The obvious place to begin is with differing opinions about policy content. Many senators and representatives have definite views about the substance of American foreign policy. These views often differ substantially from the preferred policies of the president and his senior advisers. To the degree that legislators are committed to these views, they are likely to employ their constitutional and statutory authorities to make them prevail. And those who specialize in international issues tend to have particular substantive interests. Richard Fenno's comparative study of House committees found that members of Foreign Affairs usually sought to join because of commitment to "good public policy," whereas those on other committees were more likely to stress other goals such as "influence within the House" or "re-election." [12]

If a viewpoint becomes widely shared and persists over a period of years, it can become particularly influential. A dramatic example is the consensus that developed against the Vietnam War, a consensus that not only produced the War Powers Resolution and the Indochina bombing ban, but also led to a subsequent prohibition against U.S. involvement in the Angolan civil war. Under Carter, congressional opinion was generally more conservative than that of the administration on political-military issues, as in the fifties and early sixties. This is one reason why Carter's SALT II treaty got such a cool Senate reception, and why the hardening of his foreign policy after the Soviet invasion of Afghanistan was generally welcomed on Capitol Hill. Under Ronald Reagan, by contrast, the general congressional view has been less hard-line than the administration's, especially on Central America and U.S.-Soviet relations, and the congressional resistance he has met reflects this difference of view. [13]

Another way that substantive views in Congress make themselves felt is more idiosyncratic—through "pockets of conviction" coupled with energy, persistence, and political skill. The impact of Senator Henry Jackson (D-Wash.) on strategic arms policy in the seventies is one major example. More recently, Senators William S. Cohen (R-Maine) and Sam Nunn (D-Ga.) and Representatives Les Aspin (D-Wis.) and Albert Gore, Jr. (D-Tenn.) joined to press the Reagan administration to moderate its arms control stand. (Gore was elected to the Senate in 1984.) Such personal efforts usually require a committee or subcommittee power base. And they are effective, often, because they are exceptional. Most senators and representatives lack the time or the interest to give foreign policy issues this kind of sustained attention. Thus those who do can have a disproportionate impact, both on the actions of Congress and those of the executive branch.

Electoral Interests

A second source of conflict is the electoral pressures on senators and representatives. They must worry not only about overall U.S. policies, but also about their own visible role in the policy process and how the public perceives their stands. Most want to be re-elected; a substantial minority aspires to broader-constituency public offices (some representatives to the Senate, some senators to the White House). In David Mayhew's persuasive formulation, these electoral needs drive legislators to concentrate on three types of activity affecting how they appear to their constituents: credit claiming, advertising (of one's name), and position taking on public issues (to strengthen identification with stances favored in the legislator's support coalition).[14] Foreign Relations is one of the Senate's most prestigious committees not so much because of its legislative power—which is comparatively modest—but because it offers a "bully pulpit" for members to gain visibility and reputation on international issues.

In credit claiming, advertising, and position taking activities, a senator's or representative's primary stake is not in how overall U.S. policies actually turn out; what matters instead is what the member appears to be saying and doing about them. In 1979, presidential aspirant Howard Baker (R-Tenn.), whose support of the Panama treaties as Senate Minority Leader exposed him to right-wing attack, took a strong anti-SALT II position in order to recoup. In 1981, Democrats signaled their human rights commitment by requiring that President Reagan certify progress in El Salvador every six months. In some instances it may even be in a legislator's interest not to control policy, because then he risks being blamed if the policy fails. Henry Jackson, for example, won congressional support for and reluctant Ford administration acquiescence in his proposal to link trade concessions to Soviet policies on Jewish emigration.[15] When Russia renounced the bilateral trade agreement and emigration declined, Jackson was vulnerable to charges that his amendment had been impractical and counterproductive.

An example of presidential awareness of members' thirst for the public limelight was President Eisenhower's hope in the 1950s that Ohio Senator John Bricker could be induced, through creation of some sort of "Bricker Commission," to put aside his widely supported amendment to restrict presidential treaty-making power. The president was convinced that "all Bricker wants is something big in public with his name on it."[16] In 1978 junior senator Dennis DeConcini (D-Ariz.) won temporary notoriety by conditioning his support of the Panama treaties on a reservation declaring the U.S. right to "the use of military force in Panama" to keep the canal open after it went under Panamanian control. This condition triggered a predictable uproar in Panama and almost led to its rejection of the treaties; only after a compensating Senate reservation reiterated U.S. "adherence to the principle of non-intervention" did Panamanian President Omar Torrijos agree to final ratification.[17]

Linked to legislators' electoral interests is their need to respond to interest groups. Industries seek protection from imports. A strong, attentive Jewish constituency and a newly emergent Greek-American lobby seek to affect Middle Eastern and Mediterranean policy. On noneconomic international issues, such pressures are less important than on most domestic issues. Legislators need not always accede to such pressure, especially where countervailing forces exist, but they must respond to them in some way. And on issues like energy policy, a matter of domestic economic regulation with considerable foreign policy import, legislators may find that the need to cope with pressures and counterpressures is what most drives their decision.

Legislators are also influenced by party loyalties. It seldom pays for an administration to define a controversial foreign policy issue in partisan terms; this is likely to lose more votes than it gains. But there remains some predisposition to support a president of one's own party, as evidenced by shifting alignments on foreign aid legislation under Democratic and Republican presidents.[18] Moreover, legislators must be sensitive to party sentiment in order to avert primary challenges or to bolster their prospects for winning nominations for "higher" offices. And Senate and House leaders must retain the confidence of their party colleagues.

Institutional Factors

A separate source of executive-congressional conflict is the particular features of Congress as a policy-influencing institution. One such feature is the unsuitability of congressional "handles" to the conduct of day-to-day foreign policy. Congress can, of course, prevail on any single issue through its lawmaking and appropriations powers. In this sense Senator Fulbright was correct in concluding that "it was not a lack of power which prevented the Congress from ending the war in Indochina," because "Congress had the means, through its control of appropriations, to compel an early or immediate end. . . ."[19] But Congress could not legislate a more nuanced approach, such as a particular negotiating strategy, to terminate the war. Nor can it for other issues. The money power has practical limitations because, as Thomas Schelling observed more than a decade ago, most major foreign policy choices are of the "non-budgetary sort."[20] Relations with particular countries are comprised of a stream of day-to-day decisions and communications; inevitably these involve executive discretion.

In the fifties a freshman Republican representative asked President Eisenhower which committee he should join—Foreign Affairs or Ways and Means. Eisenhower advised the latter, noting that "on taxes Ways and

Means was king, but that on foreign relations he was." [21] A key reason is that taxes can be controlled by legislation establishing rules of general applicability, and executive discretion—while it does exist—is usually limited in this area. Congress can also limit executive foreign policy discretion by establishing binding rules (for example, a requirement imposed in 1974 that 70 percent of food aid must go to the neediest nations), and by fixing policy toward specific countries on specific issues (for example, embargoing arms sales to Turkey that same year). But the policy costs can be severe; rules often outlast the circumstances justifying their creation. A law that restored balance to U.S. food aid allocations in 1974 and 1975 helped to distort them in 1976, when more grain was poured into Bangladesh despite overloaded ports and storage capacity.[22] And the Turkey prohibition locked the United States into an unproductive and potentially damaging policy stalemate when the Ankara government responded in kind. Congress responded by lifting the embargo in 1978.[23]

Legislators often recognize, of course, that discretion is desirable in principle. But in practice they are not the ones who get to exercise it, and administration officials—faced with their own sets of pressures—may well employ their discretion to get around what Congress intends. The response on the Hill may then be to tighten the rules. This is particularly likely when trust between the two branches is low, as has typically been the case since 1970.

A related problem with congressional handles on foreign policy is that legislative action is public action. It may often be desirable that U.S. pressure be exercised more discreetly—a "quiet" suspension of arms sales, for example, or low-key representations of human rights. But again, this involves executive action, and to the degree that such pressure is being applied quietly, members of Congress cannot be sure that it is really being exerted seriously at all.

Another institutional source of conflict is the decentralization of congressional policymaking power, which is rooted in the formal equality and separate constituencies of members. Combined with the weakness of national parties, these alone give individual members considerable leeway in what they *say* about policy issues. Often conflicting or counterproductive signals overseas are the result, as illustrated when Panamanians or Saudi Arabians read (or even hear on live radio) how certain senators characterize their countries and their leaders in the heat of policy debates.

More significant than words in generating conflict, however, is the dispersion of actual influence over issues. This is the product, in part, of a series of internal reforms dating from the 1910 revolt against Speaker Joe Cannon but accelerating sharply in the early 1970s. Procedural democracy and subcommittee proliferation have weakened committee chairmen. As partial compensation, there have been gains in the strength of party leaders, whose direct role in shaping the specific substance of legislation traditionally has been much less than their influence over floor scheduling and members' committee assignments. But on key votes, administration lobbyists generally work to deliver the votes themselves rather than expecting Hill leaders to do so.

Negotiating with 100 or 435 individuals is not a simple task, but today an administration needs to deal directly with an increasing number of members. Complicating the task is the weakening of party and ideological ties, and the lack of a broad-based national foreign policy consensus. Thus the Carter administration had to mobilize votes issue by issue during the 95th Congress. In the United States Senate, it won five major foreign policy-related victories in 1978: Panama, arms sales to the Mideast, lifting the Turkey embargo, the energy program, and foreign assistance. Only eleven senators said "yes" on all five, and only one was consistently opposed.

The Proliferation of Congressional Staffs

Finally, executive-congressional conflict arises from the increased role of foreign policy staff aides on Capitol Hill. Between 1947 and 1976 the number of personal and committee staff members increased more than fivefold.[24] Only a minority of the personal staff members handles substantive issues, and only a minority of these handles international matters. But expansion in these categories has at least paralleled the total increase. Between 1970 and 1979, for example, the number of staff aides serving on the four major foreign policy/national defense committees more than doubled—from 108 to 236. And in 1975 junior senators were given additional funds to hire people to support them in their committee work. Today most senators have at least one foreign policy specialist on their personal staffs—something that was very rare 20 years ago. And while the exponential growth in congressional staffs had run its course by the late seventies, more recent statistics suggest a leveling off, not a decrease.

Staff aides provide members of Congress with close-at-hand expertise, which strengthens their capacity to engage knowledgeably on issues. One mid-seventies treatment dubbed them "the New Equalizers." [25] But staff aides also reflect and exacerbate the decentralization of the Congress because in most cases their power springs from a relationship with a single legislator. This is true by definition for personal staffs. It is usually also true for committee aides, since without the confidence of an important committee member they tend to be limited to routine functions. This does not mean, however, that the interest of each aide is identical to that of his or her legislative patron. Indeed, as legislators' schedules become more burdened, and the number of staff members increases, substantive and political communication between legislator and aide becomes progressively more difficult. The legislator has less feel for the nuances of "his" issues; aides have, out of necessity, considerably greater freedom in day-to-day action, and this makes them independently influential actors. Overburdened legislators tend to deal substantively with one another through their staff members, making the Congress a less collegial place than it was 20 or 30 years ago.

Do staff aides use their influence to mediate interbranch conflict or to generate it? Obviously, they do both. Foreign policy experts on Capitol Hill can work with executive branch officials to facilitate compromise on particular issues, though sometimes at the cost of pushing the legislator a bit to one side—he doesn't always "speak the same language" or have the time to learn it. Substantive staffs can also provide a capacity for advance planning. In 1977, for example, pro-SALT Senate aides organized interchanges with executive branch counterparts on strategic arms control. This was followed by a similar effort by their bosses; a group of 17 senators began meeting semimonthly in the office of Majority Whip Alan Cranston (D-Calif.) to prepare for the anticipated ratification debate.

But often staff members are not so much objective analysts as conduits for information packaged by special interests. As one of the best informed analysts of staff politics concluded, "Congress has become just as incapable of evaluating the biases in the information from its own staffs as it has from sources outside Congress." [26] Moreover, entrepreneurial staff members have strong stakes in generating new proposals that challenge executive policies; there is a "web of self-interest binding Members and their staffs to the fate of 'their' common programs; Members want bills with their names on them; the staff wants to 'case a shadow.' " [27] Henry Jackson's amendments on Soviet trade and strategic arms were vehicles not just for the senator but for his influential national security aide, Richard Perle, as well. In fact, a staff member typically has much stronger stakes in pushing any particular proposal than does his boss since the legislator will have a number of policy aides and a number of initiatives pending.

Ultimately, of course, a staff member's impact is limited by the willingness of his or her boss to become involved in particular substantive issues. But usually staff pressure is toward increasing such involvement. This generates more executive-congressional conflict, for better and for worse. As a result, activist staffs often increase the workload of members of Congress, though one frequent argument for staffs is that they help relieve that burden.

Managing Conflict

Ideally, suggestions for coping with executive-congressional foreign policy conflict would be preceded by some statement of what the optimal level of conflict is. In practice, this seems impossible. Substantively, the answer varies with one's degree of satisfaction with prevailing policies. Politically and procedurally, one can point to a range of advantages and disadvantages of executive-congressional conflict, but there is no easy formula to aggregate them.

Congress fuels decentralization in American foreign policymaking, thereby contributing to innovation and policy entrepreneurship. Conflict raises the level of public consciousness about issues, generates information, and often brings to prominence previously neglected interests. The threat of a congressional rebuff may constrain the executive in the short run, but it also may make policy more soundly based in the longer run, for this threat forces the executive into a more active public explication of its policies and helps limit the gap between those policies and public understanding.

Sometimes diplomatic benefits accrue from executive-congressional conflict. Panama certainly conceded more in the canal negotiations because of the need for Senate ratification, and more than once a "threat" of unfavorable congressional action has induced Japan to make trade concessions. Last but not least, policy conflict helps to protect us from arbitrary government power.

But executive-congressional conflict can also do serious damage to foreign policy. One detrimental byproduct is *tactical inflexibility*. The more an administration is hemmed in by congressional restrictions, the less it can pursue subtle policies or conduct delicate negotiations with particular countries and regions. Another negative byproduct is *policy unpredictability*. Foreign officials increasingly respond to U.S. diplomats: "Ah yes, no doubt that is your government's intention, but what will Congress do?" [28] Such uncertainty undermines presidential credibility and U.S. diplomatic credibility generally. It is one thing to be constrained by a Congress whose will one knows or can reasonably predict. In 1967 Lyndon Johnson could check quietly with former Senate Armed Services chairman Richard Russell (D-Ga.) on how far he should commit the United States to reversion of Okinawa to Japan; when the chairman counseled caution, Johnson could limit himself to moderate steps without advertising his impotence. But it is quite another matter to get comparably authoritative signals today.

These consequences of executive-congressional conflict are part of the enormous larger problem of achieving purposive and coherent foreign policies, such as are necessary to make headway on urgent world problems like arms control and international economic recovery.[29] My own judgment is that by the mid-seventies the policy costs of conflict and decentralization were substantially exceeding the gains. Others will disagree. In any case, prescriptions for conflict management must respond to its sources, and each of the *roots* of conflict analyzed earlier suggests *routes* to its resolution that can be pursued by official "conflict managers": the leaders of both branches, but primarily the president and his senior foreign policy aides.

Dealing with Substantive Differences

If conflict arises from differing substantive policy preferences, policy leaders have three options: they can *adjust* by acceding to, or compromising with, opposing views; they can seek to *persuade* others to change their views;

or they can seek to *override* their adversaries by mobilizing a winning coalition against them. In practice, leaders often employ some combination of all three.

Adjustment can be tactical or strategic. In the first instance, a concession is made on specifics without changing the central policy thrust, as when the Reagan administration accepted the proposals of the relatively liberal House Foreign Operations Subcommittee in 1981 as the price for getting any aid appropriations bill through Congress. A strategic adjustment involves something larger: an administration substantially changing its policy because of domestic constraints, or shelving a particular goal because it cannot win congressional acceptance or is unwilling to invest the political capital required to get it. An example of the first was the Vietnam policy shift begun in 1968 after the Tet offensive; an earlier example of the second was the deferral of serious China policy moves until "the second Kennedy administration." [30] Even if one prefers the president's goals to those of his adversaries, strategic adjustment is often very desirable. Better to devote one's energies to goals that are domestically sustainable than to begin with a sweeping set of initiatives, only to see most of them undermined by domestic strife.

Persuasion can be direct, through substantive communication with the legislators themselves, or indirect, through efforts to change public or elite opinion and thus the weight of arguments legislators read in the press and hear from their constituents. In April 1983, President Reagan sought to increase congressional funding of his controversial Central America policies through a nationally televised address to a joint session of Congress. The direct audience was the members. But Reagan was successful, to a modest degree, because legislators felt his rhetoric made headway in the broader national market.

A third option for policy leaders in dealing with substantive differences is to override their adversaries. When executive initiative is involved, this may mean simply going ahead with an action on the calculation that Congress won't later reverse it. Or if the issue is before the legislature, it means outvoting those whose support cannot be won at acceptable cost. (In some cases, of course, the prospect of being outvoted will make legislators more amenable to substantive bargaining.)

To help cope with serious policy differences in 1983, the Reagan administration created two highly visible, bipartisan commissions: one headed by Lt. Gen. Brent Scowcroft on strategic arms; another under Henry Kissinger for Central America. The former put together a package of policy changes—on weapons and arms control—which persuaded Congress to continue funding the beleaguered MX missile, at least for 1983. The latter was less successful in its effort to win broad congressional support for increases in economic *and* military aid to the Central American region.

Coping with Political Interests

To the degree that substantive lines are clearly drawn and views are deeply held, policy conflict is a zero-sum game; one cannot simultaneously ratify the Panama treaties and keep the canal. But since policy actors have other, nonsubstantive interests, understanding these interests offers a route to conflict management that allows leaders to win substantive gains by helping legislators get nonsubstantive benefits. The political needs of senators and representatives can be understood and recognized as legitimate, rather than condemned. Leaders can seek ways of responding to these interests to build up support for their policies.

If politicians depend on self-advertising and credit claiming, then leaders can consider credit sharing. Rather than portraying policy gains as the achievement of a few lonely individuals, as Nixon and Kissinger were wont to do, an administration can share the limelight with legislative leaders whose support is important to its goals. The classic example is the role of Senate Majority Leader Arthur Vandenberg from 1947 to 1949. Dean Acheson's description of the process is still worth quoting:

> Arthur Vandenberg . . . was born to lead a reluctant opposition into support of governmental proposals that he came to believe were in the national interest. . . . One of Vandenberg's stratagems was to enact publicly his conversion to a proposal, his change of attitude, a kind of political transubstantiation. The method was to go through a period of public doubt and skepticism; then find a comparatively minor flaw in the proposal, pounce upon it, and make much of it; in due course propose a change, always the Vandenberg amendment. Then, and only then, could it be given to his followers as true doctrine worthy of all men to be received. . . . [The stratagem's] strength lay in the genuineness of his belief in each step.[31]

And, Acheson goes on to explain, the Truman administration happily supported Vandenberg's formula for marrying his political interest to the administration's foreign policies.

Similarly, the Carter administration needed Majority Leader Byrd and Minority Leader Baker on Panama and wisely shared credit with them. Each enacted publicly his conversion to the treaties in a way that underscored the importance of his role. But because power in today's Senate is less centralized, meeting leaders' political interests is not enough. Thus more than 40 senators—with administration encouragement—went to Panama to see for themselves. No fewer than 78 cosponsored the Byrd-Baker "leadership amendments" that incorporated in the treaty language concessions that Torrijos had made on the interpretation of U.S. defense rights. And when all this proved insufficient, the Carter administration reluctantly accepted the DeConcini reservation that brought Panama to the verge of repudiating the treaties.[32]

Even when a foreign government refuses to make concessions, legislators can claim credit for influencing U.S. implementation of an accord. To induce key senators to abandon their opposition to selling Airborne Warning and Control System (AWACS) planes to Saudi Arabia, for example, Reagan encouraged them to help draft a presidential letter to the Majority Leader clarifying the terms of the sales.[33]

Another way that leaders can help legislators cope with politically difficult issues is to take some of the heat for them. Both Byrd and Baker played this role on Panama, and Baker did so on AWACS. Such a role can be particularly valuable on issues where there is strong interest-group pressure. One reason why Carter's special trade representative, Robert Strauss, quickly became popular on Capitol Hill was that he was perceived as coping very adroitly with industry pressures, thus shielding legislators from their full force. And Strauss's office was an institution Congress had established for that precise purpose. Executive lobbyists can also help by seeing to it that before an issue comes up for a vote a sympathetic legislator hears from important interests in support of his (and the administration's) position. For example, when Ford administration officials wanted to get Byrd to play an active role in moving the Trade Act of 1974 to enactment, they persuaded the United Mine Workers to cable him that they found the bill acceptable.[34]

A similar rule applies to ethnic and other specific interest groups. The more key executive officials are on good working terms with them and can maintain their understanding and basic confidence, the less they are likely to press legislators to override administration actions. To the degree such groups have strong substantive views, of course, it may be very difficult to maintain that confidence while pursuing policies that they oppose. Middle East policy supplies the most obvious contemporary example.

Finally, executive leaders can exploit the political vulnerability of legislators, especially their fear of being blamed for a dramatic policy failure or disarray. President Nixon had a bent for putting forward a *fait accompli* (bombing Cambodia or promising credits and most-favored nation trade status to Russia), which Congress could not reverse without publicly repudiating administration policy generally and thus undercutting "American commitments." This might be called the "chicken" approach to executive-congressional relations; it seems founded on the belief that even if Congress is not in on the policy takeoffs, a majority will not wish to risk being blamed for crash landings. Similarly, Ronald Reagan bought some time for his Central America policies with a not very subtle political threat. "Who among us would wish to bear responsibility for failing to meet our shared obligation?" he asked. He doubted "that a majority in the Congress or the country [would] stand by passively while the people of Central America are delivered to totalitarianism and we ourselves are left vulnerable to new dangers." [35]

Institutional Problems:
The Limits of Consultation and Centralization

Congressional foreign policy leverage depends ultimately on handles that are blunt instruments—cutting off funds, rejecting or amending painfully negotiated treaties. The costs to foreign policy of actually employing these instruments are often severe, and this is recognized on both ends of Pennsylvania Avenue. Yet by the time Congress comes to act on an issue, the executive branch may be locked into a particular course and unwilling—perhaps unable—to change it. The stage is then set for a counterproductive interbranch power struggle.

The alternative, almost universally supported, is consultation among executive and legislative leaders as policies are taking shape.[36] This approach enables congressional views to be incorporated more smoothly and continuously. At its best, consultation offers a trade. Legislators get earlier entrée to issues and some degree of influence over them in return for some commitment to mobilize congressional backing for the policies that emerge; they advise as well as consent. Executive leaders give up some of their autonomy in exchange for strengthening the political base for their policies and reducing the dangers of being blind-sided on the Hill. Such consultation sometimes involves actual congressional involvement in negotiations; 26 senators, for example, went to Geneva in 1977 and 1978 as official advisers to the SALT II negotiating team.

But in practice consultation can quickly become complicated. One obvious problem is who should consult with whom. Close consultation can only work among a fairly limited number of people; otherwise, it becomes too cumbersome and too public. But whom does one choose in Congress? If the leaders of the chamber and/or the relevant committees can speak reliably for the Congress on a given issue, that is fine. Scrupulous, detailed consultation with the Senate Finance and House Ways and Means Committees, for example, preceded Carter's formal submission of his proposed Trade Agreements Act of 1979 and led directly to its overwhelming enactment.[37] But Senate Foreign Relations was not comparably representative of the Senate on SALT. Nor is it always clear who represents the executive. Senior House International Relations Committee members protested in June 1978 that Carter administration divisions had generated confusion "as to what is U.S. policy on such issues as Soviet-American relations and Africa."[38] They weren't sure who, Secretary of State Cyrus R. Vance or national security assistant Zbigniew Brzezinski, could authoritatively consult with them.

There are other problems with consultation. Theoretically, an administration does not simply co-opt congressional leaders but allows them real policy influence. But if the president and his senior advisers cannot convey a clear and consistent sense of where they want to go and some political credibility concerning their ability to get there, they will discourage those inclined to cooperate and encourage those inclined to challenge. An administration may find that its genuine efforts to share information and influence win not cooperation but contempt.

Finally, the day-to-day costs of consultation may be greater to politicians than they appear at first glance. One cost is in time and attention—overtaxed resources that legislators must allocate with care. Thus, like busy people everywhere, "their own responsibilities force them to live and operate in the short run." [39] Consequently, legislators are reluctant to give detailed attention to a particular issue until they have to. Not surprisingly, those who consulted with senators on Panama in early 1977 found it difficult to get them to focus on the specifics that became so crucial in early 1978. The same was true on SALT a year later.

Even more important, perhaps, early engagement has costs in limiting political flexibility. Even those who expect ultimately to support particular treaties often find it safer to wait until the texts are completed and the initial political reaction comes in. Moreover, it should be emphasized that executive officials, including the president, may eschew consultations for similar reasons: they may want to maintain *their* flexibility. It is hard enough to manage an issue with a foreign country and within the executive branch without opening it up to congressional participation as well.

One means of encouraging prior consultation by the executive has been the legislative veto. In laws enacted in 1974 and 1976, Congress subjected certain presidential decisions on trade policy and arms sales to congressional override, thus encouraging the administration to check congressional sentiment before it proceeded. Similar provisions were included in the War Powers Resolution of 1973 and the Nuclear Non-Proliferation Act of 1978. Legislative vetoes have proved less constraining than advance prohibitions written into law, and they do less collateral damage because they do not single out particular countries for negative treatment. And Congress has never actually vetoed a presidential foreign policy action, although Reagan had to lobby very hard to sustain his sale of AWACS aircraft to Saudi Arabia in 1981. However, the Supreme Court declared such veto provisions unconstitutional in its *Chadha* decision of June 1983. [40]

Decentralization is another institutional problem of congressional foreign policymaking. Here the counterprescription is obvious: strengthening congressional leadership. As already noted, recent reform has been mainly in the opposite direction, moving power from the committee to the subcommittee and individual member. The weakening of committee chairmen and the strengthening of the House caucus has opened up the possibility of increased power for chamber political leaders. Speaker Tip O'Neill was able to expedite energy legislation by creating, in early 1977, an Ad Hoc Select Committee on Energy. [41] The Speaker has also been given new powers over committee assignments and referrals of bills. However, as Lawrence Dodd has noted, there is strong tension between the desires of members of Congress to maintain power for their institution—which point toward centralization—

and members' interests in power for themselves individually—which pull them toward decentralization.[42]

Another means of combating congressional decentralization, in theory at least, would be giving the foreign policy committees greater authority and substantive reach. Ways and Means under Chairman Wilbur Mills provides a possible model—that of screener and broker for the whole House on issues within a broad jurisdiction.[43] The Bolling Committee report of 1974 sought to move House Foreign Affairs in this direction. The application of this approach to current foreign policy, however, presents numerous problems. First is that of jurisdiction, which passes to Armed Services on military issues and to other substantive committees on most international economic questions. Second, the expanded role would require committees that reasonably reflect the range of views in their parent chambers, whereas Foreign Relations in the Senate and Foreign Affairs in the House tend to attract atypically liberal, internationalist legislators. Third, such a "solution" is dependent on the strength and political style of the chairman. Fourth and most important, many members today would view such a proposal not as a solution but as the sort of problem from which they had at long last freed themselves.

Finally, there is the possibility of establishing a new congressional focal point for foreign policy consultation and integration: the oft-proposed Joint Committee on National Security along the lines of the Joint Economic Committee, or Graham Allison and Peter Szanton's proposal for a Committee on Interdependence in each house, without direct legislative authority but drawing its membership from the major standing committees.[44] While such proposals probably wouldn't hurt, it is uncertain how much they would help if the committees lack leverage within the Congress itself, as they certainly would without legislative jurisdiction. Thus, one analyst has argued the need to go further, to establish, by constitutional amendment, a Congressional Security Council empowered to "exercise congressional authority under specified emergency conditions." [45] But others worry that such a body might be too easily co-opted by the president, becoming "an instrument rather than a critic of executive authority." [46]

Since significant centralizing reforms are presently impractical, probably the best route for executive and congressional leaders is to build personal political alliances stretching across a range of issues. If leaders can work systematically and reciprocally to strengthen one another, some centralizing impact may be felt. The Reagan administration gained enormously in 1981-1984 from its effective alliance with Senate Majority Leader Howard Baker.

Rationalizing Congressional Staffs

What should be done about congressional staffs? The average level of subject matter competence among congressional foreign policy aides is probably considerably higher than among congressional substantive staff members taken as a whole. But they must respond to similar pressures because they work in the same basic environment.

If the magnitude of staffs generates conflict, one reform would be to reduce staff size. The only practical way to do this would be to cut overall staff funds available to legislators and committees, since the control of each over allocation of its funds will remain pretty near absolute. Another approach, not necessarily inconsistent with the first, is to concentrate on changing the balance among types of staff members to increase the ratio of experienced, nonpartisan substantive professionals to partisan advocates. These professionals would serve on standing committees and be custodians of process as well as experts trusted on both sides of the aisle; they would, of course, have their own views on issues, but would subordinate these to their primary tasks of supplying expertise and helping manage committee decision processes. Partisan advocates would remain on personal staffs and on investigatory subcommittees, but in reduced numbers. One oft-cited congressional model of staff professionalism is the Joint Committee on International Revenue Taxation, which has long supplied high quality, and highly respected, tax expertise for the tax writing committees of the two chambers.[47]

But it is far easier to brainstorm about what roles staff members should play than to make such roles work out in practice. Committee staffs get their authority from their relationships with the key committee members; responding to members' needs may pull aides into advocacy roles, whatever reformers might intend. Or if a committee staff holds to a nonpartisan, process role, most of the action may well pass to the personal staff aides, for the effectiveness of a "neutral" staff supplying expertise and managing process depends on a centralized committee decision process and a relatively strong chairman who values and enforces these staff roles. Thus, decentralization of committees means a decentralized advocacy process among members that fuels staff advocacy in turn.

A final approach to staffing, again not inconsistent with the aforementioned, is to strengthen staff institutions that serve Congress as a whole, in order to expand the quality and quantity of analysis at Congress's disposal. To this end, the Congressional Research Service has been upgraded, the General Accounting Office has moved from a relatively narrow auditing focus to program evaluation, the Congressional Budget Office conducts macroeconomic and budget analyses, and the Office of Technology Assessment studies subjects with important science and technology content.

The problems these institutions face, however, are well known. Too often they must serve 535 masters, and yet their distance from these masters makes it difficult to establish the relations of trust necessary for involvement in members' urgent current concerns. They conduct valuable studies, some of which are drawn upon by specific legislators and committees. But with partial exception of the Congressional Budget Office, they do not supply the sort of visible, integrative analysis that can itself give structure and coherence to congressional debates.

Conclusion

Since executive-congressional conflict has multiple causes, there is no convenient single solution. The root of the problem is that Americans want things that are, in practice, contradictory. We agree on the need for coherent and purposive policies, but often disagree very strongly about the content of those policies. And we value our democratic political process in which differing policy goals and means contest.

The foreign policy problem is not to avoid executive-congressional conflict, but to manage it. Certain general remedies—institutionalizing consultation, strengthening staff expertise on Capitol Hill—are difficult to implement or have mixed effects. Others—strengthening leadership institutions—go against recent congressional reform trends. Nevertheless, this chapter has tried to suggest, through analysis and illustration, how a better understanding of congressional interests and institutions can help in getting livable resolutions of foreign policy issues. And unless we decide to amend our Constitution,[48] such coping mechanisms are the best we can hope for.

NOTES

1. Victor C. Johnson, "Congress and Foreign Policy: The House Foreign Affairs and Senate Foreign Relations Committees" (Ph.D. diss., University of Wisconsin, 1975), pp. 33-34.
2. J. William Fulbright, "American Foreign Policy in the 20th Century Under an 18th Century Constitution," *Cornell Law Quarterly* 47 (Fall 1962): 7.
3. Compare, for example, the above-cited article with "Congress and Foreign Policy" written by J. William Fulbright in July 1974. This later article appeared in the *Report of the Commission on the Organization of the Government for Conduct of Foreign Policy* (Murphy Commission), Appendix L, June 1975, pp. 58-65.
4. Letter from William M. Capron to Senator Frank Church, quoted in "Eating Crow at Mike's," *Washington Monthly*, September 1970, p. 50.
5. For a detailed description of this "revolution," see Thomas Franck and Edward Weisband, *Foreign Policy by Congress* (New York: Oxford University Press, 1979). For a careful, sympathetic analysis of how one of its major products has worked out in practice, see U.S. Congress, House, Committee on Foreign Affairs, "The War Powers Resolution," committee print by John H. Sullivan (Washington, D.C.: Government Printing Office, 1982).
6. There was even a third Fulbright formulation, arguing for "leaving to the executive the necessary flexibility to conduct policy within the broad parameters approved by the legislature." See J. William Fulbright, "The Legislator as Educator," *Foreign Affairs* (Spring 1979): 726.
7. See I. M. Destler, "Trade Consensus, SALT Stalemate: Congress and Foreign Policy in the Seventies," in *The New Congress*, ed. Thomas Mann and Norman

Ornstein (Washington, D.C.: American Enterprise Institute for Public Policy Research, 1981).

8. Richard Neustadt, *Presidential Power* (New York: Signet, 1964), p. 42.

9. Nelson W. Polsby, "Policy Initiation in the American Political System," in *Perspectives on the Presidency*, ed. Aaron Wildavsky (Boston: Little, Brown & Co., 1975), p. 229; and Alton Frye, "Congress and President: The Balance Wheels of American Foreign Policy," *Yale Review* 69 (Autumn 1979): 6-7.

10. Alexander Hamilton, James Madison, and John Jay, *The Federalist Papers* (New York: Modern Library), no. 70, p. 454.

11. Ibid., p. 455.

12. Richard F. Fenno, Jr., *Congressmen in Committees* (Boston: Little, Brown & Co., 1973), pp. 9-13.

13. Murrey Marder, "Hill Fights Reagan for Soul of Foreign Policy," *Washington Post*, September 2, 1984, p. 1.

14. David R. Mayhew, *Congress: The Electoral Connection* (New Haven: Yale University Press, 1974), Part I.

15. A detailed account appears in Paula Stern, *Water's Edge: Domestic Politics and the Making of American Foreign Policy* (Westport, Conn.: Greenwood Press, 1979).

16. Emmet John Hughes, *The Ordeal of Power* (New York: Atheneum Publishers, 1963), pp. 143, 144. Eisenhower added: "We talk about the French not being able to govern themselves, and we sit here wrestling with Bricker Amendment."

17. See I. M. Destler, "Treaty Troubles: Versailles in Reverse," *Foreign Policy* 33 (Winter 1978-1979): 45-65.

18. A comparison of relatively close House votes on foreign economic assistance from 1966 to 1981 yields the following: During the Johnson administration 68 to 78 percent of Democrats voted aye, compared to 29 to 39 percent of Republicans. Under Nixon and Ford, Democratic support dropped to the 54 to 67 percent range, while Republican support rose to 39 to 59 percent. Two Carter administration votes examined in 1977 show Democratic support at 62 and 70 percent, Republican at 39 and 44 percent. Similar votes under Reagan in 1981 found Democratic backing down to 56 and 59 percent, Republican up to 53 and 49 percent.

19. Fulbright, "Congress and Foreign Policy," p. 59.

20. Thomas Schelling, "PPBS and Foreign Affairs," Senate Government Operations Subcommittee on National Security and International Operations, 1968, p. 2.

21. Fenno, *Congressmen in Committees*, p. 30.

22. See I. M. Destler, *Making Foreign Economic Policy* (Washington, D.C.: The Brookings Institution, 1980), pp. 77-82.

23. Ellen B. Laipson, "Congressional-Executive Relations and the Turkish Arms Embargo," Congressional Research Service for the House Foreign Affairs Committee, Congress and Foreign Policy Series, No. 3, June 1981.

24. Norman J. Ornstein, Thomas E. Mann, Michael J. Malbin, and John F. Bibby, *Vital Statistics on Congress, 1982* (Washington, D.C.: American Enterprise Institute for Public Policy Research, 1982), chap. 5.

25. Frederick Poole, "Congress v. Kissinger: The New Equalizers," *Washington Monthly*, May 1975, pp. 23-32.

26. Michael J. Malbin, "Congressional Committee Staffs: Who's in Charge Here?" *The Public Interest* (Spring 1977): 19. For Malbin's full analysis, see Michael J.

Malbin, *Unelected Representatives: Congressional Staff and the Future of Representative Government* (New York: Basic Books, 1980).

27. Malbin, "Congressional Committee Staffs," p. 38.
28. John Lehman, *The Executive, Congress and Foreign Policy: Studies of the Nixon Administration* (New York: Praeger Publishers, 1976), p. x.
29. These problems are addressed more broadly in I. M. Destler, *Presidents, Bureaucrats, and Foreign Policy* (Princeton, N.J.: Princeton University Press, 1972 and 1974); and Destler, Leslie H. Gelb, and Anthony Lake, *Our Own Worst Enemy: The Unmaking of American Foreign Policy* (New York: Simon and Schuster, 1984).
30. Roger Hilsman, *To Move a Nation* (New York: Doubleday & Co., 1967), chap. 24.
31. Dean Acheson, *Present at the Creation: My Years at the State Department* (New York: W. W. Norton & Co., 1969), p. 223.
32. Destler, "Treaty Troubles," pp. 60-61.
33. I. M. Destler, "Reagan, Congress, and Foreign Policy in 1981," *President and Congress: Assessing Reagan's First Year*, ed. Norman J. Ornstein (Washington, D.C.: American Enterprise Institute for Public Policy Research, 1982), p. 75.
34. Destler, *Making Foreign Economic Policy*, p. 186. On the executive-congressional relations of trade, see also Robert A. Pastor, *Congress and the Politics of U.S. Foreign Economic Policy: 1929-1976* (Berkeley: University of California Press, 1980), Part II.
35. See I. M. Destler, "The Elusive Consensus: Congress and Central America," in *Central America: Anatomy of Conflict*, ed. Robert S. Leiken (New York: Pergamon Press [for the Carnegie Endowment], 1984), pp. 319-335.
36. For a number of proposals to improve executive-congressional consultation, see "Congress and Foreign Policy," *Report of the Special Subcommittee on Investigations of the House Committee on International Relations*, January 2, 1977.
37. For an insider's account, see Robert Cassidy, "Negotiating About Negotiations," in *The Tethered Presidency*, ed. Thomas M. Franck (New York: New York University Press, 1981), pp. 264-282.
38. Letter of June 7, 1978, to President Jimmy Carter from 14 members of the House International Relations Committee, released by the committee. (The committee was renamed "Foreign Affairs" in 1979.) On similar problems in the Reagan administration, see Alexander Haig, *Caveat: Realism, Reagan, and Foreign Policy* (New York: Macmillan, 1984).
39. Charles O. Jones, "Why Congress Can't Do Policy Analysis," *Policy Analysis* (Spring 1976): 261.
40. On the adverse implications of this decision for interbranch conflict management, see James L. Sundquist, "The Legislative Veto: A Bounced Check," *The Brookings Review* (Fall 1983): 13-16; and I. M. Destler, "Dateline Washington: Life After the Veto," *Foreign Policy* (Fall 1983): pp. 181-186.
41. See Bruce Oppenheimer, "Congress and the New Obstructionism: Developing an Energy Program," in *Congress Reconsidered*, 2nd ed., edited by Lawrence C. Dodd and Bruce I. Oppenheimer (Washington, D.C.: CQ Press, 1981), pp. 275-316.
42. Lawrence C. Dodd, "Congress and the Quest for Power," in *Congress Reconsidered*, 1st ed., edited by Lawrence C. Dodd and Bruce I. Oppenheimer (New York: Praeger Publishers, 1977), pp. 289-297.

43. See John F. Manley, *The Politics of Finance* (Boston: Little, Brown & Co., 1970); and Fenno, *Congressmen in Committees*. On the Bolling Committee, see Roger H. Davidson and Walter J. Oleszek, *Congress Against Itself* (Bloomington, Indiana: Indiana University Press, 1977).
44. Graham Allison and Peter Szanton, *Remaking Foreign Policy: The Organizational Connection* (New York: Basic Books, 1976), pp. 110-111.
45. Dodd, "Congress and the Quest for Power," p. 303. A similar proposal, concerning decisions to employ nuclear weapons, appears in Jeremy J. Stone, "Presidential First Use Is Unlawful," *Foreign Policy* (Fall 1984): 106-112.
46. Arthur Schlesinger, Jr., "The Role of the President in Foreign Policy," *Murphy Commission Report*, Appendix L, p. 40.
47. Malbin, "Congressional Committee Staffs," pp. 20-25. Malbin puts forward the idea of "dual staffing"; committees might have a "core of nonpartisan professionals on the staff, supplemented by partisan slots controlled by the majority and minority."
48. For some interesting constitutional reform proposals, see Lloyd N. Cutler, "To Form a Government," *Foreign Affairs* (Fall 1980): 126-143.

16. THE LEGISLATIVE VETO IN THE 1980s

Joseph Cooper

One of the most significant institutional developments in twentieth century American politics has been the emergence and growth of the legislative veto. First initiated in the 1930s, usage of the veto exploded in the 1970s with the result that it became an increasingly influential factor in both foreign and domestic policymaking.

This pristine, unfettered era of the legislative veto's history was ended abruptly by the Supreme Court in late June of 1983. In a sweeping decision, *Immigration and Naturalization Service v. Chadha,* the Court ruled that one-house or simple resolution forms of the veto were unconstitutional.[1] Two weeks after the *Chadha* decision, the Court affirmed without comment two Appeals Court decisions against the veto, one of which outlawed two-house or concurrent resolution forms of the mechanism.[2] Neither concurrent nor simple resolutions are presented to the president for his approval, and simple resolutions represent the action of a single house of the Congress. Thus, in both these instances, the Court based its rulings on the provisions of Article I, Sections 1 and 7, which stipulate that the process of lawmaking must involve *bicameral approval* and *presentment to the president for his consent or veto.*

As important as these judicial decisions are, they have not ended controversy over the legislative veto nor foreclosed its future use. This chapter examines one dimension of the continuing controversy: the merits of and need for the veto as an institutional mechanism. Although a host of legal or constitutional issues still remain, these issues will be addressed only for purposes of specifying the constraints that now limit congressional options with respect to the veto.[3] To a greater degree than the legal issues, the institutional issues force analysts to come to terms with the basic character and current needs of representative government in the United States; they involve questions of politics in their highest and broadest sense and, as such, provide an appropriate focus for a chapter in this volume.

The Context of Controversy

To begin, it is necessary to place the legislative veto in more detailed perspective. This section briefly reviews the structural components of the veto, identifies its main forms, summarizes its history, and analyzes the limits imposed by *Chadha*. With this information as background, the impacts of the mechanism, the political system's need for it, and the range of options still available to the Congress are assessed in the sections that follow. The chapter concludes with a review of developments since *Chadha* and some observations on the future of the legislative veto.

The Veto and Its Forms

The legislative veto may be defined as a statutory mechanism that renders the implementation or the continuing implementation of decisions or actions, authorized by the statute, subject to some further form of legislative review and control for a specified time period. For example, in the decade preceding the *Chadha* decision, simple and concurrent resolution forms of the veto were applied to control rulemaking by officials in a number of departments and independent agencies. The Federal Trade Commission (FTC) provides a good illustration. A 1980 act reauthorizing the agency required that FTC rules lay before the Congress for 90 days before going into effect, during which time Congress could negate or disallow any such rule through the passage of a concurrent resolution.[4] To cite another, but quite different, example of veto control before *Chadha,* the War Powers Resolution of 1973 limited the president's ability to introduce American armed forces into hostilities without a formal declaration of war to ninety days. During this time period, Congress was authorized to require the withdrawal of the forces through the passage of a concurrent resolution. In addition, the president was denied authority to maintain the forces beyond the time period unless Congress passed a joint resolution or bill to that effect.[5]

In short, then, when veto review is included as part of an enabling statute, executive decisions or actions authorized by the statute cannot go into effect or remain in effect unless Congress approves or does not disapprove them within a specified time period. All forms of the legislative veto share this basic generic characteristic of making delegated executive power or discretion *directly contingent* on further legislative review and control. Nonetheless, before the recent Supreme Court decisions, forms of the veto could and did vary greatly depending on how choices along several dimensions of structure were made and combined.[6]

First, a wide range of options existed with respect to the agent or agents charged with the exercise of veto power. Congress thus has vested veto power in one house, both houses, committees, subcommittees, a committee chair, blends of committee and house action, and even blends of one- and two-house action.

Second, the manner in which the decisionmaking process operates has been and remains open in a number of key respects. Two of the most important are whether veto review subjects decisions or actions to approval or disapproval within a specified time period and whether veto review is a condition for implementing authorized decisions or actions ("before-the-fact" review) or a means of terminating decisions or actions already in effect ("after-the-fact" review). In the first five decades of the veto's existence, the Congress preferred negative forms, although approval forms were also quite common. However, reliance on "after-the-fact" rather than "before-the-fact" review has been infrequent. In addition, several other aspects of operation are important and have varied: whether veto proposals are submitted by or through the president, whether veto proposals are amendable once submitted, and whether veto proposals are protected by provisions that limit debate and ensure access to the floor.

Third, until the *Chadha* decision in 1983, the formal mechanisms or instruments through which veto action was implemented varied. Approval or disapproval was often expressed by simple, concurrent, or committee resolutions—that is, by forms of action not subject to the president's veto power. However, from its very beginnings, veto review also operated through waiting period or "report and wait" procedures, in which the enabling statute simply requires that proposed decisions or actions lie before Congress or its committees for a specified number of days before taking effect. Although left unstated, formal congressional action to veto or negate the proposed decision or action has to take the form of a regular bill and, if passed by both houses, be submitted to the president for his approval.

Aside from these traditional instruments of action, Congress has invented several variants in response to criticism of the veto on legal grounds. In the 1950s Congress tied the committee resolution form to the appropriations process by making funds to implement certain executive decisions or actions contingent on securing the approval of designated committees. Since the 1950s, however, this form has been used only sporadically. In the 1970s a new form emerged as both usage of the veto and criticism of it on legal grounds accelerated. Under this form, authority to approve or disapprove is expressly stipulated in the statute, but it must be exercised through the passage of joint resolutions or bills, both of which are subject to the president's veto power. Once the joint resolution form appeared, Congress began to combine concurrent and joint resolution forms of veto review in especially important areas of executive decisionmaking, such as impoundment and war powers.[7]

With increased usage, the variety of options that existed for structuring veto review led to a profusion of forms. Students of the history of the veto have identified more than a dozen different forms. However, our purposes in this chapter can adequately be served by a relatively simple classification scheme organized in terms of the two factors the Supreme Court has found so critical to the veto's constitutionality: submission to the president for his approval and bicameral consideration.

We shall thus distinguish between *congressional forms* and *law forms* on the basis of these criteria. *Congressional forms* are those in which veto action is not subject to the president's veto power and may be taken by portions of the Congress as well as by both houses. *Law forms* are those in which veto action follows regular legislative procedures and involves both bicameral agreement and submission to the president for his approval.

Within these basic categories, congressional forms can be distinguished further in terms of the agent or agents vested with veto power. Law forms are necessarily two-house forms, but can be distinguished in terms of whether approval or disapproval within a specified time period is explicitly or only implicitly provided for in the enabling statute.

Table 16-1 is organized according to the categories defined above. It provides summary data on the forms of vetoes embodied in veto provisions enacted into law between 1932 and 1982. The table indicates three aspects of structural use that are especially worth noting: the heavy degree of reliance on various congressional forms, the popularity of the waiting period form, and increased use of the joint resolution form as the decade of the 1970s ended.

Patterns of Veto Usage

The veto's rise to a position of importance in the operations of the federal government did not occur quickly or evenly. Yet however sluggish and haphazard the process of development, the results by the early 1980s were quite impressive.[8]

Table 16-1 Veto Provisions Classified by Form, 1932-1982

	1932-1978	*1979-1982**
Congressional Forms		
One-House	71	24
Two-House	65	23
Committee	69	26
Other	0	5
Totals	205	78
Law Forms		
Joint Resolution or Bill	9	11
Waiting Period or Advance Notification	238	no data
Totals	247	11

* As of August 5, 1982.

SOURCE: Clark Norton, *1978 Congressional Acts Authorizing Congressional Approval or Disapproval of Proposed Executive Actions* (Washington, D.C.: Congressional Research Service, 1979), pp. v-vi; M. S. Cavanagh et al., *Congressional Veto Legislation: 97th Congress* (Washington, D.C.: Congressional Research Service, 1982), pp. 1-7; and Barbara Craig, *The Legislative Veto: Congressional Control of Regulation* (Boulder, Colo.: Westview Press, 1983), p. 18.

The veto mechanism was invented in the 1930s as a stratagem for facilitating the president's ability to reorganize the executive branch. However, only a few dozen veto provisions were enacted in the 1930s and 1940s. Moreover, about two-thirds of these provisions dealt with projects and contracts of various types and immigration matters. Perhaps the two most important uses concerned executive reorganization plans, the original and crystallizing application, and the licensing of nuclear materials for production or use.

In the 1950s and 1960s veto usage expanded. More than 100 veto provisions were passed, although project and contract uses continued to account for almost half of all provisions, and minor governmental operations uses for nearly another quarter. Hence, veto provisions in important policy areas remained restricted in number and range, despite including matters such as Department of Defense and National Aeronautics and Space Administration (NASA) reorganizations, presidential action on Tariff Commission recommendations, the apportionment of highway funds among the states, foreign agreements regarding military uses of atomic energy, and termination of federal grants and loans for failure to comply with the Civil Rights Act of 1964.

Although veto usage had grown considerably in the 1950s and 1960s, in the 1970s it simply exploded. Roughly three-quarters of the 500 veto provisions enacted into law over the last half-century were enacted in the 1970s. And with this explosion in veto usage came scores of new applications in important policy areas. Table 16-2 provides some illustrative examples.

It is thus not surprising that Justice Byron R. White, in his dissent to the Court's decision in *Chadha* outlawing one-house vetoes, stated that the "prominence of the legislative veto mechanism in our contemporary political system and its importance to Congress can hardly be overstated. It has," he noted, "become a central means by which Congress secures the accountability of executive and independent agencies."[9] Indeed, the Court decisions in mid-1983 outlawing congressional forms of the veto affected more than 200 separate vetoes in 126 laws.[10]

The Veto After *Chadha*

As formulated in *Chadha,* the crux of the constitutional issue with respect to the veto mechanism is whether its exercise constitutes "lawmaking" in the sense intended by Article I of the Constitution. The Court held that it did, and thus ruled against forms of the veto that did not involve bicameral approval and presentment to the president. However, its reasoning and conclusions are not as clear and unavoidable as they may appear. Veto resolutions are not original acts of lawmaking, but rather derive their legal effect from enabling statutes which are passed as regular laws. Furthermore, officials in departments and agencies routinely make highly discretionary and binding policy decisions under the authority of enabling statutes as well.

Table 16-2 Selected Veto Provisions Passed Between 1970 and 1982

Defense Policy: War Powers (1973) Export of Defense-Related Goods or Technology (1975) Arms Sales (1976)	*Consumer Policy:* All FTC Rules (1980) All Consumer Product Safety Commission Rules (1981)
Foreign Policy: Foreign Assistance in Violation of Human Rights (1975) Cooperative Agreements Regarding Nuclear Fuel, Facilities, and Technology (1978)	*Energy Policy:* Rationing Plans, Strategic Reserves, and Oil Exports (1975) Reimposition of Natural Gas Price Controls (1978) Oil and Gas Bidding Systems for Outer Continental Shelf (1979)
Trade: Presidential Proposals for Import Relief, Waiver Extensions, and Non-discriminatory Treatment (1974) Curtailment of Export of Agricultural Commodities (1979)	*Environmental Policy:* Sales and Withdrawals from Public Lands (1976) EPA Rules Regarding Hazardous Substances (1980) EPA Rules Regarding Pesticides (1980)
Education Policy: All Department of Education Rules (1974, 1978, and 1979) Enrollment Periods in Veterans' Educational Assistance (1976) Schedule of Family Contributions for Pell Grants (1981)	*Miscellaneous:* Impoundment (1974) Federal Reserve Board Changes in Interest Rate Differentials Between FDIC and FSLIC Banks (1975) Farm Credit Administration Rules (1980)

SOURCE: 103 S.Ct. 2811-2816.

Hence, to a significant degree the case against the veto rests on the ability to distinguish *executive decisionmaking* under powers delegated by a prior piece of legislation from *congressional action* under veto provisions authorized by a prior piece of legislation.

The position of the Court in *Chadha* involved two interrelated arguments.[11] On the one hand, Chief Justice Warren E. Burger argued that action through veto resolutions was "essentially legislative" in character and effect because it altered legal rights in a binding fashion. He concluded that Congress can take such actions only through the regular legislative process, that is, through forms of decisionmaking that involve bicameral approval and presentment to the president. According to Burger, once Congress has passed a law, it cannot exercise further policy discretion except by returning to the regular legislative process. On the other hand, Burger argued that once

Congress delegated discretionary authority to officials in departments or agencies, the exercise of such discretion became "presumptively" executive. Therefore, the exercise of such discretion was not "legislative" or even "quasi-legislative" and it was not a relevant consideration in deciding the status of the veto.

In sum, Chief Justice Burger ultimately relied upon a sequential or procedural approach to legislative and executive power rather than an inherent function approach; that is, he emphasized the *stages* of decision-making, rather than the *substance* or character of the decisions themselves as his main criterion of legislative and executive power. Given the result that Burger wanted, he was wise to do so, even though the inherent function approach has traditionally provided the justification for establishing agencies and commissions independent of and outside the executive branch. In the case of the veto, any exclusive or even primary emphasis on the character of the decisions would have either vindicated all vetoes over matters of broad policy importance or threatened the legality of the wholesale delegations of discretionary authority to officials in departments and agencies that the Court has countenanced for years, despite the explicit Article I provisions that state that all legislative power is vested in Congress. However, Burger's application of a procedural or sequential approach is so rigid that it renders his use of this approach simplistic and highlights the moribund state of the nondelegation of legislative power doctrine.[12]

It should be apparent, then, why—in the context of a modern administrative state and the various convolutions the Court has undergone to legitimize it—the *Chadha* decision is not persuasive to many observers.[13] Nonetheless, our concern here is with the limits it imposes on veto usage, limits the Congress will have to observe for the identifiable future and perhaps forever. Given the decision and its rationale, two points can be made regarding the leeway that remains to Congress.

First, whereas the Court has explicitly or implicitly outlawed all congressional forms of the device, including one-house, two-house, and committee forms, there appears to be no constitutional bar to the waiting period or joint resolution forms of the veto. Chief Justice Burger suggests this to be the case in a footnote to his opinion, and it represents the consensus of members of Congress and high executive officials in the aftermath of *Chadha*.[14] Nor is this a surprising result. The same logic that outlaws congressional forms validates law forms.

Second, ironically enough, the rationale of the *Chadha* decision widens the constitutional potential of one specific type of congressional form which hitherto has seen only limited use—house or committee vetoes tied to the appropriations process. If the distinction between legislative and executive power is procedural or sequential, then bars to the prospective appropriation of funds established on the basis of simple, concurrent, or committee resolutions can be defended strongly as internal acts of rulemaking and integral aspects of Congress's historic right to appropriate or not as it sees fit.

Thus, the way appears open for using statutes or House and Senate rules to authorize the consideration of veto resolutions on certain topics and to instruct the Appropriations Committees to include provisos in appropriations bills barring funds for objects or purposes disallowed by such resolutions.

The Merits of the Veto

Throughout its history, and with growing intensity in recent years, critics have attacked the legislative veto on policy or institutional grounds. They have argued that the veto mechanism distorts the decisionmaking process and that Congress does not need the device to protect its constitutional role. Up to now, such criticism has focused on congressional forms. However, the logic of the argument applies to *all* forms and *all* uses of the device. If this argument is correct, there is no need to examine congressional options in the wake of *Chadha*. Rather, the legislative veto should simply be abandoned. Hence, the qualitative effects of the veto on governmental decisionmaking at the national level and the political system's need for the mechanism must be assessed before questions of how Congress should employ the veto can be addressed.

The Case Against the Veto

The criticism directed at congressional forms has focused on the use of one- and two-house vetoes to control the exercise of rulemaking power in a variety of important policy areas. The critique has been multifaceted, but its most important dimension concerns the veto's impact on effective decision-making in the public interest.

Critics of the veto argue that the consequences of controlling rulemaking through congressional forms were invariably inimical to sound and demo-cratic decisionmaking. According to these critics, congressional forms pro-vided committees with a substantial increase in leverage, with negotiating power "with teeth," since even under one- and two-house vetoes, rules were first referred to committees and could be endangered by committee decisions to bring resolutions of disapproval to the floor.[15] Such leverage, the critics claim, forced officials to negotiate the final content of rules with committee leaders. Equally if not more important in their view, these negotiations both displaced the fair, open, impartial, and expert processes of decisionmaking that would have otherwise governed under the "notice and comment" provisions of the Administrative Procedure Act, and intro-duced a second round of politics in which covert, intense, and particular-istic pressures were brought to bear. The critics therefore conclude that the result of relying on congressional forms was both to promote *ad hoc*, arbitrary, and irrational policy outcomes, and to provide the special inter-ests, which operate through and dominate committees, with excessive and unfair advantage.

This negative view of congressional forms can be found in the writings of lawyers such as Harold Bruff, Ernest Gellhorn, and Antonin Scalia, and political scientists such as Robert Gilmour and Barbara Craig.[16] The logic of their attack on the veto mechanism clearly applies across different categories of usage and is not limited simply to rulemaking. What is perhaps not immediately as clear is that it applies to *law forms* of the veto as well as to *congressional forms*. Let us pause for a moment to explain why, since many observers remain uncertain about differences in the impacts of these two basic types of veto. Indeed, even some critics of congressional forms favor use of the waiting period form, and others contrast congressional forms and regular legislative procedures in attacking the effects of congressional forms on representative government.[17]

Joint resolutions of approval or negation also provide committees with substantial leverage. To be sure, in contrast to one- and two-house vetoes, they are subject to presidential veto. In addition, in contrast to one-house vetoes, they require bicameral approval. Nonetheless, while these requirements reduce committee leverage, they do not eliminate it overall or prevent it from varying according to the politics of particular circumstances. Under joint resolution forms, as under one- and two-house forms, officials have to negotiate with committees and take careful heed of both the short-run and the long-run costs of opposing them. Indeed, joint resolutions of approval may often provide committees with greater leverage than one- and two-house vetoes since in such instances officials must organize positive majorities in both houses rather than simply avoid disapproval in one or both houses. Moreover, the fact that amendments can be offered freely under joint resolution forms, whereas they were usually barred under congressional forms for reasons of constitutionality, adds substantially to committee leverage. In any event, the basic point is clear: the practical differences between one- and two-house vetoes and joint resolution forms are not great enough to render these forms immune to the criticisms leveled at congressional forms.

The situation with respect to the waiting period form is similar. Formally, this type of veto is highly distinguishable from congressional forms and it appears not to have the same consequences. However, the waiting period form flags matters for congressional attention and institutionalizes opportunities for intervention and negotiation. Given the continuing dependence of officials on committees for both authority and funds, such opportunities can provide substantial leverage whenever committees choose to exercise it. In fact, as shown even in case studies conducted by the veto's critics, the leverage exercised by committees under the waiting period form can approach or even match the leverage exercised under one- or two-house forms of the veto.[18]

In sum, then, if providing congressional committees with opportunities for intervention and leverage in the process of execution is bad, then the critique applies to law forms of the veto as well as to congressional forms. Committee leverage over executive officials rests on the powers of Congress and on the influence of committees in their parent bodies, not on the presence or absence of regular procedures.

The Case for the Veto

The issue, however, is whether congressional participation in the administrative process through the veto is necessarily or generally as bad as the veto's critics claim. The answer is no. The veto's critics exaggerate the virtues of executive decisionmaking and fail to appreciate the role and benefits of politics in a democratic order.

Two points may be made to counter the executive biases of the veto's critics. First, "special" interests are just as much at home in the process of execution as in the legislative process. Moreover, it is arguable whether more diffuse and less well-financed interests have easier access to agencies and commissions or to congressional committees. Undoubtedly, it varies with circumstances. Thus, black and white contrasts rest on bias and presumption. The claim that notice and comment procedures render the administrative process "open" while special interest domination renders committee operations "closed" fails to take account of the policy blinders and commitments administrators bring to their jobs, the high costs in terms of time, attention, and money that participation in the administrative process involves, and the responsiveness of elected representatives to broad and diffuse interests that criss-cross large numbers of individual constituencies.[19]

Second, in areas in which important questions of public policy are at issue, it is not obvious that administrators are wiser or more devoted to the public interest than legislators. Indeed, the basic belief of constitutional democratic orders is that they are not. Nor is it obvious that the quality of executive decisionmaking does not benefit from forcing "experts" to pay more heed to views of "where the shoes are pinching" that conflict with their own viewpoints and preferences. Moreover, though the provisions of the Administrative Procedure Act and subsequent requirements for decisionmaking "on the record" have served to "judicialize" the rulemaking process, this result is no unmixed blessing for representative government. When important policy decisions are involved, judicialized procedures may narrow and inhibit full and responsible consideration of all the factors and issues involved.[20]

Similarly, the antipolitical biases of the veto's critics are identifiable and may be countered. First, committees are not pathological entities in the Congress, but instruments of division of labor that contribute to institutional effectiveness. Otherwise, they would not have been invented and could not continue to exist. This is not to say that gaps or differences between the committees and the whole cannot and do not occur; but committees are responsive to the whole and can be disciplined by the whole. More specifically with respect to the veto, under one- and two-house forms as well as all law forms, the leverage of committees rests in large part on their demonstrated ability to induce the whole to accept the resolutions or bills they choose to bring forward.[21]

Second, because they are parts of the Congress rather than the whole, committees are not wholly or primarily the home of special interests. Such reasoning is as fallacious in the case of Congress as it would be if applied to executive agencies. To be sure, instances can be cited in which the veto has been used by committees for purposes many would disapprove, for example the rejection by concurrent resolution of a proposed FTC rule requiring used car dealers to disclose defects. However, other instances can be found in which the positions of opponents and proponents of the used car veto would be reversed, such as use of veto review by committees to block coal leasing on the public lands and oil and gas leasing in wilderness areas and along state coastlines.[22]

The point is that the committee system and the veto mechanism are not the instrument of any fixed, limited, and parochial set of groups, but rather of the broad congeries of interests and viewpoints, which for various political reasons enjoy better access to and influence in Congress than the executive at particular moments in time. That critics of the veto fail to see this is attributable to the simplistic way in which they often equate constituent pressure and special interests. As a result, for many of these critics the leverage committees have exercised through the veto on behalf of federal assistance for middle-class college students, housing assistance for disadvantaged senior citizens, or nondiscriminatory treatment of female athletes becomes mere warfare for special interests. If so, one wonders what the public interest is and how it is to be found.[23]

Yet, this equation and the conclusions drawn from it reveal something basic about the underlying assumptions of the veto's critics: they lack faith in politics and political processes of accommodation as the central means of locating and formulating the public interest. Rather, they see the public interest as some entity above politics that is best identified by judicious and expert administrators, at least once Congress has acted through law. Since the process of execution as well as the legislative process now involves highly discretionary and important policy decisions, any sequential or procedural distinction in this regard lacks relevance and persuasiveness. Even so, it is no accident that the arguments of the veto's critics against congressional forms apply to law forms as well. In truth, despite what some critics of the veto contend, they apply to the legislative process in general since committees have as great—if not greater—power *vis-à-vis* the whole in the regular legislative process, and they can and do use this power to influence both administrative proposals for law and administrative choices in carrying out the law.[24] Indeed, in the light of the informal patterns of relationship that have long prevailed among committees and agencies generally, the irony of the critics' position is striking. They combine a belief in the perniciousness of committees with opposition to veto arrangements that would render these relationships subject to control by the whole Congress.

One final point remains to be made concerning the impacts of the veto mechanism. Critics have focused on only a portion of veto uses while explicitly or implicitly condemning veto usage generally. Yet, in many nonrulemaking areas it is even harder to posit a yawning gap between committee preferences and the desires of the whole, even harder to picture the veto as an instrument of special interests rather than the Congress as an institution. Note, for example, the enactment of congressional forms of the veto to tie foreign aid to human rights, to limit the president's ability to impound funds, to control arms sales, to restrict nuclear proliferation, and to limit executive discretion in rewarding and punishing trading partners around the world. Indeed, even with respect to congressional forms designed to control various types of projects and contracts, the veto does not represent any strengthening of special interests, but rather a choice to provide the executive with more flexibility while still providing for congressional control.[25]

In conclusion, then, our intent is not to argue that committees or political processes do not err. The legislative process is not without its warts. But then the administrative process is not the paragon of fairness, wisdom, and objectivity that the veto's critics assume either. The issue thus reduces to one of balance and trust. The basic question to be answered is whether representative government in the United States. gains or loses by the introduction of a second round of politics in areas where substantial discretionary authority is exercised by presidents and other high officials. The critics of the veto prefer to rely on executive wisdom and power, and the logic of their case against congressional forms in the rulemaking area applies to all uses and all forms. Our contention is that their position does not accord with the basic faith, genius, or realities of constitutional democratic government in the United States. Thus, the view presented here is quite different. The veto should not be treated as an anathema, which concern for the public interest would consign to some congressional scrapheap as soon as possible. Rather, it should be treated as an instrument that like all other instruments can be misused but when properly used has substantial potential for good.

The Need for the Veto

The conclusion that the veto mechanism should be treated as an instrument, not an anathema, leads immediately to consideration of the need for the device. Critics of the veto do not avoid this question, but they treat it in a somewhat secondary fashion. Obviously, if the veto is venal, it is not necessary. Nonetheless, most of the veto's critics feel obliged to address the question of need directly and to suggest alternatives. And well they should, given the number and importance of the veto provisions that have been enacted and the growth of executive power since the 1930s.

All critics of the veto have argued that Congress should abandon congressional forms and do a more craftsmanlike job of lawmaking instead.

As befits the logic of their critique, many of these critics contend that better lawmaking combined with reliance on its traditional oversight mechanisms will suffice to protect Congress's role and power in the political system. Harold Bruff and Ernest Gellhorn are good cases in point.[26] In addition, Robert Gilmour and Barbara Craig argue that in the area of foreign policy, the device has been ineffective and is therefore not needed.[27] Gellhorn argues that the device is ineffective as an oversight mechanism generally.[28] Antonin Scalia agrees, but contends that the problem of combining executive power and congressional control is insoluble unless the nation resolves to have the federal government do less.[29] Finally, the American Bar Association (ABA) supports use of the waiting period form to control important rules, and Gilmour and Craig support limited use of joint resolutions of approval for the same purpose.[30]

Alternatives to the Veto

Let us begin by considering the need for greater congressional influence or control over delegated authority and the alternatives suggested by the veto's critics. In truth, these critics do not deny the need to increase congressional effectiveness; virtually all admit that a serious problem exists. The issue is thus reduced to the alternatives to the veto and the veto's effectiveness.

Interestingly enough, all alternatives except better lawmaking are easily disposed of, often on the basis of considerations raised by opponents of the veto themselves. First, critics of the veto, such as Bruff, Gellhorn, and Scalia, are well aware of the *ad hoc* character and limited reach of oversight through appropriations, investigations, and confirmation of personnel. They themselves lack faith that these traditional weapons have much potential for raising oversight to some qualitatively superior level of performance, and they understand that the constraints derive from time pressures, substantive complexity, political divisions, and career interests.[31]

Their judgments in this regard are powerfully reinforced by past experience. In fact, Congress has not stood still; in recent decades it has substantially augmented its capacity for oversight through traditional mechanisms. Congress has expanded staff, established a host of oversight subcommittees, increased the number of provisos in appropriations bills, and required periodic review and reauthorization of programs in a variety of policy areas.[32] Nonetheless, such actions have not deterred it from expanding veto usage as well. Nor is this attributable wholly or primarily to personal or institutional aggrandizement. Rather, it is largely attributable to the range of authority delegated to officials in agencies and commissions, new and more conflictual patterns of politics, and the difficulties of after-the-fact control through traditional mechanisms.[33]

Take, for example, the area that is most salient to the veto's critics: rulemaking. It is true that rulemaking applications of the veto exploded in the 1970s. But note the following facts: in the years from 1955 through 1960, the number of new pages of public laws totaled 6,057 and the number of pages added in the *Federal Register* totaled 4,569. The comparable figures for 1973 through 1978 are 11,338 and 32,337![34] Similarly, whereas 37 new regulatory laws were passed between 1956 and 1965, 119 were passed between 1966 and 1975.[35] In short, there was an explosion in regulatory authority and administrative rulemaking as well, an explosion that could not be contained or controlled by adjusting funding levels, adding provisos, requiring periodic reauthorization, or confirming personnel.

Second, substituting a single law form for the array of congressional forms that were previously relied upon is not a viable alternative either logically or practically. Despite the presumptions of the ABA, the waiting period form is not an innocent mechanism in terms of the logic of the attack on congressional forms. Rather, as argued above, this form is subject to the same objections that the Bar Association has leveled at congressional forms. Nor can Gilmour and Craig exempt the joint resolution of approval form from the criticism they direct at all other congressional and law forms. It is true that this form is closest to regular lawmaking procedures; still, the more critical point is that it too endows committees with substantial leverage. Indeed, as explained above, this form may often favor committee power more than any of the negative, two-house congressional or law forms. These defects in logic are matched by defects in practical efficacy. The proponents of the veto could not and would not accept reliance on a single form. And with good reason. No one form possesses the combination of strength and flexibility needed to justify exclusive use under all the varying needs and circumstances that exist. Even if the veto's critics could surmount their inconsistencies and disagreements, reliance on a single law form would cripple the veto's ability to play a significant role in meeting Congress's varied oversight needs.

Third, and last, Scalia's conclusions are insightful, but hardly realistic. Undoubtedly, the volume and complexity of the responsibilities the federal government has assumed are a prime factor in expanding executive power and straining congressional control. Yet, to ask the federal government to do less to a degree that would obviate the need for enhanced oversight capacity in areas where the veto has been used ignores realities that cannot be ignored. Is the federal government to refrain from arms sales, trade negotiations, aiding schools and students, regulating pollution and hazardous substances, using military force abroad, and regulating private use of public lands? If not, and if traditional means of control are often inadequate, then the problem recurs. In short, nineteenth century solutions are not appropriate for twentieth century problems.

The issue of alternatives thus comes down to whether Congress can improve its lawmaking performance to such a point as to make use of the veto mechanism unnecessary. At least some of the critics of the veto understand the substantive and political difficulties involved. Once again, they are not sanguine about the possibilities of any substantial increase in congressional control through better lawmaking. Nonetheless, they believe that choice of this alternative is demanded by democratic ideals, and that the public has a right to insist on laws which provide clear and directive standards for executive action and a firm basis for holding officials accountable for results, no matter what the pressures or difficulties.[36]

Yet, in truth, reliance on better lawmaking as an alternative to the veto is neither practical nor wise. To be sure, Congress can do a better job of clarifying its intent. Nonetheless, what still remains in question is how much and to what effect. After all, the primary barriers here do not derive from willful irresponsibility or laziness, but the conditions of modern government in contemporary America.

First, in highly complex and turbulent areas of policy, it is difficult, if not impossible, to state intent except in highly broad terms since precise issues and problems cannot be anticipated. Note arms sales, for example. Second, to the degree that clearer and more directive standards can be provided, sizable room for administrative discretion still remains. Note EPA rules, for example. It is no accident that in recent decades the rate of increase in *Federal Register* pages far exceeds the rate of increase in statute pages or pages per statute.[37] The traditional "cure" is to try to write the laws in even greater detail, because in the end power lies in control of the concrete, not the abstract. However, even if Congress had the time and the resources to follow this course in some general or comprehensive fashion, which is doubtful, the cure often could be worse than the disease. For to limit authority by specifying details can well be to hamstring the executive, and in so doing, to vitiate Congress's ability to achieve the broader goals that led it to delegate authority in the first place. Third, given the current state of the congressional party system in which allegiance is weak, power decentralized, conflict intense, and alignments volatile, attempts to write clear standards or detailed provisions may well result in defeat of the legislation. The price of passage may thus be vagueness, but delegation of authority for action nonetheless needed to protect the national interest. Note, for example, gasoline rationing contingency plans in the late 1970s.[38]

Clearly, this is a case in which insistence on adhering to the critics' ideal version of the needs of democratic orders does more damage to these needs than Congress's pragmatic willingness to delegate broad authority under veto control. The dilemma Congress often confronts as it seeks to deal with its daily workload is simply not amenable to solution through better lawmaking, although admittedly the quality of lawmaking can be improved. To deny Congress access to the veto when it encounters one or more of the constraints outlined above is thus to restrict it and the political system to highly counterproductive choices. Congress can delegate the broad authority needed for effective action in vital areas of national responsibility, but without adequate control. It can refuse to delegate authority so as to preserve control through obstruction, although inaction at best may be only a temporary palliative that breeds more intense needs and even harsher demand for action in the future. Or it can pepper the authority it delegates with detailed instructions and restrictions so as to protect its control, although such provisions may well vitiate executive effectiveness and Congress's ability to achieve its basic policy goals.[39]

In contrast, the veto frees Congress from such Hobson's choices. Its great virtue is that it permits the two essential yet conflicting needs of the modern democratic state, executive leadership and legislative control, to be reconciled and mutually satisfied. To be sure, the mechanism is no panacea, it may be misused, and it may at times entice Congress into doing a poorer job of lawmaking than it would otherwise do. Still, the point remains that in a variety of policy areas the veto provides the only or the best means of maintaining the exacting balance between consent and action that the Constitution intends and upon which the continued viability of our republic depends. Hence, some part of wisdom lies in accepting the limits of practical reality. Pristine notions of a legislature that legislates and an executive that executes were not fully descriptive or functional in the nineteenth century; they are even less so today.

The Effectiveness of the Veto

One final issue remains—the claim that the veto is not needed because it is ineffective. One part of the argument relates to time. Especially with respect to rulemaking, the contention is that effective control through the veto requires more time and attention than Congress can devote without severely damaging its general legislative responsibilities.[40] A second part of the argument relates to patterns of implementation. Gilmour and Craig argue that in foreign policy areas, the veto provisions contained in statutes have not in fact been much used and therefore that the mechanism is not effective. They conclude that Congress would be better advised to develop relations of trust and comity with the executive than to pursue an adversarial approach through the veto.[41] Gellhorn's objection is more basic. He argues that the veto is a negative mechanism which, like other oversight mechanisms, has been applied in an *ad hoc*, limited, and particularistic manner. He concludes, "The legislative veto, therefore, is unlikely to rescue Congress from itself." [42]

Ironically enough, the arguments relating to patterns of implementation counter the arguments relating to time. *Ad hoc* or sporadic implementation of veto power equates to selective implementation, and such implementation allows Congress to pick and choose its objects of control in terms of their political salience. If Congress properly exploits all the veto forms that remain available, this is quite a practical strategy for it to continue to pursue. Indeed, it will require far less time than the alternative most intensely favored by the veto's critics: better lawmaking across the board.

As for the more substantive objection, there is no necessary connection between *ad hoc* or sporadic implementation and ineffectiveness. The impact of the veto depends on the importance of the outcomes it affects, not the frequency of its use. Moreover, the veto's ability to affect outcomes does not derive solely from actual implementation or even threats to implement it; rather, the very existence of the device sensitizes officials to anticipate and forestall congressional criticism. Thus, it is a mistake to dismiss the veto in an area such as arms sales, as Gilmour and Craig do, because disputes between the branches have occurred relatively infrequently. The more important considerations are these: the disputes focused on those arms sales that were highly controversial, that is, sales to Middle Eastern and Persian Gulf nations; in these cases Congress secured important concessions and even informally blocked some sales; and, last but not least, as one past administrator of the program put it, the veto "provided a keystone for an important structure of notification and consultation that in the vast majority of cases resolved major differences." [43] Similarly, although Gilmour and Craig also dismiss the war powers veto because of lack of implementation, it was involved recently in authorizing American troops in Lebanon. In addition, the veto has played a role in military decisions with respect to Grenada and El Salvador.[44]

The differences between these areas and rulemaking, where actual veto usage also encompassed only a small proportion of possible cases, are accordingly far less weighty than Gilmour and Craig recognize. Moreover, Congress understands, if some of the veto's critics do not, that relations of trust and comity with the executive may be aided—rather than undercut—by mechanisms which increase its power, and that the influence it derives from such relations invariably atrophies in any particular instance in which sharp disagreements over policy needs and objectives persist.

In contrast, Gellhorn's argument is at heart normative, not empirical. In his view, ad hoc or sporadic veto review is ineffective because it is bad, because it gives too much power to committees and allows Congress to avoid confronting broad policy issues. Thus, the veto is ineffective because it does not fit Gellhorn and other critics' ideal view of proper legislative operations. Indeed, if anything, the critics' critique of the impact of the veto on rulemaking implies that it is too effective.

In the preceding section of this chapter, the validity of the critics' equation of committee leverage and action inimical to the public interest was questioned. Here their anticommittee views may be questioned in terms of their consequences for congressional power as well. Gellhorn's presumptions regarding legislative operations are reminiscent of John Stuart Mill's maxims regarding the proper role of a legislature. Mill saw legislatures as ill-fitted to deal with the details of either legislation or administration. He therefore enjoined them not to seek to govern, but rather to serve as deliberative forums for the discussion of important issues.[45] Such presumptions, however, are more appropriate to parliamentary systems than to our separation of powers framework of government. After a brief experiment with ministerial government in its early decades, Congress rejected such a mode of operations. It has relied on committees, and not shied from involving itself in details ever since. Its instincts in doing so were and remain correct, if measured in terms of maintaining legislative power and autonomy. Thus, criticism of this mode of operation that rests implicitly on other ideals should at least be revealed for what it is. Then the question can be focused on the real issue: whether preserving congressional power through the veto is good or functional for the separation of powers framework upon which our government is based. The answer for all the reasons outlined above is most decidedly yes.

Strategies and Options

If the veto is neither bad nor unnecessary, this analysis suggests two basic strategies for the Congress to follow as well as some guidelines for selecting options within these strategies. These strategies are constrained by the *Chadha* decision, but they are designed to exploit the leeway that remains to preserve the efficacy of the veto mechanism.

Extending Law Forms

Because Congress has no choice but to operate within parameters set by the Court, its main response to *Chadha* should be to substitute law forms of the veto for congressional forms. In so doing, it should be attentive to the costs and benefits of different types of law forms of the veto.

Negation by joint resolution or by bill under waiting period requirements provides greater opportunities for the conservation of time and effort, two very scarce resources in a late twentieth century Congress of more than 500 members. Issues can be selected in terms of their political importance, and only cursory attention need be devoted to matters that are noncontroversial. The cost, of course, is the need for a two-thirds majority if the president and Congress disagree, which reduces the power of the mechanism and Congress's leverage in applying it. Approval by joint resolution provides for greater legislative control. However, it requires Congress to pass on each and every matter subject to veto review. The results are likely to be quite costly in terms of floor time, even if special calendars or procedures are invented to expedite consideration.

In addition, different types of law forms affect congressional power for reasons beyond the size of the majority required to exercise control through veto review. Under negative law forms, proposed decisions or actions go into effect unless opponents can organize a majority on the floor to strike them down. Under affirmative law forms, proponents have to organize the floor majorities. Negative law forms thus provide the president and other officials with greater leverage. Moreover, the leverage is usually even greater under waiting period forms than joint resolution forms. In the former case common practice has been to provide only for a waiting period and not to include provisions for discharge and limited debate with respect to the bill, while the opposite has been true with respect to veto resolutions.

In sum, then, congressional leverage tends to increase as one moves from waiting period requirements to negation by joint resolution to approval by joint resolution. However, because time costs also increase, so too do constraints on use in terms of flexibility and range of control.

These are the primary effects associated with different law forms, but they do not operate in isolation. Rather, they may be augmented or depressed by supplementary aspects of structure which are also matters of choice. As outlined previously, these additional structural variables include: whether expedited procedures are provided to facilitate access to the floor and to limit debate; whether provisions for amendability are permitted; whether the submission of proposals is vested in the president or required to be forwarded through him; and the length of the time period.

The primary effects of the main law forms and the secondary effects of choices among remaining structural options are outlined in Table 16-3. This table indicates that the possibilities for variation in law forms are much broader than they may at first appear, and that opportunities for fine-tuning and experiments in design exist.

In fact, the use of law forms to compensate for the loss of congressional forms might well not be a viable strategy if this were not true. Congress needs a mix of law forms to replace the highly variegated mix of congressional forms outlawed by *Chadha*. In the case of these outlawed forms, the mix emerged over time, and time will be required for any mix of law forms to emerge. However, even at this early stage some broad guidelines can be suggested on the basis of the primary effects of basic forms and the secondary effects of subsidiary structural options.

In general, Congress should design and apply law forms of the veto by balancing time pressures against the degree of control that abstractly would be desirable. The joint resolution of approval form is best suited to areas of substantial political importance where relatively limited numbers of proposed actions or decisions need to be considered. Arms sales or war powers provide a good example. Given the pressure of other business and the variety of special calendars that already exist, wholesale or even widespread use of this form would be a mistake. However, the range or scope of the approval form can be extended somewhat by including provisions for limited debate and non-amendability so that matters can be voted up or down fairly quickly. Such provisions, to be sure, involve costs for congressional leverage, but they make approval forms viable for the control of matters such as appropriations recisions.

At the other end of the scale, waiting period forms are most appropriate for areas of limited importance that involve large numbers of proposed actions or decisions. Control over various types of projects and contracts provide good examples. The power of the waiting period form can be extended by lengthening the time period required for veto review beyond the normal 60 or 90 days, while allowing the committee to waive it whenever it sees fit. This increases the power of the form and its suitability for use in important areas

Table 16-3 Law Forms of the Veto: Primary and Secondary Effects of Various Designs

Law Forms of the Veto	Expedited Procedures		Amendability		Longer Time Period		Submissions by or Through President	
	Leverage	Time	Leverage	Time	Leverage	Time	Leverage	Time
Joint Resolution: Approval	+	−	+	+	+	+	+	−
Joint Resolution: Negation	+	−	+	+	+	+	−	−
Waiting Period	0	0	0	0	+	+	−	−

Secondary Effects of Structural Options

Primary Effects of Law Forms

Congressional Leverage — Time Costs

Key: ↑ = increase in primary effect
       + = augments primary effect
       − = depresses primary effect
       0 = no variation in structural option

of policy. Possible uses here include disposals of government interests or properties or private use of the public lands. However, increases in time period also intensify problems of delay in executive action, and this cost also must be borne in mind.

Joint resolutions of negation are appropriate for the broad middle range in which the matters to be controlled are too important to be left to waiting period control and too numerous to be subjected to individual approval. The scope of this form in terms of encompassing large numbers of issues can be extended by requiring nonamendability. Appropriation deferrals might thus be appropriate for negation by joint resolution, as would various trade policy items and rulemaking insofar as it is not controlled by the appropriations form of the veto that is recommended in the next section.

In conclusion, then, in applying law forms of the veto Congress must rely heavily upon negative rather than approval forms of the device. A rifle rather than a shotgun approach is generally preferable for approval forms, although it also may be feasible in some cases to combine approval and negative forms.[46]

Preserving Congressional Forms

Reliance on law forms should not be Congress's only response to *Chadha*. On balance, law forms cannot combine power and efficiency as effectively as congressional forms. Rather, joint resolutions of approval involve costs in terms of time that one- and two-house vetoes avoid, and negative law forms involve costs in terms of leverage that one- and two-house vetoes also avoid. Congress therefore should exploit the weaknesses in the *Chadha* opinion both to preserve the congressional form for the immediate future and to induce the Court to rethink its decision in a context far less narrow and prejudicial to the veto than *Chadha*, which involved private immigration rights.

Both objectives can be met by tying the veto to the appropriations process and experimenting with such vetoes to control selected areas of rulemaking. As noted earlier, the procedural or sequential approach to legislative power adopted in *Chadha* is particularly vulnerable to implementing the veto through appropriations bills. Similarly, usage with respect to rulemaking is desirable because it highlights the discretionary nature of the subject matter to be controlled and forces the Court to face the inconsistencies *Chadha* involves for adjusting the parameters of a separation of powers framework to the realities of a modern administrative state. Procedurally, appropriations vetoes are not difficult to design. Either statutes or House and Senate rules can be used to permit floor consideration of resolutions of disapproval with respect to proposed or pending administrative rules and to bar the appropriation of funds to implement any such rules that are disapproved.

Conclusion

In the year that has elapsed since the *Chadha* decision, proposals to substitute joint resolution forms of the veto for congressional forms have been advanced in a variety of important policy areas. Thus far, none of these proposals has been enacted, but more than a dozen have been included as provisions in bills that have passed one or both houses. Most of these proposals have been cast as joint resolutions of approval, and they have involved topics such as consumer protection rules, bans on the export of technology and agricultural commodities, MX missile production, nuclear proliferation, executive reorganization, military aid to El Salvador, sale of the Conrail System, the export of Alaskan oil, and District of Columbia self-government. In addition, proposals to substitute or introduce joint resolution forms have figured prominently in a Senate attempt to amend the War Powers Act, in a close floor vote on certain Environmental Protection Agency (EPA) rules, and in conflict over the reauthorization of the FTC.[47]

Three other related developments are worth noting. First, Louis Fisher has identified more than two dozen instances since *Chadha* in which Congress has enacted congressional forms of the veto. With a few exceptions, these instances involve committee vetoes over the reprogramming or use of appropriated funds.[48] Clearly, Congress does not believe that its Appropriations Committee will be challenged in areas in which they traditionally have exercised control either formally on the basis of provisions in statutes or informally on the basis of understandings with administrators. In addition, these enactments may indicate that many members believe that control through the appropriations process is not vulnerable to the reasoning in *Chadha*. However, in contrast to the appropriations form of the veto recommended above, these vetoes are committee vetoes and typically require officials to secure advance approval for their actions rather than simply barring the prospective use of appropriated funds for a certain purpose.[49]

Second, events suggests that, as predicted, the demise of congressional forms of the veto will lead to a strengthening of informal patterns of control through committees and to increased reluctance to delegate broad authority to executive officers.[50] Third, Department of Justice officials have stated that the time period provisions involved as parts of one- and two-house vetoes remain valid. Thus, for example, in arms sales, the former two-house veto has been transformed into waiting period control.[51]

What then, does all this portend for the future? Clearly the veto is not going to disappear. Indeed, even in this first post-*Chadha* year it has figured in three of the hottest issues before Congress: Stinger missile sales in the Middle East, the production of MX missiles, and military aid to El Salvador.[52] Still, as in the past, use and development is going to be *ad hoc* and controlled by the circumstances of particular situations. There is no consensus in the Congress on the merits of the mechanism or its proper use. The enactment of veto provisions thus will be contingent on a variety of factors that will be situationally determined: the degree of hostility or distrust present toward the president and/or other prominent officials, the effectiveness of other formal and informal alternatives, the character of the political divisions over the substantive issues, and the number and mix of veto forms already in existence. In this last regard, Congress's initial instinct after *Chadha* to reach for the joint resolution of approval form will have to be moderated if it intends to rely heavily on the veto mechanism. This reaction, although understandable, will be self-defeating unless disciplined by the same talent for eclecticism and inventiveness that Congress displayed before *Chadha*.

The ultimate fate of the veto is therefore difficult to predict. Indeed, it is even possible, if Congress enacts an appropriations form of the veto in a major policy area, that the courts will again play a significant role. This much, however, can be said: there is more reason to believe that the veto has a significant future than to doubt it. Moreover, whatever the veto's future, its fate is of high importance. This esoteric and strange mechanism continues to have profound implications for the division of power between the branches. Its fate will thus substantially affect the character of representative government in the United States as our republic enters its third century.

NOTES

1. 103 S.Ct. 2764 (1983).
2. See *Process Gas Consumers Group v. Consumer Energy Council*, 103 S.Ct. 3556 (1983), and *United States Senate v. FTC*, 103 S.Ct. 3556 (1983).
3. These issues include the legal status of past actions taken under the authority of veto provisions, whether delegated authority conditioned by veto provisions can continue to be exercised without them, and the validity and implications of the *Chadha* decision itself. See Kathleen Sylvester, "After *Chadha*, A Legal Void," *National Law Journal*, April 23, 1984, pp. 1, 8.
4. P.L. 96-252 (May 28, 1980).
5. P.L. 93-148 (November 7, 1973).
6. The analysis that follows is based on Joseph and Ann Cooper, "The Legislative Veto and the Constitution," *George Washington Law Review* 30 (1962): 476-470; Joseph Cooper and Patricia Hurley, "The Legislative Veto: A Policy Analysis," *Congress and the Presidency* 10 (1983): 6-9; Clark Norton, *Congressional Review, Deferral, and Disapproval of Executive Actions: A Summary and an Inventory of Statutory Authority* (Washington, D.C.: Congressional Research Service, 1976), pp. 1-10; and M. S. Cavanagh et al., *Congressional Veto Legislation: 97th Congress* (Washington, D.C.: Congressional Research Service, 1982).
7. P.L. 93-344 (July 12, 1974) subjects expenditure deferrals to negation by concurrent resolution, but requires that recisions be approved by joint resolution. On war powers, see note 4.
8. The historical analysis relies upon H. Lee Watson, "Congress Steps Out: A Look at Congressional Control of the Executive," *California Law Review* 63 (1975): 995-1029; Barbara Craig, *The Legislative Veto: Congressional Control of*

Regulation (Boulder, Colo.: Westview Press, 1983), pp. 15-27; Joseph Cooper, "The Legislative Veto: Its Promise and Its Perils," *Public Policy* 7 (1956): 158-165; and the sources cited in note 6. The percentage of veto provisions passed in the 1970s is derived from a table in Craig, *Legislative Veto*, p. 18.

9. 103 S.Ct. at 2792 (1983).

10. James Sundquist, "The Legislative Veto: A Bounced Check," *The Brookings Review* 2 (1983): 13.

11. 103 S.Ct. at 2780-2788 (1983).

12. See "The Supreme Court, 1982 Term," *Harvard Law Review* 97 (1983): 185-193. See also Joseph Cooper, "Congress and the Legislative Veto," *Center for Strategic and International Studies Working Paper*, Washington, D.C., November 30, 1983.

13. See E. Donald Elliott, "INS v. *Chadha*: The Administrative Constitution, the Constitution, and the Legislative Veto," in *The Supreme Court Review*, ed. Philip B. Kurland et al. (Chicago: University of Chicago Press, 1983), pp. 125-176.

14. 103 S.Ct. 2776 (1983), fn. 9. See also U.S. Congress, House, Committee on Foreign Affairs, *U.S. Supreme Court Decision Concerning the Legislative Veto*, 98th Cong. 1st sess., 1983, pp. 63 and 77.

15. Robert Dixon, "The Congressional Veto and Separation of Powers: The Executive on a Leash," *North Carolina Law Review* 56 (1978): 445.

16. See Harold Bruff and Ernest Gellhorn, "Congressional Control of Administrative Regulation: A Study of Legislative Vetoes," *Harvard Law Review* 90 (1977): 1369-1440; Antonin Scalia, "The Legislative Veto: A False Remedy for System Overload," *Regulation* 3 (1979): 19-26; Robert Gilmour, "The Congressional Veto: Shifting the Balance of Administrative Control," *Journal of Policy Analysis and Management* 2 (1982): 13-25; and Craig, *Legislative Veto*, pp. 123-138.

17. Richard Smith and Guy Struve, "Aftershocks of the Fall of the Legislative Veto," *American Bar Association Journal* 69 (1983): 1262; and Cooper and Hurley, "Legislative Veto," pp. 20-21.

18. See Craig, *Legislative Veto*, pp. 45-62; and Robert Gilmour and Barbara Craig, "After the Congressional Veto: Assessing the Alternatives," *Journal of Policy Analysis and Management* 3 (1984): 389.

19. On the role of special interests in the administrative process, see Joseph Cooper and William West, "The Congressional Veto and Administrative Rulemaking," *Political Science Quarterly* 98 (1983): 285-304; and Glenn Robinson, "The FCC: An Essay on Regulatory Watchdogs," *Virginia Law Review* 69 (1978): 189-193, 197-203. See also John Chubb's study of energy policymaking in the 1970s, an area in which numerous vetoes were enacted. He concludes that participation in bureaucratic policymaking was "generally biased in favor of concentrated interests," whereas legislative participation was more pluralistic and competitive. John Chubb, *Interest Groups and the Bureaucracy* (Stanford, Calif.: Stanford University Press, 1983), pp. 258-264.

20. West and Cooper, "Congressional Veto," p. 294. On the virtues of politicians versus experts, see Lloyd Cutler and David Johnson, "Regulation and the Political Process, *Yale Law Journal* 84 (1975): 1395-1419.

21. See Cooper and Hurley, "Legislative Veto," pp. 17-18; Heinz Eulau and Vera McCluggage, "Standing Committees in Legislatures: Three Decades of Research," *Legislative Studies Quarterly* 9 (1984): 219-243; and Arthur Maass,

Congress and the Common Good (New York: Basic Books, 1983), chaps. 5-6.

22. See *National Journal,* October 30, 1982, p. 1858, and May 26, 1984, p. 1036; and *Time,* September 26, 1983, p. 17.

23. For treatment of these cases by the veto's critics, see Bruff and Gellhorn, "Congressional Control of Administrative Regulation," pp. 1382-1385, 1388-1390, 1412-1414; and Craig, *Legislative Veto,* pp. 54-59. In contrast, see West and Cooper, "Congressional Veto," p. 297.

24. Cooper and Hurley, "Legislative Veto," pp. 18, 20-21.

25. For a review of veto provisions enacted before *Chadha* in nonrulemaking areas, see Congressional Research Service, "Studies on the Legislative Veto," *Committee Print Prepared for U.S. House Committee on Rules,* 96th Cong. 1st sess. (Washington, D.C.: Government Printing Office, 1980). See also Louis Fisher, "Congress and the President in the Administrative Process," in *The Illusion of Presidential Government,* ed. Hugh Heclo and Lester Salaman (Boulder, Colo.: Westview Press, 1981), p. 27.

26. Glen Robinson et al., *The Administrative Process* (St. Paul, Minn.: West Publishing Co., 1980), p. 80. See also John Bolton, *The Legislative Veto: Unseparating the Powers* (Washington, D.C.: American Enterprise Institute for Public Policy Research, 1977), pp. 15-24; and Craig, *Legislative Veto,* p. 146.

27. Gilmour and Craig, "After the Congressional Veto," pp. 384-386, 390.

28. Ernest Gellhorn, "The Role of Congress," in *Communications for Tomorrow: Policy Perspectives for the 1980s,* ed. Glen Robinson (New York: Praeger Publishers, 1978), pp. 445-460.

29. Scalia, "False Remedy," p. 26.

30. Smith and Struve, "Aftershocks," p. 1262. See also *Brief of American Bar Association on Amicus Curiae in INS v. Chadha,* Supreme Court of the United States, October term, 1981, pp. 24-25.

31. See Harold Bruff, "Presidential Power and Administrative Rulemaking," *Yale Law Journal* 88 (1979): 456-459. See also Scalia, "False Remedy"; and Gellhorn, "Role of Congress."

32. Allen Schick, "Politics Through Law: Congressional Limitations on Executive Discretion," in *Both Ends of the Avenue: The Presidency, the Executive Branch, and Congress in the 1980s,* ed. Anthony King (Washington, D.C.: American Enterprise Institute for Public Policy Research, 1983), pp. 170-184; and Maass, *Congress and the Common Good,* chaps. 2, 7-8, 10, 12.

33. See Schick, "Politics Through Law," pp. 154-170; Cooper and Hurley, "Legislative Veto," pp. 14-18; and Cooper and Cooper, "Legislative Veto and the Constitution," pp. 508-512. See also Allen Schick, "Congress and the 'Details' of Administration," *Public Administration Review* 36 (1976): 516-528.

34. For statute pages, see Norman J. Ornstein et al., *Vital Statistics on Congress, 1982* (Washington, D.C.: American Enterprise Institute for Public Policy Research, 1982), p. 137. For *Register* pages, see U.S. Congress, Senate, Committee on Judiciary, *Hearings Before the Subcommittee on Administrative Practice and Procedure,* 95th Cong., 2nd sess., 1978, p. 1033.

35. Ronald Penoyer, *Directory of Federal Regulatory Agencies* (St. Louis, Mo.: Center for the Study of American Business, 1981), pp. 13, 93-121.

36. See Craig, *Legislative Veto,* p. 146; Scalia, "False Remedy," pp. 24-26; and Gellhorn, "Role of Congress," p. 460.

37. Ornstein et al., *Vital Statistics on Congress, 1982,* pp. 137, 139.

38. See James Sundquist, *The Decline and Resurgence of Congress* (Washington, D.C.: The Brookings Institution, 1981), pp. 344-367. See also Elliott, "INS v. *Chadha*," pp. 150-156; and Maass, *Congress and the Common Good*, pp. 194-197.

39. See Sundquist, "Bounced Check," pp. 13-16; I. M. Destler, "Dateline Washington: Life After the Veto," *Foreign Policy* (1983): 181-186; and Schick, "Politics Through Law," p. 177.

40. Scalia, "False Remedy," p. 25. See also Gilmour and Craig, "After the Congressional Veto," p. 390.

41. Gilmour and Craig, "After the Congressional Veto," p. 384.

42. Gellhorn, "Role of Congress," p. 459.

43. For a full record of disputes over arms sales, see the foreign policy sections of the *Congressional Quarterly Almanac* for the years 1975 to 1983. Matthew Nimetz, former undersecretary of state, is the administrator quoted. See U.S. Congress, Senate, Committee on Foreign Relations, *Legislative Veto: Arms Export Control Act*, 98th Cong., 1st sess., 1983, p. 37.

44. See *National Journal*, May 19, 1984, pp. 989-993. For further evidence of the importance and benefits of pre-*Chadha* veto provisions in foreign policy areas including human rights, nuclear proliferation, arms sales, and war powers, see Thomas Franck and Edward Weisband, *Foreign Policy by Congress* (New York: Oxford University Press, 1979), pp. 61-115.

45. John Stuart Mill, *On Representative Government* (New York: Macmillan, 1947), chap. 5.

46. Such a mix has been proposed recently in both the House and Senate as a means of subjecting all proposed administrative rules to veto control. See *Congressional Quarterly Weekly Report*, October 29, 1983, p. 2236.

47. See H.R. 1314, 2668, 2867, 2970, 3231, 3932, 3648, 5119, and 5167, 98th Congress. See also S. 979, 861, and 1342, 98th Congress.

48. See Louis Fisher, *One Year After INS v. Chadha: Congressional and Judicial Developments*, Congressional Research Service typed report, June 23, 1984. See also *Congressional Quarterly Weekly Report*, October 29, 1983, p. 2235.

49. See Cooper and Cooper, "Legislative Veto and the Constitution," p. 469, fn. 7. See also Fisher, "Congress and the President in the Administrative Process," pp. 26-29, for a discussion of formal and informal control through committees plus a pre-*Chadha* example of the type of appropriations veto suggested earlier in the text.

50. The mechanism for strengthening informal control that appears to be gaining momentum is prior notification. Such requirements are, in effect, waiting period forms that operate through committees. See *Congressional Quarterly Weekly Report*, October 29, 1983, p. 2236; and March 3, 1984, p. 521. For evidence on sentiment regarding delegations of discretionary authority, see S. 675, 452, and 1545, 98th Congress.

51. See testimony of Deputy Attorney General Edward C. Schmults in Committee on Foreign Affairs, *U.S. Supreme Court Decision Concerning Legislative Veto*, p. 63; and *Congressional Quarterly Weekly Report*, March 17, 1984, p. 612.

52. *Congressional Quarterly Weekly Report*, March 28, 1984, pp. 667-668; May 12, 1984, p. 1090; and June 2, 1984, pp. 1291, 1304-1306.

Part VI

CONGRESS AT WORK:
CLOTURE AND BICAMERALISM

17. CHANGING TIME CONSTRAINTS ON CONGRESS: HISTORICAL PERSPECTIVES ON THE USE OF CLOTURE

Bruce I. Oppenheimer

The congressional process operates under time constraints. As any student in an introductory American government course knows, a bill must pass the House and Senate in identical form within the two-year period that comprises a Congress before it can be sent to the president for his signature. If the two-year period expires before this process is completed, the bill must begin anew in the next Congress regardless of how far it previously had progressed.

Surprisingly, political scientists, with several important exceptions, have not found the exploration of time limitations on the Congress of particular interest. Lewis Froman in his insightful book *The Congressional Process* notes that the legislative process is "lengthy and time-consuming with many opportunities for delay." [1] James Sundquist analyzes legislative decision-making through the Eisenhower, Kennedy, and Johnson years, and his case studies provide numerous examples of where time simply ran out before all the requisite majorities could be built.[2] And Representative Richard Bolling (D-Mo.) argues that pushing the 1957 civil rights bill early in the 85th Congress was crucial to its eventual success. The timing made opponents' delaying tactics less likely to succeed.[3]

All three studies were written in the 1960s when the constraints on Congress were less severe than they are now. The two-year term remains the same, but the press of time is greater. With more committee hearings, roll call votes, and complex legislative issues, Congress now operates year round. Not only does a bill require the support of a majority at each decision point through the legislative process in order to "beat the clock," but it also must compete with other bills for a place—for time—on the various decisionmaking agendas. Congress rarely has the luxury it once possessed of staying in session an extra week or month to finish important legislation. Now it is common for an old Congress to end just in time for the new one to begin.

The author would like to thank Joseph Cooper and Roger Davidson for their advice and assistance and the Dirksen Congressional Leadership Research Center and the University of Houston Center for Public Policy for supporting this research.

As I will demonstrate in this chapter, Congress is in an environment where time pressures critically affect the behavior of its members, the work of its leaders, and the rules and procedures under which it operates. Understanding the time constraints on the operation of the institution is crucial for a better understanding of how Congress works today and why it has changed. To illustrate the growing importance of time, I have selected Senate Rule 22, the cloture rule, as the prime focus of analysis.

There are good reasons for choosing the cloture rule for particular attention. First, as a time management tool cloture provides a procedure for ending debate in an organization where the right of unlimited debate was once the norm. Thus, one might expect its application to be sensitive to institutional time pressures. Second, the frequency of efforts to invoke cloture and the success of those efforts have considerably increased since 1961. By examining changes in time constraints on Congress, we will be able to evaluate the accuracy of commonly held explanations for why cloture is used more frequently. And finally, the amendment of Rule 22 in 1975—whereby three-fifths of the Senate membership, as opposed to two-thirds of those present and voting, was required to invoke cloture—gives us an opportunity to consider the effects of time problems on the Senate's decision to liberalize its cloture rule after numerous efforts to do so had failed. Before cloture and its uses are analyzed, some observations about time constraints on Congress need to be made.

The History of Time Constraints

Congress in the late twentieth century is under more severe time constraints than at any point in its history. Time difficulties are not totally new to the institution, however. Pressures in the political and social environment have periodically forced Congress to deal with problems of time. For example, in the early part of the nineteenth century most members of Congress were not full-time politicians. In a largely agrarian society, they could not afford to stay in Washington for long stretches of time. Crops needed planting and harvesting. Small businesses required regular attention. And transportation to and from their homes and Washington was slow and arduous. Moreover, Washington was far from a pleasant place to reside.[4] As the workload of the national government gradually increased, the press to complete congressional business expeditiously so that members could return to their regular vocations grew. This time pressure clearly contributed to the development and reliance on a committee system.[5]

During the 1870s and 1880s, Congress again faced a time and workload problem. In the House of Representatives the legislative calendar became quite crowded, but the leadership lacked the authority to move important legislation ahead of minor bills. This played into the hands of obstructionists who could consume floor time on minor bills as members became anxious to return home. Decisions about what legislation would be considered was often made by the Appropriations Committee chairman because that committee's spending bills were privileged. Eventually, under the leadership of Speaker Thomas Reed (R-Maine), the Speaker was given considerable control over scheduling floor proceedings in response to the ability of the minority to obstruct the House.[6]

In reaction to a slightly different type of time constraint problem, the Senate in 1917 enacted a substitute amendment to Rule 22 that established the first procedure for limiting debate—the cloture resolution. During the lame duck session of the 64th Congress (1915-1917), a group of 12 progressives conducted a 23-day filibuster on President Woodrow Wilson's bill to arm merchant ships. With the end of the Congress at hand, the opponents were able to run out the clock to defeat the bill. When the new Congress convened, the first order of business of the Senate was the adoption of a resolution providing for cloture on a spending measure if it received the support of two-thirds of those present and voting.

These instances suggest that time constraints may result from a variety of causes either internal or external to the institution. When the time constraints became significant, the House and Senate often adjusted to this organizational stress.

To a greater or lesser degree, every Congress faces time pressures that provide members who wish to defeat a measure with opportunities for obstruction or delay. These time constraints are likely to be the greatest at particular periods during a normal Congress. I would suggest the following:

1. The later in a Congress it is, the more important time becomes. Early in a Congress, time exists to overcome obstacles and the means to do so may allow considerable choice. Late in a Congress, choices are limited because time is not available. Moreover, those presenting the obstacle know their advantage and can extract a higher price for its removal.

2. The later in a session of a Congress or the closer to a major recess it is, the more important time becomes. Any time a break is forthcoming, there is a wish to finish up as much pending business as possible. Sponsors of legislation know that events can occur during break periods that may displace their bills on the agenda when Congress returns. For example, a bill that reaches the floor before a break may pass quite quickly and move on, but if it is delayed then, it may languish once Congress returns. Those placing obstacles in the path of legislation possess the upper hand in bargaining. Members wishing to complete other business are not likely to tolerate a given piece of legislation tying up the proceedings for very long.

3. When a particularly urgent legislative issue needs to be addressed, time becomes more crucial. This can lead to a variety of machinations, but the bargaining advantage again tends to rest with the opponents of congressional action.

By comparison, time considerations are normally less vital early in a Congress, early in a session, immediately following a recess, and with important but not urgent issues. The paradoxical feature of time constraints is that they present the need to complete work quickly yet play into the hands of those who wish for delay or defeat.

The Growth of Time Constraints

Although every Congress is likely to find it has certain periods when time constraints are severe and we can point to periods when Congress was faced with time problems resulting from internal and external environmental conditions, Congress now finds itself in an era when it is working under time constraints nearly all the time. Put quite simply, the workload of Congress since the early 1960s has grown to such an extent that, with rare exceptions, it consumes the entire two-year cycle of a Congress and often key work, such as the passage of appropriations bills, remains incomplete at the end.

From the 72nd Congress (1931-1933) through much of the 76th Congress, second session (1939), no session of Congress from start to finish ran more than eight months; they averaged about six months. Until World War II was in full swing in Europe, Congress normally completed business no later than June of an election year. In the 1950s the sessions lengthened to an average of 7 months, in the 1960s to 10 months, and in the 1970s to 11 months. With the exception of the 98th Congress, first session, they have remained at that level.[7] The Christmas and New Year holidays consume nearly a month betweeen the end of the first session and the beginning of the second session, so Congress is operating year round.

True, it is not formally in session all of this time. Recesses have become more clearly fixed in the congressional schedule. And the total number of days in session has not increased as dramatically as the overall length of the Congresses, going from about 250 days in the House and 275 in the Senate on average in the 1950s to 325 in the House and 350 in the Senate in the 1960s and 1970s.[8] But the demand for these regularized recesses in a re-election-oriented legislature may have actually increased, thus contributing to the consumption of available time.

One additional indicator of the increased length of Congresses is the number of pages in the *Congressional Record.* (See Table 17-1.) Although not an exact index of the time consumed by a Congress, it does give some sense of the tremendous growth of floor activity.[9] The printing of the *Record,* always considered a major publication feat, has become a truly incredible effort since the 1960s.

The growing size of the *Congressional Record* mirrors other indicators of a more time-constrained institution: more committee and subcommittee meetings, more recorded votes, and more bills under consideration.[10] The work demands and time pressures on Congress have multiplied in recent decades. In addition, Congress has continued to add to its work responsibil-

Table 17-1   Pages in the *Congressional Record,* 72nd-97th Congresses

Congress	Pages	Congress	Pages
72nd (1931-1932)	21,444	85th (1957-1958)	36,487
73rd (1933-1934)	18,936	86th (1959-1960)	38,873
74th (1935-1936)	25,709	87th (1961-1962)	45,087
75th (1937-1938)	21,411	88th (1963-1964)	49,730
76th (1939-1940)	26,423	89th (1965-1966)	57,548
77th (1941-1942)	19,811	90th (1967-1968)	68,755
78th (1943-1944)	20,804	91st (1969-1970)	85,803
79th (1945-1946)	23,326	92nd (1971-1972)	85,011
80th (1947-1948)	22,032	93rd (1973-1974)	85,384
81st (1949-1950)	30,866	94th (1975-1976)	77,650
82nd (1951-1952)	23,529	95th (1977-1978)	78,364
83rd (1953-1954)	27,278	96th (1979-1980)	66,900
84th (1955-1956)	28,368	97th (1980-1981)	52,533

NOTE: Pages for index and extension of remarks are excluded.

ities. The congressional budget process, implemented in 1975, increased the workload. In addition to 13 or more appropriations bills, any tax bills, and debt ceiling increases, the House and Senate must use substantial committee and floor time to write and enact two budget resolutions and a reconciliation bill each year. And there is little to indicate that the budget process has speeded Congress's work on appropriations.

In January 1979, the Senate debated changes in its rules to limit the amount of time available for debate once cloture was invoked. At that time several senators stressed the changing time constraints on the Senate. Edmund Muskie (D-Maine), a 20-year veteran of the Senate, observed how conditions had changed:

> There is just so much time in the calendar year. We have now reached the bottom of time. There is no more left. I have been here when the Senate was in session on New Year's Eve, on New Year's Eve with the work of the Senate uncompleted. The prospect of reaching the end of a calendar year with important work which cannot then be completed before the year is over is frightening.[11]

What frightened Senator Muskie and others so much was the realization that the rules, norms, and procedures of the Senate had been seriously disrupted by the pressures of time. It was certainly no accident that the debate centered on further modifications of Rule 22; in a time-constrained environment, cloture has taken on new significance. An examination of the changing use of the cloture rule can tell us much about the effects of time constraints on Congress.

The Cloture Rule

The most striking feature about cloture has been the change in the frequency of its use. As the data in Table 17-2 indicate, cloture was rarely used before the 1960s. Moreover, a careful examination of the cloture votes prior to 1961 shows how limited the circumstances were in which these efforts to cut off debate were made. Astute senators were even unaware, at times, of how the cloture rule worked. During the debate surrounding the filing of a cloture petition on the 1922 tariff bill, discussion centered on how cloture was implemented. Senate Minority Leader Oscar W. Underwood (D-Ala.), renowned for his skillful use of rules and procedures, admitted during discussion with a colleague about the floor procedure concerning amendments once cloture was invoked, "I have not read the rule for some time." [12] In fact, it had been a year and a half since the previous cloture vote, and it would be three and a half years until the next one. As Patty D. Renfrow notes, cloture votes between 1917 and 1937 "were infrequent, and they were waged against a diffuse set of issues." [13] Cloture votes were taken on issues ranging in importance from the acquisition of land for governmental buildings in the District of Columbia to the Versailles Treaty. By comparison, from 1938

Table 17-2   Use of Success of Cloture, 66th-97th Congresses

Congresses	Cloture Invoked	Cloture Defeated	Total Cloture Votes
66th-71st (1919-1931)	4	6	10
72nd-76th (1931-1940)	0	3	3
77th-81st (1941-1950)	0	8	8
82nd-86th (1951-1960)	0	2	2
87th-91st (1961-1970)	4	22	26
92nd-Early 94th* (1971-1975)	16	38	54
94th-97th (1975-1980)	35	53	88

* The 94th Congress is split at the point in 1975 when the Senate changed Rule 22 to allow three-fifths of the Senate, instead of two-thirds of those present and voting, to invoke cloture. Except for the period from 1949 to 1958 when two-thirds of the Senate was required for cloture, the two-thirds present and voting was generally required for cloture from 1919 until the change in 1975.

until the 1970s, cloture votes were taken almost exclusively on civil rights or related issues, although they remained infrequent, Renfrow finds.

In this and other studies of cloture, scholars have tended to concentrate on the causes and consequences of the increase in cloture votes in the late 1960s and 1970s. Their findings can be summarized as follows. First, Senate liberals began to use the filibuster to stop conservative legislation.[14] Prior to the 1962 vote on the Comsat bill, the filibuster was the preserve of conservatives, particularly Southern Democrats. Second, by this time the norms of the Senate had broken down.. Members were no longer restrained in their use of the filibuster, and it became a popular way to derail legislation on all kinds of issues. Third, in an effort to cut off debate, the leadership began to try multiple cloture votes. Thus, the Senate, Renfrow contends, "was more inclined to spend time to acquire the necessary votes in favor of cloture in order to defeat filibusters" rather than yield to those conducting the filibuster.[15] Finally, it is argued that the increased use of the filibuster made it a less effective weapon. Rule 22 was changed in reaction to the overuse of filibusters. Cloture was then invoked more frequently.

Unfortunately, these explanations are not totally satisfactory and in some cases are misleading if not incorrect. Renfrow and other scholars have not always asked the best questions about changes in the use of cloture, and therefore the conclusions they have reached have been incomplete. Southern Democrats were not the only ones to engage in filibusters prior to 1962, nor did they always oppose cloture efforts.

The tendency to equate filibusters and cloture votes is part of the error. During the 1938-1961 period, when civil rights dominated the cloture votes, there were other filibusters by northerners on which no cloture votes were taken. These include at least two famous ones: the attempt by Glen Taylor (D-Idaho) to stop the override of President Harry S. Truman's veto of the Taft-Hartley bill in 1947 and the filibuster of the Tidelands oil bill by Wayne Morse (I-Ore.) in 1953. True, Taylor, Morse, and their allies disclaimed any intent of carrying on what Morse labeled "the ultimate filibuster—a filibuster which seeks to prevent any vote from ever occurring on a measure."[16] In addition, prior to 1938 few southerners participated in filibuster efforts except when it was part of a Democratic party position in the Senate. Instead, they often voted for cloture, signed cloture petitions, and even favored those petitions.

The belief that southern opposition to cloture is part of a historical tradition is a myth probably dating back to the 1890s when southerners filibustered the Force bill that provided for the imposition of federal troops in the South to supervise elections. This resulted in an unsuccessful effort to pass a Senate cloture rule. At various times, appeals were made to southerners based on recollections of the Force bill debate. During the 1925 debate on approval of U.S. participation in the World Court, Senator James Reed (D-Mo.) pleaded: ". . . I am looking at some southern Senators now whose very liberties were preserved once by freedom of debate in the Senate."[17] His appeal had little effect: senators representing the 11 states of the Confederacy voted 18 to 4 in favor of cloture.

More importantly, cloture votes increased significantly in the 1960s and 1970s, even when those involving filibusters by liberals are not counted. Certainly the fact that liberals as well as conservatives more freely engaged in filibusters is part of the reason for the growth in cloture votes, but it is not a very satisfactory explanation.

Much the same is true for the circuitous argument that filibusters increased because the norms of the Senate broke down. The evidence given for the breakdown in Senate norms often includes the increase in filibusters. This may be correct, but it is a bit of a truism. What we would really like to know is why senators decided to use the filibuster more often. The breakdown in Senate norms may have been a precondition for more filibusters, but that does not explain why senators selected this behavior (that is, filibustering and the use of cloture votes).

It is correct that the increased number of cloture votes as presented in Table 17-2 is more dramatic because of the more frequent use in recent years of multiple cloture votes. When we look at issues on which cloture votes occurred (see Table 17-3), the change is more modest, but it is still sizable. The question remains: Does the greater frequency of filibusters alone explain the move to multiple efforts to invoke cloture. And if so, has the Senate leadership resorted to other tactics to stem this tide?

Finally, if one is to argue that filibusters have become less effective weapons than they were prior to the 1970s (based on the greater success rate of cloture votes and the change in the cloture rule), how then does one explain the increase in the use of filibusters and cloture? The figures on cloture vote success seemingly would discourage filibusters. Are we to assume that senators are irrational in their use of the filibuster? Or are the conclusions inaccurate or incomplete?

The Other Side of the Coin

Instead of asking why the use of cloture and the number of filibusters have increased in recent decades, we may find it more informative to ask why cloture was used so rarely for nearly a half century. After all, before 1961 only 23 cloture votes were taken.

The answer to this reformulated question is both straightforward and revealing. There were few cloture votes because time was a less important factor in the legislative process than it is today. Without severe time pressures, there was no great need to limit debate. And those who engaged in filibusters could rarely hold the process hostage. In turn, the incentives for filibusters were fewer. Without time pressures, the Senate in many situations could wait out a filibuster by a single or even a dozen or so members. Therefore, the filibuster became a tactic that could be successful only on those occasions when the Senate faced time constraints or on major issues on which

Table 17-3 Issues on Which Cloture Votes Were Taken, 66th-97th Congresses

Congresses	Issues on Which Cloture Was Successful in Ending Debate	Issues on Which Cloture Vote(s) Did Not End ·Debate	Total Issues on Which Cloture Vote(s) Occurred
66th-71st (1919-1931)	4	6	10
72nd-76th (1931-1940)	0	2	2
77th-81st (1941-1950)	0	6	6
82nd-86th (1951-1960)	0	2	2
87th-91st (1961-1970)	4	12	16
92nd-Early 94th* (1971-1975)	15	9	24
94th-97th (1975-1980)	27	11	38

* As in Table 17-2, the splitting of the 94th Congress is done to separate cloture votes before and after the change from two-thirds present and voting to three-fifths of the membership. Issues are defined by the same legislation within the same Congress.

a sizable number of its members were intensely committed (such as civil rights).

A careful examination of cloture votes between 1917, when the cloture rule was adopted, and 1937 reveals the importance of time constraints to filibuster efforts. Of the 11 cloture votes taken, seven took place during lame duck sessions in January and February following an election. With a new Congress scheduled to begin in early March, time pressures were strong. An eighth cloture vote occurred late in the second session of the 69th Congress. The bill was a relatively minor one on migratory-bird refuges although states rights issues were involved. Numerous other bills were discussed at length during the 10 days that the bird refuge bill was the pending order of business. The cloture vote appears to have been the best way to free the Senate to consider far more critical legislation. Senators were clearly more concerned with other business than with the fate of migratory birds. Thus, 8 of the 11 cloture votes came when time constraints were significant.

In the cases of the three other cloture votes, the Senate voted for cloture, after considerable debate, on two: the Versailles Treaty and the World Court.

Only on the tariff bill of 1922 was there neither time pressure nor a successful cloture vote. The bill, H.R. 7456, which had already passed the House, was before the Senate for 10 weeks before a cloture petition was filed. There were more than 2,000 amendments pending to the bill, and the Democratic leadership charged that only amendments of the majority party had been considered. When asked by Senator Irvine Lenroot (R-Wis.) ". . . when, in his judgment, the bill will pass the Senate if there be no limitation on debate," Minority Leader Underwood responded:

> I will say to the Senator candidly—that I do not know, but I should be very much delighted if we come to a final vote by August. I do not want to stay here. I am not in favor of the bill—I hope it can be defeated—but I realize under our system of parliamentary government that the majority party have a right to enact their laws and submit them to the country. . . . I can only say that I have earnestly hoped that there might be no undue delay in the matter, and I know that I have not indulged in any undue delay.[18]

Cloture was defeated on a vote that was largely along party lines. Debate continued through July and most of August 1922 in an unair-conditioned Senate chamber. The House, which had adjourned, returned on August 18. The Senate passed the bill on August 19. A conference was organized, and the Senate took up a soldiers' compensation bill that had been held up since June 12. The tariff bill marathon was over.

The Senate was rarely under time pressure in the early 1920s. Usually it could manage to extend a session for a day, a week, a month, or even more to finish important business. Hence, the need for a cloture vote to shut off debate was infrequent. And the "ultimate filibuster" (Morse's phrase) was normally not an effective tactic either. The workload, far more manageable than today, enabled the Senate to debate a bill at great length. In the same Congress that endured the Washington summer while debating the tariff bill, the Senate had already spent nearly three months on a tax bill and two months on the four-power treaty. True, proponents of the measures, such as Senator Frank Kellogg (R-Mich.), complained about "delays and delays and delays" on the part of Democratic senators, but enough time was available to be generous with bill opponents.[19] In the end, majorities normally prevailed.

Following the formation of the conservative coalition in the late 1930s and until the early 1960s, Congress remained relatively free of severe time constraints. Except the years during World War II, when it was necessary for Congress to formally stay in session continuously, the sessions grew gradually longer. Nevertheless, the press of business did not as yet create serious time binds. And cloture was used no more frequently from 1938 through 1960 than it had been in the first 20 years of the rule.[20] Only 12 cloture votes were taken. However, some features of these votes significantly differed from those of the 1917-1937 period. First, in no case did the Senate succeed in invoking cloture. Second, the cloture votes were largely limited to civil rights legislation. Nine of the votes dealt with antilynching, antipoll tax, or fair employment legislation. Two of the other three cloture votes were not in reaction to true needs to end debate.[21] Third, only three of the twelve votes took place under the time pressure of lame duck or late session activities.

These differences are important because they indicate that even when time constraints were not severe the filibuster was used successfully to defeat legislation in the Senate. But at least a sizable minority in the Senate had to find the issue significant enough to engage in a filibuster. (In fact, on five of the civil rights cloture votes, more senators opposed cloture than voted for it.) To southern senators, civil rights bills met that criterion. Thus, they formed a large enough nucleus to transform the Senate environment from one with few or no time constraints to one with severe time pressures. They were sufficient in number and intensity that, with the support of others who opposed cloture on general principles, their threat to keep the Senate at a standstill was a believable one.[22]

The differences I have described in the cloture votes during these two periods should not distract us from the basic similarity between them. In both periods, cloture votes were few because the filibuster was still not a feasible tactic except in selected circumstances.

Why did the 1938-1960 period not contain cloture votes similar to those between 1917 and 1937, a time when periodic time pressures existed? On this some reasonable speculation is available. During most of the latter period there were few conservative initiatives, and often those would be blocked elsewhere in the process by Northern Democrats or by Presidents Roosevelt and Truman. Moreover, as the debates during the Morse and Taylor filibusters demonstrate, many liberals were reluctant to use filibusters because they feared that they would give the filibusters on civil rights bills greater legitimacy. But perhaps most importantly, those who engaged in civil rights filibusters may well have deemed it wise to reserve them for that issue. Excessive use of the tactic on lesser legislation during time-constrained periods at the end of Congress might fuel the fire of those who sought to ease the cloture requirements.

In discussing why restrictions on debate had not been necessary in the Senate, Senator Patrick Moynihan (D-N.Y.) referred to the early days of Franklin Roosevelt's first term:

> Why has that period recalled by some as the most constructive and by others as the most destructive moment in our history become known as "the 100 days"? Because that is how long Congress was in session when Roosevelt was first here. They came in March and went home in June. The whole structure of government was different when, in 100 days, we could enact the New Deal and go home in June. That Senate could leave the arrangements for extended debate to the most random kind of procedure. There was nobody, for practical purposes, in the history of the U.S. Senate who had ever run out of time.

I would like to repeat that: For practical purposes, in the 150 years up until that time, no Senator had ever run out of time. They always adjourned with another 2 or 3, or 4, 5, 6, or 7 months left in the calendar year, with their work done.

In such a setting, unrestricted debate was not only an honorable provision, but a practical one. If someone wanted to be heard longer on a subject that he cared about, as Senators should, he could say, "Let's not go home; it is June 15, we can stay here until June 17, and you can finish hearing me." [23]

For much of the period until the 1960s, conditions had changed incrementally. But as those increments continued to lengthen Congresses, the Senate began to lose flexibility. And with major increases in the Senate workload in the 1960s and 1970s, the luxury of unlimited debate became something the Senate found more difficult to afford. Greater time constraints created a different incentive structure. The filibuster strategy in a highly time-constrained environment became viable for those wishing to delay, defeat, or bargain for alterations in legislation. With the Senate increasingly under time pressure, a filibuster or the threat of one could be usefully employed at any time in a Congress—not just at the end. A few senators or even a single one could hold the Senate hostage. A sizable minority of the Senate was no longer necessary to make the threat credible. Accordingly, an issue that was of intense interest to only one senator could present the potential for a filibuster. The group pressures formerly needed to sustain or restrict the use of filibusters were lacking. In sum, any filibuster could be an "ultimate filibuster" preventing "any vote from ever occurring on a measure."

Cloture Votes in the 1960s

The changes that made the filibuster a more effective weapon did not come about immediately. Time constraints on Congress did not suddenly increase. And senators did not recognize all at once that conditions were conducive for the filibuster. But the 87th Congress (1961-1962) does present a watershed or threshold when time pressures began to be sufficient to encourage more filibusters. After a period of consolidation during the Eisenhower presidency, the Kennedy administration submitted an activist legislative agenda to Congress.

The 87th Congress marked the point at which the Senate began to be in session regularly for more than 300 days. (In fact, it met during a nine-month period in each session.) And it was also the Congress in which the number of pages in the *Congressional Record* began a sizable climb upward, increasing by more than 6,000 pages from the 86th Congress. (See Table 17-1.) By the last Congress of the 1960s, the 91st, which met on 384 days over a 22-month period, the page total leveled off at its high of nearly 86,000 pages.

Correspondingly, it is within the 87th Congress that the number of cloture votes began to rise. After only two cloture votes in the five preceding Congresses, there were four in the 87th Congress and a total of 26 over the five Congresses of the 1961-1970 period, more than in the entire previous history of cloture.

Although civil rights was still the dominant issue area and most cloture votes were on major issues, the subject area of cloture votes did broaden. Included among the 26 votes were three on a labor issue (the repeal of Section 14b of the Taft-Hartley bill); two each on the supersonic transport and on the abolishment of the Electoral College; and one each on Comsat, a legislative reapportionment constitutional amendment, and the nomination of Abe Fortas to be chief justice of the United States. In addition, at various times five cloture votes were taken on efforts to amend Rule 22. Southern Democrats remained the most frequent users of the filibuster, but they were not the only ones. Moreover, some Southern Democrats actually began to vote for cloture.

If one examines Table 17-3, it may not be obvious at first that senators who chose to filibuster in the 87th through 91st Congresses met with the success of their predecessors in the 66th through 86th. On the 16 issues that comprised the 26 cloture votes between 1961 and 1970, cloture was invoked on four, which was four more than in the preceding 30 years. What is important, however, is that on 12 issues cloture was not invoked—also more than in the preceding 30 years. In a more time-constrained environment, the success rate of cloture improved, but due to the growing incentives to filibuster the number of successful filibusters also increased.

The Senate Responds

The response of the Senate leadership to the increase in filibusters took several forms. Majority Leader Mike Mansfield (D-Mont.), with the strong insistence of President Lyndon B. Johnson, pressed the sizable minority engaged in filibusters on some bills—especially key civil rights legislation such as the Civil Rights Act of 1964 and the Voting Rights Act of 1965—to the limit. Mansfield placed other business on hold until enough votes could be garnered for cloture after the opponents and their tacit supporters were exhausted and the necessary compromises were made. But this strategy, which in the case of the 1964 bill involved round-the-clock sessions over much of a 57-day period, proved impractical as a routine response. It was difficult to organize and unpopular with senators, who preferred to sleep in places other than the Senate cloakroom. Moreover, such a response used enormous amounts of time and delayed the entire Senate agenda at a point when time was becoming a luxury commodity.

Using multiple cloture votes was a second strategy. For the leadership to yield to those filibustering after a single vote only strengthened the incentives to filibuster. Sometimes close together and at other times with sizable gaps, the majority party leadership often made at least two cloture efforts and in one case held votes on four cloture resolutions.[24] Again, timing and compromises led to the switching of some votes. On the whole, however, multiple cloture votes gave the leadership a way of showing bill sponsors the seriousness of its efforts.

A third albeit a somewhat later response to the increased number of filibusters was the track system. Prior to implementation of the track system, the Senate was confined to considering a single piece of legislation on the floor. A filibuster delayed not only the bill being debated but all other legislation awaiting floor consideration. Following the defeat of a cloture motion on an equal jobs opportunity bill in 1972, Majority Leader Mansfield suggested that the Senate spend the first part of each day on the equal employment bill and then move on to other legislation.

In a time-constrained environment, this two-track procedure removes some of the pressure filibusters create. It is not always successful, however, because it requires that the leadership gain unanimous consent of the Senate.[25] Some senators have criticized the leadership for using the two-track system because they believe it makes it easier to sustain a filibuster and relieves the pressure on senators to vote for cloture.

The final response to the increase in filibusters was the renewal of efforts to make cloture easier by changing Rule 22. The rule was eventually changed in 1975, but the pressure and the support for altering it grew during the 1960s. As presiding officer of the Senate, Vice President Hubert Humphrey moved the Senate closer to a position whereby debate over a change in its rules could be ended by a majority vote.

The question rested on an interpretation of whether the Senate was a continuing body because two-thirds of its membership carried over from one Congress to another, or whether the Senate began anew with the start of each Congress. If it was a continuing body, any change in rules would be subject to existing rules, including the cloture provisions. But under the latter interpretation, the Senate's rules would not carry over from Congress to Congress; accordingly, a majority vote could cut off debate on the adoption of a set of Senate rules at the start of a new Congress.

In 1957 Vice President Richard Nixon had suggested that a Senate majority could adopt its own rules, but no vote was ever taken on the Nixon opinion. And in 1963 Vice President Johnson put the question of the Senate's ability to change its rules before the Senate but did so in such a way that the question itself was subject to debate and the two-thirds cloture requirement. Vice President Humphrey put a similar question before the Senate in 1967 when a point of order was raised against a motion by Senator George McGovern (D-S.D.).

McGovern's motion combined the adoption of new rules with an end to debate on their adoption by majority vote. Cloture reformers under these circumstances simply needed to muster a majority to table the point order (that is, a motion not subject to debate). The motion to table, however, was defeated 37-61. Then at the start of the 91st Congress in January 1969, Humphrey, as outgoing vice president, ruled that a majority of the Senate had the right to end debate on a change in Senate rules. The Senate reversed the ruling, but the margin was narrowed to 45-53.

In addition to rulings from the chair, Senate support for invoking cloture on resolutions to amend Rule 22 grew. At the start of the 92nd Congress four cloture votes were attempted. The last of them obtained a 55-39 majority— still short of the two-thirds requirement.

The Filibuster Gets Out of Hand

Despite the serious time and workload problems facing the Senate in the early 1970s, Rule 22 remained unchanged. As these conditions became more acute, the filibuster became an even more attractive weapon for senators wishing to defeat legislation. The Senate took 10 cloture votes each year from 1971 to 1973. In 1974 the number of cloture votes jumped to 21, corresponding to filibusters on 11 different issues. From the beginning of the 92nd Congress in 1971 until Rule 22 was changed in 1975, there were 54 cloture votes, nearly as many as in the previous 55 years combined. The filibuster had become a free-for-all, and Rule 22 was not sufficient to discourage it. The range of issues on which filibusters took place broadened to include nearly every policy area. And during the Nixon and Ford presidencies, many of the filibusters were by Northern Democrats who after 1971 recanted their previous criticism of Rule 22.[26] Conversely, some Southern Democrats found themselves voting for cloture for the first time in careers that spanned more than two decades. Although there was greater success in invoking cloture, often it was achieved only after substantive concessions were made to those filibustering.

The task of managing Senate business became more difficult if not impossible for the leadership. In reaction to the pressures of time and the use of the filibuster, Senate leaders often resorted to filing cloture petitions as soon as there was even the slightest threat of a filibuster. Because of the two-day delay after a petition is filed before a vote can be taken, the leadership frequently filed a second petition even before the first cloture vote. Ironically, one effect of the need to file immediately for cloture was that debate on a bill was sometimes limited to a greater extent when a filibuster was threatened than it would have been if there were no filibuster. In between cloture votes other legislation was often considered.

By the beginning of the 94th Congress (1975-1976), it became clear to many senators that Rule 22 would have to be revised if the Senate was to operate effectively once again. Senators James Pearson (R-Kan.) and Walter Mondale (D-Minn.) led the fight to change the rule. In their proposal, S.Res. 4, cloture would require the support of three-fifths of those senators present and voting instead of two-thirds. Vice President Nelson Rockefeller gave the reform position a boost when he ruled that a majority of the Senate could end debate on S.Res. 4. And unlike the 1969 ruling by Humphrey, Rockefeller's ruling was sustained when appealed. The vote was 51-42.[27]

Bargaining then began between the reformers and conservatives, led by Senator Russell Long (D-La.), who recognized the need for change in the cloture requirements but preferred more modest revisions. Long proposed that cloture require three-fifths of the Senate (60 members) instead of three-fifths of those present and voting, that the change be in effect only for the 94th Congress, and that his compromise be offered only if two-thirds voted to invoke cloture. In return, Long agreed to help rally other senators behind the change. With the agreement reached, the filibuster against the rule change, led by Senator James Allen (D-Ala.), was ended with two identical cloture votes of 73-21. (The first was needed to proceed to consideration of S.Res. 4 and the second to end debate on it.) On each of these, seven Democrats from the states that comprised the Confederacy supported cloture.

To the surprise of its critics, Rule 22 as revised did make it easier to invoke cloture. The Senate has found it less difficult to satisfy the 60-vote requirement for cloture than the earlier requirement of two-thirds of those present and voting. The success rate on cloture votes (Table 17-2) and especially on cloture issues (Table 17-3) has improved.

Despite the greater success of cloture after 1975, the incentive to filibuster did not decline markedly. Between the change in Rule 22 (which subsequently became effective not only for the 94th Congress but for future Congresses) and 1982, there was an average of 11 cloture votes involving an average of nearly five legislative issues each year. Those who wished to use the filibuster found another means for delay with Rule 22—the post-cloture filibuster. Senate rules allow for consideration of any germane amendments that are offered prior to cloture. By presenting numerous amendments prior to cloture, demanding their consideration after cloture is invoked, and using other dilatory tactics, senators are able to continue their filibusters even after cloture is invoked.

Like the filibuster, the post-cloture filibuster has been an available tactic since the establishment of the cloture procedure in 1917. However, prior to 1975 it was rarely employed. Post-cloture filibusters are an option only when cloture has already been invoked and only when time for legislative business is short. Both conditions were most unusual prior to the 1970s. Moreover, Walter Oleszek contends that members believed post-cloture delays "violated the spirit of fair play." [28] But if Oleszek is correct, fair play considerations were suspended once the preconditions for a post-cloture filibuster—time constraints and the invoking of cloture—became frequent.

Senator Allen was the first to take full advantage of the post-cloture filibuster, which was used on three occasions in 1976 and once in 1977. Before adjournment for the 1976 election, his post-cloture filibuster nearly defeated a bill requiring the courts to pay attorneys' fees for the winning side in civil rights lawsuits.[29] Only three weeks before, Allen's post-cloture filibuster resulted in the weakening of an antitrust enforcement bill.[30]

A year later, liberal Democratic senators Howard Metzenbaum (Ohio) and James Abourezk (S.D.) led a post-cloture filibuster of a natural gas deregulation bill. More than 500 amendments were pending to the bill when cloture was invoked on September 26. By demanding that amendments be read, asking for roll call votes on amendments, and requesting quorum calls, Metzenbaum and Abourezk were able to hold the Senate hostage for a week. On October 3, after all-night sessions failed to break their resolve, Majority Leader Robert Byrd (D-W.Va.), in cooperation with the Senate's presiding officer, Vice President Walter Mondale, began calling up the amendments and having them ruled out of order as dilatory. The post-cloture effort was defeated, but Byrd was severely criticized as being dictatorial.[31]

In reaction to post-cloture filibusters, the Senate again amended Rule 22 in February 1979, early in the 97th Congress. The change places a 100-hour cap on Senate action after cloture (including procedural motions and votes). It also limits each senator to calling up not more than two amendments until every other senator has been given the chance to do the same.

Despite this reform, post-cloture filibusters still menace the Senate. In a time-constrained environment, the possibility that the Senate will be kept from voting on a bill for 100 hours is no small matter. The threat of a post-cloture filibuster is serious. At 10 hours a day, it can consume 10 days of floor activity. And should the leadership seek to use all-night sessions to bludgeon those conducting the post-cloture filibuster, along with the rest of the Senate, it would still take more than four exhausting days.

At the end of the lame duck session of the 97th Congress, North Carolina Republicans Jesse Helms and John East filibustered a gasoline tax bill. Peer pressure proved insufficient to restrain them from using the full prerogatives the rules allow. Overwhelming cloture votes of 89-5, 87-8, and 81-5 on the bill and the conference report, as well as verbal attacks from weary Senate colleagues, did little to convince Helms and East that their efforts were hopeless. Upon adopting the conference report, the Senate adjourned on December 23. But it was hardly in a holiday spirit.

During the 98th Congress, efforts to limit the use of filibusters continued. In response to a request from Majority Leader Howard Baker (R-Tenn.), former senators James Pearson (R-Kan.) and Abraham Ribicoff (D-Conn.) completed a year-long study of Senate operations. They recommended, among other things, that debate on a motion to consider legislation be limited to one hour (under existing rules, a motion to consider legislation can be filibustered), that senators be allowed to offer only two amendments after cloture is invoked, and that only a single vote be allowed on an amendment after cloture.[32] But Rule 22 was not changed during the 98th Congress, perhaps because, for a variety of reasons including the stalemate of split party control, it was less time constrained than any recent Congress or because of other controversial items in the Pearson-Ribicoff recommendations.

It is doubtful that the shorter 98th Congress marks the beginning of a new congressional era in which time problems are reduced. Outgoing Senate majority leader Baker's recommendations for a return to the bygone days when service in the Congress was not a member's prime occupation and sessions lasted six months have not received serious consideration. It may be impossible and not entirely desirable to turn the clock back more than 50 years in terms of congressional operations. Nevertheless, Baker's pleas highlight the time problem. The Senate finds itself in an organizational environment where the incentives of obstructionists of every political persuasion to filibuster—before and after cloture—remain strong.

Other Effects of Time Constraints

An understanding of the importance of time in the legislative process can lead to insights about aspects of congressional operations other than cloture and filibusters. Competition for this nonexpanding commodity has increased to such an extent that other behaviors have been significantly affected. Attention to the matter of time constraints may help us find answers to two previously troublesome questions.

First, why do legislative proponents build larger than minimum winning coalitions? Game theorists suggest that legislators seek to build minimum winning coalitions to maximize the gain that each member of the coalition will achieve. Of course, legislators operate under conditions of imperfect information. Therefore, to ensure success they may build coalitions that are at least slightly larger than the ones needed to win passage of legislation.

In the congressional process today, however, minimum coalitions may be a secondary consideration of legislators. Their major problem is that each piece of legislation is competing with every other piece of legislation for scarce time on a range of decisionmaking agendas through which legislation must pass. To present legislation with the backing of only a minimum winning coalition may slow the rate at which it is scheduled on these agendas.

A hypothetical example may help to illustrate this point. Suppose Representative X goes to the Speaker and asks him to schedule a bill for floor consideration. The Speaker then may question him about how controversial the bill was in committee. If Representative X answers that it was reported out by a narrow 19-18 vote, the Speaker may be extremely reluctant to schedule it. He may respond "it's too controversial" or "it may not pass" or, most likely, "it's going to take up more floor time than we can afford given the other legislation we have to consider." On the other hand, if the member's response to the Speaker is that the bill was reported out of committee by a 36-1 vote and in his opinion any minority position in the committee report could be handled by votes on a few amendments, the Speaker's attitude may be considerably more favorable. If the member is confident enough about his bill, he may even suggest to the Speaker that it could be considered under suspension of the rules when debate would be limited to 40 minutes and a two-thirds vote would be needed for passage.

Without serious time constraints, the incentive to build larger than minimum winning coalitions normally would be lacking. But today, in an era of extreme time pressures, large coalitions are a prerequisite for moving most legislation through the process.

A second question relates to logrolling, a bargaining process in which two or more members exchange support on issues of prime interest to each. This is believed to be a common procedure in Congress. Why then do so many members claim, "I won't vote for something I oppose in order to gain support for something I favor"? Some may properly point out that members do not like to admit to this type of logrolling. Certainly to some extent that may be true. But many members do engage in logrolling, although not the type that is typically envisioned. Logrolling in a time-constrained environment often involves the trading of time priorities; legislators agree to an exchange on the movement of legislation through decisionmaking points they control. An example will clarify how this form of logrolling works.

A veteran of more than three decades in the House and an individual known for his candor told me that he never voted for legislation he opposed. He said he did engage in frequent logrolling, especially in recent years. He then related this story. The representative wanted a particular bill moved through the Senate expeditiously. The legislation was on the agenda controlled by a particular senator who favored it and would eventually move it along. The problem for the representative was how to get the senator to give the bill top priority. Through a lobbyist, the representative learned that the senator had a similar interest in a piece of legislation that was on an agenda controlled by the representative. The representative favored the bill that was of interest to the senator and would eventually move it along, but other legislation had higher priority. The representative announced that nothing would move on his agenda until the legislation that he was interested in was speeded up in the Senate. The expected result occurred. According to the representative, the senator immediately "did what he was eventually going to do and I scheduled the hearing on his legislation at our next meeting."

The representative claimed that this kind of interchamber logrolling was very frequent but rarely cited by congressional scholars. Strong incentives exist for logrolling in a time-bound process with multiple decision points and many members in control of agendas as committee or subcommittee chairs. As with the building of coalitions, the emphasis is on moving legislation quickly through the numerous decision points. With crowded agendas, the problem is not merely gathering majority support but competing with other items on each agenda that also may have majority support. Because of Congress's heavy workload and shortage of time, a low priority on the legislative agenda as well as organized opposition may doom legislation to delay or defeat.

Conclusion

The time pressures under which Congress operates in the late twentieth century place boundaries on the congressional process that previously existed only for brief periods. These pressures explain why cloture votes, so rare for 40 to 50 years, have become much more frequent since the 1960s. The impact of changing time constraints on coalition building and logrolling in Congress has not been discussed in this chapter as fully as their impact on cloture, nor have these cases been given much empirical verification. Nevertheless, they also underscore the growing importance of time as a factor in explaining congressional behavior.

In the case of cloture and the filibuster, the Senate attempted to adjust to the stresses that time constraints were placing on it by changing Rule 22 in 1975 and 1979. There is little indication that these changes in cloture have done much to discourage filibusters, although they may have prevented them from becoming more frequent. By comparison, the House—with a more elaborate set of rules and without the Senate tradition of unlimited debate—has had greater success in coping with time pressures. The adoption of more complex rules providing for the terms under which individual bills will be debated is becoming an accepted feature in the House, although some members complain of these "gag" procedures.

In the past, Congress was able to adapt to institutional stresses by changing its norms, rules, and procedures. The norms of reciprocity and comity, the development of a committee system, the growth of specialization, the formalization of party leadership roles, and many other changes occurred in response to stresses on the House and Senate. To get its work done, Congress altered the legislative process, and with good reason we may expect it to find solutions to its current time and workload problems. But, as in the past, those solutions will have costs in terms of the freedom of action of individual members and the influence of Congress in the struggle over policy.

NOTES

1. Lewis A. Froman, Jr., *The Congressional Process* (Boston: Little, Brown & Co., 1967), p. 17.
2. James L. Sundquist, *Politics and Policy* (Washington, D.C.: The Brookings Institution, 1968).
3. Richard Bolling, *House Out of Order* (New York: Dutton, 1965), pp. 180-185.
4. James S. Young, *The Washington Community, 1800-1828* (New York: Columbia University Press, 1966).
5. See Joseph Cooper, *The Origins of the Standing Committees and the Development of the Modern House* (Houston, Texas: William Marsh Rice University, 1971). Although Cooper is explicitly concerned with workload and expertise problems, his writing makes clear that time constraints are a driving force in the development of the committee system.
6. William A. Robinson, *Thomas B. Reed, Parliamentarian* (New York: Dodd, Mead & Co., 1930), pp. 102-123, 175-234.
7. The first session of the 98th Congress ended on November 8, 1983—the earliest completion of a first session since 1965.

8. Figures are based on data presented in Norman J. Ornstein, Thomas E. Mann, Michael J. Malbin, and John F. Bibby, *Vital Statistics on Congress, 1982* (Washington, D.C.: American Enterprise Institute, 1982), pp. 130-133.

9. Of course, much of the material printed in the *Record* is not actually spoken on the floor of the House and Senate. And the tendency to include such material has increased.

10. Ornstein, Mann, Malbin, and Bibby, *Vital Statistics, 1982*, pp. 126-141.

11. *Congressional Record*, daily edition, January 9, 1979, p. 51415.

12. *Congressional Record*, July 6, 1922, p. 9982.

13. Patty D. Renfrow, "The Senate Filibuster System, 1917-1979: Changes and Consequences" (Paper presented at the annual meeting of the Southern Political Science Association, Atlanta, Georgia, November 6-8, 1980), p. 8.

14. Ibid., p. 30. On liberals' use of the filibuster, see Gary Orfield, *Congressional Power: Congress and Social Change* (New York: Harcourt, 1975).

15. Renfrow, *The Senate Filibuster System*, pp. 30-32.

16. *Congressional Record*, April 24, 1953, p. 3766.

17. Ibid., January 22, 1925, p. 2590.

18. Ibid., July 5, 1922, p. 9985.

19. Ibid., p. 10002.

20. It is important to note that for a 10-year period from 1949 to 1959 Rule 22 required two-thirds of the membership of the Senate, not just two-thirds of those present and voting, to invoke cloture. This may have further dampened any efforts to present cloture petitions.

21. One cloture vote on a British loan agreement resolution occurred even though no formal filibuster was under way. Three days after cloture was defeated, the resolution passed the Senate easily because its major opponent, Theodore Bilbo (D-Miss.), had gone home to run for re-election. In the other case cloture on a labor dispute bill was defeated 77-3 after an agreement had been worked out, and the sponsor of the cloture motion had tried to withdraw it.

22. See Raymond E. Wolfinger, "Filibusters: Majority Rule, Presidential Leadership, and Senate Norms," in *Readings on Congress*, ed. Raymond E. Wolfinger (Englewood Cliffs, N.J.: Prentice-Hall, 1971), pp. 286-305. Wolfinger contends that other hurdles in the congressional process easily may have blocked all but one of these civil rights bills even if a majority cloture rule had existed. Thus, civil rights proponents, especially the less vigorous ones, may well have recognized the futility of an extended effort to invoke cloture.

23. *Congressional Record*, daily edition, January 9, 1979, p. 51415.

24. Most but not all cloture efforts during this period had the backing of the majority party leadership.

25. Walter J. Oleszek, *Congressional Procedures and the Policy Process*, 2nd ed. (Washington, D.C.: CQ Press, 1984), pp. 157-158.

26. Orfield, *Congressional Power*.

27. *Congressional Quarterly Weekly Report*, March 1, 1975, p. 448.

28. Oleszek, *Congressional Procedures*, p. 190.

29. *Congressional Quarterly Weekly Report*, September 25, 1976, p. 2614.

30. Ibid., September 4, 1976, p. 2424.

31. Oleszek, *Congressional Procedures*, p. 191.

32. *Congressional Quarterly Weekly Report*, April 9, 1983, p. 696.

18. BICAMERALISM IN CONGRESS: THE CHANGING PARTNERSHIP

Edward G. Carmines and Lawrence C. Dodd

The U.S. Congress stands out as one of the most distinctive national legislatures in the world. This distinctiveness is evident in both its extensive policymaking role and its formal separation from the executive. Yet nowhere is the uniqueness of Congress seen more clearly and consequentially than in its bicameral nature: two separate chambers sharing legislative power.[1] While other national legislatures have two separate houses, their upper chambers have faded in importance and prestige, leaving the lower house the pre-eminent legislative institution.[2] In the United States, by contrast, the power and status of the Senate rivals and perhaps surpasses the House. It is this prominence of the upper house that gives our bicameralism special significance.

In this essay we will examine the bicameral nature of the U.S. Congress, focusing especially on the changing relationship between the House and Senate. How could the Senate, originally the less prestigious chamber, increase in power and prestige to such an extent that it challenges the House for legislative pre-eminence? The House is, after all, the legislature of the people, the body that is theoretically closer to the common man and more representative of the majority will. The ability of a less representative institution such as the Senate to challenge the more democratic body is an intriguing puzzle in an age enamored of democratic rule.

A related concern is the relative power and role of the two chambers today. Are the two houses equal partners, or are there forces favoring the power and prestige of one over the other? And what consequence does the bicameral relationship, whether an equal or unequal partnership, have for the operation of Congress? To address these questions, we shall look first at the constitutional design of bicameralism and trace its historical evolution. We shall then examine the changing state of bicameralism in the contemporary period, giving special attention to its prospects in the emerging post-industrial era.

Larry Dodd wishes to thank the Hoover Institution at Stanford University for its financial and clerical support during the preparation of this chapter.

Bicameralism: The Constitutional Design

The fact that the U.S. Congress is composed of two chambers sharing power is hardly an accident or afterthought. It was a deliberate choice by the members of the Constitutional Convention in 1787 and an integral element of the theory of government articulated at the convention and outlined in the *Federalist Papers*.[3] The framers of the Constitution sought to create a national government strong enough to rule decisively and yet sufficiently limited so that it would not abuse its powers over the people. How to form a government that was both authoritative and nontyrannical—this was the great dilemma confronting the framers. Their solution was threefold.

First, they gave the national government extensive responsibilities for taxation, interstate and foreign commerce, and foreign policy, while reserving other powers for the states; this grant of power helped ensure a national government with strong but not exclusive policymaking authority. Second, they constructed a government in which authority and power did not reside in a single individual or institution but was dispersed widely throughout various institutions. Third, the framers placed the government on a popular, democratic base. Article II of the Constitution thus granted the essential powers of government to Congress[4] and specified that the members of the House of Representatives be directly elected by the people.

The extensive policymaking responsibilities of Congress together with its democratic base made it the great institutional centerpiece of American government. Yet this very importance made Congress a focus of additional concern to the founding fathers. As Madison wrote, "A dependence on the people is, no doubt, a primary control on the government; but experience has taught mankind the necessity of auxiliary precautions."[5]

Madison and other founders feared that Congress, as an elective institution with taxing and spending powers, might accumulate governmental power in its own hands and dominate the executive and judiciary. Their concern thus shifted from how to separate governmental power among different branches of government to ways to build constraints into Congress itself. This concern led them to create a bicameral legislature. The framers of the Constitution decided that the way to control legislative authority was to divide it, just as they divided government itself.

Madison stated the rationale for separation this way:

> In republican government the legislative authority necessarily predominates. The remedy for this inconvenience is to divide the legislature into different branches: and to render them by different modes of election and different principles of action, as little connected with each other as the nature of their common functions and their common dependence on the society will admit.[6]

By dividing the Congress into the House and Senate and requiring that any legislation be passed by both chambers in an identical form, the framers again put into practice their basic principle of government: different institutions sharing power in order to check and balance one another. Bicameralism was one of the primary "auxiliary precautions" against unlimited governmental authority, in this case legislative authority.

As an auxiliary precaution, bicameralism was intended to control the behavior of the House of Representatives. From the beginning of the Constitutional Convention, the framers recognized that an elective and representative assembly—a House of Representatives—would be an essential element of the new government. When they discussed their fear of the legislature, they meant their fear of this elected representative assembly. The problem, as Hamilton put it, was that the House, as the sole legislative chamber, might be "a full match if not an overmatch for every other member of the government."[7]

If selected directly by the people, as seemed necessary given the democratic spirit of the American Revolution, the House might be overly responsive to popular sentiments and enact legislation that was both dangerous and unwise. Moreover, like legislative assemblies in the colonies, the House of Representatives presumably would require a strong Speaker for proper leadership of its members and coordination of its activities. The Speaker's role would be further enhanced, Madison feared, by the dearth of legislators competing for power in the House.[8]

Because of the difficulty of long distance travel and communication in the rural, agrarian society of the late eighteenth century, and the importance of local as opposed to national issues, Madison expected most legislators to serve only one or two terms in Congress before retiring to state and local politics. A legislator interested in national politics and willing to remain in the capital faced few House colleagues interested in competing with him for influence or challenging the expansion of his power. An ambitious individual, confronting such a vacuum and skillful at building personal alliances, could win the Speakership and gather to it resources that would allow him to control the House. Such a Speaker, unconstrained by his colleagues, could use the taxing and spending powers of the House to dominate national politics itself.[9]

The founding fathers created the Senate to provide an internal congressional check on these potential tyrannical tendencies of the House and its Speaker. By having senators selected by state legislatures, not by mass electors, the founders hoped the Senate would provide a dignified, stabilizing counterforce to the House.

The vice-president was chosen to be the presiding officer of the Senate to facilitate closer ties with the executive branch. Senators were given lagged, six-year terms so they would have time to consider public policy carefully and offset any hasty actions taken by House members. Presumably because of their greater wisdom and maturity, senators were given prerogatives in the ratification of treaties and the approval of executive and judicial appointments. In sum, the Senate was to be an "anchor against popular fluctuations," the chamber that would act with "more coolness, with more system and with more wisdom, than the popular branch." [10]

The framers designed the House to be a truly representative institution. Its members, selected simultaneously for two-year terms, were elected from districts drawn in proportion to the nation's population. Only the members of the House could initiate revenue legislation, reflecting the framers' great concern that the people determine their own taxes. This provision gave the House a claim to pre-eminence in all financial matters.

The essence of bicameralism, then, was two distinct, independent chambers with different sizes, terms of office, constitutional responsibilities, and constituencies. The House seemed destined to be the most prestigious and powerful body because of its elective status, its pre-eminence in fiscal matters, and its presumed capacity to generate strong and forceful leadership. The Senate lacked full democratic legitimacy because the people played a more indirect role in the selection of its members. The Senate also lacked a strong, elected presiding officer. Nevertheless, it did possess unique roles, particularly in foreign policy, that could sustain its power in legislative affairs.

These distinctions between the House and Senate rested in part on expressed constitutional provisions that could be changed only by amendment. A degree of stability thus was built into the operation of bicameralism, with the House and Senate unable to alter differences in their length of office, their modes of selection, or their distinct constitutional powers. But the actual operation of bicameralism also depended on the nature of the society in which it operated.

The existence of a rural and agrarian society led the framers to expect that the elected House would have high turnover, a strong Speaker, and potentially a tyrannical bent. These expectations fueled the drive for bicameralism and a nonelective Senate. They also convinced the framers that the House, despite its much larger size, would maintain a cohesive organization equal to and possibly superior to the Senate, particularly since the Senate would not have a strong presiding officer. Similarly, the framers assumed that America would remain relatively isolated by the oceans from foreign entanglements. Influence over foreign policy would be of modest importance, they thought, and thus could be given to the Senate without violating the principle of popular government.

Two centuries have now passed since the founding fathers designed the bicameral Congress. Their world—a small nation on the eastern seaboard, dominated by an agrarian economy and rural lifestyle, isolated by the oceans from foreign wars—has vanished. In its place is an industrial and, more recently, a post-industrial nation of continental size and great international power. These societal transformations have necessarily altered the operation of bicameralism and eroded the constitutional design.

The Evolution of Bicameralism
in the Nineteenth Century

The evolution toward modern bicameralism began in the nineteenth century when the Civil War activated the move away from an agrarian economy and toward an industrial order. The response of Congress to these environmental changes tells us a great deal about the flexibility of our bicameral arrangements and about the types of factors most likely to produce substantial alteration in the roles of the House and Senate today.

The Agrarian Era

In the early decades of the Republic, the House eclipsed the Senate in status and influence, much as the founding fathers had expected. The Senate was seen as "an honorific nothing." In fact, prior to the Civil War one did not make a long-term career out of Senate service, "except perhaps as a fluke." [11] The House, by contrast, experienced perhaps its greatest period of pre-eminence during the Speakership of Henry Clay. So prestigious was the House that John Quincy Adams chose a career there following his presidency.

The ascendancy of the House during the first half of the nineteenth century resulted from several factors. Senators' unelected status and statewide responsibilities naturally built a barrier between them and the public. The Senate lacked full democratic legitimacy, whereas the House was the very embodiment of democratic principles. In addition, the Senate did not develop a strong internal organization, whereas the House, experiencing the high turnover that Madison had predicted, invested great power in its Speaker. The strong organization of the House enabled it to provide legislative leadership to the nation, which reinforced the prestige it gained as the nation's most democratic institution.

There were other reasons for the ascendancy of the House during this period. First and foremost, the House drew its membership from every byway in the country and thus was close to the pulse of the people. The large number of House members gave the House and its leadership a capacity to gauge and influence public opinion that neither the Senate nor the president could match. The president, as one individual with a small staff, had no direct means to reach the public in a rural society that lacked modern man's communication and rapid transportation systems. Senators, unelected and serving states rather than small districts, were also more isolated from the public than were House members.

In these early years the constitutional power of the House loomed large. The Senate's distinctive constitutional powers over treaties and nominations were defused by the physical isolation of the nation and the small size of the government. By contrast, the primacy of the House in fiscal affairs allowed it to claim broad influence over budgetary politics and shape the domestic policies of the day. This more critical policy focus of the House—together with its greater prestige as an elected body, strong organization, and closeness to the public—made it the dominant partner in Congress.

The Civil War ended the first era of American politics, the agrarian era. The debates over slavery highlighted the importance of the Senate as a forum for the discussion of national issues, greatly increasing its prestige. The war and its aftermath spurred the rise of a mass production economy and new transportation systems such as the intercontinental railroad. The technological revolution also produced faster ships to cross the oceans and facilitate the trade of the goods made possible by industrialization. The Civil War thus drastically altered the environmental conditions presumed by the founders and unleashed a new period of American history, a period referred to by Samuel Huntington as the "post-agrarian era" of American politics.[12]

The Post-Agrarian Era

The post-agrarian era stretches roughly from the end of Reconstruction in the 1870s to the first decade of the twentieth century. For the first time the country was preoccupied with creating an industrial base, building its urban centers, developing a system of interstate and international commerce, and debating the proper role of the government in economic and foreign affairs.

Perhaps the most significant political impact of post-agrarianism was the increased power of Congress and greater attractiveness of congressional service. During the agrarian era many policy problems, even on national topics such as commerce, were local problems best addressed by local governments and state legislatures. But with the growth of industrialization and interstate commerce the country's policy problems became increasingly national in scope and subject to congressional regulation. Congress became more central to the daily lives of citizens and a more attractive arena in which to gain and exercise power. Therefore, politicians began seeking long-term careers in Congress and turnover declined.[13]

The new policy issues of the post-agrarian era influenced the Senate perhaps more than the House because of the Senate's constitutional prerogatives in foreign affairs and greater interest in national concerns. In addition, the expanding role of government increased the size of the federal bureaucracy and created many new governmental positions whose occupants were subject to Senate approval. The resulting expansion in the patronage controlled by senators made the Senate more influential in state and national politics.

Environmental changes in the late nineteenth century benefited the House as well. The rise in international trade made tariff legislation the most critical issue of the day. The House, with its special constitutional powers in revenue matters, thus was able to expand its role in national policymaking. In fact, two chairs of Ways and Means, the revenue-writing committee in the

House, were the only two members of Congress to be elected president during this period. The election of Representative James Garfield in 1880 and Representative William McKinley in 1896, together with the nomination of Representative James Blaine as the Republican party's presidential candidate in 1884, clearly demonstrate the high standing of the House at that time.

The late nineteenth century was a golden era for the bicameral Congress. As Woodrow Wilson wrote in 1885, Congress was in ascendancy in American politics, dominating the presidency and the courts.[14] Both the House and the Senate possessed constitutional powers that were critical to national policymaking, and both were well organized.[15] Each asserted its unique constitutional powers and played a clear role in making national policy.

Congress thus was more dominant and bicameralism was more balanced than the framers had planned. Yet underlying this period of congressional ascendancy were forces that eventually would undercut the power of Congress and alter its bicameral partnership. For example, the House, adjusting to the doubling, tripling, and quadrupling of the nation's population, increased its seats from 243 in 1860 to 435 in 1913. During the same time the number of senators increased from 72 to 96, reflecting the admission of 12 new states to the union. By the early twentieth century the size of the House had greatly outstripped that of the Senate. This made the House a much more difficult institution to manage and decreased the prestige associated with service in it.

Nevertheless, turnover declined and careerism increased in the House as well as in the Senate. The move toward careerism came first in the Senate, where the average length of service rose from four years in 1880 to more than eight years by the early 1900s.[16] In the House, careerism lagged behind by about 15 years until the 1896 realignment greatly increased the number of safe districts in the country.[17] In both chambers, careerism was accompanied by decentralizing pressures. The number of legislators who wanted to hold positions of power grew, and the dominance of party leaders was questioned. Careerism threatened to reverse the founders' assumption that high turnover would produce centralized congressional leadership and sustain the governing capacity of the House and Senate.

The calls for decentralization were largely unsuccessful in the late nineteenth century; the existence of strong national parties, the modest number of careerists, and the strong procedural powers of congressional leaders combined to thwart the reformers. Moves toward fragmentation of the committee system were early warning signals, however, of the difficulties Congress could face if turnover continued to decline.

The post-agrarian era thus was a paradoxical one. It was the great era of congressional power. Congress had the institutional cohesion and constitutional authority to dominate national policy. The growing importance of foreign policy and patronage enabled the Senate to emerge as a more equal partner to the House. It was also a time when the House extended its influence, tariff policy was the most important national issue, and the Ways and Means Committee served as an "incubator" for presidents.

In short, Congress had become a powerful force in domestic and foreign affairs. Yet the very rise of Congress to prominence was attracting careerist legislators whose desire for personal power threatened to fragment the institution and undermine its capacity to make decisions. Moreover, the nation's population explosion had swelled the size of Congress, which further complicated congressional policymaking. These tensions erupted with the coming of the industrial era during the first two decades of the twentieth century.

Bicameralism in the Industrial Era

The Progressive movement and World War I spurred on the industrialization of America. The Progressives brought to national politics a great concern for the democratization and decentralization of government, thus providing a philosophical and reformist argument for careerist legislators who wanted to decentralize power in Congress. The Progressives also favored a more active and powerful role for the federal government, including protection of the environment, the regulation of industry as well as commerce, and the use of the individual income tax to raise revenues. This expanded role of government fueled a continued rise in the power of Congress and reinforced the attractiveness of congressional service.

World War I, like the Civil War, increased the nation's need for the rapid and reliable production of war materiel. The government's efforts to meet these needs strengthened the country's commitment to new technologies, the development of its industrial base, the urbanization of its citizenry, and the economic interdependence of its various regions. The war also solidified the view of the national government as an active force in international politics.

Thus, the first two decades of the twentieth century marked a second great watershed period analogous to the Civil War and Reconstruction. By 1920 the nation was an industrial and urban society in which government revenues, derived from an income tax, financed social programs to protect consumers, the young, and the environment. Internationalism versus isolationism was the central political debate of the period. Women, beneficiaries of the Progressives' commitment to democracy, had the right to vote. In short, the outlines of modern America were in place. The coming of this new America transformed both Congress and its bicameral arrangements.

Restructuring Bicameralism

The new political agenda of the industrial era made the Congress more critical to the daily life of the country than ever before and ensured that more politicians would seek long-term congressional careers. As a result of the growing number of careerist legislators and the Progressives' efforts to democratize government, party leaders in Congress in the early twentieth century faced serious threats to their centralized control of power. By 1910 the reformers were powerful enough to challenge the leadership and win. Speaker Joe Cannon was stripped of much of the authority that had enabled the Speakership to lead and coordinate the House over the preceding century. Senate leaders were also weakened during this period, although in a less public and formal manner.[18]

This weakening of the power of congressional leaders marked the end of bicameralism as the founders conceived it. They instituted a bicameral legislature in the late eighteenth century because they feared that the House would elect a strong leader and play too strong a role in American politics. Two legislative chambers, they felt, would provide the division of authority needed to rein in the power of the legislature. But with the demise of strong central leadership and the subsequent rise of committee government, fragmentation and immobilism resulted. Rather than a restraint on an aggressive Congress, bicameralism now became an inducement toward weakness, a constitutional provision that helped increase the leverage of the executive and judiciary over the legislative branch.

The decline of central leadership had its greatest influence on the procedures and power of the House.[19] With 435 members, the House could not operate effectively under informal procedures of cooperation and mutual adjustment. It needed formal mechanisms that could plan and coordinate the flow of business and rule with authority. Without strong central leadership, the House was faced with a variety of often competing centers of power—the weakened Speaker, the Rules Committee, the Ways and Means Committee, the Appropriations Committee, and numerous specialized substantive committees. The smaller Senate was better able to adjust to the weakening of party leadership and thus improved its leverage over the House.

The Senate also benefited from other developments. Passage of the Seventeenth Amendment in 1913 made the Senate an elective body and removed the most substantial constitutional difference between it and the House. The Senate was then able to claim full legitimacy as a democratic institution. The second development was the nation's emergence as an economic and military power with extensive international interests and responsibilities. As America's international involvement increased, the Senate's special constitutional role in foreign policy became more important. The Senate's power was demonstrated most notably by its rejection in 1918 of the Versailles Treaty, a decision based in part on President Woodrow Wilson's failure to consult the Senate adequately during his negotiation of the treaty. The rejection of the Versailles Treaty revealed more clearly than on any previous occasion the power of the Senate in foreign policy.

In earlier decades the large size of the House and its local access had enabled it to be the superior institution at communicating with and persuading the public, but the rise of new communication technologies—mass circulation national newspapers, radio, and eventually television—tilted the power of communication toward the Senate and the presidency. These mass media were drawn to the Senate because of its small size, which allowed them to focus on individual senators, and because senators' large constituencies and more national and international focus provided the media with a wider audience. Media attention made national personalities out of senators and a notable debating forum out of the Senate. Individual senators and the Senate as a body could convey their opinions to the public more easily than could the larger House and its more parochial and anonymous members.

The House, for its part, was not without its strategies of influence. What House members lacked in national prominence, for example, they tried to make up for by outstripping senators in technical knowledge about legislation. The special influence they lacked in the area of foreign policy, they sought to balance by asserting dominance over revenue and appropriations legislation. And the House remained the truest reflection of the nation's pluralistic population. It was the essential arena in which coalitions were built and compromises reached among the spokesmen for the nation's distinctive local and regional interests.

The very parochialism of the House provided it with a certain stability. House members knew their districts, cultivated personal ties with their constituents, and established long-term support that senators, riding above the fray, could not match. In the process of developing their careers, House members lost whatever tinge of radicalism they may have had in the early years of the Republic. Representatives became spokesmen for the dominant economic and social interests in their districts, and their politics tended to be conservative. Senators, in building coalitions among minorities throughout their states, often held more liberal and controversial views.[20]

Contrasting the House and Senate

Industrial America thus produced a bicameralism very different from that foreseen by the framers of the Constitution. They had expected a radical, elected, aggressive, and powerful House that would be constrained by a conservative and appointed Senate. The industrial era produced an elected and powerful Senate that was often better organized, more visible, and even on occasion more liberal than the large, unwieldy, and parochial House.

These unforeseen developments, arising from the constitutional and environmental changes early in this century, have led the House and Senate to develop in very different ways over the past 60 years. The differences in the day-to-day life of the two houses influence how new environmental changes will affect bicameral arrangements today. Thus, before examining the effects that post-industrialization have on bicameralism, we will compare the electoral and institutional politics of the House and Senate during the industrial era.

Electoral Politics. Electoral differences between the two houses since ratification of the Seventeenth Amendment are rooted first and foremost in the fact that representatives serve for two years and senators for six. House members thus must always be prepared to face public evaluation of their decisions. Senators, according to an old adage, have two years to be statesmen, two years to be legislators, and then two years to be politicians running for re-election. As a result of constant electoral pressures, representatives are presumed to be more responsive to short-term changes in public opinion than senators.

This responsiveness is reinforced by the small size of House districts, relative to states, which allows members (in fact, may require them) to engage in personalized campaigns and develop specialized home styles that fit their constituencies.[21] The small size and homogeneity of most districts lead representatives to stress local issues and constituency service. And the personalized and parochial nature of House campaigns produce relatively safe seats.[22] These factors inhibit the House from taking a national approach to issues and have thereby limited its leadership on national issues.

The electoral circumstance of senators is quite different. Senatorial candidates campaign statewide and run for office only every six years. They rely less than House members on personal campaign appearances and friendships. Their diverse and mobile audience is reached through extensive use of mass media.[23] As a result, the theme of Senate elections is more likely to be national in character. Over the past several decades, national political forces have had a reasonably strong impact on their electoral fortunes.[24]

The electoral differences between the House and Senate reinforce the effects of their constitutional differences. The Senate has benefited from the growing importance of foreign affairs, not solely because of its unique constitutional role in this area, but also because statewide elections provide Senate candidates with the incentive and opportunity to look beyond narrow local questions to national and international issues. Six-year terms also give senators sufficient freedom from short-term electoral politics that they can pursue wider interests.

House members, tied to local districts and facing re-election every two years, have a primary incentive to focus on local problems that affect their constituents rather than on national and international concerns. So long as the local constituency gets its federal funds and constituents receive satisfactory casework, House incumbents usually can win re-election without great difficulty. Questions of ideology and national policy thus are likely to affect Senate races more than House races.[25]

Institutional Politics. These electoral and constitutional distinctions between the House and Senate have led to quite different patterns of institutional behavior. Some of the characteristics of Senate elections—specifically, their tendency to be more ideological, policy-oriented, and national than House elections—help give the Senate a special role in national policymaking. As Nelson Polsby has observed, "The essence of the Senate is that it is a great forum, an echo chamber, a publicity machine." He goes on to state that "in the Senate the three central activities are (1) cultivating national constituencies; (2) formulating questions for debate and discussion on a national scale (especially in opposition to the President); and (3) incubating new policy proposals that may at some future time find their way into legislation." [26]

It is the grand design of national public policy rather than the nitty-gritty details of legislation that is of prime concern to most senators. The detailed expertise on legislative matters that is needed to produce sound legislation is usually provided by the House. Its established division of labor—that is, the tendency of members to focus their main attention and energies on their few committee assignments—leads to technical expertise that far exceeds the more generalist Senate.

Thus, a related distinction between the two chambers concerns the basic organizational structure of the House and Senate. The House is predominantly a committee-centered body. With 435 members, it simply could not consider legislative matters on the floor without the extensive prior use of committees. Members get to know other members often through their being colleagues on the same committee. The consideration of legislation on the floor is usually dominated by members of the relevant substantive committee. Committees, in short, are essential to the workings of the twentieth-century House.

While the Senate also is organized around committees, they are far less important to the typical senator than to the typical House member. Not only do most senators serve on many more committees than representatives, but senators may develop an interest in an issue that lies beyond their committee assignments. Moreover, the Senate is a flexible enough institution that individuals find it easy to pursue wide-ranging concerns. In other words, if the House is organized to fulfill the goals of its members through committees, the Senate accommodates its members by its individualist orientation. It is the individual senator who is the essential driving force of the contemporary Senate.[27]

There is a final institutional difference between the House and Senate that partly originates in their differing electoral environment and institutional character—the emergence of the Senate as a presidential incubator. This development no doubt reflects the media-dominated, national, and public-policy-oriented nature of Senate campaigns.[28] Given how most senators become senators—namely, by becoming television celebrities who can comment on any national or international problem—it is not surprising that many are seen as potential presidential material. Indeed, so many senators aspire to the presidency that Alan Ehrenhalt of Congressional Quarterly believes the Senate as an institution may be adversely affected. It is a substantial strain, he observes, to be in the Senate and running for president.[29]

Conclusion

As we have seen, the coming of an industrial society has generated a House and a Senate that differ greatly from those of earlier times and from each other. The Senate has emerged as the more prestigious and influential body. Its elected status, longer term, constitutional prerogatives in foreign policy, availability as a forum for national debate and leadership, and special role as a presidential incubator have combined to increase its prestige. The House has developed as a chamber devoted to technical expertise, personalized constituency service, and responsiveness to local political interests. The greater relative status of the Senate is shown, among other ways, in its tendency to dominate conference committee decisions despite the greater legislative expertise of House members.[30]

These patterns have been evident in the House and Senate for most of this century, and they remain strong today. But the history of bicameralism demonstrates that even the strongest and most dominant patterns are subject to change when the underlying social and economic environment is transformed. Post-industrialism appears to be precisely such a change. In the final section we will consider its effects on the electoral procedures, institutional politics, and policy agenda of the House and Senate.

Post-Industrial Change and the New Bicameralism

Post-industrialism involves the rise of a high-tech society in which agriculture and industry are automated and most people work in service jobs in areas such as education, communication, and health care. The post-industrial revolution, which first took hold during the 1960s, is well under way in America today. The majority of the public is involved in service occupations, and technical advances are being made in mass communications, transportation, computer technology, and robotics.[31]

At the domestic level, these changes are associated with the growing call for government to facilitate the transition to a high-tech economy and to ensure a decent and equitable quality of life for an increasingly mobile population. They also are associated with a deep clash of political values over the moral choices that the technological advances of post-industrialism produce. At the international level, these changes involve the development of nuclear and space-age technologies. Post-industrialism also depends upon developing good relations with Third World nations whose cheap labor force and extensive natural resources are essential to the economies of post-industrial nations.[32]

As the history of earlier eras makes clear, societal transformations of the magnitude of these post-industrial changes will alter the conduct of politics and the nature of bicameralism. Such environmental changes introduce new policy problems, thereby potentially transforming the policy roles of one or both houses. They revolutionize campaign techniques, alter institutional procedures, and change the attractiveness of House and Senate careers. It is not yet clear whether post-industrialization will affect the House-Senate partnership as dramatically as did the moves from an agrarian to a post-agrarian to an industrial society. The post-industrial era is still in its early stages; the space race and Vietnam War in the 1960s spurred it on, but it is not yet fully consolidated as the dominant economic and social force in American life. Nevertheless, broad outlines of the impact of post-industrialism are becoming increasingly apparent.[33]

Post-industrialism has complicated congressional politics by dramatically increasing the number and widening the scope of issues that legislators must confront. The growing complexity and unfamiliarity of the policy agenda have led members to create specialized committees and subcommittees to deal with the new issues, thereby further fragmenting Congress. These changes, in turn, undercut Congress's ability to provide strong and coherent policy leadership and thereby created a demand for central committees to improve policy coordination in areas such as budgetary politics. Post-industrialism threatens to continue the decline, begun in the industrial era, in the policy influence of Congress. It confronts Congress with problems of organization and decisionmaking that are far more difficult than those of the industrial era. Will the House and Senate respond to these new problems in constructive ways and with equal degrees of success?

Electoral Politics

Let us address this question by first examining elections and mass communications. The mass communications revolution of the post-industrial era provides House and Senate candidates with a greater opportunity than in the past to contact constituents. The expense of television somewhat limits its utility in House races, particularly since districts often fail to correspond to a natural media market. House candidates generally find a highly direct and personal campaign much more practical and efficacious than TV ads.[34] Television is far more efficient in statewide constituencies because it allows candidates to reach voters whom they probably could not contact through personal campaigning.[35] Television also influences Senate races through the greater coverage that it gives to the Senate as an institution and to the policy positions of senators. As we have already noted, television has made household names out of many Senate candidates. House members, by contrast, have remained more enmeshed in local politics.

House members' attention to their districts has been aided by developments in rapid transportation, mass mailing techniques, and the computerization of casework activity.[36] These developments allow House members to maintain an almost constant presence in and attention to their districts. Home several weekends a month, anxious to solve their constituents' problems with the federal government, members of the House are personal ombudsmen for their constituents in Washington.[37]

The recent technological advances in communication and transportation thus have had different implications for the House and Senate. Television has increased senators' visibility, status, and national orientation, and it has led them further away from a personalized relationship with their constituents. Yet television can prove to be a double-edged sword because it is a resource available not only to senators but also to their challengers who can afford it. In fact, television may so raise the prestige and visibility of Senate service that it increases the number of serious challengers and gives them a resource with which to defeat Senate incumbents.

With respect to House elections, the high-tech revolution has served primarily to strengthen incumbents rather than challengers. Their small districts, frequent trips home, and rapid response to casework allow incumbents to develop close ties with many constituents. Moreover, mass transportation, mass mailings, and computerized casework enable them to develop a personal relationship with constituents and provide a direct, personal service that challengers cannot match. House elections thus are typically less competitive than Senate elections.[38]

These basic differences between the House and Senate generate other contrasts. Because of senators' greater need for media advertising and larger constituencies, Senate elections are much more expensive than House campaigns. Unless the candidate is wealthy, he or she will require a major infusion of funds to run a competitive race. Under these circumstances, political action committees (PACs), especially those with a national orientation, are likely to be key sources of funds and quite visible participants in the electoral process. In short, nationally organized groups are more likely to focus on Senate than House elections.[39] Therefore, the themes of Senate elections are national in character. More than House contests, they tend to center on the clash between the candidates' ideologies and national policy positions and are less likely to hinge on local issues and constituent service.

Thus, national political forces have a reasonably strong impact on Senate elections.[40] As a result, Senate elections are becoming more competitive and volatile while House races are experiencing a high degree of incumbent security. The decline in the competitiveness of House elections is tied, in part, to the greater ease with which members can return to their districts, to their increased resources for casework activity, and to their abilities to create home styles that mesh closely with the character of their districts. The greater competitiveness of Senate races, by contrast, is tied to the visibility of senators and the availability of mass communications resources to well-financed challengers. Home style and constituent service are bonds between House members and their constituents that challengers find hard to break. A senator's media image and policy visibility are viable targets for a well-funded challenger.

These contrasts between the competitiveness of House and Senate elections have great significance for careerism within the two houses and thus for politics within the two institutions. Members of the House, less threatened by electoral defeat, can concentrate on pursuing personal power within the House, thereby further fragmenting its centralized structure. Members of the Senate, more threatened by electoral challenge and more likely to be in their first term, must pay attention to getting re-elected and are less free than they might otherwise be to build up personal power in the Senate. These differences in career behavior have significant consequences for the overall operation of the two institutions.

Institutional Politics

The Senate has historically been known as an individualized institution with a highly fragmented power structure. This characterization remains largely true today and can be seen in senators' use of filibusters to assert their policy stands. Nevertheless, significant recent developments orient the individualistic Senate toward more cooperation and compromise than one now witnesses in the House. For example, increases in Senate turnover limit power struggles within the institution. Junior senators bargain from positions of weakness and vulnerability rather than strength and dominance. As a result, they have an incentive to respond to the wishes of senior legislators and party leaders if they are to succeed in the Senate. This motivation increases the likelihood that senators will work together.

Senators' incentives to work with party and ideological leaders are reinforced by national lobby groups. Increasingly critical to the funding of Senate elections, lobbies encourage senators whom they have helped to operate as cohesive groups, often in support of key committee or party leaders. The intense pressure from lobby groups can inhibit the ability of senators to focus on parochial and idiosyncratic concerns and force them to be attentive to the national forces that helped elect them.

Finally, the growing competitiveness and cost of Senate elections have forced senators to concentrate more collective attention on financing elections. During the late 1970s the Republican party in the Senate skillfully used its congressional campaign committee to collect contributions for Republican incumbents who were in trouble and Republican challengers who had a chance of winning office. Through state-of-the-art fund-raising techniques the committee has been able to build a large war chest. This party-directed fund-raising campaign, now undertaken by Senate Democrats as well, encourages party members to cooperate with the leaders who dispense party funds and thus creates additional impetus for cohesiveness and cooperation in the Senate.[41]

These forces toward cooperation and cohesiveness do not negate the natural individualism of the Senate nor the policy conflict that has come with the rise of the post-industrial agenda. The Senate is undoubtedly a more complex and unwieldy institution than it was in earlier decades. Nevertheless, the foregoing factors, together with the Senate's small size, have saved it from being crippled by the effects of post-industrialism.

The experience of the House has been rather different. The effects of post-industrialism have been to decrease the competitiveness of House elections and increase incumbent security. These developments have freed members to pursue positions of power for themselves, thereby producing a highly fragmented system of committees and subcommittees and a weakening of its most vital Ways and Means Committee.[42] This fragmentation, together with the large size of the House, have made it a very difficult institution to operate.[43]

To streamline the legislative process, the House has turned to electronic voting procedures. These procedures, however, may have robbed House leaders of their flexible control of the voting process while producing formal means that dissidents can use to increase roll call votes and thereby obstruct House business. Furthermore, to improve its declining image and prestige, the House recently began to televise its proceedings. The TV broadcasts have given self-interested careerists and dissidents a powerful new resource for gaining personal visibility and engendering conflict.

Although the coming of post-industrial technologies has helped House members in their personal quests for re-election and power, it has eroded the governance of the House itself. Senators, by contrast, have suffered in terms of their personal electoral security while the Senate as an institution may have benefited. The consequences of these patterns can be seen by focusing on the changing policy roles of the two institutions, particularly in the areas of budgetary and fiscal policy.

The Changing Roles of the House and Senate

In response to the need for planning that grows out of post-industrial change, the contemporary Congress has created a centralized budgetary process. Budgetary reform was in many ways a more salient concern in the Senate than in the House, largely because of the Senate's greater interest in national policy and the House's reluctance to alter its existing committee system. As the Senate and House pursued their own political ends during the design of the new budget system in 1974, two very different budget committees emerged.[44]

In the House, legislators were quite concerned that the new budget committee might alter power relations among members and committees. As a result, a weak committee was created that lacked the capacity to act decisively. Requirements that members from key existing committees be included on the budget committee and that no member serve longer than four years weakened the new committee. Its members lacked a real incentive to establish the committee's power and develop strong control of the budgetary process. By contrast, the Senate created a committee with permanent membership that possessed the incentive to play a strong, cohesive role in budgetary affairs.

This contrast between the House and Senate budget committees has had important consequences for the power of the two houses. The Senate's well-organized structure and more cohesive membership have allowed it to develop a strong role in monetary matters and a fair degree of prominence in the area of revenue policy—an area that the Constitution sets aside as the greater responsibility of the House. Not only is post-industrial change aiding the Senate by magnifying the importance of foreign policy, but it also appears to be increasing the role of the Senate in fiscal affairs.

The expanded role of the Senate is seen not only in the general budget-making process but also in the actual initiation and drafting of revenue legislation. Going against all constitutional and historical precedents, the House in 1982 allowed the Senate Finance Committee to initiate a major revenue bill. Although there were several reasons for this decision, a major one was simply the difficulty of organizing and controlling the House Ways and Means Committee. Thus, a precedent was set, and the Senate added a growing role in revenue matters to its pre-eminence in foreign policy.[45]

Has overall control of revenue policy shifted from the House to the Senate? It is much too early to tell with any certainty, but the possibility of such a shift is disturbing. Historically, the House has taken a constitutional prescription that is rather limited in character—"all bills for raising revenue shall originate in the House" (Article 1, Section 7)—and built around it a justification for House pre-eminence in monetary matters and thereby in domestic legislation. This strong role of the House was made possible, at least in part, by its capacity to organize effectively and assert its authority. This was true both in the nineteenth century with a strong Speaker and in the twentieth century with strong Ways and Means and Appropriations committees. If the House now loses that organizational capacity, it has little to fall back on to ensure its policy dominance in this area—only a constitutional prescription to initiate legislation, a prescription that the Senate may find easy to finesse.

The vulnerability of the House becomes more apparent when one compares its revenue authority to the Senate's special powers. With respect to treaties and nominations, the Senate is given the sole congressional power of advice and consent. Even if the Senate has extensive problems handling this responsibility, the House cannot act in its stead. But the Senate faces no similar difficulty should the House become unable to operate effectively in budgetary and fiscal matters.

The Senate has all of the constitutional power of the House in monetary matters save the authority to initiate revenue legislation. Should the House face severe organizational problems, the Senate could increase its role dramatically by providing policy leadership in fiscal matters while taking care to abide by technical niceties in the formal introduction of final bills. Should the governing capacity of the House weaken and that of the Senate increase, the House could experience an erosion in its power that would be hard to contain since its historic dominance of budgetary and domestic matters is built on such a slender constitutional thread.

Conclusion

As we have seen, the history of bicameralism is one of change. The Constitution outlines only the broad contours of the House-Senate partnership, contours that can be shaped by the ebb and flow of environmental forces. As society moved from the agrarian era of the founding fathers to an industrial order, the politics of bicameralism altered, with the Senate becoming a more equal and vital partner to the House.

Now the move into a post-industrial, hi-tech world again may be transforming bicameralism. The electoral and institutional changes fueled by the coming of post-industrialism over the past two decades appear to be weakening the governing capacity of Congress while strengthening the power of the Senate relative to the House. What are the possible consequences of this new relationship?

First, conflict between the House and Senate may increase. Previous alterations in the power relations of the two houses did not involve a struggle between them over their joint powers or a usurpation by one house of the power of the other. The historic rise of the Senate was largely tied to the growing importance of its unique powers in foreign policy. But now the Senate has reached into a domain that constitutionally and historically has been the province of the House—namely, fiscal and monetary policy. Even though this development comes in large part as a result of its own disorganization, the House may see it as unwarranted and unacceptable and try to obstruct and undermine Senate leadership in this area.

Second, the responsiveness of Congress to short-term shifts in public opinion may decline. The Senate, increasingly the more influential body and the one with more competitive elections, is re-elected in full only every six years. The House, with its two-year terms that allow the public to register immediate displeasure, seems to be increasingly insulated from electoral upheaval and declining in its policy influence. The public thus confronts a weakened House whose two-year elections seem almost meaningless and a stronger Senate whose more competitive elections are spread out over six years. Neither institution appears to offer short-term control of public policy through the electoral process. Nevertheless, both institutions are subject to electoral change in the long run, and the focus of the legislature on long-term policy analysis may have its own benefits in terms of policy deliberations and risk-taking.

Finally, Congress may become more national in focus and deliberative in nature. The growing prominence of the Senate—in budgetary and fiscal matters, for example—may focus attention on the national and international consequences of social and economic policy. Similarly, the more deliberative nature of the Senate should focus attention more on debate over public policy and less on the technical details in the drafting of legislation.

Thus, Congress appears to be changing in important ways, moving toward a more conflict-ridden and nationally oriented institution. This institution will be relatively immune from short-term electoral change and preoccupied with deliberation over policy directions. The Senate will be the more dominant institution while the House will suffer from organizational problems. The challenge to the new Congress will be to ensure representation of and responsiveness to the people.

The rise of the Senate and the weakening of the House shift power away from popular representation based on population. This shift may be temporary, but it is significant. Congress is the nation's central democratic institution, and when alterations in the power and performance of the House and Senate undermine its representativeness and responsiveness, as would be the case with a decline in the influence of the House, it is cause for concern. Students of Congress must carefully examine the factors that underlie this decline and consider measures to reverse it. They also must study the Senate more closely than in the past and identify the norms and procedures that can best assist it in fulfilling its leadership role in the post-industrial era.

NOTES

1. Jean Blondel, *Comparative Legislatures* (Englewood Cliffs, N.J.: Prentice-Hall, 1973); Gerhard Loewenberg and Samuel C. Patterson, *Comparing Legislatures* (Boston: Little, Brown & Co., 1979); and John E. Schwarz and L. Earl Shaw, *The United States Congress in Comparative Perspective* (Hinsdale, Ill.: Dryden Press, 1976). For recent discussions of bicameralism in Congress, see Richard F. Fenno, Jr., *The United States Senate: A Bicameral Perspective* (Washington, D.C.: American Enterprise Institute for Public Policy Research, 1982); Lawrence D. Longley and Walter J. Oleszek, "The Three Contexts of Congressional Conference Committee Politics: Bicameral Politics Overviewed" (Paper presented at the annual meeting of the American Political Science Association, Chicago, Illinois, 1983); and Jeffrey L. Pressman, *House vs. Senate* (New Haven, Conn.: Yale University Press, 1966).

2. For a discussion of whether an upper chamber exists or not in 28 democratic countries, and if so how its members are elected, see David Butler, "Electoral Systems," in *Democracy at the Polls,* ed. David Butler, Howard R. Penniman, and Austin Ranney (Washington, D.C.: American Enterprise Institute for Public Policy Research, 1981), pp. 12-19. In footnote 1 on page 8, Butler states, "Only in the United States ... is the upper chamber as important as the lower chamber."

3. For interpretations of this theory of government, see Robert Dahl, *A Preface to Democratic Theory* (Chicago: University of Chicago Press, 1963); and Vincent Ostrom, *The Theory of a Compound Republic* (Blacksburg, Va.: Public Choice, 1971).

4. Bob Eckhardt and Charles L. Black, Jr., *The Tides of Power: Conversations on the American Constitution* (New Haven: Yale University Press, 1976).

5. James Madison, Alexander Hamilton, and John Jay, *The Federalist Papers* (New York: New American Library, 1961), p. 322.

6. Ibid., p. 322.
7. Ibid., p. 403.
8. Ibid., p. 309; pp. 334-335.
9. Ibid. See also Robert Scigliano, *The Supreme Court and the Presidency* (New York: Free Press, 1971); and Gordon S. Wood, *The Creation of the American Republic, 1776-1787* (Chapel Hill: University of North Carolina Press, 1969).
10. James Madison, *Notes of Debates in the Federal Convention of 1787* (New York: W. W. Norton, 1969), p. 83.
11. H. Douglas Price, "Congress and the Evolution of Legislative Professionalism," in *Congress in Change,* ed. Norman J. Ornstein (New York: Praeger Publishers, 1975), pp. 5-7.
12. Samuel P. Huntington, "Postindustrial Politics: How Benign Will It Be?" *Comparative Politics* 6 (January 1974): 163-192.
13. See Nelson W. Polsby, "The Institutionalization of the U.S. House of Representatives," *American Political Science Review* 62 (1968): 144-168; Randall B. Ripley, *Power in the Senate* (New York: St. Martin's Press, 1969), p. 43; and Morris P. Fiorina, David W. Rohde, and Peter Wissell, "Historical Change in House Turnover," in *Congress in Change,* pp. 24-57.
14. Woodrow Wilson, *Congressional Government* (1885; reprint, Baltimore: Johns Hopkins University Press, 1981).
15. See George R. Brown, *The Leadership of Congress* (Indianapolis: Bobbs-Merrill Co., 1922); Richard Bolling, *Power in the House* (New York: Capricorn, 1968); and David J. Rothman, *Politics and Power* (New York: Atheneum Publishers, 1969).
16. Ripley, *Power in the Senate,* p. 43.
17. Price, "Congress and the Evolution of Legislative 'Professionalism,'" p. 9.
18. Kenneth W. Hechler, *Insurgency: Personalities and Politics of the Taft Era* (New York: Columbia University Press, 1940), pp. 27-82; Brown, *The Leadership of Congress,* pp. 195-197, 275.
19. Brown, *The Leadership of Congress,* pp. 106-107, 248-249.
20. For discussion of the Senate's greater tendency toward liberalism, see Lewis A. Froman, Jr., *The Congressional Process: Strategies, Rules and Procedures* (Boston: Little, Brown & Co., 1967). This tendency also may refer to the Senate's greater responsiveness to national ideological swings, which during the industrial era reflected the rise of Democratic liberalism. The Senate, as the truer reflector of the nation's ideological moods, thus could also swing more decisively to the right in a period of conservative resurgence. The important point is that the Senate may be more prone to radical swings in temperament than the founding fathers expected of the House.
21. Fenno, *The United States Senate,* pp. 12-25; Fenno, *Home Style* (Boston: Little, Brown & Co., 1978); and Charles O. Jones, *Every Second Year* (Washington, D.C.: The Brookings Institution, 1968).
22. Morris Fiorina, *Congress: Keystone of the Washington Establishment* (New Haven: Yale University Press, 1977).
23. Fenno, *Home Style,* pp. 9-12.
24. Warren Lee Kostroski, "Party and Incumbency in Postwar Senate Elections: Trends, Patterns, and Models," *American Political Science Review* 67 (December 1973): 1213-1234.

25. Barbara Hinckley, "House Reelections and Senate Defeats: The Role of the Challenger," *British Journal of Political Science* (October 1970): 628-642; and Thomas E. Mann and Raymond E. Wolfinger, "Candidates and Parties in Congressional Elections," *American Political Science Review* 74 (September 1980): 617-632.

26. Nelson W. Polsby, "Strengthening Congress in National Policymaking," in *Congressional Behavior,* ed. Nelson W. Polsby (New York: Random House, 1971), p. 7.

27. Richard F. Fenno, Jr., *Congressmen in Committees* (Boston: Little, Brown & Co., 1973).

28. Robert L. Peabody, Norman J. Ornstein, and David W. Rohde, "The United States Senate as Presidential Incubator: Many Are Called But Few Are Chosen," *Political Science Quarterly* 91 (Summer 1976): 237-258.

29. Alan Ehrenhalt, "The Moulting Season in the U.S. Senate," *Congressional Quarterly Weekly Report*, March 15, 1983, p. 535.

30. For more on conference committee politics, see David Vogler, *The Third House* (Evanston, Ill.: Northwestern University Press, 1971); John Ferejohn, "Who Wins in Conference Committee?" *The Journal of Politics* 37 (November 1975): 1033-1046; Gerald S. Strom and Barry S. Rundquist, "A Revised Theory of Winning in House-Senate Conferences, *American Political Science Review* 71 (June 1977): 448-453; and Longley and Oleszek, "Conference Committee Politics."

31. Daniel Bell, *The Coming of Post-Industrial Society* (New York: Basic Books, 1973); and Huntington, "Postindustrial Politics."

32. Lester C. Thurow, *The Zero Sum Society* (New York: Basic Books, 1980); and Lawrence C. Dodd, "Congress, the Constitution, and the Crisis of Legitimation," in *Congress Reconsidered,* 2nd ed., edited by Lawrence C. Dodd and Bruce I. Oppenheimer (Washington, D.C.: CQ Press, 1981), pp. 400-411.

33. See, for example, Paul Lenchner, "Postindustrialization and the New Congress" (Paper presented at the annual meeting of the Southern Political Science Association, Atlanta, Georgia, 1979); and John S. Saloma III, *Congress and the New Politics* (Boston: Little, Brown & Co., 1969).

34. For general discussion of Congress and the media, see Michael Robinson, "Three Faces of Congressional Media," in *The New Congress,* ed. Thomas E. Mann and Norman J. Ornstein (Washington, D.C.: American Enterprise Institute for Public Policy Research, 1981), pp. 55-96.

35. Fenno, *The United States Senate,* pp. 9-12.

36. See, for example, Stephen E. Frantzich, "Computerized Information Technology in the U.S. House of Representatives," *Legislative Studies Quarterly* 4 (1979): 255-280.

37. Fiorina, *Congress: Keystone of the Washington Establishment*; and John R. Johannes, *To Serve Our People: Congress and Constituency Service* (Lincoln, Neb.: University of Nebraska Press, 1984).

38. Hinckley, "House Reelections and Senate Defeats"; and Mann and Wolfinger, "Candidates and Parties."

39. Marjorie Random Hershey, *Running for Office: The Political Education of Campaigners* (New York: Chatham House, 1985).

40. Kostroski, "Party and Incumbency."

41. *Congressional Quarterly Weekly Report,* November 1, 1980, pp. 32-38.

42. Steven S. Smith and Christopher J. Deering, *Committees in Congress* (Washington, D.C.: CQ Press, 1984).
43. Barbara Sinclair, *Majority Leadership in the U.S. House* (Baltimore: Johns Hopkins Press, 1983).
44. John W. Ellwood and James A. Thurber, "The Politics of the Congressional Budget Process Re-examined," in *Congress Reconsidered*, 2nd ed.; and Allen Schick, *Congress and Money: Budgeting, Spending and Taxing* (Washington, D.C.: The Urban Institute, 1980).
45. Pamela Fessler, "Spending Cuts, Record Tax Hike Pass Senate," *Congressional Quarterly Weekly Report,* July 24, 1982, p. 1747.

CONTRIBUTORS

David W. Brady is the Herbert Autrey Professor of Social Sciences at Rice University. He received his Ph.D. in political science from the University of Iowa in 1970. His publications include *Congressional Voting in a Partisan Era: A Study of the McKinley Houses* (1973), *Public Policy and Politics in America*, 2nd ed. (1984), *Public Policy in the Eighties* (1983), and numerous articles in professional journals. He has recently completed a Project 87-funded manuscript on critical elections in the U.S. House of Representatives.

Charles S. Bullock III is the Richard B. Russell Professor of Political Science at the University of Georgia. He received his Ph.D. from Washington University, St. Louis, and has done research on Congress, civil rights, and policy implementation. He is the coauthor of *Law and Social Change* (1972), *Racial Equality in America* (1975), *Coercion to Compliance* (1976), *Public Policy and Politics in America*, 2nd ed. (1984), *Public Policy in the Eighties* (1983), *Implementation of Civil Rights Policy* (1984), and *Government in America* (1984).

Bruce Cain is Associate Professor of Political Science at the California Institute of Technology. He received his Ph.D. from Harvard University and is the author of *The Reapportionment Puzzle* (1984).

Edward G. Carmines, Professor of Political Science at Indiana University, specializes in the areas of American politics and methodology. He received his Ph.D. from the State University of New York, Buffalo, and is the coauthor of *Statistical Analysis of Social Data* (1978) and *Measurement in Social Science* (1980), as well as numerous articles in professional journals. His current research focuses on the effects of political issues on the evolution of mass party alignments. During 1982 and 1983 he was a Visiting Scholar at Nuffield College, Oxford.

Melissa P. Collie is a visiting Assistant Professor at Stanford University and has been an Assistant Professor at Rice University, where she received her Ph.D. in political science in 1984. She is the author of articles on congressional elections and legislative voting behavior in the *American Political Science Review* and *Legislative Studies Quarterly*.

Joseph Cooper is Dean of Social Sciences and Lena Gohlman Fox Professor of Political Science at Rice University. He has served as Staff Director of the U.S. House Commission on Administrative Review and as the Program Chair for the 1985 American Political Science Association meeting. He is the author of a monograph on the development of the committee system and of numerous articles on congressional structures, processes, and politics.

Roger H. Davidson is Senior Specialist in American Government and Public Administration at the Congressional Research Service of the U.S. Library of Congress. He teaches government and politics at the University of Maryland and is the author of *The Role of the Congressman* (1969) and coauthor of *Congress in Crisis* (1966), *On Capitol Hill* (1972), *Congress Against Itself* (1977), *Congress and Its Members*, 2nd ed. (1985), and *A More Perfect Union*, 3rd ed. (1985).

Christopher J. Deering is Associate Professor of Political Science at The George Washington University. He received his Ph.D. from the University of California, Santa Barbara, and served as a Brookings Institution Research Fellow (1977-1978) and an APSA Congressional Fellow (1984-1985). He is the coauthor of *Committees in Congress* (1984).

I. M. Destler is a Senior Fellow at the Institute for International Economics, Washington, D.C. He received his Ph.D. from the Woodrow Wilson School of Public and International Affairs, Princeton University. He is the author of *Presidents, Bureaucrats, and Foreign Policy* (1972) and *Making Foreign Economic Policy* (1980), and the coauthor of *Our Own Worst Enemy: The Unmaking of American Foreign Policy* (1984). He did the original research and writing for his chapter in this collection while a Senior Associate at the Carnegie Endowment for International Peace.

Lawrence C. Dodd, Professor of Political Science at Indiana University, received his Ph.D. from the University of Minnesota. He is the author of *Coalitions in Parliamentary Government* (1976) and the coauthor of *Congress and the Administrative State* (1979). He has served as President of the Southwestern Political Science Association (1979-1980), as a Congressional Fellow (1974-1975), and as a Hoover National Fellow (1984-1985).

John W. Ellwood, Associate Professor at the Amos Tuck School of Business Administration, Dartmouth College, received his Ph.D. in political science from Johns Hopkins University. He has taught at the University of Virginia and the Woodrow Wilson School of Public and International Affairs, Princeton University. He served as a Congressional Fellow (1974-1975) and as the special assistant to the director of the Congressional Budget Office (1977-1980). He is the author of *Reductions in U.S. Domestic Spending: How They Affect State and Local Governments* (1982).

Robert S. Erikson is Professor of Political Science at the University of Houston. He received his Ph.D. from the University of Illinois. He is the coauthor of *American Public Opinion: Its Origins, Content, and Impact,* 2nd ed. (1980), and the author of numerous articles on congressional elections.

John Ferejohn is Professor of Political Science at Stanford University, where he also received his Ph.D. His research interests include Congress and public policy, congressional elections, and theories of legislative behavior. He is the author of *Pork Barrel Politics* (1974), and the coauthor of a forthcoming study on legislators and constituencies in the United States and Great Britain.

Morris P. Fiorina is Professor of Political Science at Harvard University. He received his Ph.D. from the University of Rochester and has written extensively on American politics, especially in the areas of representation and electoral accountability. His books are *Representatives, Roll Calls, and Constituencies* (1974), *Congress: Keystone of the Washington Establishment* (1977), and *Retrospective Voting in American National Elections* (1981).

Gary C. Jacobson is Professor of Political Science at the University of California, San Diego. He received his Ph.D. from Yale University in 1972. He is the author of *Money in Congressional Elections* (1980) and *The Politics of Congressional Elections* (1983), and the coauthor of *Strategy and Choice in Congressional Elections,* 2nd ed. (1983).

Burdett A. Loomis, Associate Professor of Political Science at the University of Kansas, received his Ph.D. from the University of Wisconsin and served as a Congressional Fellow (1975-1976). Coeditor of *Interest Group Politics* (1983), he has written on congressional careers and organizations. In 1984 he directed American University's Congressional Management Project.

Bruce I. Oppenheimer is Associate Professor of Political Science at the University of Houston. He received his Ph.D. from the University of Wisconsin and has been both a Brookings Fellow (1970-1971) and a Congressional Fellow (1974-1975). His publications include *Oil and the Congressional Process* (1974) and articles on the House Rules Committee and energy policy. He is the primary author of *A History of the Committee on Rules* (1983).

Norman J. Ornstein is Resident Scholar at the American Enterprise Institute and Series Editor of public television's "Congress: We the People." He was a Congressional Fellow (1969-1970) and worked to reorganize the Senate's committee system in 1976 and 1977. He currently serves as a consultant on political coverage to the Public Broadcasting System and to CBS News. His books include *Congress in Change: Evolution and Reform* (1975), *Interest Groups, Lobbying and Policymaking* (1978), *Vital Statistics on Congress,* 1984/1985 edition, and *The New Congress* (1981). His essay in this collection is part of a broader study of the U.S. Senate that Ornstein, Peabody, and Rohde will publish with CQ Press.

Robert L. Peabody is Professor of Political Science at the Johns Hopkins University. He has served as Associate Director of the American Political Science Association's Study of Congress project and as Staff Assistant to former House Speaker Carl Albert. He is the author of numerous books on Congress, including *Leadership in Congress* (1976); editor of *Education of a Congressman* (1972); coauthor of *To Enact a Law: Congress and Campaign Finance* (1972) and *Congress: Two Decades of Analysis* (1969); and coeditor of *New Perspectives on the House of Representatives,* 3rd ed. (1977).

David E. Price is Professor of Political Science and Policy Sciences at Duke University. He received his Ph.D. from Yale University, where he taught until 1973. His publications include *Who Makes the Laws?* (1972), *The Commerce Committees* (1975), *Policy-Making in Congressional Committees* (1979), and *Bringing Back the Parties* (1984). He has served as a legislative aide to the late Senator E. L. Bartlett (D-Alaska), Staff Director of the Democratic National Committee's Commission on Presidential Nomination (Hunt Commission), and Executive Director and Chairman of the North Carolina Democratic Party.

David W. Rohde is Professor of Political Science and department chairperson at Michigan State University. He is a former APSA Congressional Fellow. He received his Ph.D. at the University of Rochester and is the author of a variety of articles on congressional reform and congressional elections. He is a coauthor of *Change and Continuity in the 1980 Elections,* rev. ed. (1983).

Catherine E. Rudder, Associate Director of the American Political Science Association, received her Ph.D. at Ohio State University. She has worked for two members of the House Committee on Ways and Means and has written about tax policy since serving as a Congressional Fellow (1974-1975).

Barbara Sinclair is Professor of Political Science at the University of California, Riverside. She received her Ph.D. from the University of

Rochester and has served as a Congressional Fellow (1978-1979). Her writings on the U.S. Congress include *Congressional Realignment* (1982) and *Majority Leadership in the U.S. House* (1983).

Steven S. Smith is Assistant Professor of Political Science at Northwestern University. He received his Ph.D. from the University of Minnesota, served as a Congressional Fellow (1980-1981), and currently is a member of the editorial board of the *American Journal of Political Science*. He is the author of numerous articles on congressional politics and the coauthor of *Committees in Congress* (1984).

Gerald C. Wright teaches at Indiana University and was formerly the Political Science Program Director at the National Science Foundation. He received his Ph.D. at the University of North Carolina, Chapel Hill. His publications include *Electoral Choice in America: Party, Image and Incumbency in State and National Elections,* as well as numerous articles in professional journals.

SUGGESTED READINGS

Aberbach, Joel D. "Changes in Congressional Oversight." *American Behavioral Scientist* 22 (1979): 493-515.

Abramowitz, Alan J. "A Comparison of Voting for U.S. Senators and Representatives in 1978." *American Political Science Review* 74 (1980): 637-640.

Arnold, R. Douglas. *Congress and the Bureaucracy.* New Haven, Conn.: Yale University Press, 1979.

Asher, Herbert B. "The Learning of Legislative Norms." *American Political Science Review* 67 (1973): 499-513.

Asher, Herbert B., and Herbert F. Weisberg. "Voting Change in Congress: Some Dynamic Perspectives on an Evolutionary Process." *American Journal of Political Science* 22 (1978): 391-425.

Bacheller, J. M. "Lobbyists and the Legislative Process: The Impact of Environmental Constraints." *American Political Science Review* 71 (1977): 252-263.

Bauer, Raymond A., Ithiel de Sola Pool, and Lewis A. Dexter. *American Business and Public Policy.* New York: Atherton, 1963.

Bibby, John F., and Roger H. Davidson. *On Capitol Hill,* 2nd ed. Hinsdale, Ill.: Dryden, 1972.

Bolling, Richard. *House Out of Order.* New York: E. P. Dutton, 1965.

____ . *Power in the House.* New York: E. P. Dutton, 1965.

Born, Richard. "Changes in the Competitiveness of House Primary Elections, 1956-1976." *American Politics Quarterly* 8 (1980): 495-506.

Brady, David W. *Congressional Voting in a Partisan Era: A Study of the McKinley Houses.* Lawrence, Kansas: University of Kansas Press, 1973.

Brady, David W., Joseph Cooper, and Patricia A. Hurley. "The Decline of Party in the U.S. House of Representatives, 1887-1968." *Legislative Studies Quarterly* 4 (1979): 381-407.

Bullock, Charles S., III. "House Careerists: Changing Patterns of Longevity and Attrition." *American Political Science Review* 66 (1972): 1295-1305.

____ . "House Committee Assignments." In *The Congressional System: Notes and Readings,* 2nd ed. Edited by Leroy N. Rieselbach. North Scituate, Mass.: Duxbury Press, 1979.

____ . "Redistricting and Congressional Stability, 1962-1972." *Journal of Politics* 37 (1975): 569-575.

Clausen, Aage R. *How Congressmen Decide.* New York: St. Martin's Press, 1973.

Clem, Alan L., ed. *The Making of Congressmen: Seven Campaigns of 1974.* North Scituate, Mass.: Duxbury Press, 1976.

Collie, Melissa. "Incumbency, Electoral Safety and Turnover in the House of Representatives, 1952-1976." *American Political Science Review* 75 (1981).

Cooper, Joseph. "Strengthening the Congress: An Organizational Analysis." *Harvard Journal on Legislation* 2 (1975): 301-368.

——. *The Origins of the Standing Committees and the Development of the Modern House.* Houston, Texas: William Marsh Rice University, 1971.

Cooper, Joseph, and David W. Brady. "Toward a Diachronic Analysis of Congress." *American Political Science Review* 75 (1981).

——. "Institutional Context and Leadership Style: The House from Cannon to Rayburn." *American Political Science Review* 75 (1981).

Cover, Albert D. "Contacting Congressional Constituents: Some Patterns of Perquisite Use." *American Journal of Political Science* 24 (1980): 125-134.

——. "One Good Term Deserves Another: The Advantage of Incumbency in Congressional Elections." *American Journal of Political Science* 21 (1977): 523-541.

Cover, Albert D., and David R. Mayhew. "Congressional Dynamics and the Decline of Competitive Congressional Elections." In *Congress Reconsidered,* 2nd ed. Edited by Lawrence C. Dodd and Bruce I. Oppenheimer. Washington, D.C.: CQ Press, 1981.

Davidson, Roger H., David M. Kovenock, and Michael K. O'Leary. *Congress in Crisis: Politics and Congressional Reform.* Belmont, Calif.: Wadsworth, 1966.

Davidson, Roger H., and Walter J. Oleszek. *Congress Against Itself.* Bloomington, Ind.: Indiana University Press, 1977.

——. *Congress and Its Members.* Washington D.C.: CQ Press, 1985.

Dexter, Lewis A. *How Organizations Are Represented in Washington.* Indianapolis: Bobbs-Merrill Co., 1969.

——. *The Sociology and Politics of Congress.* Chicago: Rand McNally, 1969.

Dodd, Lawrence C. "Congress and the Quest for Power." In *Congress Reconsidered,* 1st ed. Edited by Lawrence C. Dodd and Bruce I. Oppenheimer. New York: Praeger Publishers, 1977.

——. "The Expanded Roles of the House Democratic Whip System." *Congressional Studies* 6 (1979).

Dodd, Lawrence C., and Richard L. Schott. *Congress and the Administrative State.* New York: John Wiley & Sons, 1979.

Eckhardt, Bob, and Charles L. Black, Jr. *The Titles of Power: Conversations on the American Constitution.* New Haven, Conn.: Yale University Press, 1976.

Edwards, George C., III. *Presidential Influence in Congress.* San Francisco: W. H. Freeman, 1980.

Erikson, Robert. "Is There Such a Thing as a Safe Seat?" *Polity* 8 (1976): 623-632.

——. "The Advantage of Incumbency in Congressional Elections." *Polity* 3 (1971).

Eulau, Heinz, and Paul Karps. "The Puzzle of Representation." *Legislative Studies Quarterly* 2 (1977): 233-254.

Fenno, Richard F., Jr. *Congressmen in Committees.* Boston: Little, Brown & Co., 1973.

——. *Home Style.* Boston: Little, Brown & Co., 1978.

——. "If, as Ralph Nader Says, Congress Is 'the Broken Branch,' How Come We Love Our Congressmen So Much?" In *Congress in Change,* edited by Norman J. Ornstein. New York: Praeger Publishers, 1975.

_____ . *The Power of the Purse.* Boston: Little, Brown & Co., 1966.

_____ . *The United States Senate: A Bicameral Perspective.* Washington, D.C.: American Enterprise Institute for Public Policy Research, 1982.

Ferejohn, John A. *Pork Barrel Politics.* Stanford, Calif.: Stanford University Press, 1974.

Fiorina, Morris P. *Congress: Keystone of the Washington Establishment.* New Haven, Conn.: Yale University Press, 1977.

_____ . *Representatives, Roll Calls and Constituencies.* Lexington, Mass.: Lexington Books, 1974.

Fiorina, Morris P., David W. Rohde, and Peter Wissel. "Historical Change in House Turnover." In *Congress in Change,* edited by Norman J. Ornstein. New York: Praeger Publishers, 1975.

Fishel, Jeff. *Party and Opposition.* New York: David McKay Co., 1973.

Fisher, Louis. *The Constitution Between Friends: Congress, the President and the Law.* New York: St. Martin's Press, 1978.

_____ . *President and Congress: Power and Policy.* New York: Free Press, 1972.

Fowler, Linda. "Candidates' Perceptions of Electoral Coalitions." *American Politics Quarterly* 8 (1980): 483-494.

Fox, Harrison W., Jr., and Susan Webb Hammond. *Congressional Staffs: The Invisible Force in American Lawmaking.* New York: Free Press, 1977.

Frantzich, Stephen E. "Computerized Information Technology in the U.S. House of Representatives." *Legislative Studies Quarterly* 4 (1979): 255-280.

Freeman, J. Leiper. *The Political Process.* New York: Random House, 1955.

Froman, Lewis A., Jr. *The Congressional Process: Strategies, Rules and Procedures.* Boston: Little, Brown & Co., 1967.

Goehlert, Robert U., and John R. Sayre. *The United States Congress: A Bibliography.* New York: Free Press, 1982.

Goldenberg, Edie N., and Michael W. Traugott. *Campaigning for Congress.* Washington, D.C.: CQ Press, 1984.

Goodwin, George, Jr. *The Little Legislatures.* Amherst: University of Massachusetts Press, 1970.

Harris, Joseph. *Congressional Control of Administration.* Washington, D.C.: Brookings Institution, 1964.

Hayes, Michael I. "Interest Groups and Congress: Toward a Transactional Theory." In *The Congressional System: Notes and Readings,* 2nd ed. Edited by Leroy N. Rieselbach. North Scituate, Mass.: Duxbury Press, 1979.

Henry, Charles P. "Legitimizing Race in Congressional Politics." *American Politics Quarterly* 5 (1977): 149-176.

Hershey, Marjorie R. *The Making of Campaign Strategy.* Lexington, Mass.: Lexington Books, 1974.

Hinckley, Barbara. *Stability and Change in Congress.* New York: Harper & Row, 1971.

_____ . "The American Voter in Congressional Elections." *American Political Science Review* 74 (1980): 641-650.

_____ . *The Seniority System in Congress.* Bloomington, Ind.: Indiana University Press, 1971.

Hoadly, John F. "The Emergence of Political Parties in Congress, 1789-1803." *American Political Science Review* 74 (1980): 757-779.

Holtzman, Abraham. *Legislative Liaison.* Chicago: Rand McNally, 1970.

Huitt, Ralph K., and Robert L. Peabody. *Congress: Two Decades of Analysis*. New York: Harper & Row, 1969.

Huntington, Samuel P. "Congressional Responses to the Twentieth Century." In *The Congress and America's Future*, 2nd ed. Edited by David B. Truman. Englewood Cliffs, N.J.: Prentice-Hall, 1973.

Hurley, Patricia, and Kim Quarle Hill. "The Prospects for Issue-Voting in Contemporary Congressional Elections." *American Politics Quarterly* 8 (1980): 425-448.

Jackson, John. *Constituencies and Leaders in Congress*. Cambridge, Mass: Harvard University Press, 1974.

Jacobson, Gary C. *Money in Congressional Elections*. New Haven, Conn.: Yale University Press, 1980.

——— . *The Politics of Congressional Elections*. Boston: Little, Brown & Co., 1983.

Jacobson, Gary C., and Samuel Kernell. *Strategy and Choice in Congressional Elections*. New Haven, Conn.: Yale University Press, 1983.

Jewell, Malcolm E. *Senatorial Politics and Foreign Policy*. Lexington: University of Kentucky Press, 1962.

Jewell, Malcolm E., and Samuel C. Patterson. *The Legislative Process in the United States*, 3rd ed. New York: Random House, 1977.

Johannes, John R. *Policy Innovation in Congress*. Morristown, N. J.: General Learning Press, 1972.

Jones, Charles O. "Representation in Congress: The Case of the House Agricultural Committee." *American Political Science Review* 55 (1961): 358-367.

——— . *The Minority Party in Congress*. Boston: Little, Brown & Co., 1970.

——— . "The Role of the Congressional Subcommittee." *Midwest Journal of Political Science* 6 (1962): 327-344.

——— . "Will Reform Change Congress?" In *Congress Reconsidered*, 1st ed. Edited by Lawrence C. Dodd and Bruce I. Oppenheimer. New York: Praeger Publishers, 1977.

Keefe, William J. *Congress and the American People*. Englewood Cliffs, N. J.: Prentice-Hall, 1980.

Keefe, William J., and Morris S. Ogul. *The American Legislative Process*, 4th ed. Englewood Cliffs, N.J.: Prentice-Hall, 1977.

Kingdon, John W. *Candidates for Office*. New York: Random House, 1968.

——— . *Congressmen's Voting Decisions*. New York: Harper & Row, 1973.

Kuklinski, James H. "District Competitiveness and Legislative Roll Call Behavior: A Reassessment of the Marginality Hypothesis." *American Journal of Political Science* 21 (1977): 627-638.

LeLoup, Lance T. *Budgetary Politics*. Brunswick, Ohio: Kings Court Press, 1977.

LeLoup, Lance T., and Steven Shull. "Congress Versus the Executive: The 'Two Presidencies' Reconsidered." *Social Science Quarterly* 59 (1979): 704-719.

Loewenberg, Gerhard, and Samuel Patterson. *Comparing Legislatures*. Boston: Little, Brown & Co., 1979.

Lowi, Theodore J. *The End of Liberalism*. New York: W. W. Norton & Co., 1969, 1979.

Maass, Arthur. *Congress and the Common Good*. New York: Basic Books, 1983.

Maisel, Louis S. *From Obscurity to Oblivion: Running in the Congressional Primary*. Knoxville, Tenn.: University of Tennessee Press, 1982.

Manley, John F. *The Politics of Finance*. Boston: Little, Brown & Co., 1970.

Mann, Thomas E. *Unsafe at Any Margin: Interpreting Congressional Elections.* Washington, D.C.: American Enterprise Institute for Public Policy Research, 1978.

Mann, Thomas E., and Norman J. Ornstein. *The New Congress.* Washington, D.C.: American Enterprise Institute for Public Policy Research, 1981.

Mann, Thomas E., and Raymond E. Wolfinger. "Candidates and Parties in Congressional Elections." *American Political Science Review* 74 (1980): 617-632.

Matthews, Donald R. *U.S. Senators and Their World.* New York: Vintage Books, 1960.

Mayhew, David R. *Congress: The Electoral Connection.* New Haven, Conn.: Yale University Press, 1974.

____ . *Party Loyalty Among Congressmen.* Cambridge, Mass.: Harvard University Press, 1966.

Nelson, Garrison. "Partisan Patterns of House Leadership Change, 1789-1977." *American Political Science Review* 71 (1977): 918-939.

Norpoth, Helmut. "Explaining Party Cohesion in Congress: The Case of Shared Party Attributes." *American Political Science Review* 70 (1976): 1157-1171.

Ogul, Morris S. *Congress Oversees the Bureaucracy.* Pittsburgh: University of Pittsburgh Press, 1976.

Oleszek, Walter J. *Congressional Procedures and the Policy Process,* 2nd ed. Washington, D.C.: CQ Press, 1984.

Oppenheimer, Bruce I. *Oil and the Congressional Process: The Limits of Symbolic Politics.* Lexington, Mass.: Lexington Books, 1974.

____ . "Policy Effects of U.S. House Reform: Decentralization and the Capacity to Resolve Energy Issues." *Legislative Studies Quarterly* 5 (1980): 5-30.

____ . "The Rules Committee: New Arm of Leadership in a Decentralized House." In *Congress Reconsidered,* 1st ed. Edited by Lawrence C. Dodd and Bruce I. Oppenheimer. New York: Praeger Publishers, 1977.

Orfield, Gary. *Congressional Power: Congress and Social Change.* New York: Harcourt Brace Jovanovich, 1975.

Ornstein, Norman J. *Congress in Change: Evolution and Reform.* New York: Praeger Publishers, 1975.

Ornstein, Norman J., and Shirley Elder. *Interest Groups, Lobbying and Policymaking.* Washington, D.C.: CQ Press, 1978.

Ornstein, Norman J., and David W. Rohde. "Shifting Forces, Changing Rules, and Political Outcomes: The Impact of Congressional Change on Four House Committees." In *New Perspectives on the House of Representatives,* edited by Robert L. Peabody and Nelson W. Polsby. Chicago: Rand McNally, 1977.

Parker, Glenn R. "The Advantage of Incumbency in House Elections." *American Politics Quarterly* 8 (1980): 449-464.

____ . "Some Themes in Congressional Unpopularity." *American Journal of Political Science* 21 (1977): 93-110.

____ . *Studies of Congress.* Washington, D.C.: CQ Press, 1984.

Parker, Glenn R., and S. L. Parker. "Factions in Committees: The U.S. House of Representatives." *American Political Science Review* 73 (1979): 85-102.

Payne, James L. "The Personal Electoral Advantage of House Incumbents, 1936-1976." *American Politics Quarterly* 8 (1980): 465-482.

Peabody, Robert L. *Leadership in Congress: Stability, Succession and Change.* Boston: Little, Brown & Co., 1976.

Peabody, Robert L., and Nelson W. Polsby, eds. *New Perspectives on the House of Representatives,* 3rd ed. Chicago: Rand McNally, 1977.

Peters, John G., and Susan Welch. "The Effects of Charges of Corruption on Voting Behavior in Congressional Elections." *American Political Science Review* 74 (1980): 697-708.

Pierce, John C., and John L. Sullivan. *The Electorate Reconsidered.* Beverly Hills, Calif.: Sage Publications, 1980.

Polsby, Nelson W. *Congress and the Presidency.* 3rd ed. Englewood Cliffs, N.J.: Prentice-Hall, 1976.

——. "Institutionalization in the U.S. House of Representatives." *American Political Science Review* 62 (1968): 144-168.

Polsby, Nelson W., Miriam Gallagher, and Barry Rundquist. "The Growth of the Seniority System in the House of Representatives." *American Political Science Review* 63 (1969): 787-807.

Powell, Lynda W. "Issue Representation in Congress." *Journal of Politics* (1982).

Price, David E. *Who Makes the Laws?* Cambridge, Mass.: Schenkman Publishing Co., 1972.

Price, H. Douglas. "Congress and the Evolution of Legislative Professionalism." In *Congress in Change,* edited by Norman J. Ornstein. New York: Praeger Publishers, 1975.

Ragsdale, Lyn. "The Fiction of Congressional Elections as Presidential Events." *American Politics Quarterly* 8 (1980): 395-398.

Reid, T. R. *Congressional Odyssey: The Saga of a Senate Bill.* San Francisco: W. H. Freeman, 1980.

Rieselbach, Leroy N. *Congressional Politics.* New York: McGraw-Hill, 1973.

——. *Congressional Reform in the Seventies.* Morristown, N. J.: General Learning Press, 1977.

——. ed. *Legislative Reform: The Policy Impact.* Lexington, Mass.: Lexington Books, 1978.

——. *The Roots of Isolationism.* Indianapolis: Bobbs-Merrill & Co., 1966.

Ripley, Randall B. *Majority Party Leadership in Congress.* Boston: Little, Brown & Co., 1969.

——. *Party Leaders in the House of Representatives.* Washington, D.C.: The Brookings Institution, 1967.

——. *Power in the Senate.* New York: St. Martin's Press, 1969.

Ripley, Randell B., and Grace N. Franklin. *Congress, the Bureaucracy and Public Policy.* Homewood, Ill.: Dorsey Press, 1980.

Rohde, David W., and Kenneth A. Shepsle. "Democratic Committee Assignments in the U.S. House of Representatives." *American Political Science Review* 67 (1973): 889-905.

Rothman, David J. *Politics and Power.* New York: Atheneum, 1969.

Rudder, Catherine E. "Committee Reform and the Revenue Process." In *Congress Reconsidered,* 1st ed. Edited by Lawrence C. Dodd and Bruce I. Oppenheimer. New York: Praeger Publishers, 1977.

Saloma, John S., III. *Congress and the New Politics.* Boston: Little, Brown & Co., 1969.

Schneider, Jerrold E. *Ideological Coalitions in Congress.* Greenwood, Conn.: Greenwood Press, 1979.

Schwarz, John E., and L. Earl Shaw. *The United States Congress in Comparative Perspective.* Hinsdale, Ill.: Dryden Press, 1976.

Seidman, Harold. *Politics, Position, and Power,* 2nd ed. London: Oxford University Press, 1975.

Shepsle, Kenneth A. *The Giant Jigsaw Puzzle.* Chicago: University of Chicago Press, 1978.

Sinclair, Barbara Deckard. "Determinants of Aggregate Party Cohesion in the U.S. House of Representatives." *Legislative Studies Quarterly* 2 (1977): 155-175.

——. *Majority Leadership in the U.S. House.* Baltimore: Johns Hopkins University Press, 1983.

Smith, Steven S., and Christopher J. Deering. *Committees in Congress.* Washington, D.C.: CQ Press, 1984.

Stone, Walter J. "The Dynamics of Constituency: Electoral Control in the House." *American Politics Quarterly* 8 (1980): 399-424.

Sundquist, James L. *The Decline and Resurgence of Congress.* Washington, D.C.: The Brookings Institution, 1981.

——. *Politics and Policy.* Washington, D.C.: The Brookings Institution, 1968.

Truman, David B. *The Governmental Process.* New York: Alfred A. Knopf, 1951.

Turner, Julius. *Party and Constituency: Pressures on Congress,* rev. ed. Edited by Edward V. Schneier, Jr. Baltimore: Johns Hopkins Press, 1970.

Unekis, Joseph, and Leroy N. Rieselbach. *Congressional Committee Politics: Continuity and Change.* New York: Praeger Publishers, 1984.

Uslaner, Eric M. "Policy Entrepreneurs and Amateur Democrats in the House of Representatives." In *Legislative Reform: The Policy Impact,* edited by Leroy N. Rieselbach. Lexington, Mass.: Lexington Books, 1978.

Vogler, David J. *The Third House.* Evanston, Ill.: Northwestern University Press, 1971.

——. *The Politics of Congress.* Boston: Allyn & Bacon, 1974.

——. *The Third House.* Evanston, Ill.: Northwestern University Press, 1971.

Wahlke, John C., Heinz H. Eulau, W. Buchanan, and L. C. Ferguson. *The Legislative System: Explorations in Legislative Behavior.* New York: John Wiley & Sons, 1962.

Wayne, S. J. *The Legislative Presidency.* New York: Harper & Row, 1978.

Weisberg, Herbert F. "Evaluating Theories of Congressional Roll Call Voting." *American Journal of Political Science* 22 (1978): 554-577.

Westefield, L. P. "Majority Party Leadership and the Committee System in the House of Representatives." *American Political Science Review* 68 (1974): 1593-1604.

Wildavsky, Aaron. *The Politics of the Budgetary Process.* Boston: Little, Brown & Co., 1964.

Wilson, Woodrow. *Congressional Government.* Gloucester, Mass.: Peter Smith, 1885, 1973.

Wolfinger, Raymond E., and Joan Heifetz Hollinger. "Safe Seats, Seniority, and Power in Congress." *American Political Science Review* 59 (1965): 337-349.

Young, James S. *The Washington Community, 1880-1828.* New York: Columbia University Press, 1966.

INDEX